THE
WORLD'S
HISTORY

THIRD EDITION

VOLUME II: SINCE 1100

THE
WORLD'S
HISTORY

THIRD EDITION

VOLUME II: SINCE 1100

HOWARD SPODEK

PEARSON

Prentice
Hall

Upper Saddle River, N.J. 07458

Editorial Director: Charlyce Jones Owen
Executive Editor: Charles Cavaliere
Development Editor: Elaine Silverstein
Editorial Assistant: Shannon Corliss
Executive Marketing Manager: Heather Shelstad

Pearson Education LTD.
Pearson Education Australia PTY, Limited
Pearson Education Singapore, Pte. Ltd
Pearson Education North Asia Ltd
Pearson Education, Canada, Ltd
Pearson Educación de Mexico, S.A. de C.V.
Pearson Education–Japan
Pearson Education Malaysia, Pte. Ltd

This book was designed and produced by
Laurence King Publishing Ltd, London
www.laurenceking.co.uk
Every effort has been made to contact the copyright holders, but should there be
any errors or omissions, Laurence King Publishing Ltd would be pleased to insert
the appropriate acknowledgment in any subsequent printing of this publication.

Editor: Richard Mason
Picture Researcher: Emma Brown
Design: Newton Harris Design Partnership

Front cover: The Great Exhibition, Crystal Palace, London, 1851. Engraving.
Guildhall Library, London.

10 9 8 7 6 5 4 3 2 1
ISBN 0-13-177317-8

BRIEF CONTENTS

CONTENTS

MAPS

PICTURE CREDITS

LITERARY CREDITS

Every effort has been made to obtain permission from all copyright holders, but in some cases this has not proved possible. The publishers therefore wish to thank all authors or copyright holders who are included without acknowledgement. Prentice Hall and Laurence King Publishing apologizes for any errors or omissions in this list and would be grateful to be notified of any corrections that should be incorporated in the next edition.

Cambridge University Press: *The Journals of Captain James Cook on His Voyages of Discovery* by James Cook, edited by J. C. Beaglehole, 2 vols. (Cambridge University Press, for the Hakluyt Society, 1955, 1961).

Columbia University Press: *Introduction to Contemporary Civilization in the West*, 2 vols. (Columbia University Press, 1954); *Sources of Chinese Tradition: From 1600 Through The Twentieth Century*, vol. 2, edited by William Theodore de Bary and Richard Lufrano (Columbia University Press, 2000).

Faber & Faber Ltd.: 'The Waste Land', *Collected Poems 1909–1962* by T. S. Eliot (Harcourt Brace Jovanovich, 1936).

Grove/Atlantic Press Inc.: *The Gandhi Reader*, edited by Homer Jack (Grove Press, 1956).

Harcourt Brace Inc.: 'The Century's Decline', *View with a Grain of Sand* by Wislawa Szymborska (Harcourt Brace, 1995).

Hodder Murray Publishers: *Ibn Khaldun, An Arab Philosophy of History* by Ibn Khaldun, translated by Charles Issawi (John Murray, 1950).

Houghton Mifflin Company: *The Human Record: Sources of Global History*, vol. 2, edited by Alfred J. Andrea and James H. Overfield (Houghton Mifflin, 3rd edition, 1998).

Jawaharlal Nehru Memorial Fund: *Glimpses of World History* by Jawaharlal Nehru (Oxford University Press India, 1982); *Hind Swaraj or Indian Home Rule* by Mohandas Karamchand Gandhi (Navajivan Press, 1938).

The New Press: *Truth and Lies: Stories from the Truth and Reconciliation Commission in South Africa* by Jillian Edelstein (The New Press, 2001).

Random House Inc.: *A Higher Kind of Loyalty* by Liu Binyan (Pantheon Books, 1990).

University of California Press: *Canto General* by Pablo Neruda, translated by Jack Schmitt (University of California Press, 1991).

A. P. Watt Ltd.: 'The White Man's Burden', *Rudyard Kipling: Selected Poems*, edited by Peter Keating (Penguin Twentieth-Century Classics, 1993); 'The Second Coming' by W. B. Yeats, cited in *Literature of the Western World*, edited by Brian Wilkie and James Hurt (Macmillan, 1984).

SUPPLEMENTS

The World's History comes with an extensive package of supplementary print and multimedia materials for both instructors and students, many of which are available free to qualified adopters.

FOR THE INSTRUCTOR

- The *Instructor's Manual/Test-Item File* includes chapter outlines, overviews, key concepts, discussion questions, suggestions for useful audiovisual resources, and approximately 1500 test items (essay, multiple choice, true/false, and matching).

- The *Instructor Resource CDROM*, compatible with both Windows and Macintosh environments, provides instructors with such essential teaching tools as hundreds of digitized images and maps for classroom presentations, PowerPoint lectures, and other instructional material. The assets on the IRCDROM can be easily exported into online courses, such as WebCT and Blackboard.

- *Test Manager* is a computerized test management program for Windows and Macintosh environments. The program allows instructors to select items from the test-item file to create tests. It also allows online testing.

- The *Transparency Package* provides instructors with full color transparency acetates of all the maps, charts, and graphs in the text for use in the classroom.

- A *Correlation Guide to the Advanced Placement Exam* provides strategies and suggestions for using *The World's History* in AP World History courses.

FOR THE STUDENT

- *History Notes* (Volumes I and II) provides practice tests, essay questions, and map exercises to help reinforce key concepts.

- *Documents in World History* (Volumes I and II) is a collection of 200 primary source documents in global history. Questions accompanying the documents can be used for discussion or as writing assignments.

- Produced in collaboration with Dorling Kindersley, the world's most respected cartography publisher, *The Prentice Hall Atlas of World History* includes approximately 100 maps fundamental to the study of world history—from early hominids to the twenty-first century.

- *World History: An Atlas and Study Guide* is a four-color map workbook that includes over 100 maps with exercises, activities, and questions that help students learn both geography and history.

- *Reading Critically About History* is a brief guide to reading effectively that provides students with helpful strategies for reading a history textbook.

- *Understanding and Answering Essay Questions* suggests helpful analytical tools for understanding different types of essay questions, and provides precise guidelines for preparing well-crafted essay answers.

- Prentice Hall is pleased to provide adopters of *The World's History* with an opportunity to receive significant discounts when copies of the text are bundled with Penguin Classics titles in world history. Contact your local Prentice Hall representative for details.

MEDIA RESOURCES

- **Key** Prentice Hall's New Online Resource **OneKey** lets instructors and students in to the best teaching and learning resources—all in one place. This all-inclusive online resource is designed to help you minimize class preparation and maximize teaching time. Conveniently organized by chapter, OneKey for *The World's History, Third Edition* reinforces what students have learned in class and from the text. Among the student resources available for each chapter are: a complete, media-rich, interactive e-book version of *The World's History, Third Edition*; quizzes organized by the main subtopics of each chapter; over 200 primary-source documents; and interactive map quizzes.

    For instructors, OneKey includes images and maps from *The World's History, Third Edition*; instructional material; hundreds of primary-source documents; and PowerPoint presentations.

- *Prentice Hall OneSearch with Research Navigator: History 2005* This brief guide focuses on developing critical-thinking skills necessary for evaluating and using online sources. It provides a brief introduction to navigating the Internet with specific references to History web sites. It also provides an access code and instruction on using Research Navigator, a powerful research tool that provides access to three exclusive databases of reliable source material: ContentSelect Academic Journal Database, the New York Times Search by Subject Archive, and Link Library.

- The *Companion Website*™ (www.prenhall.com/spodek) works in tandem with the text and features objectives, study questions, web links to related Internet resources, document exercises, interactive maps, and map labelling exercises.

- *Prentice Hall World History Image Library* Bringing together hundreds of images—many of which have never before been digitized—this innovative new CDROM organizes images of fine art, culture, photographs, posters, cartoons, and manuscripts from around the world into thematic units, allowing instructors to efficiently export the material into customized PowerPoint lectures or other presentation platforms. In addition, interactive global maps showing change over time allow instructors to visually portray the large patterns of world history.

- *World History Documents CD-ROM* Bound into every new copy of this textbook is a free World History Documents CD-ROM. This is a powerful resource for research and additional reading that contains more than 200 primary source documents central to World History. Each document provides essay questions that are linked directly to a website where short-essay answers can be submitted online or printed out. A complete list of documents on the CD-ROM is found at the end of the text.

PREFACE

Why History?

The professional historian and the student of an introductory course often seem to pass each other on different tracks. For the professional, nothing is more fascinating than history. For the student, particularly one in a compulsory course, the whole enterprise often seems a bore. This introductory text is designed to help the student understand and share the fascination of the historian. It will also remind professors of their original attraction to history, before they began the specialization that has almost certainly marked their later careers. Furthermore, it encourages student and professor to explore together the history of the world and the significance of this study.

Professional historians love their field for many reasons. History offers perspective and guidance in forming a personal view of human development. It teaches the necessity of seeing many sides of issues. It explores the complexity and interrelationship of events and makes possible the search for patterns and meaning in human life.

Historians also love to debate. They love the challenge of demonstrating that their interpretations of the pattern and significance of events are the most accurate and the most satisfying in their fit between the available data and theory. Historians also love the detective work of the profession, whether it is researching through old archives, uncovering and using new sources of information, or reinterpreting long-ignored sources. In recent years historians have turned, for example, to oral history, old church records, files of photographs, cave paintings, individual census records, and reinterpretations of mythology.

Historical records are not simply lists of events, however. They are the means by which historians develop their interpretations of those events. Because interpretations differ, there is no single historical record, but various narrations of events each told from a different perspective. Therefore the study of history is intimately linked to the study of values, the values of the historical actors, the historians who have written about them, and of the students engaged in learning about them.

Professional historians consider history to be the king of disciplines. Synthesizing the concepts of fellow social scientists in economics, politics, anthropology, sociology, and geography, historians create a more integrated and comprehensive interpretation of the past. Joining with their colleagues in the humanities, historians delight in hearing and telling exciting stories that recall heroes and villains, the low born and the high, the wisdom and the folly of days gone by. This fusion of all the social sciences and humanities gives the study of history its range, depth, significance, and pleasure. Training in historical thinking provides an excellent introduction to understanding change and continuity in our own day as well as in the past.

Why World History?

Why specifically world history? Why should we teach and study world history, and what should be the content of such a course?

First, world history is a good place to begin for it is a new field for professor and student alike. Neither its content nor its pedagogy is yet fixed. Many of the existing textbooks on the market still have their origins in the study of western Europe, with segments added to cover the rest of the world. World history as the study of the inter-relationships of all regions of the world, seen from the many perspectives of the different peoples of the earth, is still virgin territory.

Second, for citizens of multicultural, multiethnic nations such as the United States, Canada, South Africa, and India, and for those of the many other countries such as the United Kingdom and Australia which are moving in that direction, a world history course offers the opportunity to gain an appreciation of the national and cultural origins of all their diverse citizens. In this way, the study of world history may help to strengthen the bonds of national citizenship.

Third, as the entire world becomes a single unit for interaction, it becomes an increasingly appropriate subject for historical study. The noted historian E.H. Carr explained that history "is an unending dialogue between the present and the past". The new reality of global interaction in communication, business, politics, religion, culture, and ecology has helped to generate the new academic subject of world history.

Organization and Approach

The text, like the year-long course, links *chronology*, *themes*, and *geography* in eight units, or parts of study. The parts move progressively along a time line from the emergence of early humans to the present day. Each part emphasizes a single theme—for example, urbanization or religion or trade—and students learn to use all eight themes to analyze historical events and to develop a grasp of the chronology of human development. Geographically, each part cover the entire globe, although specific topics place greater emphasis on specific regions.

REVISIONS TO THE THIRD EDITION

Readers of the first and second editions will find that this third edition builds on the strengths of the first two while adding new materials and new perspectives. Every aspect of the book's program has been exhaustively reviewed and revised. The pedagogical features were carefully examined. Revised and new, more useful elements were added including Review Questions, Key Topics, a running in-text glossary, up-to-date, annotated bibliographies, interactive maps, and Turning Point essays, which use visual sources to help the reader move from the themes of one part to the new themes of the next. The text has been reworked extensively to produce a narrative with improved coverage of gender issues, trade, technology and capitalism, the Islamic world and its influence, Africa and Latin America.

ORGANIZATIONAL CHANGES

Theme and Chronology

One of the most important organizational principles of this text from the beginning has been its emphasis on a thematic introduction to world history. Readers generally applauded this approach, but warned that sometimes it led us to neglect chronology. As in the first two editions, one theme is highlighted in each of the eight parts of the textbook, and the parts trace major chronological eras in the world's history, from the evolution of humans to the early 21st century. In this edition we have addressed much more effectively the problem of keeping chronology clear even as we continue to concentrate on themes. Readers should find this attention to consistent chronology—with much less of the moving back and forth in time periods that characterized earlier editions —also an important improvement.

Reorganization and New Materials

Readers familiar with the earlier editions will notice revisions and reorganization throughout the text, from beginning to end. The most striking difference appears in the final unit. It has been entirely reorganized, divided into two separate parts. The first of these looks at the world from the early twentieth century until about 1980, following much of the structure of the original and continuing to use the theme of "The Human Uses of Technology." A new unit has then been added that analyzes issues since about 1980 analyzed through the new theme of "Identity." Arguing that human action comes, in part, out of the sense of who we are, it examines new issues of religious, national, gender, and age identity. In each case it asks how new technologies, especially of communication, have affected these identities, and how these identities have affected technology. The final chapter will examine these new identity issues in several different regions of the world. Another major change is the addition of a new chapter, number 13, which examines European Visions 1000–1776. This chapter, along with Chapter 12 now forms a bridge between the pre-modern and modern worlds, and between volumes 1 and 2 in the paperback edition.

Historiography

A fundamental principal of the first two editions was the emphasis on the three questions: "What Do We Know?" "How Do We Know It?" and "What Difference Does It Make?" Teachers and students, both at the university level and, increasingly, in Advanced Placement courses appreciated the attention to these three historiographical issues, but they often found them cluttering the text. Discussions of the work and arguments of various historians appeared frequently, but inconsistently. In this edition each feature has been given a clearer place so that faculty and students can use them more effectively. In general, the main narrative conveys the "What Do We Know?" materials. Separate, color-coded, boxed features—usually two in every chapter—carry the "How Do We Know?" materials, demonstrating how historians sift through source materials and debate their interpretation. Questions accompany each of these "How Do We Know?" features to encourage students to appreci-ate the work of the historians in producing the records we have today. Additional color-coded boxed features in each chapter will introduce relevant primary sources for further analysis. Finally, each chapter ends with a discussion of "What Difference Does It Make?: Legacies to the Future." In another new feature, a set of questions end each chapter to guide students in their analyses of the material.

New Layout and Design

Readers will also see immediately a streamlined, cleaner design. A larger format provides for a more aesthetically-pleasing presentation, while the abundance of special feature boxes that filled the earlier editions have been reduced. More importantly, the basic material of many of the boxes has been incorporated into the narrative text. The text is now set in single-column, which allows for a more spacious layout. Each chapter now opens with a two-page spread that features an illustration embodying the core theme of each chapter.

CONTENT CHANGES

Within each part, materials have been updated, revised, and added. Examples of some of the more notable changes and additions include: a discussion of the fossils of early hominids discovered in Chad; additional materials on early urbanization in India and Africa; new evaluations for the decline of the Roman empire; consideration of the Gnostic gospels and their significance in understanding early Christianity; the assimilation of Islam into African empires in the

10th through the fifteenth centuries. Part Five, on world trade, 1000 to 1776 and Part Six, on migration and demography, 1200–1750, have been restructured into a single unit on the movement of goods, ideas, and people. The Scientific Revolution of the sixteenth, seventeenth, and eighteenth century gets more coverage. The Industrial Revolution has been placed into a wider context, more clearly setting the stage for the events that began to unfold in late eighteenth-century England. As noted, the twentieth century is now given expanded coverage, and divided into two chronological periods, each with its own theme. The region-by-region analysis presented in the closing chapters of the first two editions has been replaced by a more thematic consideration of global issues in the late twentieth century, more in keeping with the thematic approach of the rest of the text. Throughout the book increased prominence has been given to issues of gender.

In updating the book to cover most recent events, new materials have been added to reflect new developments, for example: the increasing importance of China in world trade; of religious/cultural militancy in India; of economic recovery in Southeast Asia and decline in parts of Latin America; of the global economy; of responses to the global AIDS epidemic, especially in Africa; of breakthroughs and cautions in cloning and applications of genome research; of the attacks on America of September 11, 2001, the American response; and global reactions to both the attacks and the American responses.

Chapter-by-Chapter Revisions

Chapter 1 incorporates the results of the most recent archaeological research, and new information on the discovery of a fossil skull in Chad that may extend hominid evolution 2.5 million years back in time

Chapter 2 includes improved coverage on the Sumerians and their contributions to the development of early civilizations.

Chapter 3 has been dramatically reorganized to treat various aspects of ancient Egyptian history to fit the thematic trajectory of the chapters. It contains new material on daily life and an extended analysis of gender roles in society. Much of the material previously included in this chapter has been moved to Chapter 5 on the rise of empires.

Chapter 4 has been revised to better connect themes within the Parts. In keeping with the overall desire to improve coverage of gender issues, more information is supplied on women in Chinese societies. The chapter now also contains more information on the Zhou.

Chapter 5 has been reorganized to include the Egyptian empire as among the early empires. The section on Alexander the Great has been brought up-to-date and expanded. In addition the coverage of gender has been improved.

Chapter 6 has been revised for improved readability and also includes a more detailed discussion of gender in the ancient world. It also includes fresh material on the decline of the Roman Empire.

Chapter 7 has been reorganized to present a clear discussion of China's earliest ideologists. It also has improved coverage of gender.

Chapter 8 contains a much clearer discussion of Indian culture, and includes additional thoughts on the comparison of different imperial systems.

Chapter 10 adds new materials on the controversial Gnostic gospels and their significance for the interpretation of Christianity.

Chapter 11 clarifies the chronology of the early caliphate and the wars of succession. It includes a reorganized and expanded section on Islam, which more clearly highlights gender issues in Islam and compares them with other religions.

Chapter 12 has been thoroughly revised. It is far more comprehensive on trade networks, and their significance, especially sea-borne networks.

Chapter 13 has been thoroughly revised to examine more fully the background to European overseas expansion. Medieval European history has been moved here and conceptually placed in a global context, including the decline of Mediterranean trade and the rise of Atlantic exploration. It also looks at the Medieval European revival of trade and its relationship to Renaissance ideas, and new worldviews in general.

Chapter 14 has been completely revised, with more attention to the nation-state and fuller discussion of "the great divergence," analyzing the economic restructuring of the world in which western Europe rose to prominence over China.

Chapter 15 has been restructured for greater clarity and clearer comparison of the various kinds of population movements, free, indentured, enslaved, settler, and conquest.

Chapter 16 adds more extensive coverage of the scientific revolution and clarifies issues of comparison among the several major political revolutions of the time.

Chapter 17 expands the discussion of the historical background to the industrial revolution, adds information on indentured labor, reorders the material for greater clarity and stronger indication of the connection among economic, political, and social relationships.

Chapter 18 has been restructured and updated for more careful consideration of the relationships between capitalism, the industrial revolution, imperialism, and responses to the imperial outreach.

Chapter 19 has been extensively revised and contains an enhanced discussion of the contests over the uses of technology. Greatly expanded coverage of World War I and the global depression, and their significance. The chronology has been restructured for greater clarity.

Chapter 20 includes extensive revisions to cover the ideologies of the combatants in World War II, the war and its consequences, including the early confrontations of the cold war.

Chapter 21 has been thoroughly revised to cover the cold war, the end of colonialism, the rise of newly independent nations, and the creation of a third world bloc.

Chapter 22 contains additional materials on Mao's planning, on Gandhi's work on behalf of industrial unions, and on problems and hazards of technology.

Chapter 23 is a new thematically-based chapter covering key identity issues of the late-twentieth and early twenty-first centuries, especially those created by the end of the cold war and the increasing network of economic globalization, but also considering the cultural identities that are emerging as a result of these changes.

Chapter 24 is a new chapter of brief case studies of contemporary themes in five geographical areas: the integration of the European Union, the dissolution of Yugoslavia, continuing warfare between Israelis and Palestinians, the Truth and Reconciliation Commission in South Africa, and the economic revival of contemporary China. Also coverage of global criminal networks.

PEDAGOGICAL ENHANCEMENTS

This edition retains many of the pedagogical features of the previous editions, including source boxes and timelines. We have introduced several new pedagogical features including a list of key topics at the beginning of each chapter, chapter review questions at the end of each chapter, one–two interactive maps per chapter, a running glossary of items highlighted in the text that appears in the margins as well as at the back of the book, and "Turning Points" essays at the end of each part use visual sources to highlight the key themes in each part. Each of these features is designed to make the text more accessible to students. Collectively, these materials provide a rich, comprehensive and challenging introduction to the study of world history and the methods and key interpretations of its historians.

- Substantially revised, the **Introduction** describes the key themes of the text and the methods historians use to practice their craft.
- The timelines have been completely redesigned to make the information easier to read and are now called **At a Glance**.
- New **Turning Points** essays illustrate visually the connections between one part and the next. In some cases, the **Turning Points** tell their own story as well, notably in the bridge into the twentieth century that uses the modern Olympic Games to illustrate and introduce many of the issues that are to follow.
- The **How Do We Know?** features have been separated from the text and placed in color-coded boxes. There are usually two in every chapter. Each **How Do We Know?** feature aims to help the student examine primary source materials, and each one ends with pertinent, thought-provoking questions.
- Each chapter ends with a discussion of legacies to the future, namely, **What Difference Does It Make?**
- This edition also continues the emphasis on the use of **Primary Sources**, for these are the kinds of materials from which the historical record is argued and fashioned. Each chapter usually has two primary sources, clearly highlighted in color-coded feature boxes.
- The **Bibliography** for each chapter has been thoroughly revised and up-dated to reflect current scholarship. In addition, each item in the bibliography is now annotated to direct students with their reading.
- Each chapter begins with a list of **Key Topics** that provide an overview of the chapter.
- Each chapter now ends with **Review Questions** to help students to re-examine the material. The questions are also useful for classroom debates and could serve as essay topics.
- The introduction to each of the eight **Parts** now includes more specific key references to the chapters that follow.
- **World History Documents CD-ROM.** Bound into every new copy of this textbook is a free World History Documents CD-ROM. This is a powerful resource for research and additional reading that contains more than 200 primary source documents central to World History. Each document provides essay questions that are linked directly to a website where short-essay answers can be submitted online or printed out. A complete list of documents on the CD-ROM is found at the end of the text.

Maps and Illustrations

To aid the student, extensive, clear and informative charts and maps represent information graphically and geographically. Several new maps have been added to provide better geographical context in the narrative. New to this edition one map in most chapter is now interactive. A wide range of illustrations, many in color, supplement the written word. For the third edition we have added more than 130 new illustrations.

One element that has not changed in this new edition is the mental image I keep before me of my own children—albeit at a younger age, since by now their knowledge in so many fields surpasses my own—and of my students. I write for them.

ACKNOWLEDGEMENTS FOR THE THIRD EDITION

Prentice Hall has taken an active role in the preparation of this edition. The wise interventions of Charlyce Jones-Owen, Editorial Director; the copy-editing of Marty Green and Elaine Silverstein, Developmental Editors; the content editing of Nancy Fitch, Professor of History at California State University, Fullerton; and the advice compiled from many external reviews by Charles Cavaliere, Executive Editor, have all resulted in many of the improvements evident in this edition. Laurence King Publishers in London continue to provide the excellent work in the production of the text and I am deeply indebted to them. Lee Ripley Greenfield, Director of College and Fine Arts, has assured that this transoceanic venture has proceeded reasonably smoothly, aided by Lesley Henderson, Senior Editor, Richard Mason, Senior Managing Editor, Nick Newton, Designer, and Emma Brown, Picture Researcher. Without them, there would be no third edition, and I am grateful for their patient and firm guidance and wise diplomacy. I have also benefited immensely from the kindness of many teachers and students who have used this book and took time to write to me with their advice and suggestions. I thank them and hope that they will see the benefits of their experience and wisdom in this edition.

Grateful acknowledgments are also extended to the following reviewers of the third edition: Wayne Ackerson, Salisbury University; Ewa Bacon, Lewis University, Illinois; Maurice Borrero, St. John's University; Stuart Borsch, Assumption College; Kenneth M. Chauvin, Appalachian State University; Jorge Cañizares-Esguerra, State University of New York, Buffalo; Nupur Chaudhuri, Texas Southern University; Mark Gunn, Meridian Community College; Phyllis Jestice, University of Southern Mississippi; Frank Karpiel, College of Charleston; David Kenley, Marshall University; Ane Lintvedt, McDonogh School; Angus Lockyer, Wake Forest University; John Langdon, University of Alberta; Louis McDermott, California Maritime Academy; Susan Maneck, Jackson State University; Michael Pavkovic, Hawaii Pacific University.

ABOUT THE AUTHOR

Howard Spodek received his B.A. degree from Columbia University (1963), majoring in history and specializing in Columbia's newly designed program in Asian Studies. He received his M.A. (1966) and Ph.D. (1972) from the University of Chicago, majoring in history and specializing in India. His first trip to India was on a Fulbright Fellowship, 1964–66, and he has spent a total of some seven years studying and teaching in India. He has also traveled widely throughout the United States, Latin America, Asia, Africa, and Europe. He has been a faculty member at Temple University since 1972, appointed Full Professor in 1984. He was awarded Temple's Great Teacher award in 1993.

Spodek's work in world history began in 1988 when he became Academic Director of a comprehensive, innovative program working with teachers in the School District of Philadelphia to improve their knowledge base in world history and facilitate a rewriting of the world history program in the schools. Immediately following this program, he became principal investigator of a program that brought college professors and high school teachers together to reconsider, revise, and, in many cases, initiate the teaching of world history in several of the colleges and universities in the Philadelphia metropolitan area. Those projects led directly to the writing of the first edition of the current text (1997).

Howard Spodek has published extensively on India, including *Urban-Rural Integration in Regional Development* (1976); *Urban Form and Meaning in South-East Asia* (editor, with Doris Srinivasan, 1993); and a wide array of articles, especially on urbanization—and on women's development issues—in India. He has written on his experiences with world history faculty at the college and high school levels in articles in The History Teacher (1992, 1995). In addition he wrote and produced the documentary film, *Ahmedabad* (1983). He has received funding for his research, writing, teaching, and film from Fulbright, the National Endowment for the Humanities, the National Science Foundation, the American Institute of Indian Studies, and the Smithsonian Institution.

INTRODUCTION: THE WORLD THROUGH HISTORIANS' EYES

THEMES AND TURNING POINTS

Most readers of this textbook have probably not taken many courses in history. Few are (thus far) planning to major in history, much less become professional historians. A lot therefore rides on this single text. It must present a general introduction to world history that interests, engages, and even fascinates the reader through its subject matter, its narrative, and its analysis. It must open the eyes, minds, and hearts of students who come to this course believing that history is only about the past, and mostly a matter of learning names, dates, and places. It must introduce them to the methods and "habits of mind" of the historian. It must demonstrate how knowledge of the contents and methods of world history—and of this book in particular—will broaden their horizons and also have practical usefulness.

"Usefulness" is not always associated with the study of history. Indeed, in everyday conversation, the phrase "that's history" means that an event is no longer significant. It may once have been important, but it is not now. From this point of view, "history" is a record of people and events that are dead and gone. For the historian, however, the opposite is true. The past has made us who we are, and continues to influence who we are becoming. In this sense, the past is not dead, just as people whom we have known personally and who have influenced our lives are not "dead," even though they may no longer be with us. This text will highlight ways in which the past continues to have profound effects on the present and future. It will help us understand who we have become.

History does not provide specific answers to today's problems, but it does provide examples and case studies that help us improve our thinking. Generals study past wars to understand how modern battles may be fought; economists study past periods of growth and recession to understand how we can encourage the former and avoid the latter. Understanding the ways in which families and relationships have functioned in the past helps us find ways to make our own families and relationships more satisfying today.

World history gives us the largest possible canvas on which to carry out these studies. We cannot, however, study everything that ever happened. We must choose what to include and what to exclude. We must choose strategies that maximize our ability to understand our lives today in the context of the whole range of human experience.

In this text we choose two fundamental organizing principles as our framework for the study and teaching of world history. First, we choose a series of eight chronological turning points, each of which changed the patterns of human life. Second, we explain the importance of each of these changes in terms of the new themes they introduced into human experience. These two elements—chronological turning points and interpretive themes—go together.

This text is organized around eight turning points and themes. Others might also have been chosen, but these turning points represent eight of the most important transformations in human life. The thematic analysis of these turning points encourages students to grapple with the origins and continuing presence of eight of the most significant themes in life: the biological and cultural qualities that make humans the special creatures that we are; the settlements we create and live in; the political power that we assemble and sometimes oppose; the religious systems through which many people find meaning in their individual lives and communities; the movement of trade and people that has linked the peoples of the world ever more closely, sometimes in cooperation, sometimes in competition, and sometimes in conflict; the political, industrial, and social revolutions, especially of the seventeenth through the twentieth centuries; the continuing technological developments that continue to re-shape our world; and the quest for personal and group identity, so prevalent in our own times.

Because real life does not fit neatly into exact chronological periods, there will be significant overlap among the turning points. Readers may argue that the themes are also not limited to single chronological periods. For example, political regimes, religious systems, and economic organizations appear at all times in history. This argument is, of course, correct: "everything is related to everything else," and in reality each chronological period will include several themes. We have chosen, however, to highlight particular themes in particular historical periods so that students will understand these themes more thoroughly and learn to employ them as tools of analysis in forming their own understanding of our world.

CHRONOLOGICAL TURNING POINTS AND PART THEMES

PART ONE. TURNING POINT: The emergence of the first humans. Biological and early cultural evolution, 5 million B.C.E. to 10,000 B.C.E.
THEME: Historians and anthropologists search for and interpret artifacts and records to determine what is human about humans.

PART TWO. TURNING POINT: Creating settlements, first agricultural villages and, later, cities. 10,000 B.C.E. to 1000 C.E.
THEME: Settlements—villages, towns, and cities—are created to meet community needs.

PART THREE. TURNING POINT: The creation of early empires, 2000 B.C.E. to 1100 C.E., from Sargon of Assyria through Alexander the Great, Qin and Han China, Republican and Imperial Rome, and India of the Mauryas and Guptas.
THEME: Imperial political power is generated, increased, consolidated, and resisted.

PART FOUR. TURNING POINT: The creation and diffusion of global religions: Judaism, Christianity, Islam, Hinduism, and Buddhism. 2500 B.C.E. to 1500 C.E.
THEME: Spiritual feelings are mobilized into powerful religious systems, some of which attain global scope.

PART FIVE. Global movement of goods and people, and the linking of continents; 1000–1776.
THEME: The flows of goods and people are channeled into global networks.

PART SIX. TURNING POINT: Revolutions, both political and industrial, 1640–1914.
THEME: Vast, abrupt changes in political and economic systems create new social values and systems affecting individuals, families, and communities.

PART SEVEN. TURNING POINT: Technological change and its human control; 1914 to 1980.
THEME: New technological systems—both simple and complex—are instituted to improve or threaten human life.

PART EIGHT. TURNING POINT: The formation of new identities; global, national, regional, cultural, and personal, 1975 to the present.
THEME: Increasingly tight-knit webs of communication, trade, and power bring diverse individuals and groups into contact, forcing them to constantly reconsider their identities.

Global Scope

The scope of this text, and of each turning point and theme within it, is global. For example, the study of the industrial revolution in Europe includes its funding—in part—from the wealth that poured into Europe from its New World conquests of people, land, gold, and silver, and from African slave labor; its global extensions in the form of imperialism in Asia, Africa, Australia, and Latin America; and the interactions of colonizers and colonized in response to the new opportunities and challenges.

SOCIAL SCIENCE METHODS, COMPARATIVE HISTORY, AND THE STUDY OF VALUES

Comparative History and the Methods of the Social Sciences

The global, interactive, and comparative format of this text provides also an introduction to social science methodology. The methods of the social sciences are embedded in the structure of the book. Because each part is built on comparisons among different regions of the world, the reader will become accustomed to posing hypotheses based on general principles and to testing them against comparative data from around the world.

This method of moving back and forth between general theory and specific case study, testing the degree to which the general theory and the specific data fit each other, is at the heart of the social sciences. For example, in Part 2 we will explore the general characteristics of cities, and then examine how well the generalizations hold up through case studies of various cities around the world. In Part 3 we will seek general theories of the rise and fall of early empires based on comparisons of China, Rome, and India. In Part 4 we will search for commonalities among religious systems through a survey of five world religions. In Part 8 we begin with an analysis of new issues of political and cultural identity and then examine their significance in a series of six brief case studies in different regions of the world. These comparisons enable us more clearly to think about and to understand the workings of cities, empires, and religions not only of the past, but also of our own time and place.

Multiple Perspectives

The text highlights the importance of multiple perspectives in studying and interpreting history. The answers we get—the narrative histories we write—are based on the questions we ask. Each part suggests a variety of questions that can be asked about the historical event that is being studied and a variety of interpretations that can emerge in the process of answering them. Often there is more than one "correct" way of understanding change over time and its significance. Different questions will trigger very different research and very different answers. For example, in Part 5 we ask about the stages and processes by which Western commercial power began to surpass that of Asia. This question presupposes the fact that at earlier times Asian power had been superior and raises the additional questions why it declined and why European power advanced. In Part 7 we ask how the industrial revolution affected and changed relationships between men and women; this question will yield different research and a different narrative from questions about, for example, women's contributions to industrialization, which is a useful question, but a different one.

Through the systematic study of the past in this thematic, comparative framework, students will gain tools for understanding and making their own place in the world today. They will not only learn how the peoples of the world have gotten to where we are, but also consider the possibility of setting out in new directions for new goals.

Evaluating Values

This form of analysis will also introduce a study of values. In order to understand the choices made by people in the past, we must attempt to understand the values that informed their thinking and actions. These values may be similar to, or quite different from, our own. In order to understand the interpretations introduced by later historians, we must understand the historians' values as well. These, too, may be similar to, or different from, our own. Historians usually had personal perspectives from which they viewed the past, and these perspectives influenced their interpretations. Finally, in order for student-readers to form their own understanding of the past, and to make it more useful in their own lives, they must also see how their own values influence their evaluation of past events.

For most of the past century, social scientists spoke of creating "value free" disciplines. Today, most scholars believe that this is impossible. We cannot be "value free." On the contrary, we must attempt to understand the values that have inspired historical actors, previous historians, and ourselves. Coming to an understanding of the values of others – historical actors and historians who have studied them – will help readers to recognize and formulate their own values, a central part of a liberal arts education.

HISTORY AND IDENTITY

History is among the most passionate and bitterly contentious of disciplines because most people and groups locate a large part of their identity in their history. Americans may take pride in their nationality, for example, for having created a representative, constitutional democracy that has endured for over 200 years (see Part 7). Yet they may be saddened, shamed, or perhaps incensed by the existence of 250 years of slavery followed by inequalities in race relations continuing to the present (see Part 6). Christians may take pride in two thousand years of missions of compassion toward the poor and downtrodden, yet they may be saddened, shamed, or even incensed by an almost equally long record of religious warfare and of persecution of those whose beliefs differed from their own (see Part 4).

As various ethnic, religious, class, and gender groups represent themselves in public political life, they seek not only to understand the history that has made them what they are, but also to persuade others to understand that history in the same way, to create a new consciousness. Feminist historians, for example, find in their reading of history that patriarchy, a system of male-created and male-dominated institutions, has subordinated women. From available data and their interpretation of them, they attempt to weave a persuasive argument that will win over others to their position.

Some will not be persuaded. They may not even agree that women have been subordinated to men, but argue that both genders have shared in a great deal of suffering (and joy) throughout history (see Parts 1 and 7). The historical debates over the origins and evolution of gender relationships evoke strong emotions because people's self-image, the image of their group, and the perceptions others hold of them are all at stake. And the stakes can be high.

CONTROL OF HISTORICAL RECORDS

From earliest times, control over the historical records and their interpretation has been fundamental to control over people's thoughts. The first emperor of China, Qin

Shihuang (r. 221–207 B.C.E.), the man who built the concept of a united China that has lasted until today attempted to destroy all knowledge of the past:

> He then abolished the ways of ancient sage kings and put to the torch the writings of the Hundred Schools in an attempt to keep the people in ignorance. He demolished the walls of major cities and put to death men of fame and talent. (deBary, I: 229).

Lenin addressing troops in Sverdlov Square, Moscow, May 5, 1920. The leaders of the Russian Communist revolution crudely refashioned the historical record to suit the wishes of the winners. After Lenin's death in 1924, his second-in-command Leon Trotsky (pictured sitting on the podium in the left-hand picture) lost to Josef Stalin the bitter power struggle that ensued. Not only was Trotsky banished from the Soviet Union, but so was his appearance in the official archives (see doctored picture below).

So wrote Jia Yi (201–168? B.C.E.), poet and statesman of the succeeding Han dynasty. Shihuang wished that only his interpretation of China's past, and his place in it, be preserved. Later intellectuals condemned his actions—but the lost records were irretrievable (see Part 3).

In similar fashion, the first great historian of the Christian Church, Eusebius of Caesarea (c. 260–339) in his accounts of the early Christians in the Roman Empire, chose carefully to include elements that he considered of "profit" to his mission, and to exclude those that were not.

> It is not for us to describe their miserable vicissitudes [in persecution] … just as it is not a part of our task to leave on record their faction-fights and their unnatural conduct towards each other, prior to the persecution. That is why we have decided to say no more about them than suffices for us to justify God's Judgment … We shall rather set forth in our whole narrative only what may be of profit, first, to our own times, and then to later times. (MacMullen, p. 6).

Historical Revision

Interpretations of events may become highly contested and revised even after several centuries have passed. Colonial governments seeking to control subject peoples sometimes argued that the conquered people were so backward that they benefited from the conquest. Later historians, with more distance and more detachment, were often less kind to the colonizers. Some 1900 years ago the historian Tacitus was writing bitterly of the ancient Romans in their conquest of England: "Robbery, butchery, rapine, the liars call Empire; they create a desolation and call it peace" (*Agricola*, 30)

In our own era, the many nations that have won their freedom from colonialism echo similar resentments against their foreign rulers and set out to revise the historical record in keeping with their newly won political freedom. Jawaharlal Nehru, the first prime minister of independent India (1947–64), wrote in 1944 from the prison cell in which he had been imprisoned for his leadership of his country's independence movement:

> British accounts of India's history, more especially of what is called the British period, are bitterly resented. History is almost always written by the victors and conquerors and gives their viewpoint; or, at any rate, the victors' version is given prominence and holds the field. (Nehru, p. 289)

Philip Curtin, historian of Africa and of slavery, elaborates an equally critical view of European colonial accounts of Africa's history:

> African history was seriously neglected until the 1950s … The colonial period in Africa left an intellectual legacy to be overcome, just as it had in other parts of the world. … The colonial imprint on historical knowledge emerged in the nineteenth and early twentieth centuries as a false perspective, a Eurocentric view of world history created at a time of European domination … Even where Europeans never ruled, European knowledge was often accepted as modern knowledge, including aspects of the Eurocentric historiography. (Curtin, p. 54)

Instead, Curtin continues, a proper historiography must:

> show the African past from an African point of view … For Africans, to know about the past of their own societies is a form of self-knowledge crucial to a sense of identity in a diverse and rapidly changing world. A recovery of African history has been an important part of African development over recent decades. (p. 54)

Religious and ethnic groups, too, may seek to control historical records. In 1542, the Roman Catholic Church established an Index of Prohibited Books to ban writings it considered heretical. (The Spanish Inquisition, ironically, stored away many records that later scholars used to recreate its history and the history of those it persecuted.) More recently, despite all the evidence of the Holocaust, the murder of 6 million Jews by the Nazi government of Germany during World War II, a few people have claimed that the murders never took place. They deny the existence of such racial and religious hatred and of its consequences, and ignore deep-seated problems in the relationships between majority and minority populations.

The significance of the voyages of Columbus was once celebrated uncritically in the United States in tribute both to "the Admiral of the Ocean Sea" himself and to the courage and enterprise of the European explorers and early settlers who brought their civilizations to the Americas. In South America, however, where Native American Indians are more numerous and people of European ancestry often form a smaller proportion of the population, the celebrations have been far more ambivalent, muted, and meditative.

In 1992, on the 500th anniversary of Columbus' first voyage to the Americas, altogether new and more sobering elements entered the commemoration ceremonies, even in the United States. The negative consequences of Columbus' voyages, previously ignored, were now recalled and emphasized: the death of up to 90 percent of the Native American Indian population in the century after the arrival of Europeans; the Atlantic slave trade, initiated by trade in Indian slaves; and the exploitation of the natural resources of a continent until then little touched by humans. The ecological consequences, which are only now beginning to receive more attention, were not all negative, however. They included the fruitful exchange of natural products between the hemispheres. Horses, wheat, and sheep were introduced to the Americas; potatoes, tomatoes, and corn to Afro-Eurasia. Unfortunately, the spread of syphilis was one of

Indians giving Hernán Cortés a headband, from Diego Duran's *Historia de las Indias*, **1547.** Bent on conquest and plunder, the bearded Spaniard Cortés arrived on the Atlantic coast of Mexico in 1519. His forces sacked the ancient city of Tenochtitlán, decimated the Aztec people and imprisoned their chief, Montezuma, before proclaiming the Aztec Empire "New Spain." By stark contrast, this bland Spanish watercolor shows local tribesmen respectfully paying homage to the invader as if he were a god; in ignoring the brutality exercised in the colonization of South America, the artist is, in effect, "rewriting" history. (*Biblioteca National, Madrid*)

the consequences of the exchange; scholars disagree on who transmitted this disease to whom (see Part 5).

Thugs sometimes gain control of national histories. George Orwell's satirical novel *Animal Farm* (published in 1945) presented an allegory in which pigs come to rule a farm. Among their many acts of domination, the pigs seize control of the historical records of the farm animals' failed experiment in equality and impose their own official interpretation, which justifies their own rule. The rewriting of history and suppression of alternative records by the Communist Party of the former Soviet Union between 1917 and 1989 reveals the bitter truth underlying Orwell's satire (see Part 8).

Although the American experience is much different, in the United States, too, records have been suppressed. Scholars are still trying to use the Freedom of Information Act to pry open sealed diplomatic archives. (Most official archives everywhere have twenty-, thirty-, or forty-year rules governing the waiting period before certain sensitive records are opened to the public. These rules, which are designed to protect living people and contemporary policies from excessive scrutiny, are the general rule everywhere.)

WHAT DO WE KNOW? HOW DO WE KNOW IT? WHAT DIFFERENCE DOES IT MAKE:

So, historical records are not simply lists of events. They are the means by which individuals and groups develop their interpretations of these events. All people develop their own interpretations of past events; historians do it professionally. Because interpretations differ, there is no single historical record, but various narrations of events, each told from a different perspective. Therefore the study of history is intimately linked to the study of values.

To construct their interpretations, historians examine the values—the motives, wishes, desires, visions—of people of the past. In interpreting those values, historians must confront and engage their own values, comparing and contrasting these values with those of people in the past. For example, they ask how various people viewed slavery, or child labor, or education, or art and music in societies of the past. In the back of their minds they compare and contrast those older values with values held by various people today and especially with their own personal values. They ask: How and why have values changed or remained the same through the passage of time? Why, and in what ways, do my values compare and contrast with values of the past? By learning to pose such questions, students will be better equipped to discover and create their own place in the continuing movement of human history. This text, therefore consistently addresses three fundamental questions:

> What Do We Know?
> How Do We Know It?
> What Difference Does It Make?

Even when historians agree on which events are most significant, they may differ in evaluating why the events are significant. One historian's interpretation of events may be diametrically opposed to another's. For example, virtually all historians agree that part of the significance of World War II lay in its new policies and technologies of destruction: nuclear weapons in battle and genocide behind the lines. In terms of interpretation, pessimists might stress the continuing menace of these legacies of terror, while optimists might argue that the very violence of the war and the Holocaust triggered a search for limits on nuclear arms and greater tolerance for minorities. With each success in nuclear arms limitation and in toleration, the optimists seem more persuasive; with each spread of nuclear weapons and each outbreak of genocide, the pessimists seem to win.

The study of history is thus an interpretation of significance as well as an investigation of facts. The significance of events is determined by their consequences. Sometimes we do not know what the consequences are; or the consequences may not have run their course; or we may differ in our assessments of the consequences. This play between past events and their current consequences is what historian E.H. Carr had in mind in his famous description of history as "an unending dialogue between the present and the past" (Carr, p. 30).

TOOLS

The study of history requires many tools, and this text includes most of the principal ones:

- Primary sources are accounts that were produced at the time an event occurred. Those who produced them were eyewitnesses with direct knowledge of what happened. The core of historical study is an encounter with primary materials, usually documents, but including other artifacts—for example, letters, diaries, newspaper accounts, photographs, and artwork. Every chapter in this text includes representative primary materials.
- Visual images, a strong feature of this book, complement the written text, offering non-verbal "texts" of the time. These are often central pieces of evidence. For example, in Chapter 9 we illustrate the influence of Hinduism and Buddhism in Southeast Asia through the temple architecture of the region.
- Maps place events in space and in geographical relationship to one another.
- Chronological timelines situate events in time and sequence.
- Brief charts supply summaries as well as contextual information on topics such as religion, science, and trade.

Review Questions

- Please review the eight themes and turning points selected here. From what you already know of world history, do these seem well-chosen? Would you select different or additional themes and turning points for your account? If so, which ones and why?
- Examine how one of the values in which you believe has come from historical experience, either your own experience or that of relatives and friends, or the experience of groups to which you belong.
- When you tell other people about yourself, what "records" from your past do you highlight? Which ones do you leave out of the story, or even conceal? Are there any that you would like to destroy? Can you destroy them? How does the audience you are speaking to affect your choice of "records"?

Suggested Readings

BASIC, COMPREHENSIVE, INTRODUCTORY MATERIALS

Carr, E.H. *What Is History?* (Harmondsworth, Middlesex: Penguin Books, 1964). A classic introduction to the study of history and historiography from the point of view of a master.

Tosh, John. *The Pursuit of History: Aims, Methods, and New Directions in the Study of Modern History*, 2nd ed. (London: Longman, 1991). Excellent, comprehensive introduction to the study of history, with discussions of many different kinds of historical study, their methods and purposes.

MORE SPECIALIZED MATERIALS

Bennett, Judith M. "Medieval Women, Modern Women: Across the Great Divide," in David Aers, ed., *Culture and History, 1350–1600: Essays on English Communities, Identities, and Writing* (New York: Harvester Wheatsheaf, 1992), 147–75. Discusses continuity, in contrast to change, in women's history.

Curtin, Philip D. "Recent Trends in African Historiography and Their Contribution to History in General," in Joseph Ki-Zerbo, ed., *General History of Africa, Vol. I: Methodology and African Pre-History* (Berkeley: University of California Press, 1981), 54–71. An excellent introduction to this fine series commissioned by the United Nations.

deBary, William Theodore, et al., comps. *Sources of Chinese Tradition*. 2nd ed. 2 vols. (New York: Columbia University Press, 1999, 2000). THE anthology of materials on the subject.

Lerner, Gerda. *The Creation of Patriarchy* (New York: Oxford University Press, 1986). A controversial study of patriarchy in ancient Mesopotamia by a distinguished historian of the United States. Lerner re-tooled to study this fundamental feminist question.

MacMullen, Ramsay. *Christianizing the Roman Empire (A.D. 100–400)* (New Haven: Yale University Press, 1984). Excellent analysis of the factors leading to Christianity's success in the Roman Empire. Gives major role to government support.

Nehru, Jawaharlal. *The Discovery of India* (Delhi: Oxford University Press, 1989). A history of his country, written in jail during the freedom struggle by the man who became India's first prime minister.

Orwell, George. *Animal Farm* (New York: Harcourt, Brace, 1946). A classic satire on government by thugs; aimed at the USSR.

Tacitus, Cornelius. *Tacitus' Agricola, Germany, and Dialogue on Orators*, trans. Herbert W. Benario (Norman: University of Oklahoma Press, 1991). One of ancient Rome's great historians who understood the cruelty underlying the power of empire.

Religion to Trade

Moving from the theme of religion in Part 4 to the theme of trade in Part 5 may seem a big jump. Are not matters of the spirit quite separate from matters of commerce? In Christianity, did not both the Gospel of Matthew (6:24) and of Luke (16:13) quote Jesus as saying, "No servant can be the slave of two masters … You cannot serve God and Money"? Did not Matthew quote Jesus as saying, "It is easier for a camel to pass thorough the eye of a needle than for a rich man to enter the kingdom of God" (Matthew 19: 23-24). Christian clergy were sworn to lives of poverty.

As the Church became wealthy at various times in its history, reformers lamented its departure from the ascetic standards of its early years. Martin Luther proclaimed his reformation of the Church in the mid-fifteenth century in part as a protest against the Church's sale of "indulgences," documents granting forgiveness of sin in exchange for donations to the Church. Luther argued that money could not take the place of honest penance.

Lucas Cranach the Elder, The Pope's Selling of Indulgences, 1521. Woodcut.

A bishop blessing the annual market, St. Denis, near Paris, 14th century. Miniature. (*Bibliothèque Nationale, Paris*)

Church might bless their economic interests. See for example the illustration (*left*) depicting a bishop blessing the annual market at St. Denis, near Paris.

Other religions generally began with a more accommodating view of the relationship of religion and trade. The Book of Genesis portrays Judaism's founder, Abraham, as a semi-nomadic owner of flocks of sheep and goats, and a man who bargained actively in purchasing a burial site for his wife. In more systemic terms, the rabbis interpreted the Biblical injunction against taking interest as applying to loans among friends and family members; they devised methods of allowing modest interest to be taken on commercial loans. Islam, which views Abraham also as the first Muslim, worked out similar practical methods of discriminating between personal loans and business loans. Islam's great Prophet, Muhammad, was himself a businessman married to a businesswoman. Many mosques are constructed with business properties adjacent to them, the rent of which goes to support the mosque. See the illustration below.

Large and popular religions must, however, have some flexibility in their belief systems, and we find in Christianity many examples of the accommodation of spiritual and financial interests. The Church became wealthy because many people tithed, they gave ten percent of their earnings to the Church. In exchange, the

H. Griffiths, *Mosque of Bajazet with the Seraskier's Gate*, Istanbul, c. 1850. Engraving. (*Stapleton Collection, England*)

Hinduism designates the pursuit of "artha," wealth and power, as an important life goal, and sets aside the longest stage of the life cycle to the practicalities of administering a household. One whole caste category, the vaishyas, is composed of business people. In parts of India, especially Gujarat, at New Year's time, businessmen invite brahmin priests to bless their account books for the coming year in an elaborate ceremony called chopada puja, or the worship of the account books. The illustration on this page indicates that as Hindu businessmen have traveled overseas in modern times, they have continued this custom of integrating business practice with religious ritual.

His Holiness Pramukh Swami Maharaj sanctifying books of account during the Chopada Puja ceremony at the Shri Swaminarayan Mandir, Neasden, London.

QUESTIONS

1. To what degree have religious and business leaders accommodated one another – or failed to find such accommodation?
2. What have been the terms of the accommodation?
3. How have the members of each group benefited or lost out from the accommodation or the failure of accommodation?

5

The Movement of Goods and Peoples 1000–1776

CHANNELS OF COMMUNICATION: THE EXCHANGE OF COMMODITIES, DISEASES, AND CULTURE

We have frequently noted the importance of trade in regional and world economies. Trade linked the oldest centers of urban civilization—Mesopotamia, the Indus valley, and the Nile valley—as we noted in Part 2. In Part 3 we saw that empires sought to protect the principal transportation routes and that emperors sought to capture their profits. In Part 4 we noted that world religions spread along the same routes as trade and that religions were often carried by merchants. Both Buddhism and Islam spread to eastern Asia via the overland silk routes, and to Southeast Asia via the shipping lanes of the Indian Ocean. The exchange of ideas and cultures went hand-in-hand with the exchange of commodities.

In this Part trade is our central focus. In Chapter 12 we explore the role of traders and their relationships with political rulers from about 1100 to about 1500. We study the geography of the principal trade routes. They were not yet fully unified, and certainly not yet global, but they were linked together and capable of delivering goods from one end of Afro-Eurasia to the other. The transportation networks of those days required considerable coordination by merchants from various parts of the world, and considerable off-loading and re-loading of merchandise to move it from one region to the next—but they could deliver the goods.

Epidemics sometimes accompanied trade missions. The most devastating of them, the "Black Plague" of the mid-fourteenth century, wiped out more than one-third of the population in many places from China to western Europe, dramatically restructuring relationships of wealth and power in its wake. Security was critically important along the trade routes, as were the Mongol descendants of Chinggis Khan in providing that security along the silk routes of Central Asia. We read personal accounts of great traders and travelers like Marco Polo and Ibn Battuta. We close with an examination of the expansion of trade in Europe, the growing importance of traders, the resurrection of cities and trade routes and the cultural renaissance that these movements inspired.

Chapter 13 explores some of the oceans and seas of the world. For thousands of years, the Indian Ocean, the Red Sea, the Persian Gulf, the Arabian Sea, the Bay of Bengal the Mediterranean Sea, and the South China Sea, had been principal highways of seaborne trade. But the Atlantic and Pacific Oceans had not. Some evidence suggests that an occasional, rare voyage might have crossed these vast bodies of water, but establishing regular contact awaited Columbus' four voyages across the Atlantic 1492–1504, and Magellan's circumnavigation of the earth, 1519–22. The chapter charts the background of the voyages that provided the first continuous linkage of the three continents of North and South America, and Australia,

Marco Polo, from *Romance of Alexander*, c. 1340. The great world traveler is shown setting sail for China from Venice in 1271. Europe was eager for news of the Mongol Empire—potential allies against the ancient Muslim enemy—and a steady stream of intrepid merchants and missionaries brought back amazing reports of the Khan's court. The exotic reminiscences of Marco Polo are, however, by far the most famous. (*Bodleian Library, Oxford*)

to the core area of Afro-Eurasia and examines the astonishing results of these voyages.

Chapter 14 describes trade becoming global and the rulers of nation-states encouraging their merchants to participate in it. The Spanish and Portuguese came first, followed by the Dutch, French, and English. The search for wealth inspired the creation of new economic institutions and the reform of cultural and religious thought. In 1776 the Scottish philosopher and economist Adam Smith published *The Wealth of Nations*, signaling the arrival of a new philosophy of economic organization called capitalism, an economic system in which the means of production are privately owned and goods and services are exchanged according to levels of supply and demand in markets. Smith applauded the work of private businesspeople who pursued their own profit, and proclaimed them the chief engine of progressive change in world history. He opposed both governmental and religious control of trade—the existing system—and

proposed instead free trade, mostly unregulated markets, and independent merchant-capitalists.

Smith's word was not final, and the market-based, supply-and-demand philosophy of capitalism is still debated today—reviled by some, extolled by others—significant to virtually all considerations of economic systems and to many questions of politics, culture, and religion as well. The final section of chapter 14 indicates how the economic and political leadership of a variety of countries, from Russia in the west to Japan in the east, responded to the new wealth and power of western Europe.

ESTABLISHING WORLD TRADE ROUTES

THE GEOGRAPHY AND PHILOSOPHIES OF EARLY ECONOMIC SYSTEMS
TRADE AND TRADERS: GOALS AND FUNCTIONS
1000–1500

KEY TOPICS

- World Trade: An Historical Analysis
- Trade Networks
- Trade in the Americas before 1500
- Trade in Sub-Saharan Africa
- Muslim and Jewish Traders
- Asia's Complex Trade Patterns
- The Mongols

Today, long-distance, international trade forms a substantial part of the world's commerce and includes even the most basic products of everyday food and clothing. In earlier times, however, long-distance trade represented only a small fraction of overall trade, mostly supplying luxury goods—silks, gold, spices, and the like—for the wealthy upper classes. Because these goods were extremely valuable relative to their weight, merchants could carry them over hundreds or even thousands of miles and still sell them for handsome profits. Some commercial goods, like raw wool and cotton, were also traded over medium distances, a few hundred miles. The transportation costs were justified because these raw materials became more valuable after importation and manufacture into finished products.

Before 1500, by far the largest share of trade was local—food crops traded for local hand manufactures or raw materials. These goods were necessities, but they had little value in relationship to their weight: the cost of transportation was a substantial part of their final price. They were, therefore, traded over only short distances. Often, they were bartered in exchange for other local goods rather than sold for money in more distant markets. This local exchange of goods is a fundamental part of local and regional history, but the study of world history focuses on long-distance trade and its importance in knitting together distant regions of the world.

Trade provides an index of economic vitality. It stimulates economic growth; people produce goods and provide services only if markets exist for them. Anyone who has ever looked for a job has experienced this economic truth. If jobs exist, people can find work; if jobs do not exist, they remain unemployed and economically unproductive. Similarly, both production and consumption are limited by the availability of markets. If markets are easily accessible, products can be bought and sold easily; if not, then trade, production, and consumption stagnate.

WORLD TRADE: AN HISTORICAL ANALYSIS

Historians studying world trade seek to understand its purposes, conditions, and regulations. We ask about social as well as economic values. For example: What benefits have different systems of trade achieved? Which systems have benefited which

Opposite **Boucicault Master, Trade in the Gulf of Cambay (detail), India, 1410. Vellum.** As the main port of northeastern India, Cambay excited the wonder of painters and artists in far-off Europe. This illustration from the *Livre des Merveilles* (*The Book of Wonders*) (1410) represents Cambay's ships and traders in European guise, not surprisingly because the artist had never been to the city. (*Bibliothèque Nationale, Paris*) members of society? Which systems have harmed which members of society? What have been the trade-offs in benefits and losses under each system? These questions, of course, are not only historical. The present-day debates over the "globalization" of trade—the opening of more and more countries of the world, and more and more products, to import and export trade—demonstrate their enduring significance. The street demonstrations in Seattle in 1999, and subsequently in other cities around the globe, against the World Trade Organization, which attempts to expand, facilitate, and regulate international trade, reveal the intense passions underlying these debates today.

To what degree do governments regulate or control economic markets? To what degree should they? In a completely **free market economy**, conditions of trade would not be regulated at all. Prices would vary only in terms of the relationship between the **supply** of goods and the economic **demand** for them, and businesspeople would be free to seek their fortune as they choose. Societies, however, do regulate trade to some degree in order to serve the greater good of the society. For example, governments may wish to ensure that everyone has enough food for survival. They may therefore decide that agricultural production should be expanded and industrial production limited. In time of scarcity—in wartime, for example—governments may ration food and essential commodities to ensure that everyone has access to at least minimum quantities. By taxing some items at high rates and

free market economy An economic system in which the means of production are largely privately owned and there is little or no government control over the markets.

supply and demand In economics, the relationship between the amount of a commodity that producers are able and willing to sell (supply), and the quantity that consumers can afford and wish to buy (demand).

AT A GLANCE : MEDIEVAL WORLD TRADE

DATE	POLITICAL/SOCIAL EVENTS	TRADE DEVELOPMENTS	EXPLORATION
1050 C.E.	■ Almoravids destroy Kingdom of Ghana (1067)		
1100 C.E.		■ Age of Great Zimbabwe in southern Africa	
1150 C.E.		■ Paper-making spreads from Muslim world to Europe	
1200 C.E.	■ Foundation of first Muslim empire in India ■ Chinggis Khan establishes Mongol Empire (1206–1405) ■ Collapse of Mayan civilization in Central America; rise of Incas in Peru ■ Rise of Mali, west Africa		
1250 C.E.	■ Osman I founds Ottoman dynasty in Turkey (1290–1326) ■ Emergence of Empire of Benin ■ Mongols fail to conquer Japan (1281)		■ Marco Polo arrives in China (1275)
1300 C.E.	■ Height of Mali (Mandingo) Empire under Sultan Mansa Musa		■ Ibn Battuta's travels in East Asia and Africa (c. 1330–60)
1350 C.E.	■ Ming dynasty in China (1368)		
1400 C.E.	■ Ottoman Turks establish foothold in Europe at Gallipoli	■ China reconstructs and extends Grand Canal	
1450 C.E.		■ Decline of Kilwa and Great Zimbabwe in southeast Africa (c. 1450)	
1500 C.E.	■ Zenith of Songay Empire of the middle Niger region (1492–1529) ■ Hernán Cortés and Spanish conquistadors defeat Aztecs and seize Mexico (1519–21) ■ Francisco Pizarro and Spanish conquistadors defeat Incas and seize Peru		

others at low rates, governments promote or limit various kinds of production and trade. Business may be more regulated or less regulated, but it is never completely unregulated.

In the earliest societies, such as Egypt, Mesopotamia, and China, government officials, often in alliance with priests, had more power than did private merchants, and trade was highly regulated. Nevertheless, considerable evidence suggests that market economies based on private profit did exist from earliest times. This trade for private profit was embedded in deeper political, social, religious, and moral structures of society. Long-distance private trade flourished most profitably in major port cities around the world. The merchants who carried on this port-city trade were often foreigners, with some independence from local political and social structures. They tended to occupy marginal positions in the host society, but central positions in the international trade networks.

TRADE NETWORKS

These long-distance merchants encouraged and brokered trade between the society in which they were living and far-flung networks of international merchants. They formed "trade diasporas," networks of interconnected commercial communities living and working in major trade cities throughout Africa, Europe, and Asia. As historians of trade have pointed out, trade diasporas appear in the archaeological record as early as 3500 B.C.E.

World trade routes. Between 1100 and 1500 a relay system of trade by land and sea connected almost all populous regions of Eurasia, as well as north and east Africa. Long-distance traders carried goods along their own segments of these routes, and then turned them over to traders in the next sector. The western hemisphere was still separate, and had two major trade networks of its own.

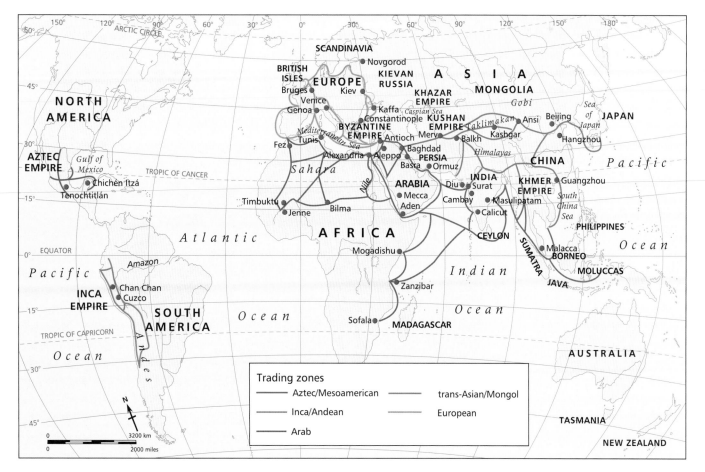

Some of them have endured for millennia. During the height of the Roman Empire, for example, traders from Rome sailed the waters of the Mediterranean Sea and the Indian Ocean. On rare occasions they continued all the way to China. Usually, these traders were not ethnically Roman. Most frequently they were descendants of the major trading communities of the eastern Mediterranean: Jews, Greek-speaking Egyptians, and Arabs. Roman trade left a heritage of these diaspora traders—in the form of small religious communities of Jews, Christians, and Muslim Arabs—living along the southwest coast of India long after the sack of Rome in 410.

Typically, the visiting merchants who carried the trade were marginal to their host societies rather than embedded within them. They were not unregulated by the hosts, nor were they totally subordinated. They were expected to take a reasonable profit in exchange for the benefits they brought to the port city.

TRADE IN THE AMERICAS BEFORE 1500

In the western hemisphere, two major trade networks had developed. The northern network served primarily the area that is Mexico today, although in those years it was ruled by several different groups. The southern network ran north–south both along the Pacific Coast and inland along the spine of the Andes Mountains. East–west routes rose to altitudes of 15,000 feet, linking the coastal settlements with those of the mountains. There was little traffic between North and South America and virtually none between the eastern and western hemispheres, except for rare voyages, such as that of Leif Eriksson, the Viking explorer who reached Newfoundland about the year 1000 (see Chapter 13).

Trade in the Inca Empire

In the Andes Mountains of South America, a significant and long-lasting hub of civilization grew up after 600 C.E. By the time the Incas consolidated their empire in the early fifteenth century, the mountain peoples generated extensive trade, connecting

Photograph of a *quipu*. In the Inca empire, which extended from Ecuador to central Chile, trading was facilitated by an extensive road network. This *quipu*, a device of knotted string used to record dates and accounts, would have been a handy aid to the traveling South American businessman in the early 1400s.

Pre-Columbian America. Pre-Columbian America had two great regions of trade and political power. In the north, the Aztec kingdom, centered on Tenochtitlán, dominated. The adjacent Maya of Central America were in decline. In South America, about 1500, the Inca dominated the Andes mountain regions, linking them together through an extensive system of roads.

settlements over hundreds of miles north to south and linking together some 32 million people.

Trade was important up and down the mountainsides. With peaks rising up to 20,000 feet, these mountain slopes hosted several different ecological zones, encouraging product differentiation and trade. The valleys below provided sweet potatoes, maize, manioc, squash, beans, chili peppers, peanuts, and cotton. The hills above produced white potatoes, a cereal grain called quinoa, coca, medicines, feathers, and animal skins. The highland people specialized in manufacture and crafts, including gold working.

The state and its semi-divine rulers controlled this trade between the ecological zones. Under Inca rulers, from the early 1400s until the Spanish conquest in 1535, many of the best of the 15,000 miles of roads through the Andes were open only to government officials.

Trade in Central America and Mexico

In the Yucatán peninsula of Central and North America, the Mayan peoples had flourished from 200 B.C.E. to 900 C.E. Mayan traders flourished relatively independently, amassing a disproportionate share of wealth. Archaeologists suggest that the increasing wealth of the traders created social tensions and that ultimately the traders were brought under the control of the hierarchical state, creating a new set of unequal relations dominated by kings rather than merchants.

By the time the Spanish arrived in the 1520s, the Maya had weakened in the Yucatán, and the Aztecs dominated the valley of Mexico. The Spanish conquistadors wrote vivid accounts of the great marketplace of the Aztec capital, Tenochtitlán. As the Spanish leader Hernán Cortés summarizes in one of his letters:

> This city has many squares where trading is done and markets are held continuously. There is also one square twice as big as that of Salamanca, with arcades all around … There are streets of herbalists where all the medicinal herbs and roots found in the land are sold. There are shops like apothecaries', where they sell ready-made medicines as well as liquid ointments and plasters. There are shops like barbers', where they have their hair washed and shaved, and shops where they sell food and drink. (*The Second Letter*, pp. 103–104)

The market met every fifth day, with perhaps 40,000 to 50,000 merchants swarming in, rowing their canoes across the lake to the island on which Tenochtitlán was built. In many ways, the market was like the great fairs that were held in medieval Europe, drawing merchants from distant corners of the kingdom and beyond.

But how independent were these Tenochtitlán merchants? The Spanish described the city's market as being under tight government control. In addition to officers who kept the peace, collected taxes, and checked the accuracy of weights and measures, a court of twelve judges sat to decide cases immediately.

A guild of traders, called *pochteca*, carried on long-distance trade, which expanded steadily through the fifteenth century. They led trade expeditions for hundreds of miles, exchanging city-crafted obsidian knives, fur blankets, clothes, herbs, and dyes for such raw materials as jade, seashells, jaguar skins, feathers from forest birds, and, in the greatest volume, cotton from the Gulf coast. They were to marry only within the guild, and, though they were commoners, they could send their sons to temple schools and they had their own courts.

Because the American Indians had not invented the wheel, goods were carried by pack animals—and by humans. Boats were used on streams and rivers. Along the South American coast, near the equator, the Incas sailed boats constructed of balsa wood, while the Mayans paddled canoes through the river systems of the Yucatán.

The traders often gathered both goods and military intelligence for the ruling Aztec families. Royal troops protected them and sometimes used attacks on traveling *pochteca* as a justification for punishing the attackers and confiscating their lands. The *pochteca* lived in their own wards in the towns, had their own magistrates, and supervised the markets on their own. Their main god, Yiacatecutli, seemed akin to the Toltec god Quetzalcoatl, and this, too, suggests that they were to some degree foreigners living in a trade diaspora, with a high degree of independence from the state and temple.

The two major civilizational hubs functioned independently of one another and both were, of course, virtually completely cut off from Afro-Eurasia. When Europeans arrived in the sixteenth century brandishing new weapons, commanding new military organizations, and transmitting new diseases, the American residents were unprepared for the challenges.

TRADE IN SUB-SAHARAN AFRICA

Africa south of the Sahara was also well-integrated into webs of trade relationships. In West Africa, traders dispatched caravans of goods on camel back across the Sahara, linking the forest cultivators and miners in the south with the merchants and rulers of the Mediterranean coast. In East Africa traders along the coast procured gold and ivory from the interior of the continent and sold them to the seafaring merchants of the Indian Ocean.

West Africa

The domestication of the camel in the second to fifth century C.E. opened the possibility of regular trans-Saharan trade. Oases provided the necessary rest and watering points for caravans, as well as producing dates, a major commodity of trade. The

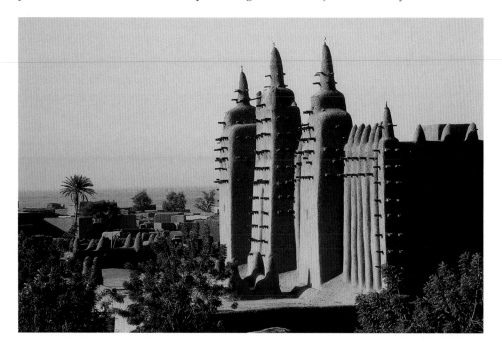

Mosque at Jenne, Mali, first built fourteenth century C.E. The spectacular mud-brick mosques found in the major towns of the African savanna states, such as Jenne and Timbuktu, point to the acceptance of Islam by the merchant and ruling classes in the thirteenth and fourteenth centuries. The mud, which washes away in the rain, needs continual renewal—hence the built-in "scaffolding" of the structure.

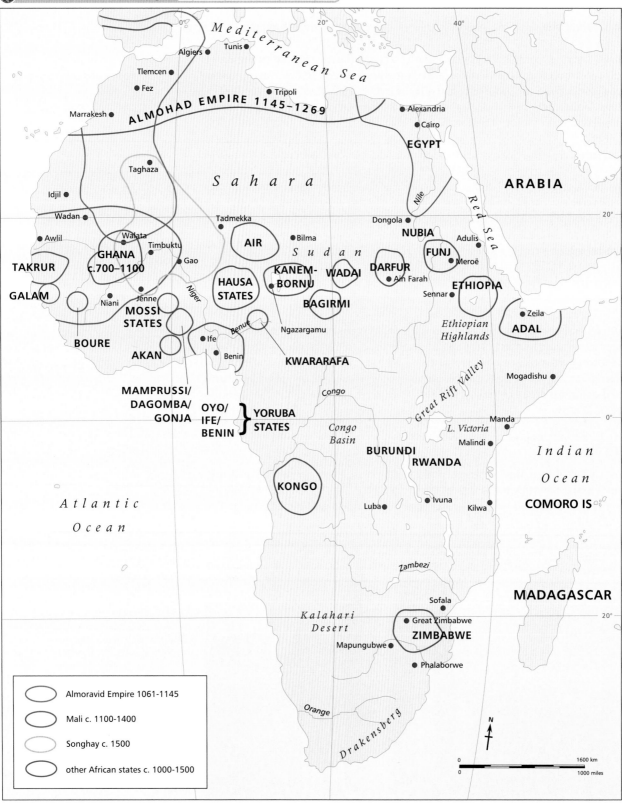

For an interactive version of this map, go to: http://www.prenhall.com/spodek/map12.3

African kingdoms. Many states appeared in 1000–1500 in northern and western Africa, their power based on control over long-distance trade—gold, ivory, and slaves moving north; metalware, textiles, and salt carried south. Ghana, Mali, and Songhay are discussed in the text. These states, protected from marauders by the Sahara, could usually maintain their independence.

earliest written records of this trans-Saharan trade begin with the arrival of Muslim traders in the eighth century.

For the most part, African political units were local, but three large empires in succession arose around the northern bend in the Niger, near Timbuktu, where the **sahel**, the arid fringe of the desert, meets the vast Sahara itself. These three empires—Ghana (about 700 to about 1100), Mali (about 1100 to about 1400), and Songhay (about 1300 to about 1600)—kept the trade routes open and secure. In contrast with most governments in other parts of the world that amassed wealth and power by controlling land and agriculture, these empires drew their power from control over trade, traders, and trade routes.

Gold, slaves, cloth, ivory, ebony, pepper, and kola nuts (stimulants) moved north across the Sahara; salt, dates, horses, brass, copper, glassware, beads, leather, textiles, clothing, and foodstuffs moved south. Gold was the central attraction. In the fourteenth century, the gold mines of West Africa provided about two-thirds of the gold used to finance trade in the eastern hemisphere. In 1324, when the Muslim emperor of Mali, Mansa Musa (r. 1307–32), passed through Cairo on his way to Mecca, he dispensed so much gold in gifts to court officials and in purchases in the bazaar that local prices in Cairo were inflated for years to come. A European map of 1375 showing a seated Mansa Musa as ruler of Mali is noted as follows: "So abundant is the gold found in his country that he is the richest and most noble king in all the land."

There were many natural break-points for the north–south trade: From the Mediterranean coast to the northern fringe of the desert, trade was borne by pack horse; across the desert, via oases, by camel; across the arid sahel and the grassy savanna lands south of the Sahara again by pack animal; and finally, through the tropical forest, impenetrable to larger animals and afflicted with the lethal tsetse fly, it was borne by human porters. For the most part, locally dominant trade groups carried the trade from one market center to the next in short relays. A few trading communities, however, notably the Soninke and, especially, their Mande-speaking Dyula branch, established trade diasporas that negotiated with the rulers.

East Africa

In the fourth century, the kingdom of Axum in Christian Ethiopia dominated the trade of the Red Sea and to some extent the Arabian Sea. With the rise of Islam, however, Arab traders gained control of the flow of merchandise and Arab armies began restricting Ethiopian power. After the ninth century, and south of the Horn of Africa, Arab merchants provided the main trading link between East Africa and the Indian Ocean. The first major port to spring up had been Manda, followed in the thirteenth century by Kilwa. The ruling Arab dynasty along the coast also seized control of the port of Sofala further to the south. Through local African merchants they exchanged goods with the peoples of the interior, especially at the trading post of

sahel "Shore"—the northern and southern edges of the Sahara Desert. A semi-arid region of Africa, extending from Senegal eastward to the Sudan.

Great Zimbabwe. The biggest and most celebrated of several stone enclosures in east Africa dating from the tenth to fifteenth centuries, Great Zimbabwe provided raw materials for trade at the coastal settlements, especially gold, copper, tin, and iron, and was also a trading post for luxury goods—Islamic pottery and cowrie shells were dug up at the site.

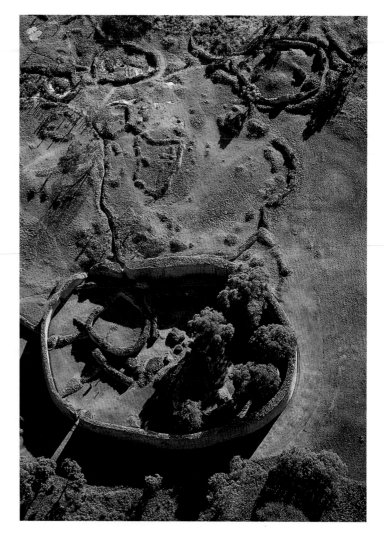

Great Zimbabwe. Here they found abundant supplies of valuable metals such as gold and copper (often cast into ingots) and animal products: ivory, horns, skins, and tortoise shells. Slaves were also an important commodity. Great Zimbabwe was the largest and most remarkable of all the developing towns. Architecturally, it featured a 100-acre stone enclosure and another 100 smaller enclosures in the surrounding region.

From these inland sources, goods were transported to the coastal ports and shipped onward to Arabia and India in exchange for spices, pottery, glass beads, and cloth. In the port cities of Africa's east coast, the Swahili language of the nearby African peoples received from these Indian Ocean traders a strong admixture of Arabic vocabulary, enriching Swahili and ensuring its place as the dominant language of the coastal trade.

MUSLIM AND JEWISH TRADERS

Muslim Arab traders played critical roles in the development of African trade networks, from north to south across the Sahara and overseas from the East African coast to various ports along the shores of the Indian Ocean. Their religion and ethnicity formed the basis of community and trust necessary for conducting business in a world that had no international courts or legal systems. A much smaller group, Jews, too, were able to carry on international trade across the entire eastern hemisphere from China to western Europe and Africa. For Jews, like Arabs, religion and ethnicity were the underlying basis of their trade diaspora. Within their overseas communities they quickly learned whom they could trust and this enabled them to establish highly efficient trade networks. Other groups of global traders also formed commercial networks on the basis of shared religion and ethnicity, although they were generally less extensive geographically, for example Christian Armenians, Jain and Hindu Gujaratis from western India, and Fukienese from the southeast coast of China. Small overseas Muslim trade communities also often attracted local traders to assimilate to Islam, as happened especially in Indonesia and southeast Asia. The other trading communities generally stayed within their own social and religious networks, enjoying trade relations with local groups, but not encouraging their conversion.

Statuette of Semitic trader, Chinese, 10th century. Traders from the Roman Empire traveling the silk routes were likely to be Jews from the Fertile Crescent, Greek-speaking Egyptians, and other Levantines. They and their descendants eventually settled along the trans-Asian routes, which most likely explains the Chinese derivation of this glazed porcelain Semitic peddler, made during Tang dynasty times. (*The Seattle Art Museum*)

Jewish Traders

During the period of Tang-Abbasid control over the silk route—the eighth and early ninth centuries—Jews had once again emerged as a preeminent trading community throughout the diaspora linking Europe and China. The emigration of Jews to many far distant points of settlement facilitated their trade connections. Their religious diaspora supported their trade diaspora. Charlemagne's ninth-century European empire employed them to carry trade in southern Europe. Baghdad, astride many of the key trade routes in western Asia, held the most prominent Jewish community in the world at the time, but there were also small Jewish communities in Calicut and Cochin in south India and in Kaifeng, China. When the Portuguese explorer Vasco da Gama reached Calicut in 1498, a local Jewish merchant was able to serve as interpreter. Cairo, Egypt, one of the world's great trade centers, also sheltered a very significant Jewish community.

Muslim Traders

With the rise of Islam (see Chapter 11), and especially after the Abbasid caliphs shifted their capital to Baghdad in 762, Muslim traders dominated the routes through the Indian Ocean. Ethnically, most were Arabs and Persians. In the thirteenth century, as the Muslim sultanate of Delhi came to rule most of India, many of the Hindu ocean-going traders, especially those in the western Indian region of Gujarat, converted to Islam. Along with their trade goods, they carried their culture and religion. Distant merchants who encountered them in order to trade, slowly also absorbed elements of Islam. In regions as distant as Malaysia and Indonesia local merchants began to assimilate to the religion of these oceanic traders. When the ruler of Malacca converted to Islam, about 1400, the trading circuit of Muslim merchants was complete.

Islam encouraged trade. The *hajj* (pilgrimage), advocated for every Muslim at least once during his or her lifetime, demanded international travel; trade connections flourished with the *hajj*. A Muslim trade colony had operated in Sri Lanka from about 700 C.E. Arab traders sailed with the monsoon winds first to India, then on to Southeast Asia, and some even on to the southeast coast of China. Catching the proper seasonal winds in each direction and using their **lateen** (triangular) sails to maximum effect, sailors could complete a round trip from Mesopotamia to China in less than two years. Carried not by military power but by traders, Islam came to be the dominant religion in Indonesia (the most populous Muslim country in the world today), and to attract tens of millions of Chinese adherents. The entire length of the Indian Ocean

lateen A triangular sail affixed to a long yard or crossbar at an angle of about 45 degrees to the mast, with the other free corner secured near the stern. The sail was capable of taking the wind on either side.

Anon., *King Edward I Returns from Gascony*, **1470. Miniature.** This is an example of a ship with lateen sails. Europeans adapted these sails from Arab models because they enabled ships to tack against the wind as well as run with it. (*British Library, London*)

HOW DO WE KNOW?

The Records in the Cairo Genizah

Information on Mediterranean cultures and their trade connections into the Indian Ocean, from the tenth through the thirteenth centuries, has come to historians from the Cairo Genizah (Hebrew for a repository of old papers), studied by Solomon Goitein from the 1950s through the 1980s. Jewish law requires that the written name of "God" not be destroyed but stored for later burial; the Genizah was the storage point in Cairo for such documents for several centuries. Because paper was scarce and often re-used, the manuscripts in the Genizah include massive bundles of notes and manuscripts on secular as well as sacred aspects of life: on trade and commerce, on social organization in general, and on the Jewish community in particular. Marriage contracts "state in

detail and with great variety the conditions regulating the future relations of the newly married, and thus constitute a precious source for our knowledge of family life" (I:10). Wills and inventories of estates are "veritable mines of information" (I:10). Letters of correspondence, both personal and business, "form the largest and most important group [of manuscripts]. They are our main source not only for our knowledge of commerce and industry, but also for various other subjects, such as travel and seafaring" (I:11). "There are hundreds of letters addressed to various authorities containing reports, petitions, requests for help, demands for redress of injustice, applications for appointments, and a great variety of other matters" (I:12). Religious responsa are frequent, questions and answers between commoners and sages concerning religious philosophy, doctrine, and

practice. Most women were illiterate, but they dictated many letters to scribes: "We hear the female voice guiding the male pen" (I:12). For the most part the writing is in Arabic, but transcribed in Hebrew letters. These centuries-old manuscripts have proven to be a gold mine for historians studying the life of Cairo, its citizens, and their external connections throughout the Mediterranean Sea and the Indian Ocean.

- Given the nature of the Genizah repository, what kinds of records do you think would be most fully represented? Least well represented?
- How might records of family life and records dictated by women help to fill out the records of business transactions?
- How important was Cairo as a trade center at this time?

littoral, from East Africa through India and on to Indonesia, housed a Muslim, largely Arab, trading diaspora.

ASIA'S COMPLEX TRADE PATTERNS

As the largest continent, with the largest population and the oldest civilizations, it is not surprising that Asia developed complex trade networks thousands of years ago. As early as 1250, a set of interlinked trade networks connected the main population and production centers of Asia, Africa, and Europe. The earlier map (p. 377) illustrates their vast and comprehensive geographic coverage. From east to west, Japan and China were linked by land routes to Central Asia and by sea lanes to the Indian Ocean. Both land and sea routes continued westward to Arabia, western Asia, and on to the Mediterranean and Europe. Well-developed sea traffic linked also to the East African coast, where land routes extended into the African continent. North–south routes ran through China, Central and West Asia, and Europe, and from the Mediterranean across the Sahara by camel. At this time there was not yet any central transportation headquarters or company that could carry goods all the way from East Asia to western Europe, for example, but arrangements could be made for even this long voyage to be completed stage by stage.

The Polynesians of the South Pacific

The Polynesians are Austronesian-speaking peoples who migrated from south China and Southeast Asia perhaps 6000 years ago to Taiwan, the Philippines, and eastern Indonesia (see Chapter 1). Those who settled in the islands adjacent to these areas became known as Melanesians. Those who continued on eastward became known as

Polynesians. These Polynesians continued to sail eastward in single and double canoes, 100 to 150 feet long, made of wooden components fitted together and held in place by ropes and cords of fiber. These ships, with their single, square, woven-mat sails, could carry not only men and women but also food supplies and even live animals. In these simple, elegant craft, the Polynesians began vast ocean voyages that would take them as far northeastward as Hawaii (400 C.E.), as far southeastward as Easter Island (400 C.E.), and as far southwestward as New Zealand (750 C.E.). They became the greatest seafaring peoples of pre-modern times. Students of Polynesian history marvel both at the enormous stone statues erected on some of the Polynesian islands, most spectacularly on Easter Island, and at the accomplishments of their sea voyages. Polynesians apparently visited every island within the huge triangle of Hawaii, Easter Island, and New Zealand. Nevertheless, despite traveling through thousands of years and thousands of miles, the Polynesians preserved several remarkably similar elements of culture throughout their domains. Anthropologists note the similarities across the islands of Polynesia of tools, names of plants, terms of kinship, and artistic styles.

Were Polynesians capable of sailing across the Pacific and establishing contact with the Americas? Apparently so. The Hawaiian Islands are closer to the Americas than to Asia, and Easter Island is only 2200 miles off the coast of South America. Indeed, many scholars argue that this contact was accomplished, citing the sweet potatoes and manioc of Polynesia as their evidence. But, whatever the capabilities of the Polynesians and their canoes, and whatever the source of these food supplies, the Polynesians did not establish permanent connections to the Americas. Apparently they were not interested in sailing for the sake of exploration, but only to find places in which to settle, raise families, and obtain necessary food supplies. Although they were among the greatest sailors in human history, they apparently did not sail just for the excitement of the voyage, but rather for more specific and immediate needs.

Malay Sailors in the South China Sea and the Indian Ocean

Extraordinary as the Polynesian sailors were, apparently they adopted their sails from the Malay sailors of the South China Seas probably late in the first millennium B.C.E. These sailors left four major legacies to world seafaring, one primarily in their own neighborhood, the other three of much wider significance. The first was the most important: cargo ships—*jongs*, or junks as they are usually called in English. These ships with multilayered hulls, two to four masts, two rudders, and a normal capacity of 400 to 500 tons, seem to have inspired the junks used by Chinese merchant sailors to the north. Second, their balance-lug square sails seem to have inspired a series of adaptations and inventions, from the sails used by the Polynesians, to the sails used by Arab sailors, later modified to triangular sails, called lateen sails. (Other authorities believe that the balance-lug sail developed on the Nile River, also in the first millennium B.C.E., and they argue that this Egyptian invention was the background source for the Arab lateen

Johannes Baptista van Doetechum, *A Chinese Junk*, from *Jan Huyghen van Linschoten: His Discourse of Voyages into the East and West Indies*, 1579–92. **Engraving.** Apparently first an invention of the Malay sailors of the South China Sea, and adapted by the Chinese, these ships could carry more than a thousand tons of cargo and hundreds of sailors. (*Private Collection*)

sails.) These lateen sails were subsequently copied by European sailors in the Mediterranean and used for their voyages in the Atlantic. The balance-lug sail could be turned to face into the wind or to tack against it, allowing sailors to set their course with much greater maneuverability. As the sail was turned, from an angle it appeared to be triangular, and sailors learned that a triangular sail would work equally well. Thus the lateen sail was born and ultimately carried to the sailing paths of the world.

Third, the Malay sailors learned the patterns of the seasonal monsoon winds of the Indian Ocean and learned to sail with them. The rain-laden monsoon winds are attracted from the Indian Ocean inward toward Central Asia during the summer months, when the continental interior is much hotter than the oceans around it, and blow outward from the continent toward the ocean in the cooler months, when the ocean is warmer than the interior. The Greeks, too, learned how to use the monsoon winds of the Indian Ocean effectively in the first few centuries B.C.E. Whether from the Malays or the Greeks, the knowledge of the wind patterns soon reached all the sailors of the Indian Ocean, including the Europeans when they arrived in 1498.

Finally, using their ship technology and knowledge of the winds, Malay sailors made regular voyages of 3000 miles across the Indian Ocean—probably via the Maldive, Seychelles, and Comoro islands—to the large island of Madagascar, 250 miles off the coast of East Africa, where they established themselves as the majority population, as they remain to this day. The Malay sailors brought to Madagascar bananas, coconuts, taro, and their language, which also continues as the dominant language of the island.

Along with their settlements, the Malay sailors established sea routes from East Africa to China. They carried frankincense and myrrh from East Africa, Arabia, southwest Iran, and the Makran Coast of India to present day Vietnam and China. From Timor, 1800 miles to the southeast of Vietnam, they brought aromatic woods, especially sandalwood. From the "Spice Islands," the Moluccas, 1000 miles east of Java, they brought cloves, nutmeg, and mace. For more than a thousand years they were the master sailors of the South China Sea.

Sailors and Merchants of the Indian Ocean

The great crossroads of the world's shipping lanes in the period 1100–1500 was the Indian Ocean. Its waters encompass three distinct geographical sectors, each with its own cultural orientation. The western sector sweeps from the East African coast across Arabia and continues on to the west coast of India. From the time of Alexander the Great and the Roman Empire, Greek sailors participated in this trade. By the first century B.C.E. Greek sailors had learned to use the monsoon winds to navigate these waters swiftly and effectively. From the fourth to the eighth centuries, following the decline and fall of the Roman Empire, two new groups dominated this western region of the Indian Ocean: sailors from Axum (modern Ethiopia and Eritrea), and its Red Sea port of Adulis, and sailors from Sassanian Persia, an empire that was in the ascendant in western Asia at the time.

From the eighth to the sixteenth century, Arab Muslim traders and sailors became masters of the western Indian Ocean sea lanes. This was the area made famous by the legendary exploits of Sinbad the Sailor. As Islam inspired the people of Arabia to undertake expeditions of conquest by land beginning in the seventh century (see Chapter 11), Arab sailors also began to assume prominence in the Indian Ocean trade. Among the Arabs living at the southern end of the Arabian peninsula, some had experience with sea trade, but those to the north, the majority, did not. As Arab armies moved still further north, however, they came into contact with, conquered, and learned from previous masters of the Indian Ocean, the Sassanians of Iran. Mastering

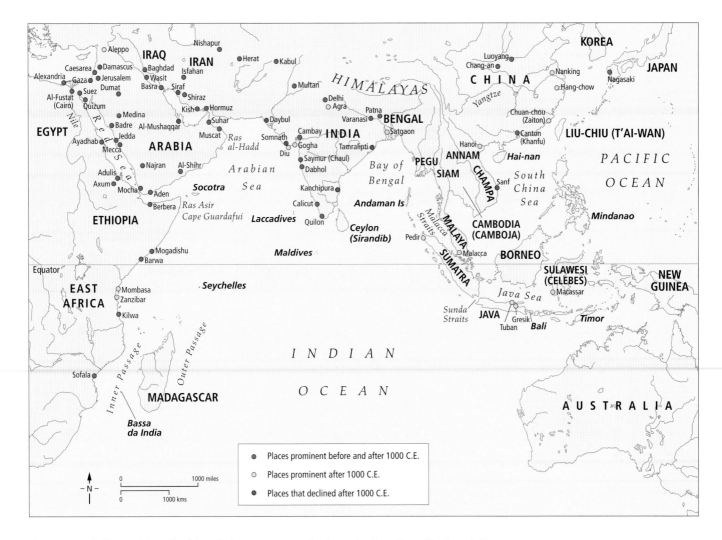

Trading ports and cities, Indian Ocean, 618–1500 C.E. The Indian Ocean was the pivot of long-distance seaborne trade from the Mediterranean to the South China Sea. Each of its port cities housed a rich diversity of merchants of many ethnicities and cultures.

these new skills, and inspired by their own expansionism, Arab sailors displaced the Sassanians. In 762 C.E. the new Abbasid dynasty built a new capital in Baghdad, in the heartland of Mesopotamia. In this land that had participated in sea trade for millennia, the Arabs' concern for oceanic trade increased further.

As they increasingly participated in sea trade, Arab sailors became true masters of the Indian Ocean trade. Lacking wood in Arabia, they depended on others to build their ships, or obtained teak from southern India to build their own. For reasons that remain unclear, they did not use metal nails in ship construction, but "stitched" the wooden planks together with coir—the fiber of coconut husks—or other fibers. Like the Malay and the Greek sailors before them, they learned to sail with the monsoon winds. The Arab Muslim Ahmad Ibn Majid included extensive recommendations on travel dates appropriate to the monsoon winds in his comprehensive fifteenth-century guide to navigation throughout the Indian Ocean. For example:

Travelling from Bengal and connected regions [begins] in the 40th day of the year [1st January] and its end is the 70th day [31st January]: it is no good travelling later than that if bound for Hormuz or Yemen or the Hijaz. Travelling to Ceylon and the Maldives is possible until the 70th and 80th days although it is a gamble in some years by the 80th and the same from Malacca, Pegu, and Siam. But from Java, Sumatra, Malacca, and Tanasari to Bengal, sailing takes place from the 90th to the 140th days.

The pattern of emporia trade in the Indian Ocean, c. 1000–1500. Trade goods did not travel on a single ship the whole length of this region. Rather, they would be loaded at a port in one of the three regions, off-loaded and reloaded in the next for shipment to the third region.

The rise of Arab Muslim sea traders was a remarkable transformation for this ethnic and religious group. The Arabs had been quite accustomed to trade—Muhammad himself was a camel driver and leader of caravans—but trade by sea was different. They took to this new way of life eagerly and came to dominate the sea lanes from the Mediterranean coast in the west all the way east to Guangzhou (Canton) and Hangzhou in China, frequently displacing previous communities of sailors.

In the eastern waters of the Indian Ocean, for example—from India and the Bay of Bengal to Indo-China and the Malacca Straits—Indian sailors and merchants, largely Hindu, had predominated. East of the Malacca Straits, these sailors entered into the South China Sea, attracted by China's wealth and luxury products. Despite the geographical distance of their homes from this region, they came to surpass in importance the more local Chinese and East Asian merchants.

Until the tenth century, much of the cultural influence in this region came from India, as evidenced in the many astonishingly large and beautiful temple complexes of this region—for example, Borobudur and Prambanan in Java, Angkor Wat in Cambodia, Pagan in Burma, and the Cham Shaivite temple of central Vietnam. These Buddhist and Hindu temples marked centers of cultural as well as political and economic dominance. From the seventh to the tenth century, south Sumatra was home to the Buddhist Srivijayan maritime empire, the largest and most powerful of the Indian-influenced Southeast Asian kingdoms.

Boucicault Master, Trade in the Gulf of Cambay, India, 1410. Vellum. Merchants and travelers carried exciting tales of their adventures, but when European painters sought to represent these wonders they could only fill in their imagination with scenes from their own experience. Hence this illustration looks more like a European town than an Indian city port. (*Bibliothèque Nationale, Paris*)

By the end of the thirteenth century, however, Muslim traders, mostly from India, began their trade and proselytization through the entire Southeast Asian archipelago of islands—today's Indonesia, Borneo, Celebes, the Moluccas, and the Philippines. By the fourteenth century, most of the ocean-going merchants appear to have been Muslims, either Arabs or Indian converts from Hinduism, and their descendants. On the basis of their economic strength as traders they attracted local peoples and encouraged them to assimilate to Islam. When the ruler of Malacca converted, about 1400, Muslim supremacy in Indian Ocean trade reached its zenith. From west to east, Muslim merchants dominated the major ports. In Indonesia and the Malaysian

SOURCE

The Arabian Nights

Arab Muslim traders of the Indian Ocean fill the pages of some of the best loved tales of world literature. The Thousand Nights and One Night, *also called the* Arabian Nights, *fables originally written in Persian during the years of the Abbasid Empire (750–1258), include the tales of the seven voyages of Sinbad (Sindbad) the Sailor, who won a fortune through a series of hazardous (if unbelievable) adventures at sea. The adventures, supposedly told night after night by Scheherazade to the emperor, Haroun al-Rashid (r. 786–809), as a ploy to postpone her scheduled execution, are fanciful, but Sinbad's descriptions of his departures on each of his voyages are based on the reality of Indian Ocean shipping. This translation from the beginning of the third voyage is by Richard F. Burton who brought the complete tales to the English-speaking world in the late nineteenth century.*

I returned from my second voyage overjoyed at my safety and with great increase of wealth, Allah having requited me all that I had wasted and lost, and I abode awhile in Baghdad-city savouring the utmost ease and prosperity and comfort and happiness, till the carnal man was once more seized with longing for travel and diversion and adventure, and yearned after traffic and lucre and emolument, for that the human heart is naturally prone to evil. So making up my mind I laid in great plenty of goods suitable for a sea voyage and repairing to Bassorah [Basra], went down to the shore and found there a fine ship ready to sail, with a full crew and a numerous company of merchants, men of worth and substance; Faith, piety and consideration. I embarked with them and we set sail on the blessing of Allah Almighty and on His aidance and His favour to bring our voyage to a safe and prosperous issue and already we congratulated one another on our good fortune and bon voyage. We fared on from sea to sea and from island to island and city to city, in all delight and contentment, buying and selling wherever we touched, and taking our solace and our pleasure, till one day … [and here begin the fabulous adventures of the third voyage]. (*The Thousand Nights and One Night*, Vol. 4, pp. 2031–2)

Arab trader, illustration from the *Maqamat* **of al-Hariri, 12th century.** Regional shipping routes linked into the oceanic, intercontinental routes. This ship, with Arab passengers and Indian, and perhaps African, crew, sailed the Persian Gulf connecting Mesopotamia and the Indian Ocean.

peninsula Islam displaced the Hindu and Buddhist cultures that had already taken root, and today both Malaya and Indonesia are primarily Muslim countries.

Arabs did not sail further, into the Atlantic or Pacific Oceans, simply because they had no need. They sailed at will throughout the most valued seas of the world that they knew. They had no problem of access. While Europeans were beginning to attempt to find new routes to India and China in the fifteenth century, the Arabs were already there.

China

By 1500 China was the most economically advanced region in the world, a magnet for world trade. China is so huge, however, that its internal trade far outweighed its external trade. It is so rich and varied in its productivity that others came to China to obtain its products far more regularly than the Chinese traveled abroad in search of the products of others. China's policies towards trade have, nevertheless, altered through the centuries we are considering here, partly as a result of changes in imperial leadership, partly in response to external pressures. Even though it created a highly integrated system of internal markets and reached extraordinary levels of agricultural and industrial productivity under the Song Dynasty, China was defeated by Mongol invaders and had to abandon a large part of its territories, relocate to the south, and reconstruct its economy. The Ming Dynasty overthrew the Mongols and undertook a series of spectacular ocean voyages. Then, in another change of policy, later Ming emperors forbade the Chinese to trade overseas. Nevertheless, overseas merchants continued to pour in, eager to do business with the Central Kingdom.

International Trade. As early as the fourth century C.E. the Chinese also participated in the trade of the South China Sea and the Indian Ocean, although probably only as far west as Sri Lanka. Their oceanic trade activity increased with the rise of the Tang dynasty (618–907 C.E.). During much of this period, the Abbasid Empire (750–1258) was at its height, and helped to protect the sea lanes of the Indian Ocean. But with the decline of both empires in the ninth century, the Chinese largely withdrew from this oceanic trade and concentrated instead on inland issues, in accord with their geographical position centered on the Yellow River valley and the north. After 1127, however, they returned to oceanic enterprise, when the Song dynasty was driven from north China by the invasions of the Tatars and other northern peoples. As they moved south, establishing a new capital at Hangzhou, about 100 miles from the modern-day port-metropolis of Shanghai, they turned their attention back to the sea. With various northern groups in control of the old overland silk routes, sea-borne trade was an obvious transportation and communication alternative. For this purpose, the Chinese mastered the craft of building large ships and merchants created new patterns of commercial exchange, including sophisticated credit systems. In addition to a merchant marine, China constructed a powerful navy.

Ink and watercolor print showing silk manufacture, Chinese, early 17th century. During the Song dynasty (960–1279), long-distance trade across Central Asia dwindled. Maritime trade, with its very much safer and cheaper routes, now offered a viable alternative, and silk, along with porcelain and tea, continued to attract the merchants of the world. Unwinding filaments from silkworm cocoons in order to make yarn was considered women's work, as this Ming dynasty print suggests. (*Victoria & Albert Museum, London*)

In 1368, a new dynasty, the Ming, came to power. Especially in the early years of the dynasty, Ming emperors adopted policies of expansionism by land and self-assertion by sea. The Ming Emperor Yung-lo (r. 1402–24) dispatched a series of seven spectacular ocean voyages under the Muslim eunuch, Admiral Zheng He. The first voyage set out in 1405 with sixty-two large junks, 100 smaller ships, and 30,000 crew. The largest ships were 450 feet long, displaced 1600 tons, held a crew of about 500, and were the largest ships built anywhere up to that time. They carried silks, porcelains, and pepper. The first expedition sailed as far as Calicut, near the southwest tip of India. In six further missions between 1407 and 1433, Zheng He sailed to ports all along the Indian Ocean shores, at least twice reaching the East African ports of Mogadishu, Brava, Malindi, and Kilwa. Interested in exotic treasures that could not be found in China, Emperor Yung-lo seemed most pleased with a giraffe sent to him by the sultan of Malindi on the fourth voyage, in 1416–19. These colossal expeditions demonstrated both the skill of Admiral Zheng He and the vision of Emperor Yung-lo. On the basis of these accomplishments, many historians believe that the Chinese would have been able to cross either the Atlantic or the Pacific Ocean—had they wished. But they did not push their expeditions any further and, in 1433, the Ming emperor terminated the great, state-sponsored Indian Ocean voyages.

Why did the emperor terminate these voyages? Why did China not dispatch its own missions to Europe, and even to the western hemisphere? It appeared to have the

SOURCE

Chinese Ships in South Indian Harbors: An Account by Ibn Battuta

The fourteenth-century traveler Ibn Battuta (1304–68) did not usually comment on ships and sailors. He was far more interested in his encounters with people on land. In the south Indian port of Calicut, however, he was so impressed with the capacity and design of the Chinese ships in the harbor that he gave a remarkable description. He notes that while the Chinese allowed only Chinese ships to dock in their ports, the pilots and crew were not necessarily Chinese:

We traveled to the city of Calicut, which is one of the chief ports in Malabar [the southwest coast of India], and one of the largest harbors in the world. It is visited by men from China, Sumatra, Ceylon, the Maldives, Yemen, and Fars [Persia], and in it gather merchants from all quarters ... there were at the time thirteen Chinese vessels, and we disembarked. Every one of us was lodged in a house and we stayed there three months as the guests of the infidel [Zamorin ruler of Calicut], awaiting the season of the voyage to China. On the Sea of China traveling is done in Chinese ships only, so we shall describe their arrangements.

The Chinese vessels are of three kinds; large ships called *chunks* [junks], middle-sized ones called *zaws* [dhows], and small ones called *kakams*. The large ships have anything from twelve down to three sails, which are made of bamboo rods plaited like mats. They are never lowered, but turned according to the direction of the wind; at anchor they are left floating in the wind. A ship carries a complement of a thousand men, six hundred of whom are sailors and four hundred men-at-arms, including archers, men with shields and arbalests, who throw naphtha. Each large vessel is accompanied by three smaller ones, the "half," the "third," and the "quarter." These vessels are built only in the towns of Zaytun and Canton. The vessel has four decks and contains rooms, cabins, and saloons for merchants; a cabin has chambers and a lavatory, and can be locked by its occupant, who takes along with him slave girls and wives. Often a man will live in his cabin unknown to any of the others on board until they meet on reaching some town. The sailors have their children living on board ship, and they cultivate green stuffs, vegetables and ginger in wooden tanks. The owner's factor [representative] on board ship is like a great *amir* [nobleman]. When he goes on shore he is preceded by archers and Abyssinians with javelins, swords, drums, trumpets, and bugles. On reaching the house where he stays they stand their lances on both sides of the door, and continue thus during his stay. Some of the Chinese own large numbers of ships on which their factors are sent to foreign countries. There is no people in the world wealthier than the Chinese. (Ibn Battuta, pp. 234–6)

technological capability to do so. Why did Chinese emperors choose only to receive European shipping—rather than to dispatch their own ships—beginning with the Portuguese in 1514?

Many answers appear plausible. The Ming turned their energies inward, toward consolidation and internal development. At first they pushed the Mongols further north from the Great Wall, but an invasion of Mongolia failed in 1449. Thereafter, the Ming limited their military goals, rebuilt the Great Wall, and restricted their forces to more defensible borders.

In 1411 the Ming reconstructed and extended the Grand Canal from Hangzhou in the south to Beijing in the north. The canal was the cheapest, most efficient means of shipping the grain and produce required by the northern capital. The man-made inland waterway also reduced the importance of coastal shipping, enabling the Ming emperors to turn their backs on the seas and ocean. The faction of eunuchs, dedicated court servants like Zheng He, who urged the government to continue its sponsorship of foreign trade, lost out in palace competition to other factions that promoted internal development. International private shipping was also curtailed.

The Ming government limited contacts with foreigners and prohibited private overseas trade by Chinese merchants. In 1371, coastal residents were forbidden to travel overseas. Recognizing the smuggling that resulted, the government issued further prohibitions in 1390, 1394, 1397, 1433, 1449, and 1452. The repetition of this legislation reveals that smuggling did continue, but, for the most part, private Chinese sailors were cut off from foreign trade. The government defined the expeditions of Zheng He as political missions that sought tribute to China from outlying countries. Although products were exchanged on these voyages, officially trade was not their goal. So, while both private and government trade flourished in the interior of China, and while thousands of Chinese emigrated to carry on private businesses throughout Southeast Asia, China's official overseas trade virtually stopped. Zheng He's expeditions stand out as spectacular exceptions to generally restrictive policies.

These decisions to limit China's international trade, both official and private, proved enormously costly. Chinese society became introverted and, although economic growth continued, innovation stagnated. Under the Song dynasty (960–1279) Chinese technology had been the most innovative in the world. Creativity continued under the Mongols, but by about the beginning of the Ming dynasty, China became more conservative. Military technology improved but then it, too, stagnated. China had invented gunpowder before 1000 C.E., but used it only sporadically. Ming cannon in the early fifteenth century were at least equal to those anywhere in the world, but metal was in short supply, limiting further development. The Ming fought few battles against fortress cities, where cannon were most useful, so they also saw little need to invest further in developing this heavy weaponry. No enemies appeared against whom they needed such weapons. In fighting against invasions from the north, the crossbow was of more importance to the infantrymen, who made up China's armies of a million and more soldiers. At first, when China was itself very advanced, these decisions to limit further military innovation seemed not so consequential. Later, however, they would render the country vulnerable to newly rising powers.

Internal Trade. When Marco Polo arrived in China in 1275, the splendor and wealth of the country overwhelmed him. He described its ruler, Kublai Khan, as "the mightiest man, whether in respect of subjects or of territory or of treasure, who is in the world today or who ever has been, from Adam our first parent down to the present moment." Polo correctly informed the West that China in the late 1200s was the richest, most technologically progressive, and largest politically unified country in the world.

The foundations of China's wealth had been in place for centuries. We have already read in Chapter 7 of China's generally growing population, territory, power, and wealth through its successive dynasties from Qin to Tang. Under the Song dynasty (Northern Song, 960–1126; Southern Song, 1127–1279), China underwent an economic revolution. A revolution in agriculture underpinned the advance: better soil preparation and conservation; improved seeds that often allowed more than one crop per season; better water control and irrigation; and more local specialization of crops. The new techniques were implemented most intensively in the lower Yangzi valley, as the Song moved south from China's historic northern base around the Yellow River. Indeed, they maintained regional capitals, two of which served as national capitals: Kaifeng in the north and Hangzhou in the south, near the mouth of the Yangzi. Thanks to the invention of woodblock printing in the ninth century under the Tang dynasty, ideas could spread in China more rapidly than anywhere else. One of the first uses of print had been to conserve and spread religious concepts; the oldest printed book extant in the world is a copy of the Buddhist *Diamond Sutra* from 868. Now the new method of printing was put into the service of disseminating the new farming methods.

Agricultural improvements—plus China's traditional excellence in textile production and remarkable innovations in the most advanced coal and iron industry in the world—inspired a trade revolution. Common people became involved in the mass production of goods for sale. Domestically this included the production of military goods for the Song army of over one million men; internationally it emphasized traditional silks and porcelain ceramics now supplemented with the export of iron and steel products. Trade became monetized, with copper as the principal currency. Chinese currency was so popular in Japan at this time that it became the most important medium of trade. Chinese ships sailed as far as East Africa, returning with exotic goods, such as gold, ivory, tortoise-shell, rhinoceros horns (regarded as aphrodisiacs), leopard skins, ambergris, and some slaves. Large numbers of Song coins were excavated in Zanzibar in 1888. Ships returning from Southeast Asia also brought luxuries: aromatic herbs and spices, rhinoceros horns, pearls, and camphor. From Arabian lands came frankincense.

In 1024, in Sichuan province, China, paper money was printed for the first time in the world. (Sometimes the government printed an excess of paper money, giving rise to inflation.) Merchants invented new credit mechanisms to facilitate trade. Government control of trade, quite marked under the Tang, was sharply reduced in favor of greater market freedom and trade made up an increasing share of government revenue. Customs offices in the nine official ports, especially the largest, Canton and Zaitun (Quanzhou), collected import taxes of 10 to 15 percent of the value of goods. In 1128, maritime trade brought in 20 percent of China's total cash revenues. Merchants were valued for the taxes the state could collect from them. Those who paid the most were rewarded with official rank.

The great luxury products of China—silk, porcelain, and tea—continued to attract thousands of foreign merchants as they had since Tang times. Many were Muslim Arabs. A few Lombards, Germans, and French were also present. They were treated as welcome guests, and special quarters in the port cities were set aside for them. In issues that involved no Chinese but only these foreigners, they could apply their own laws. Shops with foreign goods and foreign schools catered to their interests. Nevertheless, these merchants followed Chinese commercial rules, and many became quite Sinicized in their manners. When they ended their sojourn in China, they were feted with large farewell feasts.

The international merchants were at the peak of a highly integrated national system of trade and commerce, a system that was built on domestic and international water transport. To integrate the system of waterways, portage of goods was arranged at points of dangerous rapids and cataracts. To ensure smooth passage, double locks were installed on the man-made Grand Canal, which extended from Hangzhou in the

River traffic at Qing Ming festival, Kaifeng, by Zhang Zeduan, Song dynasty scroll. The multitude of Chinese junks on the Yellow River suggest the well-developed channels of trade in northern China. (*National Palace Museum, Taiwan*)

SOURCE

River Trade in China

Just as the vast and profitable trade in silk depended ultimately on the hard work of millions of spinners and weavers and their families, so river trade in China depended, at least partially, on the investments of common people. The three sources below support that assertion. The first is from Marco Polo attesting to the abundance of river trade in China. The second is from Pao Hui, writing in the thirteenth century about the financing of overseas river trade. The third is a Song dynasty scroll illustrating the multitude of Chinese junks sailing on the Yellow River at Kaifeng.

First, Marco Polo writing of the Yangzi River:

I assure that this river runs for such a distance and through so many regions and there are so many cities on its banks that truth to tell, in the amount of shipping it carries and the total volume and value of its traffic, it exceeds all the rivers of the Christians put together and their seas into the bargain. I give you my word that I have seen in this city [I-ching] fully five thousand ships at once, all afloat on this river. Then you may reflect, since this city, which is not very big has so many ships, how many there must be in the others. (cited in Elvin, pp. 144–5)

Then compare Pao Hui on the financing of river trade in Southern Song China:

All the people along the coast are on intimate terms with the merchants who engage in overseas trade, either because they are fellow countrymen or personal acquaintances. Leakage [of copper currency] through entrusting occurs when the former give the latter money to take with them on their ships for the purchase and return conveyance of foreign goods. They invest from ten to a hundred strings of cash, and regularly make profits of several hundred per cent. (Shiba Yoshinobu, p. 33)

Finally, examine Zhang Zeduan's twelfth-century scroll painting, Going on the River at the Qingming Festival. *At this time, the city of Kaifeng, situated on the Yellow River and at the crossroads of some of China's most important canals, was the hub of water-borne traffic for all of northern China. Inland Kaifeng and Hangzhou, on the coast, were China's most important regional capitals. They formed the apex of a regional system of urbanization that unified the whole country.*

Market towns sprang up throughout China, enabling virtually every rural family to sell its products for cash and to buy city goods. In turn, the small market towns were linked to larger cities, which provided more specialized products and access to government administrators. Here, families could buy and sell, arrange a marriage, determine the latest government rulings, hear about new farming possibilities, learn the dates and the results of academic examinations. These towns were so widespread that nearly every farm family lived within reach of one.

At the base were the rural families, struggling to survive by producing commodities demanded by the traders. Hand manufacture, especially of cotton and silk cloth, often supplemented farm production in rural areas. Invention made the process more productive. In particular a reeling machine, invented around the eleventh century, drew several silk filaments at once from silkworm cocoons immersed in boiling water. It then drew the filaments through eyelets and hooks and finally banded them into silk thread.

The rural producers were integrated into the market system either through direct, personal access or through brokers who supplied raw materials and bought the finished product. Women were the chief producers in this supplemental rural industry. They also carried the finished product to market. Conditions of production and of marketing could be savage. Xu Xianzhong's "Prose Poem on Cotton Cloth" presents the harshness of both aspects. It is not clear whether the

women in the marketplace are selling their cloth, or themselves, or both:

Why do you ignore their toil? Why are you touched
Only by the loveliness that is born from toil?
...
Shall I tell you how their work exhausts them?
By hand and treadle they turn the rollers of wood and iron,
Feeling their fibre in between their fingers;
The cotton comes out fluffy and the seeds fall away.
The string of the cotton bow is stretched so taut
It twangs with a sob from its pillar.
They draw out slivers, spin them on their wheels
To the accompaniment of a medley of creakings.
Working through the darkness by candlelight,
Forgetful of bed. When energy ebbs, they sing.
The quilts are cold. Unheard, the waterclock flows over.
...
When a woman leaves for market
She does not look at her hungry husband.
Afraid her cloth's not good enough, She adorns her face with cream and powder,
Touches men's shoulders to arouse their lust,
And sells herself with pleasant words.
Money she thinks of as a beast its prey;
Merchants she coaxes as she would her father.
Nor is her burden lifted till one buys.
(Elvin, pp. 273–4)

south to administrative centers, including Beijing, in the north; this system helped to link the agricultural wealth of the south with the administrative cities of the north. Tugboats with human-powered paddle-wheels serviced the main ports. Chinese oceangoing ships, equipped with axial rudders, watertight bulkheads, and magnetic compasses, gained a reputation as the best in the world.

THE MONGOLS

The Song dynasty (960–1279) developed the waterways of China, but the great Central Asian overland silk routes had declined after the ninth century along with the Abbasid and Tang dynasties that had protected and encouraged them. Under the Mongol Empire (1206–1405), the largest land empire ever known, traffic on the silk routes revived.

The two million Mongols who inhabited the plateau region of Central Asia were divided into several warring tribes, each led by a *khan*. The land was poor and the climate harsh. The Mongols shepherded their cattle, sheep, and goats in a circular pattern of migration called transhumance: in the brief summers they moved their herds northward to pasture; in winter they turned back south. They spent most of their waking hours on horseback and mastered the art of warfare from the stirrups, with bow and arrow as well as sword by their side.

The "Pax Mongolica"

Cultural historians credit the Mongols with little permanent contribution because they were absorbed into other, more settled and sophisticated cultures. But they did establish, for about a century, the "Pax Mongolica," the Mongolian Peace, over a vast region, in which intercontinental trade could flourish across the reopened silk route. Reports from two world travelers, Ibn Battuta (1304–68) of Morocco and Marco Polo (1254–1324) of Venice, give vivid insights into that exotic trade route.

During his thirty years and 73,000 miles of travel, Ibn Battuta commented extensively on conditions of travel and trade. For example, in Central Asia Ibn Battuta encountered a military expedition of Oz Beg Khan (d. 1341), the ruler of the khanate of the Golden Horde:

> We saw a vast city on the move with its inhabitants, with mosques and bazaars in it, the smoke of the kitchens rising in the air (for they cook while on the march), and horse-drawn wagons transporting the people. (Dunn, p. 167)

yurts A portable dwelling used by the nomadic people of Central Asia, consisting of a tentlike structure of skin, felt, or hand-woven textiles arranged over wooden poles, simply furnished with brightly colored rugs.

The tents of this camp/city were Mongol **yurts**. Made of wooden poles covered with leather pelt, and with rugs on the floor, the yurts could be disassembled quickly for travel.

Later, Ibn Battuta was granted his request to travel with one of Oz Beg Khan's wives along the trade route as she returned to her father's home in Constantinople to give birth to her child. Ibn Battuta reported that the princess traveled with 5000 horsemen under military command, 500 of her own troops and servants, 200 female slave girls, 20 Greek and Indian pages, 400 wagons, 2000 horses, and about 500 oxen and camels. They crossed from Islamic Mongol territory to Christian Byzantium.

Marco Polo was a merchant in a family of merchants, and his account of his travels to and in China was thus particularly attuned to patterns of trade. His numerous descriptions of urban markets support the idea of an urban-centered trade diaspora. For example, consider Marco Polo's description of Tabriz in northwest Persia:

HOW DO WE KNOW?

The Mongol Empire

Because it was the largest contiguous land empire in history, understanding the entire Mongol Empire requires language competence in Mongolian, Chinese, Persian, Arabic, Turkish, Japanese, Russian, Armenian, Georgian, and Latin. No scholar can be expected to master all of these languages, but serious scholars are expected to know at least one or two of them and to use others in translation. Surprisingly, Mongolian may not be the most important. Before Chinggis Khan, the language was not written and there are no archives of the Mongol Empire, at least none that have survived. The only major historical text in Mongolian is The Secret History of the Mongols, and, although some scholars think it inauthentic, it is our principal source for the biography of Chinggis Khan. Another text from the days of Chinggis Khan, the Altan Debter, or Golden Book, is lost, but Persian and Chinese historians mention it, and their references show the book to be consistent with, although not the same as, The Secret History.

Chinese and Persian texts are the next most important, discussing Mongol rule over the two empires flanking, and captured by, the Mongol Empire. In China, the major text is the official dynastic history of the Yuan, or Mongol, dynasty. In Persia, several authors are important, most notably Rashid al-Din. Until his time, the Mongol conquest posed a problem for Muslim historians: The conquest of the Abbasid Empire was not supposed to happen. Muslims were to conquer others, as they had done with great consistency; they were not supposed to be conquered themselves. During Rashid al-Din's time, however, the Mongols converted to Islam. Rashid al-Din must have understood this well, since he himself had converted from Judaism. Rashid al-Din wrote the history of the Mongol Empire which, he said, marked a new era in world history. Later, he wrote Jami' al-tawarikh, a Collection of Histories, recording the history of all the peoples touched by the Mongols from the Chinese in the east to the Franks in the west. It was the first example of the form of a world history. For the last twenty years of his life, until he was assassinated as the result of a court intrigue in 1318, Rashid al-Din served as principal adviser to the Il-Khan ruler of Persia.

Distant Europe held relatively little importance for the Mongols, but a number of European sources discuss their conquests. These included men such as Giovanni de Piano Carpini, who was sent by Pope Innocent IV to visit the Khans, and William of Rubruck, who visited the Mongols at the behest of the king of France, Louis IX. The most comprehensive account is by Matthew Paris, who chronicled European reactions to the Mongol advances from his post at St. Albans, England, but the most popular came from travelers, of whom the most famous was Marco Polo.

- Mongolian may not be the most important language in the study of the Mongolian empire, yet the most important biography of Chinggis Khan is in Mongolian. How do you explain this paradox?
- Why are Chinese and Persian important languages for studying the Mongol Empire?
- Would you consider Rashid-al-Din's Collection of Histories a history of the world? Why or why not?

The people of Tabriz live by trade and industry; for cloth of gold and silk is woven here in great quantity and of great value. The city is so favourably situated that it is a market for merchandise from India and Baghdad, from Mosul and Hormuz, and from many other places; and many Latin merchants come here to buy the merchandise imported from foreign lands. It is also a market for precious stones, which are found here in great abundance. It is a city where good profits are made by traveling merchants. The inhabitants are a mixed lot and good for very little. There are Armenians and Nestorians, Jacobites and Georgians and Persians; and there are also worshippers of Mahomet, who are the natives of the city and are called Tabrizis. (Marco Polo, p. 57)

Central Asian routes challenged travelers and their animals. Despite the Pax Mongolica, merchants still had to be prepared to defend themselves from attack. As Marco Polo recounts:

Among the people of these kingdoms there are many who are brutal and bloodthirsty. They are forever slaughtering one another; and, were it not for fear of the government … they would do great mischief to traveling merchants. The government imposes severe penalties upon them and has ordered that along all dangerous routes the inhabitants at the request of the merchants shall supply good and efficient escorts from district to district for their safe conduct on payment of two or three groats for each loaded beast according to the length of the journey. Yet, for all that the government can do, these brigands are not to be deterred from frequent depredations. Unless the merchants are well armed and equipped with bows, they slay and harry them unsparingly. (Polo, p. 61)

For those merchants and statesmen who did reach Beijing, the Khan maintained a massive service industry to provide hospitality. Polo noted, in particular, an army of prostitutes:

I assure you that there are fully 20,000 of them, all serving the needs of men for money. They have a captain general, and there are chiefs of hundreds and of thousands responsible to the captain. This is because, whenever ambassadors come to the Great Khan on his business and are maintained at his expense, which is done on a lavish scale, the captain is called upon to provide one of these women every night for the ambassador and one for each of his attendants. They are changed each night and receive no payment; for this is the tax they pay to the Great Khan. (Polo, p. 129)

Almost everything we know about Marco Polo's life is based on the colorful account he left us of his travels through Asia. Little is known of his childhood years in Venice or his education. Marco's father and uncle, both Venetian merchants, traveled from their home in 1260 on a trade mission as far as the northern end of the Caspian Sea. Then war broke out, and their route back home was blocked. But the route eastward was open, so the brothers traveled on to Beijing, where Chinggis Khan's grandson, Kublai Khan (1215–94), ruled.

The Great Khan invited the men to return with more information on Christianity and a delegation from the pope. The information and delegation never materialized, but in 1271 the two brothers, along with the seventeen-year-old Marco, set out for China again. They arrived in 1275 and remained there for seventeen years. How exactly they occupied themselves during this time is unclear from Marco's account, but it was not uncommon for foreigners to find employment in the Mongol state. Kublai Khan, it appears, was so enchanted by Marco's tales of foreign lands that he sent him on repeated reconnaissance trips throughout the empire. The Polos eventually set off for home in about 1292, reaching Venice in 1295 and reuniting with relatives and friends who had believed them long-since dead.

Soon after his homecoming, Marco was captured in battle by Genoese sailors and imprisoned. He dictated the tales of his travels to his fellow prisoner Rustichello, a writer of romances. Europe now had its most complete and consistent account up to that date of the silk route and of the fabulous Chinese empire of Kublai Khan. Marco's *Travels* was soon translated into several European languages, introducing to Christian Europe a new understanding of the world.

For seven centuries scholars have hotly debated the authenticity of Marco Polo's account. No original copy of *The Travels* exists, and scholars have been faced with some 140 manuscript versions that were copied in various languages and dialects from scribe to scribe before the invention of printing. Frances Wood, head of the China Department at the British Library, has asked, *Did Marco Polo Go to China?* (1996). Wood emphasizes the arguments against. Polo did not mention any of the phenomena that should have caught his attention during his reported time in China: Chinese writing, tea, chopsticks, foot binding, the Great Wall. Despite his claims to frequent meetings with Kublai Khan, Marco Polo is not mentioned in any Chinese records of the time. Wood concludes that Polo's work is actually based on materials gathered from others and that he himself never traveled beyond the Black Sea. As a travel narrative, Wood asserts, the book was a fabrication, but as an account of what was known of China at the time, it was a very rich and very influential source of information. Many commentators are therefore equally adamant that Polo did complete all the travels that he claimed, and the debate over the extent of Marco Polo's own travels continues.

Chinggis Khan

Chinggis (Genghis) Khan Temujin, later called Chinggis (Genghis) Khan, was born about 1162 into one of the more powerful and more militant Mongol tribes. His father, chief of his tribe, was poisoned by a rival tribe. About three generations before Temujin's birth, one of his ancestors, Kabul Khan, had briefly united the Mongols, and Chinggis made it his own mission to unify them once again. He conquered the surrounding tribes, one by one, and united them at Karakorum, his capital. Although skilled at negotiation, Chinggis was also infamous for his brutality. Historian Rashid al-Din (1247–1318), writing almost a century after his conquests, reports Chinggis Khan's declaration of purpose, emphasizing women as the spoils of warfare:

> Man's greatest good fortune is to chase and defeat his enemy, seize all his possessions, leave his married women weeping and wailing, ride his gelding, and use the bodies of his women as a nightshirt and support, gazing upon and kissing their rosy breasts, sucking their lips which are as sweet as the berries of their breasts. (cited in Ratchnevsky, p. 153)

Chinggis defeated the Tartars and killed all surviving males taller than a cart axle. He defeated the rival Mongol clans and boiled alive all their chiefs. In 1206, an assembly of all the chiefs of the steppe regions proclaimed him Chinggis Khan—"Universal Ruler." He organized them for further battle under a pyramid of officers leading units of 100, 1000, and 10,000 mounted warriors, commanded, as they grew older, by his four sons. Promotion within the fighting machine was by merit. Internal feuding among the Mongols ended and a new legal code, based on written and recorded case law, called for high moral standards from all Mongols.

Chinggis turned east toward China. On the way he captured the Tangut kingdom of Xixia, and from Chinese engineers he mastered the weapons of siege warfare: the mangonel and trebuchet, which could catapult great rocks; giant crossbows mounted on stands; and gunpowder, which could be launched from longbows in bamboo-tube rockets. In 1211 Chinggis pierced the Great Wall of China, and in 1215 he conquered the capital, Zhongdu (modern Beijing), killing thousands.

Chinggis departed from China to conquer other kingdoms. His officials and successors continued moving south, however, until they

Chinggis Khan, from Rashid al-Din's world history, 13th century. Chinggis Khan's conquests had as much impact on West Asia as they did on China. This Persian illustration of Chinggis pursuing his enemies comes from a history, which some consider to be the first world history, written by Rashid al-Din (1247–1318), a Persian administrator employed by Mongol Il-Khans in Iran. (*Bibliothèque Nationale, Paris*)

captured all of China, establishing the Mongol dynasty, 1276–1368. They conquered Korea, large parts of Southeast Asia as far as Java, and attempted, but failed, to take Japan as well. The planned assault on Japan in 1281 was stopped by *kamikaze*, divine winds, which prevented the Mongol fleet from sailing.

Chinggis himself turned west, conquering the Kara-Khitai Empire, which included the major cities of Tashkent and Samarkand. He turned southward toward India, reaching the Indus River and stationing troops in the Punjab, but he was unable to penetrate further. Turning northwest, he proceeded to conquer Khwarizm. In the great cities of Bukhara, Nishapur, Merv, Herat, Balkh, and Gurgan, millions were reported killed, an exaggeration, but still an indication of great slaughter. Chinggis went on to capture Tabriz and Tbilisi.

After Chinggis's death in 1227, his four sons continued the expansion relentlessly. In the northwest they defeated the Bulgars along the Volga and the Cumans of the southern steppes and then entered Russia. They took Moscow, destroyed Kiev, overran Moravia and Silesia, and set their sights on the conquest of Hungary. To the terrified peoples in their path, it looked as if nothing could stop the Mongols' relentless expansion. But in 1241, internal quarrels did what opposing armies could not: they brought the Mongol advance in Europe to a halt. During the dispute over succession that followed the death of Chinggis's son Ogedei (1185–1241), the Mongols withdrew east of Kiev. They never resumed their westward movement, and central and western Europe remained untouched.

The Mongol successor states. After the death of Chinggis Khan's grandson Mongke in 1259, the Mongol world devolved into four successor states. Kublai Khan's emerged as the most powerful, but only after a long struggle with Song China. In Central Asia, the Chagatai dominated the eastern steppe; the Golden Horde became established in southwest Russia; and the Il-Khan in Persia ruled from Kabul to Anatolia.

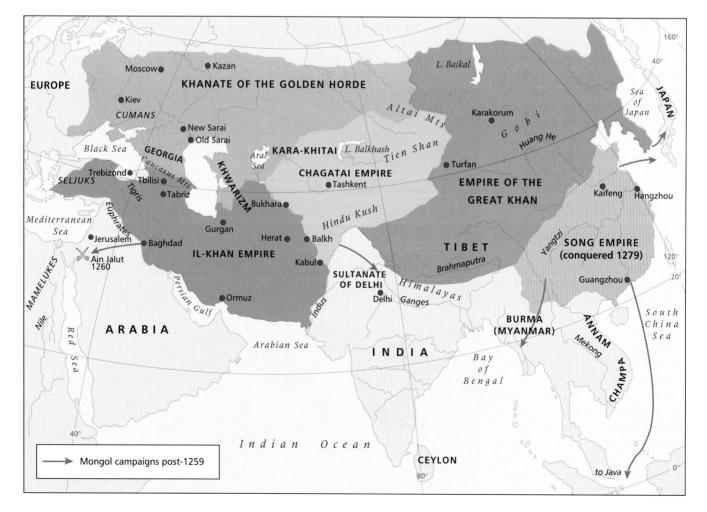

In the southwest, under Chinggis's grandson Hulegu (*c.* 1217–65), the Mongols captured and destroyed Baghdad in 1258, ending the five-century-old Abbasid dynasty by killing the caliph. But in the next year, Mongke, Chinggis's grandson and the fourth and last successor to his title as "Great Khan," died while campaigning in China, and many of the Mongol forces withdrew to attend a general conclave in Karakorum to choose his successor. In 1260, Mongol forces were defeated by a Mamluk army at the battle of Ain Jalut, in modern Jordan, and never again pushed further to the southwest.

The End of the Mongol Empire

Mongol rule was extensive but brief. At their apogee, 1279–1350, the Mongols had ruled all of China, almost all of Russia, Iran, Iraq, and Central Asia. The huge empire was administered and ruled through four separate geographical *khanates*, or sub-empires, each under the authority of a branch of Chinggis Khan's family. Over time central authority declined and the four khanates separated, each becoming an independent empire.

The Mongols could not govern their empire from horseback, and they were soon absorbed by the peoples they had conquered. They intermarried freely with the Turks who had joined them as allies in conquest. In Russia, Mongols and Turks merged with Slavs and Finns in a new Turkish-speaking ethnic group, the Tartars. In Persia and China they assimilated into local culture, converting to various religions, including Christianity, Buddhism, and Confucianism. In most of the areas inhabited by Muslims, the Mongols and their Turkish allies typically converted to Islam.

As the four segments of Chinggis's empire went their own separate ways, slowly they were driven from their conquests. By 1335 the male line of Chinggis and his grandson Hulegu died out in the Il-Khan Empire in Persia. The Ming dynasty defeated and evicted the Mongol (or Yuan) rulers in 1368. The Chagatai khanate was destroyed by Timur the Lame (Tamerlane) after 1369. The Russians pushed out the Golden Horde (named not, as one might think, for their numbers, but for their tents, *Ordu* in Turkish) more slowly. The last Mongol state in the Crimea was conquered only in the eighteenth century.

Plague and the Trade Routes

In addition to commerce and religion, disease also followed the trade routes. An unexpected side effect of the Pax Mongolica was the spread of a plague—called the Black Death—that devastated Eurasia's population in the 1300s. Until recently this mortal disease was believed to be the bubonic plague, but research within the last decade suggests that it may have been a different, unknown, disease. Whatever the disease was, it apparently followed the Mongols from Central Asia into China in 1331 and decimated its population. China's population, estimated at 123 million in 1200, dropped to 65 million in the census of 1393. Part of the decrease was caused by warfare between Chinese and Mongols, but a large part must also have been caused by the plague.

Along the silk routes, after the mid-fourteenth century, the presence and the role of the Mongols declined, probably also as a result of plague deaths. The plague reached the Crimea in 1346. There, plague-infested rats boarded ships, disembarking with the disease at all the ports of Europe and the Near East.

Within the next five years, in Europe, where the plague was new and people had no natural immunity, one-third of the population died. The ravages of the plague fore-shadowed further, even worse epidemics that would sweep across the continents of

The routes of the plague. The central and east Asian stability imposed by Mongol rule—the "Mongol Peace"—brought mixed benefits. Trade flourished, and travelers such as Ibn Battuta and Marco Polo were able to write remarkable accounts of the lands they visited. At the same time, however, vectors for other travelers, such as the rats that carried bubonic plague, also opened up. The Black Death, originating in Central Asia, was one of a succession of plagues that followed the trade routes by land and sea, decimating parts of Europe and China.

the New World, as groups of people who had not previously been exposed to one another's diseases began to meet for the first time (see Chapter 14).

From Mongol to Ming: Dynastic Transition

During the ninety years of Mongol rule, 1279–1368, China's population plummeted from a high of 100 million to just over 50 million. Despite the splendor of Kublai Khan in his capital at Beijing, the Chinese economy did not serve everyone equally well. Marco Polo told of especially bitter poverty and class division in south China where the Han Chinese of the Southern Song dynasty experienced Mongol rule as cruel and exploitative:

> In the province of Manzi almost all the poor and needy sell some of their sons and daughters to the rich and noble, so that they may support themselves on the price paid for them and the children may be better fed in their new homes. (Polo, p. 227)

Revolution simmered until 1368, when the Ming dynasty overthrew the Mongols and ruled for almost three centuries, until 1644.

Under the Ming dynasty, the population increased sharply. By 1450 it had reached 100 million again, and by 1580 the population was at least 130 million. Plagues and rebellions again caused the population to fall back to 100 million by 1650, but from that trough it rose consistently into present times.

The population settled new territories as it grew. The origins of the Chinese Empire had been in the Yellow River valley in the north (see Chapter 4). At the time of the Han dynasty, more than 80 percent of the population of China lived north of the Yangzi valley. Under the late Tang dynasty, the population was divided about equally between north and south. Warfare with the Mongols in the north drove more migrants south, and at the height of the Mongol dynasty up to 90 percent of the population lived in the south. Economically, the south produced rice, cotton, and tea, three of China's most valuable products, not available in the northern climate. Closer to the sea lanes of Southeast Asia and the Indian Ocean, the south also developed China's principal ports for international commerce. The Song built a powerful navy and Chinese merchants carried on regular trade with Southeast Asia, India, and the Persian Gulf. After the Mongols were defeated, however, migration began to reverse. By about 1500, 75 percent lived in the south, and movement back to the north was continuing.

LEGACIES TO THE PRESENT
WHAT DIFFERENCE DO THEY MAKE?

The years shortly before and after 1500 marked a turning point in world trade patterns. Before 1500 trading routes criss-crossed Africa, Europe, and Asia. These routes connected with one another, but they were not unified into a single system of trade. Long-distance trade goods would travel in stages from one set of routes to the next, carried first by one set of traders and then transferred to another, as goods were transported to their final destination. The most important long-distance traders were the Muslim Arab sailors and merchants of the Indian Ocean routes and beyond to the ports of China. Chinese traders dominated the East Asian waterways and occasionally, and spectacularly, sailed into and across the Indian Ocean. At this time, few European traders journeyed into Asia. In the thirteenth century, Mongol rulers provided protection along the old silk routes, reopening these land passages through Central Asia.

The western hemisphere had two sets of regional routes—mostly unconnected with each other—one centering on Mesoamerica, the other on the Andes Mountains of South America. Except for rare voyages, the American routes and the Afro-Eurasian routes remained separated from each other by the vast expanses of the Atlantic and Pacific Oceans.

As European traders grew more powerful after 1500, they attempted to subordinate pre-existing regional systems to their own centralized control from European head-quarters. Within a single generation they seized control of the Americas. Asian powers, however, were much less vulnerable and they tended to pay little attention to the newly arriving Europeans. China and Japan mostly kept them out. European control increased as northwestern Europe industrialized after 1750 (see Chapter 16). Then the European traders, and their governments, supported by new productivity at home, as well as new ships and new guns, began to declare supremacy in global trade. They challenged the legacies of Arab and Chinese supremacy in the east, and Native American isolation in the west, and began to introduce new regimes of trade and domination into world history.

Review Questions

- What is a "trade diaspora"? What was the importance of trade diasporas to the spread of world trade before 1500? What advantages did Jews and Muslims have for exercising world trade in the period 1000–1500?
- What were the principle inter-regional trading networks in 1300?
- What is a lateen sail? Where did it originate? What is its significance?
- How would you compare the relative importance of inland and overseas trade for China in the fifteenth century?
- How did the Mongol Empire facilitate world trade?

- Trace the rise of Arab seafaring to show how it came to be predominant in the Indian Ocean and South China Sea.

Suggested Readings

PRINCIPAL SOURCES

Abu-Lughod, Janet L. *Before European Hegemony: The World System A.D. 1250–1350* (New York: Oxford University Press, 1989). A résumé of the principal trade routes around 1250. Unfortunately omits African routes.

Adas, Michael, ed. *Islamic and European Expansion* (Philadelphia: Temple University Press, 1993). Key collection of historiographical essays on major topics in world history, 1200–1900. Articles by Eaton and Tucker on Islam, and McNeill on "gunpowder empires" are especially helpful for this unit.

Chaudhuri, K.N. *Trade and Civilization in the Indian Ocean: An Economic History from the Rise of Islam to 1750* (Cambridge: Cambridge University Press, 1985). A survey of goods, traders, ships, regulations, and competition among those who sailed and claimed to control the Indian Ocean.

Cortés, Hernán. *Letters from Mexico*, trans. from the Spanish and ed. by Anthony Pagden (New Haven: Yale University Press, 1986). Newest edition of Cortés' letters.

Curtin, Philip. *Cross-Cultural Trade in World History* (Cambridge: Cambridge University Press, 1984). Classical statement of the significance and ubiquity of trade diasporas.

Dunn, Ross. *The Adventures of Ibn Battuta* (Berkeley: University of California Press, 1986). Dunn uses Ibn Battuta and his travels as the center-point of an analysis of Islamic life throughout the Islamic ecumene in the fourteenth century.

Elvin, Mark. *The Pattern of the Chinese Past* (Stanford: Stanford University Press, 1973). Primarily economic history, focused heavily on the central questions of why China did so well economically until about 1700, and then why it did so badly after that time.

ADDITIONAL SOURCES

The Book of the Thousand Nights and a Night: A Plain and Literal Translation of the Arabian Nights Entertainment, 6 vols. in 3, trans. by Richard F. Burton (New York: Heritage Press, 1946).

Bentley, Jerry H. *Old World Encounters* (New York: Oxford University Press, 1993). Survey of the range of cross-cultural, long-distance encounters—especially through trade, religion, and culture—throughout Afro-Eurasia from earliest times to about 1500. Engaging.

Chaudhuri, K. N. *Asia Before Europe* (Cambridge: Cambridge University Press, 1990). Survey of the economic and political systems of Asia before the impact of colonialism and the industrial revolution. Comprehensive, comparative, and thoughtful.

Columbia College. Columbia University. *Introduction to Contemporary Civilization in the West*, Vol. I (New York: Columbia University Press, 2nd ed., 1954). Very well-chosen, long source readings from leading thinkers of the time and place. Vol. I covers *c.* 1000 to 1800.

Crosby, Alfred W. *Ecological Imperialism: The Biological Expansion of Europe, 900–1900* (Cambridge: Cambridge University Press, 1986). The biological—mostly destructive—impact of European settlement around the world, a tragedy for native peoples from the Americas to Oceania.

Frank, Andre Gunder and Barry K. Gills, eds. *The World System: Five Hundred Years or Five Thousand?* (London: Routledge, 1993). In this somewhat tendentious, but well argued, account, globalization is nothing new.

Ghosh, Amitav. *In an Antique Land* (New York: Knopf, 1993). A novel, travelogue, historical fiction of Indian Ocean exchanges in the twelfth century and today. Captivating. Much of the tale is based on the research in Goitein's study, below.

Goitein, Shelomo Dov. *A Mediterranean Society: The Jewish Communities of the Arab World as Portrayed in the Documents of the Cairo Genizah*, 6 vols. (Berkeley: University of California Press, 1967–83). Extraordinary research resulting from the examination of a discovered treasury of about ten thousand documents from about 1000–1300. Despite the title, gives insight into a variety of communities of the time.

Hanbury-Tenison, Robin. *The Oxford Book of Exploration* (New York: Oxford University Press, 1994). An excellent collection of primary sources on exploration.

Hourani, George Fadlo. *Arab Seafaring in the Indian Ocean in Ancient and Early Medieval Times* (Princeton: Princeton University Press, 1951, reprinted 1995). The standard introduction. Examines the trade routes and the ships prior to and after the coming of Islam.

Ibn Battuta. *Travels in Asia and Africa 1325–1354*, trans. and selected from the Arabic by H.A.R. Gibb (New Delhi: Saeed International, edition 1990). Selections from the writings of one of the greatest travelers in history.

Ibn Majid, Ahmad. *Arab Navigation in the Indian Ocean Before the Coming of the Portuguese*, trans., introduced, and annotated by G.R. Tibbetts (London: Royal Asiatic Society of Great Britain and Ireland, 1971). Translation of Ibn Majid's classic fifteenth-century guide for navigators, along with very extensive discussion by Tibbetts placing the author and work in context and discussing contemporary theories of navigation.

Komaroff, Linda and Stefano Carboni, eds. *The Legacy of Genghis Khan: Courtly Art and Culture in Western Asia, 1256–1353* (New York: Metropolitan Museum of Art and New Haven: Yale University Press, 2002). Lavishly illustrated catalogue of blockbuster art exhibit, with numerous interpretive essays as well.

Levathes, Louise. *When China Ruled the Seas: The Treasure Fleet of the Dragon Throne, 1405–33* (New York: Oxford University Press, 1996). Scholarly study of the expeditions of Zheng He.

Ma, Laurence J.C. *Commercial Development and Urban Change in Sung China (960–1279)* (Ann Arbor: Department of Geography, University of Michigan, 1971). Careful, scholarly, detailed research monograph.

Menzies, Gavin. *1421: The Year China Discovered America* (New York: William Morrow, 2003). Menzies brings together many scraps of evidence in concocting the argument that Zheng He actually did sail to America. The evidence does not hold.

Polanyi, Karl, Conrad M. Arensberg, and Harry W. Pearson, eds. *Trade and Market in the Early Empires* (Chicago: The Free Press, 1957). Fundamental argument by historical anthropologists that early trade was mostly regulated by rulers and priests.

Polo, Marco. *The Travels*, trans. from the French by Ronald Latham (London: Penguin Books, 1958). One of the most fascinating and influential travelogues ever written.

Ratchnevsky, Paul. *Genghis Khan: His Life and Legacy*, trans. and ed. by Thomas Nivison Haining (Oxford: Blackwell, 1991). The current standard biography of the personally elusive Chinggis Khan.

Raychaudhuri, Tapan and Irfan Habib, eds. *The Cambridge Economic History of India*. Vol. 1: *c.* 122–*c.* 1750 (Cambridge: Cambridge University Press, 1982). Collection of articles of fundamental significance.

Risso, Patricia. *Merchants and Faith. Muslim Commerce and Culture in the Indian Ocean*. (Boulder: Westview Press, 1995). Among the questions explored: "What difference did it make to be a Muslim?"

Schele, Linda and David Freidel. *A Forest of Kings: The Untold Story of the Ancient Maya* (New York: William Morrow and Co., 1990). The story of the deciphering of the Mayan ideographs and the histories of warfare that they reveal, by two of the leading researchers.

Shaffer, Lynda Norene. *Maritime Southeast Asia to 1500* (Armonk, NY: M.E. Sharpe, 1996). Useful survey on the voyages, trade goods, markets, towns, and government of the region—from earliest times.

Shiba Yoshinobu. *Commerce and Society in Sung China*, trans. by Mark Elvin (Ann Arbor: Michigan Abstracts of Chinese and Japanese Works on Chinese History, 1970). Scholarly source materials with annotations from the economic transformation of the Song dynasty.

Skinner, G. William. "Marketing and Social Structure in Rural China," *Journal of Asian Studies* XXIV, No. 1 (November 1964), 3–43. Classic account of the interlocking structure of urban development in China from local market towns through national capitals of trade.

Toussaint, Auguste. *History of the Indian Ocean*. Trans. from the French by June Guicharnaud (Chicago: University of Chicago Press, 1966). Broad historical sweep of exploration, trade, cultural exchange, fighting, and rule in and of the Indian Ocean from earliest times to the 1960s. Very useful survey.

Wood, Frances. *Did Marco Polo Go to China?* (Boulder, CO: Westview Press, 1996). One of the more recent, and lucid, statements of the controversy.

◎ World History Documents CD-ROM

EUROPEAN VISIONS

ECONOMIC GROWTH, RELIGION AND RENAISSANCE, GLOBAL CONNECTIONS 1100–1776

KEY TOPICS
- The Atlantic
- The Decline of Trade in the Mediterranean
- Trade and Social Change in Europe
- The Renaissance
- A New World
- Oceania

Until 1492 no continuous links connected the eastern and western hemispheres although there had certainly been some voyages between them. The expeditions of Leif Eriksson and other Vikings from Scandinavia around the year 1000 are well known, documented, and authenticated in the artifacts they left behind in their temporary settlements on the northeast coast of North America. Some of the foods of Polynesia—sweet potatoes and manioc—that apparently came from South America present evidence of other contacts, even more fleeting, across the Pacific. Permanent contact between the two major continental landmasses of the world was established, however, only with Christopher Columbus' conquest of the Atlantic Ocean in 1492. The consequences for the people of both hemispheres were enormous.

We have seen that three groups had the capacity to cross the oceans prior to Columbus' expedition. Polynesians and South Americans apparently made contact in some fashion, but neither felt the need to continue their brief encounter. Arab traders of the Indian Ocean probably had the shipping capacity to make the voyage to the Americas, but they also had no need. The Indian Ocean with its neighboring Mediterranean Sea and South China Sea provided all the trading opportunities they required. The Chinese, who were capable of dispatching fleets as far as East Africa, had the capacity, but the imperial decision to terminate these voyages ended their explorations. The Europeans, except for the Vikings, also did not venture out so long as the ports of the Middle East provided access to the great markets of Asia. Only when that access was reduced and profits were curtailed, and when their own economies and technologies grew stronger, did their imaginations expand. Even then, the western Europeans who set off exploring were not looking for new lands, but only for new routes to well-known markets. Columbus did not realize that he had discovered two new continents. In this chapter we discuss the great voyages of exploration of Columbus, Vespucci, Magellan, Tasman, and Cook, who opened new oceanic perspectives to an incredulous world.

THE ATLANTIC

From the eighth until the twelfth century, the European north Atlantic was primarily the province of marauding sailors and raiders from the north. These Vikings were the ancestors of today's Norwegians, Swedes, and Danes. They were also colonizers, fishermen, and traders. One group from Norway began to settle Iceland around 870 and Greenland about 982. Under Leif Eriksson they reached Newfoundland in North America about 1000 and established a settlement there as well, but it did not endure. Danes and Norwegians plundered along the entire Atlantic coast of Europe, with

Opposite **French caravel, 1555. Watercolor on paper.** The sturdy caravel, adapted by Europeans from the Arab ships of the Indian Ocean, became the ship of choice for oceanic exploration. Columbus and Vasco da Gama both sailed in caravels. By arming his caravel with cannon, Gama transformed it into a weapon of war.

CHAPTER 1

The Arrival of King Sweyn and Danish Troops in England, 11th century. Vellum. Sweyn Forkbeard (c. 987–1014), a formidable Viking warrior from Denmark, created a Danish North Sea empire, gaining control over Norway (1000) and conquering England (1013). He is shown here disembarking from his warship.

especially early and devastating attacks on Lindisfarne off the northern coast of England (793), Dorestad in Frisia (834), and Nantes in France (842), where they murdered the bishop and all his clergy. In 859 they sailed through the Strait of Gibraltar and attacked ports along the Mediterranean. Arabs from North Africa and Spain were launching similar attacks in the Mediterranean at about the same time.

These Vikings were also traders and colonizers who often fostered urban development and trade in the places they conquered. They founded the town of Dublin, in Ireland, in 841, and they conquered much of northern England, establishing the kingdom of York in the 870s. Vikings also conquered the French territory of Normandy in the late eighth century, from where in 1066 their leader, William of Normandy (William the Conqueror), conquered England. The Normans, as these "Northmen" came to be known, also founded a kingdom in southern Italy and Sicily and established a principality in Antioch.

The Swedes turned eastward across the Baltic Sea and founded trading cities along the river systems of Russia, establishing their capital first at Novgorod in the early ninth century and in Kiev in 882. They proceeded all the way south to the Black Sea, where they traded with the Byzantine Empire. The Swedish settlements became catalysts for the formation of the political and economic organization of the Slavic people in whose midst they were established. Kiev became the capital of the first Russian state; its people were called the "Rus." Historians continue to debate whether that term refers to the Vikings, the Slavs, or the hybrid group that emerged as the Slavic majority assimilated the Viking minority. By about 1000 the fierce Vikings became more peaceful, and their raids ceased as their home regions of Scandinavia developed into organized states and accepted Christianity. They lost interest in further exploration westward across the ocean.

Voyages across the north Atlantic, except those of the Vikings, are not recorded historically and are unlikely to have occurred. In the south Atlantic even less travel took place. There is no known crossing of the south Atlantic. Africans carried on only limited coastal shipping and Europeans were frightened of the unknown hazards of the west African coast, especially south of Cape Bojador. In addition, they recognized that the prevailing winds on the African coast blew from north to south and they feared that while they might be able to proceed to the south they might not be able to return north.

THE DECLINE OF TRADE IN THE MEDITERRANEAN

As Arab armies swept across the Middle East and North Africa, they hesitated before taking to sea battles in the Mediterranean Sea. Nevertheless, in 643 they captured

Alexandria, the most important port in the eastern Mediterranean, and in 655 they engaged and defeated a fleet of the Byzantine Empire at Dhat al-Sawari, off the southwestern coast of modern Turkey. They established their dominion by land along the eastern and southern coasts of the Mediterranean and had enough sea power in the eastern Mediterranean to hold their own against the Byzantine Empire, and even to expand. By about 950 they held parts of southern Italy as well as major islands in the Mediterranean: Cyprus, Crete, and Sicily. The southern and southeastern Mediterranean had become a "Muslim lake." The Byzantine Empire continued, however, to control the northeastern shores of the Mediterranean, and various Frankish and Germanic Christian powers held the north-central coast. The Mediterranean Sea, and its coastline, were divided into three major cultural and political spheres of control: Muslim to the south and southeast, Byzantine to the northeast, and Roman Catholic to the northwest. The Mediterranean is so large and so diverse that such divisions seem natural enough. (Look carefully at the accompanying map of the Mediterranean Sea on page 429 to see the many islands and peninsulas and the many smaller seas that mark its inlets.)

Scandinavian and Arab Muslim, and East Slav invasions, 9th–10th centuries. Europe was subjected to repeated invasions that temporarily weakened the continent but then increased its power. The Vikings settled and developed Scandinavia, and their interaction with the Slavs gave shape to Russia. The Muslims brought with them an understanding of the culture of ancient Greece and Rome that Europeans had forgotten. (Adapted from *The Times Atlas of World History*, 5th edition. London. Times Books.)

Three developments followed these divisions. First, the Mediterranean once again became a war zone. Battles between the Christians of southern Europe and the Muslims of the Middle East and North Africa persisted from the eighth century until 1571, when the naval Battle of Lepanto, in Greek waters, fixed generally accepted zones of control between them. Second, trade continued but oscillated with the fate of Europe's internal economy and with warfare in the Mediterranean. Finally, in the southeastern Mediterranean, where land separated the Mediterranean Sea from the Indian Ocean—where today the Suez Canal provides that link—the European merchants felt blocked. The valuable and profitable merchandise coming from the Indian Ocean basin—the spices of India and Indonesia; the silk and porcelain of China; and the gold and ivory and slaves of East Africa—were controlled by Middle Eastern Muslim traders. The eastern Mediterranean trade blockage is often seen as a religious confrontation. On several occasions, for example, popes forbade Catholics to trade with Muslims. But

AT A GLANCE : MEDIEVAL WORLD TRADE

DATE	POLITICAL/SOCIAL EVENTS	TRADE DEVELOPMENTS	EXPLORATION
1050 C.E.	■ Normans under William I invade England (1066) ■ Seljuk Turks take Baghdad ■ Franks invade Anatolia and Syria and found Crusader states	■ Venice dominates Adriatic; trading ports set up throughout eastern Mediterranean (1000–1100)	
1100 C.E.		■ Wool trade flourishing between England and Flanders	
1150 C.E.	■ Salah al-Din, sultan of Turkish Syria and Egypt, retakes Jerusalem (1187) ■ St. Francis of Assisi (1181–1226) ■ St. Dominic (1170–1221) ■ St. Clare of Assisi (1194–1253)	■ Market fairs in the Champagne region, France	
1200 C.E.		■ Rise of craft guilds in towns of western Europe ■ Foundation of Hanseatic League (1241)	
1250 C.E.		■ Increasing Venetian links with Central Asia and China (1255–95) ■ Revolt of craftspeople in Flanders	
1300 C.E.	■ Hundred Years War between England and France (1337–1453) ■ Bubonic plague in Europe (1346–50)	■ West Africa provides two-thirds of the gold of the eastern hemisphere	
1350 C.E.	■ Ghettoization of Jews in western Europe ■ Ashigawa Shoguns dominate Japan (1338–1573)	■ Revolts of urban workers in Italy and Flanders	
1400 C.E.	■ Ottoman Turks establish foothold in Europe at Gallipoli	■ Great Chinese naval expeditions reach east coast of Africa and India under Zheng He	■ Portugal's Prince Henry the Navigator sponsors expeditions to West Africa
1450 C.E.	■ Printing of Gutenberg's Bible (1455) ■ War of the Roses in England (1453–85) ■ Turks capture Constantinople (1453) ■ Jews driven from Spain (1492) ■ Treaty of Tordesillas (1494)	■ Medici family in Florence: Giovanni, Cosimo, Lorenzo	■ Bartholomeu Dias sails round Cape of Good Hope (1488) ■ Columbus reaches the Americas (1492) ■ Vasco da Gama reaches the Malabar coast, India (1498)
1500 C.E.	■ Machiavelli, *The Prince* (1513) ■ Muslims in Spain forced to convert or leave	■ Portugal sets up trading port of Goa, in India (1502); Portuguese ships armed with cannon	■ Ferdinand Magellan's voyage round globe (1519–22)

For an interactive version of this map, go to: http://www.prenhall.com/spodek/map13.2

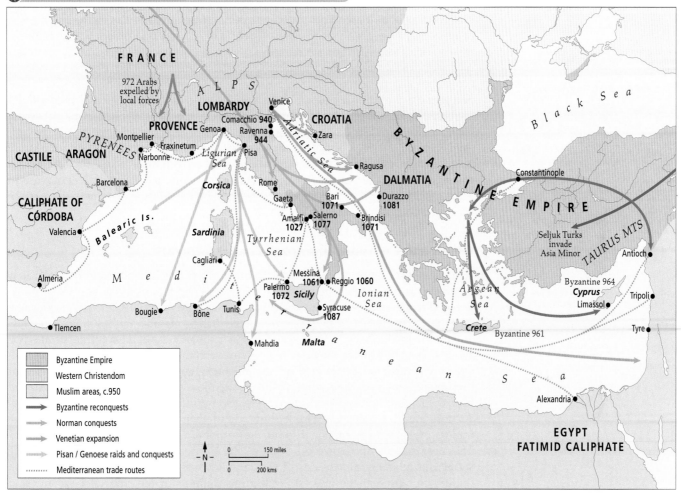

Map legend:
- Byzantine Empire
- Western Christendom
- Muslim areas, c.950
- → Byzantine reconquests
- → Norman conquests
- → Venetian expansion
- → Pisan / Genoese raids and conquests
- ······ Mediterranean trade routes

0 150 miles
0 200 kms
– N –

these prohibitions were generally disregarded. More critical was the competition for profits among the many different groups of traders. The Muslim traders themselves were not a unified group. Most were Arabs, but many of the Egyptian traders were Mamluks, and later Seljuk and Ottoman Turks invaded the area as well. Among the European trading communities, many felt that the city-state of Venice, with its skilled merchants and sailors, controlled the eastern Mediterranean trade in spices, cotton, and silk textiles for its own advantage. Religious and ethnic differences may have exaggerated the tensions among the traders, but the main contest was the competition for profits.

In search of higher profits and easier access to trade commodities, some merchants and some princes began seeking alternative routes to the Indian Ocean. This search took on special intensity in western Europe, which was geographically farther from the Middle East and closer to the Atlantic. Beginning in 1277, a maritime route between Italy and Spain in the Mediterranean and England and Flanders in northwestern Europe brought regular trade to the north Atlantic seacoast of Europe. Also, European trade generally was picking up in the early fifteenth century, as the continent recovered from the devastation of the plague. One search now began to explore the southern Atlantic Ocean for routes around the coast of Africa to India; another sought routes directly across the north Atlantic.

European resurgence in the Mediterranean, c. 1000. After centuries of attacks from Vikings and Muslims, the Europeans of the Mediterranean began to fight back effectively, but the Mediterranean continued as a zone of intermittent warfare between Christians and Muslims until the Battle of Lepanto, 1571. (Adapted from *The Times Atlas of World History*, 5th edition. London. Times Books.)

TRADE AND SOCIAL CHANGE IN EUROPE

The popularity of Marco Polo's accounts of his travels reflects the increasing interest of western Europeans in international trade. The Vikings and others were opening a new world of trade in the eastern fringes of Europe by the mid-1200s, and at about this time western Europeans were beginning to emerge from localized, agrarian, manorial economies and from the localized political systems of administration and order that had marked the Middle Ages. This was a period in which agricultural productivity increased and additional lands were brought under the plow as forests were cut down. New wealth enriched the towns and stimulated trade within Europe, while the crusades brought new opportunities for renewed commerce across the Mediterranean to ports of the Middle East and the merchandise that arrived there from Asia. This rebirth of long-distance trade in Europe aggravated the frustrations of the traders of western Europe with the problems of doing business in the Middle East and the eastern Mediterranean generally.

Guilds and City-states Confront Rural Aristocrats

guild A sworn association of people who gather for some common purpose. In the towns of medieval Europe, guilds of craftsmen or merchants were formed in order to protect and further the members' professional interests and for mutual aid.

As business increased, local traders and manufacturers formed trade organizations called **guilds**. These guilds regulated prices, wages, the quality and quantity of production and trade, and the recruitment, training, and certification of apprentices, journeymen, and masters. The guilds also represented their members in town governments and thus helped to keep industrial and commercial interests at the forefront of the civic agenda. The guilds were the principal organization through which the merchants successfully confronted the landed aristocrats and won legal rights and privileges for their businesses and their cities. Guild members were mostly males, but widowed heads of households and workshops were also included among the voting members.

Most guilds were organized locally, within their hometowns, but international traders organized international guilds corresponding to their commercial interests. The most famous and powerful of them, the Hanseatic League, though lacking the social and religious dimensions of a true guild, was founded in the mid-thirteenth century to represent the interests of leading shippers of the cities of Germany and the Baltic Sea. Headquartered in the city of Lübeck, the League established its own commercial trading posts as far west as London and Bruges (modern Belgium), and as far east as Novgorod in Russia. Throughout the region, it lobbied for legal systems that favored its members. Ships belonging to the League carried grain, timber, furs, tar, honey, and flax westward from Russia and Poland, and woolen goods eastward from England. From Sweden they carried copper and iron ore. In the fourteenth century about 100 towns were affiliated with the League. As states such as the Netherlands (United Provinces), England, and Sweden grew powerful, they asserted their control of the Baltic and the League began to die a natural death after dominating the commerce of its region for almost two centuries.

Opposite **Italian School, The Oar Makers, 18th-century painting of a medieval guild sign.** By the thirteenth century, as the advantages of corporate organizations over individual enterprise loomed larger, specific craftsmen's guilds began to appear—in this case, that of the oar makers. Guilds issued regulations that covered everything from protecting the welfare of deceased members' families to ensuring quality of production. (*Museo Correr, Venice*)

Economic and Social Conflict within the City

In two regions of western Europe, north Italy and Flanders, the manufacture of textiles came to dominate the urban economies. In Florence, between 200 and 300 workshops provided a livelihood for one-fourth of the city's population, producing a total of 100,000 pieces of woolen cloth each year. Other cities of northern Italy, though smaller, had similar workshops. The economies of Flanders and the neighboring regions of northern France and what is now Belgium were increasingly dominated by the production of textiles.

HOW DO WE KNOW?

Fernand Braudel Begins the Historical Study of Oceans

Fernand Braudel (1902–1985) was studying for his doctorate in Paris in the 1920s, specializing in the Mediterranean foreign policy of Phillip II of Spain, when he decided to change course:

I was already beginning to move outside the traditional bounds of diplomatic history when I began to ask myself finally whether the Mediterranean did not possess … a history and a destiny of its own, a powerful vitality, and whether this vitality did not in fact deserve something better than the role of a picturesque background … (The Mediterranean, p. 1)

Braudel left his studies of diplomatic history and joined the group of young Parisian scholars—the "Annales" School—that was transforming the study of history from narrowly political questions to encompass much broader issues of geography, ecology, social structures, and "mentalités," or attitudes. As his work progressed, he became one of the school's most prominent leaders.

Braudel's first great historical work was The Mediterranean and the Mediterranean World in the Age of Phillip II, in two volumes, first published in 1949. Here Braudel worked out in practice his concept of three time frames always operating simultaneously: most deeply rooted, the longue durée, extending back even to geologic times and establishing the fundamental conditions of material life, states of mind, natural environment, and geography; the middle time frame of social, economic, and political organization; and the short term, the time of an individual life, the time frame of most conventional historical study of events. Implementing this concept of diverse time frames, Braudel began with the physical and human geography of the Mediterranean basin, went on to its political systems, and ended with the specific policies of Philip II and other rulers of his time. He examined general population figures, the everyday food that people ate, the houses they lived in, the clothes they wore, the fashions they affected, the technology they used, their money and media of exchange, and the cities they built and used. His work revolutionized the way many historians understood their discipline.

Two generations later, K.N. Chaudhuri encountered Braudel and his work. Chaudhuri explains the impact of that meeting on his own historical research and writing:

The idea that the study of a civilization might be named after a sea originated with Fernand Braudel. Arab geographers were aware a thousand years ago of the relationship between different oceans and the Bilad al-Islam [the lands of Islam]. In our own times, Braudel remains one of a select group of French historians and geographers who have perceived with rare clarity the connection between the sea and the people who lived around its shores. For him the interaction between space, the passage of solar time, and the identity of civilizations constitutes one of the most important latent forces of history … a whole generation of historians have learnt their craft from this great teacher. (Trade and Civilization, p. 1)

Chaudhuri then began writing Trade and Civilisation in the Indian Ocean, which he named in tribute to Braudel's pioneering work on the Mediterranean. Other scholars have followed this lead, and its comprehensive perspective has influenced many more.

- What was Braudel's motivation for leaving his studies of diplomatic history to study the Mediterranean Sea?
- What was new about his work?
- In light of Chaudhuri's comments, what questions that Braudel was asking about the Mediterranean might be useful to ask about other great bodies of water?

Left **Aerial view of present-day Delft, west Netherlands.** Here, gabled medieval townhouses are seen surrounding the bustling market square in Delft. Since the late 1500s the town has been famous for its pottery and porcelain known as delftware. Dutch products began to compete in European markets with porcelain imports from China.

Right **Painting of Hertogenbosch, Netherlands, 1530.** Compare today's photograph of a medieval square on market day *(left)* with this view of a cloth market in another Dutch town painted in 1530. The layout and construction of the stalls are virtually identical.

The new organization of textile production created a complex class structure with some possibility of upward mobility. Capitalist traders organized the manufacture. They estimated the market demand for production and supplied workers with the raw materials and equipment necessary to meet it. Below them, guild masters and the aspiring journeymen and apprentices within the guilds held the best positions among the manual workers: shearing the sheep; fulling the cloth (that is, shrinking and thickening it by moistening, heating, and pressing it); and dyeing the wool. Weavers, carders, and combers were lower on the pay and social scales, and of these, only the weavers were likely to organize a guild. Below all these, an army of poor people washed, warped, and spun the wool. Female and child laborers, employed at even lower pay and in worse conditions than the men, enabled working families to survive. Latent class antagonisms between employer and employee occasionally broke out in open conflict.

Revolts broke out in the Flemish cities of Douai, Tournai, Ypres, and Bruges at the end of the thirteenth century. The leaders were usually craftsmen, and they usually demanded that guild members be allowed to participate in government. The proletariat, the workers outside the guild organizations, could hope only that increased wages, shorter hours, and better conditions of work might trickle down to their level as well.

In the fourteenth century, class antagonisms increased. Increasingly impoverished workers, suffering also from plagues, wars, and bad harvests, confronted increasingly wealthy traders and industrialists. Workers were forbidden to strike and, in some towns, forbidden even to assemble. Nevertheless, a limited class consciousness was growing, especially in Florence, the greatest industrial center of western Europe. In 1345 ten wool-carders were hanged for organizing workers.

New Directions in Philosophy and Learning

On the basis of merchant wealth in the cities, a Renaissance—a rebirth in thought, literature, art, manners, and sensibilities—arose throughout central and western Europe. Most historians see the Renaissance emerging in the fourteenth century with the rise of trade and the increasingly favorable emphasis placed upon the profit motive in western Europe. Historians of the Church, however, detect the roots of this transformation as early as the mid-eleventh century—a period usually referred to as the High Middle Ages—when a shift occurred in religious as well as secular values.

Philosophers in the eleventh century began to suggest that pure faith was not enough to attain salvation. They spoke of additional values that opened the way to a new understanding and experience of the world. St. Anselm (1033–1109) stressed the need for an intellectual basis for faith. Peter Abelard (1079–1142) emphasized the need for a rational approach to the interpretation of texts. St. Bernard of Clairvaux (1090–1153) sought to combine love and spirituality with faith. Meanwhile, the new wealth and power of their Church offended some Roman Catholics, and they challenged the Church to live up to its early ideals of compassion for the poor and simplicity in everyday living. New orders of priests and nuns began to form as a way of returning to these early ideals: Franciscans followed the teachings of St. Francis of Assisi (1181–1226), Dominicans followed St. Dominic (1170–1221), and the "Poor Clares", an order of nuns, followed St. Clare of Assisi (1194–1253).

The same era witnessed an intellectual opening to the Arab world, especially through links in Spain. Christian scholars began the systematic translation of Arabic texts into Latin, reestablishing the link with the ancient Roman and Greek texts that the Arabs had preserved and developed, and that the European world had lost. The works of Avicenna (Ibn Sina) (980–1037), Averroes (Ibn Rushd) (1126–98), and the Jewish philosopher Maimonides (1135–1204) helped restore the emphasis upon logic and philosophy that Aristotle had taught.

Universities were founded to preserve, enhance, and transmit knowledge. Most emphasized practical disciplines: medical studies at Salerno and legal studies at Bologna; theological studies at Paris. All were founded before 1200. Later, students and professors from Paris crossed the English Channel and founded the University

Simone Martini, *St. Francis*, c. 1320. Fresco. Church of S. Francesco, Assisi. St. Francis of Assisi (*c.* 1182–1226) gave away all his possesssions to the poor. When his father disowned him, he stripped naked and, cloaked in a robe given by the Bishop of Assisi, went from place to place begging for food, offering service, and preaching. The religious order that he founded became the largest in Europe.

French School, *Avicenna*, 18th century. Oil on canvas. Ibn Sina, called Avicenna by Christian Europeans, was one of the foremost Islamic students of Aristotle's work. He influenced Church scholars, who re-learned Greek scholarship through him. (*Bibliothèque de la Faculté de Médecine, Paris*)

of Oxford about 1200, with Cambridge following shortly afterward. By 1300 there were about a dozen universities in western Europe; by 1500, nearly one hundred.

Curricula usually centered on theology, but they included grammar, dialectic, rhetoric, arithmetic, music, geometry, and astronomy. The theology curriculum, in particular, required the approval of the Church. This could be problematic, as illustrated by the case of St. Thomas Aquinas (1225–74). St. Thomas was the greatest Christian theologian of his age and paved the way for the new ideas of the Renaissance. Contentiously, he also welcomed the rationality of Aristotle. While many Church leaders rejected Aristotelian logic as contradicting the teachings of the Church, Aquinas saw no conflict. Instead, he declared that logic and reason, as taught by Aristotle, and faith, as taught by the Church, were complementary. In places where they did

Theological lecture at the Sorbonne, Paris, 15th century. Ms illumination. Sponsored by the Church, universities were founded primarily for the study of theology, but some included specializations in medecine and law. All the students were male and most were quite serious-minded. (*Bibliothèque de Troyes*)

HOW DO WE KNOW?

Islamic Influences on the European Renaissance

Arab thinkers, their translations of classical Greek works, and their comments on them, helped inspire the European Renaissance. Ibn Rushd's (Averroes') Arabic translations of and commentaries on Aristotle revealed that philosopher's works to western Europeans who had lost contact with the originals. In addition to his philosophy, Ibn Sina's (Avicenna's) Qanun (Canon) of medicine remained central to European medical thought for centuries. Al-Khuwarizmi's work in mathematics remained influential for centuries, and lives on in our lexicon today in the word algorithm, based on his name. From the tenth to the twelfth century Arabs, Christians, and Jews lived in such proximity, and even harmony, in parts of Spain—the home of these three scholars—that linguistic borrowing back and forth became common. Poetic and prose forms were also borrowed, especially from Arabic literature to Latin and the Romance languages. European scholars, such as Gerard of Cremona, sought out the best in Arabic thought in order to translate it. We have also seen that Europeans adapted Arab technology, such as the caravel, which gave them access to the oceans of the world.

Despite this rich harvest of culture and technology from the Arab world, we have the harsh, even hysterical judgment of Petrarch (1304-1374), one of the greatest Italian poets of the Renaissance, often called "the father of humanism":

I implore you to keep these Arabs from giving me advice about my personal condition. Let them stay in exile. I hate the whole lot ... You know what kind of physicians the Arabs are. I know what kind of poets they are. Nobody has such winning ways; nobody, also, is more tender and more lacking in vigor, and, to use the right words, meaner and more perverted. The minds of men are inclined to act differently; but, as you used to say, every man radiates his own peculiar mental disposition. To sum up: I will not be persuaded that any good can come from Arabia. (Cassirer, et al., p. 142.)

What has happened between the early welcome given to Arabic learning and its bitter, summary rejection by Petrarch? Several interpretations are possible: First, Arabic influence was always greatest in Spain, where Muslims ruled much of the country for centuries, in some regions for almost eight centuries. Other European countries were less influenced. Even in Spain, as Christians began to reconquer the country, they began to focus on Muslims as political and religious enemies rather than as cultural colleagues. A similar change over time occurred throughout the Christian world as the launching of the crusades, after 1095, crystallized a new political antagonism between the two religious communities. The passing of time also brought new cultural currents to Europe, the development of new vernaculars especially in the Romance languages, such as Spanish, Italian, and French, broadening and deepening the base of culture, and making it more nationalistic. The Western Europeans also developed their own intellectual competences and institutions, reducing their reliance on others. The European Renaissance took Western Europeans in new directions.

Scholars sometimes designate three different periods as "renaissances" in Western Europe. The first was the Carolingian Renaissance, initiated by Charlemagne, about 800; the second was the Renaissance of the High Middle Ages, about the middle of the eleventh to the middle of the thirteenth centuries, significantly influenced by Muslim scholarship and learning; the third was the best known, and most influential, the Renaissance of the mid-fourteenth to the mid-sixteenth centuries. Each of the later renaissances built on the earlier ones, but also discarded some of their qualities. In Petrarch's dismissal of Arabic poetry and of Arabs generally we see a dramatic transformation in the attitudes of Christian thinkers, as their own religious and philosophical traditions become less open, and more hostile, to the influences of other cultures.

- The fourteenth century Renaissance took place primarily in Italy and in northwestern Europe. Why do you think it did not take place in Spain, where so much earlier cultural development took place?
- Petrarch turned against Arabic learning, but not against the early Greek philosophers. Would such a division have been possible in twelfth-century Spain? Why or why not?
- Arabic learning could be seen as more successful because it continued to hew to traditional paths, whereas Western Christian scholarship could be seen as a failure for turning in new directions. Would you accept such a characterization?

appear to conflict, however, he conceded that divine truths must take precedence: "Some divine truths are attainable by human reason, while others altogether surpass the power of human reason." Clerics should attempt to reach truth through reason, but when that proved too difficult, divine truths as revealed through the Church were the most reliable guide in showing the true path in life.

Aquinas was ahead of his time. For more than fifty years, the Franciscan order banned the reading of his works. Universities at Paris and Oxford condemned many of his doctrines. But within a century, Aquinas' synthesis of logic and faith, of Aristotle and the Church, became the standard orthodoxy of Roman Catholicism. Although Aquinas gave divine revelation precedence over human reason, on the eve of the

Renaissance he opened the door of the Church to the importance of reason in all human endeavors.

No matter how rigorous the rules and regulations of the universities, the assembly of dozens of inquisitive and exuberant young male students led to challenges to authority and quests for individualism. The "Golliard Poets" took their name from the biblical Goliath, a kind of early anti-Christ. These poets reveled in the pleasures of youth and ridiculed the conventions of sobriety, solemnity, and sanctity. They wrote parodies that were usually irreverent and sometimes obscene, for example, a *Drunkard's Mass*, a *Glutton's Mass*, and an *Office of Ribalds*. They mocked the most sacred beliefs of their time, declaring "I believe in dice … and love the tavern more than Jesus." They declared their blessings for one another: "Fraud be with you."

Today most scholars agree that these many changes in religious and philosophical attitudes opened the way to the European Renaissance, a philosophical and artistic movement that reached its greatest creativity in the two centuries stretching from the mid-1300s through the mid-1500s.

Disasters of the Fourteenth Century: Famine, Plague, and War

Paradoxically, the Renaissance was ushered in not only by an increase in scholarship and cultural borrowing, but also by extraordinary disasters that afflicted Europe in the fourteenth century. The area was plunged into famine, civil upheavals, and, worst of all, a plague that halted its general economic prosperity and its population growth for a century. These catastrophes led to a reshuffling of classes and a reevaluation of values, which provided receptive soil for a renaissance.

For some four hundred years, beginning about 900, Europe's rural population had been increasing in size and density as farmers chopped down forests and brought new land under the plow. However, scarcity of resources then resulted, and by the mid-thirteenth century parts of central Italy, for example, began to suffer depopulation. In addition, in the fourteenth century the climate turned wetter and colder, the winters more severe, reducing harvests. Consequently, the resistance to disease was reduced among populations everywhere.

The plague had begun in Asia and China's population had dropped from about 123 million in 1200 to about 65 million in 1393. When the plague reached Europe by way

Sheep in pen being milked, Luttrell Psalter, 14th century. Woolen-cloth merchants had congregated in Flanders from an early stage, and by the twelfth century the industry there needed English wool to function to capacity. Prior to medieval times overland traders could transport only small and valuable objects over long distances; by the fourteenth century the emergence of sea routes meant that bulk goods, such as wool and grain, could be traded internationally. (*British Museum, London*)

SOURCE

Giovanni Boccaccio Describes the Plague

Giovanni Boccaccio (1313–75) captured the horror of the plague in the introduction to his otherwise droll and humanistic classic of the era, The Decameron:

In the year of Our Lord 1348 the deadly plague broke out in the great city of Florence ... At the onset of the disease both men and women were afflicted by a sort of swelling in the groin or under the armpits which sometimes attained the size of a common apple or egg. Some of these swellings were larger and some smaller, and all were commonly called boils. From these two starting points the boils began in a little while to spread and appear generally all over the body. Afterwards, the manifestation of the disease changed into black or livid spots on the arms, thighs, and the whole person ... Neither the advice of physicians nor the virtue of any medicine seemed to help ... almost everyone died within three days of the appearance of the signs—some sooner, some later ...

The calamity had instilled such horror into the hearts of men and women that brother abandoned brother, uncles, sisters, and wives left their dear ones to perish and, what is more serious and almost incredible, parents avoided visiting or nursing their very children, as though these were not their own flesh. (xxiii–xxiv)

The Triumph of Death, French, 1503. This sixteenth-century work recalls the enormous loss of life caused by the Black Death of 1348. Brought back from East Asia by Genoese merchants, the bubonic plague is estimated to have killed between 20 and 50 percent of Europe's inhabitants. Contemporary medicine was impotent in the face of the disease, whose onset meant almost certain death. (*Bibliothèque Nationale, Paris*)

of trading ships in 1348, it killed off a third of Europe's population, reducing it from 70 million in 1300 to only 45 million in 1400.

Social Unrest Follows the Plague

Peasants who survived the plague benefited from the labor shortages that followed, gaining higher wages and access to more land, freedom from labor services, and geographical mobility. They began to form a new class of property-owning farmers. Together with urban industrial workers and guild members, they rioted more frequently and boldly against kings and nobles who attempted to raise taxes to fund their wars.

In urban areas, too, the new scarcity of workers encouraged those who survived to demand higher wages, better working conditions, and more civic rights. In industrialized Florence, the *Ciompi* (the lowest class of workers, named for the neighborhood of Florence in which they lived), revolted, supported by lower level artisans. In 1378 they presented their demands to the officials of Florence. They wanted open access to the guilds, the right to unionize, a reduction of worker fines and punishments, and the right "to participate in the government of the City." They gained some of their goals, but the powerful business leaders of the city ultimately triumphed. By 1382 the major guilds were back in control, and soon a more dictatorial government under the Medici family was installed. Similar revolts occurred in Flanders, but on a smaller scale, and with no more success. The dissolution of the norms of everyday life, and the certainties of the class structure, inspired a reassessment of fundamental values and institutions that may have helped carry Renaissance values of individualism and a humanistic perspective to the common people as well as the elites.

THE RENAISSANCE

The central motivating philosophy of the Renaissance was **humanism**, the belief that the proper study of man is man. Renaissance humanism held strongly to a belief in God, but assigned Him a less overwhelming, less intimidating role in human life and action. Asserting the importance of the individual, it challenged the monopoly of the Church over the interpretation of cultural life. In his *Oration on the Dignity of Man*, Giovanni Pico della Mirandola (1463–94) places in the mouth of God Himself the most succinct statement of this humanistic perspective of the Renaissance:

I have given you, Adam, neither a predetermined place nor a particular aspect nor any special prerogatives in order that you may take and possess these through your own decision and choice. The limitations on the nature of other creatures are contained within my prescribed laws. You shall determine your own nature without constraint from any barrier, by means of the freedom to whose power I have entrusted you … I have made you neither heavenly nor earthly, neither mortal nor immortal so that, like a free and sovereign artificer, you might mold and fashion yourself into that form you yourself shall have chosen.

According to this typical Renaissance perspective, God gives mankind the power to shape its own destiny.

New Artistic Styles

Renaissance art continued to emphasize religious themes, but it also began to reveal the influence of humanistic and commercial values. Masaccio's painting of *Trinity with the Virgin* (1427) demonstrates the evolution of geometric perspective in painting, suggesting not only a new artistic technique but also a new relationship of individuals to space.

Renaissance in Italy, 1300–1570. From 1300–1570 in Italy, artists and intellectuals worked to fuse the Christian tradition (originating in antiquity but developed during the Middle Ages) with the Greco-Roman tradition in a movement fundamental for the later evolution of the modern civilization of the West: the Renaissance. This map shows the principal places that are associated with the names of important figures.

By the fifteenth century, artistic and commercial sensibilities had joined together. *The Arnolfini Wedding Portrait*, painted in 1434 in Flanders by Jan van Eyck, depicts in a realistic setting and clothing the marriage of a businessman, probably an Italian stationed in Flanders, and his perhaps already pregnant wife. Renaissance artists frequently merged their concerns for secular business affairs with their concerns for a spiritual life.

The richest fruits of Renaissance creativity matured in Florence, where the illustrious Medici family provided lavish patronage. The family's fortune had been built by

humanism A term applied to the intellectual movement initiated in Western Europe in the fourteenth century by such men as Petrarch and Boccaccio and deriving from the rediscovery and study of Classical, particularly Latin, literary texts.

Left **Masaccio, *Trinity with the Virgin, St. John, and Donors*, 1427.** During the Renaissance, people began to rethink their relationship to God and the world around them; at the same time, artists were developing a new means of depicting reality. According to some art history scholars, Masaccio's monumental fresco is the first painting created in correct geometric perspective (the single vanishing point lies at the foot of the cross). (*S. Maria Novella, Florence*)

Below **Jan van Eyck, *The Arnolfini Wedding Portrait*, 1434.** Giovanni Arnolfini, an Italian merchant living in Flanders, commissioned this pictorial record of his marriage. On the far wall, van Eyck has written in Latin "Jan van Eyck was here," much as a notary would sign a document. (*National Gallery, London*)

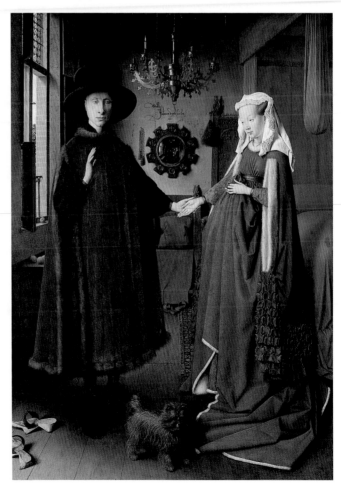

Right **Michelangelo Buonarroti, Sistine Chapel Ceiling (post restoration), 1508–12. Fresco.** Renaissance humanism praised the ability of human beings to be creative and original, yet it continued to be anchored in classical, religious imagery. Pope Sixtus IV commissioned Michelangelo to use his imagination in painting the Sistine Chapel ceiling in the Vatican, Rome, with biblical scenes. (*Vatican Museums and Galleries, Vatican City*)

Leonardo da Vinci, *Vitruvian Man,* **c. 1492. Pen and ink on paper.** Renaissance artists studied the proportions of the human body carefully and represented it accurately. Leonardo's drawing suggests the geometric perfection of the body, relating it both to the circle and the square, and thus to a perfect and harmonious cosmos. (*Galleria dell'Accademia, Venice*)

the merchant-banker Giovanni de' Medici (1360–1429), and was enhanced by his son Cosimo (1389–1464) and grandson Lorenzo (1449–92). In this supportive environment creative artists developed and expressed their genius. They included Michelangelo (1475–1564), the sculptor of such masterpieces as *David*, *Moses*, and the *Pietà*, and the painter of the Sistine Chapel ceiling in Rome; Leonardo da Vinci (1452–1519), scientific inventor and painter of the *Mona Lisa*; and Niccolò Machiavelli (1469–1527), author of *The Prince*, a harsh, and hard-nosed philosophy of government. At the same time, the general population of the city of Florence enjoyed high standards of literacy and expressiveness.

Developments in Technology

Creativity flourished in the practical arts as well as the fine arts, and it contributed substantially to the rise of merchant power. In 1317 merchants in Venice established regular commercial voyages through the Strait of Gibraltar and northward along the Atlantic coast to France and Flanders. Many innovations resulted from amalgamating local techniques with those encountered in the course of trade, especially with Arab civilization. Improvements in sailing technology included a new design in the ships themselves. In the thirteenth century the caravel of the Mediterranean, with its triangular, or lateen (Latin) sails, used mostly by Arab sailors, was blended with the straight sternpost and stern rudder of northern Europe. The caravel could also be rerigged with a square sail for greater speed in a tail wind. The astrolabe, again an Arab invention, helped sailors determine their longitude at sea. The rediscovery in the early fifteenth century of Ptolemy's *Geography*, written in the second century C.E., and preserved in the Arab world, helped to spark interest in proper mapping. (An error in longitude in Ptolemy's map led Columbus to underestimate the size of the globe by about one-third and to think that he could reach East Asia by sailing across the Atlantic.)

Cannon, especially when mounted on ships, gave European merchants firepower not available to others. Although the Chinese had invented gunpowder centuries before, the Europeans put it to practical use in warfare in the fourteenth century to become the masters of gunmaking. By the early 1400s they were firing cannonballs. The Ottoman Turks employed western European Christians to build and operate the cannons they used in 1453 to besiege and conquer Constantinople. The Turkish rulers of Persia also employed European gunners and gun manufacturers, and copied their works. By the late 1400s European warring powers were competing energetically in an "arms race" to develop the most powerful and effective cannons and guns. Leonardo and others worked on the mathematics of the projectiles. When Portuguese ships began to sail into the waters of the Indian Ocean after 1498, claiming the right to regulate commerce, their guns and cannons sank all opposition. Some historians have designated this era the Age of Gunpowder Empires.

The Chinese had also invented the principle of movable type and the printing press, but, again, European technology surpassed them in implementation. Movable type was better suited to Europe's alphabetic languages than to Chinese ideographs. By 1455, in Mainz, Germany, Johannes Gutenberg (*c.* 1390–1486) had printed the first major book set in movable type, the Bible. By the end of the century at least 10 million individual books in some 30,000 different editions had been produced and distributed.

In fourteenth-century Italy, two centuries after the decimal system had been absorbed from India via the Arab world, businesspeople began to develop double-entry bookkeeping. This facilitated the accurate accounting of transactions and the efficient tracking of business profits and losses. In 1494 Luca Pacioli (*c.* 1445–*c.* 1514), a Franciscan friar and mathematician, first published the method in systematic form.

The cannon. From the 1450s, innovations in weapons changed the nature of warfare. The most dramatic changes affected the cannon, as shown here in *Four Books of Knighthood*, 1528.

The Church Revises its Economic Policies

In establishing its independent power, the urban business community confronted not only landed aristocrats on the one hand and organizations of urban workers on the other, but it also faced an often hostile clergy. From its earliest times, the Church had taken a dim view of the quest for private profit and wealth. St. Augustine perpetuated the disdain. In the High Middle Ages theologians seriously debated whether it was possible for a merchant to attain salvation.

The Church forbade Christians to take and give interest on loans. For this reason, Jews carried out much of the business of moneylending. In fact, Jews were so much a part of the merchant classes in early medieval northern Europe that a traditional administrative phrase referred to "Jews and other merchants." Church laws forbidding Jews to own land also pushed them into urban life and commerce. By the end of the thirteenth century, Christian rulers forced Jews to live in ghettos, specific areas of the cities to which they were confined each night. In European society, Jews were stigmatized four times over: alien by religion, foreign by ancestry, moneylenders by occupation, and segregated by residence. Nevertheless, Jews were tolerated as an economically vital trade diaspora until local people mastered the intricacies of business. After that, Jews

Rodrigo Aleman, *The Conquest of Granada on January 2, 1492*, Toledo Cathedral, late 15th century. The conquest of Granada by the Catholic King Ferdinand II and Queen Isabella I of Spain marked the final victory of the *reconquista*, the Christian recovery of all of Spain from Muslim rule. Here the Moorish king Boabdil is handing over the keys to the town.

were often persecuted, sometimes murdered, and repeatedly exiled—from England in 1290, from France in 1394, from Spain in 1492, and from many German cities.

As commerce increased, the Church began to revise its opposition to business and businessmen. St. Thomas Aquinas addressed the issue directly in his *Summa Theologica*. Aquinas justified commerce: "Buying and selling seem to be established for the common advantage of both parties." He wrote of a "just" price, determined by negotiation between buyer and seller. Neither Church nor government needed to regulate prices: "The just price of things is not fixed with mathematical precision, but depends on a kind of estimate, so that a slight addition or subtraction would not seem to destroy the equality of justice." Profit was allowed if its uses were deemed appropriate: "Nothing prevents gain from being directed to some necessary or even virtuous end, and thus trading becomes lawful." Traders were allowed compensation for their labor: "A man may take to trade … and seek gain, not as an end, but as payment for his labor." Aquinas elaborated similar interpretations to allow interest on commercial loans.

Most of the dynamism of western European trade through the fifteenth century emanated from the relatively secular city-states of Flanders and Italy, but in the Iberian peninsula, Portugal and Spain created a powerful new merger of the desire to spread missionary Catholicism with the desire for economic profit. The Portuguese crown dispatched sailing missions along the African coast that ultimately reached the Cape of Good Hope, turned north into the Indian Ocean and onward to India, and were poised to continue on to China. The newly unified government of Spain commissioned Christopher Columbus to sail westward in search of a new route to the Indies. Instead he discovered a "New World."

A NEW WORLD

Portugal was particularly well situated geographically to explore the Atlantic coast of Africa as the opening step in finding an alternative route to India. At first, however, the main goal was to achieve supremacy over the Muslims who controlled the southern shores of the Mediterranean. King John I (*c.* 1385–1435) launched a crusade to capture at least part of North Africa from Muslim control. In 1415 he succeeded in taking Ceuta, a local trading center on the African side of the Strait of Gibraltar. John thought he would achieve both spiritual and economic gain, but once the trans-Saharan caravans saw that Ceuta had fallen to Christians, they turned their trade to other coastal cities.

John's third son, Prince Henry (1394–1460), later called the Navigator, expanded on his father's goals. He, too, wished to defeat Muslim power, but he thought the best

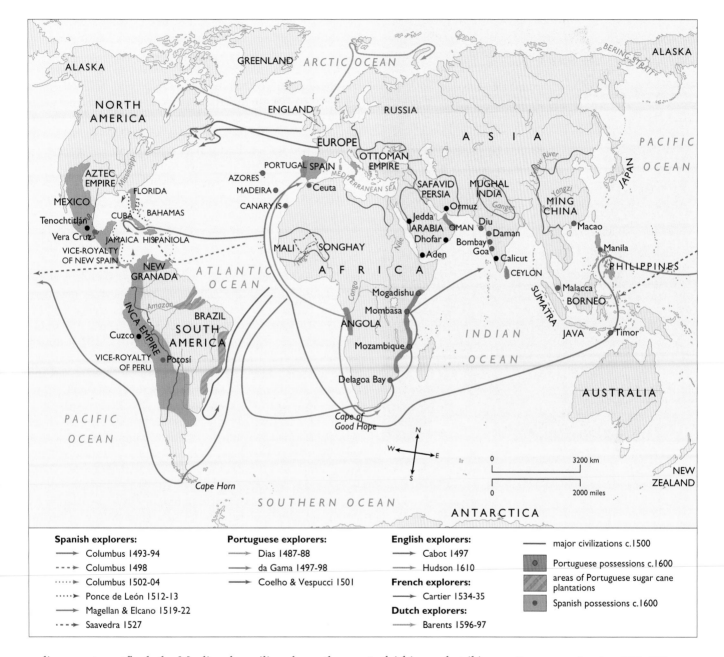

Spanish explorers:

→ Columbus 1493-94

--→ Columbus 1498

····→ Columbus 1502-04

······→ Ponce de León 1512-13

→ Magellan & Elcano 1519-22

--·→ Saavedra 1527

Portuguese explorers:

→ Dias 1487-88

→ da Gama 1497-98

→ Coelho & Vespucci 1501

English explorers:

→ Cabot 1497

→ Hudson 1610

French explorers:

→ Cartier 1534-35

Dutch explorers:

→ Barents 1596-97

——— major civilizations c.1500

⬚ Portuguese possessions c.1600

▨ areas of Portuguese sugar cane plantations

▪ Spanish possessions c.1600

policy was to outflank the Muslims by sailing down the coast of Africa and striking them from the south. Legends of a Christian king, Prester John, sometimes said to rule in Mesopotamia, sometimes in Africa, led Henry, first, to believe that he would find an ally. Second, Henry was curious about the possibility of oceanic exploration. Finally, he believed that it might be possible to reach India by sailing around Africa, although no-one in Europe had any idea of the size and shape of that continent. At the southwestern tip of Portugal he established a center for the study of navigation and the building of ships. He gathered a staff of experts, who tested existing navigational tools, such as the magnetic compass, astrolabe, and compass, and created new geographical and mathematical tables. They constructed caravels modeled on Arab ships, with lateen sails, which could sail with the wind or tack against it, so they would be able to return, no matter what the direction of the prevailing wind. Caravels with lateen sails

European exploration, 1450–1600.
Spanish and Portuguese explorers and traders had established settlements in South America and the Caribbean by 1600, and commercial depots on the coasts of Africa, India, the Pacific islands, China, and Japan—at a time when English, Dutch, and French explorations of North America had just begun.

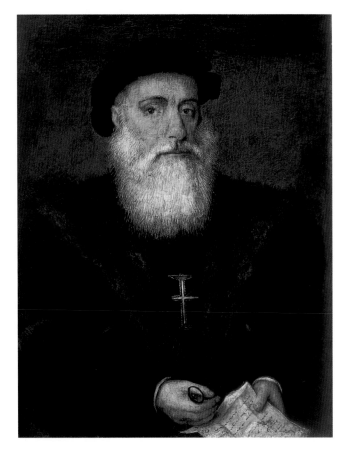

Portuguese School, *Vasco da Gama*, **c. 1524.** Gama's 1497–9 expedition on behalf of the Portuguese Crown completed the sea link from Europe around Africa to India. On his next voyage, 1502–3, he established the policy of using military force to create Portuguese power in the Indian Ocean.

became standard for voyages of Atlantic exploration, including those of Christopher Columbus almost a century later.

Slowly, Prince Henry's men attempted a series of explorations, each reaching just a little further down the African coast. They feared the shoals of the coast, and so sailed out to the west, farther out into the ocean, and allowed the northern winds to blow them south, further down the coast. On an expedition in 1444 they captured some 200 Africans and brought them back to Portugal for sale as slaves. Prince Henry died in 1460, but the project continued. As the Portuguese expeditions rounded the hump of west Africa, they proved their profitability as they reached what they called the grain coast, the ivory coast, the gold coast, and the slave coast—each named for its principal exports to Portugal. In 1488, Bartolomeu Dias (*c.* 1450–1500) reached the southern tip of Africa and turned northward for 300 miles. He would have continued onward—toward India—with his two caravels, but his crew refused to go further. The route, however, now lay open.

Dias' career intersected with that of Christopher Columbus (1451–1506). Columbus was in Lisbon seeking support for his intended exploration westward across the Atlantic just as Dias returned. Dias' report made clear that an alternative route to India had been found: there was no need to risk the transatlantic attempt. The Portuguese crown rejected Columbus' appeal, and so he went to Spain, where he was successful. In 1492 he discovered a transatlantic passage, which he thought had carried him to Japan (Cipangu), or at least its vicinity. Meanwhile, disputes at court and domestic problems delayed further Portuguese sailing, and it was not until 1498 that Vasco da Gama (*c.* 1460–1524) made his epic voyage around the coast of Africa to India. In sailing around Africa, Gama chose not to hug the coast but to sail far out into the Atlantic, as far as the Cape Verde Islands, and ride the winds back to the southern tip of Africa. Once he began the voyage northward, there was another touch of irony. The sea captain who guided him from East Africa to India was, according to legend, Ahmad Ibn Majid, the most famous navigator of his day. Thus, Ibn Majid, quite unknowingly, conveyed to India the first of the European Christians, who would soon displace the Arab Muslim merchants and sailors of the Indian Ocean.

Gama made a triumphal return to Lisbon, although he brought back only two of his four ships and only 55 of his 170 men survived. On his return visit in 1502, Gama initiated the policies of destroying ships, persons, and property, and of seizing goods that marked the early centuries of Portuguese conduct in Asia. His ships were armed with cannon, and he was prepared to use them. For example, he confronted a large dhow carrying pilgrims to Mecca. He burned the ship, apparently killing all the people on board, and seized from it 12,000 ducats and goods worth another 10,000. When Gama returned to Lisbon this time, he left behind a permanent armed naval force of five ships to begin to claim control of the waters of the Indian Ocean. In India and the Indian Ocean, Portuguese navies subsequently destroyed the Muslim fleet in 1509, conquered Hormuz at the entrance to the Persian Gulf, established Goa as the capital of Portuguese activities in Asia, captured Malacca in 1511, and opened oceanic trade with the lands of east and Southeast Asia. Wherever they went, they actively sought converts to Christianity, often by force. By establishing its new trade routes to the east, Portugal achieved its economic goals. In 1503 the price of pepper in Lisbon was one-fifth the price in Venice, and thus trade in the eastern Mediterranean between Venice and Alexandria was undermined.

By 1488, when Columbus' plea to the Portuguese court for support was aborted by Dias' voyage, Columbus had already been trying for three years to gain backing for his venture. He was known in Portugal, for he had sailed on various Portuguese ships as far north as the Arctic Circle, south almost to the equator, east to the Aegean, and west to the Azores. Finally, in Spain he received from the newly merged thrones of Ferdinand of Castile and Isabella of Aragon the backing he needed. In his voyage, Columbus depended on two geographical estimates and he got both wrong. He underestimated the total circumference of the earth and he overestimated the total east–west span of the Eurasian continent. The globe was bigger than he thought, and so was the oceanic distance that he had to traverse. And nowhere in his figures was there the space for two continents of which he and the people of Europe knew nothing, despite Leif Eriksson's voyages. When Columbus arrived in the New World, he thought he had reached islands off the eastern coast of Asia. Although he found only a little gold, he believed—and promised his patrons—that an abundance of it yet awaited him. He promised also a virtually limitless supply of cotton, spices and aromatics, timber, and slaves. He characterized the people of the lands he had come upon as ready for conversion to Christianity. He reported all these observations in a letter addressed to Ferdinand and Isabella.

Six months later Columbus embarked on a much larger expedition with seventeen ships, 1200 men, including six priests to carry on the work of conversion, and enough supplies to establish a permanent settlement. The expedition, however, yielded no serious commercial gains and it took Columbus two years to gain support for a third expedition, in 1498, with only six ships. For the first time, he landed on the continental landmass, in what is today Venezuela. Even at the end of his life, after yet another, fourth voyage that brought him to Central America, Columbus recognized neither the enormity of his mistake nor the enormity of his discovery. He never realized that he had not found China, Japan, India, or islands off the coast of Asia. Nor did he realize that he had discovered a "New World."

Amerigo Vespucci (1454–1512) of Florence was the first person clearly to recognize Columbus' error and his success. In 1499, sailing with a Spanish fleet after Columbus' third expedition, Vespucci traveled some 1200 miles along the coast of South America. He recognized clearly that this was a continental landmass, but he did not yet realize which one. In a second voyage, 1501–2, this one under the flag of Portugal, he traveled some 2400 miles down the coast of South America. He reported carefully on all that he saw: humans and their customs and tools, animals, plants, and hints of great treasures. Unlike Columbus, however, Vespucci was cautious: "The natives told us of gold and other metals and many miracle-working drugs, but I am one of those followers of Saint Thomas, who are slow to believe. Time will reveal everything" (Boorstin, p. 250). On his return to Spain, Vespucci was asked by Queen Isabella to establish a school for pilots and a clearing house for information brought back from the New World. In 1507 the clergyman and mapmaker Martin Waldseemüller published a new map of the world as known at the time, and on it he named the new western areas "America." In 1538, Gerardus Mercator published his large and influential map of the world designating two new continents as North America and South America. Vespucci himself died in 1512 of malaria, contracted on his voyages.

Only the eastern coast of the Americas was known to Europeans when Vasco Nuñez de Balboa (1474–1517) followed the guidance of one of his Native American allies, crossed the Isthmus of Panama, climbed a peak, and, in 1513, became the first European to see the Pacific Ocean. Four years later, Balboa was falsely accused of treason toward the king of Spain and was beheaded. With the recognition that the Americas

SOURCE

The Journal of Columbus' First Voyage to the Americas

Columbus kept a day-by-day journal of his first voyage. Columbus' original has been lost, but fortunately the priest Bartolomé de Las Casas (1474–1566) prepared an abstract that he used in writing his own Historia de las Indias. *Columbus' leading biographer in English, Samuel Eliot Morison, calls the abstract, "The most important document in the entire history of American discovery." This account of what Columbus saw and how he related to it is written sometimes in the first person of Columbus, sometimes in the third person, as the voice of Las Casas. Note especially the overwhelming importance given to religion:*

Prologue: Your Highnesses, as Catholic Christians and Princes devoted to the Holy Christian Faith and the propagators thereof, and enemies of the sect of Mahomet and of all idolatries and heresies, resolved to send me, Christopher Columbus, to the said regions of India, to see the said princes and peoples and lands and the disposition of them and of all, and the manner which may be undertaken their conversion to our Holy Faith, and ordained that I should not go by (the usual way) to the Orient, but by the route of the Occident, by which no one to this day knows for sure that anyone has gone …

12 October 1492: At two hours after midnight appeared the land, at a distance of two leagues … Presently they saw naked people, and the Admiral went ashore in his barge, and [others] followed. The Admiral broke out the royal standard, and the captains [displayed] two banners of the Green Cross, which the Admiral flew on all the vessels as a signal, with an F and a Y, one at one arm of the cross and the other on the other, and over each letter his or her crown … and said that they should bear faith and witness how he before them all was taking, as in fact he took, possession of the said island for the King and Queen …

15 October: It was my wish to bypass no island without taking possession, although having taken one you can claim all …

22 October: All this night and today I was here, waiting to see if the king here or other people would bring gold or anything substantial, and many of this people came, like the others of the other islands, as naked and as painted, some of them white, others red, others black, and [painted] in many ways … any little thing I gave them, and also our coming, they considered a great wonder, and believed that we had come from the sky …

1 November: It is certain that this is the mainland and that I am before Zayto [Zaytun] and Quisay [Hangzhou], [two great port cities of China] 100 leagues more or less distant the one from the other …

6 November: If they had access to devout religious persons knowing the language, they would all turn Christian, and so I hope in Our Lord that Your Highnesses will do something about it with much care … And after your days (for we are all mortal) … you will be well received before the eternal Creator …

12 November: Yesterday came aboard the ship a dugout with six young men, and five came on board; these I ordered to be detained and I am bringing them. Afterwards I sent to a house which is on the western bank of the river, and they brought seven women, small and large, and three boys. I did this because the [Indian] men would behave better in Spain with women of their country than without them …

27 November: Your Highnesses ought not to consent that any foreigner does business or sets foot here, except Christian Catholics, since this was the end and the beginning of the enterprise …

22 December: The Indians were so free, and the Spaniards so covetous and overreaching, that it was not enough that for a lace-tip or a little piece of glass and crockery or other things of no value, the Indians should give them what they asked; even without giving anything they [the Spaniards] wanted to get and take all, which the Admiral had always forbidden …

23 December: In that hour … more than 1000 persons had come to the ship, and that all brought something that they owned, and that before they come within half a crossbow shot of the ship, they stand up in their canoes with what they brought in their hands, saying "Take! Take!" (Morrison, pp. 41–179)

were continental in size, and that another ocean lay between them and Asia, Charles V of Spain commissioned Ferdinand Magellan (*c.* 1480–1521) to sail west, find a passage around the southern tip of South America, and proceed across the Pacific—no matter how big it was—and reach the Spice Islands of East Asia. Magellan set out in 1519 with five ships and about 250 sailors from several different European countries. The voyage became the first circumnavigation of the globe, yielding the first accurate picture of the full magnitude of the planet and completing the picture of most of its main contours. It took just twelve days less than three years. Only eighteen men completed the trip. Magellan himself was killed in a skirmish with Mactan tribal warriors in the Philippine island of Cebu.

OCEANIA

One inhabited continent remained unmapped. Europeans had touched on the northern and western coasts of Australia, but without gaining a clear idea of the continent's size, shape, or character. In 1642, the Dutch East India Company commissioned Abel Tasman (c. 1603–59), a Dutch navigator, to explore the continent. On two voyages, Tasman circumnavigated Australia without actually exploring it. In the process, he also discovered the island later named Tasmania. In 1768, the British government commissioned James Cook (1728–79) to carry out astronomical observations in Tahiti as well as to explore the south Pacific in search of a Great Southern Continent which had been rumored to exist, but whose existence was not proved. He sailed on the *Endeavour*, a sturdy 368 ton, 98 feet long ship, of the sort used to carry coal. He took along with him the young scientist Joseph Banks (1743–1820), who made vast contributions to botany and zoology on the basis of his findings on this voyage. Indeed because of Banks' discoveries, one of the most important harbors in southeast Australia was named Botany Bay. Cook charted the coasts of New Zealand and explored the eastern coast of Australia, but he found no other continent. His voyage of two years and eleven months became the second circumnavigation of the earth. On a second, even more adventuresome voyage, 1772–5, Cook saw the mist, fogs, and icebergs of the Antarctic Ocean, but never landed on or even saw the continent, although he reached within 75 miles of its coast. With these major oceanic adventures, and others, the main contours of the world's oceans and landmasses became known, and, at least geographically speaking, all humanity had come to live in a single, interconnected world.

LEGACIES TO THE FUTURE
WHAT DIFFERENCE DO THEY MAKE?

Voyages of exploration, trade, conquest, and settlement evoke a sense of wonder at the courage, daring, and skill of the captains and sailors who embarked on them, and the governments and businesspeople who organized and financed them. Each participant was called by a different set of values: the desire to chart the unknown; the pressure to find a new home; the quest for profit; the urge to proselytize; the lust for conquest; the competition for superiority. Often, many of these motives were mixed together. Their legacy has left us with admiration for the conquest for the skill of individual European captains to sail into the unknown with such limited ships and equipment. The legacy of these people is the achievement of a geographically known and integrated globe. It is not, however, a single, simple legacy, but a variegated set of mixed legacies that includes competition, greed, self-righteousness, and violence in the achievement of global integration. Few participants prepared for oceanic voyages with the greater good of the entire world at heart. Most, instead, sought benefits for themselves, their region or nation, or their religious group. They looked out on a huge and diverse world from relatively narrow and often self-interested perspectives.

By 1500 European traders had established a permanent connection between the eastern and western hemispheres for the first time, following Columbus' voyages across the Atlantic and Magellan's circumnavigation of the world. Inspired by the early explorations of Prince Henry the Navigator around the west coast of Africa, Portuguese sailors rounded the Cape of Good Hope and opened new routes into the Indian Ocean. These explorations followed centuries of western European economic expansion, national consolidation, and intellectual renaissance. Explorers were motivated by their mixed desire for knowledge, profit, national aggrandizement, and Christian proselytizing.

Review Questions

- Of the groups—Polynesians, Malays, Indians, Chinese, Arabs, and Europeans— discussed in this chapter and in Chapter 12, why do you think that the Europeans were the first to circumnavigate the globe?
- How did the Portuguese displace the Arabs as the predominant maritime power in the Indian Ocean?
- Why do you think that Columbus could not, or did not, recognize that he had not reached East Asia? (There is no single correct answer to this question.)
- What were the demographic, economic, and social effects of the plague in the fourteenth century?
- What was the European Renaissance? To what did degree did it develop from contacts with non-European peoples?

Suggested Readings

PRINCIPAL SOURCES

Adas, Michael, ed. *Islamic and European Expansion* (Philadelphia: Temple University Press, 1993). Key collection of historiographical essays on major topics in world history, 1200–1900. Articles by Eaton and Tucker on Islam, and McNeill on "gunpowder empires" are especially helpful for this section.

Boorstin, Daniel J. *The Discoverers* (New York: Random House, 1983). Extremely well-written, engaging history of four kinds of invention and discovery. One is maritime, mostly European explorers and cartographers 1400–1800.

Chaudhuri, K.N. *Trade and Civilization in the Indian Ocean: An Economic History from the Rise of Islam to 1750* (Cambridge: Cambridge University Press, 1985). A survey of goods, traders, ships, regulations, and competition among those who sailed and claimed to control the Indian Ocean.

Crosby, Alfred W. *Ecological Imperialism: The Biological Expansion of Europe, 900–1900* (Cambridge: Cambridge University Press, 1986). The biological—mostly destructive— impact of European settlement around the world: a tragedy for native peoples from the Americas to Oceania.

Curtin, Philip. *Cross-Cultural Trade in World History* (Cambridge: Cambridge University Press, 1984). Classical statement of the significance and ubiquity of trade diasporas.

SECONDARY SOURCES

Aquinas, St. Thomas. *Summa contra Gentiles* and *Governance of Rulers* (excerpts) in *Introduction to Contemporary Civilization in the West*, cited below. Aquinas defined the field of thirteenth-century Roman Catholic theology—and beyond.

Bloch, Marc. *Feudal Society*, 2 vols. (Chicago: University of Chicago Press, 1961). Classic, if dated, comprehensive view of the workings of feudalism in western Europe.

Boccaccio, Giovanni. *The Decameron*, trans. by Frances Winwar (New York: Modern Library, 1955). Delightful tales, set against the background of the plague raging through western Europe in the 1340s.

Braudel, Fernand. *Capitalism and Material Life, 1400–1800*, trans. from the French by Miriam Kochan (New York: Harper and Row, 1973). Comprehensive survey of the beginnings of the modern capitalist system in Europe.

———. *The Mediterranean and the Mediterranean World in the Age of Phillip II*, 2 vols, trans. Sian Reynolds (New York: Harper and Row, 1973). Comprehensive survey of the beginnings of the modern capitalist system in Europe.

Cassirer, Ernst, Paul Oskar Kristeller, and John Herman Randall, jr. eds. *The Renaissance Philosophy of Man* (Chicago, IL: University of Chicago Press, 1948).

Chaudhuri, K. N. *Asia Before Europe* (Cambridge: Cambridge University Press, 1990). Survey of the economic and political systems of Asia before the impact of colonialism and the industrial revolution. Comprehensive, comparative, and thoughtful.

Cohn, Samuel K., Jr. *The Black Death Transformed: Disease and Culture in Early Renaissance Europe* (London: Arnold, 2002). Studies and summarizes the research on the nature of the plague and its longer term effects.

Columbia College. Columbia University. *Introduction to Contemporary Civilization in the West*, Vol. 1 (New York: Columbia University Press, 2nd ed., 1954). Very well-chosen, long source readings from leading thinkers of the time and place. Vol. I covers about 1000–1800.

Fernandez-Armesto, Felipe. *Columbus* (New York: Oxford University Press, 1991). Careful, sensitive biography of the man and his times.

Frank, Andre Gunder and Barry K. Gills, eds. *The World System: Five Hundred Years or Five Thousand?* (London: Routledge, 1993). In this somewhat tendentious, but well argued, account, globalization is nothing new.

Gabrieli, F. "The Transmission of Learning and Literary Influences to Western Europe,' in Holt, P.M., Ann K.S. Lambton, and Bernard Lewis, eds. *The Cambridge History of Islam, Vol. 2B: Islamic Society and Civilization* (Cambridge, MA: Cambridge University Press, 1970, pp. 851–89). Comprehensive summary of the influence of Islamic learning on Europe, especially good on contrasting different time periods.

The Hammond Atlas of World History ed. Richard Overy (Maplewood, NJ: Hammond, 1999). Excellent, standard historical atlas.

Havighurst, Alfred F., ed. *The Pirenne Thesis: Analysis, Criticism, and Revision* (Lexington, MA: D.C. Heath, rev. ed. 1969). Well-selected pieces from Pirenne, his critics, and supporters. Well introduced, supported, and summarized, although mostly European in orientation.

Hohenberg, Paul M. and Lynn Hollen Lees. *The Making of Urban Europe, 1000–1950.* (Cambridge: Harvard University Press, 1985). Brief, but comprehensive text on the significance of cities to the history of Europe. Special attention to the social development of cities and their residents.

Kee, Howard Clark, *et al. Christianity: A Social and Cultural History* (New York: Macmillan, 1991). An accessible and insightful introduction to a huge subject.

Lindberg, Carter. "The Late Middle Ages and the Reformations of the Sixteenth Century," in Kee, *et al. Christianity*, pp. 257–423. Excellent survey.

Levenson, Jay A. *Circa 1492: Art in the Age of Exploration* (Washington: National Gallery of Art, 1991). Catalogue of an astounding art exhibit, covering the arts in all the major regions in the world at the time of Columbus' voyages.

Morison, Samuel Eliot, trans. and ed. *Journals and Other Documents on the Life and Voyages of Christopher Columbus* (New York: The Heritage Press, 1963). The crucial documents.

Nicholas, David. *The Evolution of the Medieval World* (New York: Longman, 1992). Useful survey.

Pirenne, Henri. *Medieval Cities: Their Origins and the Revival of Trade*, trans. from the French by Frank D. Halsey (Princeton: Princeton University Press, 1925). Classic statement of the importance of free merchants to the rise of commercial cities and the development of the modern world. Dated, and more limited than claimed, but pathbreaking and enormously influential.

——. *Mohammed and Charlemagne*, trans. from the 10th French edition by Bernard Miall (New York: W.W. Norton, 1939). Key revisionist text citing the Islamic victories in the Mediterranean as the end of Roman Europe and the beginning of rebirth in the north under Charlemagne.

Polanyi, Karl, Conrad M. Arensberg, and Harry W. Pearson, eds. *Trade and Market in the Early Empires* (Chicago: The Free Press, 1957). Fundamental argument by historical anthropologists that early trade was mostly regulated by rulers and priests.

Reynolds, Susan. *Fiefs and Vassals* (Oxford: Clarendon Press, 1994). Scholarly, influential examination of "feudalism," arguing that the word is misused to cover too wide a variety of regional and temporal patterns.

Subrahmanyam, Sanjay. *The Career and Legend of Vasco da Gama* (Cambridge: Cambridge University Press, 1997). The most thorough available account of the man, his contributions, and the historical puzzles surrounding them, presented in overwhelming scholarly detail.

Tuchman, Barbara. *A Distant Mirror: The Calamitous Fourteenth Century* (New York: Knopf, 1978). Engaging history of a century filled with war and plague.

Wills, John E., Jr. "Maritime Asia, 1500–1800: the Interactive Emergence of European Domination," *American Historical Review* XCVIII, No. 1 (February 1993), 83–05. Survey of European entrance into and domination of Indian Ocean and Chinese sea lanes.

World History Documents CD·ROM

THE UNIFICATION OF WORLD TRADE

NEW PHILOSOPHIES FOR NEW TRADE PATTERNS, 1500–1776

KEY TOPICS

- The Expansion of Europe and the Birth of Capitalism
- The Empires of Spain and Portugal
- Trade and Religion in Western Europe: The Protestant Reformation and the Catholic Reformation
- The Nation-State
- Russia's Empire under Peter the Great
- Diverse Cultures, Diverse Trade Systems
- The Influence of World Trade: What Difference Does It Make?

THE EXPANSION OF EUROPE AND THE BIRTH OF CAPITALISM

By 1500, ocean voyages of exploration and trade had brought the eastern and western hemispheres together, initiating a new phase of world history. During the next three centuries most of the regions of the world began to enter into a single system of trade and exchange. The organization of this emerging system generally followed the economic principles of **capitalism**, being dedicated to the pursuit of private economic profit through the private ownership of wealth and the means of producing wealth.

Capitalism claimed to allow individuals to exchange their products and labor in free, unregulated markets. It had little place for the restrictive rules of Church and government. Free-market exchange would determine the prices of goods and labor by reaching a balance between supply and demand. These market prices would then influence what would be produced and what would be consumed. The lure of the market would encourage people to invest their capital, or accumulated wealth, in economic activities that might earn profits (or suffer losses). Despite these free-market claims and their desire to be free of regulation, capitalists frequently persuaded governments to support and assist them in their money-making projects. In exchange, capitalists lent their financial support to government.

Major west European governments had been following principles of **mercantilism**, the belief that government should regulate trade—especially by restricting the outflow of gold and silver—for the greater strength of the state. Slowly these governments were persuaded that allowing businessmen more freedom of trade would in fact benefit the state even more by generating more taxable wealth. Capitalists and the governments worked together to achieve the goals of both: protection and encouragement for the businessmen, taxes for the state.

Western European businessmen led in sponsoring new international trade initiatives that emphasized private profit and national aggrandizement. As a result, the trading centers of northwestern Europe grew ever larger. By 1700, London had a population of 550,000, Paris, 530,000, Lisbon, 188,000, and Amsterdam, 172,000. Each of

capitalism An economic system characterized by private or corporate ownership of the means of production and by private control over decisions on prices, production, and distribution of goods in a free, competitive market of supply and demand.

mercantilism An economic policy pursued by many European nations between the sixteenth and eighteenth centuries. It aimed to strengthen an individual nation's economic power at the expense of its rivals by stockpiling reserves of bullion, which involved government regulation of trade.

Opposite **Imam Quli Khan's soldiers in boats being repulsed by the Portuguese at Hormuz. Miniature, seventeenth century.**

these cities was both a national capital and a major trading center. Economic and political interests reinforced one another.

In western Europe, overseas trade was restructuring public life, but it was not equally important in other parts of the world. In several very large empires, government by itself continued to be a formidable force and more important than private business. The largest city in Europe, for example, was not an Atlantic Ocean port but Constantinople (modern-day Istanbul), the capital of the Ottoman Empire. It, too, was an important commercial city, serving the eastern Mediterranean and the Middle East, but it owed its size—700,000 residents—and importance more to its political role than to its trade. In India, China, Japan, and Southeast Asia, too, government authorities generally dominated business interests. There were exceptions, but government control was the pattern.

Each major region of the world also had a very different experience in confronting the new international world system of trade being fashioned by the Europeans. The Americas, for example, succumbed almost immediately. The Chinese, on the other hand, remained somewhat independent of the system until the mid-nineteenth century, and in some ways China actually dominated the system. Even though the Chinese and Indians were not the shippers carrying the goods overseas, it was their products and their economies that evoked a very large proportion of international trade. Chinese products—especially tea, silk, and porcelain—were the objects of a great deal of the trade. The Europeans sailed in order to get them—as well as the spices and textiles of India and Indonesia, and the gold and, later, some 10 million enslaved people of Africa. Almost half the silver of the New World mines went to China to pay for exports to Europe. Asians and Africans may not have sailed as widely and aggressively as Europeans did after 1500, but it was the goods of Asia and Africa that motivated the European voyages. Later, as in the Americas, Europeans would seek ever greater control over the terms of trade. Finally they would impose colonial rule, in part to create new terms of trade more favorable to themselves. In many respects, these societies let others dominate ocean trade because of geographical factors as well as the belief that they produced everything they needed at home.

THE EMPIRES OF SPAIN AND PORTUGAL

The Ottoman conquest of Constantinople in 1453 gave it control of the eastern Mediterranean trade and encouraged the Atlantic countries to seek new routes to Asia, inspiring Columbus' and Vasco da Gama's voyages of exploration. The first European nations to dominate the new overseas trade and colonization were the Spanish and the Portuguese. Both faced directly on the Atlantic Ocean. Portugal's rulers saw the Atlantic as their front door to the world. Spain's rulers, just consolidating their country in 1492, saw it as a new route to riches, power, and proselytization.

Spain's New World Conquests

The four voyages of Christopher Columbus between 1492 and 1504 revealed to the Spanish crown some of the opportunities for agricultural development, religious conversion, and exploitation of resources in gold and silver to be found in the Americas. Spanish settlers began to colonize the islands of the Caribbean and the north coast of South America. In response to tales of great riches, Spanish conquistadors marched inland to conquer what they could. In 1519, Hernán Cortés began his expedition from Veracruz with 600 Spaniards, a few guns, and sixteen horses. Because the Aztecs under Moctezuma II engaged in frequent wars and collected extensive tribute from various

SOURCE

Adam Smith on Capitalism

By the late eighteenth century, as European economies were expanding, they became the subject of discussion and debate among businesspeople, political leaders, and philosophers. Adam Smith (1723–90) had already established his reputation as a moral philosopher before he turned to writing what became his most famous work. In 1776 Smith published The Wealth of Nations, *a book of a thousand pages, the first systematic explanation of a newly emerging philosophy of economics, later called capitalism.*

In contrast to the mercantilist views of his day, Smith argued that national wealth was not to be measured by treasuries of precious metals, but rather by quantities of productivity and of trade. He opened his great work with an illustration from a pin factory where a division of labor into specialized tasks of production increased output dramatically. Smith further argued that when workers specialize in what they do best, and then exchange their products in the market, productivity increases. The competitive free market guides production: Goods that consumers want to buy attract higher prices, and producers supply them in order to earn good profits; unwanted goods earn no profits, and producers stop producing them. This law of supply and demand in the market, argues Smith, leads to the production of the amounts and kinds of goods that suit the wishes of consumers and the capacity of producers. According to Smith's Law of Accumulation, profits are reinvested in further production.

Smith reached a new and surprising conclusion: Wealth comes not from the command of a ruler, nor the regulations of the clergy, nor the altruism of members of the community, but as a result of people pursuing their own economic self-interest and exchanging the fruits of their labor in the market.

> It is not from the benevolence of the butcher, the brewer, or the baker that we expect our dinner, but from their regard to their self-interest. We address ourselves, not to their humanity, but to their self-love, and never talk to them of our necessities, but of their advantages. (Smith, p. 14)

Although Smith did not use the term, today we call the system he analyzed capitalism—that is, most wealth, or capital, rests in private, non-governmental hands, and economic decisions on price, supply, and demand are made through the free market rather than by government decision. Critics of this capitalist market system, in which buyer and seller negotiate freely over prices, equated capitalism's self-interest with greed, but Smith explained how competition transformed self-interest into community benefit: If a greedy producer charges too much for his goods, someone else will undercut him and lower prices will result; if he pays his employees too little, they will abandon him and seek work elsewhere. Out of the conflicting self-interests of individual members of the society, paradoxically, social harmony will emerge. Smith, who was a professor of moral philosophy at the University of Edinburgh, disagreed with those who said that rulers or priests must regulate the economy to achieve equity. Like an "invisible hand," the impersonal market would do the job.

Believing that the free, unregulated market would correct most economic imbalances, Smith opposed government intervention. He argued for a hands-off government policy of **laissez-faire** *toward the market—that is, let people do as they choose. But he did recognize that some necessities for economic growth were beyond the powers of any single, small producer. "The erection and maintenance of the public works which facilitate the commerce of any country, such as good roads, bridges, navigable canals, harbors, et cetera, must require very*

different degrees of expense" (Vol. 5, p. 1), and therefore Smith urged government to promote these public works. He believed that education was fundamental to economic productivity. Private education was more effective than public education, but government-supported public education was better than none.

Smith recognized, of course, that the market did not always succeed in balancing supply and demand. Huge businesses that formed virtual **monopolies** *could control whole industries and manipulate market forces. Their size gave them unfair leverage and Smith wanted them broken up. The* Wealth of Nations *attacked the British East India Company, the joint stock company that monopolized virtually all of Britain's trade in Asia and had even become the acting government of Bengal in India. Smith argued that its monopoly should be broken. His plea, however, did not bring about a change.*

Capitalism was the prevailing economic philosophy in Britain in the years of its economic supremacy in the nineteenth century, and the new system spread to many other countries as well. As we shall see in the following chapters, many critics blamed capitalism for the inhumanity and cruelty of the slave trade, the seizure of colonies overseas, and the vulnerability of workers at home. Smith understood these problems, but argued that they were corruptions of the market system rather than natural products of it. He condemned slavery as a form of kidnapping and theft of human beings, rather than a free-market exchange. Similarly he deplored the European destruction of the Native American states and populations as a violation of human ethics:

> The savage injustice of the Europeans rendered an event which ought to have been beneficial to all ruinous and destructive to several of those unfortunate countries. (Smith, p. 416)

laissez-faire An economic policy of non-interference by government in the working of the market and the economic affairs of individuals.

monopoly The exclusive control over the production or supply of a particular commodity or service for which there is no substitute.

Emperor Atahualpa arrested by Francisco Pizarro in 1532. When Pizarro landed on the northern coast of Peru on May 13, 1532 he brought with him a force of 200 men with horses, guns, and swords. The Inca Emperor Atahualpa, backed up by thousands of troops, felt he had little to fear from the Spanish and, as this contemporary Peruvian drawing shows, he accepted Pizarro's seemingly friendly invitation to meet accompanied only by his bodyguards. It was a trap, and Pizarro arrested and later executed him.

tribes living in the region, Cortés was joined by thousands of Native Americans from the various states through which he passed, who wished to overthrow the powerful Aztec empire at Tenochtitlán, modern-day Mexico City. Cortés' small force entered the city without a struggle on November 8, 1519, possibly helped by a woman, Malinche or Marina, who became his mistress and translator. The peace didn't last, however, and after the Spaniards massacred several Aztec leaders during a festival, the population revolted. They killed Moctezuma believing that he had collaborated with Cortés, and they forced the conquistadors to leave the city on June 30, 1520. Cortés suffered heavy losses, perhaps as many as two-thirds of his men and several horses, but the Spaniards reached Tlaxcala, where their new Native American allies nursed them back to health and helped them plan to retake Tenochtitlán. The Spaniards conquered the capital city again on August 13, 1521 after a bitter four-month siege, and the empire fell to them. In the next twenty years they captured the Yucatán and most of Central America, although revolts continued in the region. Cortés became ruler of the Kingdom of New Spain, reorganized in 1535 as the Vice-Royalty of New Spain.

In South America, the Inca Empire of the west coast and Andes Mountains became accessible to Spanish conquistadors after Vasco Nuñez de Balboa found a portage across the Isthmus of Panama in 1513. Now the Spanish could transport their ships from the Atlantic coast overland across the Isthmus and sail south along the Pacific Coast to Peru. Rumors of great stores of gold encouraged these voyages. Like the Aztecs, the Inca were divided. In 1525, after the death of Huayna Capec, possibly from smallpox, a civil war broke out between two of his sons—Huáscar and Atahualpa—over who should rule the empire. Fighting was fierce and ended only in 1532, when Atahuallpa captured Huáscar and executed him In the same year, Francisco Pizarro, leading a force of some two hundred men, captured Atahualpa. Although given a room full of gold as ransom for the emperor's life, Pizarro nevertheless feared a revolt and killed him. In 1533 he captured the Inca capital, Cuzco. The Spanish conquistadors fought among themselves for years until Spain established the Vice-Royalty of Peru in the mid-sixteenth century as the South American counterpart to the Vice-Royalty of New Spain in the north. Revolts against the Spaniards continued until they captured and beheaded the last Inca emperor, Tupac Amarú, in 1572.

How had a few hundred Spanish soldiers and their Indian allies succeeded in overthrowing the two largest empires in the Americas? The conquered Native Americans:

Inca–Spanish wooden drinking vessel, Peru, c. 1650. This painted Inca ritual drinking vessel made of wood, known as a *kero*, represents people of three different cultures: to the left, an Inca dignitary; in the center, a Spaniard playing a trumpet; and on the right, one of the earliest depictions of a black African in South America, a man playing a drum.

• were divided and fought among themselves. The Native Americans were not a single united people, but many different, competitive, and even warring peoples. In conquering the

AT A GLANCE : THE INTERCONNECTING WORLD

DATE	EUROPE	THE AMERICAS	ASIA AND AFRICA
1500	■ Communero revolt in Spain (1520–21) ■ Luther excommunicated (1521)	■ Four voyages of Christopher Columbus (1492–1504) ■ Cortés conquers Tenochtitlán (1521)	■ Portuguese establish trading posts in East Africa (1505) ■ Portugal captures Goa, India (1510) ■ Portuguese missionaries arrive in China (1514)
1525	■ Henry VIII becomes head of new Anglican church (1534) ■ First stock exchange in Antwerp (1538) ■ Calvin establishes Presbyterian theocracy in Geneva (1541)	■ Pizarro captures Inca emperor Atahualpa (1532) ■ Potosí silver mine discovered (1545)	■ Mughals invade India (1526) ■ St. Francis Xavier arrives in Japan (1549)
1550	■ Council of Trent (1545–63) ■ End of Hundred Years War (1558) ■ Tobacco first introduced into Europe (1559); potato (c. 1565)	■ Portuguese begin sugar cultivation in Brazil (c. 1560)	■ Akbar consolidates Mughal Empire (1556–1605) ■ Spanish capture Manila, Philippines (1571) ■ Portuguese establish colony in Angola (1571)
1575	■ Spanish Armada defeated by England (1588) ■ Henry IV of France issues Edict of Nantes (1598)		■ Matteo Ricci arrives in China (1582) ■ Japan invades Korea (1592)
1600	■ Dutch, English, and French East India companies founded ■ Holland wins independence from Spain; Bank of Amsterdam established (1609)		■ Tokugawa shoguns begin consolidation of Japan (1603) ■ Christianity outlawed in Japan (1606) ■ Dutch found Batavia (Jakarta), Indonesia (1619)
1625	■ Portugal declares independence from Spain (1640) ■ Russia captures Siberia (1649)		■ Manchus conquer China and form Qing dynasty (1644)
1650	■ English Navigation Act (1651) ■ Louis XIV of France, the "Sun King" (1643–1715)		■ Dutch capture Cape of Good Hope (1652)
1675	■ War of the League of Augsburg (1688–97) ■ Bank of England created (1694)		■ Qing dynasty establishes "Canton system" (1683)
1700	■ Peter the Great founds St. Petersburg (1704) ■ War of the Spanish Succession (1702–13) ■ Act of Union creates Great Britain (1707)		■ Edo, Japan, has 1 million people
1725	■ War of Austrian Succession (1740–8)		
1750	■ Seven Years War (1756–63) ■ Adam Smith, *The Wealth of Nations* (1776)	■ War of American Independence (1775–81)	■ After English victory at Plassey, English gain Bengal (1757)

dominant groups—Moctezuma's Aztecs in Mexico and Atahualpa's Inca in Peru—the Spanish found many allies among the enemies of these groups. In addition, the Inca were weakened by their own civil war.

● lacked the Spaniards' military technology and organization. The Spanish introduced firearms, steel armor and weapons, and horses—animals that had never previously been seen in the Americas. The Spaniards also fought differently from the indigenous populations, shooting from a distance rather than engaging in the hand-to-hand warfare practiced by the Aztecs.

World exploration. The limitations on sea routes through the Middle East drove the trading nations of western Europe to seek alternate maritime passages to Asia. European navigators and cartographers rapidly built a map of the globe which included, by sailing west, the "New World" of the Americas and, by sailing south, a passage around Africa, linking with the Arab trading routes of the Indian Ocean. The voyages of the Ming Chinese admiral Zheng He were undertaken to demonstrate China's strength even more than for trade.

- were demoralized when their commanders-in-chief, Moctezuma II in Mexico and Atahualpa in Peru, were captured. The Indian empires were highly centralized so that the capture and murder of their leaders left them disorganized. Less centralized and more remote groups, like the Araucanians of central Chile, held out far longer, winning a revered place in Latin American history and poetry.
- succumbed to European diseases, such as smallpox. The Native Americans had no immunity to these diseases that were new to the Americas. The diseases proved far more deadly than the warfare.

Legend had it that the Indians also viewed the Spanish as gods returning to their homelands and therefore deserving of obedience rather than resistance, but recent scholarship has dispelled this myth as a fiction later created by the Spanish.

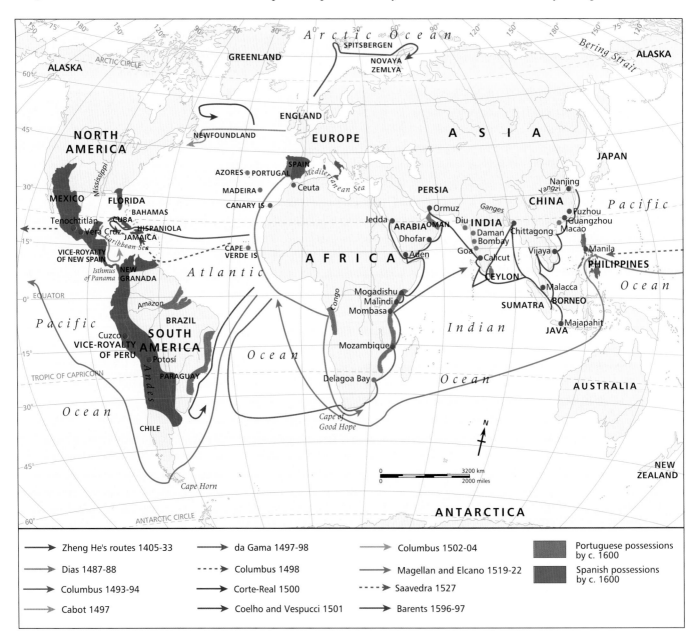

→ Zheng He's routes 1405-33	→ da Gama 1497-98	→ Columbus 1502-04	▨	Portuguese possessions by c. 1600
→ Dias 1487-88	----▶ Columbus 1498	→ Magellan and Elcano 1519-22	▨	Spanish possessions by c. 1600
→ Columbus 1493-94	→ Corte-Real 1500	----▶ Saavedra 1527		
→ Cabot 1497	→ Coelho and Vespucci 1501	→ Barents 1596-97		

Making the Conquests Pay. After the conquests, the Spanish began to reorganize the economies of the Americas. They established the *encomienda* system, assigning the taxes and the labor of local Indian populations to Spanish colonists who were also to convert them to Christianity, if possible. The Indians were enslaved under conditions of great cruelty. The *encomienda* system was first established on the island of Hispaniola, where in twenty years the Indian population fell from several million to 29,000. Humane voices, especially of priests such as Bartolomé de Las Casas, opposed the *encomienda* system, but it continued until so many Indians died that it could function no longer. In most of Mexico and Peru the system had ended by the late 1500s, but it operated for another century in Venezuela; for another two centuries, until 1791, in Chile; and until the early 1800s in Paraguay.

The systems that replaced it were not much more humane. The *repartimiento* system in central Mexico and the similar *mita* system in Peru forced Indians into low-paid or unpaid labor for a portion of each year on Spanish-owned farms, in mines and workshops, and on public works projects. These systems, too, were forms of unofficial slavery. Not all labor was coerced, however. Spanish-owned plantations or *haciendas*, agricultural estates producing commercial crops and livestock, employed both free and indentured labor. The *haciendas* often produced commercially the newly imported products of the eastern hemisphere—wheat, cattle, pigs, sheep, chickens, horses, and mules—in addition to the indigenous local crops of maize, potatoes, and manioc (cassava).

Perhaps the worst conditions existed in silver mines, which also used paid labor at very low wages. The immense Potosí mine in Upper Peru (today's Bolivia) employed 40,000 Indian miners in the seventeenth century. Tunnels were dug that destroyed the landscape, and working conditions were inhuman. Children were forced to crawl through cracks and were often made to work without breaks.

As sugar plantations were introduced into the Caribbean islands and into Portuguese-held Brazil, Indian laborers were unable or unwilling to perform the gang labor of the cane fields, so slaves were imported by the millions from Africa. African slaves also worked the tobacco, cacao, and indigo plantations.

From the Spanish perspective, the most valuable products of the Americas throughout the sixteenth century were gold and silver. The mine at Potosí, discovered in 1545, was the largest silver mine in the world. Smaller mines were opened in Mexico in 1545 and 1558. In 1556 a new method of separating silver from ore by using mercury, available from Almadén in Spain, was discovered. Between 1550 and 1800 Mexico and South America produced more than 80 percent of the world's silver and more than 70 percent of its gold. The precious metals were exported each year from Latin America eastward to Europe and westward to

encomienda A concession from the Spanish crown to a colonist, giving him permission to exact tribute from a specified number of Indians living in a certain area.

repartimiento A system by which the Spanish crown allowed colonists to employ Indians for forced labor.

mita A system of forced labor in Peru, begun under Inca rule, by which Indian communities were required to contribute a set number of laborers for public works for a given period.

hacienda A large rural estate in Spanish America, originating with Spanish colonialization in the sixteenth century.

Plan of Potosí and the Cerro Rico (Rich Hill), Upper Peru. This seventeenth-century painting shows Potosí and the hills in which the lucrative silver mines were located. The mines at Potosí employed some 40,000 poorly paid Indian laborers and tens of thousands of horses—shown in this painting ascending and descending the hills—to transport the material and drive the machinery.

the Philippines, where the Spanish had captured Manila in 1571 and established it as their chief trade center for East Asia. They were ultimately used to pay for European purchases of silks, tea, textiles, and spices from India and China. Between one-third and one-half of all American silver produced between 1527 and 1821 found its way to China. The Mexican peso became a legal currency in China. Asian traders demanded payment in gold and especially silver because Europe itself produced very little of interest to them.

Merchant Profits. The gold and silver mines of the Americas brought enslavement and poverty to the Native Americans, and they benefited the Spaniards less than the merchants of Antwerp, Genoa, Amsterdam, London, and Paris. The Spanish did not have the commercial infrastructure to employ their newly captured resources in profitable investments, and they lacked the ships to carry the trade generated by the new finds of gold and silver. The experienced merchants of the trade cities of Europe organized the necessary commercial services. They exchanged the raw metals for cash and bills of exchange, provided loans to tide over the period from the arrival of one shipment of silver to the next, arranged the purchase of goods needed by the Spanish, and supplied the necessary shipping. In the sixteenth century, the most important of these commercial centers was Antwerp (Belgium), with its skilled and wealthy merchants from Antwerp and from England, France, Portugal, Italy, Spain, and Germany.

Warfare and Bankruptcy. Many regions of Europe at this time were "owned" by particular families, who had the responsibility to protect them and the rights to tax them and bequeath them to others. These families often intermarried—and whole countries changed rulers. Charles V (r. 1515–56) inherited Spain and the Spanish colonies in Africa, the Americas, Naples, and Sicily from his mother's parents, Ferdinand of Aragon and Isabella of Castile. From his father's family, the House of Burgundy, he inherited the Netherlands and the German lands owned by the Habsburg family. Charles was the most powerful ruler in Europe.

Charles V had been raised in Flanders by his father's family of the House of Burgundy. He spoke no Spanish, and his pride and foreignness alienated the Spanish. He appointed foreign courtiers from Flanders to offices in Spain, and he used Spanish wealth to fund his political programs in central European territories. Spaniards revolted. The nobles wanted to stop the drain of money to central Europe and the assignment of offices to foreigners. They wanted Charles to return to Spain. As civil order broke down, artisans and business classes in Castile revolted against the great landholders in the Communero revolt of 1520–21. The revolutionaries held conflicting goals, and as they fought one another to exhaustion Charles easily retained his hold on government.

But when Charles entered into wars against the Ottoman Turkish Empire in eastern Europe and on the Mediterranean, and into the Christian religious wars of Catholic versus Protestant in northern and central Europe (see next section on the Protestant Reformation and the Catholic Reformation), he bankrupted even the silver-rich treasury of Spain. After Charles's abdication in 1556, his son Philip II (r. 1556–98) continued the politics of warfare and suffered much the same fate. Even his military victories were financial defeats.

Portugal's Empire

Isabella and Ferdinand united their thrones, creating modern Spain in 1492, but the western third of the Iberian peninsula, Portugal, remained a separate state. For sixty years, from 1580 to 1640, it was incorporated into Spain, but otherwise it has remained separate until today. In terms of worldwide exploration and trade, Portugal, under the leadership of Prince Henry the Navigator (1394–1460), who sponsored many voyages along the coast of Africa, had entered the field earlier and more vigorously than Spain.

Portugal in Africa. Portugal sought souls for Christianity, gold for its national treasury, grain and fish for its domestic food supply, and slaves for its new sugar plantations. Portuguese entrepreneurs, having seen sugar plantations in the eastern Mediterranean, planted their own on Madeira and other islands in the Atlantic Ocean off the coast of Africa. (Spanish landlords and businessmen did the same in the Canary Islands.) These new plantations needed laborers. Portugal went to Africa to obtain them.

In 1415 Portugal captured Ceuta on the Moroccan coast of North Africa, one of the major points of the trans-Saharan trade in gold and slaves. Then, to get closer to the sources of supply, Portuguese ships, supported by the crown, sailed down the coast of West Africa, rounding Cape Bojador in 1434 and continuing on to the Gold Coast in 1472. Bartholomeu Dias reached the Cape of Good Hope and continued northward, sailing his slim, long caravels, a few hundred miles up the east coast of Africa in 1488. As the Portuguese explored they also built fortresses—such as El Mina in modern Ghana—as assembly and shipping points for their purchases of slaves and gold. For

The first European trading empires about 1750. European seaborne intercontinental trade was dominated by Spain and Portugal in the sixteenth century. The Spanish rapidly colonized Central America, the Andes mountain regions, and the Philippines. The Portuguese concentrated on the coasts of Brazil, east and west Africa, and the Arabian Sea ports of India. A century later the Dutch, English, and French followed, establishing settler colonies in North America and South Africa and fortified trading posts along the coasts elsewhere.

The fortress of São Jorge da Mina (later called El Mina), African Gold Coast, 1482. Built at the order of King John II of Portugal in 1482, this fortress—like many others—provided a fortified trading post designed both to protect Portuguese trade from rival Europeans and to serve as a supply base. At the beginning of the sixteenth century trade was in gold and kola nuts with imports of American crops such as maize and cassava, and trans-shipment of slaves. It was not until the late seventeenth century that the export of slaves became the main trade on the Gold Coast.

the most part, the Portuguese remained in their coastal enclaves of fortresses, trading posts, and Christian missionary outposts.

At some points, however, the Portuguese did venture inland to explore, trade, evangelize, and attempt to conquer. From El Mina, on the Gold Coast, for example, they went inland to trade directly with Mane and Soninke merchants. In the Kongo, they converted King Nzinga Mbembe (1507–43) and many of his people to Christianity, although the Portuguese slave trade in the Kongo ultimately alienated people from their king. He wrote to the king of Portugal, on humanitarian grounds, that the slave trade was destroying the Kongo as its people turned predatory towards one another. He wanted the trade stopped. His plea was ignored. The Portuguese, and the Kongolese themselves, desired the profits of the trade.

In Angola, on the west coast, the Portuguese went directly inland to bring slaves to the coast, and claimed the region as their colony in 1484. By 1500, Lisbon was receiving some 1500 pounds of gold and 10,000 slaves each year from west Africa. On the east coast of Africa, they sacked the Swahili trading city of Kilwa to gain control of the Indian Ocean trade and claimed Mozambique for its rich gold supplies. Although the Portuguese mostly stayed in coastal enclaves like Sofala, and established an outpost on Mozambique Island, they also traveled inland along the Zambezi River.

Portugal in Brazil. In 1500, a Portuguese expedition headed for India was blown off course in the Atlantic and landed briefly in Brazil. The Portuguese claimed the land but did little to develop it until pressed by competition from other European powers. By the mid-sixteenth century they had established some coastal towns, including a colonial capital at Salvador, introduced Jesuit missionaries, and planted the first of the plantations that would make Brazil the first of the huge plantation colonies in the Americas. By 1700 Brazil had 150,000 slaves—half its total population—working its sugar plantations.

By this time, other nations had developed sugar plantations in the Caribbean, contesting Brazil's leadership and undercutting prices and profits. In 1695, however, gold and diamonds were discovered in the interior mountains of Brazil (in the state later named Minas Gerais, General Mines), and by the mid-eighteenth century Brazil was mining some 3000 tons of gold each year, mostly through slave labor. Unfortunately, as often happens with windfall profits from the discovery of raw materials, Portugal and Brazil spent the profits on goods from other countries, especially Britain, without developing new economic enterprises of their own. When the gold began to run out in the mid-eighteenth century, Brazil and Portugal found themselves in debt to Britain, but hooked on British imports, without further means of paying.

Portugal in the Indian Ocean. Throughout the sixteenth century, even taking into account the emerging sugar profits from Brazil, Portugal's main overseas interests lay in Asia. In 1498 Vasco da Gama had extended Portugal's voyages of exploration eastward. Departing from the east coast of Africa, with the assistance of a local pilot who knew the route, he sailed into one of the world's liveliest arenas of trade, the Indian Ocean and the west coast of India (see Chapter 13). Almost immediately the Portuguese introduced armed violence into trade relations that had been peaceful. In 1500 an armed Portuguese expedition under Pedro Alvarez Cabral (c. 1468–1520) was under instructions from the government to establish a fort and trading post at Cochin, India, to promote relations with other "Christian kingdoms" in India, and to impede Muslim shipping to the Red Sea. Cabral had numerous armed engagements with ships in the Indian Ocean and in ports on India's southwest coast. In fighting at Calicut, fifty-four of Cabral's men were killed and substantial goods were lost. In response, Cabral bombarded Cochin, killing between 400 and 500 people and destroying considerable goods and property.

When da Gama returned on his second voyage in 1502 he came with twenty-one armed ships to assert Portuguese power in the Indian Ocean. Seven years later, at the Battle of Diu, Portuguese cannon devastated a combined Egyptian–Gujarati–Calicut fleet. Under Governor Afonso de Albuquerque (1509–15) Portugal captured Goa in 1510, Malacca in 1511, and Hormuz in 1515. At the height of their Indian Ocean power, Portugal held some fifty ports, with Goa serving as their Indian Ocean capital. The Portuguese imposed a system of passes in the Indian Ocean. To the extent that they could enforce it, the Portuguese forced ocean traders to pay them a tax of passage—previously unheard of—and demanded that many of them put into port at Portuguese centers, especially Goa. The Portuguese were making money as much from their own kind of piracy as from trade. Their reputation for violence spread.

By the end of the century, however, it became clear that the Portuguese could not maintain their coercive system. Many of their own merchants operated as private traders despite the official state monopoly; Portuguese officers were often corrupt; their military was not well disciplined; and they lacked the manpower to actually enforce the controls that they asserted over Indian Ocean traders. Most of all, beginning in the seventeenth century, the much larger ocean-going nations of the Netherlands, England, and France entered the Indian Ocean waters in substantial force, and tiny Portugal was no match for them. Portugal remained in the East, but only as a minor power.

Evaluating the Spanish and the Portuguese Empires

Critics who claim that Europe's wealth was built on the exploitation of people overseas certainly have some justification, but the experiences of Spain and Portugal demonstrate that exploitation alone was not enough. To build and sustain wealth, countries must be able to use wealth effectively. They must conceive and implement policies of economic growth. They require banks and instruments of exchange to store and transmit money. They need commercial intelligence to create and evaluate strategies for investing capital sensibly and profitably. They must develop efficient means of transporting goods and people. They must not allow their commercial aims to be excessively deflected by warfare. Both Spain and Portugal lacked these facilities. Both societies, too, were hierarchical societies, where prestige belonged to those in the nobility, the aristocracy. It was common in both Spain and Portugal for people to use whatever mercantile wealth they accumulated to buy into the nobility and buy land, then cease to engage in trade and commerce. Thus, both countries built enormous global empires in the sixteenth century based on their ocean explorations (see Chapter 13), but by the end of the sixteenth century both these empires were on the wane, first challenged and then surpassed by the Netherlands, France, and England, countries that established successful commercial communities.

Culturally, Spain and Portugal were far more successful. The influence of their languages and cultures remains dominant in Latin America until today, and they continue to have an effect on areas as far as the Philippines (for Spain) and Angola, Mozambique, Goa, and tiny Macao (for Portugal). But as economic and political powers, Spain and Portugal, despite their early, extraordinary successes, were soon eclipsed by the commercially astute nations of northwest Europe.

TRADE AND RELIGION IN WESTERN EUROPE: THE PROTESTANT REFORMATION AND THE CATHOLIC REFORMATION

Charles V and his son Philip II fought against Protestant countries in wars explicitly devoted to matters of religion. These wars siphoned off vast treasures that Spain brought from the Americas and diverted her from economic and commercial growth. To understand the choice that Spain made, we must analyze the warfare between Catholics and Protestants that divided Europe in the sixteenth and seventeenth centuries. We will also consider scholarly arguments over the extent to which religious philosophies have a direct impact on national economic development.

The Reformation

Catholicism had won the hearts, spirits, and tithes of the overwhelming majority of the population of western and central Europe. By 1500 the Church had become so wealthy and powerful that several reformers charged the Church with straying from Jesus' early simplicity and his message of compassion for the poor.

Martin Luther (1483–1546), a pious German monk who lived in a monastery in Wittenberg and taught in the university there, shared these criticisms of the Church's wealth and further asserted that it claimed too much power over individual conscience. Luther doubted the importance of sacraments and authority. He kept his doubts private, however, until in 1517 a friar came to Wittenberg selling **indulgences**, which offered exemption from punishment for sins in exchange for donations to the Church. Outraged, Luther posted on the door of the castle church **ninety-five theses**, or statements of his belief, asserting the importance of faith and grace alone. Priests, he wrote, were not needed to mediate between humans and God. Pressed to recant, Luther refused, declaring "it is neither right nor safe to act against conscience."

indulgences In the Roman Catholic church, the remission from the punishments of an absolved sin, obtainable through good works or special prayers and granted by the Church through the merits of Christ and the saints. The sale of indulgences in the late medieval church led to widespread abuse.

ninety-five theses Luther's exposition of his beliefs and his differences with the Catholic Church, posted publicly as a challenge to Church authority.

For an interactive version of this map, go to: http://www.prenhall.com/spodek/map14.3

The Reformation in Europe. The tide of religious reform was felt throughout Europe and changed its political map. The early commitment of most of northern Europe to Calvinism, Lutheranism, or Anglicanism was counterbalanced by the recovery to Catholicism of France and Poland. Counter-Reformation zeal, combined with political confrontation and dynastic rivalry, culminated in the Thirty Years' War (1618–48), fought across Europe's heartland at enormous cost.

When Pope Leo X excommunicated Luther, several local rulers in Germany protected him. They used the occasion to assert their independence of Charles V, who was not only king of Spain but also Holy Roman Emperor, with powers over Germany. From this time, Luther often aligned himself with local rulers. When a revolt of peasants against their landlords swept Germany in 1524, Luther urged the local princes to suppress the revolt by force, and thousands were killed. The kings of Denmark and Sweden and many of the princes of Germany adopted this branch of Protestantism, which is called Lutheranism in America, making this region of northern Europe the heartland of the new denomination. Printing presses using movable type, introduced into Europe by Johannes Gutenberg about 1450, helped to spread the new message as well as new German translations of the Bible, making the sacred text available to ordinary readers who could not read Latin, the language of earlier Christianity, and freeing them from dependence on priestly readings and interpretations.

In Geneva, Switzerland, John Calvin (1509–64) preached another doctrine of reform. Like Luther, Calvin spoke of justification by faith and the supremacy of individual

John Calvin weighing the Bible against Popish Pomp. Calvin had studied the writings of the first generation of reformers such as Martin Luther and accepted without question the idea of justification by faith alone and the biblical foundation of religious authority. This contemporary woodcut shows him weighing what he saw as the extraneous ceremonial trappings and overweening bishops of the Catholic Church against the simple truth of the Bible.

conscience. He denied the authority of the Church. Calvin went beyond Luther in arguing that God grants His grace to whomever He chooses, regardless of individual behavior. Unlike Luther, Calvin rejected alliances with government, although he did create a religious community that dominated the government of the city of Geneva. Calvinism spread widely in western and central Europe, and in New England, without the patronage of any political authority. (In the United States Calvinism is the dominant faith of Presbyterianism, named for its elected leaders or presbyters.)

A third major strand of reform arose in England, where King Henry VIII (r. 1509–47) broke from the Church not for reasons of doctrine, but to claim authority for England over the entire Catholic establishment within the country—churches, monasteries, and clergy—and to gain for himself a divorce, which the Church had forbidden, from the first of his six wives. Henry had no doctrinal quarrel with Rome. He simply wanted to head the English Church himself, and in 1534 Parliament named him "Protector and Only Supreme Head of the Church and Clergy of England," a title that was passed in slightly modified form to later English sovereigns. In England, Henry's new church was called Anglican. (Its followers in the United States are called Episcopalians.)

Each of the three reform movements rejected the authority of the pope, stressed the freedom of individual conscience in matters of faith, and permitted their clergy to marry. Collectively, these various protests against the power and doctrine of the Catholic Church were called Protestantism or the Protestant Reformation.

The Catholic Reformation (the Counter-Reformation)

Its religious monopoly challenged, the Catholic Church countered with the Council of Trent to intensify its own efforts at internal reform. The Council met irregularly for eighteen years, 1545–63, reaffirming the basic doctrines of Catholicism. It reasserted the necessity of the celibacy of the clergy and encouraged greater religious devotion among them. It created new religious orders to purify the Church and transmit its teachings. In 1534 Ignatius Loyola (1491–1556) founded the Society of Jesus, which was especially dedicated to education, secular as well as religious, and to carrying the message of the Church around the world. From 1540 Francis Xavier (1506–52) introduced the Jesuit vision to India, Indonesia, and Japan, baptizing thousands of new Christians. In Paris in 1625, Vincent de Paul (1581–1660) began his work among the wretched of the slums, a humanitarian mission that continues around the world today.

The Catholic Church was fighting for an international, universal vision of the world under its own leadership, while the various Protestant movements encouraged separate national states. In response, several of the new national states encouraged the Protestant movement.

HOW DO WE KNOW?

Weber and Tawney on Religion and Capitalism

The social scientist Max Weber (1864–1920), writing The Protestant Ethic and the Spirit of Capitalism in the early twentieth century, argued that Protestantism's emphasis on individual achievement and divine grace tended to promote economic enterprise and capitalism. Weber claimed that Protestant ministers urged their followers to demonstrate their virtue through devotion to thrift, discipline, industriousness, and business.

> Striving for wealth is objectionable only when it has the aim of a carefree and merry existence. But as exercise of duty in a calling it is not only morally permitted but actually commanded . . . Worldly Protestant asceticism acted effectively against the spontaneous enjoyment of wealth; it limited consumption, especially that of luxuries. On the other hand, it eliminated traditional inhibitions against the acquisition of property; it burst the bonds of the profit motive by not only legalizing it, but even viewing it as directly willed by God . . . He desired rational and utilitarian use of wealth for the purposes of the individual and the community. (Columbia University, pp. 84, 89)

According to Weber, Protestantism encouraged entrepreneurs to dedicate themselves to making money and laborers to finding satisfaction in hard work.

> The bourgeois entrepreneur could, and felt that he ought to, follow his economic self-interest in the certainty of being in God's good grace, and of being visibly blessed by Him. This remained true as long as he observed the formal rules of the game, kept his morals spotless, and did not make objectionable use of his wealth. In addition, the power of religious asceticism made available to him sober, conscientious, eminently capable workers who regarded their labor as their divinely ordained purpose in life. Even more, it gave him the comforting assurance that the unequal distribution of the goods of this world was the direct consequence of God's Providence which followed out His unknown aims by these distinctions as well as by this selective show of grace. (Columbia University, p. 93)

Weber extended these arguments to assert that ultimately Protestant religious leaders had made the pursuit of profit through hard work into the essence of religion.

Subsequent authors, however, notably the British social historian R.H. Tawney, rejected Weber's arguments. Capitalist thought and practice had preceded Protestantism, and some Catholic areas, such as northern Italy and parts of France, were strongly capitalistic, while some Protestant areas, notably in north Germany, were not. "There was plenty of the 'capitalist spirit' in fifteenth-century Venice and Florence, or in south Germany and Flanders, for the simple reason that these areas were the greatest commercial and financial centers of the age, though all were, at least nominally, Catholic" (Tawney, p. 262, n. 32). It was difficult to show any historically consistent correlation between religious doctrines and economic policy.

Tawney's most significant quarrel with Weber, however, was over Weber's argument that religion had ceded the central place in life to the pursuit of economic gain, at least temporarily. Weber was not pleased with this transformation, but he claimed to observe it. Tawney, on the contrary, argued that moral issues concerning the welfare of the entire society always underpin economic ones. They never become secondary.

> A reasonable estimate of economic organization must allow for the fact that, unless industry is to be paralyzed by recurrent revolts on the part of outraged human nature, it must satisfy criteria which are not purely economic . . . natural appetites may be purified or restrained, as, in fact, in some considerable measure they already have been, by being submitted to the control of some larger body of interests. (Tawney, p. 233)

Debates over the relationship between religious doctrine and business practice continue unabated and unresolved until today in relation to religion in general and to all major religions in particular. These debates continue also outside the Western world. Today when East Asian economies are flourishing, Confucian traditions are praised for encouraging development. A century ago, the same traditions, interpreted differently, had been blamed for a lack of development.

- Can you cite examples of religious sentiments influencing economic actions?
- Can you cite examples of economic actions having no relation to religious, moral, or social concerns?
- Do you side with Weber's argument that to a large degree the pursuit of economic growth has taken precedence over religious, moral, and social concerns? Or would you agree with Tawney that, in the long run, economic issues must always be subordinated to larger issues?

The Dutch Republic, France, and England

Spanish Defeats. Inspired by Protestant doctrines and chafing under Spanish rule, the Netherlands, including today's Holland and Belgium, rose in revolt against control by the Habsburg family. Although geographically small, they were among the wealthiest of Philip's possessions. They were offended by the excessive quantity and deficient quality of the Spanish administrators sent to govern them. They also feared that Philip would extend to the Netherlands and all non-Catholics the Spanish Inquisition, a royal court originally established to combat Islam and Judaism in Spain. Many of the peoples of the Netherlands had left Catholicism for new Protestant movements, and many Protestants from other countries had come seeking asylum. In the Netherlands, Protestants and Catholics had reached an accommodation and neither community wished to see that harmony destroyed by the Inquisition. Philip's government refused to pay attention, and the Netherlands erupted in fury. A civil war ensued in which thousands were killed, property was destroyed, and churches were desecrated. By 1576, however, the Netherlands had suffered enough, and representatives of all the Netherlands united across religious lines to expel the Spanish.

In the same year, Queen Elizabeth I of England (r. 1558–1603), the daughter of Henry VIII, officially and publicly aligned her country with the rebels in the Netherlands and began to pursue a policy of alliance with Protestant forces throughout Europe. In reply, Philip II prepared to invade England. In 1588 the Spanish Armada set sail for England with 130 ships, 30,000 men, and 2400 pieces of artillery. In an astonishing reversal, the Armada was destroyed by the English and by a fierce storm, which was quickly named "the Protestant wind."

Spain entered a century-long decline. The northern Netherlands won its independence in 1609, although Spain did not fully and formally acknowledge it until 1648, after years of intermittent warfare. In 1640 Portugal, which had been united with Spain since 1580, declared its independence once again, and constituent units of Spain, especially Catalonia in the northeast, fought costly, if unsuccessful, wars for independence. Philip III (r. 1598–1621) and Philip IV (r. 1621–65) were incompetent rulers; Charles II (r. 1665–1700) was mentally incapable of ruling. And finally, about mid-century, the stream of silver from the Americas dried up, dwindling from 135 million pesos in the decade 1591–1600 to 19 million in 1651–60. Spain had squandered a fabulous windfall of silver and gold. England, France, and the Netherlands emerged as the rising powers of Europe; their self-confidence and their economies flourished; and their merchant classes organized to travel the world.

The Dutch Republic: Seaborne Merchant Enterprise. In the early seventeenth century, the Dutch had the most efficient economic system in Europe. The Dutch Republic bordered the North Sea, reclaimed land from its waters, and lived from its largesse. Fishing was the Republic's great national industry. One out of every four Dutch persons was reliant on the herring industry—catching, salting, smoking, pickling, selling—and others depended on cod fishing and whaling. With their windmills and their dikes, the Dutch reclaimed land from the sea—364,565 acres between 1540 and 1715—and also from inland lakes—another 84,638 acres. With such an investment of capital and energy the Dutch worked their land carefully and efficiently. They developed new methods of crop rotation, planting turnips in the fall to provide winter food for humans and sheep. At other times of year they raised peas, beans, and clover to restore nitrogen to the soil. With these cropping patterns, the Dutch no longer had to leave one-third of their land fallow each year. They farmed it all, increasing productivity by 50 percent. In addition, the Dutch built one of the largest textile industries in Europe, based on wool from their own sheep and on huge quantities imported from England.

On the seas and in the rivers, the Dutch were sailing 10,000 ships as early as 1600, and for the next century they dominated the shipping of northern Europe. From the Baltic they brought timber and grain to Amsterdam and western Europe. In exchange, from the ports of Portugal, Spain, and France they carried salt, oil, wool, wine, and, most of all, the silver and gold of the New World. Often they warehoused in Amsterdam the trade goods en route to other ports, earning additional profits on the storage. They used substantial amounts of the timber themselves to build the most seaworthy, yet economical, ships of the day.

The Dutch also developed commercial institutions to underpin their dominance in trade. The **bourse**, or stock exchange, was opened in Amsterdam in the mid-sixteenth century as the Dutch were gaining control of the Baltic trade, and it was reopened in 1592 as they captured a dominant role in supplying grain to Mediterranean countries. In 1598 they initiated a Chamber of Insurance; in 1609 the Bank of Amsterdam was established. This bank accepted coins from all over the world, assessed their gold and silver content, and exchanged them for gold florin coins that were fixed in weight and value and became the standard everywhere. The Dutch government guaranteed the safety of deposits in the national bank, thereby attracting capital from through-out Europe. Depositors were able to draw checks on their accounts. For two centuries, until the French Revolution in 1789, Amsterdam was the financial center of Europe.

In 1602 Dutch businessmen founded the Dutch East India Company, a joint stock company dedicated to trade in Asia. The Company captured several Portuguese ports, but concentrated on the most lucrative of all the East Asian centers, Java and the Moluccas, the Spice Islands of today's Indonesia. In 1619 the Dutch East India

bourse stock exchange

Andries van Eertvel, *The Return to Amsterdam of the Fleet of the Dutch East India Company*, 1599. The Dutch East India Company was founded in 1602 to create a monopoly over Dutch trade and to seize control of the Portuguese trade routes in the Indian Ocean. The company owned a fleet of ships armed with cannon which carried pepper, indigo, raw silk, saltpeter, and textiles from India to western Europe. In the later 1600s, large-scale exports of textiles were also carried from India to Africa in payment for slaves going to the Caribbean. (*Johnny Van Haeften Gallery, London*)

National Joint Stock Companies: Instruments of Trade and Colonization

National joint stock companies were one of the key commercial innovations of Dutch, French, and English financiers in the seventeenth century, giving them an enormous advantage in overseas trade. Forerunners of the modern business corporation, the companies sold stock publicly, sometimes for a single expedition, more commonly for all the expeditions and activities of the company. Financiers invested in expectation of the great profits that might come from successful shipping ventures. Their potential losses and liabilities were limited to the value of their investment; the rest of their personal property was protected. Individual states gave legal charters to these companies in expectation of the benefits of trade for the country. These national companies were chartered for expeditions throughout the world. Those headed toward the Americas were designated "West India Companies," those toward Asia were "East India Companies." The companies of each state usually saw themselves in competition with each other, sometimes leading to armed struggle. And their missions included colonization, and sometimes proselytization, as well as trade.

The government "Edict Providing for the Establishment of a Company of the West Indies," establishing the French West India Company in 1664, is representative of the aspirations of the state and of the merchants looking to the Americas for both settlement and trade:

> We have recognized that colonial trade and navigation are the only and true means of raising commerce to the brilliant position it holds in foreign lands; to achieve this and to stimulate our subjects to form powerful companies we have promised them such great advantages that there is reason to hope that all those who take interests in the glory of the State, and who wish to profit by honorable and legitimate means will willingly participate . . . but as it is not sufficient for these companies to take possession of the lands which we grant them, and have them cleared and cultivated by the people they send there at great expense, if they do not equip themselves to carry on . . . commerce . . . it is also absolutely necessary, in order to carry on this trade, to provide numerous ships to carry each day the goods which are to be sold in the said countries, and bring back to France those which they export. (Columbia College, *Contemporary Civilization*, I: 815–20)

Investment in the Company was open to foreigners as well as to native-born French. The Company was "obliged to introduce into the lands granted above, the number of clergy necessary for preaching the Holy Gospel, and instructing these peoples in the faith of the Catholic, Apostolic and Roman religion; and also to build churches." It also had many of the attributes of a sovereign state:

> The said Company may build forts in all places it shall judge necessary for the defense of the said country . . . may arm and equip for war such number of vessels as it shall deem fitting for the defense of the said countries and the security of the said commerce . . . may negotiate peace and alliances in our name, with the Kings and Princes of the countries where it wishes to establish its settlements and trade . . . and, in case of insult, declare war on them, attack them, and defend itself by force of arms. (ibid).

In the Indian Ocean, trade in spices was a large part of the Companies' business. Between them the English and Dutch East India Companies carried 13.5 million pounds of pepper to Europe in the peak year of 1670, the British share mostly from India, the Dutch share from Indonesia. Other goods included indigo, raw silk, saltpeter, and, increasingly, Indian textiles. There were also large-scale exports of textiles carried by Europeans from India to Africa in payment for slaves going to the Caribbean.

The Companies' ships were armed, and their representatives established fortresses and trading centers on the coasts of Asia and of the Americas, and the Companies became, in effect, miniature governments. Malachy Postlethwayt's Universal Dictionary *of 1751 wrote that the Dutch East India Company*

> makes peace and war at pleasure, and by its own authority; administers justice to all . . . settles colonies, builds fortifications, levies troops, maintains numerous armies and garrisons, fits out fleets, and coins money. (cited in Tracy, *The Political Economy of Merchant Empires*, p. 196)

In India, in the seventeenth century, the English, French, and Dutch East India Companies set up trading posts within towns. Until the end of the century, the Mughal emperors and local governments generally welcomed the foreign traders as means of stimulating the Indian economy through trade and enriching the government through taxes. Following its victories at Plassey in 1757 and Buxar in 1765, however, the British East India Company became the de facto government of the province of Bengal in India—with the rights of collecting taxes and the responsibility for providing order and administration. The Company's holdings continued to expand until it was effectively the ruler of almost all of India. The British government regulated the East India Company from its founding in 1600, and finally disbanded it and took over direct rule of India after the Indian revolt of 1857.

Company founded Jakarta, which served as its regional headquarters until 1950 when Indonesia won its independence. In 1623 they seized Amboina in the Moluccas, killing a group of Englishmen they found there, and forcing the English back to India. The profits from these possessions reinforced Dutch economic precedence in Europe.

In 1600 a group of Dutch traders reached Japan. In 1641, all other foreigners were expelled, but, because they did not engage in missionary activity, the Dutch were permitted a small settlement on Deshima Island, off Nagasaki, and for two centuries they were the only European traders allowed in Japan. In 1652, the Dutch captured from the Portuguese the Cape of Good Hope at the southernmost tip of Africa and established there the first settlement of Afrikaners, South Africans of Dutch descent.

In the Americas, the Dutch West India Company raided the shipping of the Spanish and the Portuguese, and then founded their own rich sugar plantations in Caracas, Curaçao, and Guiana. For a few decades they held Bahia in Brazil, but the Portuguese drove them out in 1654. In North America they established New Amsterdam on Manhattan Island. The English, however, conquered and annexed it and in 1664 renamed it New York.

Despite their commercial skill and success, the Dutch could not ultimately retain their supremacy. The English Navigation Act of 1651 permitted imports to England and its dependencies only in English ships or in those of the exporting country, and this effectively restricted Dutch shipping. Three indecisive, draining wars followed, from 1652 to 1674. Additional years of warfare on land against France further exhausted Dutch resources. In 1700 the Dutch Republic had a population of 2 million people; at this time the population of the British Isles was 9 million, and that of France 19 million. An aggressive, skilled small country simply could not continue to compete with two aggressive, skilled large countries.

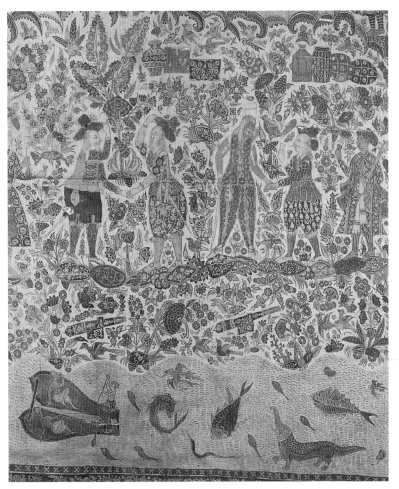

Indian cotton cloth, late seventeenth century. This detailed portrayal of Dutch traders suggests that they have come from far across the seas to trade in a rich array of goods. The Indian gentleman on the far right may find the Dutch doffing of caps and handshakes a strange form of greeting, quite different from the form used in India of joining one's hands in the "namaste" salutation.

France and Britain

France and Britain surpassed the Dutch and competed for dominance in world trade. For two centuries each pursued its own strategy of economic development—France primarily by land and Britain primarily by sea. Leadership finally went to the mistress of the waves. (The names of Britain and England are often used interchangeably. Formally, however, before the 1707 Act of Union, England and Wales were one country, Scotland another. By the Act of 1707 they were united into the single state of Great Britain.)

France: Consolidating the Nation. In the second half of the sixteenth century, France endured four decades of civil warfare because the crown was unable to control the various factions, religious groups, and regions of the country. Struggles between

Huguenot Any protestants in France in the sixteenth and seventeenth centuries. Their legal status changed according to the wishes of the monarch on the throne at the time.

Catholics and Protestants, called **Huguenots** in France, helped to fuel the warfare. So, too, did the desire of the nobles to have more independence from the king. In 1589 Henry of Navarre, a Huguenot, came to the throne as Henry IV (r. 1589–1610). Recognizing the importance of Catholicism to the majority of the French people, he joined the Catholic Church with the apocryphal comment, "Paris is worth a Mass." In 1598, however, hoping to heal the schism between the religious communities, he issued the Edict of Nantes, which gave Protestants the same civil rights as Catholics. He was not entirely successful, however, and, indeed, was assassinated by a Catholic militant. His successor, Louis XIII (r. 1610–43), following the advice of his chief minister, the Cardinal Richelieu, encouraged nobles to invest in trade by land and sea, built up France's armies, and cultivated allies among France's neighbors. Internally he captured several Huguenot strongholds in France, and concluded a truce with these French Protestants. Externally he joined with Protestant rulers in Sweden, the United Netherlands, and parts of Germany to defeat the Catholic Hapsburg Empire and increase the stature of France.

Louis XIV, in an extraordinarily long and forceful reign (1643–1715), made France the most powerful country in Europe. Under the Sun King, as Louis was known, France set the standard throughout Europe for administration, war, diplomacy, language, thought, literature, music, architecture, fashion, cooking, and etiquette. Although they had been slower than other European countries to enter transoceanic trade, the French now began to assert a global presence, trading in India, Madagascar, the American Great Lakes, and the Mississippi River; establishing colonies in the West Indies; and staking a claim to Canada. By 1690 Louis XIV had raised an army of 400,000 men, equal to the combined armies of England, the Habsburg Empire, Prussia, Russia, and the Dutch Republic. At this time, the French navy was also larger than the English, with 120 ships of the line (warships) compared to the English navy's 100. Also, as we have seen, in 1700, France had a population of 19 million, more than double that of the British Isles.

Louis XIV boasted "L'état, c'est moi" ("I am the state") by which he meant that the powers of the state rested in him alone. His leading religious adviser, Bishop Jacques-Bénigne Bossuet (1627–1704), linked the king's power to divine right, asserting that "Royalty has its origin in the divinity itself." Louis XIV continued to assert the right of the king to appoint the Catholic clergy in France, and in 1685 he revoked the Edict of Nantes in the belief that a single, dominant religion was more important than the toleration of minorities within his kingdom. This act cost France the services of many of its Protestant artisans, who fled to the Netherlands and Britain.

Economically, Louis XIV's chief economic adviser, Jean-Baptiste Colbert (1625–96), pursued a policy of mercantilism—fostering the economic welfare of one's own state against all others—by strengthening state control over the national economy even more aggressively than had Richelieu. To facilitate trade, he abolished local taxes on trade throughout central France (a region as large as England), although his government was not powerful enough to do away with these internal tariffs throughout the entire country. Colbert established a Commercial Code to unify business practice throughout the country. To improve communication and transportation, he built roads and canals, including a link between the Bay of Biscay and the Mediterranean. He set quality standards for hand manufacturers to improve their marketability and gave financial incentives to the French manufacturers of such luxury goods as silks, tapestries, glass, and woolens. Meanwhile, the needs of the army created huge national markets for uniforms, equipment, and provisions. All these policies benefited private business as well as the state, but the mercantilist insistence that the export of gold and silver weakened the national economy and that state monopolies should dominate certain economic fields, including much of foreign trade, was opposed by many business people who sought greater freedom of trade.

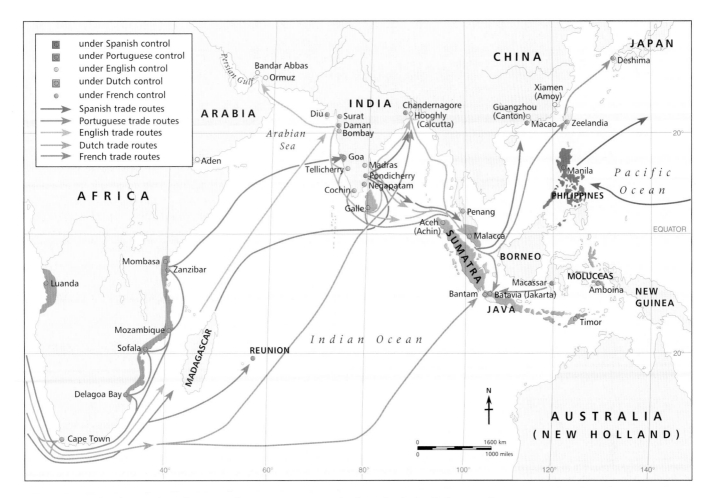

The growth of French military and economic strength disturbed the **balance of power** among the leading states of Europe and precipitated a series of wars. The War of the League of Augsburg, 1688–97, and the War of the Spanish Succession, 1702–13, reduced France's power when she was forced to cede to Britain the North American colonies of Newfoundland and Nova Scotia and all French claims to the Hudson Bay territory. Britain began to pull ahead in overseas possessions.

Britain: Establishing Commercial Supremacy. In the same wars, Britain won from Spain the *asiento*, the right to carry all the slave cargoes from Africa to Spanish America, plus one shipload of more conventional goods each year to Panama. These officially recognized trading rights also provided cover for British ships to engage illegally in the business of piracy and smuggling that flourished in the Caribbean, where buccaneers preyed on Spanish commerce.

In the eighteenth century the most valued properties in the Americas were the sugar-producing islands of the Caribbean. In the Atlantic the most valuable trade was in human cargo—the slaves who worked the sugar plantations. In Asia, control of sea lanes and of the outposts established by the various East India companies was the prize.

Competition for dominance in all three regions continued between the French and the British through four more wars in the eighteenth century: the War of Austrian Succession, 1740–48; the Seven Years' War, 1756–63; the War of American Independence (the American Revolution), 1775–81. These wars demonstrated the importance of sea power, and here the British triumphed. Around 1790, the French population

Indian Ocean trade in the seventeenth century. Prior to the sixteenth century, Arabs and other local traders had dominated Indian Ocean commerce. When the Portuguese arrived in 1498, however, European nations entered directly into these trade routes in armed ships. Controlled from headquarters in Europe, they established coastal trade enclaves throughout the region. They began to battle each other for supremacy, projecting European competition into these distant waters and shores.

balance of power In international relations, a policy that aims to secure peace by preventing any one state or alignment of states from becoming too dominant. Alliances are formed to build up a force equal or superior to that of the potential enemy.

asiento A contract between the Spanish crown and a private individual or sovereign power, giving the latter exclusive rights to import a stipulated number of slaves into the Spanish American colonies in exchange for a fee.

British power in India to 1818. The weakening of the Mughal Empire created a situation which was exploited by the English and French East India companies. They created strategic alliances with local independent princes and competed for power on land and sea. With Clive's victory at Plassey (1757) the English gained Bengal, a power base which allowed them to expand steadily, but their control over India was not secure until their final defeat of the Maratha confederation in 1818.

outnumbered the British 28 million to 16 million, and French armies outnumbered the British by an even greater ratio, 180,000 to 40,000. But the British navy had 195 ships of the line compared with France's 81.

Suffering defeats at sea, the French retreated from their colonial positions. In the Peace Settlement at Paris in 1763 at the end of the Seven Years' War they turned over their immense, but thinly populated, holdings in North America east of the Mississippi to the British and those west of the Mississippi to Spain. They kept their rich, sugar-producing islands in the Caribbean: Saint-Domingue (Haiti), Guadeloupe, and Martinique. In India, although they lost out in other locations, they kept Pondicherry on the southeast coast and a few additional commercial locations. The French navy was deployed against the British in America during the American Revolution, but it was completely crushed during the Napoleonic Wars. The British, though they lost the thirteen colonies of the United States in 1783, triumphed everywhere else because of the great strength of their navy. They held Canada. They held their islands in the Caribbean. They increased their holdings in India, and they dominated the sea lanes both across the Atlantic Ocean and through the Indian Ocean.

Institutionally, Britain surpassed all other European countries, even the Netherlands, in supporting sophisticated economic enterprise. Recognizing the importance of a stable currency, England had fixed the value of the pound sterling in 1560–61 at 4 ounces of silver, and maintained that valuation for two and a half centuries, until after World War I. Britain surpassed Amsterdam as the center of Europe's international trade. The Bank of England, created in 1694, could transact its business with a currency of fixed value. Moreover, Britain never defaulted on her debts and so earned the trust of the international financial community. In times of war as well as of peace, Britain could borrow whatever sums she needed. Politically, England developed a new system of constitutional monarchy after 1688 that gave strong support to private commercial interests, as we shall see in more detail in Chapter 15. The French later ridiculed Britain as "a nation of shopkeepers," but geographically, militarily, institutionally, politically, and agriculturally, the British were building the capacity to become the most effective businessmen in the world. They were building a nation-state and a capitalist economy.

THE NATION-STATE

The term nation-state is generally used to describe the combination of a political state with the emotional sensibility of a collective social identity. The state is a geographic territory with its own independent government, and it must have enough size and force that it is not swallowed up by another. The nation is based on some combination of shared language, religion, history, ethnicity, future aspiration, and a sense of distinctiveness from, competition with, or antagonism toward, some other nation-state or states. Nation-states may emerge from the break-up of larger empires—which may contain several nations within themselves—or from the aggrandizement of small units into larger ones through conquest or merger. Both these processes had been continuing in western Europe for centuries. Small units, like the region around Paris under Hugh Capet, were expanding into states, while large units, like Charlemagne's empire, were dissolving.

The nation-states had developed relatively efficient central governments that were capable of collecting taxes, keeping the peace, and raising and deploying armies and navies effectively in waging war. Their authority was generally recognized and accepted—even welcomed—by most of the people within their borders. That authority was different in different nation-states: England, France, and Portugal were monarchies; the Netherlands was ruled by a coalition of businessmen; Spain was a part of the larger Habsburg Empire.

Nation-states took an interest in the economic welfare of their people, although here too different states adopted different policies at different times, some capitalist, some mercantilist but with independent merchants, some state controlled. They engaged in external, overseas trade and commerce and, in this period of time, colonization. The development of overseas trade and colonization that we have studied in this chapter and in Chapter 13 was a large part of their transformation from small, locally governed units into nation-states. They also defined themselves by their relationship to one another—generally competitive, often hostile, sometimes belligerent.

By the mid-1700s the nation-states of western Europe had become the object of both fear and emulation. They were feared because of their economic and military powers. They could, and did, fight wars, conquer territories, create colonies, and dominate trade networks. Many societies and governments feared victimization by them. Consider, for example, the fate of the Aztecs, Inca, and other Native Americans. These fears led some states to keep these new nation-states at arm's length as long as they could. China and Japan remained essentially closed for centuries. It led still other governments to emulate them, to develop the strength to resist them even while becoming more like them. This was the response of Russia under Peter the Great.

The period we are now studying is critical to the formation of nation-states because in their competition over trade routes and colonies around the world, these nation-states defined themselves in relation to one another and in relation to the other civilizations with which they were engaging. This self-definition in terms of the "Other" is certainly not the only element in the definition of the nation-state, but it is important. Moreover, as the trade and colonization of European nation-states encountered other groupings of people around the world, both the Europeans and the peoples they encountered began to redefine themselves politically and culturally. The European nation-state evoked many different responses. In the rest of this chapter we shall consider some of the most important in this early era of European trade and colonial expansion.

RUSSIA'S EMPIRE UNDER PETER THE GREAT

At the end of the seventeenth century Russia had little direct contact with the market economies of northwestern Europe. The country was geographically remote by land, and by sea its principal ocean port was Archangel at the extreme north, on the White Sea, ice-bound for most of the year. The foreign trade that did exist was carried by foreign ships traveling Russia's great rivers, especially the Volga. Russia belonged to the Greek Orthodox branch of Christianity, so communication with the Church of Rome and its western European networks was also limited. Mongol rule had further isolated Russia culturally from western Europe, tying it more closely to Central Asia.

Russia began to take its modern form only after Ivan III (r. 1462–1505) overthrew Mongol domination in 1480. Muscovy, the territory around Moscow, became the core of an expanding independent state. At first, Russia expanded southeastward, defeating the khanate of Astrakhan in 1556 and capturing the Volga River basin south to the Caspian Sea with its access to the silk trade of Persia. It also expanded eastward all the way to the Pacific (1649), capturing Siberia and its rich population of fur-bearing animals.

Because of its isolation and foreign rule, Russia had only a tiny urban trading class and very few big city markets. As late as 1811, only 4 percent of its population was urban. The overwhelming majority of its people lived in **serfdom**, which bound people not directly to specific owners, but to specific land and its landlords, with little possibility for economic, social, or geographic mobility. After 1675 landlords gained the right to sell serfs off the land, even to urban owners. Occasional serf uprisings, like that led by Stepan Razin (Stenka Razin; d. 1671) in 1667, were brutally suppressed, and the gulf between free persons and serfs increased.

When Peter I, the Great (r. 1682–96 as co-emperor with his half-brother; 1696–1725 as sole emperor), became sole emperor, he saw Sweden as his principal external enemy. Sweden already held Finland and the entire eastern shore of the Baltic, bottling up Russia without any Baltic port. Worse, in a crushing blow, 8000 Swedish troops defeated 40,000 Russians at the Battle of Narva in 1700. Humiliated, Peter set out to construct in Russia a powerful state based on a powerful army and navy. In 1697, traveling under an assumed name in order to evade royal protocol, Peter had embarked on a "Grand Embassy of Western Europe," especially England and the Netherlands, but also Baltic ports and the Holy Roman Empire. He searched for allies for the wars he expected against the Turks as Russia pushed toward the Black Sea; he gathered information on the economic, cultural, and military-industrial practices of the western European powers; and for several months he even worked as a ship's carpenter in Amsterdam.

Impressed by the strength of the western European countries, Peter invited to Russia military experts from the West to train and lead his troops. He bought western European artillery and copied it. He established naval forces and reorganized the army along Western lines, in uniformed regiments, armed with muskets. He promoted mining, metallurgy, and textile manufacture, largely as means of supplying his troops. By 1703–4 Peter had started to build a new capital, an all-weather port and "window on the West," in St. Petersburg on land that he conquered from Sweden. Commercially, geographically, and architecturally, he

serf An agricultural worker or peasant bound to the land and legally dependent on the lord. Serfs had their own homes, plots, and livestock but they owed the lord labor, dues, and services. These services could be commuted to rent, but serfs remained chattels of the lord unless they were emancipated, or escaped. Serfdom declined in western Europe in the late medieval period, but persisted in parts of eastern Europe until the nineteenth century.

Left **Russia in 1682 and Peter the Great's acquisitions thereafter.**

Right **Peter the Great in armor.** Alarmed by the growing power of his western European neighbors, and by Russia's relative weakness, Peter the Great undertook to modernize his country, especially its military, economic, and cultural life. He built his program, however, on the backs of Russia's serfs.

designed St. Petersburg as a Western city. Thirty thousand died in the construction of the city from disease, drowning, or lack of food.

In 1709, when Sweden again invaded Russia, Peter was prepared. He retreated until the Swedes fell from the exhaustion of pursuing him through the severe Russian winter. Then, holding his ground at Poltava in south Russia, he defeated the remaining Swedish troops. The Swedish army was finished as an imperial force, and Russia began to seize additional Baltic possessions.

Peter's goals for Westernization were not exclusively military. He wanted Russia to be counted among the powers of Europe, and this would require cultural and economic ties as well. Peter required Western-style education for all male nobles. He established schools for their children, and sent many to study in western Europe. He demanded that aristocrats acquire the morals and tastes of Europe's elites. He made them abandon their Russian dress in favor of the clothing of western Europe, and forced the men to shave or trim their beards in the Western style, He introduced "cipher schools" for teaching basic reading and arithmetic, established a printing press, established and edited Russia's first newspaper, and funded the Academy of Sciences, which opened in 1724, a year before his death. Collectively, all these revolutionary reforms drove a wedge between the nobility and the mass of Russians.

Economically, Peter pushed for the creation of new enterprises. He built a fleet on the Baltic and encouraged exports. He organized new companies headed by groups of Russians and foreigners, and supplied them with working capital and serf laborers. He accepted the mercantilist concept of an economically strong state and saw no role for a free market in achieving it. To finance these state-organized initiatives, Peter introduced heavy taxes, which fell especially severely on the peasantry.

No democrat, Peter demanded loyalty and obedience to himself. He created a new system of administration with himself as head. He brought the Eastern Orthodox Church under state control and subordinated its clergy to his own leadership. He streamlined local and central government. He created a new "state service," including both civil and military officials, and made appointments to it completely without regard to family status, birth, or seniority. Foreigners could serve within this service, serfs could be elevated, and nobles could be demoted. All depended on performance. In 1722 he introduced a new Table of Ranks, which automatically gave noble status to officials who reached the eighth position out of fourteen. The newly elevated nobility were the chief administrators of his new policies of Westernization. These moves were revolutionary and did not survive long after Peter's death.

Peter strengthened the economic and political position of the ruling classes, the landowners, and the rising bourgeoisie while exploiting the peasantry ruthlessly. He allotted to the nobility some 175,000 serfs and 100,000 acres of land in the first half of his reign alone. Conscription, programs of forced labor, a poll tax, and indirect taxes on everything from bee-keeping to salt provoked two major uprisings in the Russian interior between 1705 and 1708. The czar suppressed them brutally. An iron-willed autocrat, Peter brought his nation into Europe and made it an important military and economic power, but millions of Russians paid a terrible price.

Peter achieved many of his goals, establishing a strong central administration, a powerful military, some commercial enterprise, international trade connections, and diplomatic contact with the nations of western Europe. He did not, however, free Russia's merchants to carry on the kinds of independent economic activity characteristic of western European commerce. And he kept the largest enterprises, like weapons

Bartolomeo Carlo Rastrelli, *The Founding of St. Petersburg*, **Russia, 1723.** This bronze relief commemorates the founding of St. Petersburg in 1704. Peter the Great intended his capital to be an all-weather port and a "window on the West." As part of his drive for Westernization he decreed that the aristocracy must abandon their Russian dress in favor of European clothes. The garb of the men depicted here indicates clearly that the edict was already in place. (*Hermitage, St. Petersburg*)

enlightened despotism A benevolent form of absolutism, a system of government in which the ruler has absolute rights over his or her subjects. It implies that the ruler acts for the good of the people, not in self-interest.

manufacture and shipping, in the hands of the state. Considered an **enlightened despot**—a ruler who advanced new concepts of intellectual inquiry and legal rights, at least for the nobility, but held on to power for himself—Peter died in 1725. Since he had killed his own son rather than permit him to sidetrack reforms, Peter was succeeded for two years by his wife and then by other family members.

In 1762 Catherine II, the Great, assumed the throne and ruled for thirty-four years. At least as despotic as Peter, Catherine won especially important victories over Poles and Turks, expanding the borders of Russia to the Black Sea. After brutally suppressing a revolt by hundreds of thousands of serfs led by Yemelyan Pugachev (1726–75), she further reduced the power of Russia's serfs.

DIVERSE CULTURES, DIVERSE TRADE SYSTEMS

Ottomans and Mughals

Two powerful empires, the Ottoman and the Mughal, were rising in Asia at about the same time as Spain and Portugal were advancing in Europe and overseas. Indeed, there was some connection. In 1600 all four empires were approaching the height of their powers. By 1700 all were in severe decline because of overextension, draining warfare, weak state systems, and lack of attention to technological improvements, especially in the military. All four also allowed control of their economic affairs to fall into the hands of foreigners. By the end of our period, all were subordinated to greater or lesser degree under the power of the newly risen French and British.

The Ottomans did not control their own trade and its profits. At first, because of political alliances with France, only French ships were allowed to trade with the Ottomans. After 1580, trade opened more widely and the English and Dutch entered the trade, along with Jews, Armenians, Venetians, and Genoese. The situation came to resemble Spain's, in which the empire's new riches went into the hands of foreign merchants. A shift in the balance of trade also weakened the central government. To pay for increasing amounts of imported manufactured goods the Ottomans exported more agricultural raw materials, increasing the wealth of landed estate holders and enabling them to break free of central control.

In India, between 1556 and 1605, the Mughal emperor Akbar established one of the great empires of the world. Akbar's administrative reforms brought change in trade and economies as well. City markets encouraged the production of luxury goods for the court and everyday goods for the common people and even village India joined the city-based cash economy. The markets contained a wide array of craftsmen, shopkeepers, and sophisticated specialists. Moneylenders and moneychangers were active throughout the urban system, enabling the smooth transfer of funds across the empire. Their *hundis* (bills of exchange) were accepted throughout the empire, and these financial instruments facilitated the work of government officials in collecting and transmitting in cash the taxes and rents on land. Indian cities boasted very wealthy financiers and important guild organizations. The guilds, much like those in contemporary Europe, regulated and supervised the major trades. Contrary to popular beliefs sometimes mistakenly held about India as an otherworldly culture, business flourished and prospered. After all, among the multitude of India's castes, were baniyas or vaishyas who were charged specifically with carrying on business.

Indian traders were highly mobile and therefore had some independence from the political fortunes of the rulers of the time. If a particular ruler could not defend his territory against foreign invasion or maintain internal law and order, or if he tried to extort excessive taxes, the merchant communities could leave for other cities more amenable to their pursuits. Conversely, rulers who wanted to improve their commercial prospects lured these footloose merchants with offers of free land and low taxes. Thus, even in the event of political decline or catastrophe, India's business might continue.

Indian businessmen continued to carry on coastal and ocean-going trade, but the imperial government could not support these ventures very effectively. They had no navy. In 1686, for example, the English blocked Indian trade between Bengal and Southeast Asia and even seized ships belonging to the officers and family members of the Mughal rulers. The Emperor Aurangzeb replied by land, forcing the English out of their settlement at Hoogly. But the English relocated, built a new town, Calcutta, and continued their mari-time commerce and armed competition. Furthermore, despite sophisticated economic institutions developed within family-held firms, Indian merchants did not developimpersonal business firms like the European joint stock companies. When the European joint stock companies arrived on the subcontinent, they opened a new scale of overseas operations. Finally, Indian merchants did not normally arm themselves or contract for armed forces, as did many European merchants, especially the joint stock companies. Although they might flee particular rulers, business elites did not directly challenge the power of the ruler or seek to supplant it with their own forces.

Ming and Qing Dynasties in China

The Ming dynasty in China, as we saw in Chapters 12 and 13, had largely closed China to foreign trade in favor of developing the internal economy and of defending the northern borders against Mongol and Manchu attack. They repaired the Great Wall and extended it by an additional 600 miles. Having limited the size and power of their navy, the Ming were harassed by Japanese and Chinese pirates on their coasts. The Ming responded meekly by avoiding the sea and reviving the system of inland transportation by canals. The pirate attacks increased and became minor invasions of the mainland, even up the Yangzi River. Following national unification at the end of the sixteenth century, the new Japanese government brought their pirates under control, but in 1592 Japan invaded Korea, intending ultimately to invade China. Warfare continued for years, mostly within the Korean peninsula, but also within north China, until Japan finally withdrew in 1598.

The Western presence was limited at this stage. The few Portuguese who arrived in China after 1514 were mostly Jesuit missionaries whose influence was felt far more in the culture of the court than in the commerce of the marketplace. Matteo Ricci (1552–1610), one of the most prominent of the Jesuit missionaries to China, shared with government officials in Beijing his knowledge of mathematics, cartography, astronomy, mechanics, and clocks, while hemastered the Chinese language and many of the Confucian classics. The Jesuits concentrated their efforts on winning the elites of China, and by 1700 some 300,000 Chinese had converted to Christianity.

Despite the shutdown of most international trade, China's economy expanded, at least until about 1600. China, after all, contained one-fifth of the

"Idris giving instruction to mankind on the art of weaving," Mughal period, c. 1590. In the Islamic tradition, the mythical Idris gives instruction and protection to pious and skilled weavers. Here weavers wash, dry, spin, skein, and weave their wool, while courtiers present rolls of cloth for inspection. Most production was localized, as suggested here, although a few examples of large, well organized workshops, with wage labor and centralized management, mostly under the control of Mughal courts, also existed. When pressured, weavers organized in boycotts and strikes to resist the exactions of rulers and merchants, and to defend the honor of their religion.

world's population and generated an immense internal economy. The canal system encouraged north–south trade. Using kaolin clay, Chinese artisans created porcelain more beautiful and stronger than ever. Weaving and dyeing of silk expanded near Suzhou; cotton textiles flourished at Nanjing; Hebei specialized in iron manufacture.

In the late Ming period, private sea-going trade with Southeast Asia began to flourish again, often carried by families who had sent emigrants to the region and thus had local contacts. Within China, however, local authorities on the south China coast regulated and limited this trade. Fascinating research by a modern scholar on the success of overseas Chinese merchants suggests that had the Chinese government supported its own traders at home, instead of restricting them, they too might have been effective in building overseas merchant empires. The Chinese merchants

Portuguese ships and sailors, lacquer screen, Chinese, seventeenth century. The faces of the sailors and the ship itself are not depicted as hostile, although at the beginning of the previous century the Portuguese had been expelled for aggressive actions and by mid century were restricted to coastal enclaves.

could, in terms of entrepreneurship and daring, do everything that the various Europeans could do. But they were helpless to produce the necessary institutional change in China to match European or even Japanese power. They were never the instruments of any effort by Ming or Qing authorities to build merchant empires; nor could they hope to get mandarin or ideological support for any innovative efforts of their own. (Gungwu, cited in Tracy, *The Rise of Merchant Empires*, p. 401)

When Europeans came to trade, the Chinese government restricted them to coastal enclaves. First, the Ming dynasty limited the Portuguese to Macao in 1557 (where they remained until 1999 under agreement with the current Chinese government). Nevertheless, as noted above, between one-third and one-half of all the silver of the New World ultimately went to China to pay for purchases of silk, porcelain, tea, and other products. Despite this new wealth, by the time the Dutch and British arrived in the 1600s the quality of the Ming administration had weakened.

The Qing dynasty, Manchus from north of the Great Wall, captured the government of China in 1644 and secured the southeast coast in 1683. They established the "Canton system," restricting European traders to the area around Canton (Guangzhou), and entrusting their supervision and control to a monopoly of Chinese firms called the Cohong. Because of these restrictions, and because of the vast size of China, European merchants had little effect on China.

Although most historians have emphasized the role of Europe in enlarging the world economy through its overseas voyages, some are beginning to see it was the vast internal markets of China and the wealth of its luxury goods—along with the spices of India and the Spice Islands—that attracted the Europeans. According to this perspective, the dominant economic force in the world economy between 1500 and 1776 was not the vigor of European exploration and trade but the richness of Asian markets that attracted them in the first place. The "pull" of the Chinese market attracted the "push" of the European merchants.

HOW DO WE KNOW?

How Europe Surpassed China Economically and Militarily

During the period covered in this chapter, the relative balance of power between Europe and Asia was shifting. The most remarkable shift was the slow but steady economic progress of western European nations compared to China, still the most powerful and wealthy nation of the time. We have examined the sheer prowess of European shipping, shipboard armaments, and the consolidation of their commercial classes and their nation states. Why did China not keep pace?

Mark Elvin, an economic historian, tackled this question in a classic study, The Pattern of the Chinese Past (1973), a sketch of Chinese economic and social history from earliest times. In a series of chapters Elvin praises the creativity of the Tang and Song dynasties, crediting the period from the eighth to the twelfth centuries with "revolutions" in farming, water transport, money and credit, market structure and urbanization, science and technology. But "the dynamic quality of the medieval Chinese economy disappeared . . . some time around the middle of the fourteenth century" (p. 203). Elvin gives three reasons for this disappearance: The Chinese frontier began to fill up with people and resources; commerce with the outside world decreased sharply; and philosophy became introspective, less concerned with engaging practical problems. The result was "quantitative growth, qualitative standstill," or what Elvin calls a "high-equilibrium trap." That is, economic growth continued and new natural resources were tapped, but most of the gains were eaten up by the population growth. For example, Elvin writes, in the sixteenth through the nineteenth centuries, New World crops were introduced, agricultural techniques

were improved, market networks were extended, the legal status of the peasantry was improved, and entrepreneurship and invention flourished. But the population doubled from about 200 million people in 1580 to about 400 million in 1850. "Agricultural productivity per acre had nearly reached the limits of what was possible without industrial-scientific inputs" (p. 312), and these inputs were simply unavailable. Technological innovation occurred, but resources for implementing them were scarce. Wood, clothing fibers, land, draught animals, and metals were in short supply. In this "high-level equilibrium trap," the Chinese economy worked well enough in its traditional forms that there were few incentives for making changes. More important, the changes that would have been necessary to increase production substantially would have required more capital and human resources than were available. China was stuck.

Had the West faced such a trap, and, if so, how had the West avoided it? Kenneth Pomeranz, another economic historian, gives his answers in The Great Divergence: China, Europe, and the Making of the Modern World Economy (2000). Yes, he says, "Europe, too, could have wound up on an 'east Asian,' labor-intensive path" (p. 13) in which there were few incentives and even fewer resources available to create innovations to improve productivity. Its escape was "the result of important and sharp discontinuities, based on both fossil fuels [coal] and access to New World resources" (p. 13). The fossil fuels became important only later, during the industrial revolution, but the New World resources became important almost immediately after their discovery by Europeans. The New World "relieved the strain on Europe's supply of what was truly scarce: land and energy . . . crucial factors leading out of a world of Malthusian constraints" (p. 23). The New World provided a place for some

of Europe's "excess" population. It also provided richly productive land, an abundance of gold and silver, the lucrative slave trade, and millions of slaves who created a new market for European products.

Was the lucky discovery of the New World the major differentiation between the European economic experience and the Chinese? Pomeranz also credits "war, armed long distance trade and colonization" (p. 166). The joint stock company organized for overseas trade and colonization was a significant breakthrough for the "unified management of trading voyages and cargoes too big for a single investor" (p. 171). The backing of the state for these ventures—without excessive, crippling interference—was probably another (p. 173). The use of "force to create monopolies or near-monopolies (mostly in spices)" was a third (p. 182). The competition among the European powers for trading and colonizing supremacy was a fourth element in driving their economic success (p. 194).

Between Elvin and Pomeranz we get a comprehensive, comparative survey of the factors at work in China and in Europe—ecological, demographic, and institutional—that led to China's stagnation and western Europe's dynamism in economic creativity in the era of the Ming and early Qing dynasties in China, the era of overseas exploration, trade, and early colonization in western Europe.

- When did the economic productivity and wealth of Western Europe surpass that of China?
- To what degree did the stagnation in China's economy result from a lack of planning and hard work?
- To what degree did the success of Western Europe's economy result from planning and hard work?

Tokugawa Japan

As in China, the early European influences on Japan were both economic and religious. Roman Catholicism appeared with the Jesuit priest Francis Xavier (1506–52), who arrived in 1549. Like Matteo Ricci in China, Xavier adapted to local cultural practices in dress, food, residence, and, of course, language. For their religious ideas, their culture, and trade, Europeans were at first warmly welcomed. Japan's **shogun**, or chief military administrator, Oda Nobunaga (1534–82), encouraged the Jesuits in their missionary work, and even after Nobunaga's assassination, Christianity found a foothold in Japan. As in China, converts numbered in the hundreds of thousands, and they were mostly from among the Japanese elites. (Among the European contributions to Japanese everyday life were tobacco, bread, playing cards, and deep-fat frying, which inspired the Japanese specialty of tempura.)

shogun The military dictator of Japan, a hereditary title held by three families between 1192 and 1867. Although they were legally subservient to the emperor, their military power gave them effective control of the country.

The Japanese government became apprehensive about so large a group of elite converts. There had been early signs of the change in policy. In 1597, after a Spanish ship captain boasted of the power of his king, and after Spain had colonized Manila making that power more blatant, the shogun Toyotomi Hideyoshi crucified six Franciscan missionaries and eighteen Japanese converts. In 1606 Christianity was outlawed, and in 1614 the shogun, Tokugawa Ieyasu, began to expel all Christian missionaries. Three thousand Japanese Christians were murdered. In 1623 the British left Japan; in 1624 the Spanish were expelled; in 1630 Japanese were forbidden to travel overseas. In 1637–8, in reaction to a revolt that was more a rural economic protest than a religious uprising, 37,000 Christians were killed. The Portuguese were expelled. Only a small contingent of Dutch traders was permitted to remain, confined to Deshima Island off Nagasaki. A limited number of Chinese ships continued to visit Japan each year and some diplomatic contact with Korea continued, but Japan chose to live largely in isolation.

As in China, the suppression of contact with outsiders did not cripple Japan. Its process of political consolidation continued under the three shoguns of the Tokugawa family, from the 1600 battle of Sekigahara until 1651. The country was unified and peaceful. Privately held guns were virtually banned. Agriculture prospered as the area of land under cultivation doubled, and the production of cash crops, such as indigo, tobacco (from the New World), sugar cane, and mulberry leaves as food for silk worms, increased. The population almost doubled, from 18 million in 1600 to 30 million by the mid-1700s, at which point it stabilized temporarily.

samurai A member of the warrior class of feudal Japan, who became vassals of the daimyo. Characterized by their military skills and stoical pride, they valued personal loyalty, bravery, and honor more than life. During the peaceful years of the Tokugawa shogunate (1603–1867) they became scholars, bureaucrats, and merchants. The class was officially abolished in 1871.

The new government was in the hands of the *samurai* warrior classes, who made up about 7 percent of the population. They benefited most from the improved conditions, and there were sometimes violent protests against increasing disparities in income, but standards of living and of education generally improved. City merchants, *chonin*, emerged as a newly wealthy and powerful class, dealing in the new cash commodities of farm and hand manufacture. They supplied banking, shipping, loans, and other commercial services, and founded family businesses, some of which endure even today. The Tokugawa capital Edo (Tokyo) grew to a million people by 1700, among the largest cities in the world at the time. In a reversal of the European pattern of the time, Japan was doing well despite cutting off almost all international trade.

chonin City merchants and their collective class. During the Tokugawa shogunate this class grew in wealth, power, and sophistication.

Southeast Asia

Southeast Asia was one of the great prizes of international commerce throughout our period, and foreign merchants from China, Japan, India, Arabia, and Europe were active in its markets. Yet the merchants of the region did not themselves become major factors in the international side of the trade. Foreign traders began their activities on the coast and then moved inland, taking control of local markets. They also fought among themselves. The Dutch East India Company, for example, expelled from the Indonesian archipelago not only the local merchants but also European competitors by 1640. By this time, the spice trade was beginning to level off and the Dutch were in the process of restructuring the economies of Southeast Asia, especially Indonesia, to produce such commercial crops as sugar, coffee, and tobacco. In the Philippines, the Spanish asserted similar power.

Local rulers entered into commercial agreements with the foreign traders that enriched themselves, but not their merchant communities. Commercial profits were repatriated from Southeast Asia back to Europe, creating ever more serious imbalances of power and wealth. Capitalist enterprise in the hands of merchants, backed by the state and by military power, was radiating outward from Europe; Southeast Asia had become a participant in this new system, and a victim of it.

THE INFLUENCE OF WORLD TRADE
WHAT DIFFERENCE DOES IT MAKE?

As we close this exploration of world trade in 1776, we have witnessed enormous changes from 1100, when we began, and even from 1500, when European explorers began their oceanic voyages. During these centuries, an entirely new set of trade networks opened, crisscrossing the Atlantic Ocean. Major elements in these new trade relationships included the export from the western hemisphere of enormous quantities of gold and silver to Europe and to Asia, across the Pacific, and the taking of millions of people in slavery from Africa to the plantations of the Americas.

The earlier center of ocean trade, the Indian Ocean, continued to be important, but now European traders—Portuguese, followed by Dutch, British, and French—gained control of the intercontinental segments of that trade. The variety of traders in coastal port cities around the world increased, with some exceptions, as in Japan, and the trade outposts of the Europeans were fortified militarily. Within Europe, the power of nation-states and of private traders increased, in large part because of the profits of international trade and because of the perceived need to support it with ocean-going fleets and navies. The new philosophy of capitalism explained and justified the rising power of private business at home and abroad. New religious denominations also arose, with philosophies that rationalized the new economic acquisitiveness. Competition increased in the technology of shipping, the sophistication of commercial strategies, the manufacture of armaments, and the training and disciplining of armed forces at home and overseas. Leadership passed from the Spanish and Portuguese to the Dutch, French, and British.

Throughout this era, the most powerful and wealthy of the world's empires were in Asia, but by the end of it, Europeans, hungry for profit, and often eager to spread the gospel of Christianity, were fashioning overseas empires of unprecedented extent.

Review Questions

- Define capitalism and discuss its strengths and weaknesses as an economic system as described by Adam Smith.
- What were the chief causes of the decline of the Portuguese empire and of the Spanish empire?
- What were the chief causes of the rise of the British, French, and Dutch empires?

- What is a nation-state? Why did European rulers seek to consolidate their countries as nation-states in the period 1500–1750?
- What were the goals of Peter the Great of Russia? In what ways did contact with the outside world encourage him to pursue these goals? To what extent did he accomplish them?

Suggested Readings

PRINCIPAL SOURCES

Braudel, Fernand. *Capitalism and Material Life 1400–1800*, trans. by Miriam Kochan (New York: Harper and Row, 1973). Highly influential overview of the beginning of capitalism as the guiding economic force in modern Europe.

Chaudhuri, K.N. *Trade and Civilization in the Indian Ocean* (Cambridge: Cambridge University Press, 1985). Comprehensive survey of the ecology, politics, traders, and the trade of the Indian Ocean.

Elvin, Mark. *The Pattern of the Chinese Past* (Stanford: Stanford University Press, 1973). An interpretive economic history from pre-Han to Qing China.Thoughtful analyses of successes and failures.

Kennedy, Paul. *The Rise and Fall of the Great Powers* (New York: Vintage Books, 1987). Examines histories of great power rivalries, including the western European rivalries in the age of exploration and trade. Seeks balance between military power and economic health.

McNeill, William H. "The Age of Gunpowder Empires, 1450–1800," in Michael Adas, ed., *Islamic and European Expansion* (Philadelphia: Temple University Press, 1993), 103–9. Brief survey of the effects of gunpowder on warfare and on the nations that use it in warfare.

Mintz, Sidney W. *Sweetness and Power: The Place of Sugar in Modern History* (New York: Penguin Books, 1985). Anthropological focus on the Caribbean sugar plantation, but places it also in the context of world trade patterns, advertising, and changing food choices.

Thornton, John. *Africa and Africans in the Making of the Atlantic World, 1400–1680* (Cambridge: Cambridge University Press, 1992). Sees Africans as active participants in the slave trade and other trading activities, not simply as passive recipients in the affairs of others.

Tracy, James D., ed. *The Political Economy of Merchant Empires* (Cambridge: Cambridge University Press, 1991). An excellent account of the merchant empires that emerged in the Early Modern period.

——, ed. *The Rise of Merchant Empires* (Cambridge: Cambridge University Press, 1990). Tracy brings together the papers of an exciting academic conference on the merchant empires of the age of exploration and early colonization. Specialized, but very important

coverage. "The Rise" discusses primarily the merchant activity; "Political Economy," primarily the imperial effects.

ADDITIONAL SOURCES

Bayly, C.A. *Indian Society and the Making of the British Empire* (Cambridge: Cambridge University Press, 1988). Sees the effects of British colonization in the early years through the eyes and activities of Indians.

Braudel, Fernand. *Civilization and Capitalism 15th–18th Century*. Vol. 2: *The Wheels of Commerce*, trans. by Sian Reynolds (New York: Harper and Row, 1986). Remarkable synthesis of the transformation of early modern Europe through its economy, social life, and culture. Volume 1 is published as *Capitalism and Material Life, 1400–1800*, see above.

——. *Civilization and Capitalism 15th–18th Century*. Vol. 3: *The Perspective of the World*, trans. by Sian Reynolds (New York: Harper and Row, 1986). Third volume in the series, looks more at the importance of international relations.

——. *The Mediterranean and the Mediterranean World in the Age of Philip II*, 2 vols, trans. by Sian Reynolds (New York: Harper Torchbooks, Vol. 1: 1972; Vol. 2: 1973). This study of the Mediterranean demonstrated Braudel's style of history, including geological influences, long-time institutional influences, and short-run political and personal influences. Highly influential for its style of history as well as its subject matter.

Columbia University. *Introduction to Contemporary Civilization in the West*, 2 vols. (New York: Columbia University Press, 2nd ed., 1954). A superb reader of some of the most influential thinkers, presented in long, rich excerpts.

Curtin, Philip, Steven Feierman, Leonard Thompson, and Jan Vansina. *African History from Earliest Times to Independence* (New York: Longman, 2nd ed. 1995). Excellent, textbook survey emphasizing anthropology as well as history.

Das Gupta, Ashin and M.N. Pearson, eds. *India and the Indian Ocean 1500–1800* (Calcutta: Oxford University Press, 1987). Articles on the vital trade and politics of the major actors in the Indian Ocean.

Duara, Prasenjit. *Rescuing History from the Nation* (Chicago: University of Chicago Press, 1995). A critical challenge to the ideas that the nation state is a creation of the modern West and that it has a fixed meaning.

Ebrey, Patricia Buckley. *Cambridge Illustrated History of China* (Cambridge: Cambridge University Press, 1996). Excellent basic survey. Pictures help tell the story. Some emphasis on women in Chinese history.

Gungwu, Wang, "Merchants without Empire: the Hokkien Sojourning Communities," in Tracy, *The Rise of Merchant Empires*, 400–21. Traces the overseas activities of merchants of the south China coast, whose opportunities in China were blocked by government.

Kamen, Henry. *Empire: How Spain Became a World Power, 1492–176,* (New York: Harper Collins, 2003). Analyzes the empire globally, accounting for the many non-Spanish groups that participated in constructing and administering it.

Lapidus, Ira. *A History of Islamic Societies* (Cambridge: Cambridge University Press, 2nd ed., 2002). A 1000+ page, comprehensive, well-written history.

Palmer, R.R. and Joel Colton. *A History of the Modern World* (New York: Knopf, 9th ed., 2002). Once THE major text; now considered too Eurocentric, and very Francophile, but still excellent.

Pearson, M.N., "Merchants and States," in Tracy, ed., *The Political Economy of Merchant Empires*, 41–116. Discusses the role of the state in encouraging business, mostly in Europe, but considers Asia as well.

Pomeranz, Kenneth. *The Great Divergence: Europe, China, and the Making of the Modern World Economy* (Princeton: Princeton University Press, 2000). How did Europe surpass China? An economic historian explores various explanations. He suggests: The exploitation of New World resources; coal in Britain; armed merchant exploration and trade.

Reid, Anthony. *Southeast Asia in the Age of Commerce 1450–1680.* Vol 1: *The Land Below the Winds*; Vol 2: *Expansion and Crisis* (New Haven: Yale University Press, Vol. 1: 1988; Vol.

2: 1993). Excellent collection of conference papers on foreign merchant impacts on Southeast Asia.

Rothermund, Dietmar. *Asian Trade and European Expansion in the Age of Mercantilism* (Delhi: Manohar, 1981). Survey of economic history.

Schama, Simon. *The Embarrassment of Riches* (New York: Knopf, 1987). Study of early modern Netherlands, especially its artistic production.

Smith, Adam. *An Inquiry into the Nature and Causes of the Wealth of Nations* (New York: Modern Library, 1937). The classic philosophical rationale for capitalism.

Spence, Jonathan D. *The Memory Palace of Matteo Ricci* (New York: Penguin Books, 1985). An account of the work and the significance of Matteo Ricci in China, filled with cultural information, as on the function of memory.

Steensgaard, Niels. *The Asian Trade Revolution of the Seventeenth Century* (Chicago: University of Chicago Press, 1973). Argues that most Asian traders were small scale and not well organized.

Tawney, R.H. *Religion and the Rise of Capitalism* (New York: Harcourt, Brace, & Co., 1926). Argues, against Max Weber, that Catholicism also showed substantial economic entrepreneurship and that religious and moral principles will always be included in economic considerations.

Thomas, Hugh. *Rivers of Gold: The Rise of the Spanish Empire, from Columbus to Magellan* (New York: Random House, 2004). The first thirty years of conquest seen largely through the eyes of the men who carried it out.

Weber, Max. *The Protestant Ethic and the Spirit of Capitalism*, trans. by Talcott Parsons (London, 1930). Argues that religious beliefs do have considerable impact on economic performance. Also, in the modern world, religious enthusiasm had been supplanted by economic aspirations.

Wolf, Eric. *Europe and the People without History* (Berkeley: University of California Press, 1982). Historical anthropologist demonstrates that non-European societies are not unchanging. Their recent history has been heavily influenced by the capitalist West.

World History Documents CD-ROM

1508

MIGRATION

DEMOGRAPHIC CHANGES IN A NEW GLOBAL ECUMENE, 1300–1750

KEY TOPICS
- The "New Europes"
- Slavery: Enforced Migration, 1500–1750
- Asian Migrations, 1300–1750
- Global Population Growth and Movement
- Cities and Demographics
- Migration and Demography: What Difference Do They Make?

In the past, historians have chosen most frequently to write about great individuals, major institutions, and the politics and wards of particular peoples. In the twentieth century, however, and especially in its second half, historians began to examine demographics—that is, human populations viewed collectively and usually represented in quantitative terms. They asked such questions as: When and why do populations grow and decline? What are the impacts on population of disease, war, famine, and more efficient farming methods? What is the distribution of population by age, gender, class, and household size? They utilize life expectancy and other "vital statistics" such as birth rates, death rates, and marriage rates. They may analyze the average age at marriage, and rates of childbirth, legitimacy, and illegitimacy.

Through large-scale analyses of such data demographers seek to understand and interpret patterns of change and, although the statistics may sometimes seem dry, they tell stories of fundamental structures and changes in human society. Today, most governments gather this sort of information as a matter of course. To find information on earlier periods that lack such systematic official data collection, historians search for other sources. Church registers of birth and death, travelers' estimates of sudden population expansion and of catastrophes, ships' records of passengers and cargo, for example, have all proved valuable sources. In this chapter we shall examine demographic data specifically concerned with migration, the movement of large groups of people across geographical space, from one region to another, and between countryside and city. We touched on some of these issues from the beginning with the migration of *Homo sapiens* around the globe

New topics in the study of the past are often inspired by new experiences in the present. In our own time, demographic shifts are dramatically altering our world, both in the population explosion that has doubled the earth's population in the last thirty years and in the migrations of hundreds of millions of people both from one region to another and from rural areas to cities. The United States, in particular, stresses its importance as a nation of immigrants, a pattern that has continued from before its beginnings as a nation down to our own times. In addition, the USA continues to experience massive population shifts, especially from north to south and from east to west, and also from countryside to city and from city to suburb. These demographic transformations evoke comparisons with earlier historical eras, especially the period 1500–1750, when the population of whole continents was restructured as new peoples immigrated and native populations perished. At the same time, great capital cities, some of them newly founded, also experienced enormous population growth.

There is another reason for choosing to study aggregate populations instead of individual lives. Such studies are often the closest we can come to understanding the lives of average people. They may not have left written records—most were not literate

Opposite **Albrecht Dürer, *Portrait of a Black Man*, 1508. Charcoal on paper.** Europeans saw black Africans mostly in slavery. This *Portrait of a Black Man* by the great German painter Albrecht Dürer is exceptional, portraying the subject as intelligent, clear-eyed, thoughtful, and independent of spirit. (*Graphische Sammlung Albertina, Vienna*).

(they could not read or write)—so we are not able to know their individual biographies, but through demographic studies of aggregate groups we may be able to gain a better understanding of the societies in which they lived and died.

Finally, new kinds of research often require new kinds of tools; sometimes the research is motivated by the availability of these new tools. Population history requires quantitative information and the statistical tools to work with it. Within the last generation demographers have made great strides in methodology, some of it as a result of new computers and data-processing capabilities. Their quantitative researches provide additional, new replies to the question "How Do We Know?"

Our explorations will take us to four major issues: First, the formation of "New Europes" around the globe as settlers from Europe set out in all directions—often with catastrophic consequences for native populations in each of these areas. Second, the trade in slaves that brought some 10 million people from Africa to the Americas—against a background of the longstanding historic trade in slaves in many parts of the globe. Third, very long-distance migrations of Mongols and Turks, groups of people emerging from Central Asia and invading and conquering lands from China in the east, to Russia and the Balkans in the west, to India in the south. Finally, we will analyze migrations from rural areas to cities in several different parts of the world and compare and contrast peoples' reasons for moving.

THE "NEW EUROPES"

From 1500 to 1750 internal developments within Europe began to increase the area's influence in the world and expedited the emigration of millions of Europeans to establish "New Europes" around the globe. Many of these developments were discussed in Chapter 14. These included:

- increasing powers of the traders in the diaspora cities of trade around the globe;
- increasing power of European nation-states and their support for overseas trade;
- shifting of trade to the Atlantic (rather than the Indian) Ocean;
- increasing pace of technological invention in Europe, especially in guns and ships;
- increasing discipline and order within European armies;
- importation of immense quantities of gold and silver from the New World, much of which was sent to China and India to pay for imports to Europe;
- exploitation of the labor of millions of slaves taken from Africa to work the plantations of the New World;
- spreading the message of aggressive Christianity.

Some historians see the crusades as a precursor of the massive movements of population after 1500. These religious campaigns to seize and settle the "Holy Land" lasted from 1096 until just after the last crusader kingdom was destroyed in 1291. The crusaders established commercial settlements along with their fortresses, and their new settlements also housed at least some missionaries. The crusades thus prefigured the European expansion after 1500 in including goals of conquest, settlement, economic gain, and missionary activity.

As we have seen in Chapter 14, in the sixteenth century both Spain and Portugal built enormous global empires. The voyages of Columbus revealed gold and silver reserves in the Americas, and many Europeans who followed him were prepared to kill Native Americans and to take over their lands. Cortés conquered the Aztec nation of Mexico in 1519 and Pizarro the Incas in 1533. The death and destruction that followed were monumental, but warfare was not the greatest killer: disease was even more deadly.

The Columbian Exchanges of Plants, Animals, and Disease

The peoples of the eastern and western hemispheres had had no sustained contact for thousands of years. Columbus' voyages therefore ushered in a new era of interaction. This "Columbian Exchange" brought in its wake both catastrophe and new opportunities. The catastrophe befell the Amerindians, who had no resistance to the diseases carried by the Europeans. The new opportunities came with the intercontinental exchange of new plants and animals.

The Devastation of the Amerindian Population.

Historian Alfred Crosby, a pioneer in the study of the exchange of microbes, cites the lowest currently accepted estimate of the Amerindian population in 1492 as 33 million, the highest as perhaps 50 million.

Aztec smallpox victims, sixteenth century. The Spanish conquest of the Americas owed more to the diseases they brought with them than to their armed forces. The Native Americans had never encountered these diseases, especially smallpox, and had no immunity. They died in horrific numbers—up to 90 percent in many regions. (*Peabody Museum of Archaeology and Ethnology, Harvard University*)

By comparison, Europe at the time had a population of 80 million. The death of millions of Amerindians followed almost immediately after Europeans began to arrive. At their lowest point after the coming of Europeans, the populations of the western hemisphere dropped to 4.5 million. The biggest killers in this demographic catastrophe were not guns, but diseases: smallpox, measles, whooping cough, chicken pox, bubonic plague, malaria, diphtheria, amoebic dysentery, and influenza. The populations of the New World, separated by thousands of years and thousands of miles from those of the Old, had little resistance to its diseases. Up to 90 percent of the population died.

Benefits of the Columbian Exchanges.

Ironically, but more happily, links between the hemispheres also brought an exchange of food sources, which later facilitated the multiplication of human lives. From South America, the cassava spread to Africa and Asia and the white potato to northern Europe. Sweet potatoes traveled to China, as did maize (corn), of which China is today the second largest producer after the United States. Today, the former Soviet Union produces ten times more potatoes by weight than does South America; Africa produces almost twice as much cassava as does South America.

The migration of flora and fauna went from east to west as well. Wheat was the leading Old World crop to come to the New World, but perhaps an even greater contribution came in domesticated animals: cattle, sheep, pigs, and goats. Domesticated horses, too, were imported from the Old World to the New. In the long run, these exchanges of food sources did much to increase the population of the world more than ten times, from about 500 million in 1492 to about 6 billion today. But not everyone participated in this growth. There were demographic winners and losers. Peoples of the European continent in 1492 were the biggest winners; Asians generally did well; Amerindians were among the biggest losers.

North America

By the early 1600s, Spanish supremacy in the New World was being challenged by the Dutch Republic, England, and France. All three had developed expertise in the construction of high quality ships, and all three fostered business groups skilled in

European settlement in eastern North America. Along the Atlantic coast of North America, Britain established an array of colonies. Thirteen of them revolted in 1776 to form the United States, but the northern areas remained loyal. The British restricted settlement across the Appalachian Mountains so that land was held by Indian nations and, still further west, claimed by the French. Florida was held by the British, 1763–83, but otherwise was a Spanish possession until invaded and conquered by the US in 1818.

trade and motivated by profit, with strong ties to political leadership. At first, all three concentrated on the Caribbean and its potential for profits from plantations. They seized and settled outposts: England most notably in the Bahamas and Jamaica, France in Saint-Domingue (modern Haiti), and the Dutch along the Brazilian coast and in Curaçao. Later they turned to the North American mainland.

North America had its own attractions for farmers, artisans, laborers, and agricultural workers who came to settle. Some of the earliest settlers were pushed out of Europe by the "price revolution" created by the availability of New World silver. The influx of the precious metal into Europe, and into the European trade networks in Asia, inflated prices; wages did not keep pace. Pressured by this decline in their economic condition, people living at the margins of European society sought the opportunity of new frontiers in North America.

Later, through the seventeenth and early eighteenth centuries, the European invaders into the New World came in different waves and appropriated different regions for their purposes. In Virginia they came at first looking for gold, beaver furs, deer skin, and a northwest passage to Asia. They failed in all these goals, and at first they failed even to survive. Of the first 900 colonists arriving in 1607–9, only sixty were alive at the end of the two years, most dying from famine and disease. Some 9000 came between 1610 and 1622; at the later date, only 2000 were alive. After 1618 the crown-appointed administrators of the colony offered 50 acres to any settler who would come, and by this date Virginia's tobacco crop became the staple product of its economy. Settlers continued to come, but life was difficult, attractive mostly to people of the lower social classes. Many signed on as **indentured laborers**, contracting to work for a fixed period of years, usually about seven, in exchange for ocean passage and fixed labor with a specific employer in the New World. About three-fourths of these laborers were male, and most aged between fifteen and twenty-four. Since their masters cared little for them, they were bought and sold, and sometimes worked to death, not much different from slaves. With life so cheap, at the whim of both man and nature, the further massacre of Native Americans, who were seen as alien, savage, non-Christian, and an obstacle to European invasion and expansion, became a way of life for the land-hungry settlers.

Maryland also grew tobacco, but its goals included more than mere economic profit. In 1632 the English Crown had given the land to George Calvert, Lord Baltimore, and he established here a religious refuge for Catholics, who were at that time an oppressed minority in England. Catholics formed a minority of the population of the colony, but they were legally protected. Their relationships with the Native Americans, however, were also murderous.

In New England, the first collective settlement of Europeans was the Pilgrim colony founded in 1620. Dissenters from the official doctrines of the Church of England, the Pilgrims also sought a religious haven in the New World. Their community was bound together by the Mayflower Compact, an agreement they drafted on board ship to the New World, establishing a governing body "for the general good of the colony; unto which, we promise all due submission and obedience." Of the 102 Pilgrims who landed at Plymouth, fewer than half survived the first year, but, with the help of Native Americans who befriended the settlers, the colony took root.

indentured labor Labor performed under signed indenture, or contract, which binds the laborer to work for a specific employer, for a specified time, usually years, often in a distant place, in exchange for transportation and maintenance.

EUROPEAN MIGRATION TO NORTH AMERICA

1565	Spanish settle in Florida
1604	Nova Scotia settled by French
1607	First permanent English settlement at Jamestown, Virginia
1608	"New France" in Canada settled by French
1611	Dutch settle on Manhattan Island
1619	Europeans bring first black Africans, as slaves, to Virginia
1620	Mayflower sails from Plymouth, England, with Pilgrim Fathers to found first colony in New England, at Plymouth, Massachusetts
1622	Maine settled by English
1624	New York settled by Dutch
1630	Massachusetts settled by Massachusetts Bay Co.
1634	English Catholics found Maryland
1635–8	Connecticut settled by English
1638	Rhode Island settled by groups from Massachusetts
1638	Delaware settled by Swedes
1663	Carolina settled by English
1670	Rupert's Land claimed by Hudson Bay Co.
1681	Pennsylvania settled by English Quakers
1682	French claim Mississippi area
1713	British sovereignty over Newfoundland recognized

Puritans arrive in New England. Religious freedom and economic opportunity were the two great attractions for European immigrants to the New World. Many of the immigrants from England were dissenters from the established official Church. Their independence was a background factor that later helped to inspire the American Revolution in 1776. Some of the dissenters, however, like the Puritans, were themselves intolerant toward others who settled in their communities, forcing them to conform or to leave.

In 1630 another group of settlers, the Puritans, arrived in New England. The Pilgrims wished to separate from the Church of England; the Puritans wished only to purify it. They were richer and better educated than the Pilgrims. Many had some college education. English King Charles I (whom many suspected of secret Catholicism and who conflicted with Protestant hardliners at home), eager to get them out of England, gave them a charter to establish the Company of the Massachusetts Bay. By the end of the year, 1000 had settled; within a decade, 20,000. Many more chose to settle in the sugar plantations of the Caribbean islands.

The Puritans had left England for their own religious freedom, but in New England, they denied it to others. People like Roger Williams, a minister who wanted the separation of Church and state, were forced to flee. The Puritans were narrow in their outlook, but fiercely devoted to community, discipline, work, education, and spreading their view of religion. They scorned Indians, fought them, and confiscated their land with little compunction.

The Dutch had settled the area around New Amsterdam until the English seized it in 1664 and, after a brief loss, recaptured it in 1673. The English renamed it New York, and the area developed its own polyglot, pragmatic, tolerant business ethic instituted by the Dutch.

Perhaps the most inspiring settlement was the Quaker colony of Pennsylvania, founded by William Penn, a British aristocrat who had joined the Society of Friends, as Quakers are called formally, inspired by a lecture on the Society's basic principles of freedom of conscience, non-violence, and pacifism. Pennsylvania and its first capital, Philadelphia (whose name means "brotherly love"), became known throughout western Europe for their religious toleration, and people of many countries and faiths immigrated here: "English, Highland Scots, French, Germans, Irish, Welsh, Swedes, Finns, and Swiss … Mennonites, Lutherans, Dutch Reformed, Baptists, Anglicans, Presbyterians, Catholics, Jews," and a few hermits and mystics). Indeed, even Native Americans immigrated to flee the violence against them that was endemic elsewhere. Unfortunately, the non-Quaker immigrant-invaders did not share Penn's early commitment to tolerant, peaceful inter-racial relationships with the Native Americans, regulated by legal contracts and personal contacts. After Penn's death, they too pushed Indians off the land, although with less violence than elsewhere.

While the English were establishing numerous, diverse, thriving colonies along the Atlantic Coast, from Newfoundland to South Carolina, and inland on Hudson's Bay, the French were settling, lightly, the inland waterways of the St. Lawrence River, the Great Lakes, and the Mississippi River, as well as Gulf Coast Louisiana. During the global warfare between Britain and France, the Seven Years War of 1756–63, British military forces conquered the North American mainland from the Atlantic to the Mississippi. Their victory ensured that North America would be English-speaking. French cultural influences and migration, however, continued to be felt in the region of Quebec, and it continues as a French-speaking province until today. By 1750, about four million people of European origin inhabited North America.

The Antipodes: Australia and New Zealand, 1600–1900

The English also conquered and sent migrants to the Pacific Islands. Crossing the Atlantic became relatively quick and easy, but reaching Australia and New Zealand, on the opposite side of the globe, was quite a different matter. Even their neighbors had established only minimal contacts with them. There had been some landings by Asians in the sixteenth century. They came to the north coast of Australia in search of a species of sea slug that looked like a withered penis when smoked and dried. The slugs became Indonesia's largest export to the Chinese, who valued them as aphrodisiacs.

Spanish copies of Portuguese charts suggest that Portuguese sailors had landed on and mapped the northern and eastern coasts of Australia, and that the Spanish may also have known about them, but no continuing contact resulted. In the early 1600s, a few Dutch sailors reached parts of the coast, several wrecking their ships in the process. Between 1642 and 1644, under commission from the Dutch East India Company, the Dutch commander Abel Tasman (c. 1605–59) began the systematic exploration of New Zealand, the sea—later named for him—that separates Australia from New Zealand, the island that was later named Tasmania, and the north coast of Australia. He reported "naked beach-roving wretches, destitute even of rice . . . miserably poor, and in many places of a very bad disposition" (cited in Hughes, p. 48). With such unpromising descriptions reaching England, and the general decline of Spanish, Dutch, and Portuguese power, Australia remained virtually untouched by Europeans for a century and a half, and the pattern of immigration from Europe lags behind the pattern going to the western hemisphere by a similar amount of time.

In 1768, the English Captain James Cook (1728–79) set out on a three-year voyage, which took him to Tahiti to record astronomical observations; to Australia to determine the nature of the "Southern Continent" reported by Tasman; to map New Zealand; and, thanks to the zeal of a young amateur botanist, Joseph Banks (1743–1820), to report on the natural resources of all these distant lands. The success of Cook's three-year voyage was made possible by discoveries of proper food supplements to prevent scurvy among the sailors and of new instrumentation to chart longitude and thus

SOURCE

Captain Cook Encounters the Aboriginals of Australia

Abel Tasman's description of the fierce Maori of New Zealand discouraged Europeans from further explorations of those islands. A similarly dismal, and racist, report on Australia was written by the only European to have visited it, William Dampier, who had come to the north coast from New Holland (Indonesia) in 1688:

> The inhabitants of this country are the miserablest people in the World . . . They have great Heads, round Foreheads, and great Brows. Their Eye-lids are always half closed, to keep the Flies out of their Eyes . . . therefore they cannot see far.
>
> They are long-visaged, and of a very unpleasing aspect; having no one graceful feature in their faces.
>
> They have no houses, but lye in the open Air, without any covering; the Earth being their Bed, and the Heaven their Canopy . . .
>
> I did not perceive that they did worship anything. (cited in Hughes, p. 48)

Captain Cook's view was the absolute contrary:

> They may appear to some to be the most wretched people upon Earth, but in reality they are far happier than we Europeans; being wholly unacquainted not only with the superfluous, but the necessary Conveniencies so much sought after in Europe, they are happy in not knowing the use of them. They live in Tranquility which is not disturb'd by the Inequality of Condition: The Earth and sea of their own accord furnishes them with all things necessary for life, they covet not Magnificent Houses, Houshold-stuff, etc., they live in a warm and fine Climate and enjoy a very wholesome Air, so that they have very little need of Clothing and this they seem to be fully sencible of, for many to whome we gave Cloth etc. to, left it carlessly upon the Sea beach and in the woods as a thing they had no manner of use for. In short they seem'd to set no Value upon any thing we gave them, nor would they ever part with any thing of their own for any one article we could offer them; this in my opinion argues that they think themselves provided with all the necessarys of Life and that they have no superfluities. (Cook, Vol. I, p. 399)

Cook took with him on the voyage a young botanist, Joseph Banks. Bank's descriptions of the Aboriginals presented them as timid, without property, and few in number. Although Banks was not proposing colonization, those who wished it could find encouragement in his comments. Banks and his associate Daniel Solander brought back from the three-year trip some 30,000 specimens representing 3000 species, of which 1600 had never before been seen by European scientists. Not all of these were from Australia, but in honor of the work of Banks and Solander, Cook named his principal harbor in Australia "Botany Bay."

Australia was distant from Europe, but based on Cook's discoveries, it seemed to hold rich promise for future encounters.

establish location at sea. Cook's descriptions of the people he encountered in Australia differed sharply from those of Tasman. He found them peaceful—unlike the Maori of New Zealand. This sealed the fate of Australia.

On the basis of Cook's report, the British government decided that Australia could serve as the "dumping ground" it had been seeking for the prisoners who were overcrowding the jails at home. (Until the Revolutionary War, the American colonies had served this purpose.) British settlement in Australia thus began in the form of penal colonies. From 1788, when the first shipload of convicts arrived, until the 1850s, "transportation" to Australia was the only alternative to hanging for British prisoners. Under the "assignment system," convicts were assigned for the duration of their sentences to particular masters, about 90 percent of them private individuals, about 10 percent government officials superintending public works projects. Conditions among the prisoners were extremely harsh, and sexual relationships in particular reflected both the demography and the harshness. Men outnumbered women among the prisoners by a ratio of 6 to 1; in the cities, 4 to 1; in the countryside, 20 to 1. Both prostitution and rape were common among the women; homosexuality flourished among the men. Beginning in 1835, new prison acts in Britain began to provide for prisons at home and the use of Australia as a prison colony quickly declined. By 1868, the last convict ship unloaded its cargo—Irish prisoners deposited in Western Australia.

The early British colonization of Australia began at Botany Bay, adjacent to Sydney, and then at other points along the southeast coast, the best watered and most fertile part of Australia. Because mountains flanked close against the coast and fresh water was scarce, progress inland was problematic, and settlement by Europeans was slow, based on commercial agriculture in wool, dairy cattle, and sugar cultivation.

In the 1850s and again in the 1890s, however, gold was discovered and newcomers rushed in. The advent of faster shipping stimulated wheat exports, and refrigeration increased the frozen meat trade after 1880. Even so, the population in 1861 was only 1,200,000; by 1901 it had climbed to 3,800,000.

The coming of Europeans, even in small numbers, destroyed the fragile ecology of aboriginal civilization, which survived only in the center and far north of the

A government jail gang, Sydney, New South Wales, eighteenth century. After they lost their colonies in the American Revolution and their prison colonies among them, the British were searching for a new dumping ground for their convicts. Australia met their needs. The first shipload of convicts arrived in 1788. (*Private Collection*)

A model war canoe, Gisbourne, New Zealand, eighteenth century. Until the end of the eighteenth century, a Maori war canoe was the most prized and decorated clan possession.

continent. As in other "New Europes," European diseases killed off the overwhelming majority of the Aboriginals. In addition, their hunting grounds were displaced by the sheep and cattle, the fences and the pasturage of the British settlers. Finally, the savagery and the explicit policies of the British, both official and unofficial, overwhelmed them. A large proprietor of sheep and cattle

> narrated as a good thing, that he had been one of party who had pursued the blacks, in consequence of cattle having been rushed by them, and he was sure they shot upwards of a hundred . . . [H]e maintained that there was nothing wrong in it, that it was preposterous to suppose they had souls. (Hughes, p. 277)

At first, the Australian Aborigines, who lived nomadically by hunting and gathering, retreated in the face of white advances, but later they began to resist, to defend their ancestral territories as best they could with bows and arrows and spears against British weaponry. They resisted in some places for up to ten years, stealing British guns and learning to use them, attacking sheep, cattle, horses, and homes. British response to the resistance was intensified by the belief that the Aborigines could neither be attracted nor compelled into productive work for the British. In 1788, when Europeans first arrived to settle Australia, there had been perhaps 300,000 Aborigines. By 2000, the 19 million inhabitants of Australia were 92 percent European, 7 percent Asian, 1 percent aboriginal. Today, most of Australia's 50,000 full-blooded Aborigines, and many of its 150,000 part-Aborigines, live on reservations in arid inland regions.

The devastation caused by the arrival of British settlers was repeated in New Zealand. The Maori, an East Polynesian people, had arrived and settled in New Zealand about 750 C.E. They had lived there for almost a thousand years, probably in isolation, until Tasman reached New Zealand's west coast in 1642. The Maori killed four members of his party and prevented his landing. More than a century later, James Cook explored New Zealand for four months and found the Maori brave, warlike, and cannabalistic. Joseph Banks, who was on the voyage, wrote: "I suppose they live intirely [*sic*] on fish, dogs, and enemies".

The people may have been fierce, but the seals and whales in the coastal waters, and the flax and timber on the land, attracted hunters and traders from Australia, America, and Britain. The first missionaries came in 1814 to convert the Maori. Warfare against and among the Maori was made more deadly by weapons introduced by Europeans. Diseases accompanying the European arrival, especially tuberculosis, venereal diseases, and measles, cut the Maori population from about 200,000 when Cook arrived to perhaps 100,000 in 1840 and to 42,000 by the end of the century. In 1840, British settlers signed a treaty with a group of Maori chiefs that gave sovereignty to the British Crown. Although they declared equal rights under law for Maoris and Europeans, in practice they enforced racial inequality. The British confiscated Maori lands on North Island and precipitated wars that drove the Maori from some of New Zealand's richest lands.

Captain Hobson signing the Treaty of Waitanga with Maori chiefs, 1840. The treaty was intended to secure the annexation of New Zealand to the British government, while guaranteeing the constitutional rights of the Maoris. But language difficulties and cultural differences caused misinterpretation of the fine print and the settlers' sense of racial superiority over the "natives" eventually precipitated wars and the forfeiture of Maori lands.

South Africa, 1652–1902

The Dutch East India Company sent the first European settlers to South Africa in 1652 to set up a base at Cape Town to facilitate shipping between Europe and Asia. The Company soon invited Dutch, French, and German settlers to move inland and to establish ranches in Cape Colony. By 1700, the Europeans held most of the good farmland in the region; by 1795, they had spread 300 miles north and 500 miles east of Cape Town. The colony then had a total population of 60,000, of which one-third were whites. Most of the African peoples were of two main ethnic groups—the Khoikhoi herdsmen and the San hunters—with some from other African groups, and some peoples of mixed ancestry.

In 1795, Britain took control of the Cape Colony from its Dutch settlers to prevent it from falling to France, which had conquered the Netherlands during the Wars of the French Revolution. In 1814, the Dutch formally gave the Cape to the British, and the first British colonists arrived in 1820. The continuing struggle for land and power among the British, Dutch, and Africans is discussed in Chapter 16.

SLAVERY: ENFORCED MIGRATION, 1500–1750

Most of the migrations of Europeans were of free peoples, who moved by choice. But throughout the seventeenth and eighteenth centuries, Africa contributed more immigrants to the New World than did Europe. These Africans came as slaves, taken as captives and transported against their will.

Trading in African slaves was not new. The Romans had included Africans among their slaves and, as we have seen in Chapter 12, since about the seventh century C.E. Arab camel caravans had carried gold and slaves northward across the Sahara to the Mediterranean in exchange for European cotton and woolen textiles, copper, and brass. On its east coast, Africa had been long integrated into the Indian Ocean trade by Muslim and Arab traders. They exported from Africa gold, slaves, ivory, and amber and imported cotton and silk cloth.

British settlement in Australia, New Zealand, and South Africa. British expansion in the scramble for empire, driven by land hunger and mineral wealth, was unparalleled. In addition to the riches of India, British colonists ousted the Dutch from Cape Colony, grasped the habitable littoral of southeast Australia (initially colonizing it with prisoners and other social outcasts), and laid claim to the world's most southerly inhabitable territory, New Zealand, as a promised land for its burgeoning early nineteenth-century population.

For an interactive version of this map, go to: http://www.prenhall.com/spodek/map15.3

The African slave trade. A trade in sub-Saharan African slaves dated from the Roman Empire, and had been lucratively developed by Arab merchants from the eighth century. But the impact of western European entrepreneurs, seeking cheap labor for the Americas, was unparalleled. The millions of Africans who survived the Middle Passage by boat from Africa to the Americas between about 1550 and the late nineteenth century formed a new African diaspora in the New World.

Portuguese and, later, other European ships reoriented the trade routes of Africa to the Atlantic coast. Caravans continued to cross the desert, but far more trade now came to the new coastal town fortresses constructed at such places as St. Louis, Cape Coast, Elmina, Bonny, Luanda, Benguela, and on São Tomé Island. Here, Africans brought gold and slaves to trade to the European shippers. The number of slaves sold rose from under a thousand a year in 1451–75, when Portugal began to trade in slaves from the West African coast, to about 7500 a year in the first half of the seventeenth century, to about 50,000 a year throughout the eighteenth and first half of the nineteenth centuries. In all, the transatlantic slave trade carried some 10 million people from Africa to the western hemisphere to work as slaves, generally on sugar, tobacco, and cotton plantations.

The slaves took on economic importance in direct proportion to the expansion of the sugar plantation economy of the Caribbean after 1650. In the 1700s, the plantations reached their maximum productivity and profitability. Between 1713 and 1792 Britain alone imported £162 million of goods from the Caribbean, almost all of it sugar. This was half again as much as all British imports from Asia during the same period. France held the richest single sugar colony in the Caribbean, Saint-Domingue, (modern Haiti).

The slaves often fared poorly on the sugar plantations of the Caribbean and Brazil, where owners often believed it was cheaper to work them to death and buy replacements from among those coming from Africa rather than to feed, clothe, and house them adequately to sustain life. In North America, which concentrated on producing other crops and where planters encouraged their reproduction, they often fared much better.

Reinterpreting the Slave Trade

From the fifteenth to the nineteenth centuries, many individual states were taking form on the African continent.

A slave market, from *Al Magamat (The Meetings)*, fourteenth century. Muslims owned and traded slaves from the earliest days of the Islamic religion. Their trade in slaves included Africa, southeastern Europe, Arabia, and the lands surrounding the Indian Ocean. Islamic law governing the treatment of slaves made the practice relatively humane; slaves were used more frequently for domestic service than for gang labor. (*Bibliothèque Nationale, Paris*)

The largest, like the Songhay empire of West Africa, was about the size of France or Spain. Medium-sized states, the size of Portugal or of England, were more numerous, including the Oyo Empire in Nigeria, Nupe, Igala, and Benin in the lower Niger Valley, the Hausa states of northern Nigeria, and Kongo, in central Africa. Slavery and the slave trade were important to the rise and decline of these states. First, in a region where land was not privately owned, slaves represented the main form of wealth. A rich state held many slaves. Second, the slaves were a source of labor, a means for their owners to increase wealth. Third, the trade in slaves was a means of still further increasing wealth, either for the state itself or for private traders. Long before Europeans arrived on the Atlantic coast, slavery was big business in these African states.

This prevalence of slavery in Africa helps to explain a turn-about in the interpretation of the slave trade. In this interpretation Africans are seen as active participants who helped build up this important trade. When European traders offered new opportunities, African businessmen, who were already active in the internal slave trade, joined in, continuing to control the trade up to the water's edge. Europeans lacked the military strength, the immunity to disease, and the knowledge of the terrain to enter the interior of the continent. They stayed in coastal enclaves, while Africans captured the slaves and brought them to be purchased. Occasionally, African rulers attempted to limit the trade, but both African and European traders seemed beyond their control. The lure of profit increased as the demand for slaves multiplied in the next two centuries.

Some of the trading communities of Africa—ethnic groups that traditionally facilitated and controlled trade—probably profited, including the Jahaanke of the Gambia–River Niger region; the Juula of northern Ghana, Côte d'Ivoire, and Upper Niger River; the Wolof of Senegal; and the Awka and Aro of Iboland in Nigeria. A new community of African–Portuguese traders was also born as Portuguese and Africans along the coast bonded and had children.

HOW DO WE KNOW?

How Many Slaves?

Philip Curtin's The Atlantic Slave Trade: A Census, *published in 1969, remains the landmark study on the demographics of the slave trade. Curtin examined the existing estimate of 15 million as the number of slaves carried from Africa to the New World and concluded that it had been accepted with little basis in research. Curtin undertook a fundamental investigation of the numbers, limiting himself to data already published rather than undertaking original archival searches of his own. The accounts included import records of specific African and American ports, shipping records, and projections based on historical slave populations in the Americas. From these records, Curtin produced the first systemic analysis of the quantity of slaves from Africa landed in the Americas.*

First he analyzed the structure of the plantation economy that produced the sugar, and stressed six key points:

- *it relied on slave labor;*
- *it was organized as an early large-scale capitalist enterprise with gangs of laborers;*
- *its owners held "feudal," legal rights over the workers;*
- *it supplied a crop for export to distant European markets but often did not grow its own food; it was completely reliant on international trade for profits and for necessities;*
- *"political control over the system lay on another continent and in another kind of society";*
- *in its organization, the sugar plantation was a forerunner of factory labor.*

Curtin begins his analysis with the importation of slaves into Europe, including Sicily, Portugal, Spain, and Italy, as well as to the sugar-producing islands off the coasts of these countries. Evaluating and revising the statistics of previous demographers for the period 1450–1500, Curtin estimates that 50,000 Africans were imported as slaves into Europe and 25,000 into the Atlantic

islands of Madeira, Cape Verde, and the Canaries. Another 100,000 were transported off the African coast to São Tomé.

Based primarily on the records of asientos, shipping licenses issued by Spanish authorities to foreign firms between 1521 and 1773, and government records, especially from Britain, Curtin estimates that up to 1865 the entire import of Africans to Spanish America was 1,552,000, with 702,000 of these going to Cuba. For the entire period from 1640 to 1807 (when the British outlawed the slave trade), Curtin estimates that 1,665,000 people were imported as slaves to the British West Indies. To the French West Indies Curtin estimates that 1,600,200 were imported between 1664 and 1838, and that in Portuguese America, these numbers were more than double. To Brazil alone, with its massive sugar plantations in Bahia, Curtin accepts the estimates of two earlier demographers, who suggested a figure of about 3,646,800. To the Dutch West Indies, 500,000 people were imported as slaves; to the Danish West Indies, now the American Virgin Islands, 28,000. Imports to the United States and pre-1776 North America totaled about 399,000.

Thus, Curtin's 1969 estimate for the total importation of slaves to the Americas was 9,566,000. Overall, "more Africans than Europeans arrived in the Americas between, say, 1492 and 1770" (p. 87). Curtin noted that, although his estimates could well be off by as much as 50 percent, they were, nevertheless, "correct enough to point out contradictions in present hypotheses and to raise new questions for comparative demography and social history" (p. 93).

Curtin also explored the effects on reproduction of the slave trade. Only about one-third of the slaves sold overseas were women, so that in Africa population losses to the next generation were proportionately limited, but in the Americas, with fewer females, the slaves did not reproduce their own numbers. Even these rates of reproduction were, however, different in different areas.

North America, for example, imported relatively few slaves because those that were imported had relatively high birth rates. They reproduced more abundantly than slaves elsewhere.

The USA and Canada imported only 4.2 percent of all the slaves imported into the Americas, about 400,000 out of 9,566,000.

> *Contrary to the parochial view of history that most North Americans pick up in school, the United States was only a marginal recipient of slaves from Africa. The real center of the trade was tropical America, with almost 90 percent going to the Atlantic fringe from Brazil through the Guianas to the Caribbean coast and islands. (p. 74)*

Birth rates among the North American slaves were proportionately higher than elsewhere. No one knows quite why:

> *Rather than sustaining the regular excess of deaths over births typical of tropical America, the North American colonies developed a pattern of natural growth among the slaves ... By the end of the eighteenth century, North American s lave populations were growing at nearly the same rate as that of the settler populations from Europe ... Historians have neglected [this] almost completely, even though it has an obvious and important bearing on such recent historical problems as the comparative history of slavery in the New World. Nor have demographic historians yet produced a complete or satisfactory explanation of this phenomenon. (p. 73)*

Two different hypotheses have attempted to explain the higher rates of reproduction in North America. The first, and perhaps most obvious, was that slaves in North America may have been better treated than elsewhere. Second, slaves in North America apparently breast fed their children for only one year, in contrast to the two years more typical in the Caribbean. Breast-feeding has a contraceptive effect that would have reduced birth rates more in the Caribbean than in the USA.

Additional demographic inquiries have followed Curtin's Census. *For example,*

HOW DO WE KNOW? (continued)

Curtin pointed out that the location of the most active slave trading varied over time, according to the law of supply and demand. Where slaves were plentiful, often because of warfare and the seizing of captives who could be sold into slavery, prices fell; then more European slavers arrived to take advantage of the low prices, increasing demand, raising prices, and encouraging European slavers to look elsewhere. The marketplace shifted as prices oscillated. The result seems to be that no area was constantly a supplier, but that each area had time t o recover some of its population losses. On the other hand, no area remained

immune to the economic attractions of the market. The sale and purchase of slaves infected the entire coastline. Later historians have sought to locate more precisely the geographical source of slaves exported from Africa. Paul Lovejoy, for example, found that of the 5.5 million exported in the hundred years between 1701 and 1800, the three largest sources were west central Africa, with 2 million, the Bight of Biafra, with 814,000, and the Senegambia, with 201,000 (Lovejoy, p. 50)

Curtin's work initiated continuing statistical research for greater precision, but we now have a clear, empirical basis

for understanding the general dimensions of three centuries of Atlantic trade in human beings.

- Philip Curtin's studies of the slave trade say very little about moral issues. What is the importance of information about the systems and statistics of plantation slavery separate from the consideration of moral issues?
- Please give examples of ways in which the slave trade was subject to the economic laws of supply and demand.
- What regions of the Americas imported the most slaves?

The effects of the slave trade on the total economy of Africa remain much disputed. Some scholars, following the pioneering work of Walter Rodney in his *How Europe Underdeveloped Africa* (1972), continue to cite dire economic consequences. Some more recent writers, however, suggest that the slave trade, despite its enormous absolute size, was small relative to the total size of Africa's population and internal economy and therefore had little effect. This debate over size and significance continues.

No one, however, can estimate the lost opportunities for African development represented by the export of so many millions of its strongest and most resilient men and women. Crosby points out ironically that Africa received new crops such as maize, manioc, and cassava as part of the Atlantic exchange. These became staple foods and may actually have increased the population more than the export of slaves depleted it. And, of course, slavery established a new population of African–Americans throughout the western hemisphere.

ASIAN MIGRATIONS, 1300–1750

Just as Europeans were transforming the Americas and other parts of the world through their migrations, Asians were moving into other parts of the world they conquered. In Chapters 12 and 13, we analyzed the geographical patterns and economic institutions of trade and traders, and found that they developed differently in Europe and in Asia. The differences became especially sharp as the Europeans set out on their voyages of transoceanic exploration and trade across the Atlantic. Now we shall see that patterns of migration also differed sharply between Europe and Asia—and yet there were striking similarities.

We focus especially on the vast, successive waves of immigrant conquerors that swept out of Central Asia between 1300 and 1750 and created three new empires and several new ruling dynasties within the already existing empire of China. Turkic-speaking invaders founded the Ottoman Empire that sprawled across western Asia, southeastern Europe, and North Africa; the Safavid Empire in Persia; and the Mughal Empire in South Asia; while in China the Mongol descendants of Chinggis Khan and, later, the Manchus introduced new dynasties to the existing empire.

The conquests of the western Europeans and the Central Asians show remarkable similarities. The time frame for these invasions and conquests is roughly parallel. (The Ottoman conquests, blocking access to the eastern Mediterranean and the Middle East, provided the inspiration for the Europeans to launch their overseas explorations.) The distances they traveled, across thousands of miles, were equally vast. Both were ultimately motivated by a desire to conquer and subdue that frequently led to ruthless cruelty. Both imposed new cultures on the peoples they conquered—but the degree of this imposition was starkly different.

The contrasts are altogether quite remarkable. The Asians traveled over land. Although they could be very violent, they did not so utterly destroy the peoples they conquered, perhaps because unlike the Amerindians, the people Asians conquered had immunity to each other's diseases because of their long contact with each other. Since the Asian conquerors were mostly immigrants on horseback with little experience of sedentary societies, they were limited in the degree to which they could influence their subjects. Over time they tended to adopt the more sophisticated and efficient ruling ideologies and institutions of the peoples they conquered. They did not displace existing societies with new ones largely of their own design. In large measure they were assimilated by the peoples they defeated. And by the early eighteenth century, as western Europe was increasing in power and wealth, most of the Asian empires were in decline.

The Ottoman Empire 1300–1700

The Ottoman Empire was named for Osman, a Turkish leader whose military victory in 1301 established its foundation in northwest Anatolia. As the Ottomans expanded from this local base they confronted the Byzantine Empire to the west and the Seljuq Turks—another Turkic-speaking group—to the east. Through the thirteenth and fourteenth centuries they expanded their holdings, capturing much of Anatolia and crossing into Europe to take Gallipoli in 1354. The Ottoman Empire rose to prominence at

Eurasian empires, 1300–1700. Eurasia on the eve of European expansion was dominated by a complex of huge, interlocking, land-based empires, linked by overland trade routes, and by the Arab trading ecumene of the Indian Ocean. The four empires highlighted here were land-based, inward-looking, and ill-prepared for the challenge of European imperialism that would arrive by sea and, over the next four hundred years, effectively undermine them.

the same time as Spain and Portugal did in western Europe (see Chapter 14) and was at its height in 1600. By 1700, however, it had begun to decline.

Three groups led and sustained the Turkish invasions: **gazis**, Turkish warriors inspired by Islam to conquer territories and bring them under **Dar al-Islam**, a government hospitable to Islam; **Sufis**, members of religious orders, often practicing mystical and ecstatic rituals, who accompanied the troops and introduced Islam within the conquered regions; and **janissaries**, slaves captured or bought from among the conquered populations, usually from among the Christians of the Balkans, to be converted to Islam and serve in the elite Turkish armies and, occasionally, in the administration. In 1527 the slave infantry numbered about 28,000. In conquering Anatolia, Turks displaced the local agricultural communities and became the majority population.

After establishing a foothold in Europe, the Ottomans invited Turkish warriors into the Balkans and occupied northern Greece, Macedonia, and Bulgaria. At the Battle of Kosovo in 1389 they secured Serbia and took control of the western Balkans. Demographically, however, the invaders were not so numerous in this region nor did they force widespread conversion. A census of 1520–30 showed that about one-fifth of the Balkan population was Muslim, about four-fifths was Christian, and there was a small Jewish minority, many of whom moved to the empire after they were expelled from Spain in 1492.

Under Mehmed II, "The Conqueror" (r. 1451–81), the Ottomans moved on to conquer Constantinople in 1453 and then the remainder of Anatolia, the Crimea on the north of the Black Sea, and substantial areas of Venice's empire in Greece and the Aegean. They began the process of rebuilding Constantinople into a great capital city, and by 1600 it had become the largest city in Europe with 700,000 inhabitants. The capital attracted a great influx of immigrant scholars to its **madrasas**, religious schools, and its bureaucratic jobs, which required Islamic learning and knowledge of the law.

Selim I (r. 1512–20) decisively defeated the Shi'a Safavid Empire in Persia at the Battle of Chaldiran in 1514. He turned next against the Mameluke Empire of Egypt, conquering its key cities of Aleppo and Damascus, and its capital, Cairo. These victories also gave the Ottomans control of the holy cities of Jerusalem, Mecca, and Medina, and of both coasts of the Red Sea.

Suleiman (Süleyman) I, "the Magnificent" (r. 1520–66), returned to battle in Europe, adding Hungary to his empire and pushing to the gates of Vienna. As they entered central Europe, the Ottomans confronted the Habsburg Empire. Alliances here crossed religious lines, with Catholic France sometimes joining with the Muslim Ottomans in alliance against the Catholic Habsburgs. In a series of battles, which collectively formed a kind of world war, the Ottomans were defeated at sea in 1571 at Lepanto, off the coast of Greece, by a coalition of the papacy, Venice, and the Habsburgs. Finally, in 1580, a peace treaty confirmed the informal boundaries that endure in the Mediterranean until today between

gazi A warrior or war leader in Islam, sometimes used as a military title among the Turks.

Dar al-Islam Lands under the jurisdiction of Muslim rulers and law; by extension, lands in which Muslims are free to practice their religion.

Sufi In Islam, a member of one of the orders practicing mystical forms of worship that first arose in the 8th and 9th centuries C.E.

janissary A member of the elite corps of Ottoman footsoldiers.

madrasa A traditional Islamic school of higher education, principally of theology and law, literally a "place of study." The madrasa usually comprised a central courtyard surrounded by rooms in which the students resided and a prayer room or mosque, where instruction took place.

Siege of Beograd (Belgrade) by Mehmed II, sixteenth-century Persian manuscript. After the setback of defeat by Central Asian conqueror Tamerlane in 1402, the Ottoman Empire rebuilt, consolidated, and extended its power. A major watershed was passed when Sultan Mehmed II conquered Constantinople (Istanbul) in 1453, making it the third and last Ottoman capital city. This Turkish empire endured for 600 years (1300–1922) and at its height spanned three continents. (*Topkapi Palace, Istanbul*)

predominantly Christian Europe to the north and west, and predominantly Muslim North Africa and West Asia to the south and east.

Battles on land continued until 1606, when the peace treaty of Zsitva Torok confirmed Ottoman rule over Romania, Hungary, and Transylvania, but recognized the Habsburgs as their equals. Financially and militarily drained by two centuries of warfare with the Habsburgs in the Balkans and southeastern Europe, the Ottomans halted their expansion into these areas in 1606. In 1683, a last attempt to seize Vienna failed. North of the Black Sea, where Russia, Poland, and the Ottomans fought, the empire had greater success, taking control of substantial parts of the Ukraine in 1676. These victories, however, marked the maximum extent of Ottoman dominance in the region. Russia had built up its military power under Peter I, the Great (r. 1682–1725), and consolidated it under Catherine II, the Great (r. 1762–96), and now, in the mid-1700s, pushed the Ottomans back. Attempting to regain lost territory, throughout the late 1700s the Ottomans once again brought in western European experts to retrain their military, as they had in capturing Constantinople, but this effort was too little, too late. The Ottoman Empire had fallen too far behind the western Europeans and the Russians both economically and militarily, and they could no longer catch up.

Through both immigration and natural increase, the population of the Ottoman Empire seems to have more than doubled, from 12–13 million in 1520–30 in the early years of the rule of Suleiman I (at a time when Spain may have had 5 million inhabitants; England 2.5 million; Portugal 1 million) to 17–18 million in 1580, to possibly 30–35 million by 1600. This doubling, or even tripling, of the empire's population was consistent with the general population increase of the Mediterranean basin, which rose from 30–35 million in 1500 to 60–70 million in 1600.

India: The Mughal Empire, 1526–1707

The Mughals, a mixture of Mongol and Turkish peoples from Central Asia, rose to power a little later than the Ottomans, beginning their invasion of India in 1526. Under four generations of commanding emperors—Akbar (r. 1556–1605), Jehangir (r. 1605–27), Shah Jahan (r. 1627–58), and Aurangzeb (r. 1658–1707)—they dominated most of the subcontinent, ruling it from splendid capitals that they built in the north, and from mobile tent-cities that they occupied while fighting throughout the subcontinent. Although they continued to rule in name until 1858, the Mughals began to decline as a result of Aurangzeb's extended military campaigns, which wasted the financial and human resources of his empire and also antagonized the Hindu majority population over whom the Mughals, who were Muslims, ruled.

In 1526 Babur (Zahir-ud-Din Mohammad, 1483–1530), a descendant of Timur on his father's side and of Chinggis Khan on his mother's side, invaded India and conquered Delhi and Agra, establishing himself as sultan. His son, Humayun, was defeated in battles with Afghans and driven out of India, but he fought his way back through Afghanistan and into north India before his death. The task of continuing the conquest and consolidating its administration fell to Humayun's son, Akbar (1542–1605), perhaps India's greatest ruler.

Akbar, Emperor of India. Born in 1542, Akbar was reared in exile with his father, the Mughal ruler Humayun, in the rugged terrain of Afghanistan. His childhood was dominated by physical pursuits, and he grew up without learning to read and write, although he loved to have others read to him. Akbar's father Humayun succeeded in returning to India and re-establishing his authority in Delhi when he fell down a staircase and died. Akbar acceded to the throne at age fourteen.

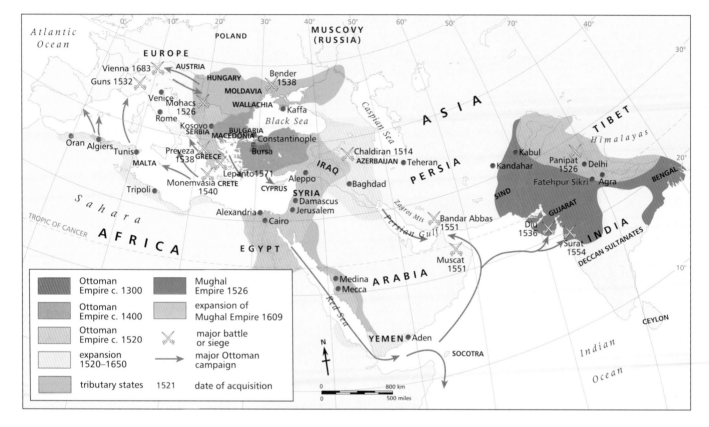

Ottoman and Mughal Empires, 1300–1700. As the Mongols ceased their advance, some of the peoples who had traveled with them began to assert their power. The Ottoman Turks began to establish their new empire, which conquered Constantinople in 1453 and thrust into southeastern Europe as well as the Mediterranean coast. Babur, a Mughal, began the conquest of India in 1526 and his grandson Akbar proceeded to construct one of the largest, most powerful, and most cultured empires of his day.

Four years later, he began to govern on his own as absolute monarch. Raised on stories of his ancestors, Timur the Lame and Chinggis Khan, and of his grandfather, Babur, Akbar now set about creating an empire of his own. He showed no mercy to those who would not submit to his rule. In 1568 protracted fighting in the Mewar district culminated in a siege of the historic fortress of Chitor and ultimately the massacre of its entire population of 30,000 inhabitants. In 1572–3 Akbar conquered Gujarat, gaining control of its extensive commercial networks and its rich resources of cotton and indigo. Then came Bengal to the east, with its rice, silk, and saltpeter. Kashmir to the north, Orissa to the south, and Sind to the west followed. Each new conquest brought greater riches.

A great conqueror, Akbar spent years on the move with his troops, but he also built new capitals for himself, first at Agra (where his grandson later built the Taj Mahal), later at Fatehpur Sikri nearby. With his chief revenue officer, Todar Mal, he established an administrative bureaucracy modeled on a military hierarchy. He surveyed each region of India down to the village level, evaluated its fertility, and thus established the land revenue each was to pay. His administrators collected the payment in cash. These reforms brought village India into a cash economy, while city markets encouraged the production of luxury goods for the court and everyday goods for the common people. Mughal officials, aware that their wealth would revert to the emperor at death, lived a life of lavish consumption.

Akbar understood immediately that as a foreigner and a Muslim in an overwhelmingly Hindu country, he would have to temper conquest with conciliation. He allowed the fiercely independent Hindu Rajputs, who controlled the hilly territory of Rajasthan, to keep their ancestral lands, and he offered them roles in his government and armies. In return they paid tribute to him, supplied him with troops, and gave him their daughters in marriage alliances, since Muslims could practice polygamy. He appointed Hindus to a third of the posts in his centralized administration, although two-thirds went to Muslims who immigrated in large numbers from Iran, Afghanistan, and Central Asia to the expanding Mughal court. In 1562 Akbar discontinued the practice of enslaving prisoners of war and forcing them to convert to Islam. In 1563 he abolished a tax on Hindu pilgrims traveling to sacred shrines. The next year, most importantly, he revoked the **jizya**, the head tax levied on non-Muslims. Between 20 and 25 percent of India's population became Muslim, most through conversion, the rest the result of immigration from outside.

Akbar encouraged and participated personally in religious discussions among Muslims, Hindus, Parsis (Indians who followed Zoroaster, their name means "Persians," where Zoroaster had his greatest influence), and Christians. (Jesuits visiting the court mistook his enquiries into Catholic doctrine as a willingness to convert.) Sufis spread their message in Hindi, a modern derivative of Sanskrit, the sacred language of Hindus. At the same time they inspired the creation of the Urdu (camp) language, the language of common exchange between the invaders and the resident population. Urdu used the syntactical structure of Hindi, the alphabet of Arabic and Persian, and a vocabulary of words drawn from Sanskrit, Persian,

Abul-Fazl presenting his book of the Akbarnama to Akbar, c. 1600. Surrounded by his courtiers, the emperor Akbar receives from his principal administrator, Abul-Fazl, the Akbarnama, an array of Mughal miniature paintings which illustrate the military, diplomatic, economic, and administrative life of Akbar's empire and government. Note the diversity in appearance and dress of the courtiers. Abul-Fazl himself was an Indian Muslim educated in Persian fashion, while Akbar was a soldier of Turkish and Mongol descent. At its best, such diversity was a mark of strength in the Mughal court. (*Chester Beatty Library, Dublin*) and Arabic. Akbar, in particular, encouraged these kinds of cultural **syncretism** and the mixing of groups. These new practices and mixing groups encouraged still more individuals to migrate to India.

In 1582 he declared a new personal religion, the Din-i-Ilahi, or Divine Faith, an amalgam of Islamic, Hindu, and Parsi perspectives. He also incorporated some concepts of Divine Rights, declaring himself the vice-regent of God and appointing himself ultimate arbiter on disputes concerning Islamic law. Elaborate ceremonials at court emphasized the emperor's supremacy, and he was careful to encourage reverence among the common people as well. Orthodox Muslims, however, saw Akbar's pronouncements as heresies and went into opposition. Several were jailed.

In 1600, at the height of Akbar's rule, the population of India reached 140–150 million, with about 110 million contained within the Mughal Empire, about the same population as China and twice that of the Ottoman Empire at its largest. The population increase that occurred all over Afro-Eurasia at this time affected India as well, and the population of the subcontinent in 1800 probably reached about 200 million.

During a reign that spanned half a century, Akbar presided over a glittering court, in which the fine arts, literature, and architecture flourished. He transformed himself from conquering despot of a foreign religious minority to respected emperor of all Hindustan. In a half century of rule, 1556–1605, Akbar had established one of the great empires of the world.

Akbar's great-grandson, and third successor, Aurangzeb (Alamgir, 1658–1707), continued the Mughal conquest almost to the southern tip of the country. But Aurangzeb forsook Akbar's tolerance. He imposed a poll tax on Hindus and desecrated their shrines and statues, antagonizing them and fomenting resentment. Aurangzeb's military adventures in the south overextended his armies and overtaxed the peasantry to the point of revolt. Hindu Marathas in western India and **Sikhs** in the north, as well as the Afghan Nadir Shah, who invaded from Iran in 1739, rose against the Mughal Empire. By the middle of the eighteenth century, the empire lay weak and open to new invaders from western Europe—the British and the French.

Safavid Persia, 1400–1700

In the thirteenth century the Mongols and Turks first devastated and then repopulated Persia. At first the invaders systematically exterminated the populations of the cities they confronted; others, hearing of the massacres, fled. The invading Mongols and Turks then settled on the land, reducing to serfdom those who remained behind, and

jizya A tax levied on non-Muslims who were considered monotheistic people-of-the-book and therefore to be protected: Jews, Christians, and, later, Zoroastrians and Hindus.

syncretism The mixture of different religious traditions. The term is also used to refer to hybridity in other areas, such as art and culture.

Sikhs Members of a religious community founded in the Punjab region of North India by Guru Nanak in the sixteenth century. Sikhism combines *bhakti*, devotional Hinduism with Islamic Sufism. In the face of the militant opposition of its neighbors, Sikhs also became a militant armed group.

MIGRATION 1200–1930

1211	Chinggis (Genghis) Khan conquers China
1301	Osman establishes the foundation of the Turkish Empire in northwest Anatolia
1370–1405	Timur the Lame's victories over Iran, northern India, Anatolia, and northern Syria
c. 1450	Portugal begins to trade in slaves from the West African coast
1453	Ottoman Empire conquers Constantinople beginning big thrust into Europe
1500–1888	About 9.6 million slaves are transported to the Americas
1521–35	Hernán Cortés captures most of Mesoamerica and the Yucatán for Spain
1533	Francisco Pizarro defeats Incas; establishes Spanish colony in South America
1565–1605	Akbar establishes Mughal Empire, gaining dominion over two-thirds of India
1607	English found colony in Virginia in North America
1600	Ottoman Empire population (*c.* 30–35 million) has more than doubled in sixty years
1619	First African slaves brought to British North America
1620	*Mayflower* sets sail for New World
c. 1640	Russia gains control over most of North Asia
1652	Dutch settlers set up a base at Cape Town, South Africa
1680–1800	Chinese imperial expansion to most of Central Asia
1788	British settlement of Australia
1840	Britain annexes New Zealand
1820–1930	50 million Europeans migrate to North and South America, Australia, and New Zealand

The Defeat of Pir Padishah by Shah Rukh in 1403, Persian, 1420–30. Shah Rukh, son of Timur the Lame, was a direct ancestor of the Safavid Persians. During his reign, he had to deal with several rebellions, including one by the Sarbadars, a brigand community in Khurasan. Leading the decisive charge, Shah Rukh's army commander beheads one of the rebel cavalrymen. (*Victoria & Albert Museum. London*)

taxing them into poverty. By the end of the century, however, the invaders began to assimilate Persian ways, rebuilding the cities, redeveloping the irrigation works, supporting agriculture and trade, including the silk routes to China, and adopting both the religion of Islam and the culture of Persia, with its monarchical traditions.

In 1370 the successor to the Chaghatay branch of the Mongols, Timur the Lame (Tamerlane, as Europeans called him; *c.* 1336–1405) came to power, ruling Iran, and much of northern India, Anatolia, and northern Syria from his capital in Samarqand until his death in 1405. With this further set of invasions, Turkish peoples came to constitute about one-fourth of Iran's population, which is the ratio today. The Mongol/Turkish invaders were pastoral peoples, and under their rule substantial agricultural land once again reverted to pasturage and villagers turned to nomadic existences, farming in valley bottoms and herding sheep in nearby mountain highlands.

Culturally, some of the Turks, as well as other ethnic groups in Iran, later came to accept the militantly religious teachings of Shaykh Safi al-Din (1252–1334). His followers, called Safavids, claimed political as well as religious authority. In 1501, a disciple of the teachings of Safi, Shah Isma'il (1487–1524) declared himself the hidden imam, the long-awaited political/religious messiah of Shi'ite Muslims. He occupied Tabriz and proclaimed himself the Shah of Iran.

The Safavids found it difficult to bring together the diverse peoples and interests of Iran. The greatest achievement was by Shah Abbas (1588–1629), who built up the military capacity of the country. He did this, in part, by importing European weapons, equipment, technicians, and advisers. He acquired and built muskets and artillery that were capable of matching the Ottomans. Like other Safavid rulers, he brought slaves from Georgia, Armenia, and Turkish lands to form the core of his armies. Abbas also built a great, new capital city at Isfahan. He encouraged trade and commerce there by inviting Armenian merchants as well as many artisans, including ceramicists who could produce "Chinese" porcelains. He invited some Chinese potters to teach Iranians their trade, and some of them remained and settled in Isfahan. Abbas, however, murdered competing religious leaders and groups, including other Shi'a groups as well as Sunnis and Sufis. His successors in the middle of the century gave official sanction to efforts to convert both Jews and Zoroastrians to Islam by force. But they did not succeed in bringing all the powers of his decentralized realm into a centralized monarchy.

By the end of the seventeenth century, the Safavid army was unraveling, its central administration was failing, regional powers were reasserting themselves, and Iran was in anarchy. Despite the occasional brilliant military conqueror, such as Nadir Shah (1688–1747), another Turkish/Mongol immigrant who took the throne in 1736, Iran was already moving toward partition, first internally, and later at the hands of Europeans and Russians.

China: The Ming and Manchu Dynasties, 1368–1750

In 1211 Chinggis Khan invaded and conquered China, destroying the Song dynasty in the process. His descendants established the Yuan dynasty, which ruled for a century (1271–1368) until the Ming dynasty drove them out and established its own long and successful rule (1368–1644).

By 1600 China's economy was flourishing and the country contained one-fifth of the world's population, about 150 million people. Ming border policy was to pacify and to accommodate the Mongol peoples of the north. The emperors stationed large numbers of troops there and rebuilt the Great Wall. Ming anxieties were well founded. In 1644 China was once again conquered by invaders from the north, as the Jurchen, or Manchus, of Manchuria established a new dynasty, the Qing (1644–1911). The Manchu invasions undercut China's power and sophistication, and contributed—along with natural disasters, virulent epidemics, and the failure of irrigation systems—to a catastrophic fall in China's population. The Mandate of Heaven had surely passed from the Ming.

The Qing expanded the borders of China, more than doubling the geographical size of the country. They conquered and controlled Tibet, Xinjiang, Outer Mongolia, and the Tarim Basin, the heartland of the old silk routes. One of their most important European contacts was with Russia, and disputes between the two empires were negotiated in the Treaty of Nerchinsk (1689), the first Chinese–European treaty negotiated on terms of equality. The treaty facilitated trade between China and Russia and delimited their border along the Amur River, although the border between Mongolia and Siberia was not fixed.

The country's population began to grow again in the eighteenth century. This was made possible by the introduction of new crops into China from the New World. Sweet potatoes, for example, were widespread in coastal China by the mid-eighteenth century, while maize and the Irish potato became common in the north and in the southwest at the same time. Peanuts had spread rapidly in south and southwestern China in the late Ming, and were also becoming an important crop in north China by the end of Qianlong's reign (r. 1736–95). All these crops helped to improve the health of China's rural workers and, because the crops grew well, even in poor and hilly land, they enabled the population to increase rapidly.

Attacks on the borders by land and sea. Through the fifteenth and sixteenth centuries, the Ming dynasty was bedeviled by raids and attacks from the Mongols and other barbarian peoples on China's northern frontiers. The Great Wall underwent major reconstruction in this period. Meanwhile coastal residents were forced to take to their boats to battle the pirates who attacked their settlements. (*Historiographical Institute, University of Tokyo*).

GLOBAL POPULATION GROWTH AND MOVEMENT

Population size is both the result and the cause of larger changes in society. The numbers are important.

Demographers estimate that Europe's population more than tripled between 1000 and 1700, with the greatest growth coming after the Black Death of 1348–51. The plague killed off perhaps a third of Europe's population, but it soon increased again to its former levels and then continued to multiply. The "New World" across the Atlantic provided a new home to some of the increased millions.

Meanwhile, the population of Africa was reduced, in large part by the loss of some 10 million slaves. The native populations of the Americas were devastated, with up to 90 percent of the Native American populations lost, in some areas, although numbers were slowly augmented by European migrants. The population of Asia more than held its own with about two-thirds of the world's population. Between 1000 and 1800 the proportion actually grew from 63 percent to 69 percent of the total. Although there were massive population movements of Mongols and Turks, these migrations do not register in these charts since almost all of the movement was from one location to another within Asia.

Europeans increased fastest of all. They multiplied not only within Europe but, in the words of Alfred Crosby, a leading scholar on the demographic effects of European expansion, they also "leapfrogged around the globe [to found] Neo-Europes, lands thousands of kilometers from Europe and from each other" (Crosby, p. 2). In 1800 North America held almost 5 million whites, South America about 500,000, Australia 10,000, and New Zealand a few thousand.

Then came the deluge. "Between 1820 and 1930, well over fifty million Europeans migrated to the Neo-European lands overseas … approximately one-fifth of the entire population of Europe at the beginning of that period" (Crosby, p. 5). The number of peoples of European ancestry who settled outside Europe grew from 5.7 million in 1810 to 200 million in 1910. These nineteenth-century figures take us into the times of the industrial revolution and its massive transformations, which are covered in the next part, but the demographic diffusion across the world had already begun by 1800.

The expansion of Europe was not unique in world history, yet it was probably the most numerically sizeable and geographically widespread mass migration ever seen; a migration across vast expanses of water; creating permanent links among continents of the world that had been almost entirely separate; and bringing European dominion over three continents besides its own.

CITIES AND DEMOGRAPHICS

Studies of population movement analyze not only migration across global regions, but also the movement from rural to urban areas, and from one urban area to another. Because cities serve as centers for rule, administration, economic production, trade, and cosmopolitan philosophy and art, migration into (or out of) the cities also tells us something of the transformation of society. Here, we combine demographic data with our information on the nature of the city or cities under study to assess these transformations. The movement from nomadic to urban society is one of the most striking examples.

As we know from Part 2, we expect urban occupations, diversity of population, and rates of innovation to be very different from those of the countryside. What then was happening in terms of rural–urban movement in the various regions of the world—and in the capital cities of the empires—we have been studying? Although an examination of capital cities is not decisive, it is suggestive. We expect that capitals of strong states will attract large and vibrant populations. Here we will look at four capital cities that were especially important in attracting migrants in the various empires we have examined.

Delhi/Shahjahanabad

Each Mughal emperor built his own capital. The sultans immediately preceding them had ruled from Delhi. Akbar ruled primarily from Agra, about 100 miles south of Delhi, but in 1569 he built a new capital, about 20 miles from Agra, at Fatehpur Sikri to honor a Sufi saint who had prayed there for a male heir for the emperor. By the end of the century, however, a shortage of water at the beautiful, architecturally eclectic capital forced Akbar to abandon the city and return to Agra. His son, Jahangir, preferred to rule from Lahore and he built up that Punjabi city as his capital. Akbar's grandson, Shah Jahan, rebuilt Delhi as his own capital and gave it his own name.

Built in a semicircular shape, with a radius of 10–12 miles, Shahjahanabad (City of Shah Jahan) apparently had a population reaching 2 million by the mid-seventeenth century. As a newly rebuilt city, almost all its residents were immigrants. The merchant and artisan population, in particular, was composed of foreign merchants such as Armenians, Persians, Central Asians, and Kashmiris.

Stephen Blake in his study *Shahjahanabad* describes the Delhi of Shah Jahan as recapturing the spirit of imperial authority vested in it over centuries, most recently by the Delhi sultanate. It served also as a religious center, a place of pilgrimage revered throughout India for its tombs and graves of saints and holy men. The inner city was encircled by a massive stone wall, 3.8 miles long, 27 feet high, 12 feet thick. At the convergence of the main streets stood the palace-fort, the home of the emperor, the administrative center of the Mughal Empire. The city had its splendors. The poet Amir Khusrau inscribed on the walls of the private audience hall of the emperor, above the peacock throne: "If there is a paradise on earth, it is here, it is here, it is here." Opposite it, a thousand yards west, set on a small hill, rose the *masjid-i-jami*, the Friday mosque, or chief public mosque of the city. In keeping with Islamic architectural principles, gardens with streams of water running through them to delight the eye and the ear were included in the landscaping.

The larger city housed an assembly of military camps, each under the leadership of one of the emperor's leading generals. M. Gentile, a visiting Frenchman in the mid-eighteenth century wrote: "There are many mansions of the nobles, which one can compare to small towns and in which reside the women, equipment, and bazaars (or public markets) of the nobles" (Blake, p. 179). The twentieth-century historian Percival Spear referred to Shahjahanabad's "nomadic court and its tents of stone" (Toynbee, p. 237), the architecture reminding the viewer that the

Shah Jahan leaving the Great Mosque at Delhi by elephant, seventeenth century. Akbar's grandson Shah Jahan restored and rebuilt Delhi in the 1600s to serve as the capital of the Mughal Empire. In 1739 the Persian emperor Nadir Shah conquered the city and looted its treasures, including the famous Peacock Throne. Today, with neighboring New Delhi, it is India's capital and third largest city.

Mughals "had started as nomads in the central Asian steppes, and until their last days they never forgot their origin" (p. 238). Each nobleman also built his own mosque. But the main function of the city was as the center of administrative and military power. Visitors to India observed that in reality the largest city in India was the military camp commanded by the emperor in the field. When he went to war, as Aurangzeb did for years at a time, hundreds of thousands of soldiers and camp followers accompanied him; Shahjahanabad itself was deserted.

Isfahan

In Iran, Shah Abbas (1537–1628) made Isfahan his capital in 1598. One of the largest and most beautiful cities of its time, it contained perhaps a half-million people in its 25-mile circumference. Its two most monumental features were a 2½ mile long elegant promenade, the Chahar Bagh, lined by gardens and court residences encouraged by Shah Abbas and, in the center of the city, the *maidan*, a large public square a third of a mile long by a tenth of a mile wide. The *maidan* was lined on one side by two tiers of shops, on the other sides by the royal palace, the royal mosque, and the smaller Lut-fullah mosque. The *maidan* served as marketplace, meeting place, and even as a sports-field where polo was played.

Shah Abbas fostered artisanal production and trade, and Isfahan welcomed merchants and craftsmen from around the world. In the extended bazaar, which stretched for 1½ miles from the *maidan* to the main mosque, were located shops, factories, and

SOURCE

Ibn Khaldun on Urban Life in the Fourteenth Century

The great social philosopher Ibn Khaldun of Tunis (1332–1406) described the transition from nomadic to sedentary and urban forms, and the "softening" of the invaders that occurred in the process of urbanization. Ibn Khaldun's analysis presents a very early philosophy of the flowering and decline of civilization, an analysis that other historians would later repeat. This analysis also presents Arab peoples as nomadic and rough, at first, but urbane and sophisticated after two or three generations of urban life.

It is rare that the age of the state should exceed three generations, a generation being the average age of an individual, that is forty years or the time necessary for full growth and development.

We said that the age of the state rarely exceeds three generations because the first generation still retains its nomadic roughness and

savagery, and such nomadic characteristics as a hard life, courage, predatoriness, and the desire to share glory. All this means that the strength of the solidarity uniting the people is still firm, which makes that people feared and powerful and able to dominate others.

The second generation, however, have already passed from the nomadic to the sedentary way of life, owing to the power they wield and the luxury they enjoy. They have abandoned their rough life for an easy and luxurious one …

As for the third generation, they have completely forgotten the nomadic and rough stage, as though it had never existed. They have also lost their love of power and their social solidarity through having been accustomed to being ruled. Luxury corrupts them, because of the pleasant and easy way of living in which they have been brought up. As a result, they become a liability on the state, like women and children who need to be protected …

… the rulers of a state, once they have become sedentary, always imitate in their ways of living those of the state to which they have succeeded and whose condition they have seen and generally adopted.

This is what happened to the Arabs, when they conquered and ruled over the Persian and Byzantine empires … Up until then they had known nothing of civilization. (Ibn Khaldun, pp. 117–19)

Ibn Khaldun's depiction of nomadic conquerors being ultimately absorbed and assimilated into the civilizations they conquer presents a process that is frequently repeated in world history. We have seen it in the barbarian conquests of Rome and China in Chapters 6 and 7. His portrait of the decadence and decay of civilizations does not, however, fit all cases. In India, for example, Aurangzeb provoked fatal rebellions when he tried to rule too strictly over too many people, from too remote a location. Aurangzeb's fatal flaw was not decadence but excessive zeal.

warehouses, as well as smaller mosques, *madrasas* (Islamic schools), baths, and *caravan-serais* (travelers' hostels). Up to 25,000 people worked in the textile industry alone. Chinese ceramicists were imported to train workers in Chinese porcelain manufacture, and carpets and metalwork were also anchors of Isfahan's craft production.

Despite their differences in religion, Shah Abbas and the European powers shared a common political and military opposition to the Ottoman Empire, which lay between them. In the early 1600s Shah Abbas allowed both the English and the Dutch to open trade offices in Isfahan. He also practiced religious tolerance, perhaps for reasons of practical statecraft. Augustinian, Carmelite, and Capuchin missions were established. Christian Armenians, forced by Shah Abbas to immigrate from their earlier home in Julfa to expand Isfahan's commerce, built their own suburb, called New Julfa, appropriate to their status as prosperous merchants. A Jewish quarter also grew up in the northwestern part of the city, but later in Shah Abbas' reign Jews were persecuted and forced to convert to Islam or to leave.

Shah Abbas maintained absolute command and imported soldiers who were totally loyal to him. He also kept his forces supplied with up-to-date weapons, for he understood that Iran's status and survival depended upon them, surrounded as it was by the hostile Ottoman Empire on the west, continuing threats from nomads to the north, and a powerful, if friendly, Mughal Empire on the east. In a report of 1605 to Pope Paul V, the friar Paul Simon described the Shah as ruthless, dictatorial, and militarily prepared with forces recruited from far and near:

> His militia is divided into three kinds of troops: one of Georgians, who will be about 25,000 and are mounted; the second force … is made up of slaves of various races, many of them Christian renegades: their number will be as many again … The third body consists of soldiers whom the great governors of Persia are obliged to maintain and pay the whole year; they will be about 50,000. (Andrea and Overfield, pp. 91–2)

Constantinople (Istanbul)

Constantinople had been the capital of the much-reduced Byzantine Empire when Sultan Mehmed II captured it and made it his own capital in 1453. He renamed the city Istanbul and began to recast it as the administrative center of the Ottoman Empire, which he was rapidly enlarging. In 1478 Istanbul had about 80,000 inhabitants; between 1520 and 1535, there were 400,000; and some Western observers estimated a population of 700,000 by 1600. Istanbul had become a city of Turks—58 percent of the population in the sixteenth and seventeenth centuries—but there were also Greeks, Jews, Armenians, and Tziganes.

The vast **conurbation** was composed of three major segments plus numerous suburbs. Central Istanbul housed the government center, with trees, gardens, fountains, promenades, and 400 mosques; sprawling, uneven bazaars where luxuries as well as day-to-day necessities could be purchased; and the Serai, near the tip of the peninsula, where the government officials lived in their palaces and gardens. Across the small waterway, called the Golden Horn, were the ports and major commercial establishments of Galata. Here the Western ships came; here were the Jewish businessmen; the shops and warehouses; cabarets; the French ambassador; Latin and Greek merchants dressing in the Turkish style and living in grand houses. On Galata, too, were the two major arsenals—that of Kasim Pasha and the Topkhana—marking the Ottoman commitment to military power. On the Asian side of the Straits of the Bosphorus was the third part of Istanbul, Üsküdar, a more Turkish city, and the terminus of the great land routes through Asia.

conurbation An enormous, complex city, made up of many parts, each of which is a small town or city by itself—a megalopolis.

Historian Fernand Braudel sees in Istanbul the prototype of the great modern European capitals that would arise a century later. Economically these cities produced little, but they processed goods passing through, and were the "hothouses of civilization", where new ideas and patterns arose and created an order. Braudel remarks that cities that were only political capitals would not fare well in the next century; those that were economically productive would. Beginning in the late sixteenth century, the economy of Istanbul was undercut by changes in the world economy. As trade shifted to the Atlantic and to European powers that carried their own commerce around the African continent instead of through the Middle East, the Ottoman Empire and its capital were left as a backwater. Trade deserted them.

London

By comparison with the Asian and east European capitals, London had a very different pattern of immigration and employment. While Delhi, Isfahan, and Istanbul declined during the late seventeenth and early eighteenth centuries in response to negative political and economic factors, London grew, primarily because of economic factors.

E.A. Wrigley, one of the founding members of the Cambridge Group for the History of Population and Social Structure, has examined the changing demography of London between 1650 and 1750 to analyze the city's relationship with English society and economy. Wrigley begins with London's extraordinary population growth, from 200,000 in 1600, to 400,000 in 1650 and 575,000 by 1700, when it became the largest city in western Europe, to 675,000 in 1750 and 900,000 in 1800. London dominated the development of all of England. In 1650 London held 7 percent of England's total population; in 1750, 11 percent.

Before the twentieth century, as a rule, large cities everywhere in the world were so unsanitary that death rates exceeded birth rates, so London's extraordinary population growth reflects not only births within the city, but also extraordinary immigration to compensate for high death rates. Wrigley estimates that by the end of the 1600s, 8000 people a year were migrating into London. Since the entire population of England at this time was only 5 million, London was siphoning half of England's population growth into itself.

With so high a proportion of England's population living in London, or at least visiting the city for a substantial part of their lives, Wrigley suggests that the capital must have had significant influence on the country as a whole. He suggests that the high levels of population growth in London in the seventeenth century may have been a significant factor in giving birth to the industrialization of the eighteenth.

Wrigley suggests several relevant causal relationships. The first group concerns economics: London's growth promoted the creation of a national market, including transportation and communication facilities; it evoked increasing agricultural productivity to feed the urban population; it developed new sources of raw materials, especially coal, to provide for them; it led to the development of new commercial instruments; and it had the effect of increasing productivity and purchasing power. Demographically, London's high death and immigration rates kept England's rate of population growth relatively low. Sociologically, London's growth disseminated new ways of thinking about economics and its importance. Londoners placed increasing value on production and consumption for the common person, encouraging higher levels of entrepreneurship throughout the country.

Wrigley does not here discuss the political variables, but without them London's growth could have simply led to parasitism, with the urban ruling elites commandeering the production of the countryside for their own good. Such parasitism was common in imperial capitals elsewhere, as we have seen above in the Asian capital cities. In London, however, a government increasingly dominated by commercial classes reinforced the values of production and increased consumption for the common person.

MIGRATION AND DEMOGRAPHY
WHAT DIFFERENCE DO THEY MAKE?

Numbers count. Demography helps us to discover patterns in history and to formulate questions about issues that need further study. In this chapter, we have employed the methods and insights of demography to examine four great migrations in world history between 1500 and 1750. We have explored the formation of "New Europes" around the globe, the numbers and motivations of the new immigrants, and the (often catastrophic) fate of the original inhabitants. Second, we have analyzed the size, geography, and economic consequences of the slave trade both in Africa, where people were seized, sold, and exported, and in the plantation economies that absorbed most of them. Third, we have compared the migrations and conquests of Turkic-speaking and Mongol peoples from Central Asia—establishing new empires in India, Persia, and the Middle East, and a new dynasty in China—with the trans-Atlantic migrations. Finally we have discussed the move from rural areas to cities—the spread of urbanization—and contrasted the motives for this move in more traditional political capitals of empire with those in younger, more trade-oriented capitals.

These migrations have attracted the continuing interest of demographic historians like Fernand Braudel, Philip Curtin, and E.A. Wrigley. Their research and the research of their colleagues have helped us to assess the connections between these great migrations of the past and events in our own world. They have also helped alert us to related demographic processes continuing in our own world at present: rapid population growth and its consequences for global ecology; global migrations for economic opportunity—both of highly skilled technical workers seeking high-paying jobs and of unskilled day laborers seeking subsistence work; the migration of jobs from richer, higher wage areas of the world to poorer, lower wage areas of the world—labor remaining stationary but jobs moving from one location to another; migration from rural areas to cities, and from cities to suburbs; migration of refugees fleeing warfare and oppressive governments; the global diffusion of diseases, such as AIDS, West Nile disease, and SARS that seem to originate in one location and spread rapidly around the world.

These migration issues also alert us to related policy issues that persist to our own times. One example is the debate over national and regional language policies in areas where the ethnic composition of the population is changing: In the southwestern United States, for example, the growing proportion of Spanish-speaking people forces constant reconsideration of the importance of bilingualism. Another issue is the encouraging of migration as a policy to change the ethnic composition of a region. The Chinese government, for example, steadily encourages people of Han Chinese ancestry to immigrate into Tibet and Xinjiang in order to make these two provinces more Chinese and less Tibetan and Uighur. Even worse, some governments have undertaken programs of mass murder—genocide—to rid their territories of unwanted peoples. The government of Serbia implemented "ethnic cleansing" in 1999 against Albanian Muslims as part of the battle for control of Kosovo province (with constant, conscious references on both sides to the conquest of Kosovo by the Ottoman Turks in 1389); the Ottoman Turkish government murdered more than 1.5 million Armenians in 1915. In the most extreme case, the government of Germany enforced against Jews in the 1930s and 1940s. These and other issues of demography continue to arise around the globe and alter human history. We will return to them repeatedly in our study.

Review Questions

- What were the "New Europes?" What characteristics did they share in common?
- What were the main reasons for the rise of slavery in the Atlantic Ocean basin between 1400 and 1750?
- What were the similarities and the differences between the great migrations from the eastern hemisphere across the Atlantic to the western hemisphere, 1500–1750, and the migrations from Central Asia to Turkey, Iran, and India at about the same time and slightly earlier?
- The populations of which continents were growing fastest and which slowest in the period 1000–1800? How do you explain the differences between their comparative growth (or decline) in these years?
- What were the principal reasons for the growth of most very large cities before the industrial revolution of about 1800?

Suggested Readings

PRINCIPAL SOURCES

Braudel, Fernand. *Capitalism and Material Life 1400–1800*, trans. by Miriam Kochan (New York: Harper & Row, 1973). Introduction to a whole new way of thinking about the rise of capitalism in Europe, emphasizing both institutions and natural ecology.

——. *The Mediterranean and the Mediterranean World in the Age of Philip II*, 2 vols., trans. by Sian Reynolds (New York: Harper and Row, 1973). Braudel looks at long-run ecological issues, medium-run institutional configurations, and short-run political decisions in this landmark study.

Crosby, Alfred W. *Ecological Imperialism: The Biological Expansion of Europe, 900–1900* (Cambridge: Cambridge University Press, 1986). Extremely well-written and well-argued discussion of the biological consequences of the encounters of distant civilizations with one another.

Curtin, Philip D. *The Atlantic Slave Trade: A Census* (Madison: University of Wisconsin Press, 1969). The pioneering work in quantifying the Atlantic slave trade.

——. *The Rise and Fall of the Plantation Complex: Essays in Atlantic History* (Cambridge: Cambridge University Press, 1990). Comprehensive account of the plantation organization, economy, and significance.

Hughes, Robert. *The Fatal Shore. The Epic of Australia's Founding* (New York: Knopf, 1986). Engagingly written, exciting, thoughtful presentation of Australian history from the first arrival of Europeans to about 1870 when the system of penal transportation ended.

Mintz, Sidney W. *Sweetness and Power: The Place of Sugar in Modern History* (New York: Penguin Books, 1985). Fascinating anthropological study that begins with the Caribbean sugar plantation, extends to the uses of sugar by the wealthy, the sugared cup of tea of the British industrial worker, the Chinese tea crop, and the advertising industry that brought much of this together.

Northrup, David, ed. *The Atlantic Slave Trade* (Lexington, MA: D.C. Heath, 1994; 2nd ed., 2001). Excellent selection of articles on causes, effects, demography, and economics of the slave trade and of abolition.

——. *Indentured Labor in the Age of Imperialism, 1834–1922* (Cambridge: Cambridge University Press, 1995). Comprehensive survey of the system of indentured labor that followed the abolition of the slave trade and slavery, and its demographics.

ADDITIONAL SOURCES

Andrea, Alfred J. and James H. Overfield, eds., *The Human Record: Sources of Global History*, Vol. 2 (Boston: Houghton Mifflin Co., 3rd ed., 1998). The excerpts are extremely well chosen for global and topical coverage.

Blake, Stephen P. *Shahjahanabad* (Cambridge: Cambridge University Press, 1990). Scholarly study of the capital city of Shah Jahan, demonstrating the influence of military camp architecture and design.

Cook, James. *The Journals of Captain James Cook on His Voyages of Discovery*, ed. by J.C. Beaglehole, 2 vols. (Cambridge: Cambridge University Press (for the Hakluyt Society), 1955 and 1961).

Frykenberg, R.E., ed., *Delhi through the Ages: Essays in Urban History, Culture and Society* (Delhi: Oxford University Press, 1986). Wide-ranging collection of scholarly articles from an important conference, covering Delhi from earliest times to almost the present.

Gates, Henry Louis, Jr. *Wonders of The African World* (New York: Knopf, 1999). Introduction to Africa for a general audience by a leading Harvard scholar.

Henige, David, "Measuring the Immeasurable: The Atlantic Slave Trade, West African Population and the Pyrrhonian Critic," *Journal of African History* XXVII.2 (1986), 303–13. Surveys the attempts to evaluate the effects of the slave trade and emigration on African life.

Ibn Khaldun. *An Arab Philosophy of History*, trans. by Charles Issawi (London: John Murray, 1950). In the 14th century, Ibn Khaldun of Tunis, an early social scientist, proposed a reading of history consistent with the experiences of both the nomadic and the sedentary people of North Africa and the Middle East.

Inalcik, Halil. *The Ottoman Empire: The Classical Age, 1300–1600*, trans. by Norman Itzkowitz and Colin Imber (New York: Praeger Publishers, 1973). A standard, accessible history by an eminent scholar.

Keegan, John. *A History of Warfare* (New York: Knopf, 1993). An eminent British scholar analyzes why, how, and with what weapons people have fought throughout history and across geography.

Klein, Herbert S., "Economic Aspects of the Eighteenth-century Atlantic Slave Trade," in James D. Tracy, ed. *The Rise of Merchant Empires* (Cambridge: Cambridge University Press, 1990), 287–310. Important new analyses of the slave trade, including birth rates and survival rates of slaves.

Lapidus, Ira M. *A History of Islamic Societies* (Berkeley: University of California Press, 1988). An excellent, comprehensive, global presentation.

Lovejoy, Paul E., "The Volume of the Atlantic Slave Trade: A Synthesis," *Journal of African History* XXIII (1982), 473–500. Another contribution to the demographic study.

New York Times 2003 Almanac (New York: Penguin, 2002). Standard reference work. Annual.

Robinson, Francis. *Atlas of the Islamic World since 1500* (New York: Facts on File, Inc., 1982). Excellent reference work by an outstanding British scholar. Well written, beautifully illustrated.

Rodney, Walter. *How Europe Underdeveloped Africa* (Washington: Howard University Press, 1972). Classic statement of the exploitation of Africa by the European slave trade and imperialism.

Segal, Ronald. *Islam's Black Slaves: The Other Black Diaspora* (New York: Farrar, Straus, and Giroux, 2001). A general survey of the history of the Arab slave trade in Africa and the Indian Ocean region.

Spence, Jonathan D. *The Search for Modern China* (New York: W.W. Norton and Co., 1990). A standard history, engagingly written, thorough, good on narrative and analysis.

The [London] Times Atlas of World History ed. Geoffrey Parker (London: Times Books, 5th ed., 1999).

Thornton, John. *Africa and Africans in the Making of the Atlantic World, 1400–1640* (Cambridge: Cambridge University Press, 1992). Sees Africans as active in creating their own world, including as businessmen conducting the slave trade.

Toynbee, Arnold. *Cities of Destiny* (New York: Weathervane Books, 1967). Colorful introduction to some of the most famous and influential cities. Illustrations and maps are lavish in this coffee-table book.

Willigan, J. Dennis and Katherine A. Lynch. *Sources and Methods of Historical Demography* (New York: Academic Press, 1982). Useful introduction to significance and methods.

Wolf, Eric. *Europe and the People without History* (Berkeley: University of California Press, 1982). An historical anthropologist writes revisionist history bringing third world people into history as important agents in creating the world as it is, in a generally Marxist framework

Wrigley, E.A. *Population and History* (New York: McGraw-Hill Book Company, 1969). Explains the uses of demographic study in history.

——. "A Simple Model of London's Importance in Changing English Society and Economy 1650–1750," *Past and Present* XXXVII (1967), 44–70. Demographic analysis suggests the importance of London in preparing the way for the industrialization of England.

◉ World History Documents CD-ROM

15.1 Bartolomé de las Casas: The "Black Legend" of Spain
15.2 Nzinga Mbemba (Afonso I): *Our Kingdom Is Being Lost*
15.3 Olaudah Equiano: *The Life of Olaudah Equiano*, or Gustavus Vassa: *The African*
15.4 Commerce, Slavery, and Religion in North Africa
15.5 Thomas Nelson: Slavery and the Slave Trade of Brazil

An Album of Comparisons

This picture album enables us to revisit three important places across periods of time. This before-and-after perspective yields some startling comparisons leading to a deeper understanding of the last century and a half.

Both the first two pictures are from Philadelphia, their perspective separated by three city blocks and 125 years. The first presents Philadelphia's Independence Hall, the site of the Second Continental Congress that adopted the Declaration of Independence on July 4, 1776, and of the Convention that adopted the Constitution of 1787. The second centers on Strawbridge and Clothier, a department store. Although no industry appears in the photograph, the electric trolley cars, the store itself, and the new "downtown" speak volumes about the transformation of the city. The photograph itself represents a medium invented only in the 1830s. From 1780 to 1907 the city had grown from about 25,000 to about 1,250,000 people.

Independence Hall, Philadelphia, c. 1780. Painting.

Strawbridge and Clothier Department Store, Philadelphia, c. 1907.

The illustrations from India suggest the continuous build up of British imperial power and wealth. In 1775 the British annexed Benaras to their holdings in eastern India, providing the background for this imagined, fawning reception of Warren Hastings, the British Governor General, by the Rajah of Benares. But it hardly compares with the actual triumphal splendor and majesty staged for George V and Queen Mary when they visited India. Their 1911 state visit marked a high point of imperial splendor.

The final pairing of pictures creates a great irony. François Biard has painted a disturbing image of the traffic in people, as they are inspected, purchased, branded, and whipped. To the rear right of the market, located on the African coast, rows of shackled slaves await their turn on the block. While a white man brands one female slave, a black man whips another. Despite its touches of voyeurism and pornography, Biard's painting unequivocally condemns slavery. During the nineteenth century slavery was abolished throughout the European-controlled world. But in Africa, European colonialism sanctioned new kinds of plantation—for example, for the production of

Left Anon. Cheyle Singh, Rajah of Benares, flatters Warren Hastings, 1784. Engraving.

Above King George V and Queen Mary of England in Delhi during a State Visit (*Darbar*) to India, 1911.

François Biard, *Slave Market on the Kambia River, Africa*, n.d. Painting.

Norman H. Hardy, 'Beating rubber and beating time–to the tune of an old love song.' Illustration from the *Illustrated London News*, October 2, 1905.

rubber in the Congo—so the equivalent of slavery was simply moved back to the African continent itself. The photograph from the *Illustrated London News* represents the processing of the raw natural rubber as an energetic activity for a lively group, but the presence of the overseer suggests that the truth was much harsher, as we shall read in this part of the book.

QUESTIONS

1. These six pictures are either illustrations or photographs, photography being invented around 1840. Which medium seems more powerful to you?
2. Within each pairing, do you think the sequence of representations suggests "progress," a process much heralded in the nineteenth century, or only difference? Why? From whose perspective?

PART

6

Social Change 1640–1914

WESTERN REVOLUTIONS AND THEIR INFLUENCE

*U*nprecedented activity in global exploration, commerce, and migration began in the thirteenth century (see Parts 5 and 6). By the seventeenth century traditional political, economic, and social philosophies and organizations seemed to be increasingly obsolete. New accommodations first took form in Europe and the Americas. Later, through political colonialism, economic imperialism, and Christian missionary activity, they spread to the rest of the world. The new forms percolated into everyday life and consciousness everywhere, but each society adapted in its own way. The results were diverse and quite often unexpected.

Many of these new forms emerged from new ways of thinking about the world. First, individuals began to think about how to understand the universe through a study of the natural sciences, culminating in Sir Isaac Newton's theory of universal gravitation. Social philosophers subsequently began to apply Newton's methods to understanding the social, political, and economic worlds. Others began to apply them in ways that resulted in major political upheavals.

Explosive events, "revolutions," punctuated the years 1640–1914. One cluster of revolutions—in England, North America, France, Haiti, and Latin America—promoted new political philosophies and introduced new political structures. Many historians refer to them collectively as constituting the "Age of Democratic Revolution."

Francisco de Goya, *Execution of the Defenders of Madrid, 3rd May, 1808,* **1814.** Goya, a Spaniard, saw the French revolution and the Napoleonic wars that followed through the prism of their violence. The bitter warfare at the French invasion of Spain, and the Spanish resistance, inspired this agonized painting. (*Prado, Madrid*)

Beginning about the same time, a series of innovations in economic organization and the uses of machinery dramatically increased the quantity and quality of economic productivity. Most historians name this transformation the "Industrial Revolution." These revolutions in politics and economics were accompanied by equally dramatic social changes, which affected the individual, the family, the neighborhood, and the community. Many of these transformations originated in western Europe, but ultimately people all over the world were affected and formulated their own varied responses, adaptations, and rejections. For purposes of analysis, this part will consider these three transformations sequentially: political change in this chapter, industrial change in Chapter 17, and social change in Chapter 18.

POLITICAL REVOLUTIONS IN EUROPE AND THE AMERICAS

THE BIRTH OF HUMAN RIGHTS IN THE AGE OF ENLIGHTENMENT, 1649–1830

KEY TOPICS

- Political Revolution
- Human Rights in the Age of Enlightenment
- England's Glorious Revolution, 1688
- The *Philosophes* and the Enlightenment in the Eighteenth Century
- Revolution in North America, 1776
- The French Revolution and Napoleon, 1789–1812
- Haiti: Slave Revolution and the Overthrow of Colonialism, 1791–1804
- The Abolition of Slavery and the Slave Trade
- The End of Colonialism in Latin America: Independence and Disillusionment, 1810–30
- Political Revolutions: What Difference Do They Make?

POLITICAL REVOLUTION

A revolution is a fundamental and often rapid change in the way a system operates—whether political, economic, intellectual, or social. A political revolution, for example, not only removes some people from office and replaces them with others, it also changes the fundamental basis on which the new leaders come to power, the authority they claim, and their mission in office. Leaders of revolutions usually state their goals in terms of high, non-negotiable principles. As revolutionary struggles unfold and as different groups rise and fall, however, they may lurch from one political position to another relatively swiftly and often violently.

In a major revolution several groups may participate and cooperate in the struggle to replace an existing government. Each group may have its own goals, and these goals may be in conflict. As their joint movement appears to be nearing success and it becomes likely that a new government will replace the old, the differences among the various participating groups will emerge. Each group will seek fiercely to incorporate its own programs and personnel into the new government and even to dominate it. This struggle to control the new government may be even more brutal, violent, chaotic, and unpredictable than the battle to overthrow the old. The stakes are high. Major revolutions can have significant, lasting consequences, not only for participants in that place and time but also for people of later generations and far-flung locations.

The first three political revolutions we will consider all share these characteristics of major revolutions. The "Glorious Revolution" of 1688 in England, the revolt of the American colonies against British rule in 1776, and the French Revolution of 1789

Opposite **Francisco de Goya,** *The Sleep of Reason Produces Monsters*, **1797. Engraving.** Goya (1746–1828) creates a terrifying scene challenging a key tenet of the Enlightenment: that human reason will produce progress. The title, *The Sleep of Reason Produces Monsters*, is seen within the etching itself and suggests that when the mind's defenses are down, as in sleep, we are prey to internal monsters.

removed one set of rulers and replaced them with another; changed the basis of authority of the state and its relationship to its citizens; and proposed new missions for the state. By "state" we mean the entire mechanism of government, its officers, its institutions, and its organization. All of these revolutions were fought in the name of principle. The English revolution was considered "bloodless," although it was the culmination of a lengthy period of national violence and civil warfare. The American and French revolutions precipitated lengthy wars.

All three of these revolutions have been characterized as "democratic" because they increased the participation of more (but not all) of the people in government. All of them at some time tried to balance two additional, competing goals: they sought to protect the rights of propertied people while increasing the power of the state (although not of the king). These goals were not, and to this day are not, fully

AT A GLANCE : THE AGE OF REVOLUTIONS

DATE	EUROPE	NORTH AMERICA	LATIN AMERICA
1640	■ Galileo dies; Newton is born (1642) ■ Civil wars in England (1642–6; 1647–9) ■ Execution of King Charles I of England (1649) ■ Restoration of English monarchy (1660) ■ Royal Society of London founded (1662)		■ Portugal takes Brazil from the Dutch (1654)
1670	■ The "Glorious Revolution" in England (1688) ■ The English Bill of Rights (1689) ■ John Locke's *Second Treatise on Government* (1689) ■ *Philosophes*: Diderot (1713–84); Voltaire (1694–1778); Rousseau (1712–78); Montesquieu (1689–1755)		
1760	■ Tennis Court Oath (June 20, 1789) ■ French Revolution (1789–99) ■ "March of the Women" (1789) ■ "Great Fear" (1789) ■ "Second French Revolution" (1791–9)	■ British levy taxes on Americans in the Stamp Act (1765) ■ American Declaration of Independence (1776); War (1775–83) ■ Constitution (1789)	■ Revolts against European rule in Peru, Colombia, and Brazil (1780–98) ■ Tupac Amaru revolt, Peru (1780)
1790	■ "Reign of Terror" (1793–5) ■ Napoleon seizes power (1799); Emperor (1804) ■ Napoleon issues Civil Code (1804) ■ Napoleon invades Russia; finally defeated (1812)	■ Bill of Rights ratified (1791) ■ Louisiana Purchase from France (1803)	■ Toussaint L'Ouverture leads slave revolt against French in Saint-Domingue (Haiti) (1791) ■ Haiti proclaims independence (1804) ■ Joseph Bonaparte, King of Spain (1808) ■ Bolívar and San Martin lead revolts against Spain (1808–28) ■ Paraguay declares independence (1810–11)
1820	■ Congress of Vienna (1814–15) ■ Reform Act extends voting franchise in Britain (1832) ■ Britain abolishes slavery in its empire (1833)	■ President Andrew Jackson evicts Cherokee Indian Nation: "Trail of Tears" (1838) ■ Warfare with Mexico ends in victory for America (1848) ■ United States abolishes slavery (1863, 1865)	■ Mexico wins independence (1821) ■ Prince Pedro declares Brazil independent (1822)

compatible. Individual rights to private property and the rights of the state often conflict. So we must be careful in our understanding of the "democracy" that emerged from these revolutions.

Collectively, for Europeans and Americans, the revolutions that occurred in the years between 1688 and 1789:

- situated the authority of government on earth rather than in heaven and thus increased the influence of the secular over the otherworldly;
- rejected the theory that governments were based on a **divine right of kings** in favor of the theory that governments derive their just powers from the consent of the governed;
- encouraged the creation of an effective bureaucracy to administer the affairs of government;
- emphasized the principle of individual merit, of "a career open to talent," rather than promoting people on the basis of personal and hereditary connections;
- helped to solidify the nation-state as the principal unit of government;
- extended effective power over the state to classes of people hitherto excluded, especially to men of the professions and business;
- encouraged the growth of business and industry for private profit;
- inspired the revolutionary leaders to export their new ideologies and methods to new geographical areas, sometimes by force; and
- precipitated wars of heretofore unknown degrees of military mobilization, geographical extent, and human destructiveness.

"Liberty," "equality," "fraternity," "natural rights," "the pursuit of happiness," "property," and "no taxation without representation" were the battle cries of these various revolutions. As frequently happens, the results were often unintended, unanticipated, and ironic. The political forms that actually resulted did increase human freedom for many people in many countries, but they often coexisted with slavery, patriarchy, colonialism, and warfare.

To understand these ironies more fully, we examine two further revolutions that were inspired in part by these first three. In 1791, the slaves of Haiti, a French colony, revolted and abolished slavery. The French reluctance, and later refusal, to sanction the revolution against slavery—despite their own revolution for human rights—demonstrated the serious shortcomings in that revolution. Then, in the first three decades of the nineteenth century, all the colonies of Spain and Portugal in Latin America fought for and won their independence. But the triumphant generals of the revolution fought among themselves as their dreams of vast, unified, powerful nations dissolved into the reality of smaller, weaker states. And the triumphant **creole** elite—the descendants of the European settlers in these colonies—suppressed indigenous peoples, people of mixed Spanish-Amerindian ancestry (**mestizos**), and African-Americans, thereby spreading disillusionment throughout the continent.

divine right of kings A political doctrine influential in the sixteenth and seventeenth centuries. It held that the monarch derived his authority from God and was therefore not accountable to earthly authority. James I of England (1603–25) was a foremost exponent.

creole In the sixteenth to eighteenth centuries, a white person born in Spanish America of Spanish parents.

mestizo A person of mixed race. In Central and South America it usually denotes a person of combined Indian and European descent.

HUMAN RIGHTS IN THE AGE OF ENLIGHTENMENT

Philosophical Rationales

The philosophy justifying England's Glorious Revolution of 1688 developed over many years. Thomas Hobbes (1588–1679), one of England's leading political philosophers, seemed to justify the enormous, existing power of the king over the citizens. In his most influential work, *Leviathan*, of 1651, he declared: "Nothing the sovereign representative can do to a subject, on what pretence soever, can properly be called injustice, or injury." But Hobbes was simultaneously providing a rationale for limiting the king's power. He declared that the king could claim his authority not by virtue of special, personal rights, nor by virtue of representing God on earth, but because "Every subject is author of every act the sovereign doth." In other words, the king has authority to the extent that he represents the will of the people.

Hobbes and the "State of Nature." Hobbes, like others of his time, was trying to understand the English monarchy in terms of its origins. He postulated the myth of a prehistoric, individualistic, unruly, "state of nature," which people had rejected in order to create a society that would protect them individually and collectively. Uncontrolled by law and a king, Hobbes wrote, "the life of man [is] solitary, poor, nasty, brutish, and short … During the time men live without a common power to keep them all in awe, they are in that condition which is called war; and such a war, as is of every man against every man." To escape such lawlessness, men had exchanged their individual liberties for social and political order. Their (mythical) **social contract**, not divine appointment, had created monarchy in order to serve the people.

social contract A mythical, unwritten agreement among early people in a "state of nature" to establish some form of government. This "contract" generally defines the rights and obligations of the individuals and of the government.

Locke and the Enlightenment. The philosophical accomplishments of the Glorious Revolution are even more closely associated with the writings of John Locke (1632–1704), who had fled England in 1683 for the Netherlands, returning only after the revolution was complete. While he was in the Netherlands, Locke wrote his most important essay on political philosophy, *Second Treatise on Government*, although it was not published until 1689, after the Glorious Revolution had been implemented and Locke felt it safe to return to England. Since Locke's philosophy parallels not only the English revolution but also many subsequent ones, his arguments deserve attention.

Like Hobbes, Locke argued that government is a secular compact entered into voluntarily and freely by individuals. If there are to be kings, they too must live under the constitution. Locke, like Hobbes, based his argument on a mythical, prehistoric, "state of nature," which people forsook in order to provide for their common defense and needs. He, however, stressed the importance of common consent in the earlier mythical contract. The legitimacy of the contract continues only as long as the consent continues. If they no longer consent to the contract, the people have the right to terminate it. Going beyond Hobbes, Locke explicitly proclaimed the right of revolution in his *Second Treatise on Government*:

> There remains still in the people a supreme power to remove or alter the legislative, when they find the legislative act contrary to the trust reposed in them. For all power given with trust for the attaining of an end, being limited by that end, whenever that end is manifestly neglected, or opposed, the trust must necessarily be forfeited, and the power devolves into the hands of those that gave it, who may place it anew where they shall think best for their safety and security. (p. 92)

Locke postulated the "equal right that every man hath to his natural freedom, without being subjected to the will or authority of any other man". "Absolute monarchy, which by some men is counted the only government in the world, is indeed inconsistent with civil society". Majority rule is Locke's basis of government: "the act of the majority passes for the act of the whole, and of course determines as having by the law of nature and reason, the power of the whole".

A Theory of Government by Property Owners. Locke was not, however, proposing radical democracy; he was not advocating one person, one vote. For Locke, government was for property owners. "Government," Locke proclaimed, "has no other end but the preservation of property". "The great and chief end therefore, of men's uniting into commonwealths, and putting themselves under government, is the preservation of their property". Indeed, after the initial, mythical social contract had established the government's authority, succeeding generations had signalled their continuing acceptance of that contract by allowing their property to be protected by the government. "The supreme power cannot take from any man any part of his property without his own consent. For the preservation of property being the end of government, and that for which men enter into society, it necessarily supposes and requires, that the people should have property".

Taxes, therefore, cannot be levied unilaterally or arbitrarily. "If anyone shall claim a power to lay and levy taxes on the people, by his own authority, and without such consent of the people, he thereby invades the fundamental law of property, and subverts the end of government".

Hobbes had already indicated the growing importance of property and industry to seventeenth-century England. Without peace and stability, he wrote:

> there is no place for industry; because the fruit thereof is uncertain; and consequently no culture of the earth; no navigation, nor use of the commodities that may be imported by sea; no commodious building; no instruments of moving, and removing, such things as require much force; no knowledge of the face of the earth; no account of time; no arts; no letters; no society. (p. 895)

Hobbes wanted a society of economic productivity achieved through industry, commerce, and invention. Locke saw private ownership of property and private profit as the means to achieving that end. He saw the property-owning classes of England, the men who made the Glorious Revolution, as the nation's proper leaders and administrators, and he asserted the importance of the enclosure acts by which England was dividing up the common lands of each village, turning them into private property, and

An Eyewitness Representation of the Execution of Charles I, **by Weesop, 1649.** Charles' belief in the divine right of kings and the authority of the Church of England led eventually to a civil war with Parliament—which he and his supporters lost. At his subsequent trial, the king was sentenced to death as a tyrant, murderer, and enemy of the nation and beheaded at Whitehall, London, on January 30, 1649. (*Private Collection*)

selling them. These enclosure acts were creating a new, wealthier landlord class, which turned its energies to increasing agricultural productivity. At the same time the acts forced rural people, who had owned no land of their own but who had been grazing their animals on common land, to give up their independence. Most found work with more prosperous landlords and some moved to the cities in search of new jobs.

Locke is today usually criticized for overlooking the situation of the non-propertied classes. In his mythical state of nature land had been abundant—available for the taking—and anyone could become a property owner. But in both Locke's time and our own, access to unclaimed, unowned property is not so easy. Indeed, when Locke notes that "the turfs my servant has cut ... become my property", he credits the labor of the landless servant to his landed master. In practice, Locke's theory justified the government of England by Parliament under constitutional law, which limited the power of the king and transferred it to the hands of the propertied classes—the system that was evolving in his time. Locke's is the voice of the improving landlords and the rising commercial classes who made the Glorious Revolution.

Intellectual Revolutions in Science and Philosophy

During the time between the two English political revolutions (1649 and 1688) of the seventeenth century, the Royal Society of London was founded in 1662. The study of science was beginning to be institutionalized, both as knowledge for its own sake and as technological application to practical problems. Ultimately, the new methods in science led to new ways of thinking about the world more generally. Thus, in some ways, our brief survey of the advancement of science might fit more appropriately in Chapter 13 on advances in global commerce or in Chapter 17 on the industrial revolution. But changes in scientific thinking proceeded step-by-step with changes in politics, so we examine them here in the midst of the revolution in political thought.

In his 1985 book *Revolution in Science*, Harvard University historian of science I. Bernard Cohen writes that the study of the history of science is a surprisingly new field. Although some of the scientists we shall consider here—Copernicus, Pascal, Galileo, Descartes, Newton, Harvey, Leeuwenhoek, and Linnaeus—spoke of their findings as revolutionary, the first academic historian to write of a scientific revolution seems to have been a Ph.D. candidate at Columbia University, Martha (Bronfenbrenner) Ornstein. In her 1913 dissertation she summarized the importance of the array of scientific discoveries and inventions that included the telescope, which "utterly revolutionized the science of astronomy," "revolutionary changes in optics," "Linnaeus's revolutionary work" in plant and animal classification, "the revolution in the universities" toward systematic, empirical research, and the role of scientific societies as carriers of culture. There had been, she wrote, "a revolution in the established habits of thought and inquiry, compared to which most revolutions registered in history seem insignificant".

In 1948, in a series of lectures, one of the most distinguished of professional historians, Herbert Butterfield, wrote that the scientific revolution of the seventeenth century "overturned the authority in science not only of the Middle Ages but of the ancient world ... [It] outshines everything since the rise of Christianity and reduces the Renaissance and Reformation to the rank of mere episodes, mere internal displacements, within the system of medieval Christendom". Butterfield refrained from calling this transformation a one-time revolution, since he saw it as a kind of "continuing historical, or history making force acting right up to the present time". Beginning in the 1950s, especially in *The Copernican Revolution* (1957) and *The Structure of Scientific Revolutions* (1962, 3rd ed., 1996), Thomas Kuhn turned his attention to the process of scientific investigation as a method of thought and research that constantly challenges conventional thinking and stands ready to overthrow it. Kuhn argued that most scientific research is based on small, incremental advances in human knowledge. Kuhn called this "normal science." "Revolutionary science" occurs when scientists break completely with existing explanations of their field, finding them inadequate, and create new theories that are better able to account for all the data available. Galileo and Newton created such great revolutions.

What then was this revolution in seventeenth-century science? First, the seventeenth century marked the move from the individual scientist working alone to the creation of a community of scientists, in touch with one another, sharing knowledge and ideas, and building a collective structure of thought and method. It would still be possible for a scientific genius like Leonardo da Vinci (1452–1519) to die with his work unrecognized, and even unknown, but this would be less likely. Leonardo, most famous for his paintings of *The Last Supper* and the *Mona Lisa*, also carried out research in human anatomy through the dissection of cadavers; he wrote of the circulation of the blood through the body and of the path of the earth around the sun; he drew sketches for inventions such as submarines and airplanes. But he did not circulate these scientific and technological ideas. At the time of his death they remained confined to his own notebooks and were not discovered until the twentieth century. The creation of scientific academies in the seventeenth century made it much less likely that such genius would remain hidden.

Second, science added four new qualities to its methods: mathematical formulations, quantifying and expressing relationships in nature in mathematical forms; **empiricism**, accepting the evidence of direct observation over theoretical and philosophical explanations; technological innovations in equipment, such as the telescope and microscope; and freedom of inquiry, encouraging scientists to follow their findings and their imagination regardless of received opinion and official doctrines. All of these qualities are found in the great revolution in astronomy and physics from Copernicus through Kepler and Galileo, and on to Newton. Indeed, many historians would call this *the* scientific revolution of the sixteenth and seventeenth centuries.

Nicholas Copernicus (1473–1543), an outstanding Polish astronomer, was commissioned by Pope Paul III to devise a new calendar that would correct the errors of the Julian calendar. The Julian calendar was based on a 365¼-day year, while the actual time it takes the earth to circle the sun is eleven minutes and fourteen seconds less. So the calendar year was continuously losing time, just a few minutes each year, but by the sixteenth century this amounted to about ten days. Holidays, like Christmas and Easter, began to slip backward into different seasons. The pope commissioned Copernicus to analyze the astronomy underlying the calendar.

In the sixteenth century, people accepted the model of the second-century C.E. Greek astronomer Ptolemy showing the earth at the center of the universe. The sun, the moon, the planets, and the stars went around it. As a mathematician, Copernicus began tracking the movements of all these bodies. He was able to fashion a

Map of the heavens according to Nicholas Copernicus, c. 1543. Copernicus placed the sun in the middle of his solar system with the earth circling around it. He also demonstrated the tilt and rotation of the earth's axis as it traveled in its yearly orbit. In these findings he differed from Ptolemy, the second century C.E. Greek astronomer, but he did continue to see the solar system as bounded, with an array of fixed stars and constellations marking its outer limits.

empiricism The theory that all knowledge originates in experience; the practice of relying on direct observation of events and experience for determining reality.

mathematical system that showed the earth at the center of the universe, as accepted belief had it, but he also found a much simpler, though still complicated, formula that showed the sun, not the earth, at the center of the solar system. His new formulation also showed the earth turning on its axis every twenty-four hours rather than having the entire cosmos revolve around the earth. As a rule, scientists faced with more than one workable explanation choose the simpler, and with his new, simpler model of a solar system Copernicus could explain the calendrical difficulties that had been his principal assignment. But this new explanation would land him in serious trouble with the Church, and he knew it.

The concept of the earth at the center of the universe as taught by Ptolemy had been adopted as the official doctrine of the Catholic Church because it was consistent with biblical passages (Joshua 10:13; Ecclesiastes 1:4-5) that spoke of the sun's circle around the earth. The consequences of challenging that belief frightened Copernicus, as he wrote to the pope in his letter of transmission introducing his findings:

> I may well presume, most Holy Father, that certain people, as soon as they hear that in this book about the Revolutions of the Spheres of the Universe I ascribe movement to the earthly globe, will cry out that . . . I should at once be hissed off the stage . . .
> Thinking therefore within myself that to ascribe movement to the Earth must indeed seem an absurd performance on my part to those who know that many centuries have consented to the establishment of the contrary judgment, namely that the Earth is placed immovably as the central point in the middle of the Universe, I hesitated long whether, on the one hand, I should give to the light these my Commentaries written to prove the Earth's motion . . . These misgivings and actual protests have been overcome by my friends . . . [one of whom] often urged and even importuned me to publish this work which I had kept in store not for nine years only, but to a fourth period of nine years . . . They urged that I should not, on account of my fears, refuse any longer to contribute the fruits of my labors to the common advantage of those interested in mathematics . . . Yielding then to their persuasion I at last permitted my friends to publish that work which they have so long demanded. (Kuhn, 1957, pp. 137–38)

In the end, Copernicus stuck to the principles of his mathematical commitments and his conscience. He presented the truth as he understood it, but he published his complete findings only on his deathbed. They created much less stir than might have been expected, since they were published as a mathematical study, comprehensible only to the most learned astronomers and mathematicians of his day. They became more the object of technical study than of theological debate.

The greatest astronomer of the next generation, Tycho Brahe (1546–1601), re-examined the mathematics of Copernicus and propounded a new schema that showed the sun and moon circling the earth in the middle of the solar system, and all the other planets circling the sun. It was a more complicated model, but one consistent with the data. The breakthrough that enshrined the sun-centered universe was made by Johannes Kepler (1571–1630). Kepler worked with Brahe toward the end of Brahe's life. For ten years he worked through the rich data he inherited, and finally reached a new understanding. The sun was at the center of the solar system and the planets, including earth, moved around it, but their orbits were not circles but ellipses, and they moved not at a fixed speed, but at a varying speed depending on their position on the ellipse. With these new insights, Kepler designed a model of the solar system that was simple, comprehensive, and mathematically consistent with the data available. He published his results in 1609 in *On the Motion of Mars*.

The theological argument was now clearly drawn. Kuhn writes, "Copernicanism required a transformation in man's view of his relation to God and of the bases of his morality". The earth was no longer the center of God's creation. There was no longer a fixed, heavenly location for God's throne. The perfection of the universe—with the earth at the center of a series of fixed, concentric, crystalline circles in which the planets traveled—was contaminated. Protestant leaders, believing in the literal word of the Bible and led by Luther himself, had attacked the heliocentric universe of Copernicus as early as 1539. The Catholic Church, at first allowing much more latitude to individual belief in this matter, was slower to condemn, but in 1610 the Church officially designated the Copernican model a heresy, and in 1616, *De Revolutionibus* and all other writings that affirmed the earth's motion were put on the *Index*, a list of writings that were forbidden to be taught or even read.

For many years the split between the mathematical astronomers and the Church continued rather quietly, with the mathematicians generally winning out among educated audiences. Then, in 1609, Galileo Galilei (1564–1642), the Italian astronomer, turned the newly invented telescope skyward and changed forever what we know about the heavens, how we know it, and its significance in the eyes of the nonspecialist, general public. Galileo added new empirical evidence and new technology to the toolkit of astronomy, opening new avenues of knowledge and popularizing them. The telescope had been created in the Netherlands; Galileo was the first to turn it toward the skies, and he made one discovery after another: The Milky Way is not just a dull glow in the sky but a gigantic collection of stars; the moon's surface is irregular, covered with craters and hills; the moon's radiant light is a reflection from the sun; the sun has imperfections, dark spots which appear and disappear across its surface; the earth is not the only planet with moons—Galileo observed at least four satellites circling Jupiter.

Galileo wrote, "We shall prove the earth to be a wandering body [in orbit around the sun] ... This we shall support by an infinitude of arguments drawn from nature" (Galileo, p. 45). Over and over Galileo stressed the validity of his own empirical observations. "With the aid of the telescope this has been scrutinized so directly and with such ocular certainty that all the disputes which have vexed the philosophers through so many ages have been resolved, and we are at last freed from wordy debates about it". "One may learn with all the certainty of sense evidence"; "All these facts were discovered and observed by me not many days ago with the aid of a spyglass which I devised, after first being illuminated by divine grace"; "our own eyes show us". Galileo's appeal to sense evidence, to direct observation, to empirically based information, and to its complete accessibility to anyone who looks through a telescope, found enormous resonance. He wrote for a general audience, not for university scholars; he wrote in Italian, not in Latin. The publication of Galileo's discoveries increased public interest in astronomy, and that public interest gradually turned into general acceptance.

The Catholic Church, deeply enmeshed in its cold war with Protestantism, finally turned against him. In 1633 Galileo was tried by the Inquisition and found guilty of having taught his doctrines against the orders of the Church. Under threat of torture, the sixty-nine-year-old scientist recanted his beliefs and was sentenced to house arrest in his villa near Florence for the rest of his life. (In 1992, 359 years later, Pope John Paul II officially and publicly spoke of the ruling of the Inquisition as a "sad misunderstanding which now belongs to the past," and suggested that there is no incompatibility between "the spirit of science and its rules of research on the one hand, and the Christian faith on the other" [*Philadelphia Inquirer*, November 1, 1992].)

In the same year as Galileo's death Isaac Newton was born in England, on Christmas Day, 1642. He studied at Cambridge University and became a professor of mathematics there at age twenty-six. In the course of his research, he discovered the calculus, a discovery he shared, separately, with the German mathematician Gottfried Wilhelm Leibnitz (1646–1716). A mathematical system especially useful in calculating motion along curved lines, the calculus was immediately valuable in predicting the

Newton experiments with light.
Newton's first published papers were in optics. Here he worked as an experimental scientist rather than as a theoretical mathematician. By passing the rays of the sun through a prism he demonstrated that white light was an amalgam of colored rays. Using this information he built a reflecting telescope, using a mirror to focus light and thus to avoid the chromatic aberration that appeared in a refracting telescope.

celestial course of planets and the earthly trajectory of artillery shells. Another area of Newton's early research was in optics, focusing on the spectrum of light as it passed through a prism. Then he turned his attention to the new issues raised by Copernicus, Kepler, and Galileo: Why do heavy bodies always fall toward earth even as the earth is moving through space? What moves the earth? What moves the planets and what keeps them in their orbits? Before Copernicus, Ptolemy's view of the fixed spheres of the universe answered those questions. But without those fixed spheres, how should we understand the movements of the heavens?

In finding the universal law of gravity, Newton showed that the laws of planetary motion that Kepler formulated, and the laws of earthly movement that Galileo discovered in his later career, along with additional principles of inertia of motion discovered by the French mathematician and philosopher René Descartes (1596–1650), were all consistent. The universal principle of gravitation, coupled with the principle of inertia—that a body once set in motion tends to continue moving at the same speed in the same direction—gives a form for understanding the means by which the universe holds together. Moreover, these forces of inertia and gravity are universal, operating in the same way on earth as in the wider universe. Asserting the principle of the universal law of gravity was the imaginative leap of Newton's new discovery; working out the mathematics was the toil of genius, and he produced it in 1687 in his *Mathematical Principles of Natural Philosophy*. He worked out the formula for the pull of gravity: all matter moves as if every particle attracts every other particle with a force proportional to the product of the two masses, and inversely proportional to the square of the distance between them. This force is universal gravitation.

Like all later scientists, Newton did not try to explain *why* this force worked, only *how* it worked. This new law had enormous philosophical implications, for it explained the "glue" in the Copernican system of the universe. It also had very practical consequences in the understanding and prediction of the tides. The great advances in mathematics underpinned not only theoretical research, but also practical invention in the form of time-keeping, mapping, and processes that required accuracy such as the aiming of artillery and the construction of steam engines. In light of his revolutionary contributions, Newton was named President of the Royal Society in 1703.

The discoveries in astronomy, physics, and mathematics were the leading sectors in the scientific revolution of the seventeenth century, but they were not alone. In England, William Harvey published *On the Movement of the Heart and Blood*, based on years of laboratory research and vivisection of animals, demonstrating the circulation of blood through the body. In the Netherlands, Anthony van Leeuwenhoek (1632–1723) improved the newly invented microscope, the other great advance in optics along with the telescope, to see and then create drawings of blood corpuscles, spermatozoa, and bacteria. His observations enabled him to argue that reproduction even among tiny creatures was through sexual mating, not spontaneous generation. Leeuwenhoek was a businessman in the cloth trade, not specially educated in the sciences, and his election as a Fellow of the Royal Society of London in 1680 demonstrated that amateurs were entering avidly into this new research.

Leeuwenhoek's researches expanded the knowledge of the number and variety of tiny, microscopic creatures. Carolus Linnaeus (1707–78) developed a system of classification for these and all other known creatures in nature, *Systema Naturae* (1735), including an analysis of sexual reproduction in plants. The further evolution of eighteenth-century science was well underway.

The new science both reduced and expanded human powers and self-understanding. Some, frightened, agreed with Blaise Pascal, a devout Christian French mathematician: "I am terrified by the eternal silence of these infinite spaces." But more took heart along with Alexander Pope, that a brave, new world was dawning:

> Nature and nature's law lay hid in night;
> God said, "Let Newton be," and all was light.

The new world of science swept away much superstition, at least for the time, and suggested that rationality and science could create a new world in which people would trust their senses to gather empirical information and to act upon it, a world in which the laws of nature could be discovered and calculated, a world in which science would inspire technological invention in the practical arts of making human life more productive and more comfortable. Throughout the eighteenth century, this vision of natural law and the power of human reason spilled over from science and technology to philosophy and political theory. Just as scientists began to undermine traditional ideas about the nature of the universe, philosophers began to challenge traditional ideas about the relationship between monarchy and populations.

ENGLAND'S GLORIOUS REVOLUTION, 1688

At about the time Hobbes was writing, England was in continuing revolt against its sovereigns. Religion was a burning issue, and it seemed that no sovereign could satisfy all the conflicting wishes of dissenters—Roman Catholics, Presbyterians, Puritans, and Quakers—and the official Anglican Church. Frustrations simmered but had no focus until both James I (r. 1603–25) and his son Charles I (r. 1625–49) ran out of money to administer their governments, especially the naval and military departments, and therefore convened Parliament to request additional funds. Many members of Parliament—landowners, increasingly wealthy city merchants, lawyers, Puritans and other religious dissenters, as well as Anglican clergy—were not inclined to give the kings the money they requested. They challenged royal authority, proposed increased power for an elected legislature, promotion by merit in government jobs, and, most of all, religious tolerance in private and public life. When Charles I nevertheless attempted to levy taxes without its sanction, the Parliament he had convened in 1640 came to open warfare with him and ultimately, under the leadership of Oliver Cromwell (Lord Protector of England, 1653–8), executed him. Cromwell, an ardent Calvinist and military genius, ruled in a rather arbitrary fashion until he died in 1658. He conquered rebels in both Ireland and Scotland and joined them with England to form the British Commonwealth. In spite of his conquests, neither Cromwell nor Parliament had been able to achieve a new form of effective government and the monarchy was restored in 1660. However, the Civil War established the notion that the monarchy could be abolished and in many ways provided the theoretical framework that led to the subsequent revolution of 1688.

SOURCE

Universal Suffrage vs. Property Rights

E.P. Thompson, the twentieth-century British historian, emphasized the contributions of common people to history. In his ground-breaking The Making of the English Working Class *(pp. 22–3), Thompson cites statements made in 1647 at an army council meeting that attempted to find a constitutional solution to the struggle between the king and Parliament and to determine the role of the common people in electing Parliament.*

Oliver Cromwell's son-in-law, General Ireton, proposed extending the franchise, but only to men of property, fearing that private property might otherwise be abolished: "No person hath a right to an interest or share in the disposing of the affairs of the kingdom ... that hath not a permanent fixed interest in this kingdom ... If you admit any man that hath a breath and being, Why may not those men vote against all property?"

The common soldiers replied more democratically and more bitterly. One asserted: "There are many thousands of us soldiers that have ventured our lives; we have had little property in the kingdom as to our estates, yet we have had a birthright. But it seems now, except a man hath a fixed estate in this kingdom, he hath no right ... I wonder we were so much deceived." If we are asked to fight on behalf of the government, we should have a voice in its election.

The Bill of Rights, 1689

Charles II (r. 1660–85) and his brother James II (r. 1685–90) continued to claim more powers than Parliament wished to sanction. James II, a Catholic, favored Catholics in many of his official appointments. When a son was born to James, leading nobles feared that James and his successors might reinstitute Catholicism as England's official religion a century and a half after Henry VIII had disestablished it in favor of the Church of England. They invited James II's daughter, Mary, and her husband William of Orange, ruler of the United Provinces of the Netherlands, both resolute Protestants, to return to England and assume the monarchy. In 1688 William and Mary arrived in England and confirmed their new rule by defeating the troops still loyal to James II at the Battle of the Boyne in Ireland in 1690.

Although the new king and queen had been invited primarily to resolve religious conflicts, their ascension to the throne also brought resolution to the power conflict between monarch and Parliament. The Bill of Rights that was enacted by Parliament in 1689 stating clearly principles that had been evolving for decades in the relationship between the monarchy and the people of England. It stipulated, among other clauses, that no taxes could be raised, nor armies recruited without prior parliamentary approval; no subject could be arrested and detained without legal process; and no law could be suspended by the king unilaterally. The Glorious Revolution thus not only displaced one monarch in favor of another but also limited the powers of the monarch under constitutional law. After all, this new monarch had been selected by noblemen and confirmed by Parliament. In addition, as William continued his wars against France, he had to defer to Parliament for funds. The Anglican Church remained the established Church of England, but the Toleration Act of 1689 granted Puritan Dissenters—but not Roman Catholics—the right of free public worship. Cromwell had already permitted Jews to return to England, almost 400 years after their expulsion in 1290. Parliament did not yet revoke the Test Act, which reserved military and civil offices for Anglicans only. Nevertheless, these settlements brought some resolution to the issues of religion in politics that had beset England for so long, although rebellion against the religious provisions continued in Scotland and especially Ireland.

The Reality of Government by Male Property Owners. For its time the Glorious Revolution may have been democratic because it placed the king under constitutional rule. But until 1820 fewer than 500 influential men in all of Britain, it has been estimated, could control the election of the majority of the Parliament. The 1832 Reform Act expanded the actual electorate in the British Isles from less than half million to about 800,000. Not until 1867 and 1884 did Reform Acts extend the vote to the middle and lower classes as well as to Catholics, Dissenters, and Jews. By that time the Industrial Revolution had created an entirely new class of occupations and workers who could successfully demand representation, as we shall see in the next chapter. Women got the vote in Britain only in the twentieth century.

THE *PHILOSOPHES* AND THE ENLIGHTENMENT IN THE EIGHTEENTH CENTURY

In the century between the Glorious Revolution in England and the American and French revolutions, a movement in philosophic thought emerged called the Enlightenment. Its intellectual center was in France, although key participants lived in America, Scotland, England, Prussia, Russia, and elsewhere. The French leaders of the Enlightenment were called *philosophes*, and their philosophy helped inspire the American and the French revolutions.

Following on the scientific revolution of the seventeenth century the *philosophes* believed in a world of rationality, in which collected human knowledge and systematic thought could serve as powerful tools for finding order in the universe and for solving key problems in political and economic life. Their concerns for clarity of thought, combined with the desire to solve practical problems in public life, gave them considerable influence over the restructuring of new political institutions in their age of revolution. The authors of the American Declaration of Independence and of the French Declaration of the Rights of Man and the Citizen drew much of their inspiration from the *philosophes*. The *philosophes* believed in order, but also in freedom of thought and expression. For them, public discussion and debate were the means toward finding better ideas and solutions. Indeed, the *philosophes* were in constant dialogue and debate with one another.

Travel influenced the *philosophes'* thought, opening them to a wider range of ideas. Charles de Secondat, the Baron de Montesquieu (1689–1755), traveled widely himself and presented satiric criticism of French institutions, including the monarchy and the Catholic Church, in the form of *Persian Letters*, supposedly dispatched by two visitors to France writing their observations to readers at home. Twenty-seven years later, in 1748, Montesquieu wrote his most influential work, *The Spirit of Laws*, in which he recognized that different countries need different kinds of governments, and advocated a separation of powers based on his (mis)understanding of the British system. The authors of the United States constitution later acknowledged their debt to Montesquieu's thought.

In terms of spiritual and religious beliefs, most *philosophes* were deists. They allowed that the world may have required an original creator, like Aristotle's prime mover, but once the processes of life had begun, he had withdrawn. Their metaphor was that of a watchmaker who built the mechanism, started it moving, and departed. Humanity's fate thereafter was in its own hands.

In contrast to such Catholic doctrines as original sin and the authority of the Church over human reason, the *philosophes* argued that human progress was possible through the steady and unrestricted expansion of knowledge or "enlightenment." Jean-Antoine-Nicolas de Caritat, Marquis de Condorcet (1743–94), author of the *Sketch of the Progress*

philosophes A group of eighteenth-century French writers and philosophers who emphasized the supremacy of human reason and advocated freedom of expression and social, economic, and political reform. They included Voltaire, Montesquieu, Rousseau, and Diderot, editor of the *Encyclopédie* (1751–72), which embodied many of their ideas.

of the Human Mind (published in 1795), proclaimed "the perfectibility of humanity is indefinite". The most famous academic product of the *philosophes* and the Enlightenment was the *Encyclopedia, or Rational Dictionary of the Arts, Sciences, and Crafts*, compiled by Denis Diderot (1713–84) and containing articles by leading scholars and *philosophes*. The *Encyclopedia* reaffirmed this faith in human progress based on education:

> The aim of an Encyclopedia is to collect all the knowledge that now lies scattered over the face of the earth, to make known its general structure to the men among whom we live, and to transmit it to those who will come after us, in order that the labors of past ages may be useful to the ages that will follow, that our grandsons, as they become better educated, may become at the same time more virtuous and more happy, and that we may not die without having deserved well of the human race. (Columbia University, *Contemporary Civilization*, pp. 988–9)

Diderot called for further social and political revolution. "We are beginning to shake off the yoke of authority and tradition in order to hold fast to the laws of reason". Challenging authority meant being open to multiple perspectives rather than holding a single truth, and Diderot built this concept into the structure of his volumes.

> By giving cross-references to articles where solid principles serve as foundation for the diametrically opposed truths we shall be able to throw down the whole edifice of mud and scatter the idle heap of dust. … If these cross-references, which now confirm and now refute, are carried out artistically according to a plan carefully conceived in advance, they will give to the Encyclopedia the … ability to change men's common way of thinking. (p. 996)

The *Encyclopedia* ultimately filled seventeen volumes of text and eleven of illustrations.

Another *philosophe*, François-Marie Arouet, better known as Voltaire (1694–1778), spoke out with courage and wit. His *Elements of the Philosophy of Newton* (1738) explicated new scientific evidence of the rational order and the human ability to comprehend the universe; *Philosophical Letters on the English* (1734) argued for freedom of religion, inquiry, and the press; *Essai sur les moeurs* (1756), translated as *Universal History*, gave a humanistic context to historical development and placed responsibility

Jean Huber, *The Philosophers at Supper*, 1750. Voltaire (1), Condorcet (5), and Diderot (6) are among the figures depicted in this engraving, a visual checklist of important Enlightenment thinkers. Seeing the Western world as emerging from centuries of darkness and ignorance, these Frenchmen promoted reason, science, and a respect for humanity—ideas that would underpin the intellectual case for the French Revolution of 1789. (*Bibliothèque Nationale, Paris*)

in human hands. Voltaire cried *"Ecrasez l'infame!"*—"crush the infamy" of superstition, intolerance, and the power of the clergy.

The *philosophes* were not, however, committed to popular democracy. Voltaire preferred benevolent and **enlightened despotism** to badly administered self-rule. In the best of all possible worlds, there would be an enlightened ruler like Frederick II, the Great, of Prussia (r. 1740–86), at whose court Voltaire lived for several years, or Catherine II, the Great, Empress of Russia (r. 1762–96), of whom he was a close friend, or Joseph II, Emperor of Austria (r. 1765–90). All three ruled countries in which the administration was efficient, taxes were reasonable, agricultural and handicraft production was encouraged, freedom of expression and religion was allowed, the military was strengthened, and powerful empires resulted. The enlightened despot acted in disciplined ways, subject in his or her mind to the law of nature. But the population at large had no say or vote in the administration. In other words, for these rulers, and for Voltaire, good government did not necessarily require self government.

enlightened despotism A system of government in which the ruler has absolute rights over his or her subjects, but uses this power for their benefit.

Colonial governments often claimed the mantle of the Enlightenment to justify their rule, arguing that they were utilizing knowledge and reason, to soften the use of brute force, as the foundation of their administration. In 1784 Warren Hastings, Governor General of the British holdings in India explained:

> Every accumulation of knowledge and especially such as is obtained by social communication with people over whom we exercise dominion founded on the right of conquest, is useful to the state … it attracts and conciliates distant affections; it lessens the weight of the chain by which the natives are held in subjection; and it imprints on the hearts of our countrymen the sense of obligation and benevolence. (Metcalf and Metcalf, p. 61)

Implementing this Enlightenment philosophy, Hastings founded the Asiatic Society of Bengal, dedicated primarily to the translation and analysis of ancient Indian texts.

Skepticism regarding democratic government was carried further in the works of Jean-Jacques Rousseau (1712–78), perhaps the most enigmatic and ambiguous of all of the eighteenth-century French thinkers. Rousseau questioned the primacy of intellect and human ingenuity. Like Hobbes and Locke, he wrote of the "state of nature," but, unlike them, he seemed, in some ways, to wish to return to it. His *Social Contract* (1762) lamented, "Man is born free; and everywhere he is in chains." In his *Discourse on the Origin of Inequality* (1755) he wrote:

> There is hardly any inequality in the state of nature; all the inequality which now prevails owes its strength and growth to the development of our faculties and the advance of the human mind, and becomes at last permanent and legitimate by the establishment of property and laws. (Columbia University, *Contemporary Civilization*, p. 1147)

Rousseau proposed a democracy far more radical than that of the other *philosophes*, yet he also seemed to justify a repressive tyranny of the majority. Like Locke and Hobbes, Rousseau mythologized an original social contract transforming a state of nature into a community, and he attributed great power to that community: "Each of us puts his person and all his power in common under the supreme direction of the general will". "Whoever refuses to obey the general will shall be compelled to do so by the whole body. This means nothing less than that he will be forced to be free" (p. 1153). Political philosophers have argued for more than two centuries over the paradox of Rousseau's "general will." How is the citizen "forced to be free"? Is this a proclamation of freedom, justification for suppressing minorities, or a proposal for creating a totalitarian state?

Adam Smith, whose economic ideas we have already examined, is sometimes grouped with the *philosophes*, with whom he carried on extensive discussions and correspondence. Like Locke, Smith believed it was normal for people to want to

"better their condition" materially. He saw that this attempt was not always successful, but suggested:

> it is well that nature imposes upon us in this manner. It is this deception which rouses
> and keeps in continual motion the industry of mankind. It is this which first prompted
> them to cultivate the ground, to build houses, to found cities and commonwealths, and
> to invent and improve all the sciences and arts, which ennoble and embellish human
> life. (*Moral Sentiments*, IV.1.10)

Much less optimistically, Smith recognized that private enrichment would engender
jealousy and envy. Private property, therefore, needed to be protected and this, he
agreed with Locke, was the task of government:

> Civil government, so far as it is instituted for the security of property, is in reality
> instituted for the defense of the rich against the poor, or of those who have some
> property against those who have none at all. (*The Wealth of Nations*, p. 674)

At the time of the American and French revolutions these arguments for enlightenment, rationality, experimental science, secularism, private profit and ownership,
"fellow feeling," and limitations on the power of government all clamored for changes
in politics, economics, and social life. But what would be the substance and direction
of those changes? How would they be implemented and by whom?

REVOLUTION IN NORTH AMERICA, 1776

As British settlers began to colonize North America, Australia, and South Africa in the
seventeenth and eighteenth centuries, they assumed that they shared in the rights of
all Britons. By the 1760s, however, North American settlers were beginning to resent
the control over their political and economic life exerted by rulers in Britain. British
control over American trade, restrictions on the development of American shipping,
and the resulting limitations on the development of certain kinds of manufacture, were
as galling as the issue of taxation. The 1763 British victory over the French in the Seven
Years War in North America, concluding a global cluster of wars between the two
powers for commercial and naval supremacy, ended the threat of attacks by French or
Indians, and freed the American colonists from further need of British troops. However, the British decided to maintain a large army in North America and to tax the colonies directly to pay for it. The 1765 Stamp Act levied taxes on a long list of commercial and legal documents. The colonists protested vigorously until Parliament repealed the Act because of serious rioting and a boycot of British goods.

Additional grievances against further imperious decrees of King George III built up until finally the Americans declared themselves an independent country in 1776 and fought to end British rule over them. The American Declaration of Independence set out a list of these

John Trumbull, *Signing of the
Declaration of Independence, July 4,
1776*, 1786–97. What began as a protest
against colonial trade restrictions and
the limiting of political liberty grew into
a revolutionary struggle and the birth of
a nation. The Declaration of
Independence enshrined the principles
underlying the new United States and
later influenced freedom-fighters all over
the world. (*Capitol Collection,
Washington*)

"injuries and usurpations." It reflected the American resolve to secure the same legal rights as Britons had won at home almost a century earlier. It charged the king with "taking away our Charters, abolishing our most valuable Laws, and altering fundamentally the Forms of our Governments." It declared the social contract that bound the colonies to Britain had been broken. It declared, ultimately, the right of revolution.

The American Revolution went further in establishing political democracy than had the Glorious Revolution in Britain. It abolished the monarchy entirely, replacing it with an elected government. Having declared that "all men are created equal," with unalienable rights not only to life and liberty, but also to the vague but seductive "pursuit of happiness," the revolutionaries now set out to consolidate their commitments in a new legal structure. Their leaders, men like George Washington, Benjamin Franklin, Thomas Jefferson, and James Madison, were soldiers, entrepreneurs, and statesmen of considerable erudition, common sense, restraint, and balance.

The Constitution and the Bill of Rights, 1789

After the Americans won their war for independence, 1775–81, and in 1783 achieved a peace treaty with Britain, political leaders of the thirteen colonies met in Philadelphia to establish a framework for their new nation. They drafted a new Constitution in 1789, and a Bill of Rights, which was ratified in 1791. The American Bill of Rights, the first ten amendments to the Constitution, guaranteed to Americans not only the basic rights enjoyed by the British at the time, but more: freedom of religion (and the separation of Church and state), press, assembly, and petition; the right to bear arms; protection against unreasonable searches and against cruel and unusual punishment; and the right to a speedy and proper trial by a jury of peers. The Americans established a federal system of government. The states individually set the rules for voting and many, but not all, removed the property requirements. By 1800 Vermont had instituted universal manhood suffrage, and South Carolina, Pennsylvania, New Hampshire, and Delaware extended the vote to virtually every adult white male taxpayer.

Historians of the early United States situate the more radical American approach to political liberty in at least four factors: religious, geographic, social, and philosophical. First, a disproportionate share of the settlers coming to America from Britain and Europe were religious dissenters seeking spiritual independence outside the established churches of their countries. Their widespread, popular beliefs in the importance of individual liberties carried over from religion into politics.

Second, the availability of apparently open land presented abundant individual opportunity to the new Americans (as they dispossessed Native Americans). Later, the historian Frederick Jackson Turner would extend this "frontier thesis," arguing that the relative freedom and openness of American life was based psychologically as well as materially on the presence of seemingly endless open frontier land. Third, the absence of landed and aristocratic privilege, and the strength of artisan classes in the urban population increased the demand for more democracy. Finally, eighteenth-century political thought had

The Boston Tea Party, 1773. On December 16, 1773, American colonists cheer as some radicals dressed up as Indians throw tea from British ships into Boston harbor. (*Yale University Art Gallery, New Haven, Connecticut*)

generally grown more radical, especially among the *philosophes* in France. By the time the Americans wrote their Bill of Rights, the French Revolution was well underway.

The First Anti-imperial Revolution

The American Revolution, in addition to securing British rights for Americans, was also, and perhaps more importantly, the first modern anti-colonial revolution. The trade and taxation policies imposed by Britain had pushed businessmen and artisans into opposition to British rule. Other nations, notably France, eager to embarrass Britain and to detach its most promising colonies, provided financial and military support, which helped the Americans to win their independence. One of the goals of the Revolution was to open the North American continent west of the Appalachian Mountains to settlement. The British prohibition on this westward movement had stood in stark contrast to Spanish and Portuguese settlement policy in Latin America. As the newly independent Americans migrated westward, annexing land as they went, they began to develop imperial interests that were expressed in the mystique of "Manifest Destiny." This popular belief in America's natural growth across the continent was consolidated with the huge Louisiana Purchase from France in 1803. Texans were encouraged to assert their independence from Mexico in 1836 and were then absorbed into the American Union in 1845. Warfare with Mexico in 1846–8 ended in victory for the United States and the annexation of the southwest. Other annexations of land in North America took place more peacefully, with negotiations with Britain for the Oregon country in 1844–6 and with Russia for the purchase of Alaska in 1867.

Over the centuries America served as an inspiration to anti-colonial forces. Jawaharlal Nehru, leading India's twentieth-century struggle for independence from Britain, cited the American Revolution as a model for his own country: "This political change in America was important and destined to bear great results. The American colonies which became free then have grown today [1932] into the most powerful, the richest, and industrially the most advanced country in the world".

The American Revolution, however, did not bring democracy to everyone. The greatest shortcoming was the American perpetuation of slavery. The system was finally ended only by the American Civil War, 1861–5, the bloodiest in the history of the nation. Even afterward, racial discrimination characterized American law until the 1960s and continues to mark American practice up to the present. The status of the Native American population actually worsened after the revolution, as settlers of European extraction headed west, first by wagon train and later by railroad. They slaughtered American Indians, pushed them out of the way, confined them to remote, semi-barren reservations, destroyed the buffalo herds on which their nomadic existence depended, and discouraged the preservation of their separate cultures and languages. For the indigenous Indians the effects of the revolution were exactly opposite to those of the settler-invaders: expansion became contraction, democracy became tyranny, prosperity became poverty, and liberty became confinement.

The hypocrisy of democratic statements, on the one hand, and atrocities against Indians, on the other, peaked in the presidency of Andrew Jackson (1829–37). Jackson fought against economic and political privilege and to extend opportunity to the common man, yet he ordered the United States Army to evict the Cherokee Nation from their lands in Georgia and to drive them to the "Great American Desert" in the west in direct defiance of the Supreme Court of the United States. About one-fourth of the 15,000 Indians forced onto this "Trail of Tears" died *en route*.

How did America reconcile its ideals of equality and liberty with the enslavement of blacks and the confinement of Indians at home? It did so by considering non-whites and non-Europeans as "other"—that is, as not quite equal biologically. Race was often

For an interactive version of this map, go to: http://www.prenhall.com/spodek/map16.1

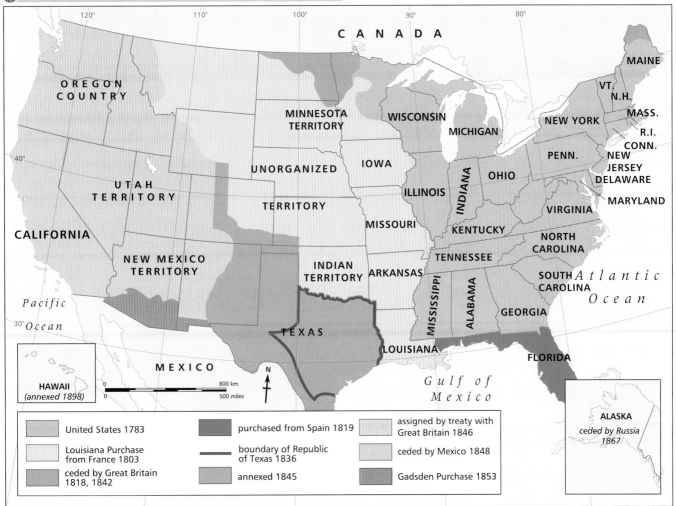

used as a definition, usually made by a quick, if approximate and sometimes inaccurate, visual measure, and often as a legal standard. The fixing of legal identity by race, which had been heretofore a flexible category, became especially common in the southern United States in dealing with slaves, ex-slaves, and free blacks. For many years, racial definition was used as a legal standard in excluding Asians from immigrating as well. If non-whites were considered not quite equal biologically, the unalienable right to liberty could be abridged. Once the revolutionary principle of equality was accepted in America and elsewhere, the battle was drawn between those who wished to narrow its application to an "in-group" while excluding "others" and those who wished to apply it to all peoples. That battle continues today, in law and in practice, in the United States and around the globe.

THE FRENCH REVOLUTION AND NAPOLEON, 1789–1812

The American Revolution, with its combined messages of colonial revolt, constitutional government, individual freedom, and equality under law, inspired many peoples at the time and over the centuries. But in comparison with European countries

The growth of the United States. The westward expansion of the United States was effected by territorial cession, acquisition, and conquest. Following independence in 1783, the Louisiana Purchase from France (1803) and the annexations of West and East Florida from Spain, doubled the nation's size. Another doubling occurred with the annexation of Texas (1845), the acquisition of Oregon (1846), and military victory over Mexico (1848), which brought the southwest. Alaska was purchased from Russia (1867). Hawaii was annexed in 1898. In all cases, European immigrants and their descendants displaced Native Americans, and in less than a century the United States had become one of the world's largest nations.

and their experiences, America and its revolution were unique. At the end of the eighteenth century, America was a country of four million people on the fringes of a continental wilderness, without traditions of class and clerical privilege, and founded in large measure by dissidents. Building on already existing British freedoms and fighting a war (with the support of several international allies) against a distant colonial government, the leaders of the revolution were an educated, comfortable elite. The French Revolution, on the other hand, was an internal revolt against entrenched feudal, clerical, and monarchical privilege within the most populous (24 million people) and most powerful European state of its time. It unleashed powerful, combative internal factions, none of which could control the direction or the velocity of revolutionary events inside or outside of France. The French Revolution immediately affected all of Europe, most of the western hemisphere, and indeed the whole world. Some would argue that the battles over its central principles continue even today. The twentieth-century Chinese leader Zhou Enlai, when asked to assess the effects of the French Revolution, legendarily replied: "It's too soon to tell."

The Origins of Revolution

The French Revolution, like the English Civil Wars of the 1640s, was triggered by the king's need for funds. Much like Charles I, King Louis XVI (r. 1774–92) decided to solicit these funds by convening leaders of the French people through the Estates-General in 1789.

From this point on, political, social, and ideological change proceeded very rapidly as political institutions, social classes, and philosophical beliefs challenged one another in a continuous unfolding of critical events. France was divided, hierarchically, into three Estates: the clergy, numbering about 100,000 and controlling perhaps 10 percent of the land of France; the nobility, perhaps 300,000 men, who owned approximately 25 percent of the land; and everyone else. The Third Estate included a rising and prosperous group of urban merchants and professionals (estimated at 8 percent of the total population), as well as working-class artisans, and the four-fifths of France who were farmers. The wealth that the king wished to tap was concentrated in the first two estates and the **bourgeoisie**, or leading urban professional and commercial classes, of the third.

bourgeoisie A French word that originally applied to the inhabitants of walled towns, who occupied a socio-economic position between the rural peasantry and the feudal aristocracy; with the development of industry, it became identified more with employers, as well as with other members of the "middle class," professionals, artisans, and shopkeepers.

The Revolt of the Third Estate

The Estates-General had not been convened since 1614, and the procedures for its meeting were disputed, revealing grievances not only against the king but also among the representatives. The nobles wished to seize the moment to make the Estates-General into the constitutional government of France, with the king subordinate to them. They wanted guarantees of personal liberty, freedom of the press and speech, and freedom from arbitrary arrest. They also wanted minimal taxation, but they might have conceded this point in exchange for greater political power. Under their proposed constitution, the Estates-General would meet in three separate chambers: one for the nobility; one for the clergy, in which the nobility also had a powerful voice; and a third for everyone else.

The Third Estate, which had long regarded the nobility as parasitic and resented their multitude of special privileges, viewed the new proposals with suspicion. The members of the Third Estate drew their inspiration for a more democratic, representative, inclusive, and accountable government from the writings of the *philosophes*, and the experience of the revolutions in England and, especially, in America. Their local spokesman and leading pamphleteer was actually a clergyman, the Abbé Emmanuel-

Joseph Sieyès (1748–1836), who wrote *What Is the Third Estate?* (1789). The tract opened with a catechism of three political questions and answers: "(1) What is the Third Estate? Everything. (2) What has it been in the political order up to the present? Nothing. (3) What does it demand? To Become Something." The leaders of the Third Estate asked for an end to the privileges that had enriched and empowered the clergy and the nobility while reducing the opportunities available to everyone else and impoverishing the French crown. Many saw the king as an ally in the struggle against the nobility. They proposed that the entire Estates-General meet in a single body, since the king had granted them as many representatives as both of the other two estates combined.

The Oath of the Tennis Court by Jacques-Louis David, 1790. In this dramatic composition, David captures the moment when the Third Estate asserted their sovereignty as the elected representatives of France. The merchants, professionals, and artisans who attended the hastily convened meeting swore to remain in session until they had drawn up a new constitution— one that would end the vested interests of the nobility and clergy. (*Musée Carnavalet, Paris*)

When the Parlement of Paris ruled that the three estates should meet separately, as the nobility had wished, the Third Estate was enraged. For six weeks its members boycotted the Estates-General when it was convened in May 1789. On June 13 a few priests joined them, and four days later the Third Estate, with its allies, declared itself the "National Assembly." The king locked them out of their meeting hall. On June 20 they met on a nearby indoor tennis court and swore the "Oath of the Tennis Court," claiming legal power, and declaring that they would not disband until a new constitution was drafted. Louis XVI, frightened by these events, and unwilling or unable to assert his own leadership, called up some 18,000 troops to defend himself from possible attack at his palace in Versailles where all these events were taking place.

The Revolt of the Poor

Meanwhile, in Paris, 12 miles away, and throughout France, mobs of people were rising against organized authority. The harvest had been poor, and the price of bread in 1789 was near record heights. Some farmers refused to pay their taxes and their manorial dues, and many city people were hungry. Beggars and brigands began to roam the countryside and move toward Paris.

In the capital, mobs stormed the Bastille, which was a combination of jail and armory. Meeting violent resistance, they murdered the governor of the Bastille, the mayor of Paris, and a number of soldiers. Hearing of events in Paris, peasants organized against remaining feudalism. Though there was little violence against people, peasants seized and destroyed documents that demanded feudal dues and taxes. In an attempt to contain these revolutionary disorders, the king, in Versailles, recognized the National Assembly, the new group formed by the Third Estate and its allies, as representatives of the people and authorized it to draft a new constitution.

The National Assembly abolished what was left of feudalism and serfdom, the tithe for the church, and the special privileges of the nobility. It issued the "Declaration of the Rights of Man and the Citizen" with seventeen articles, including:

- Men are born and remain free and equal in rights; social distinctions may be based only upon general usefulness.
- The aim of every political association is the preservation of the natural and inalienable rights of man; these rights are liberty, property, security, and resistance to oppression.
- The source of all sovereignty resides essentially in the nation …
- Law is the expression of the general will … All citizens, being equal before it, are equally admissible to all public offices, positions, and employments, according to their capacity, and without other distinction than that of virtues and talents …
- For the maintenance of the public force and for the expenses of administration a common tax is indispensable; it must be assessed equally on all citizens in proportion to their means …
- Society has the right to require of every public agent an accounting of his administration.

The Declaration further affirmed freedom of thought, religion, petition, and due process under law. It represented a triumph for the doctrines of the *philosophes*.

Meanwhile, hungry mobs in Paris continued toward insurrection. In October, led by a demonstration of housewives, market women, and revolutionary militants protesting the high price of bread, 20,000 Parisians marched to the royal palace in Versailles. This "March of the Women" broke into the palace, overwhelmed the National Guard, and forced the royal family to return to Paris where they could be kept under surveillance. In the meantime, in the countryside peasants felt an (unfounded) "Great Fear" that land-lords were attempting to block reform by hiring thugs to burn the harvest. In response, peasants attacked the estates of the nobility and the clergy, and their managers.

Over the next two years, the National Assembly drew up a constitution, which called for a constitutional monarchy; did away with the titles and perquisites of nobility and clergy; introduced uniform government across the country; disestablished the Roman Catholic clergy and confiscated the property of the Church; and convened a new Legislative Assembly, for which about one-half of adult, male Frenchmen were entitled to vote, essentially by a property qualification. Protestants, Jews, and agnostics were admitted to full citizenship and could vote and run for office if they met the property qualifications. Citizenship would be based not on religious affiliation but on residence in the country and allegiance to its government. Except for the radical—and polarizing—anti-clerical position, the actions of the French Revolution thus far seemed quite similar to those of England and America. They were consistent with the optimistic and activist world-view of the *philosophes*. The new constitution was finally promulgated in September 1791 following a wave of strikes and an official ban on labor organizations.

Contemporary colored engraving showing women marching to Versailles on 5 October 1789. Angered by reports of a luxurious banquet staged by the king, a large crowd of Parisians, mostly women, stormed Versailles and laid siege to the royal palace. Louis XVI and his family, though later executed, were at this point saved by the intervention of the French general, the Marquis de Lafayette.

International War, the "Second" Revolution, and the Terror, 1791–99

In June 1791 Louis XVI and his queen Marie-Antoinette attempted to flee France but were apprehended and, thereafter, held as virtual prisoners in the royal palace. Shocked and frightened, thousands of aristocrats emigrated to neighboring countries that were more respectful of monarchy and aristocracy. News of the abolition of feudal privilege and of the Civil Constitution of the Clergy filled the nobility and clergy across Europe with dread. Leopold II, the Habsburg emperor (r. 1790–92) and brother of Marie-Antoinette, entered into discussions with other rulers to consider war against the new French government. The French National Assembly, meeting under the new constitution, began to mobilize both in response to this threat and in anticipation of extending the revolution. In April 1792 it declared war on the Austrian monarchy, and for the next twenty-three years, France would be at war with several of the major countries of Europe.

Events careered onward at a revolutionary pace. The war went poorly and mobs stormed the royal palace attempting to kill the king and beginning the "Second French Revolution." Louis sought protection in the National Assembly and was imprisoned; all his official powers were terminated. The Assembly disbanded and called for a new National Convention—to be elected by universal male suffrage—to draw up a new constitution. Amid mob violence, the new Convention met in September 1792. Its leaders were **Jacobins**, members of a nationwide network of political clubs named (ironically) for a former convent in Paris where they had first met. They divided into the more moderate **Girondins**, named for a region of France and in general representing the provinces, and the **Montagnards**, representatives mostly from Paris, who drew their name from the benches they occupied on the uppermost left side of the assembly hall. By 361 to 359 votes, the Convention voted to execute the king in January 1793. The "Second Revolution" was well underway.

Outside the Assembly, the Paris Commune, the government of Paris, represented the workers, merchants, and artisans of the city, who were generally more radical than the Convention. They were called the **sansculottes**, "without breeches," because the men wore long trousers rather than the knee breeches of the middle and aristocratic classes. In June 1793, the Commune invaded the National Convention and forced the arrest of thirty-one Girondins on charges of treason, leaving the more radical Montagnards in control.

To govern in the midst of the combined international and civil warfare, the Convention created a Committee of Public Safety, which launched a Reign of Terror against "counter-revolutionaries." It executed about 40,000 people between mid-1793 and mid-1794. At Nantes, in the Vendée region of western France, the center of the royalist counter-revolution, the Committee intentionally drowned 2000 people. To wage war abroad it instituted a *levée en masse*, or national military draft, which raised an unprecedented army of 800,000 men, and mobilized the economic resources of France to support it.

The Committee intensified the campaign against feudal privilege, rejecting the payment of compensation to the manor lords, who lost their special rights over their tenants. It promoted instruction in practical farming and craft production, spoke of introducing universal elementary education, and abolished slavery throughout France's colonies. It introduced a new calendar, counting Year 1 from the founding of the French Republic in 1793, giving new names to the twelve months, and dividing each

SOURCE

Olympe de Gouges, "The Rights of Women"

Writing under the pen name Olympe de Gouges, Marie Gouze (1748–93) directly appropriated the language of the Revolution's Declaration of the Rights of Man and the Citizen *(1789). Her* Declaration of the Rights of Woman and the Citizen *exposed its lack of concern for the rights of women:*

> Article I. Woman is born free and remains equal in rights to man. Social distinctions can be founded only on general utility …
> Article XVII. The right of property is inviolable and sacred to both sexes, jointly or separately. (Bell and Offen, pp. 105–6)

Gouges addressed this document to the French queen, Marie-Antoinette, urging her to adopt this feminist program as her own and thus win over France to the royalist cause. In 1793 the radical Jacobins in the Assembly, condemning Gouges for both royalism and feminism, had her guillotined.

Jacobins A French revolutionary party founded in 1789. It later became the most radical party of the Revolution, responsible for implementing the Reign of Terror and the execution of the king (1793).

Girondins A French revolutionary group formed largely from the middle classes, many of them originally from the Gironde region.

Montagnards Members of a radical French revolutionary party, closely associated with the Jacobins and supported by the artisans, shopkeepers, and sansculottes. They opposed the more moderate Girondins.

sansculottes (French: "without knee-breeches") In the French Revolution, members of the militant, generally poorer classes of Paris, so-called because they wore trousers rather than the knee-breeches of affluent society.

The women of Les Halles taking Louis XVI from Versailles, 1789. Engraving. The illustration on page 542 shows the women setting out for Versailles, angry, determined, struggling. Here they return in triumph with their quarry. Contemporary cartoons and engravings told the story of the Revolution as it unfolded. (*Bibliothèque Nationale, Paris*)

month into three weeks of ten days each. The most important leader of the Committee, Maximilien Robespierre (1758–94), introduced in 1794 the Worship of the Supreme Being, a kind of civic religious ritual that alienated the Catholic majority in France.

By July 1794, however, French armies were winning wars against the other European powers, and the domestic economy seemed to be recovering. The members of the Convention, partly out of fear for their own lives, managed to end both the mob-inspired violence and the official Terror. The Convention outlawed and guillotined Robespierre. It relaxed price controls and, when working-class mobs threatened the Convention, called in the troops and suppressed the revolt. In 1795 it instituted yet another constitution, this time calling for a three-stage election of a representative government. Almost all adult males could vote for electors who, in turn, chose a

HOW DO WE KNOW?

The Historiography of the French Revolution

The study of the French Revolution remains the pre-eminent subject of French historiography, producing a seemingly endless variety of interpretations. Three approaches, however, have predominated. The first emphasizes the importance of ideas, stressing the *philosophes* as the precursors of revolution. This interpretation tends to focus on the first three months of the revolution and the significance of the "Declaration of the Rights of Man and the Citizen." R.R. Palmer's The Age of the Democratic Revolution (1959), for example, favors this reading. A second interpretation stresses the significance of class interests in the revolution, and tends to highlight the next chronological stage, as urban workers and rural peasantry escalated their protests and demonstrations. Georges Lefebvre's The Coming of the French Revolution (1939) represents this

position. A more recent interpretation (influenced by literary theory) speaks of the revolution as "discourse," an interplay of ideas and interest groups that constantly shifts, or "skids," as events unfold. As the direction of the revolution changed irrevocably with each new event—for example, the execution of Louis XVI—ideas were reassessed and classes reshuffled themselves into new alignments. François Furet's Interpreting the French Revolution (1978) is the leading statement of this point of view. Our narrative incorporates elements of all three interpretive perspectives.

There is a broader issue, too. Historians sometimes envision events as part of a long sweep of related trends. Sometimes they see them as contingencies, occurring because of circumstances that are unique and unpredictable. The French Revolution presents both aspects. On the one hand, it was an outgrowth of larger trends, the ideals of the *philosophes* and the legacies

of the British and American revolutions. On the other hand, specific events unfolded day-by-day in quite unpredictable ways; had they turned out differently—for example, had the one vote majority to guillotine the king been reversed—the outcome of the revolution might have been quite different. To understand the French Revolution, both these perspectives—the grand sweep and the contingency—are necessary.

- In your own understanding of historical change, which do you think counts for more, the ideas or interests? Why?
- In the French Revolution, what is the evidence for the importance of ideas? For the importance of interests?
- In your own understanding of historical change, which do you think counts for more, the grand sweep or contingency? Give an example from one of the revolutions other than the French Revolution that illustrates your point of view.

national legislative assembly composed of men who did have to meet property qualifications and who, in turn, chose an executive of five Directors. When the 1795 elections were threatened by insurrection, the Convention called upon General Napoleon Bonaparte (1769–1821) to protect the process.

The Directory, as the executive body was called, governed from 1795 to 1799. With the execution of the monarch, the manorial system and the privileges of the nobility and clergy had come to an end, and the Directory ratified the new peasant and commercial landowners in the possession of their new property. However, the Directory itself was unpopular and unstable, and the greater freedom benefited its opponents while at the same time enabling the Catholic Church to make a strong comeback. The elections of Directors in 1797, 1798, and 1799 were disputed, and on each occasion army officers were called in to dismiss the Directors, until, in 1799, Bonaparte, acting with the Abbé Sieyès, staged a *coup d'état* and had himself appointed First Consul. In 1802 his position was upgraded to consul for life and, in 1804, to emperor. Losing the right of free elections, France itself became a (benevolent) despotism. The process that historians usually call the French Revolution was over.

Napoleon in Power, 1799–1812

As head of government, Napoleon consolidated and even expanded many of the innovations of the revolution. To maintain the equality of classes and to systematize the administration of justice, he codified the laws of France. The Code Napoléon or Civil Code, which was issued in 1804, pressed for equality before the law and the principle of a "career open to talents," that is, all people should have access to professional advancement according to their ability, rather than by birth or social status. Uniform codes of criminal, commercial, and penal law were also introduced. The administration was organized into a smoothly functioning service throughout France.

Fearing a counter-revolution led by the Church, Napoleon reached a **concordat** with the pope. The French government continued to hold the former church lands, but agreed in exchange to pay the salaries of the clergy (including Protestants and others) and to allow the pope to regain authority over the appointment and discipline of Roman Catholic clergy. Protestants, dissenters, Jews, and others were reaffirmed in full citizenship, with all the rights and obligations that such status entailed, as long as they swore their allegiance to the state. In many conquered cities, including Rome and Frankfurt, French armies pulled down the ghetto walls that for centuries had segregated Jews. The government hired a large bureaucracy to administer the state. It selected personnel mostly on the revolutionary principle of a "career open to talent," hiring the best-qualified personnel rather than those with personal or hereditary connections.

This openness of opportunity suited Napoleon very well. He had come from Corsica, of a modest

Concordat A public agreement, subject to international law, between the pope as head of the Roman Catholic Church and a temporal ruler regulating the status, rights, and liberties of the Church within the country concerned.

Napoleon Crossing the Alps by Jacques-Louis David, c. 1800. Having chronicled the revolution with his brush, David became Napoleon's official painter. The heroic style of the portrait projects the Emperor's enormous confidence as he heads for military glory in the Italian campaigns of 1796–7. The truth of the journey was rather different: Napoleon crossed the Alps on a docile but footsure mule, not a fiery stallion. (*Palace of Versailles, near Paris*)

The empire of Napoleon. Napoleon, fired by revolutionary zeal, fought brilliantly to bring much of Europe under his dominion, often installing relatives as rulers. Napoleonic institutions were introduced to Italy, the Low Countries, Germany, and then Poland by force of arms. By 1812 Napoleon seemed invincible, but Britain's strength at sea and Napoleon's disastrous losses on land in his invasion of Russia (1812) led to his downfall.

family, and made his mark as a military officer. He had no respect for unearned authority. Nor was he formally religious. He earned his power through his military, administrative, and leadership skills. In a striking exception to the good principle of advancement by merit, however, Napoleon appointed his brothers as kings of Spain, Holland, and Westphalia, his brother-in-law as king of Naples, and his stepson as viceroy of the kingdom of Italy. He himself continued to lead the forces of France in military victories over the powers of Europe.

The Napoleonic Wars and the Spread of Revolution, 1799–1812

As a son of the revolution, Napoleon sought to spread its principles by force of arms. By 1810 he had conquered or entered into alliances with all the major powers and regions of Europe except Portugal, the Ottoman-held Balkans, and Britain. In each conquered state, Napoleon introduced the principal legal and administrative reforms of the revolution: an end to feudal privilege, equality of rights, religious toleration, codified law, free trade, and efficient and systematic administration, including statistical accounting, registration of documents, and the use of the metric system. In many areas of Europe, Napoleon was welcomed for the reforms he brought.

There were, however, flaws in Napoleon's policies, and they finally brought his rule to an end. First, Napoleon attempted to conquer Britain, and ultimately the naval power of that island nation and the land forces of its allies, especially those of Russia, proved too strong. Napoleon could not break the British hold on continental shipping and he was defeated at sea by Lord Nelson at the Battle of Trafalgar in 1805. When the Russian emperor supported Britain, Napoleon invaded Russia in 1812 and mired his army irretrievably in the vastness of that country during the bitterness of its winter. During that campaign, 400,000 of Napoleon's troops died from battle, starvation, and exposure; another 100,000 were captured.

Finally, the nations Napoleon conquered began to experience the stirrings of nationalism and the desire to rule themselves. Haiti, which had achieved virtual independence in the 1790s, resisted Napoleon's attempt to re-impose French rule and re-institute slavery in the island. Some 50,000 French troops perished in Haiti, most by diseases such as yellow fever, but many at the hands of revolutionary slaves. European peoples, too, did not want their countries to be colonies of France. By 1813 Napoleon had been defeated by his disastrous losses in Russia and by a coalition of European armies; the French were driven back to their borders. In 1814 Napoleon abdicated and Louis XVIII (r. 1814–15; 1815–24) assumed the throne of France. Napoleon escaped from exile on the Mediterranean island of Elba only to be defeated and exiled again in 1815, this time to St. Helena in the South Atlantic. The Napoleonic era was over. The Congress of Vienna, an assembly of representatives of all the powers of Europe, led by the most influential states, concluded diplomatic agreements that established a **balance of power** among them and redrew the post-war map of Europe. Political conservatism enveloped France and Europe for a generation.

HAITI: SLAVE REVOLUTION AND THE OVERTHROW OF COLONIALISM, 1791–1804

The formal philosophy and rhetoric of enlightenment and revolution proclaimed the natural desire of all humans to be free, and in the slave plantations of the Caribbean local slave revolts were common, feared, and ruthlessly suppressed. In the western sector of the island of Hispaniola in the colony of Saint-Domingue (modern Haiti), French planters had established one of the most brutal of the slave plantation systems. By 1791, 500,000 black slaves formed the overwhelming majority of the population, with 40,000 whites, many of them owners of plantations and slaves, and 30,000 free people of color, both **mulatto** and black. For decades, the slaves had escaped psychologically and culturally through the practice of **vodoun** (voodoo), a religion that blended the Catholicism of their masters with religious practices brought from Africa. Physically, they had escaped through **maroonage**, flight from the plantations to the surrounding hills. Sometimes the

balance of power In international relations, a policy that aims to secure peace by preventing any one state or alignment of states from becoming too dominant. Alliances are formed in order to build up a force equal or superior to that of the potential enemy.

mulatto In the Americas, a person of mixed race, usually with parents of European and African origin.

vodoun The popular religious cult of Haiti, as well as other areas of the Caribbean. It combines ritual elements from Roman Catholicism with theological and magical elements of West African origin.

maroonage The condition of some escaped slaves in the West Indian islands in the early eighteenth century. Following their successful escape, they sometimes established communities in inaccessible mountainous regions or forests.

The revolution in Haiti. One of the most dramatic revolutions occurred on the Caribbean island of Hispaniola. A slave revolt in 1791 in the French region, Saint-Domingue, spread rapidly, briefly penetrating and uniting with the Spanish sector, Santo Domingo. Despite interventions by French and British forces, and the incarceration and exile of its leader, Toussaint L'Ouverture, in 1802, Haiti gained its independence from France in 1804, the first successful slave revolt in history.

French lithograph of Pierre Dominique Toussaint L'Ouverture, early nineteenth century. The colony of Saint-Domingue (present-day Haiti) in the West Indies had made a fortune for the French through sugar plantations worked by African slaves. In the 1790s, under the leadership of Toussaint L'Ouverture, it became the site of a slave revolution that eventually led to independence. The former slave acquired his surname because of the ferocity with which he made an opening ("ouverture") in the enemy ranks.

econometrics The use of statistical techniques and mathematical models to analyze economic relationships. Econometrics may be applied by a government or private business to test the validity of an economic theory or to forecast future trends.

escaped slaves, maroons, established their own colonies. In the 1750s one of the maroons, François Makandal, built among the maroon colonies a network of resistance to slavery. Inspired to independence by vodoun beliefs and using poison to attack individual plantation owners, Makandal apparently planned to poison the water supply of Le Cap, the main town of northern Saint-Domingue, but he was captured and burned at the stake in 1758.

The Slave Revolt

In 1791, slave revolts broke out across Saint-Domingue. The inspiration seems to have been the natural desire for freedom, perhaps abetted by news of the American and French revolutions. One of the earliest rallying cries, delivered by the poet Boukman Dutty in Haitian–French patois, *"Coute la liberté li pale nan coeur nous tous"*—"Listen to the voice of liberty which speaks in the hearts of all of us," implied no knowledge of the European and American revolutions.

The revolt spread. From guerrilla warfare by maroon bands, it grew to general armed struggle and civil warfare. In the western part of Saint-Domingue, white planters welcomed the support of British troops who came as allies to suppress the slave revolt and also to drive out the French. The mulattoes—those of mixed race parentage—were free people, and some of them owned slaves. They now sought their own rights of representation and were divided over the issue of slavery. In the eastern part of Saint-Domingue, a new leader, Toussaint L'Ouverture (*c.* 1743–1803), a freed black, established an alliance with the Spanish rulers against both the slave system in Saint-Domingue (but not in the Spanish part of the island) and the French. Toussaint incorporated the rhetoric of the French Revolution into his own. In 1794, under Robespierre, the French National Assembly abolished slavery in all French colonies. In response, Toussaint linked himself to France as he continued his war against slaveowners, who were now aligned with the British and who resisted the new French decree. By May 1800 Toussaint had become the effective ruler of Saint-Domingue.

The Anti-Imperial Revolt

When Napoleon came to power in 1799 he reversed French policy on slavery. He dispatched 20,000 French troops to recapture the island and to reinstitute slavery as he had done in Guadeloupe in 1802. Napoleon's representative deceived Toussaint into suspending his revolution. Toussaint was imprisoned in 1802 and exiled to France, where he died the next year. Nevertheless, unified black and mulatto armies, now under many different cooperating leaders, continued the struggle against France, drove out its forces, and, once again, abolished slavery. As many as 50,000 French troops died of yellow fever, and thousands more became military casualties. On January 1, 1804, Saint-Domingue at last proclaimed its independence and its new name of Haiti, the Carib name for mountain. This completed the only known successful slave revolution in history.

THE ABOLITION OF SLAVERY AND THE SLAVE TRADE

Initially, the British tried to assist in putting down the slave rebellion in Haiti. When they failed, their subsequent decision to limit the spread of slavery by abolishing the

HOW DO WE KNOW?

Abolition: Historians Debate the Causes

Why were the slave trade, and then slavery itself, abolished in the Atlantic countries? To what extent was the spread of democratic revolution responsible? Analyses differ. Historians who emphasize the significance of the Haitian Revolution, as C.L.R. James and David Nicholls do, stress the fear that the uprising of the slaves engendered among slave owners. In the lands of the Caribbean, including northeastern Brazil, black slaves working the high-mortality plantations formed up to 90 percent of the population. Local rebellions already occurred frequently, and large-scale revolution now appeared as a real possibility. The abolition of the slave trade provided some limit on the size of the slave population, although total abolition—a much more expensive act for the slave owners—would come only later.

A second school of thought, shared by historians such as David Brion Davis and Orlando Patterson, stresses the importance of compassion as a motive. Davis emphasizes the increasing influence of humanitarian sentiment in European Christian thought from the seventeenth century:

The philosophy of benevolence was a product of the seventeenth century, when certain British Protestants, shaken by theological controversy and the implications of modern science, looked increasingly to human nature and conduct as a basis for faith. In their impatience with theological dogma, their distaste for the doctrine of original sin, their appreciation for human feeling and sentiment, and their confidence in man's capacity for moral improvement, these Latitudinarians, as they were called, anticipated the main concerns of the Enlightenment, and laid an indispensable foundation for social reform. (pp. 348–49)

The emphasis on compassion increased in reaction against the growing scale and unprecedented cruelty of slavery in the New World. Among Christian groups opposing slavery, Quakers and Methodists stood out. The birth and growth of both these denominations—Quakerism under the leadership of George Fox (1624–91) and Methodism under John Wesley (1703–91)—were contemporary with the development of mass slavery in the Americas. Other branches of Christianity had long since made peace with the institution of slavery, contenting themselves with promising a gentler existence in life after death. Quakers and Methodists, however, had to confront the reality of slavery for the first time in one of its cruelest, New World, forms. In Britain, William Wilberforce (1759–1833), a philanthropist and member of the Clapham Sect—a group of well-to-do Evangelicals—played a major part in the antislavery movement. As a Member of Parliament, he led the campaign to abolish the slave trade and to emancipate existing slaves.

The philosophes argued a third, similar but more intellectual position against slavery. They argued that slavery violated the law of nature; it was inconsistent with the nature of humankind. Montesquieu (1689–1755), in his assessments of the nature of laws and government, argued that "the call for slavery was the call of the wealthy and the decadent, not for the general welfare of mankind".

Finally, an economic critique began to develop in the eighteenth century. Slavery was not profitable to the society, certainly not to the slave, and not to the development of a more productive economy in the long run. In The Wealth of Nations Adam Smith argued that slavery, like all examples of monopoly and special privilege, inhibited economic growth. Lacking the opportunity to acquire wealth and property for himself, the slave would find it in his interest to work as little as possible. Slave owners advocated their system not so much for its economic benefits but for the power it gave them over others, despite economic losses. The leading exponents of this rationale for abolition in recent times have been Marxists, led by Eric Williams in his classic Capitalism and Slavery (1944). Many economic historians disagreed with this analysis, most notably Robert Fogel and Stanley Engerman, who published Time on the Cross in 1974, an elaborate two-volume statistical study linking economics with statistics (**econometrics**) to show the profitability of slavery. Historian Seymour Drescher arguing bluntly (1977) that abolition was "econocide," economic disaster, for Britain. Drescher sided with the humanitarian assessment: abolition was implemented despite its economic costs.

What to do without slaves? The successor system to slavery was not free labor. Indentured labor, supplied in large part by vast contract immigration from India and China, filled the labor needs of the post-slavery Caribbean as well as those of new plantation economies in the Indian Ocean in Fiji, Mauritius, and Réunion, and in south and east Africa. Although not quite slaves, indentured servants traded many of their basic economic and political rights for a number of years in exchange for their livelihood.

Finally, with the export of slave labor from Africa banned, European entrepreneurs began in the later 1800s to explore the possibilities of shifting the production of primary products to Africa itself and to employ on-site personnel to perform the necessary work. Although this system sounded like free labor, in fact the wages were so low and conditions so abysmal, that many observers saw these economic initiatives as a newer form of slavery transplanted back to Africa.

- What evidence have we seen in this chapter that the Haitian revolution played an important part in the abolition of slavery?
- What evidence do you have from this chapter, and from other studies, that would support the importance of humanitarianism in the abolition of slavery? What evidence do you have for the importance of economics?
- What is the difference between slavery and indentured labor?

slave trade in 1807 reflected, in part, their fear of further revolts. In 1833 Britain abolished slavery throughout its Empire, although "freed" slaves were required to work for their former masters for a period of time to compensate them for their loss of "property." The United States, a slave-holding country, feared that the Haitian slave revolt might spread northward and prohibited all trade with Haiti in 1806. In 1808, following Britain's lead, America outlawed participation in the international slave trade, although it abolished internal slavery only with the Civil War (1861–5). It recognized Haiti as an independent country also during that war, in 1862. Slavery was not the only issue at stake in the United States' Civil War, but each of the other issues was linked to it. Would the United States follow the model of the Northern states and become an urban, free-labor, industrial nation, or follow the Southern pattern with its rural, slave-holding plantation economy? As the North grew more populous and wealthier, the South began to feel itself an internal colony within the United States and grew increasingly resentful and rebellious. An even more central question was states' rights: Did individual states have the right to secede from the Union? The question arose primarily because the slave-holding Southern states preferred secession rather than face the possibility of abolition. When Abraham Lincoln was elected President in 1860, they feared the worst and began to secede. Lincoln, a man who would have preferred peace, recognized that to preserve the Union he would have to go to war. The American Civil War saw more than one-half million dead, the bloodiest war in the history of the country. In the midst of the war, in 1863, Lincoln issued the Emancipation Proclamation, declaring free all slaves in areas that had seceded and were fighting against the Union. In 1865, after the Union victory and Lincoln's assassination, the Thirteenth Amendment to the Constitution officially abolished slavery throughout the country. No compensation was paid. As a class, the Southern slave owners were ruined. Their way of life was finished. Elsewhere, however, the Atlantic slave trade continued at about three-quarters of its highest volume. That trade did not end effectively until slavery was abolished in 1876 in Puerto Rico, in 1886 in Cuba, and in 1888 in Brazil.

THE END OF COLONIALISM IN LATIN AMERICA: INDEPENDENCE AND DISILLUSIONMENT, 1810–30

Independence Movements

In the period 1810 to 1826 virtually all the countries of Latin America expelled their European colonial rulers and established their independence. Latin Americans drew inspiration from the intellectual and political legacies of the American, French, and Haitian revolutions, although few wanted to move so far toward democratic rights as the Europeans had done, and many were frightened by the events in Haiti.

The revolts of the early nineteenth century were led, for the most part, by creole elites, American-born direct descendants of Spanish settlers. These leaders wanted more economic and political rights for themselves, especially after Napoleon occupied Spain and installed his relatives on the Spanish throne. A series of earlier revolts, however, had been led by Amerindians and mestizos. In 1780, in Cuzco, Peru, Tupac Amaru, a mestizo with Inca ancestors, led 70,000 rebels against Spanish rule. Creoles did not join in this revolt and Tupac Amaru was captured and executed in 1783. The entire revolt was brutally crushed. The Comunero Revolt in Colombia in 1781 drove the viceroy from Bogotá but ended with only some concessions by the Spanish and internal fighting among the rebels. Mulattoes led a revolt in Bahia, Brazil, in 1798. At the time of all these revolts, Spain and Portugal were still independent, powerful countries and, with the aid of creoles and **mazombos** (American-born direct descendants of Portuguese settlers), they suppressed the revolts. In general, the creoles and *mazombos*

mazombo A direct descendant of Portuguese settlers in the Americas.

saw their fate linked more to the Spanish and Portuguese rulers than to the Amerindians or to those of mixed parentage. The Napoleonic wars in Spain, however, gave the colonies the opportunity to declare their independence, with the creoles leading the way. The revolts were bloody and successful.

In virtually every revolt, leadership was provided by a creole elite, most of whom feared the potential power of the Amerindian, mestizo, mulatto, and African majority. Such men as Father Miguel Hidalgo (1753–1811) in Mexico, Simón Bolívar (1783–1830; in northern South America, and José de San Martín (1778–1850) in southern South America, were all creoles, as were their leading generals, administrators, and supporters. They were familiar with European traditions and events, and many of them had studied in Europe. Indeed, many of the revolutions seemed to be fought for the benefit of the creoles, who actually formed less than 5 percent of the total population. Believing their own livelihood depended on low-paid and slave labor, these elites were determined to preserve the old system without Spanish and Portuguese domi-

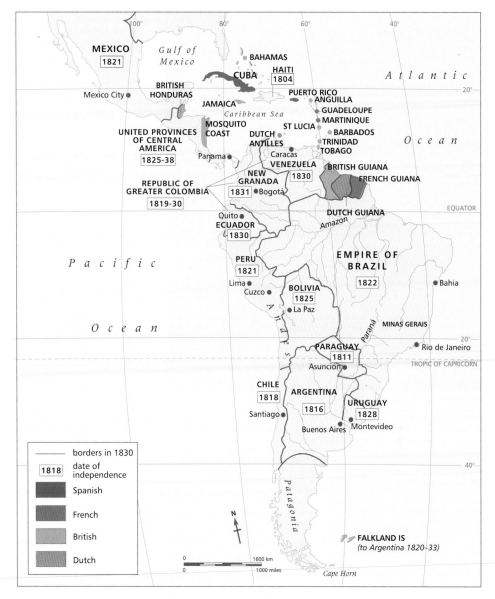

nance. Other Latin Americans, mestizos and Amerindians, gained little. On the Caribbean islands of Cuba and Puerto Rico there were no rebellions. Here the elites, frightened lest the slave revolt of Haiti be repeated on their own islands, remained loyal to Spain.

After Independence

The continent—except for Portuguese Brazil—was wrested from Spain by the sword. The greatest of the revolutionary leaders—Simón Bolívar of Venezuela in the north, José de San Martín of Argentina in the south, Antonio José de Sucré of Ecuador, and Bernardo O'Higgins of Chile—combined military excellence with intellectual, administrative, and diplomatic accomplishments.

Simón Bolívar and the Challenge of Unification. As soldier, diplomat, general, administrator, visionary, newspaper publisher, law giver, national president, dictator, lover,

Liberation movements in Latin America. The collapse of Iberian rule in Latin America was virtually complete by 1826. Sustained campaigns by Simón Bolívar and Antonio José de Sucre demolished Spanish control of Venezuela, Colombia, and Peru while, from the south, José de San Martin led the Argentine and Chilean Army of the Andes north to Lima. Liberation brought many internal power struggles and divisions, leaving the present-day South American map with an array of some twenty republics.

Antonio Salas (attrib.), *Simón Bolívar*, 1825. Bolívar was the most important military leader of the Latin American revolution. Despite a life of extraordinary adventure and accomplishment, he failed to bring about the unification of South America that he so passionately desired.

and disillusioned revolutionary, Simón Bolívar dominated public life in Latin America for most of two decades, from 1810 until his death in 1830. Son of a Venezuelen creole aristocrat, Bolívar studied in Europe from age sixteen to nineteen, primarily in Spain. On return to Caracas, his chosen bride died in their first year together, and Bolívar vowed to devote his life to politics. He returned to Europe for travel and continued study of the *philosophes*. Returning to Venezuela in 1807, he joined in the movements for independence that swept the region, especially after Napoleon's troops invaded Spain, undercutting Spanish authority and power in the Americas.

In many of his early efforts he failed. Assigned to diplomatic duty in England, he was unable to gain recognition and material support for the Venezuelan revolution. In 1811, when Venezuela lost its independence within a year of declaring it, he was serving as an army officer. In 1813 he captured Caracas and reasserted Venezuelan independence, but he was defeated and exiled in 1814. In defeat, however, he wrote visionary documents. His *Manifesto of Cartagena*, 1812, was a rallying cry for revolutionary forces to continue the struggle against Spain. His *Letter from Jamaica* of September 1815, written in exile, underlined not only Latin America's political suppression, but also its economic servitude.

Bolívar renewed his military expeditions and began to earn fabulous success, especially after he got monetary and military support from Haiti and Britain in return for freeing South American slaves. In 1819 his forces defeated the Spanish and established the Republic of Colombia with himself as president and military dictator. Within two more years they liberated Venezuela and Ecuador, filling out the borders of the federation. In Quito, Ecuador, he met Manuela Saenz, who left her husband to join Bolívar and remain by his side to the last day of his life, despite his numerous affairs and the public scandal of their own relationship.

As Bolívar made conquests from the north, various movements began their struggles for independence from the region of Rio Plate, now Argentina. One of the leaders who has emerged as one of the great military strategists of history was José San Martín. He put together a massive Army of the Andes and promised freedom to slaves who joined his forces. He later claimed they were his best soldiers. Bringing together former slaves and soldiers, he crossed the high Andes mountains with mules and llamas, successfully defeating the Spaniards in Chile and mounting attacks on Peru. He refused to rule over Chile in favor of Bernardo O'Higgins, the creole leader there, but he couldn't effectively take Peru. Ultimately, he met with Bolívar in Guayaquil, Ecuador, in 1822. No one really knows what they discussed, but after the meeting, San Martín retired to France, leaving the conquest of South America to Bolívar.

By 1825, through brilliant military action Bolívar captured Peru and Upper Peru, later named Bolivia in his honor, and became president of both.

Just as his dreams of a single united region seemed to reach fruition, however, they dissolved in warfare among his generals, who now fought for the independence of each of the constituent units. Bolívar tried to hold the federation together through dictatorial rulings, but his high-handedness further alienated his former supporters and he narrowly escaped an assassination attempt in 1828 as Manuela Saenz covered his exit. Bolívar withdrew from political leadership in 1830. A few months later he died in the agony of tuberculosis, indebted and disillusioned.

"Gran Colombia" dissolved into Colombia, Venezuela, and Ecuador. Further south, the Spanish viceroyalty of La Plata dissolved into Argentina, Paraguay, Uruguay, and Bolivia. For a decade, 1829–39, under General Andrés Santa Cruz, a mestizo, Peru and Bolivia were united, but then broke apart, to the relief of some of their neighbors. Chile, isolated by the Andes to its east, and open to the outside world via the Pacific Ocean to its west, also became a separate, independent nation. In total, eighteen nations emerged from Spanish America.

Warfare among many of the new states and the violent repression of the Indian and African-American populations (one-fourth of Brazil's population in 1850 were slaves) gave prominence and power both to national armies and to private military forces throughout Latin America. The military strongmen, or *caudillos*, came to control local areas and even national governments. Personal rule, only minimally controlled by official codes of law and formal election procedures, prevailed in many countries up to the late twentieth century. (See Pablo Neruda's epic history of Latin America in verse, p. 555.)

Mexico. Father Miguel Hidalgo led the first wave of Mexico's revolt until he was executed in 1811. Father José María Morelos (1765–1815) then took command of the revolutionary movement. Morelos sought to displace the Spanish and creole elites, to abolish slavery, and, unlike Hidalgo, to revoke the special privileges and landholdings of the Church. The early Mexican independence movement differed from that in South America because of its attack on creole elites, itself inspired by the incipient "liberation theology" of the priests Hidalgo and Morelos. Close to their parishioners, they understood that peasant poverty was a product of Spanish and creole rule. The Spanish captured and executed Morelos in 1815. By the time Mexico won its independence in 1821, its revolution was controlled by its most conservative creole elite. For two years Mexico was ruled as a monarchy, but in 1823 it was proclaimed a republic. Military leaders, businessmen, and foreign powers all struggled for control, and Mexico remained unstable for decades. Its size was also reduced by half. Central American regions, after years of rebellions, broke away from Mexico and formed a union; it dissolved in internal regional antagonisms in 1838. Texas, with waves of immigrants entering from the United States, and encouraged by the United States government, declared its independence from Mexico in 1836. Nine years later the United States annexed Texas, precipitating the Mexican–American war. In the peace settlement, America gained the territories of its current southwestern States.

Brazil. Brazil, the largest country in Latin America in terms of both geography and population, had a different method of achieving independence, and this helps to explain why it did not break apart after independence. When Napoleon invaded Portugal in 1807, the Portuguese royal family, assisted by Britain, fled to Rio de Janeiro and ruled the Portuguese Empire from the Brazilian capital for thirteen years. King Dom João (John) VI (r. 1816–26) raised Brazil's legal status to equal that of Portugal and expanded Rio as a center of trade, administration, education, and cultural institutions.

In 1821 João returned with his court to Lisbon, but left his son and heir, Prince Pedro, in Rio. When the Parliament, or Cortes, in Lisbon attempted to cut Brazil and Rio back to size, the American-born Brazilian elite, the *mazombos*, counseled defiance. In 1822 Pedro declared Brazil independent, and Portugal did little to stop

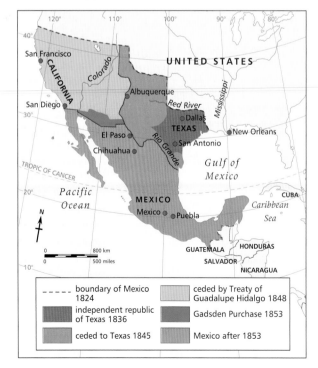

Mexico, 1824–53. In 1821 the Viceroyalty of New Spain, with its capital in Mexico City, won its independence from Spain. By 1823, the Central American countries seceded, leaving Mexico with its current southern border. Then, piece by piece, the northern areas were lost to the United States: Texas through secession from Mexico (1836) and annexation by the US (1845); some territories through warfare (1846–48); and some through purchase (1853).

Jean-Baptiste Debret, *Early Evening Refreshment in the Praca do Palaccio, Rio de Janeiro*, 1835. Lithograph. The port and capital city of Rio has long been famous for its fun-loving life and for a modicum of racial integration. But Brazil did not abolish slavery until 1888. All three of these elements are suggested in this 1835 lithograph. (*Bibliothèque Nationale, Paris*)

the move. Pedro was soon crowned "Constitutional Emperor and Perpetual Defender of Brazil," but the effective rulers of Brazil were its *mazombo* elites. Brazil was thus spared the warfare and disintegration characteristic of Spanish Latin America, but it was ruled by similar American-born descendants of Iberian families. While the former Spanish colonies became republics, Brazil became a monarchy under a member of the Portuguese royal family.

Paraguay: The New Historiography. Tiny landlocked Paraguay, with a population of 150,000, declared its independence in 1810–11 from the viceroyalty of La Plata as well as from Spain and defeated an Argentine army that had been sent to subdue it. Its dictator, José Gaspar Rodríguez de Francia, who governed until his death in 1840, has been characterized negatively by historians of several nations, including his own, but more recent revisionist studies by historians such as Richard Alan White portray Francia as a revolutionary who led his country to a period of exemplary economic and cultural independence. They suggest that Francia's negative evaluations resulted from his harsh treatment of creole elites and from his autocratic policies, but that his concern for economic development helped the Amerindians of Paraguay by keeping them isolated from exploitative world markets.

Paraguay based its revolution on self-government and land redistribution. For a half century, rulers redistributed lands of the government, the Church, and private large-scale landowners to the masses of mestizo and Indian cultivators. Paraguay became self-sufficient in food production. The government established a simple but effective education system that virtually eliminated illiteracy. The state established iron works, textile mills, and livestock industries. It did not accept foreign investment or entanglement. Paraguay's achievements in political independence, economic growth, self-reliance, and raising the standards of its native and mestizo populations, engendered envy in its neighbors and apprehension among foreign financiers.

From 1865 to 1870 Argentina, Brazil, and Uruguay, backed by loans from Britain, fought against Paraguay to destroy its populist policies. After the invaders won, they killed off the majority of Paraguay's adult male population, dismantled its political institutions, and opened its economy to foreign investment and control. Paraguay's unique experiment was over.

Religious and Economic Issues

Many of the new nations of Latin America wished to increase their own power by breaking the authority and wealth of the Catholic Church. Many confiscated church lands, refused the official collection of tithes to fund the Church, demanded a voice in the selection of clergy, and limited church control over educational facilities. To some degree, these crusades against church power reflected also Indian advocacy for a greater appreciation of indigenous cultures, both outside of Christianity and in syncretic movements to join Christian practices to existing indigenous beliefs and rituals. Mexico, which had a large Indian and mestizo population, was most eager to limit church power, and its continuing struggles were the bloodiest. Over time, in each country, individual accommodations were made between Church and state, and to this day they continue to renegotiate their positions.

Economically, until at least 1870, Latin America remained overwhelmingly agrarian, with the hacienda, a kind of feudal estate, continuing as the principal institution for organizing production and labor. The vast majority of the hacienda owners were creole, while the workers were overwhelmingly Indian and mestizo. Many Indians

SOURCE

An Epic Verse History of Latin America

In many parts of the world, historical traditions are kept alive not only in formal historical writing, but also in the arts, music, and poetry. Some of Latin America's most distinguished authors work in this tradition. The Chilean writer Pablo Neruda (1904–73), a recipient of the Nobel Prize for Literature in 1971, advanced a critical and disillusioned vision of Latin America in its first century of independence. In Canto General *(1950), Neruda's epic poem of Latin American history, he paints the Spanish settlement of the land as a harsh and tawdry process.*

The land passed between the entailed estates,
doubloon to doubloon, dispossessed,
paste of apparitions and convents
until the entire blue geography was
divided into haciendas and encomiendas.
The mestizo's ulcer, the overseer's
and slaver's whip
moved through the lifeless space.
The Creole was an impoverished specter
who picked up the crumbs,
until he saved enough
to acquire a little title
painted with gilt letters.
And in the dark carnival
he masqueraded as a count
a proud man among beggars,
with his little silver cane ...

The conquistadors of the sixteenth century had been expelled by the libertadors of the early nineteenth century, but the infrastructure of shopkeepers, clergy, administrators, and hangers-on that had become established in Latin America remained in place as the real inheritors of the revolution. Neruda scowled:

Soon, undershirt by undershirt,
they expelled the conquistador
and established the conquest
of the grocery store.
Then they acquired pride
bought on the black market.
They were adjudged
haciendas, whips, slaves,
catechisms, commissaries,
alms boxes, tenements, brothels,
and all this they called
holy western culture.

Neruda singles out the petty businessmen as the new, but unworthy, elite of Latin America. In more enterprising regions bigger businessmen and investors occupied the leadership positions. These men of practical affairs combined with craftsmen on the one hand, and with government policy makers on the other, to introduce limited industrial development in the twentieth century (see Chapter 23).

remained in villages, where their participation in any larger, external, national economy was marginal. Since ancestry counted so profoundly for each group, the ethnic and racial composition of the population, whether native-born or foreign-born, whether Indian, African, *mestizo*, or Caucasian, in large measure determined the fate and the culture of each colony.

As production for foreign markets increased, new forms of foreign domination, **neo-colonialism**, arose. The principal new power was Britain, and its method was economic investment and control. By 1824, there were 100 British commercial firms functioning in Latin America staffed by 3000 British citizens. Shipping to and from Latin America was carried primarily by British ships. Britain's economic domination of Latin American economies increased with the growing productivity and profitability of its industrial revolution at home.

In the mid-nineteenth century, Latin America was home to a mixed amalgam of philosophies and practices. From the United States and France, it inherited a legacy of revolution in the name of representative democracy and individual freedom. It inherited from Spain and Portugal a loyalty to more conservative, religious, hierarchical traditions. From Africa it inherited rich traditions of religion, food, music, and dance. From its own history of settlement it received a diverse mix of peoples from three continents, often in uneasy relationship to one another. From the international economy Latin America inherited a subordinate position, dependent on outside supply, demand, and control.

neo-colonialism The control exercised by a state or group of states of the developed world over the economies and societies of the developing world.

POLITICAL REVOLUTIONS
WHAT DIFFERENCE DO THEY MAKE?

Charles Dickens opened *A Tale of Two Cities*, his novel set against the background of the French Revolution, with the famous passage: "It was the best of times. It was the worst of times … it was the season of Light, it was the season of Darkness, it was the spring of hope, it was the winter of despair." Having examined the unfolding of this period of political revolution we can better understand Dickens' paradoxical characterization. We began with the successes of the English revolutions in establishing constitutional government. That revolution slowly expanded to include ever larger segments of the population, and to include freedom of religion among its guarantees. But that same government refused to grant the rights of Britons to its American subjects, provoking the American War for Independence. It did abolish the slave trade and slavery, but only in the early nineteenth century, and by that time, as we shall see in Chapter 17, Britain had captured extensive, non-settler colonies overseas.

The *philosophes* spoke of human perfectibility and advocated human reason. They provided rationales that inspired the American, French, and Latin American revolutions, yet many of them preferred benevolent despotism as more efficient. One of the greatest of the *philosophes*, Rousseau, has been interpreted variously as espousing a variety of government alternatives, from radical democracy to totalitarian dictatorship. And later experience would test the limits of the power of rationality in the governance of human affairs.

The War for Independence in North America freed Britain's thirteen colonies and created the United States. It introduced a limited democracy that nonetheless sanctioned attacks on Indians and permitted slavery. The most profound of all the revolutions of its time, the French Revolution, ended in class antagonism, with the monarchy restored, after much of Europe had been convulsed in more extensive warfare than it had ever seen before. Yet in the course of Napoleon's conquests, he abolished feudal privileges throughout Europe and introduced new codes of law and bureaucracies recruited on the basis of merit. Ironically, Napoleon's imperialism also provoked new nationalism among the peoples he conquered. In Haiti, in response to the slave revolt, Napoleon reversed France's stated opposition to slavery, and lost tens of thousands of soldiers to battle and disease. Haiti's successful slave revolt became a successful war for independence. Wars for independence in Latin America freed that continent from direct, political control from overseas, but power was seized by creole and *mazombo* elites who lorded it over the Native American multitudes. In addition, the new nations soon fell into economic dependence on their former colonizers.

Of all these revolutions, the French Revolution's legacies are the most ambiguous. Many scholars have looked to the radical Terror as a precursor to twentieth-century totalitarianism. Other scholars, however, have examined the revolution in terms of what it accomplished rather than what it failed to do. The French Revolution ended religious discrimination, and France went much further than England in allowing worshipers of all faiths, including Jews, to become full citizens. Though Napoleon reversed the decision, the National Convention abolished slavery, making it clear that distinctions of color and race should not matter in civic life. Still others have recognized that while class antagonisms remained, the revolution established legal equality for most males, including freed slaves and Jews, who inhabited the country. Finally, the French Revolution in many ways legitimized the notion of revolution to achieve political and social change. It inspired the Russian Revolution of 1917 and the Chinese student movement, which held a revolutionary parade at Tiananmen Square, Beijing, in support of French revolutionary ideals on the bicentenary of the storming of the Bastille on July 14, 1789. In short, the ideas of the French Revolution remain a powerful inspirational force today.

Review Questions

- What is the difference between a political revolution and a simple change of political administration?
- What were the characteristics of the "Democratic Revolutions?"
- At the celebration of the 200th anniversary of the French Revolution in 1989, the Prime Minister of England remarked that the earlier British revolution had accomplished all that the French Revolution had accomplished—without the violence. Do you agree with her assessment?
- What are the differences between a revolution against a foreign colonial government, as in the revolution of the thirteen American colonies against Britain, and a revolution against an indigenous government, as in France?
- What was the importance of the Haitian Revolution?
- Why did many of the leaders of the revolutions in Latin America feel disillusioned despite their accomplishments?

Suggested Readings

PRINCIPAL SOURCES

Burns, E. Bradford and Julie Charlip. *Latin America* (Englewood Cliffs, NJ: Prentice Hall, 7th ed, 2001).

Furet, François. *Interpreting the French Revolution*, trans. by Elborg Foster (Cambridge: Cambridge University Press, 1978). A masterful summary by one of the leading experts.

Galilei, Galileo. *Discoveries and Opinions of Galileo*, trans. by Stillman Drake (New York: Anchor Books, 1957). Gallileo's own observations and statements, fresh and clear, with helpful commentary.

Hobsbawm, Eric. *The Age of Revolution 1789–1848* (New York: New American Library, 1962). A personal, magisterial, interpretive summary, from a somewhat Marxist perspective. Excellent introduction to the period and issues.

James, C.L.R., *The Black Jacobins* (New York: Random House, 1963). A stirring account of the activities and significance of the Haitian revolution.

Knight, Franklin W. "The Haitian Revolution," *American Historical Review* 105:1 (February 2000), 103–115. A review of the most recent scholarship on the revolution.

Kuhn, Thomas S. *The Copernican Revolution* (Cambridge, MA: Harvard University Press, 1957). A case study of the methods of science in working through received interpretations and developing new ones through the experiences of Copernicus.

——. *The Structure of Scientific Revolutions* (Chicago: University of Chicago Press, 3rd edn, 1996). A generalized assessment of the methods through which scientists revise and sometimes discard older theories and develop new ones.

Lefebvre, Georges. *The Coming of the French Revolution*, trans. by R.R. Palmer (Princeton: Princeton University Press, 1947). A classic Marxist interpretation of the revolution.

Nash, Gary B., *et al. The American People: Creating a Nation and a Society* (New York: Harper and Row, 5th ed. 2003). Leading textbook account.

Palmer, R.R. *The Age of Democratic Revolution* (Princeton: Princeton University Press, 1969). A lucid, standard, comprehensive interpretive account of the revolutions covered in this chapter.

Thompson, E.P. *The Making of the English Working Class* (New York: Vintage Books, 1966). Cultural as well as economic factors that inspired working people to see themselves as a class and to struggle for rights.

White, Richard Alan. *Paraguay's Autonomous Revolution, 1810–1840* (Albuquerque: University of New Mexico Press, 1978). A controversial study presenting Paraguay as attempting to create a more democratic government that is suppressed by its neighbors.

Williams, Eric. *Capitalism and Slavery* (Chapel Hill: University of North Carolina Press, 1944). Williams portrays capitalism as promoting slavery when it is in the economic interests of slave owners, and as working for abolition when these interests change.

ADDITIONAL SOURCES

Abernethy, David B. *The Dynamics of Global Dominance: European Overseas Empires, 1415–1980* (New Haven: Yale University Press, 2000). Traces and analyzes the expansion and contraction of empire, and evaluates its legacy. The writing is thoughtful, lucid, and engaging.

Andrea, Alfred and James Overfield, eds. *The Human Record*, 2 vols. (Boston: Houghton Mifflin Co., 4th ed. 2001). Excellent selection of documents and visuals.

Boorstin, Daniel. *The Discoverers* (New York: Random House, 1983). Lucid, engaging account of the work of specific scientists and explorers and their impact on events.

Cohen I., Bernard. *Revolution in Science* (Cambridge, MA: Harvard University Press, 1985). Analyzes 450 years of major scientific revolutions and their interaction with the larger society. Magisterial yet lucid.

Columbia College, Columbia University. *Contemporary Civilization in the West*, Vol. 2 (New York: Columbia University Press, 3rd ed. 1960). Outstanding sourcebook with lengthy excerpts from highly influential thinkers and actors.

Curtin, Philip. *The Rise and Fall of the Plantation Complex* (New York: Cambridge University Press, 1989). Excellent analysis of the plantation itself and its significance to world trade and politics.

Davis, David Brion. *The Problem of Slavery in the Age of Revolution, 1770–1823* (Ithaca: Cornell University Press, 1975). Analyzes the tensions between the idea of freedom and the practice of slavery.

——. "Looking at Slavery from Broader Perspectives," *American Historical Review* 105:2 (April, 2000), 452–66. Global, comprehensive review of the literature at present.

Drescher, Seymour. *Econocide* (Pittsburgh: University of Pittsburgh Press, 1977). Argues that the abolition of slavery was an economically costly decision, taken, primarily, for moral reasons.

——. *The Problem of Slavery in Western Culture* (New York: Oxford University Press, 1966). Explores the tensions between slavery and the ideals of individual freedom and democracy.

Fick, Carolyn E. *The Making of Haiti* (Knoxville: University of Tennessee Press, 1990). A recent, comprehensive, cogent account.

Fogel, Robert William and Stanley L. Engerman. *Time on the Cross*, 2 vols. (Boston: Little, Brown, 1974). A controversial, influential, assessment of the economics of slavery.

Genovese, Eugene. *From Rebellion to Revolution* (Baton Rouge: Louisiana University Press, 1979). A study of slave revolts and their significance to abolition.

Halévy, Élie. *England in 1815* (New York: Barnes and Noble, 1961). A classic account of a society successfully avoiding revolution.

Hammond Atlas of World History ed. Geoffrey Parker (Maplewood, NJ: Hammond, 5th ed. 1999).

Hanke, Lewis and Jane M. Rausch, eds. *People and Issues in Latin American History* (New York: Markus Weiner, 2nd ed. 2000). A useful reader.

Hobbes, Thomas. *Selections*, ed. Frederick J.E. Woodbridge (New York: Charles Scribner's Sons, 1958). Primary sources.

Hobsbawm, Eric. *The Age of Empire 1875–1914* (New York: Vintage Books, 1987). Excellent, comprehensive account.

Hughes, Robert. *Goya* (New York: Knopf, 2003). Thoughtful, thorough, provocative, well-illustrated interpretation of the man and his art in their time.

Kolchin, Peter. *American Slavery 1619–1877* (New York: Hill and Wang, 1993). Comprehensive treatment, even after 1865, with comparisons to slavery in other societies.

Locke, John. *Second Treatise on Government* (Arlington Heights, IL: Crofts Classics, 1982). Primary source.

McClellan III, James F. and Harold Dorn. *Science and Technology in World History* (Baltimore: Johns Hopkins University Press, 1999). Outstanding coverage of science and technology from various parts of the world.

Márquez, Gabriel García. *The General in His Labyrinth*. trans. by Edith Grossman (New York: Knopf, 1990). Fictionalized account of the end of the life of General Simón Bolívar.

Metcalf, Barbara D. and Thomas R. Metcalf. *A Concise History of India* (Cambridge: Cambridge University Press, 2002). Especially strong on issues of identity and the importance of Muslims and of women.

Nehru, Jawaharlal. *Glimpses of World History* (New Delhi: Jawaharlal Nehru Memorial Fund and Oxford University Press, ed. 1982). Nehru wrote this socialistic account of world history from jail as a series of letters to his daughter.

Neruda, Pablo. *Canto General*, trans. by Jack Schmitt (Berkeley: University of California Press, 1991). A personal, critical assessment of Latin American history in verse by a master poet.

Nicholls, David, "Haiti: Race, Slavery and Independence (1804–1825)," in Archer, ed., *Slavery*, pp. 225–38. On the relationship of slavery to race in Haiti.

Patterson, Orlando. *Freedom in the Making of Western Culture* (New York: Basic Books, 1991). Slavery and racism conflict with the promise of freedom and democracy.

Rousseau, Jean-Jacques. *The Social Contract*, trans. by Maurice Cranston (New York: Viking Penguin, 1968). Primary source.

Smith, Adam. *The Theory of Moral Sentiments* (Charlottesville, VA: Lincoln-Rembrandt Publishers, 6th ed., 1986). Primary source.

——. *The Wealth of Nations*, Books I–III (New York: Viking Penguin Classics, 1986). Primary source.

Thompson, Vincent Bakpetu. *The Making of the African Diaspora in the Americas 1441–1900* (New York: Longman, 1987). A view that transcends the experience of individual countries to see the comprehensive picture.

Tocqueville, Alexis de. *The Old Regime and the French Revolution*, trans. by Gilbert Stuart (Garden City, New York: Doubleday Anchor Books, 1955). Classic analysis that locates precipitating factors in the revolution, and indicates that many endured long afterwards.

Turner, Frederick Jackson. *The Frontier in American History* (New York; Henry Holt, 1920). Classic interpretation of the significance to America of huge, frontier spaces in the West.

Wilentz, Sean. *Chants Democratic: New York and the Rise of the American Working Class, 1788–1850* (New York: Oxford University Press, 1984). Important contribution to working-class history.

◉ World History Documents CD-ROM

THE INDUSTRIAL REVOLUTION

A GLOBAL PROCESS, 1700–1914

KEY TOPICS

- The Industrial Revolution: What Was Its Significance?
- Britain, 1700–1860
- The Second Stage of Industrialization, 1860–1914
- Social Changes: The Conditions of Working People
- Political Reaction in Britain and Europe, 1800–1914
- New Patterns of Urban Life
- The Industrial Revolution: What Difference Does It Make?

THE INDUSTRIAL REVOLUTION: WHAT WAS ITS SIGNIFICANCE?

One of the key indices of human progress has always been the improvement in the quality and quantity of the tools that we use and the ways in which we organize production. Perhaps the most advanced civilization of pre-modern times was China of the Song dynasty (960–1279). It earned its reputation not only for its neo-Confucian high culture—its painting, poetry, and classical education—but also for its agricultural progress with new crops and more efficient harvesting. It also produced armaments—including gunpowder and siege machines—government-issued paper money, commercial ships, and extensive river and canal networks, all on a massive scale. Finally, China was technically innovative, inventing the compass, making technical improvements in the production of silk, ceramics, and lacquer, and vastly expanding printing and book production. China's advances in iron production were so extensive that deforestation became a problem in parts of the north because wood was used to smelt the ores until coal took its place. The iron was used in tools, weapons, and bridge building. Other parts of the world were, by comparison, backward in trade, commerce, and industry.

The modern industrial revolution beginning in the eighteenth century marked the transformation by which western Europe, and especially Britain, caught up with and surpassed China, and the rest of the world, in economic power and productivity. In Part 5, we surveyed some of the changes that enabled regions of western Europe to emerge from their singular concentration on agriculture as the basis of their economy; to increase their concern with commerce, trade, and exploration; to develop new technologies; and to make a general commitment to financial success and the pursuit of profit. Slowly these new economic interests led to the creation of new tools: better ships, new and improved commercial instruments and organizations, such as the joint stock company, and even the adoption and adaptation of some of China's earlier inventions, including the compass, the use of gunpowder, and movable type for printing. Business people in western Europe actively sought out new economic possibilities. They pursued them with a vigor and flexibility that were sometimes admirable, as the search for new technologies, and sometimes morally reprehensible, as in the use of millions of slaves in the creation of vast sugar plantations in the Caribbean basin, and in the extraction of gold and silver from New World sources, through coerced labor, for the benefit of European businessmen. All these economic initiatives paved the way for the industrial revolution that began in the eighteenth century.

Opposite **International Exhibition, World's Fair, South Kensington, London, 1862.** At its core, the industrial revolution substituted inanimate power for human and animal energy. Before the industrial revolution, Western Europe had lagged economically behind China and India. New machinery dramatically altered that balance.

This modern industrial revolution began with the search for profit from the manufacture of cotton textiles. The search began as European explorers and traders working in India realized that the staple cloth of India—cotton—was far more comfortable and far easier to keep clean than wool, the staple cloth of England and continental Europe. Explorers and traders began to import cotton cloth from India. Cotton cloth also became extremely important in producing clothes for the many slaves who toiled in hot climates of the Americas. As the level of imports increased, enterprising businessmen sought ways to produce the cloth in Europe. They could not grow cotton in Europe—the climate was too cold—but perhaps the cloth could be manufactured in Europe at least as economically as in India from raw cotton imported from overseas, first from India and later from the United States. Britons, after the early 1600s the most active of all Europeans in the India trade, began experimenting with new ways of manufacturing cotton cloth from the imported raw material. Their activity triggered a cascade of changes that we call collectively the "industrial revolution."

The industrial revolution began with simple new machinery and minor changes in the organization of the workplace, but these initial changes were only the first steps.

AT A GLANCE : INDUSTRIALIZATION IN THE WEST

DATE	BRITAIN	REST OF EUROPE	NORTH AMERICA
1760	■ James Watt improves Newcomen's steam engine (1763) ■ James Hargreaves introduces spinning jenny (1764)		
1780	■ Combination Act forbids workers to unionize (1799); repealed 1824		■ Eli Whitney invents cotton gin (1793)
1800	■ Luddite riots (1810–20) ■ Peterloo Massacre, Manchester (1819)		
1820	■ George Stephenson's locomotive *Rocket* (1829) ■ Factory Act forbids employment of children (1833) ■ Chartist movement calls for universal male suffrage (1838)	■ Invention of photography in France by Louis Jacques Mandé Daguerre (1839) ■ Worker revolts in Paris, Prague, Vienna, and Russia (1830)	■ First transatlantic steamship lines in operation (1838) ■ Revolver invented by Samuel Colt (1836)
1840	■ Sir Edwin Chadwick issues report on the Poor Laws (1842) ■ Friedrich Engels, *The Condition of the Working Class in England* (1845) ■ Repeal of the Corn Laws (1846) ■ Bessemer steel converter (1856) ■ Samuel Smiles, *Self Help* (1859)	■ Year of Revolutions—in France, Austria, and Prussia (1848) ■ Marx and Engels, *Communist Manifesto* (1848) ■ Siemens-Martin open-hearth steel production, Germany (1864)	■ Invention of the sewing machine (1846)
1860	■ Under Prime Minister Gladstone, Liberal government begins to provide universal state-supported education (1870) ■ Liberals under Gladstone and Tories under Disraeli compete for workers' votes ■ Trade Union Act guarantees right to strike (1871)	■ Growth of chemical industries (after 1870) ■ Massacre of the Paris Commune (1871) ■ Bismarck unifies Germany (1871) ■ Germany's SPD is first working-class political party (1875)	■ American Civil War (1861–65) ■ Richard Gatling invents the machine gun (1861) ■ Thomas Edison invents early form of telegraph (1864) ■ Invention of the typewriter (1867) ■ Canada becomes unified Dominion (1867) ■ Edison establishes private industrial development lab (1876)
1880	■ London Dock strike (1889)	■ Labor unions legalized in France (1884) ■ May 1 recognized in France as annual "Labor Day" (1890)	■ American Federation of Labor founded (1886) ■ Kodak camera (1888) ■ Homestead Steel strike (1892)

Ultimately the industrial revolution multiplied the profits of the business classes and increased their power in government and public life. It broadened and deepened in its scope until it affected humanity globally, transforming the locations of our workplaces and homes, the size and composition of our families and the quality and quantity of the time we spend with them, the educational systems we create, the wars we fight, and the relationships among nations. As a global process the industrial revolution restructured the procurement of raw materials in the fields and mines of the world, the location of manufacture, and the range of international marketplaces in which new products might be sold. As the masters of the new industrial productivity adopted this global view of their own economic activities, their ventures became imperial in scope. They marshaled the powers of their governments to support their global economic capacities. Reciprocally, the governments relied on the power of industrialists and business-people to increase their own international strength politically, diplomatically, and militarily. The balance of wealth and power in the world shifted, for the first time, toward Europe, and especially toward Britain, the first home of the industrial revolution.

BRITAIN, 1700–1860

The industrial revolution began in Britain around 1700, and although it is called a "revolution," it took over 150 years to be fully realized in 1860. During this period, the British cotton textile industry grew into the world's most productive; its railway network became the nation's principal means of inland transportation and communication; and a new fleet of steam-powered ships enabled Britain to project its new productivity and power around the globe. Economic historians agree, however, that the industrial changes were possible because agriculture in Britain—the basis of its preindustrial economy—was already undergoing a process of continuing improvement. The transformation was so fundamental that it is called an agricultural revolution.

A Revolution in Agriculture

Britain (along with the Dutch Republic, as the Netherlands was known until 1648) had the most productive and efficient commercial agriculture in Europe. Inventors created new farm equipment and farmers were quick to adopt it. Jethro Tull (1674–1741), as an outstanding example, invented the seed drill that replaced the old method of scattering seeds by hand on the surface of the soil with a new method of planting systematically in regular rows at fixed depths, a horse drawn hoe, and an iron plow that could be set at an angle that would pull up grasses and roots and leave them out to dry. New crops, like turnips and potatoes, were introduced, and farmers and large landlords initiated huge irrigation and drainage projects, increasing the productivity of land already under cultivation and opening up new land.

New laws regarding land ownership changed fundamentally the relationships between tenants and landlords. In Britain and the Netherlands peasants began to pay commercial rents to landowners in a business relationship, rather than paying fixed customary rents based on changing market values and performing labor services for them as in the past. Moreover, lands that had been held in common by the village community and had been used for grazing sheep and cattle by shepherds and livestock owners who had no lands of their own were now parceled out for private ownership through a series of **enclosure acts**.

Enclosures had begun in England in a limited way in the late 1400s. In the eighteenth century the process resumed and the pace increased. In the period 1714–1801, about one-fourth of the land in Britain was converted from community property to

enclosure acts Laws passed in England in the late 1700s to 1800s that converted public lands held in common into parcels of land to be sold to private owners.

Isaac Claesz Swanenburgh, *Spinning and Weaving Wool,*
c. **1600. Oil on wood.** This image shows the steps involved in
spinning wool for the textile industry in the Dutch Republic.
(*Stedelijk Museum, Leiden*)

private property through enclosures. The results were favorable to
landowners, and urban businessmen began to buy land as agricultural investment property. Agricultural productivity shot up;
landowners prospered. But hundreds of thousands of farmers with
small plots and cottagers who had subsisted through the use of the
common lands for grazing their animals were now turned into
tenant farmers and wage laborers. The results were revolutionary
and profoundly disturbing to the society. Peasant riots broke out as
early as the middle of the sixteenth century. In one of the uprisings,
3500 people were killed.

The process continued throughout the period of the early
industrial revolution as many of the dispossessed farmers turned to
rural or domestic industry to supplement their meager incomes.
Merchants would drop off raw cotton to workers' homes where

Seed drill, 1701. Jethro Tull (1674–1741) is a key figure of the eighteenth–century
agricultural revolution, which saw new technology harnessed to farming
techniques. Tull's machine drill employed a rotary mechanism that sowed seeds in
rows, permitting cultivation between the rows and thus reducing the need for
weeding.

women would spin it into yarn, which men would then weave into cloth, which merchants would later pick up. Later, rural workers left the land altogether and headed for new industrial jobs in Britain's growing cities. The capitalist market system transformed British agriculture and emptied the countryside, providing capital and workers for the industrial revolution. The economist Joseph Schumpeter (1883–1950) called capitalism a process of "creative destruction." In the agricultural revolution and in the industrial revolution that followed it, we see evidence of both: the often painful destruction of older ways of life and the creation of uncharted new ways.

A Revolution in Textile Manufacture

Until the mid-eighteenth century, the staple British textile had been woolens, woven from the wool of locally reared sheep. Then India's light, colorful, durable cotton textiles began to displace woolens in the market. Britain responded by manipulating tariffs and import regulations to restrict Indian cotton textiles, while British inventors began to produce new machinery that enabled Britain to surpass Indian production in both quantity and quality. The raw cotton would still have to be imported from subtropical India (and later from the southern United States and Egypt), but the manufacturing processes that turned it into cloth could be done in Britain, increasing British jobs and profits, and cutting back on cloth purchases in India, thus undercutting jobs and profits there.

When rural workers produced textiles in their home in the eighteenth century, most spinning was accomplished using a spinning wheel, first invented in India. The spinning wheel allowed women to produce fairly uniform yarn. Men wove the yarn on looms that required two men sitting next to each other passing the shuttle of the loom from left to right and back again. In 1733, John Kay (1704–64) invented the "flying shuttle," which allowed a single weaver to send the shuttle forth and back across the loom automatically, without the need of a second operator to push it. The spinners could not keep up with the increased demand of the weavers until, in 1764, James Hargreaves (d. 1778) introduced the spinning jenny, a machine that allowed the operator to spin several threads at once. The earliest jennies could run eight spindles at once; by 1770, sixteen; by the end of the century, 120. Machines to card and comb the cotton to prepare it for spinning were also developed.

Thus far, the machinery was new, but the power source was still human labor, and production was still concentrated in rural homes and small workshops. In 1769, Richard Arkwright (1732–92) patented the "water frame," a machine that could spin several strands simultaneously. Powered by water, it could run continuously. In 1779, Samuel Crompton (1753–1827) developed a "spinning mule," a hybrid that joined the principles of the spinning jenny and the water frame to produce a better quality and higher quantity of cotton thread. Unfortunately, he was too poor to patent it, but he sold designs for it to others. Now British cloth could rival that of India. Fasci-

James Hargreaves' spinning jenny. Named for his daughter, Hargreaves' invention was a spinning machine that prepared natural fibers for weaving. It thus made possible the expanded production of cotton cloth. The industrial revolution was built on relatively simple innovations like this jenny and the even earlier "flying shuttle" of John Kay, 1733.

nated by Arkwright's water frame, Edmund Cartwright (1743–1822) believed he could make a fortune by applying the principles of the technology to weaving. After some experiments, he patented the power loom in 1785, but struggled to benefit from it financially.

Meanwhile, in the coalfields of Britain, mine owners were seeking more efficient means of pumping water out of mine shafts, enabling deeper digging. By 1712, Thomas Newcomen (1663–1729) had mastered the use of steam power to drive these pumps. In 1763, James Watt (1736–1819), a technician at the University of Glasgow, was experimenting with improvements to Newcomen's steam engine, when Matthew Boulton (1728–1809), a small manufacturer, provided him with the capital necessary to develop larger and more costly steam engines. By 1785 the firm of Boulton and Watt was manufacturing new steam engines for use in Britain and for export. In the 1780s, Arkwright used a new Boulton and Watt steam engine instead of water power. From this point, equipment grew more sophisticated and more expensive. Spinning and weaving moved from the producer's home or small workshop adjacent to a stream of

The industrial revolution. In the early nineteenth century the industrial revolution spread throughout the trading nations of western Europe (and enmeshed their colonies, which provided both raw materials and markets). The earlier use of water power gave way to steam engines; coal became the power source. Canal transportation was superseded by railways, driven by steam.

For an interactive version of this map, go to: http://www.prenhall.com/spodek/map17.1

water to new steam-powered cotton textile mills, which increased continuously in size and productivity. Power looms, like Cartwright's, invented to cope with increased spinning capacity, became commercially profitable by about 1800. Increasingly, in the 1800s, power looms became one of the most important technologies of the industrial revolution.

The new productivity of the machines transformed Britain's economy. It took hand spinners in India 50,000 hours to produce 100 pounds of cotton yarn. Crompton's mule could do the same task in 2000 hours; Arkwright's steam-powered frame, available by 1795, took 300 hours; and automatic mules, available by 1825, took 135 hours. Moreover, the quality of the finished product steadily increased in strength, durability, and texture. The number of mule spindles rose from 50,000 in 1788 to 4.6 million in 1811. Cotton textiles became the most important product of British industries by 1820, making up almost half of Britain's exports.

Prior to this mechanization most families had spun and woven their own clothing by hand so the availability of machine-made yarn and cloth affected millions of spinners and weavers throughout Great Britain. As late as 1815 owners of new weaving mills continued the putting-out system, providing home-based weavers with cotton thread and paying them for the finished, woven product. When cutbacks in production were necessary, the home workers could be cut, while the large factories continued to run. The burden of recession could be shifted to the shoulders of the home producer, leaving the factory owners and laborers relatively unscathed. In 1791, home-based workers in the north of England burned down one of the new power-loom factories in Manchester. Machine-wrecking riots followed for several decades, culminating in the Luddite riots of 1810–20. Named for their mythical leader, Ned Ludd, the rioters wanted the new machines banned. Soldiers were called in to suppress the riots.

The textile revolution also generated spin-off effects around the world. India's industrial position was reversed as the country became a supplier of raw cotton to Britain and an importer of machine-manufactured cotton textiles from Britain. Britain's new mills required unprecedented quantities of good-quality cotton. Raw cotton resembled cotton balls, but it was oily and full of seeds. It was impossible to process the cotton into yarn without first cleaning it or removing the seeds from the raw cotton. In the United States, the invention of the cotton gin by Eli Whitney (1765–1825) in 1793 meant that a worker could clean 50 pounds of cotton in the time it had taken to clean one. This solved part of the supply problem. The plantation economy of the United States revived and expanded, providing the necessary raw cotton, but, unfortunately, giving slavery a new lease on life. American cotton production rose from 3000 bales in 1790 to 178,000 bales in 1810; 732,000 bales in 1830; and 4,500,000 bales in 1860. Industrialization in Britain was reshaping the world economy.

Capital Goods: Iron, Steam Engines, Railways, and Steamships

The textile industry began with a consumer product that everyone used and that already employed a substantial handicraft labor force; it mechanized and reorganized the production process in factories. Other industrial innovations created new products. Many were in the capital goods sector of the economy—that is, they produced tools to expand production rather than goods for private consumption. Britain's iron industry, which had been established since the mid-1500s, at first used wood to heat iron ore and extract molten iron, but by about 1750 new mining processes provided coal, a more efficient fuel, more abundantly and cheaply. About 1775, the iron industry relocated to the coal and iron fields of the English Midlands. A process of stirring the molten iron ore at high temperatures was introduced by Henry Cort

MAJOR DISCOVERIES AND INVENTIONS— 1640–1830

1640	Theory of numbers: Pierre de Fermat
1642	Calculating machine: Blaise Pascal
1650	Air pump: Otto von Guericke
1656	Pendulum clock: Otto von Guericke
1665–75	Calculus: Isaac Newton and Gottfried Leibnitz (independently)
1698	Steam pump: Thomas Savory
c. **1701**	Seed drill: Jethro Tull
1712	Steam engine: Thomas Newcomen
1714	Mercury thermometer: Gabriel Fahrenheit
1733	Flying shuttle: John Kay
1752	Lightning conductor: Benjamin Franklin
1764	Spinning jenny: James Hargreaves
1765	Condensing steam engine: James Watt
1768	Hydrometer: Antoine Baumé
1783	Hot air balloon: Joseph and Étienne Montgolfier
1783	Parachute: Louis Lenormand
1785	Power loom: Edmund Cartwright
1789	Combustion: Antoine Lavoisier
1793	Cotton gin: Eli Whitney
1800	Electric battery: Alessandro Volta
1807	Steamboat: Robert Fulton
1815	Miner's safety lamp: Humphry Davy
1818	Bicycle: Karl von Sauerbrun
1823	Digital calculating machine: Charles Babbage
1824	Portland cement: Joseph Aspdin
1825	Electromagnet: William Sturgeon
1826	Heliography (pre-photography): Joseph Niépce
1828	Blast furnace: James Neilson
1829	Steam locomotive: George Stephenson

(1740–1800) in the 1780s. This "puddling" encouraged the use of larger ovens and integrated the processes of melting, hammering, and rolling the iron into high-quality bars. Productivity increased dramatically. As the price of production dropped and the quality increased, iron was introduced into building construction. The greatest demand for the metal came, however, with new inventions. The steam engine, railroad track and locomotives, steamships, and new urban systems of gas supply and solid and liquid waste disposal all depended on iron for their construction. Britain produced 25,000 tons of pig iron (an extremely high quality of iron, named for the round ingots or pigs it was cast in) in 1720, 125,000 tons in 1796, and 250,000 tons in 1804. Its world market share was 19 percent in 1800 and 52 percent in 1840—that is, Britain produced as much manufactured iron as the rest of the world.

With the new steam engine and the increased availability and quality of iron, the railroad industry was born. The first reliable locomotive, George Stephenson's *Rocket*, was produced in 1829. It serviced the Manchester–Liverpool route, reaching a speed of 16 miles per hour. By the 1840s, a railroad boom swept Britain, Europe, and crossed the Atlantic to the United States, where it facilitated the westward expansion of that rapidly expanding country. By the 1850s most of the 23,500 miles of today's railway network in Britain were already in place, and entrepreneurs found new foreign markets for their locomotives and tracks in India and Latin America.

The new locomotives quickly superseded the canal systems of Britain and the United States, which had been built mostly since the 1750s as the favored means of transporting raw materials and bulk goods between industrial cities. Until the coming of the steam-powered train, canals had been considered the transportation means of the future. (The speed with which the newer technology displaced the older is one reason

George Stephenson's locomotive *Rocket*, 1829, from a chromolithographic cigarette card of 1901. On October 14, 1829, the *Rocket* won a competition for an engine to haul freight and passengers on the Manchester–Liverpool Railway. The success of Stephenson's invention stimulated a boom in locomotive construction and track laying around the world.

HOW DO WE KNOW?

Why Did the Industrial Revolution Begin in Britain?

Historians have long debated the origins of the industrial revolution. The term itself was used at least as early as 1845, in the opening of Friedrich Engels' The Condition of the Working Class in England:

> The history of the English working classes begins in the second half of the eighteenth century with the invention of the steam engine and of machines for spinning and weaving cotton. It is well known that these inventions gave the impetus to the genesis of an industrial revolution. This revolution had a social as well as an economic aspect since it changed the entire structure of middle-class society. (p. 9)

Arnold Toynbee (uncle of a twentieth-century historian with the same name) was apparently the first professional historian to use the term. In a set of lectures delivered in 1880–81, Toynbee identified 1760 as the beginning of the process. He chose this date in recognition of the inventions we have been discussing here. In 1934, John Nef, economic historian at the University of Chicago, argued that the iron industry had already been in place by the mid-sixteenth century and that date was a more appropriate choice. More recent historians, such as Fernand Braudel, have also seen the roots of industrialization stretching back for centuries. They have stressed the underlying economic, political, social, intellectual, and scientific transformations that we have discussed in the last few chapters. All these processes coalesced in the British economy in the late eighteenth century to create the industrial revolution:

- increasing productivity in agriculture;
- new merchant classes in power, and the evolution of a capitalist philosophy of economics that justified their power;
- a powerful state that supported economic development, despite the capitalist doctrine of laissez-faire that called for the state to stay out of business;
- the rise of science, with its new, empirical view of the world, and of technology, with its determination to find practical solutions to practical problems;
- a social structure that allowed and even encouraged people of different classes to work together, especially artisans, who worked with their hands, and financiers, who provided capital;
- more intense patterns of global trading for buying raw materials and for selling manufactured products;
- an expanding population that increased both the labor supply and the demand for more production;
- slave labor in plantation economies, which brought more than a century of exceptional capital accumulation;
- the discovery of massive deposits of gold and silver in the New World, which also increased capital accumulation; and
- "proto-industrialization"—that is, early forms of industrial organization that introduced new skills to both management and labor, paving the way to large-scale factory production.

This question of the origins of the industrial revolution is not purely academic. The debate carries serious implications for planning industrial development in today's world. As many newly independent nations with little industry seek to industrialize, they ask: Does industrialization mean simply the acquisition of machinery and the adaptation of advanced technology? Or must a nation also experience a much wider range of agricultural, economic, philosophical, scientific, political, and social changes? How, and under what terms, can it raise the capital necessary to begin? What are the tasks confronting a government wishing to promote industrialization? We shall examine these twentieth-century questions in Chapters 20 through 24. Those countries that have achieved high levels of industrialization —mostly the countries of Europe and their daughter civilizations overseas; Japan; and now some of the countries of East Asia (see Chapter 22)—have experienced a wide range of fundamental changes, akin to many of those that Britain experienced.

- Among the characteristics that made the industrial revolution possible, do some seem to you more important than others? Which ones? Why?
- Which processes that we usually include in the "industrial revolution" are changes in machinery and equipment? Which are changes in the social structure of the society?
- Which of these processes seem to be continuing to the present and continuing to influence contemporary economics?

historians resist predicting the future. Events do not necessarily proceed in a straight-line process of development, and new, unanticipated developments frequently displace older patterns quite unexpectedly.)

Steamships, using much the same technology as steam locomotives, were introduced at about the same time. The first transatlantic steamship lines began operation in 1838. World steamship tonnage multiplied more than 100 times, from 32,000 tons in 1831 to 3,300,000 tons in 1876. With its new textile mills, iron factories, and steam-driven transportation networks, Britain soon became the "workshop of the world."

Interior of Crystal Palace, designed by Joseph Paxton for the Great Exhibition of 1851 in London. This glass-and-iron exhibition hall, a landmark of early modern architecture, was a celebration of the powerful Victorian economy and an expression of British technological accomplishment and imperial might.

SOURCE

Conflicting Images of Early Industrial Life: The English Romantic Poets

In the century 1750–1850, Britain was transformed by industrialization. Factories, cities, and the working classes all multiplied. One response to the turmoil created by these changes was Romanticism, a new international movement in literature and the arts, which opposed the rationalism of the Enlightenment and glorified emotion. Romantic poets in Britain, such as William Wordsworth (1770–1850) and Samuel Taylor Coleridge (1772–1834), turned away from the belief in modern progress through science and rational knowledge toward nature, history, and their own inner feelings. They saw a great vision of a new aesthetic beauty emerging. Wordsworth's view of London's natural glories represents this Romantic perspective.

**Upon Westminster Bridge,
September 3, 1802**

Earth has not anything to show more fair:
Dull would he be of soul who could pass by
A sight so touching in its majesty;
This City now doth, like a garment, wear
The beauty of the morning; silent, bare,
Ships, towers, domes, theatres, and
    temples lie
Open unto the fields, and to the sky;
All bright and glittering in the smokeless
    air.
Never did sun more beautifully steep
In his first splendour, valley, rock, or hill;
Ne'er saw I, never felt, a calm so deep!
The river glideth at his own sweet will:
Dear God! the very houses seem asleep;
And all that mighty heart is lying still!
                William Wordsworth

Others, such as the poet William Blake (1757–1827), who were closer to the lives of working-class people, saw the great suffering caused by industrialization. Devoutly religious and nationalistic, Blake nevertheless condemned the people, the government, and the Church of England for tolerating "a land of poverty" in the very midst of "a rich and fruitful land." While Wordsworth looks over London from the vantage point of a bridge, Blake walks its streets and looks into the faces of its inhabitants.

London

I wander thro' each charter'd* street,
Near where the charter'd Thames does
    flow,
And mark in every face I meet
Marks of weakness, marks of woe.

In every cry of every Man,
In every Infant's cry of fear,
In every voice, in every ban,
The mind-forg'd manacles I hear.

How the Chimney-sweeper's cry
Every blackning Church appalls;
And the hapless Soldier's sigh
Runs in blood down Palace walls.

But most thro' midnight streets I hear
How the youthful Harlot's curse
Blasts the new-born Infant's tear**,
And blights with plagues the Marriage
    hearse.
                William Blake

*charter'd = licensed by the government, controlled, owned
**the infant is blind at birth, from venereal disease transmitted by the parent

No matter how upsetting Blake's view of London may be, the even more lacerated heart of the industrial revolution was actually in the Midlands and north of England, around the cities of Manchester, Birmingham, and Liverpool.

THE SECOND STAGE OF INDUSTRIALIZATION, 1860–1914

New Products and New Nations

Between 1860 and the outbreak of World War I in 1914, a "second industrial revolution" further transformed world productivity, the ways in which humans lived their lives, and the power balances among the major nations and regions of the world. The principal technological advances came in steel, chemicals, and electricity, and these were supported by organizational breakthroughs in shipping, banking, and insurance.

Steel and Chemical Industries. New technologies—the Bessemer steel converter (1856) in Britain followed by the Siemens–Martin open-hearth method of production (1864) in Germany—soon allowed iron ore to be converted to steel cheaply and abundantly. Iron is produced in blast furnaces and can be of high quality, but the final product contains some impurities. Steel production involves removing the impurities first then adding carbon to the iron ore to create a much stronger and more versatile product, which can be shaped into bars, plates, and other structural components, like girders. Germany, united as a country in 1871 under Otto von Bismarck, forged ahead. By 1900 it was producing more steel than Britain, 6.3 million tons to 5.0 million tons; in 1913, on the eve of World War I, Germany's lead had grown to 17.6 million tons against 7.7 million tons. Germany also led in the invention of a number of additional new technologies, especially the internal combustion engine, the diesel engine, and the automobile.

Chemical industries grew, especially after 1870, as synthetic substances, notably derivatives from coal, began to augment and replace the earlier reliance on natural substances from vegetables, such as alkalis and dyes. Now, synthetic, aniline dyes were made from coal tar. Both fertilizers and explosives could be made from synthetic nitrogen and phosphates. Artificial fertilizers added to a revolution in agricultural productivity, while explosives helped in the construction of engineering feats, such as the new tunnels through the Alps in Europe, the Suez Canal in North Africa, and the Panama Canal in Central America. Soda, made from the coal by-product of ammonia, was used in manufacturing both soap and glass. New drugs and insecticides enhanced the quality of life, while perfumes, and cosmetics were produced and made their way to the marketplace, as many middle-class and some working-class women, like department store clerks, sought luxury goods to add a touch of romance to their lives. Plastics, produced from coal tar acids, became available in the late nineteenth century.

Electricity. Electrical inventions sparked one another throughout Europe and across the Atlantic to the United States, as well. In 1831 Michael Faraday (1791–1867) in Britain first demonstrated the principle of electromagnetic induction by moving a metal conductor through a magnetic field to generate electricity, a process repeated regularly today in high-school classrooms. By 1850, several companies were producing simple electric generators. In the 1860s, Ernst Werner von Siemens (1816–92) in Germany developed a practical dynamo. In the United

A canal connects two oceans. The construction of the Panama Canal in 1905, linking the Atlantic and Pacific oceans, ranks as one of the greatest engineering feats of all time. The task involved removing about 175 million cubic yards of earth as well as sanitizing the entire area, which was infested by mosquitoes that spread yellow fever and malaria.

States in the 1880s, Nikola Tesla (1856–1943) invented methods to transmit power effectively over long distances, patenting the alternating current generator in 1892.

The best-known inventor of the age was the American Thomas Alva Edison (1847–1931), who acquired more than one thousand patents for his innovations, 225 of which were patented between 1879 and 1882, for incandescent light bulbs, fuses, sockets, switches, circuit breakers, and meters. Others included an early form of telegraph in 1864; the stock ticker in 1870; the phonograph based on a metal cylinder in 1877; and the wax cylinder recorder in 1888, forerunner of the vinyl record player; and the kinetoscope in 1889, a forerunner of the moving picture. More important than any single invention, however, was Edison's establishment in 1876 of (probably the first) private industrial development laboratory in Menlo Park, New Jersey, a rural area halfway between New York and Philadelphia. Until this time, invention had been largely an individual achievement, based on the skills and luck of the individual inventor. Edison's new research facility institutionalized the process of invention, and encouraged research and development and the commercialization of products like the phonograph.

Factory Production

Production, too, began to be concentrated into immense, impersonal corporations. The second industrial revolution corresponded to the era of big business. In Germany, the rising power in Europe, two large **cartels**, collaborative business associations, were formed for the production of electronic equipment: Siemens–Schuckert and Allgemeine Elektrizitäts Gesellschaft (AEG). Two others, specializing in chemical production, later merged into I.G. Farben (1925). For steel production, each major producing country had its own giants: Krupp in Germany, Schneider–Creusot in France, Vickers-Armstrong in Britain, and, largest of all, the United States Steel Corporation. These huge corporations integrated the entire process of production from raw material to finished product. They owned their own coal mines and iron works, produced steel, and manufactured such final products as ships, railway equipment, and armaments.

Industrial concentration displaced the artisan in favor of mass-production and mass-consumption. In these mass-market innovations, the United States was frequently the leader, producing the sewing machine (invented by Elias Howe in 1846); the typewriter (1867); clocks and watches, the everyday timekeepers of the new office and factory routines; the telephone, phonograph, and cinema; the bicycle, invented in its modern form in Britain by John Kemp Starley and William Sutton in 1885; and small arms, like the revolver, invented by Samuel Colt in 1836, and the rifle, invented by Oliver Winchester, and improved to a repeating rifle by Christopher Spencer in 1860.

Warfare and Industrialization

Warfare and industrialization went hand-in-hand. In the United States, for example, the Civil War (1861–5) not only restored a political union but also marked the victory of the industrializing, urban, free-labor North over the rural, plantation economy, slave-holding South. It marked a transformation that soon placed the United States among the leaders of world industrialization. Wars of white immigrants against Native American Indians, which soon turned to slaughters and forcible relocations to reservations, accompanied the new cross-continental railroads. Wars against Mexico completed the borders of the contiguous United States, and wars against Spain brought the United States its first overseas colonies.

The machine gun, invented by Richard Gatling in 1862, was improved several times. In 1883 it took on the name of the Maxim gun, for the American Hiram Maxim

cartel An association of independent producers or businessmen whose aim is to control the supply of a particular commodity or group of commodities in order to regulate or push up prices.

who created a gun that had a range of almost 1½ miles and could shoot eleven rounds per second. The Maxim won its greatest fame in Africa, where Europeans found it indispensable in their colonization efforts. In Germany, the Krupp family of steel manufacturers concentrated on producing the heavy armaments that enabled Prussia to defeat France in 1870, to forge a united Germany (see Chapter 18), and to prove a formidable combatant in both World Wars (see Chapter 19).

The Effects of the Second Industrial Revolution Worldwide

Profits from all these businesses, civilian and military, spilled over into finance capital, the purposeful reinvestment of capital into new business to reap new profits. Financiers sought new opportunities in far-flung regions of the world. The industrial development of the Americas offered huge opportunities, and Britain became the largest investor. From the 1840s, for example, the railway networks of both North and South America were in large part financed by British investors. The availability of such investment capital made the task of industrial and urban development easier in the Americas, because the necessary sums could be borrowed and repaid later.

These borrowings, and the industrialization and urbanization that came from them, encouraged the immigration that helped increase the population of North America from 39 million in 1850 to 106 million in 1900, and that of South America from 20 million to 38 million in the same period. The United States absorbed these

Machine shop, West Lynn works, USA, c. 1898. The United States led the way in mass production of household goods. In the nineteenth century, people immigrated to the big cities from rural America and from overseas to work in factories—often for low pay, with long hours and in hot, noisy conditions. The factory system expanded hugely after 1913 when Henry Ford introduced assembly-line technologies to motor-car production.

MAJOR DISCOVERIES AND INVENTIONS—1830–1914	
1831	Dynamo: Michael Faraday
1834	Reaping machine: Cyrus McCormick
1834	Photography: Louis M. Daguerre; William Henry Fox Talbot
1836	Revolver: Samuel Colt
1837	Telegraph: Samuel Morse
1839	Vulcanized rubber: Charles Goodyear
1852	Gyroscope: Léon Foucault
1853	Passenger elevator: Elisha Otis
1856	Celluloid: Alexander Parkes Bessemer converter: Henry Bessemer Bunsen burner: Robert Bunsen
1858	Refrigerator: Ferdinand Carré Washing machine: Hamilton Smith
1859	Internal combustion engine: Etienne Lenoir
1862	Rapid-fire gun: Richard Gatling
1866	Dynamite: Alfred Nobel
1876	Telephone: Alexander Graham Bell
1877	Phonograph: Thomas Edison
1879	Incandescent lamp: Thomas Edison
1885	Motorcycle: Edward Butler Electric transformer: William Stanley Vacuum flask: James Dewar
1887	Motorcar engine: Gottlieb Daimler/Karl Benz
1888	Pneumatic tire: John Boyd Dunlop Kodak camera: George Eastman
1895	Wireless: Nikola Tesla X-rays: Wilhelm Roentgen
1896	Radioactivity: Antoine Becquerel
1897	Diesel engine: Rudolf Diesel
1898	Submarine: John P. Holland Radium and polonium: Pierre and Marie Curie
1902	Radio-telephone: Reginald Fessenden
1903	Airplane: Wilbur and Orville Wright
1905	Theory of relativity: Albert Einstein
1911	Combine harvester: Benjamin Holt
1914	Tank: Ernest Swinton

investments without losing political control of its own internal development and became the most industrialized of all countries. South America, however, became an early example of neo-colonialism, in which foreign economic control leads to indirect foreign political control as well.

Canada enjoyed internal self-government within the British Empire from 1840 and became a unified Dominion, including Ontario, Quebec, Nova Scotia, and New Brunswick, in 1867. It attracted increasing immigration and investment, especially after the United States' frontier was filled in with its own immigrants. Nova Scotia and New Brunswick had joined the original provinces of Quebec and Ontario on condition that a railroad be built to link them with Quebec. More dramatically, the Canadian Pacific Railway was completed in 1885, spanning Canada from east to west. Between 1900 and 1916, 73 million acres of land were planted with wheat and other commercial agriculture. $400 million per year was invested in this sector and in the mining of coal, gold, lead, zinc, nickel, and copper.

In Russia and the Ottoman Empire, the largest investments came from France. For the six decades leading up to World War I, Russia's industrial output grew at the rate of 5 percent per year. It produced more steel than France, Italy, or Japan, and by 1914 it had 46,000 miles of railroad track and was the world's fourth largest industrial power. It could not, however, keep up with the industrial advances of the United States and Germany. Similarly, Russia's railway mileage seems less adequate when the immense expanse of the country, by far the largest in the world, is considered. The proportion of Russian industrial production remained at about 8 percent of the world total from 1880 to 1914, and most of its heavy industry was owned by foreigners.

For reasons that will be explained in Chapter 18, total foreign investment in the Ottoman Empire was much less, about $1.2 billion in 1914, and the empire's industrial base became progressively less competitive than those of western European nations. Increasingly, the Ottoman Empire was seen as the "sick man of Europe".

Overall global investments were immense, with Britain far in the lead. By 1914 Britain had invested some $20 billion, France about $8.7 billion, and Germany about $6 billion. The global age of finance capital was in full swing.

SOCIAL CHANGES: THE CONDITIONS OF WORKING PEOPLE

So far we have concentrated on the immense new productivity of industrialization, and on the abundance and the wonders of new products. But how did the workers fare? What were the conditions of life for those who worked the machines that produced this new wealth? Reports from the early years in Britain, the birthplace of the industrial revolution, relate with horrifying regularity the wretched conditions of the working class. Popular literature, official government reports, political tracts, and the cries of labor organizers repeat the same theme: In the midst of increasing national wealth, workers suffered wracking poverty and degradation. On the other hand, by the end of our period (1914), the condition of working-class people in western Europe and the United States, at least, was becoming comfortable. What had changed? How? What was the significance of the change? These questions remain important today as increasingly sophisticated machines continue to produce more abundant and more sophisticated products and more anxiety in the life of workers.

Demographic Causes and Effects of the Industrial Revolution

Many demographic studies suggest that levels of population and industrialization increased together. The population of Europe almost doubled between 1750 and 1850, from 140 million to 265 million, and then jumped another 50 percent to 400 million by 1900. At the same time, emigration carried an additional 50 million people outward from Europe, especially to the Americas, Australia, and South Africa. Much of this increase occurred before the introduction of machinery. Also, the increase seems to have been worldwide: China's population multiplied four times between 1650 and 1850. Historians now believe the main cause was the availability of new foods, such as maize, provided by the "Columbian exchange".

Demographers note two waves of change that followed the industrial revolution. First, death rates fell as people ate better and kept cleaner, and as public health measures increased the safety of the water supply, improved the sanitation of cities, combated epidemics, and taught new standards of personal hygiene. Second, parents began to realize that improved health increased the likelihood that their children would live to adulthood, and that it was not necessary to produce numerous children to ensure that two or three or four would survive. Urban birth rates went down as parents began to practice family planning. The old "iron law of wages" had argued that as income increased people would simply use the surplus to have more children; this did not continue. After years of rapid growth, by about 1900, the populations of industrial areas began to stabilize.

Winners and Losers in the Industrial Revolution

New entrepreneurs, men creating successful new industrial enterprises, often profited handsomely in this era. Their literary representative was Samuel Smiles (1812–1904), whose *Self-Help*, published in 1859, advocated self-reliance as the key to "a harvest of wealth and prosperity." Smiles described the careers of many of these self-made new men—the "industrial heroes of the civilized world"—for example, Josiah Wedgwood, a potter, son and grandson of potters, who created a new form of pottery that still bears his name. Wedgwood transformed the British pottery industry, earning great profits for himself and providing employment in his factories for 20,000 workers. As industries of all sorts expanded, each nation had its own examples of "captains of industry"—for example, four generations of the Friedrich Krupp family, manufacturers of steel and weapons in Germany; Andrew Carnegie, also in steel manufacture, in the USA; and J. Pierpont Morgan in investment banking also in the USA. In Britain, the economic and political power of the inherited nobility declined. Their wealth, based on land ownership, diminished as that of the new industrial class grew.

Handicraft workers were displaced by the new mechanization. In 1820 there were 240,000 handloom weavers in Britain; in 1840, 123,000; in 1856, 23,000. Some of these workers found jobs running the new power looms, but many could not make the transition and fell into poverty.

While attending his father's cotton mill in Manchester, Friedrich Engels (1820–95) compiled devastating accounts of *The Condition of the Working Class in England* (1845). His description of the St. Giles slum in London demonstrates the moral outrage that led him to join with Karl Marx in calling for revolution:

> Heaps of garbage and ashes lie in all directions, and the foul liquids emptied before the doors gather in stinking pools. Here live the poorest of the poor, the worst paid workers with thieves and the victims of prostitution indiscriminately huddled together … [T]hey who have some kind of shelter are fortunate in comparison with the utterly homeless. In London fifty thousand human beings get up every morning, not knowing where they are to lay their heads at night. (pp. 34–38)

Government reports, although more restrained in tone, sustained these horrific views. They called for, and got, remedial legislation. Official committees studied conditions

Putters or trolley boys, from *Mines and Miners* by L. Simonin, early nineteenth century. Until the reforms of the 1870s, owners of factories and mines were able to force children as young as five and six to work up to sixteen hours a day—often in hazardous conditions. Orphans and pauper children were especially vulnerable since capitalists merely had to keep them fed and sheltered in return for their services. The resulting disease, industrial injury, and illiteracy tended to make poor families even poorer.

in the factories and neighborhoods of Britain's growing industrial cities and in its mines. In 1831, a committee chaired by the Member of Parliament Michael Thomas Sadler (1780–1835) investigated the conditions of child labor in cotton and linen factories. It found children beginning work at the age of six, usually for twelve- and thirteen-hour days. They were often given food so wretched that, despite their hunger, they left it for pigs to eat. Workplaces were cramped and dirty all year long, and were especially damaging to health during the long nights of winter, when gas, candles, and oil lamps added their soot and smoke to the air of the factory. Still worse conditions were revealed by the Committee on the Conditions in Mines that was appointed in 1842 and chaired by Anthony Ashley Cooper, 7th earl of Shaftesbury. Children worked for fourteen hours underground each day. Legally, they could work from the age of nine, but parents needing extra income frequently brought even younger children.

Sir Edwin Chadwick (1800–90), an investigator for the Royal Commission on the Poor Laws, issued his *Inquiry into the Condition of the Poor* in 1842 after taking abundant testimony from workers in factories and mines, homes and workplaces.

Chadwick noted that the British government had already begun legislating the conditions of child labor and of tenement construction. He now urged further legislation to provide for sewage, drainage, sanitation, and a clean water supply. His report suggested that not only the poor workers but also their employers, the community, and the government would benefit. Chadwick's report helped inspire broad public support for the Public Health Act of 1848 and the creation of a Board of Health.

Gender Relationships and the Industrial Revolution

By creating factories, the industrial revolution drove a wedge between the home and the workplace that dramatically affected both. Wives who had been accustomed to working alongside, or at least in proximity to, their husbands on the farm or in the shop or workshop now found that the major source of employment was away from home. The industrial revolution forced redefinitions of identities. What should the woman's role and place be now? How should motherhood and work be balanced? In a world that expected most females to be under the protection of males, how were single women to define, and fend for, themselves? In what voice should the feminist movement address these complex issues?

As the industrial revolution began in semi-rural locations, its labor force was drawn primarily from young, (as yet) unmarried women, frequently daughters of local farmers. Some of the early factory owners built boarding houses for the women and treated them protectively, as young wards. Francis Cabot Lowell (1775–1817) built mills at Waltham, Massachusetts, on this principle. He promised the women hard work, with pay adequate to help their families and to save toward marriage. After his death, his partners extended his example by establishing a new town, Lowell, with the largest cotton mill built to that date. By the 1840s, about half the mills in New England followed this model. Factory work had its demands of order, discipline, and the clock, and the dormitory-boarding houses were somewhat crowded, but labor historian Alice Kessler-Harris quotes approvingly the very warm assessment of the Lowell experience from one of its workers in the 1830s: It was "the first field that had ever been open to her outside of her own restricted home … the first money they earned! When they felt the jingle of silver in their pocket, there for the first time, their heads became erect and they walked as if on air."

As new machinery became heavier, as factory work became more prevalent, and as economic depression pressed down on both American and British economies, the workforce shifted. Men, often farmers and immigrants, moved into the factories, displacing the women. The men demanded higher pay, which factory owners had previously hoped to avoid by hiring women. The culture of the industrializing world of that time, primarily in Britain, called for men to support their families. A young, unmarried woman might earn just enough for herself and that would be adequate. A man required a "family wage." The rising productivity of constantly improving machinery made this "family wage" possible, and it became the baseline standard for industry, although workers had to struggle for it for decades. Women were thus displaced from factory work and brought back to the home.

By the second half of the nineteenth century, "domesticity" became the desired norm for middle- and even working-class women and their families. Most middle-class women spent a great deal of time caring for their families and homes, and the new urban domesticity increased their level of security and comfort. Life expectancy, a basic index of well-being, rose rapidly for women in Britain, even slightly more than for men. It increased from forty-four years in 1890, to fifty-two in 1910, to sixty in 1920. Living standards began to rise and generally continued to rise into the twentieth century. New systems of ventilation, heating, lighting, indoor plumbing, and running hot and cold water contributed to domestic comfort and made life easier for those who could afford these services, although they often did not reach working-class neighborhoods.

Urban conditions made children less of an economic benefit, as they had been on family farms, and more of an economic burden. Family planning increased. Child-bearing became less frequent, freer from infection thanks to antisepsis, less painful with the use of anesthesia, and safer with the professionalization of the practice of medicine. The presence of children in the home also decreased as free, compulsory education, beginning as early as the 1830s and 1840s, began to take them to school for several hours each day.

With more time freed from traditional domestic responsibilities, some women began to enter into the array of white-collar jobs that were opening. The most respectable jobs provided satisfying work that also fit the culturally approved role of women as care givers and nurturers: teaching in the new school systems and nursing in the new hospitals. Other women worked as sales

Anon., "The New Machine for Winding up the Ladies," English cartoon, c. 1840. Upper-class English women wore corsets, devices made of whalebone that constricted the waist painfully, making it appear as tiny as possible and, by contrast, accentuating the hips, buttocks, and breasts. The corsets were often so tight that they interfered with women's ability to breathe properly and encouraged "swooning." The cartoonist mocks these practices.

personnel in the new department stores (where they also shopped) and as secretaries and clerks in the new offices, although this was primarily a male occupation in the nineteenth century. A very few went into professions.

While domestic concerns and new technological wonders engaged the middle classes, and were desired by the working classes, for a great number of people they were out of reach. The 15–20 percent of adult females who had to work as principal breadwinners for themselves and their families confronted more basic problems of earning a living. The value placed on domesticity as the proper role for females, and the concomitant view that men should earn a "family wage" but that women needed only supplementary income, made the plight of the working woman doubly difficult. These women, often immigrants, desperately poor, and without male support, were no longer seen, as the first industrial women workers had been, as proud and independent, but as unfortunate objects of sympathy and pity.

They found jobs where they could. Domestic service was most common, employing two to three times as many women as industry, even in industrialized countries. On the margins of society, other women earned a living through prostitution. In the second half of the nineteenth century, censuses in the largest cities, London and Paris, routinely reported tens of thousands of prostitutes walking the streets, serving in brothels, or, occasionally, employed in more comfortable settings by more prosperous clients. These women were often condemned by more conventional society, but they often found this job the only one that paid enough to enable them to support their families. Most of them worked only until about the age of twenty-five, by which time they usually found other work or were married, a rosy picture painted by the middle classes, but often contradicted by working-class experience.

The socialist wing of the feminist movement understood that class differences often inhibited solidarity among women. Karl Marx spoke of the difference between the bourgeois and the proletarian family. He wrote of the conflict between the roles of mother and of worker. With Engels, Marx condemned the "double oppression" of women by both capitalism and the family, but he praised capitalism for freeing women from being regarded as property. He encouraged women in their struggle for citizens' rights and economic independence. In *The Origin of the Family, Private Property and the State* (1884), Engels argued that the form of the family was not fixed. It had evolved substantially in the past, and he proposed further, revolutionary change:

> The peculiar character of the supremacy of the husband over the wife in the modern family, the necessity of creating real social equality between them and the way to do it, will only be seen in the clear light of day when both possess legally complete equality of rights. Then it will be plain that the first condition for the liberation of the wife is to bring the whole female sex back into public industry, and that this in turn demands that the characteristic of the monogamous family as the economic unit of society be abolished. (Engels, 137–8)

In Germany, the Social Democratic Party (SPD) created a separate organizational structure for women that enlisted 174,751 women members by 1914, the largest movement of women in Europe. The number reflects, however, not only women seeking independent expression, but also women who sought to ally themselves with their husbands as members of the party. Working women's organizations were undercut by the opposition of male unionized workers who feared that the women would take away their jobs or, at least, increase the labor pool and thus drive down wages.

POLITICAL REACTION IN BRITAIN AND EUROPE, 1800–1914

Political, Economic, and Social Reform in Britain

Britain had a growing urban, industrial population that demanded political, economic, and social change. The government, recognizing that industrialization was transforming Britain away from its aristocratic and agrarian traditions and fearful of the consequences, responded initially by trying to repress the movement for reform. The Peterloo Massacre at St. Peter's Fields in Manchester in 1819 demonstrated the government's position. A huge but peaceful demonstration by 80,000 people called for universal male suffrage, the annual election of the House of Commons in Parliament, and the abolition of the Corn Laws. The Corn Laws had raised the tariff on grain to levels that effectively banned importation, thus keeping the price of basic foodstuffs high, favoring landowners and farmers at the expense of the growing urban, industrial population. Soldiers fired on the demonstrators, killing eleven and wounding some 400. The government applauded the soldiers and passed further legislation to restrict free expression.

The mood of Parliament had changed by 1832, becoming more fearful but also more accommodating, partly because of revolutions on the European continent, and partly because of riots in Britain. Fearing the possibility of revolution, the Whig party in Parliament forced through the Reform Bill of 1832. Its most significant provision was to shift 143 seats in Parliament from rural constituencies, which were losing population and were often dominated by single families, to expanding urban constituencies. The number of voters increased by about 60 percent but still totaled only about 800,000 in all of Britain. A far greater proportion of the new voters, however, were professionals: doctors, lawyers, businessmen, and journalists. The benefits of the 1832 reforms went to the middle classes, but soon the two main parties, conservative Tories and more liberal Whigs, jockeying for power, began to craft new programs to protect and enfranchise urban working people. Some commentators at the time and afterward viewed these political moves as sincere attempts to broaden the base of British political participation. Others saw them as cynical attempts to add voters from the new middle class while leaving industrial workers unrepresented. Whatever the motivation, they were effective in forestalling revolution during extremely tense times, and over several decades they did increase the (male) electorate significantly.

In addition to political reform, Parliament addressed the demands of economic and social legislation. The Factory Act of 1833 not only forbade the employment of children under the age of nine in textile mills, it also, for the first time, provided for paid inspectors to enforce the legislation.

Parliament abolished slavery in the British Empire in 1833 and passed a new Poor Law in 1834, which provided assistance just adequate to sustain life. The law required that recipients live in government workhouses and participate in government-created work projects, but this provision was not usually enforced. In 1835 it enacted a Municipal Corporations Act, which reformed elections and administrations in large cities, enabling them to cope more successfully with the problems of growth and industrialization. In 1842 the employment of women and of children under the age of ten was forbidden in coal mines. The Ten Hour Act of 1847 extended this ruling to

The Chartists. As this contemporary cartoon implies, the sheer weight of support received by the Chartists was a powerful argument in favor of voting rights being extended to all men (though not yet women). Parliament rejected increasingly large charters, or petitions, on three occasions and it was not until 1918 that universal male suffrage was adopted in Great Britain.

cover factories and limited the hours of work for women. In practice, men's hours were also soon reduced.

On some fundamental issues Parliament moved slowly, and sometimes it refused to move at all. The Chartist movement, a national working-class movement dissatisfied with both the 1832 Reform Bill and the new Poor Law, presented a Charter or petition with more than a million signatures to Parliament in 1838 calling for universal male suffrage, an end to property qualifications for members of parliament, and equal electoral districts. The Chartists hoped to achieve reform by gaining access to politics rather than by destroying machines, as their Luddite forbears had done. Despite, or perhaps because of, a wave of violence instigated by some of the few "physical force" Chartists, the House of Commons rejected the petition. When it was resubmitted in 1842, with more than 3.3 million signatures, the Charter was rejected again, overwhelmingly, by 287 votes to 49. Parliament feared that universal suffrage would bring an end to the sanctity of property and the capitalist economic system.

In 1846, however, under a Tory government led by Robert Peel, Parliament did repeal the Corn Laws, signaling the victory of the urban constituencies and the triumph of free trade. Britain gave up its policy of self-sufficiency in food and entered fully into the international trade system to purchase its food and sell its manufactured goods. A second Reform Bill in 1867, passed by the Tory government of Benjamin Disraeli, doubled the electorate to about 2 million, about one-third of all adult males. The Bill enfranchised many urban working men, although it continued to exclude most of those agricultural and industrial workers who lived in the countryside.

The two major political parties, Liberals and Tories, now competed directly for the favor of the industrial workers. In 1870, the Liberal government of William Gladstone began to provide universal, state-supported education and, in the next year, it formally legalized labor unions. The Tories, under Disraeli's second administration, 1876–80, extended the acts regulating public sanitation and conditions of labor in factories and mines. They also regulated the conditions of housing for the poor. In 1884, under Gladstone, a third Reform Bill doubled the electorate again. Not until 1918 did Britain adopt universal male suffrage for men 21 years of age and over and extend the vote to

The Great Procession, June 18, 1910. Not only women campaigned for their right to vote: in this procession of the WSPU (Women's Social and Political Union) a hunger strikers' banner is hoisted aloft by male supporters. Emmeline Pankhurst, frustrated that politicians would not pass legislation to allow women to vote, organized the WSPU and began a militant campaign to secure women's suffrage in Britain. She used assaults on public property to call attention to her cause, and spent time in prison where she and other jailed suffragettes went on hunger strike.

women over the age of 30 who were either ratepayers or married to ratepayers.

While women finally gained the right to vote in both Britain and the United States after World War I, it was not without a long and often violent struggle. The Chartists had peacefully demanded that women obtain the right to vote in the 1840s without success. Women's suffrage committees were formed, but legislators in Parliament rejected most of their demands. Their failure to win suffrage through peaceful means led Emmeline Pankhurst and her daughter Christabel to form suffragette organizations, which became increasingly violent. Though many abhorred the violence, many more grew sympathetic to giving women the right to vote. The participation of suffragettes in the national effort in World War I softened opposition, and in 1918 British women aged thirty or over received the complete franchise. In 1928 the Representation of the People Act gave British women voting rights equal to those of men.

Emmeline Pankhurst with her daughter Christabel, 1908. These were the mother and daughter founders of the Women's Social and Political Union (1903), the most renowned of Britain's suffrage movements. Their campaigns were militant and disruptive. They set fire to public buildings, smashed windows, sabotaged mailboxes, slashed paintings in London's National Gallery, and pelted government officials with eggs. Emmeline was jailed repeatedly, and force-fed when she went on hunger-strikes.

In the United States, women turned to conventions and voluntary associations to promote suffrage. One of the most important conventions was held in Seneca Falls, New York, on July 19–20, 1848. The declaration that came out of this convention called not only for the right to vote but also for increased educational and employment opportunities for women. Other conventions followed. Women first gained the right to vote in local and school board elections in some western states and finally gained national voting rights with the ratification of the Nineteenth Amendment to the U.S. Constitution in August, 1920.

Labor Organization

Like women, who organized to obtain political rights, the working class organized to improve labor conditions. Social historian E.P. Thompson identifies the London Corresponding Society, founded in 1792, as perhaps "the first definitely working-class political organization formed in Britain." Unions were forbidden to unionize under the Combination Act of 1799, but in 1824 this law was repealed. Small trade unions took root, usually finding their greatest success among the better-off "aristocracy of labor"—the machinists, carpenters, printers, and spinners. Sometimes they would go on strike; politically they organized for suffrage campaigns; and some helped organize cooperative enterprises. Only under the Trade Union Act of 1871 was the right to strike recognized officially. Unskilled workers began increasingly to join unions, with miners and transport workers usually in the lead. They drew encouragement from the Fabian Society, a group of intellectuals centered in the Bloomsbury area of London that sought to make government and society more receptive to working-class interests without violence. They supported the London Dock strike of 1889, which demonstrated working-class strength by closing that great port. They formed the core constituency of the new Labour Party. The Party won only two seats in the 1900 elections, but in 1906 it captured twenty-nine seats and began its permanent role in parliamentary politics in Britain. By 1914, 4 million Britons held membership in trade unions.

Karl Marx and Theories of Worker Revolution. In Britain, workers created their own organizations, which then gained the support of political party leaders. Elsewhere, political leaders and theorists attempted to provide leadership in organizing much smaller groups of workers. Foremost among the theoreticians was Karl Marx (1818–83). A well-educated and trained German journalist of Jewish ancestry, Marx

WOMEN'S EMANCIPATION 1790–1928

c. 1790	Olympe de Gouges writes the polemical *Declaration of the Rights of Woman and the Citizen*
1792	Mary Wollstonecraft writes *A Vindication of the Rights of Woman*, regarded as the first manifesto of the women's movement in Britain
1794	Condorcet writes of the desirability of establishing equality of civil and political rights for men and women in *Progrès de l'esprit*
1829	*Sati* (ritual suicide by Hindu widows) is banned in India
1848	Elizabeth Cady Stanton and Lucretia Mott organize the first women's rights convention at Seneca Falls, New York
1850	Beginnings in Britain of national agitation for women's suffrage
1857–72	Married Women's Property Acts allow British women to keep their own possessions on marriage
1866	Mott founds American Equal Rights Association
1868	First public meeting of women's suffrage movement held in Manchester, England
1869	In Britain women ratepayers may vote in municipal elections; Cady Stanton is first president of US National Woman Suffrage Association
1890	Footbinding beginning to die out in China
1903	Emmeline Pankhurst founds Women's Social and Political Union
1906	Pankhurst and her daughters launch militant campaign in Britain
1913	Suffragettes protest in Washington, D.C.; International Women's Peace Conference held in the Netherlands
1914–18	Women assume responsibilities outside the home during World War I
1918	British women householders over 30 years granted the vote
1919	Constance de Markiewicz is the first woman elected to Parliament in Britain
1920	19th amendment to the Constitution gives US women the vote
1928	British women over 21 years granted the vote

called for a worker-led revolution. He organized revolutionary socialists through active campaigning, wrote polemical tracts calling for revolution, such as *The Communist Manifesto* (with Friedrich Engels) and produced three volumes of scholarly analysis and critique of the capitalist system called *Das Kapital*.

Marx began his studies in Berlin at a time when western and central Europe were alive with revolutionary sentiments—both of workers seeking new rights and of nationalists seeking greater political representation. In 1848, many of these revolutionary pressures came to a head—and were crushed. In France, a revolt against the monarchy of Louis Philippe (r. 1830–48) and the proclamation of a provisional republic was followed by the establishment of government-sponsored workshops to provide employment for the poor. A new, far more conservative government was elected, however, and it closed the workshops in Paris. The poor people of the city barricaded city streets, and the army was called out. More than 10,000 people were killed or injured in the ensuing street riots.

In Austria, protesting students and workers briefly took control of Prague and Vienna and then were suppressed in both cities by regular forces of the Austrian army at the cost of thousands of casualties. In Prussia, in the same year, worker demands for more democracy and more worker rights joined with demands for a new constitution that would lead toward the merger of Prussia with the many small German-speaking states of the former Holy Roman Empire into a new country of Germany. At first it appeared that the Prussian king Frederick William IV (r. 1840–61) would grant these demands, and a Constituent Assembly was convened in Frankfurt to write a new German constitution. In the end, however, the king reasserted his divine right to rule and rejected the constitution. Under these circumstances, the smaller states refused to join in a unified government. Conservative forces remained in control of central Europe, and Marx moved to London, where he spent the rest of his life, much of it in active scholarship in the British Museum.

Marx believed that wealth is produced not so much by capitalists, who control the finances, but by the **proletariat**—the laborers—who do the actual physical work of production. Because employers do not generally accept this point of view, workers do not receive proper compensation for their contributions. Violent revolution is the only recourse "to raise the proletariat to the position of ruling class, to establish democracy." In a stirring call to this revolution, Marx and Engels declared the Communist Party as its leader:

proletariat In Marxist theory, those who live solely by the sale of their labor.

> Let the ruling classes tremble at a Communist revolution. The proletarians have nothing to lose but their chains. They have a world to win. Workingmen of all countries, unite! (*The Communist Manifesto* p. 44)

Until the revolution would take place, Marx and Engels called for many shorter term legislative goals, including: "a heavy progressive or graduated income tax ... free education for all children in public schools ... and ... abolition of child factory labor in its present form." Many other labor groups shared these goals, and they were subsequently adopted in virtually all industrialized countries.

After the revolution would occur, Marx and Engels called for the establishment of a powerful, worker-led government to assume control of the economy, and they looked forward to a still later time when the state would be unnecessary and would "wither away". They identified the state as "the organized power of one class for oppressing another," so when workers ruled the state there would be no need for further oppression and the state would vanish. Marx and Engels gave no further description of this utopia, but it would be based on their most central and most radical tenet:

> The theory of the Communists may be summed up in the single sentence: Abolition of private property. (p. 23)

Marx's theory included a view of history that saw class struggle as perpetual: "The history of all hitherto existing society is the history of class struggles." The current form of the struggle was bourgeoisie vs. proletariat. The bourgeoisie themselves had created the proletariat by organizing the new factories that employed and exploited them. Marx condemned the sexual ethics of the bourgeoisie. Despite their official reverence for the family, Marx accused them of sexual abuse of their workers, economic perpetuation of prostitution, and wife-swapping among themselves: "Our bourgeois, not content with having the wives and daughters of their proletarians at their disposal, not to speak of common prostitutes, take the greatest pleasure in seducing each other's wives." Marx heaped scorn on religion, charging the bourgeoisie with using it as an "opiate" to divert the proletariat from its fundamental economic concerns. Marx was a materialist, arguing that economics is the basis of life; ideas and intellectual life are based on economic status: "Man's consciousness changes with every change in the conditions of his material existence, in his social relations and in his social life ... The ruling ideas of each age have ever been the ideas of its ruling class."

The proletarian revolution predicted as inevitable by Marx and Engels did not take place in the nineteenth century. (In Chapter 20 we will consider the extent to which the 1917 Russian Revolution was proletarian and Marxist and in Chapter 22 we will ask the same question about the Chinese revolution of 1949.) As we have seen, in Britain three factors worked toward a relatively peaceful resolution of class tensions. First, workers' unions began to win their demands for higher pay, shorter hours, and better working conditions. Second, political institutions expanded to assimilate the new worker organizations and accommodate many of their demands. Third, legislation favorable to workers was passed, the franchise was extended, and the Labour party took its place in Parliament.

In retrospect, some of Marx and Engels' most enduring criticisms have been cultural rather than economic. They identified five critical areas of social-cultural tension during the height of the industrial revolution:

- the problem of coping with rapid change, as *The Communist Manifesto* observed: "all that is solid melts into air";
- the alienation of factory workers from their work, as they became insignificant cogs in great systems of production;
- the alienation of workers from nature, as farmers left the countryside to find jobs in urban industries;
- the dominance of the husband over the wife in the modern family and the earlier conditions of equality ended; and
- the economic competition that drove workers as well as owners to subordinate their own humanitarian and personal goals to the unceasing economic demands of the capitalist system.

Germany, 1870–1914. Although Marx was frustrated by the revival of conservative forces in continental Europe around 1848, a new wave of labor unrest and strikes swept across the region in the late 1860s and early 1870s, signaling the growing strength of labor. In Germany chief minister Otto von Bismarck (1815–98) pursued diverse and sometimes conflicting strategies to keep working people allied to his government. He extended universal male suffrage to the North German Confederation in 1867 and then to all of Germany when he unified the country in 1871 (see Chapter 18). But he limited the power of the legislature and diluted the power of the vote because government ministers were responsible to the king, not to Parliament. When Germany's opposition Social Democratic Party became Europe's first political party based on the working classes, in 1875, Bismarck sharply restricted its organizational activities. On the other hand, declaring "I too am a socialist," he passed legislation providing workers' disability and accident insurance and, in the 1880s, the first compulsory social security system in Europe. This legislation, however, covered only male industrial workers, not women or children. Thanks to government policies, worker militancy, and its learning from Britain's painful experiences, Germany did not repeat the worst conditions of child and female labor, and of the excessive hours and brutal conditions of industrial work.

The United States, 1870–1914. In the United States, labor began to organize especially with the industrialization that began after the Civil War (1861–5). A number of craft unions joined together to form the National Labor Union in 1866. It claimed 300,000 members by the early 1870s, but it did not survive the depression of 1873. The Noble Order of the Knights of Labor, founded as a secret society in 1869, grew into a mass union, open to all workers, with 700,000 members in 1886. The leadership of the Knights of Labor could not control its members, however, and various wildcat strikes broke out, some of them violent, alienating much of the rest of the membership. America's most successful labor organization was the American Federation of Labor, a union of skilled craft workers, founded in 1886 by Samuel Gompers (1850–1924). Its membership grew to 1 million by 1900 and 2 million by 1914. Women were not allowed to join, but in 1900 the International Ladies Garment Workers Union (ILGWU), which organized male and female workers who made women's clothing, was formed—with men dominating its leadership.

A series of strikes in America throughout the 1890s led to violence, sometimes in response to falling wages, often in response to poor working conditions or paternalism, the excessive control managers and owners held over workers' lives. Hired detectives, local police, and even soldiers attacked strikers and were attacked in return. Near Pittsburgh, steel workers lost the Homestead Steel strike in 1892 as the governor of Pennsylvania sent in 8000 troops. The American Railway Union under Eugene Debs lost a strike at the Pullman Palace Car Company in Chicago when the Governor of Illinois obtained a court injunction to force the workers back to their jobs. Violence ensued, leaving scores of workers dead. In resolving a 1908 strike of hat makers, the United States Supreme Court ruled that trade unions were subject to the Sherman Anti-Trust Act, leaving their members personally liable for business losses suffered during strikes. Until this ruling was reversed in the 1930s, militant unionism was virtually dead, although the small Industrial Workers of the World (IWW), representing a radical perspective on labor organization, did form in 1905 and was responsible for several major strikes, especially in western states.

The United States did develop powerful labor organizations, mostly in the twentieth century, but it never produced a significant political party based primarily on labor. Labor organization in the United States was fragmented into craft-specific unions. In this nation of immigrants, workers also held multiple identities; their ethnic identities frequently inhibited them from building union solidarity with those of other ethnic groups. Many immigrants came to America to earn money and return home; these workers did not usually have a commitment to active unionization. Pay scales and working conditions in the United States were significantly better than in Europe, further muting worker grievances. Finally, the capitalist ideology of the country discouraged class divisions, and the government restricted labor organization.

France, 1870–1914. As we have seen, worker revolts broke out repeatedly in France, many of them inspired by the French revolutionary tradition and others by the low wages and poor working conditions that characterized French industry. Skilled

Massacre of the Paris radicals. The slaughter meted out to the Paris Commune of 1871 is graphically depicted by the Post-Impressionist painter Edouard Manet. Left-wing urban leaders tried to set up their own state-within-a-state, but the communards were put down brutally by the national government. At least 20,000 were summarily executed and over 40,000 were taken prisoner. (*Museum Folkwang, Essen*)

artisans, displaced by new industries, often organized these revolts. Even before the industrial revolution took root, worker and artisanal revolts played a leading role in the French Revolution—and were crushed along with it. They boiled over again in 1848 and were crushed again as the army killed as many as 10,000 workers in street riots in Paris. Later in the century, the revolts were increasingly dominated by industrial workers. In 1871, much of the potential leadership of a workers' movement was once again wiped out. The French national government killed at least 20,000 people and exiled another 10,000 in the Paris Commune, an uprising of urban leaders in Paris.

A decade later, however, some of the exiles from the Paris Commune returned and organization began again, this time with greater success. In 1884 *syndicats*, labor unions, were legalized. Two competing federations were formed, one calling primarily for mutual help, the other for political action. Together, they numbered 140,000 members in 1890, a figure that more than tripled to 580,000 by the end of the century. By 1909, an umbrella group, the Confédération Génerale de Travail, numbered nearly a million. In 1890, May 1 was recognized as an annual "Labor Day." French politics, however, was dominated by the wealthier business leaders. Industrial workers organized, but they commanded less influence than farmers, shopkeepers, and small businessmen.

Labor in the Non-industrialized World. Wherever they reached, the new industrial products displaced old handicraft industries and workers. The craftsmen could not compete with the speed, consistent quality, and low price of the machine-made products. Many of them were ruined. The Indian cotton textile industry provided the most striking example. In 1834–5, the highest ranking British official in India lamented, "The bones of the cotton weavers are bleaching the plains of India." Lord Bentinck's remark was especially true in Bengal, in eastern India, a region that had participated heavily in the export trade, but to some degree it was true throughout India. And as a general observation on the fate of handicraft workers, the comment correctly captured the problem globally. Some of the displaced workers could find jobs in other crafts, not yet overtaken by the new industries. Some could continue their old crafts by cutting back farther and farther on their meager profits and incomes in order to try to compete with the machines. A few could produce fine handicrafts for the specialized luxury market. Many were pushed into agricultural work, especially as their countries could no longer compete as exporters of (hand) manufactured goods and were transformed into exporters of raw materials and importers of finished manufactures. In the industrializing world artisans were also displaced, but the rapidly expanding industries could absorb many of them. The craftspeople mourned the devaluation of their handicraft skills, and the cold, standardized rhythms of the machines wore down their spirits, but they had jobs and, as industrialization increased productivity, their incomes rose.

In some of the poorest countries—most notably India and China—indentured labor overseas became an alternative to unemployment for a wide range of peoples. Between 1831 and 1921, about 2 million people made their way from India and China and, to a lesser extent from Africa, the Pacific Islands, and Japan as indentured laborers to work primarily in the sugar plantations of the Caribbean, Mauritius and Réunion in the Indian Ocean, Hawaii, Fiji, and Peru. Four factors encouraged this mass migration. First, the end of slavery forced a search for alternative labor sources. Slavery did not end all at once, with the British ban on the slave trade in 1807, nor with Britain's outlawing slavery in its colonies in 1833. It continued in the USA until 1863, in Cuba until 1886, and in Brazil until 1888, and, illegally, even until today in many locations. After the formal end of slavery, many slaves continued to labor in conditions of semi-slavery. Nevertheless, the system was finished and a new source of labor was needed to supplement the quasi-slave population that continued. Second, the production of sugar increased globally, and dramatically, throughout the nineteenth century,

SOURCE

Tariffs, Wealth, and Poverty: Reflections on America and India by Pandita Ramabai

Pandita Ramabai (1858–1922) traveled in the United States for three years, 1886–9, and on her return home published a travelogue in Marathi. Translated literally as The Peoples of the United States, *it has recently been published in English as* Pandita Ramabai's American Encounter. *In India, Ramabai was a pioneering reformer for women's education. American women impressed her for their public accomplishments individually and in the groups that they often organized. Indeed, the whole country impressed her favorably. One of the areas in which America compared most favorably with India was in its control of its own tariff policy. American industry did so well, Ramabai argues, because it closed its markets to imports that might be competitive. She criticizes the Indian people for not similarly excluding foreign competitive goods, but she does not give any indication of recognizing that America was free to set its own exclusionary tariffs; India, under British colonial rule, had no such freedom. Her audience, however, would surely have understood that. Or was Ramabai urging her fellow Indians simply to boycott foreign goods voluntarily—to just say no— even without formal tariffs? Some Indian nationalists of her time were beginning to argue for that position, and by the early twentieth century, this would be the official position of the Indian National Congress, as we shall see in Chapter 22.*

The goods which come into this country from foreign countries are charged a heavy customs duty . . . The people here take great precautions to prevent the domination of foreign countries in trade and in other matters, and to prevent their becoming slaves of others . . . This is worth remembering by the people of our country who look to England for everything, who rely entirely on England, and who use English goods to the detriment of native industries and trade. The American said that drinking the tea and wearing the clothes imported from England harms the industries of his country; therefore he would never drink such tea or wear English clothes, but would content himself with whatever good or bad clothes were available in his own country. And he also acted accordingly. That is why this country has reached such prosperity today. And what have we achieved? We have given our gold and bought pots of pewter in return; we have shut down our handlooms and started wearing cheap English clothes. Like the Indians of North America, we have succumbed to the lure of shiny, colored glass beads; and we have sold our precious gem-studded land to foreigners in return for glass beads and glass bottles filled with wine. Now we are screaming because the wine has started to claim our lives, and the fragments of broken glass have made gaping wounds in our feet. This is why our country is in such a wretched state! This clearly shows that the United States and India are on opposite sides of the globe! (Ramabai, p. 227)

from 300,000 tons in 1790 to 10 million tons in 1914. Laborers were required even beyond the number of slaves previously employed in its cultivation and harvest.

Third, imperial reach connected far-flung regions of the world, making possible this international flow of labor. Indian indentured laborers traveling to the West Indies, or Mauritius, or Fiji remained within a single imperial system, with relatively similar laws, a single language of rule, and established systems of transportation and communication. One and a third million of them made the move. Similarly, indentured laborers from France's West African colonies migrating to the French Caribbean or to Réunion moved within a single system. The 387,000 Chinese who emigrated under terms of indenture—the majority of them to Cuba and Peru—were less tied into a single empire, but they were part of the global economic system that the Europeans had developed. This was also true for the 65,000 Japanese who migrated to Hawaii. The fourth element in the indentured traffic was the technological capacity to move so many people around the globe, forth and back, because the indentures of the servants were for limited time periods, usually five to seven years, after which they might go "back home." Sometimes they were encouraged to return, sometimes not.

The indentured laborers were not displaced persons in the industrial system as the craftsmen were. Most were farm laborers to begin with, but it was the industrial system that created the mechanisms of the indenture system. And many observers compared the conditions of gang labor on sugar plantations to the rigors and routinization of the factory work floor. The overwhelming majority of the servants were male, and the absence of females was probably relieved by the knowledge that after five or seven years the servants might return home to establish family life.

Many observers thought that the women who did sign on as indentured laborers were mostly prostitutes. Some were, but most, like the men, recognized that even the low pay of the overseas indentured laborer was at least double that of the Indian or Chinese agricultural worker. They moved to try to improve their situation. Although indentured servitude had some of the attributes of temporary slavery, it had a limited time frame, and thus the prospect of freedom at the end of years of indenture. For many it was a trap. For some it was an escape.

NEW PATTERNS OF URBAN LIFE

The core habitat of industrialization was the city. During the eighteenth century, cities began a period of growth that has continued without break until today. In the largest cities, by the late 1800s this process began to include middle-class suburbanization, which was made possible by the new railroad transportation systems for goods and passengers. In the early twentieth century, automobiles, buses, and trucks enlarged the system to ever-greater dimensions.

Much of the urban growth in the nineteenth century was a direct result of industrialization. The steam engine, which could be constructed anywhere, made the location of industries more flexible. Factories sprang up near port facilities, at inland transportation hubs, in the heart of raw materials resource centers, such as the Midlands of England, or Silesia in central Europe, and near large concentrations of consumers, like the great cities of Paris and London. New industrial metropolises dotted the map.

Immigrants streamed into the new cities for jobs. Farmers became factory workers and the balance between urban and rural populations tilted continuously cityward. Within cities, the children of artisans became factory workers. Both farmers and artisans found the new industrial city shocking. They were exchanging the styles of life of

SOURCE

Diverse Perspectives

Like the proverbial elephant that appeared different to each person who approached it from a different perspective, the industrial city signified something different to each observer. Wordsworth and Blake (p. 570) had certainly seen early nineteenth-century London very differently. From the middle of the century, two additional poets from two additional cities provide still different points of view. Charles Baudelaire presents the hard-working people of Paris—indeed the city itself— as just struggling to get by at the break of a new day.

The crow of a rooster, far off, cuts
　through the hazy air.
A sea of fog bathes the buildings.
Men in agony in the workhouses
Heave their dying breath in
　undignified gasps.
The debauched return home,
　broken by their work.
The shivering dawn robed in pink
　and green
Advances slowly along the
　deserted Seine,
And somber, aging, Paris, rubbing
　its eyes,
Picks up its tools, and sets to work

While Baudelaire anguished with his city's lonely despair, in the United States, Walt Whitman sang rapturously of the dynamism of his own Manhattan, New York:

The down-town streets, the jobbers' houses of
　business, the houses of business of the
ship-merchants and money-brokers, the river-
　streets,
Immigrants arriving, fifteen or twenty thousand in
　a week,
The carts hauling goods, the manly race of drivers
　of horses, the brown-faced sailors,
The summer air, the bright sun shining, and the
　sailing clouds aloft,
The winter snows, the sleigh-bells, the broken ice in
　the river, passing along up or down
with the flood-tide or ebb-tide,
The mechanics of the city, the masters, well-form'd,
　beautiful faced, looking you straight in the eyes,
Trottoirs throng'd, vehicles, Broadway, the women,
　the shops and shows,
A million people—manners free and superb—open
　voices—hospitality—the most
courageous and friendly young men,
City of hurried and sparkling waters! City of spires
　and masts!
City nested in bays! My city!

Back Queen Street, Deansgate, Manchester. As this *Illustrated London News* drawing of housing conditions of the Manchester cotton operatives in 1862 shows, accommodation in this city could be spartan. Manchester in particular, with its high mortality rate, desperately needed the attentions of voluntary agencies that were attempting to better the living conditions of those who had been drawn to work in the new industries. Despite the fact that many workers emigrated to the United States or to British colonies overseas, the population continued to grow at a great rate, with adverse consequences for public health and housing.

farm and workshop for regimes of routinization, standardization, and regulation. The skills that they had previously mastered were of little use here. At the same time, opportunities beckoned: cultural, educational, recreational, social, and, most important, economic. In the early years of the industrial revolution, conditions of labor and of public health were abysmal; later, as productivity increased, workers organized, employers and governments paid heed, and conditions started to improve. "City lights" began to appear more attractive. The nineteenth century began the age of global urbanization.

Philosophical and sociological speculations on the nature of the city also flourished and were equally diverse. In Germany, Max Weber (1864–1920) analyzed the modern industrial city as a new creation. He contrasted, negatively, its freewheeling life and amorphous institutions against the close-knit guilds and political and religious associations of earlier self-governing European cities, especially medieval cities (see Chapter 13). Weber concluded that the sprawling industrial city—open to any immigrant who wished to come and embedded within a nation-state that controlled its life and politics—was quite different from the self-contained city of earlier times. Europe, at least, was living in a new era.

Many observers agreed that the openness of the industrial city and the lack of institutional ties among its citizens were leading to a breakdown of the social fabric and a breakdown of the individual personality. The division of labor was turning the individual into a specialist concerned only with narrow interests; the sense of personal or community wholeness was lost. And the sheer multitude of people and experiences in the city was also forcing the individual to retreat even further into a small, private niche. The urban dweller was evolving into a person swift of intellect to achieve his own needs, but lacking concern for and integration with the larger community.

Georg Simmel (1858–1918), a social psychologist in Germany, wrote in 1903 of the destabilizing effects of these new cities:

> The individual has become a mere cog in an enormous organization of things and powers which tears from his hands all progress, spirituality, and value in order to transform them from their subjective form into the form of a purely objective life … the metropolis is the genuine arena of this culture which outgrows all personal life.

Here ... is offered such an overwhelming fullness of crystallized and impersonalized spirit that the personality, so to speak, cannot maintain itself under its impact. (Sennett, pp. 58–9)

Some observers claimed to see the negative effects of urban individualism as part of an historical process that would ultimately lead to disaster. Oswald Spengler (1880–1936), a German philosopher of history, declared that the enormous "world-cities" of his day were inevitably destroying the spirit of the folk peoples that had built them. In his famous book *The Decline of the West* he argued that this destructive cycle of urban growth and decay had occurred before:

This, then, is the conclusion of the city's history; growing from primitive barter-center to culture-city and at last to world-city, it sacrifices first the blood and soul of its creators to the needs of its majestic evolution, and then the last flower of that growth to the spirit of Civilization—and so, doomed, moves on to final self-destruction. (Sennett, p. 85)

These attacks on urban life perpetuated the centuries-old cultural struggle between the cosmopolitan city of businessmen and the (perhaps imagined) homogeneous country-side of the common folk. The struggle was most extreme in rapidly industrializing Germany. German cities like Berlin had not experienced the same rise and liberation of the merchant classes as had those in Britain, the Netherlands, and France. A generation after Spengler, Germany would turn inward, filled with praise for the traditional values of "the Volk, the People"—meaning the native-born, rural people—and scorn the more diverse, cosmopolitan urbanites (see Chapter 19).

Within this array of sociological, psychological, mythological, and pathological evaluations of the industrial city, many scholars believed that quantitative statistical studies would enable both residents of the industrial city and their observers to understand most clearly the processes through which they were living and to make plans for future directions. Just as accurate measurement and assessment had helped bring in the industrial era, so they helped in its evaluation. Two men—Adna Ferrin Weber, an academic researcher, and Charles Booth, a businessman who wanted to understand the problems of urban poverty in order to combat them—launched quite different, exemplary, quantitative studies of the city that inspired public action as well as further research. Weber's study was global, looking at cities around the world, wherever statistics were available, and found clear correlations between the rate of industrialization, the growth of cities, the strength of immigration, and the increase in standard of living. Booth dispatched researchers throughout London to quantify the conditions of life among the poor. His findings inspired new social movements and legislation.

In the United States, with millions of immigrants streaming into its cities in

Gustave Caillebotte, *Paris, a Rainy Day*, 1876–77. An Impressionist's-eye-view of life in an urban setting. Although a number of studies suggest that the burgeoning urban development of the turn of the century ground down the lives of the poor, for the bourgeoisie, with leisure time on their hands, cities provided a backdrop for pleasure. (*Musée Marmottan, Paris*)

HOW DO WE KNOW?

Quantifying the Conditions of Industrial Urbanization

"The most remarkable social phenomenon of the present century is the concentration of population in cities." These words open Adna Ferrin Weber's The Growth of Cities in the Nineteenth Century, published in 1899, the first comprehensive quantitative study of the subject. A century later it remains an invaluable introduction to the central issues. In the rivalry between city and countryside, Weber generally paid tribute to the role of the city:

> In the last half-century [1848–98], all the agencies of modern civilization have worked together to abolish this rural isolation; the cities have torn down their fortifications, which separated them from the open country; while the railways, the newspaper press, freedom of migration and settlement, etc., cause the spread of the ideas originating in the cities and lift the people of the rural districts out of their state of mental stagnation. Industry is also carried on outside of the cities, so that the medieval distinction between town and country has lost its meaning in the advanced countries. (pp. 7–8)

Apart from their cultural contributions, cities and industry were needed to absorb the surplus growth of rural population. In most of Europe, except France, he writes, "the rural populations, by reason of their continuous increase, produce a surplus which must migrate either to the cities or foreign lands" (p. 67). Without cities and industrial jobs, what would happen to this surplus population? This rhetorical question implied by Weber continues to our own day.

Weber began with a statistical summary and an analysis of levels of urbanization in his own time, and traced it back through the nineteenth century. As part of his research, Weber attempted global coverage and he gathered his data from official government publications as well as unofficial population estimates from around the world. In general, he found industrialization the main reason for city growth. England and Wales, 62

percent urban, were by far the most industrialized and the most urbanized regions on earth. The next closest were Australia, at 42 percent, and various parts of Germany, at about 30 percent. In general, the largest cities were growing fastest. London, the world's largest city in 1890, held 4.2 million people; New York, the second largest, 2.7 million. The least industrialized countries were the least urbanized—below 10 percent—but most of these countries did not maintain statistical records.

In contrast to the gloom of poverty and oppression pictured by Marx and Engels a half century earlier, Weber radiated optimism about the direction of urban life, including increasing levels of longevity and personal comfort. Describing conditions that only the wealthiest could enjoy, he wrote:

> Consider the conveniences at the disposal of the fin de siècle [end of the century] housewife: a house with a good part of the old-fashioned portable furniture built into it, e.g., china cabinets, refrigerators, wardrobes, sideboards, cheval glasses [full-length, swivel mirrors], bath tubs, etc.; electric lights, telephones and electric buttons in every room, automatic burglar alarms, etc. ... [Weber then quotes another urban advocate:] Thus has vanished the necessity for drawing water, hewing wood, keeping a cow, churning, laundering clothes, cleaning house, beating carpets, and very much of the rest of the onerous duties of housekeeping, as our mothers knew it. (pp. 218–20)

A judicious scholar, Weber did not omit the many negative aspects of city life at the end of the nineteenth century. Although death rates in the city had been declining steadily, urban death rates in 1899 remained higher than rural ones in most countries. In one of the worst examples, during the decade 1880–90, when the expected length of life at birth for all of England and Wales was forty-seven years, in Manchester, one of the greatest centers of the early industrial revolution, it was twenty-nine. Industrialization exacted its costs. Nevertheless, Weber reviewed the public

health measures such as water and sewage systems and the provision of clinics that had already been effective in other places, strongly advocated more of them, and remained optimistic about the urban future—if urbanites could cooperate for the common good.

Weber's pioneering statistical work gives us one flavor of industrial urbanization at the end of the nineteenth-century. Charles Booth (1840–1916) gives quite another. Booth led a team of researchers in London, which produced the seventeen volumes of Life and Labour of the People in London. Between 1886 and 1903, Booth and his colleagues systematically visited thousands of homes throughout London, interviewing workers to discover how the working people of the metropolis labored and lived. They concentrated their efforts in East London, the most industrialized, and most distressed, area of the city. The researchers asked questions about such critical issues as occupations, levels of income and consumption, housing size and quality, quantity and quality of amenities. They began with these statistical questions and then proceeded to qualitative discussion of the neighborhoods and their character. They concluded by asking what was being done, and what could be done, to improve conditions, especially through religious institutions.

- For Weber and for Booth, what was the relationship between formal, quantitative study of the city, and action to deal with its problems?
- How might the global research of Weber be integrated with the local, community research of Booth? How might the research of one influence the research of the other?
- Based on other readings from this chapter, what, if anything, is surprising about the research findings of Weber and Booth?

Guaranty Building in Buffalo, New York, designed by Louis Henry Sullivan, 1894–96. Sullivan's designs for steel-frame construction of large buildings—made possible because steel was now readily available and the elevator had been invented—were the forerunners of today's skyscrapers. A glance at the skyline of any large American or European city will confirm that Sullivan greatly influenced twentieth-century architecture, particularly in the United States. Sullivan's working principle that form follows function applied to the tall buildings (up to ten stories in the late nineteenth century) that he designed. It was important to maximize the limited space in city centers, and the idea of carrying buildings upward instead of outward met the need.

search of industrial jobs, urban diversity was accepted, even valued, and certainly studied. The "Chicago School of urban ecology" took form about the time of World War I as scholars at the University of Chicago studied their own city, the world's fastest growing industrial metropolis of the day. To some degree, they philosophized and speculated as did the Germans, but, building on studies like those of Weber and Booth, they also launched empirical research into conditions in the city. They studied neighborhoods within the city as well as the metropolis as a whole.

The Chicago School argued that urbanites did not live their lives downtown, as so many previous scholars had implied, but in local neighborhoods, each of which had its own characteristics. Within these neighborhoods, people's lives were not so disconnected, isolated, or alienated as they might appear superficially. At the end of the day, most people went back to their own homes in their own neighborhoods, places where they had a strong sense of self and community. The variety of social and economic lifestyles multiplied with the size of the city and the diversity of its functions. Neighborhoods reflected this diversity.

A comprehensive perspective on the city would have to take account of neighborhoods as well as business districts. These commercial areas themselves were quickly increasing in size, complexity, and facilities. By the 1870s, department stores, coffeehouses, pubs, and restaurants had added urbanity to the central business district, attracting retail shoppers, window shoppers, and people with some leisure time. Theaters, concert houses, museums, the press and publishing houses, libraries, clubs, and a multitude of new voluntary associations provided culture and entertainment. They also created a "public sphere"—a setting in which citizens form and circulate their most influential civic ideas, goals, and aspirations. Here was the modern analogue of the ancient Greek *agora*.

A new transportation system made possible this specialization of commercial, cultural, industrial, and residential neighborhoods within the city. London opened its first underground railway system in 1863, the first major subway system in the world, and others followed. From the 1870s, commuter railways began to service new suburbs, and electric trolleys came into service after 1885. The availability of steel at commercial prices made possible the construction of skyscrapers, and the invention of elevators made them accessible. The first skyscrapers rose in the 1880s, beginning with ten-story buildings in Chicago.

Urban Planning: The Middle Ground of Optimists and Pessimists

Both optimists like Weber and pessimists (or realists) like Booth agreed that the industrial city had serious problems, and both agreed that serious planning was necessary to cope with them. Town planning as a profession was born. One of the central problems of the industrializing city of the early nineteenth century was crowding. Poor ventilation, inadequate sanitation, unclean water, alienation from nature, and poor health—especially tuberculosis—resulted as densities in urban cores reached, and even surpassed, 100,000 people per square mile. By the last decades of the century the electric trolley cars and commuter railways offered the means to suburbanize, and the city expanded in area as never before. At first the densities in the center did not appear to diminish, for the stream of new immigrants to the city matched and even exceeded those who were suburbanizing.

By the late 1800s, town planners began seeking comprehensive solutions to the new problem: How to provide space for population increase, allow for geographical expansion, yet continue to provide green space, while fostering participation in both the local community and the metropolis as a whole? The British reformer Ebenezer Howard (1850–1928) provided one of the first proposals in his book *Tomorrow: A Peaceful Path to Real Reform* (1898), later revised and reissued as *Garden Cities of Tomorrow* (1902). Howard's schematic plan for a "Group of Slumless Smokeless Cities" illustrates his provocative concept of a region of about 250,000 people on 66,000 acres. This would be far too miniature to cope with the problems of a London or a New York. Its intense control over the planning process also demanded political decisions that might not be possible within a participatory democracy. Nevertheless, the **garden city** concept of a core city ringed by separate suburbs, each set in a green belt, linked to one another by rapid transit, provided provocative, creative, somewhat utopian thinking for the new urban problems dawning with the new century.

garden city A planned town combining work, residential, agricultural, and recreational facilities, and surrounded by a rural belt.

THE INDUSTRIAL REVOLUTION
WHAT DIFFERENCE DOES IT MAKE?

By the beginning of the twentieth century, the industrial revolution had brought unprecedented wealth and power to those who had mastered its technologies—especially the rulers and elites of the nations of Western Europe and the United States. Applying inanimate power, where previously there had been only humans and animals, had brought new productivity. Agriculture changed first, through enclosures and changing agricultural practices, becoming both more intensive and more extensive, so that fewer farmers could feed more people, freeing—and forcing—many of their fellow workers to leave their farms for urban, industrial jobs. In the cities, steam power and later electrical power enabled factories and the new goods they produced to multiply. Families were restructured in the new urban, industrial settings, with changing relationships between husbands and wives, and more formal schooling for children. Women raised their voices, demanding an equality that they had felt on the family farm and were in danger of losing on the factory floor and in the urban household, with its smaller family groups, greater longevity, and proportionately fewer years that parents spent in raising children. Railway track and steamship lines girdled the earth, and the oceans were connected by canals. Electricity lit up the night, provided the bright lights of the city, powered telephones and telegraphs, and supplied energy to factories and homes in remote areas. With a feeling of self-satisfied triumphalism, the masters of this industrializing world conquered much of the land surface of the world and made it their colonial possession, thus bringing remote areas into the web of the industrial world, whether they wished to be there or not.

In the industrialized countries, the earlier years of poverty, insecurity, filth, and high death rates for industrial workers seemed to be passing as increasing productivity provided more material benefits, unions provided representation, and governments began to legislate in their favor—although the battles for workers' welfare were far from over. Antagonism between captains of industry and their workers continued. New kinds of social relationships formed among industrial workers as they arrived in new urban neighborhoods, with opportunities and constraints quite different from those they had known in their rural homes. They were living in a world transformed and now they were transforming themselves by building new kinds of communities along with their neighbors, friends, and co-workers.

Millions of migrants were on the move, from village to city, from country to country, and from continent to continent. Most traveled as free immigrants, but almost ten million people from poorer countries traveled as indentured laborers to supply the still-flourishing plantations of the world in the aftermath of the abolition of slavery.

The condition of many of the "free" migrants, too, was often precarious. All of these groups formed new kinds of communities in their new homes. The study of sociology was born and flourished.

The industrial revolution restructured the world profoundly, as thoroughly as the agricultural revolution had done some five thousand years earlier. Today we speak of living in a post-industrial world. Our sources of energy, our means of transportation and communication, our international and intercontinental connectivity, our cities, our political institutions, our levels of technical and professional education, our family and gender relationships are in many respects different from those at the height of the industrial revolution, yet they are all built on the transformations of that era. Those of us who live in countries that went through the industrial revolution as it unfolded still live with its infrastructure. Those of us who live in countries that did not directly experience the full weight of that revolution—in large parts of Africa and Asia, in particular—are now trying to understand what parts of that revolution we must recreate in order to cope with the modern world, and what parts we may "leapfrog," finding a new way of achieving some of the benefits of that revolution without going directly through it; establishing networks of cell phone communication, for example, and using that technology, without ever establishing a network of land lines, with all of their infrastructure and expense. While one group is emerging from the industrial revolution, another may be attempting to bypass it.

Review Questions

In answering the first five questions, you may wish to specify different perspectives for different countries and time periods.

- What would you identify as the key social changes introduced by the industrial revolution?
- To what degree do you see rural people benefiting or losing out as a result of the industrial revolution?
- How are industrialization, urbanization, and immigration related to one another?
- In which ways do you see women benefiting from the industrial revolution? In which ways to you see them losing out?
- What were the new political problems raised by the industrial revolution?
- To what degree do you think we can consider the world today as still living in a period of industrial revolution? To what degree do you think that period is past?

Suggested Readings

PRINCIPAL SOURCES

Adas, Michael, ed. *Islamic and European Expansion* (Philadelphia: Temple University Press, 1993). Excellent anthology of historiographical articles that introduce modern world history. Several articles on the period of the industrial revolution and its effects on men and women.

Headrick, Daniel R. *The Tools of Empire* (New York: Oxford University Press, 1981). The industrial revolution gave to Europeans the tools to create empire: weapons, steamships, quinine.

Marx, Karl and Frederick Engels. *The Communist Manifesto* (New York: International Publishers, 1948). The great critique of the evils of industrial capitalism and a revolutionary agenda to overthrow it.

Stearns, Peter N. *The Industrial Revolution in World History* (Boulder, CO: Westview Press, 1993). Excellent introduction to the background, development, and significance of the industrial revolution in global scope and historical time depth.

Thompson, E.P. *The Making of the English Working Class* (New York: Vintage, 1966). Thompson taught us to see the working class not only in Marxist terms but also in cultural terms, to understand their lives as more than just revolutionary fighters.

ADDITIONAL SOURCES

Andrea, Alfred and James Overfield, eds. *The Human Record*, Vol. 2 (Boston: Houghton Mifflin, 3rd ed., 1998). Excellent anthology for world history.

Bairoch, Paul. *Cities and Economic Development*, trans. by Christopher Braider (Chicago: University of Chicago Press, 1988). Heavily quantitative assessment of cities' role in economic development.

Bell, Susan Groag and Karen M. Offen, eds. *Women, the Family, and Freedom: The Debate in Documents, Vol. 1, 1750–1880* (Stanford: Stanford University Press, 1985). Excellent selection of documents on the feminist movement, with insightful commentary.

Braudel, Fernand. *Civilization and Capitalism 15th–18th Century: The Perspective of the World*, trans. by Sian Reynolds (New York: Harper and Row, 1984). Excellent, sweeping background to the industrial revolution.

Davis, Lance E. and Robert A. Huttenback. *Mammon and the Pursuit of Empire* (New York: Cambridge University Press, 1989). Stresses the importance of economic interests, private and public, in the creation of empire.

Engels, Friedrich. *The Condition of the Working Class in England*, trans. by W.O. Henderson and W.H. Chaloner (Stanford: Stanford University Press, 1968). THE explication of the horrors of early industrialization in England, written by a young businessman who became a communist because of what he saw with his own eyes.

——. *The Origins of the Family, Private Property, and the State*, ed. by Eleanor Burke Leacock (New York: International Publishers, 1973). Condemns the contemporary (1884) status of women and urges fundamental restructuring.

Hobsbawm, Eric. *The Age of Capital 1848–1875* (New York: Vintage Books, 1975). This series by Hobsbawm provides an excellent overview of the period of the industrial revolution. Global, but strongest on Europe. Critical of capitalism.

——. *The Age of Empire 1875–1914* (New York: Vintage, 1987).

Kennedy, Paul. *The Rise and Fall of the Great Powers* (New York: Random House, 1987). Great empires since 1500 have been built and preserved by careful attention to the balance between guns and butter, military expenditure and a thriving civilian economy.

Lenin, V.I. *Imperialism, the Highest Stage of Capitalism* (Peking: Foreign Languages Press, 1965). The classic view that industrial nations seek empires as marketplaces for buying raw materials and selling finished products because home markets alone are insufficient.

Perrot, Michelle. *Workers on Strike; France, 1871–1890*, trans. by Chris Turner with Erica Carter and Claire Laudet (Leamington Spa: Berg, 1987). Useful study of labor organization in industrial France.

Ramabai Sarasvati, Pandita. *Pandita Ramabai's American Encounter: The Peoples of the United States (1889)* trans. and ed. by Meera Kosambi (Bloomington: University of Indiana Press, 2003). A rare travelogue by an Indian woman, concerned with economic, social, and political development in America with special attention to women's progress.

Revel, Jacques and Lynn Hunt, eds. *Histories: French Constructions of the Past*, trans. by Arthur Goldhammer *et al.* (New York: New York Press, 1995). How French historians understand the significance of their nation's history. New interpretations for new times.

Sennett, Richard, ed. *Classic Essays on the Culture of Cities* (Englewood Cliffs: Prentice Hall, 1969). An excellent selection of classical sociological essays.

Wallerstein, Immanuel. *The Modern World-system 1: Capitalist Agriculture and the Origins of the European World-economy in the Sixteenth Century* (San Diego: Academic Press, 1974). The fullest exposition of the theory of core-periphery exploitative development, with Europe and the US as the core and Asia, Africa, and Latin America as the periphery.

Weber, Adina Ferrin. *The Growth of Cities in the Nineteenth Century: A Study in Statistics* (Ithaca: Cornell University Press, 1963). A dissertation that became a key to the quantitative understanding of urban growth worldwide.

⊚ World History Documents CD-ROM

19.1 Benjamin Disraeli: *Sybil* (1845)
19.2 Women Miners in the English Coal Pits
19.3 Sadler Report: Child Labor
19.4 Andrew Ure: *A Defense of the Factory System* (1835)
19.5 The Chartist Demands (1838)
19.6 Luddism: An Assault on Technology
19.7 Robert Owen: *Utopian Socialism* (1816)
19.8 Karl Marx and Friedrich Engels

NATIONALISM, IMPERIALISM, AND RESISTANCE

COMPETITION AMONG INDUSTRIAL POWERS 1650–1914

KEY TOPICS

- Nationalism
- The Quest for Empire
- Africa, 1652–1912
- Gender Relationships in Colonization
- Anti-Colonial Revolts, 1857–1914
- Japan: from Isolation to Equality, 1867–1914
- Nationalism and Imperialism: What Difference Do They Make?

NATIONALISM

The political and industrial revolutions of the seventeenth, eighteenth, and nineteenth centuries gave birth to modern nationalism, a commitment to building up the nation as a central part of the identity of the citizen and as a powerful force in world affairs. Like the ideals of democracy and the productivity of the industrial revolution, the belief in nationalism has continued to shape the world to this day.

The French Revolution, the Napoleonic Wars, and Nationalism

The ideology and actions of the French Revolution gave a new definition to the concept of the nation and introduced new political and cultural loyalties. In 1789, the members of the National Assembly, declaring themselves "the representatives of the people of France," proclaimed in the *Declaration of the Rights of Man and the Citizen*: "The source of all sovereignty is located essentially in the nation; no body, no individual can exercise authority which does not emanate from it expressly." This Declaration proclaimed that the people of France were forging a social contract, swearing allegiance not to a ruler, religion, or language/ethnic group but to all the people of the nation—a common political group. The Declaration seemed to take for granted the primordial elements of French nationality—a common language, history, geography, and vision for the future. It ratified a new national identity for France. The French state took to itself new, unprecedented powers. It had the authority to tax in the name of the nation, the very authority that Louis XVI had sought for himself when he had convened the Estates General. Asserting the authority to draft virtually the entire adult male population of the country for the army in the new *levée en masse*, France conscripted an army numbering hundreds of thousands. Backed by this army, France swept across Europe between 1791 and 1815, not only to conquer others but also to promote its idea of nationalism. French armies imposed their imperial governments on the nations they conquered, and, after the promulgation of the Napoleonic Code in 1804, they imposed their legal system as well. The new message seemed

Opposite **Kobaysgu Kiyochika, The Sino-Japanese War in Korea, 1894. Engraving.** Japanese forces are shown firing down on their Korean enemy as a journalist makes notes in the foreground. (*Victoria & Albert Museum, London*)

clear: A people organized under a national banner of its own making could act with unprecedented power to tax, to fight, to legislate, to conquer, and to rule.

French nationalism and French military power evoked the nationalism of other countries in response, especially in Britain and Russia. Russia's nationalism expressed itself in the power to resist, to stage a strategic retreat until Napoleon's French army was mired, frozen, and starved in the depths of Russia's winter, and then to fight back. The British, by contrast, mobilized their navy and army immediately to confront the French and ultimately to prevail. The wealth generated by the early stages of its industrial revolution enabled Britain to finance these armed struggles.

These wars demonstrated that nations could mobilize powerful forces militarily, economically, and politically. Disorganized nations, on the other hand, lay open to conquest. At least in part as a response to the power that France demonstrated in its Napoleonic Wars, new nations asserted their independence in many regions of the

AT A GLANCE : THE WORLD BEYOND THE INDUSTRIALIZED WEST

DATE	OTTOMAN EMPIRE	INDIA, S-E ASIA & CHINA	AFRICA
1800		■ Sir Stamford Raffles establishes Singapore for the British (1819) ■ Shaka seizes leadership of the Zulu kingdom near the Cape Colony (1816)	■ British forces drive Napoleon from Egypt (1801); Muhammad Ali assumes rule (1807)
1820	■ Greece wins independence; Serbia, Wallachia, and Moldavia gain autonomy (1829) ■ French gain control of Algeria from empire (1830) ■ Muhammad Ali renders Egypt effectively independent (1832)	■ Java War, Dutch vs. Indonesians (1825–30) ■ Dutch introduce cultivation system in Indonesia (1830) ■ First Opium War (1839–42): China cedes Hong Kong to the British	■ Great Trek north by the Boers (Afrikaners) (1834–41) ■ French invade Algeria (1830); warfare with al-Qadir (1841)
1840	■ Crimean War (1853–4) ■ Westernization encouraged in the Hatt-i Humayun edict (1856)	■ Taiping Rebellion begins (1850); suppressed 1864 ■ "First War for National Independence" in India (1857) ■ Russians seize Amur River region (1858) ■ Second Opium War (1856–60): Beijing occupied by French and British	■ David Livingstone lands along Angola coast for first African expedition (1841)
1860	■ Young Turks go into exile (1876) ■ Russian attack through the Balkans reaches Istanbul (1877)	■ Russians seize Maritime Provinces (1860) and Ili valley in Turkestan (1871–81)	■ Suez Canal opens (1869) ■ Diamonds and gold discovered in the Cape Colony region ■ Egyptian *khedive* forced to add European representatives to his cabinet (1878)
1880		■ France seizes all of Indochina (1883–93) ■ Germany annexes Eastern New Guinea and the Marshall and Solomon Islands (1880s) ■ Japan defeats China in warfare (1894–5) ■ Boxer Rebellion (1898–1900) ■ Ethiopia defeats Italian forces at Adowa (1896)	■ Bismarck's Berlin Convention apportions Africa among competing powers (1884) ■ General Kitchener retakes Sudan in Battle of Omdurman (1898) ■ Rhodesia (now Zimbabwe and Zambia) named after Cecil John Rhodes (1898) ■ Boer War (1899–1902)
1900	■ Italy takes Libya from weakened empire (1911)	■ India's first steel mill at Jamshedpur, Bihar (1911) ■ Subcontinent has 35,000 miles of railroad track (1914)	■ Maji-Maji revolt against German rule in Tanganyika (1905–07) ■ Belgian Parliament takes over control of the Congo (1908) ■ British form Union of South Africa (1910) ■ Natives Land Act closes 87 percent of South African land to African ownership (1913)

world in the early nineteenth century. In the Balkans, Greece achieved its independence from the Ottoman Empire in 1829, and other break-away regions soon followed. The regions of South America claimed their independence of Spain and Portugal. Canada asserted its unity and its autonomy from Britain. Italy and Germany successfully created unified countries out of disparate petty states. And the United States survived a civil war to re-assert its unity as a powerful, expanding nation.

The Periphery of Western Europe

Nationalists—people who asserted their wish and responsibility to create, strengthen, and consolidate their nations—were most active on the periphery of western Europe. In southeastern Europe, revolts in the Balkans broke out from 1815 onward in the name of individual nationalities. The first successful revolt was that of the Greek peoples against the Ottoman Empire. Greece won its independence in 1829 with the backing of military forces dispatched by Britain, France, and Russia. At the same time, other Ottoman territories also gained autonomy: Serbia, Wallachia and Moldavia in present-day Romania, and Egypt. The western European powers supported these aggressive nationalisms in the Balkans and northeast Africa because they diminished the power of the Ottoman Empire while increasing their own leverage within the regions.

Nationalism always has two faces. As a positive force, it promises to empower the masses of a nation with freedom and evoke their collective participation in building new futures. As a negative force, it threatens to compel the masses to serve the state and to turn one nation against another in destructive warfare. The Balkans have seen both these faces. Some nationalist movements won independence and the possibility of greater freedom and creativity. On the other hand, a century of simmering nationalism throughout the region climaxed in 1914 when a Serbian nationalist assassinated the Crown Prince of Austria-Hungary in Sarajevo after the Emperor Franz Joseph annexed Bosnia—a territory Serbia desired for itself—in 1908. The major powers of Europe soon took sides, and World War I began (see Chapter 19). And, as we shall see in Chapter 24, nationalism in the Balkans continues today as a potent and often violent force.

In Chapter 16 we noted the revolutions in Latin America. Continent-wide revolts broke down into individual national movements, undermining the unifying visions of Simón Bolívar and José de San Martín. Nationalism did not represent everyone within Latin America. Although nationalists spoke in the name of "the people," they mostly represented specific groups: lawyers, journalists, teachers, and military officials. Nationalism in South America was a "top-down" movement of elites.

In Canada, the Report to the British government by the Earl of Durham in 1839 led to the unification of mostly English-speaking Upper Canada, today's Ontario, with mostly French-speaking Lower Canada, today's Quebec. Lord Durham urged the institution of responsible government over domestic affairs and the rapid development of railways and canals to consolidate the nation. The British Government quickly accepted and implemented the Durham Report. In 1867, Britain established the Dominion of Canada, increasing the scope of parliamentary democracy and adding the eastern maritime provinces to the core of Quebec and Ontario. Tensions between the British and French regions of Canada diminished, but they have not disappeared. Nevertheless, Canadian nationalism has continued to prevail over regionalism.

The United States, a land of immigrants from its inception, had established itself as a nation based on an oath binding all of its diverse citizens to the common good. Americans declared in their Constitution:

We, the People of the United States, in Order to form a more perfect Union, establish Justice, insure domestic Tranquility, provide for the common defence, promote the general Welfare, and secure the blessings of Liberty to ourselves and our Posterity, do ordain and establish this Constitution for the United States of America.

With this Constitution the United States declared that the nation was not necessarily an array of people who shared a common history, geography, language, race, ethnicity, religion, and language. A nation could be formed on the basis of a new vision of the present and future and adherence to a common law.

Foreign observers, like Alexis de Tocqueville (1805–59), commented on the newness of America and its lack of history. A substantial proportion of America's institutions, and of its population, was drawn from the British Isles, but immigrants came from all over the world. Some were excluded from full citizenship, including African-American slaves, Native American Indians, and women. But the pattern for future inclusion was also being set. Many, but not all, new immigrants could join this nation, and, after slaves were freed, so could they, although racism remained a powerful force. Native Americans remained torn between allegiances to Indian nations and the American nation. Despite these divisions, the American Constitution illustrated the degree to which a nation was constituted by the will of its people, and especially of its leaders, rather than by primordial historical legacies.

In 1861, the American nation was faced with a struggle for survival when the eleven Confederate States of America seceded from the Union. The Confederacy claimed greater rights for constituent states, especially the right to sanction slavery, and it favored agrarian rather than industrial economic policies. Some 500,000 men were killed in the Civil War that followed. Immediately following the war, the victorious central government instituted generous policies favoring reconciliation (often at the expense of the recently freed ex-slaves), although later these policies became more punitive. After the war, with unity secure, and Northern business leaders asserting great powers, the industrial and economic expansion of the United States set a pace exceeding that of any other nation.

Italy and Germany

In the heart of Europe, nationalism grew in hard soil. The great powers of Austria, Prussia, Russia, France, and Britain suppressed new national uprisings by peoples within their empires. At their meeting to draft the peace settlements at the Congress of Vienna in 1814–15 after the Napoleonic Wars, they set limits on national movements in central Europe. Led by Prince Clemens von Metternich (1773–1859), foreign minister of Austria, conservative leaders of the major European powers were successful in quelling powerful nationalistic uprisings in Poland, Prussia, Italy, and Hungary between 1846 and 1849. (Belgium did gain national independence, from the Dutch, in 1830.) In western Europe, Irish nationalism became increasingly important as the Irish wanted to abrogate the Act of Union of 1801 that made Ireland a part of Great Britain and to preserve the Gaelic language. Under the leadership of Daniel O'Connell, Young Ireland organized hundreds of thousands of people until the British arrested him on conspiracy charges. Only in the 1850s did nationalism win major victories in lands under these empires. Then Italy and Germany began successfully to unite their several divided regions to form new nations. In each country, cultural nationalism preceded political mobilization.

Before 1870, neither Italy nor Germany existed as the unified nations we know today. Each was divided up into many petty states under the control of different rulers. In Italy, the largest single state was the kingdom of Sardinia-Piedmont, but other states

For an interactive version of this map, go to: http://www.prenhall.com/spodek/map18.1

The unification of Italy and Germany.
The middle years of the nineteenth century saw popular forces drawing together the disparate territories of central Europe into modern nation states. In Germany the political, military, and economic strength of Prussia had been growing for over two centuries, and Bismarck's wars with Denmark (1864), Austria (1866), and France (1870) eventually secured the union. In Italy the expansion of Piedmont–Sardinia into Lombardy, Venetia, and Rome, and Garibaldi's march through the south, united the nation.

were controlled by other rulers. The area around Venice was controlled by Austria, and the region around Rome by the pope. Most of the small states of Germany had been included within Charlemagne's empire, founded in 800 C.E., and then within its successor institution, the Holy Roman Empire. Each of these states had its own ruler and even its own system of government. The largest, Austria, was in itself a significant state. The smallest had only a few thousand inhabitants. In addition, to the east lay Prussia, a powerful state that was beginning to think of itself as the leader of the German-speaking peoples.

As nation-states formed in western Europe and demonstrated the economic, political, military, and cultural power that came from unity, regional leaders in Italy and Germany also sought unification for themselves. A common language and clearly demarcated geographical borders were considered vital elements in national unity, and were helpful to Italy in consolidating its peninsular nation. Germany, however, lacked clear natural geographic boundaries and faced the question as to which German-speaking states would be included within the new country and which would be excluded.

Giuseppe Mazzini (1805–72) provided a prophetic vision for Italy. In 1831 he founded Young Italy, a secret association urging Italian unification and independence from foreign control by the French, Austrians, and Spanish. Mazzini's *On the Duties of Man* expressed his nationalistic, democratic, and humanistic views:

Anon., **Giuseppe Garibaldi meets Victor Emmanuel II, King of Sardinia, c. 1860.** Several different leaders contributed to the creation of the modern nation of Italy. Garibaldi led armed "red shirts" and freed southern Italy to join the Italian nation. The core of the new Italy was the Kingdom of Sardinia-Piedmont under King Victor Emmanuel II.

O my brothers, love your Country! Our country is our Home, the House that God has given us, placing therein a numerous family that loves us, and whom we love; a family with whom we sympathize more readily, and whom we understand more quickly, than we do others; and which, from its being centred round a given spot, and from the homogeneous nature of its elements, is adapted to a special branch of activity. (Columbia University, p. 570)

When Mazzini's cultural view was joined to the political organization of Camillo Cavour (1810–61), prime minister of Sardinia-Piedmont in 1852 under King Victor Emmanuel II, the nationalist movement was poised for political victory. Cavour formed a brief alliance with Napoleon III of France against Austria. This enabled the king to annex Lombardy. The adjacent regions of Parma, Modena, and Tuscany joined by plebiscite, in which the population could either agree or disagree to accept a decree issued by their rulers. In 1860, the popular mercenary Giuseppe Garibaldi (1807–82) led 1150 followers, wearing red shirts, into the south Italian Kingdom of the Two Sicilies, which collapsed and subsequently also joined Piedmont after a plebiscite. Venetia, the region around Venice, was added after a war in which Italy allied with Prussia against Austria. Finally, Rome was annexed in 1870 after French troops were withdrawn to fight against Prussia. Through the various contributions of Mazzini, Cavour, Garibaldi, Victor Emmanuel II, Napoleon III, war, and popular votes, Italy had become a unified nation.

At about the same time, prime minister Otto von Bismarck of Prussia (1815–98) was unifying the multitude of small German states

BISMARCK

French cartoon portraying Prince Otto Eduard Leopold von Bismarck, Prime Minister of Prussia, 1870. Political figures have traditionally been treated irreverently by cartoonists, but this caricature is savage. The French were outraged by Bismarck's ambitions to get the Prussian prince Leopold on to the Spanish throne—a key factor in the war between the two countries.

HOW DO WE KNOW?

What is Nationalism?

For most people in today's world, nationality is an important part of personal identity, and historians find nationalism to be a central concern of the past two centuries. Some stress the significance of particular forms of nationalism, others argue that national identity is, and can be, constantly shaped and reshaped. In this sense historians of national identity are similar to historians of gender identity: They not only wish to understand where we have been, they also want to use these explorations of the past as a means to search for alternative futures.

One of the first historians and philosophers of nationalism, the Frenchman Joseph-Ernest Renan (1823–92), captured the twofold nature of nationalism in his 1882 lecture "What is a Nation?" It looks both backward and forward in creating a unified vision. Nationalism requires a fundamental shared history in the lives of the citizens, but the past alone is not enough for constructing a nation. That task requires also a vision of what the nation might become and a political commitment to constructing such a future. More dramatically, in considering the nation as a "spiritual principle," Renan asserted his belief that in his time nationalism was displacing religion as a central concern:

A nation is a spiritual principle, the outcome of the profound complications of history; it is a spiritual family not a group determined by the shape of the earth. We have now seen what things are not [by themselves] adequate for the creation of such a spiritual principle, namely, race, language, material interest, religious affinities, geography, and military necessity. What [else] then is required? ...

A nation is therefore a large-scale solidarity, constituted by the feeling of the sacrifices that one has made in the past and of those that one is prepared to make in the future. It presupposes a past; it is summarized, however, in the present by a tangible fact, namely, consent, the clearly expressed desire to continue a common life.

More recently, anthropologist Benedict Anderson has referred to the nation as an "imagined political community," stressing the importance of human imagination, creativity, and persuasion—all expressed through the public media—as the means by which the idea of the nation is created, refined, and disseminated. "It is imagined because the members of even the smallest nation will never know most of their fellow-members, meet them, or even hear of them, yet in the minds of each lives the image of their communion" (Anderson, p. 15). For Anderson, as for Renan, the nation is not so much an entity existing in nature as it is an institution created by leaders who are successful in gaining acceptance for their idea of the nation.

In addition to Renan's "spiritual principle," modern nationalism comprises two additional elements. First, at least since the French Revolution, the modern nation exists in a world of other nations, frequently competitive with one another. To some degree, each nation defines itself in its relationship with others. Second, at least since the French Revolution and the industrial revolution, the nation has been the vehicle for the spread of trade networks and capitalism throughout the world. The significance of the nation in achieving economic goals has given great power to national identity.

- How well does Renan's concept of the nation as a "spiritual family" fit the nationalism expressed in the American Constitution? and the nationalism of the various Italian and German spokesmen?
- How might a nation express its desire to continue a common life? How might it reject that desire?
- How does Renan's concept of a "spiritual family" compare with Anderson's idea of an "imagined community?" Are they actually referring to the same relationship but with different words, or are their concepts different?

into a single German nation under William I (King of Prussia 1861–88, Emperor of Germany 1871–88). The cultural basis of German unity was solidly established. The brothers Jakob and Wilhelm Grimm, founders of the modern science of linguistics, analyzed the various dialects of German and collected fairy tales from all parts of the region, publishing them in 1812 as a unifying folklore for the nation. A series of philosophers and historians, including J.G. von Herder (1744–1803), J.G. Fichte (1762–1814), Georg Wilhelm Friedrich Hegel (1770–1831), Leopold von Ranke (1795–1886), and Heinrich von Treitschke (1834–96), urged Germany to fulfill its natural destiny, just as Mazzini had done in Italy.

From 1828 a customs union, *zollverein*, that created a free trade area throughout many of the German states, had already established an economic foundation for unification. Increasing industrialization provided the financial and military underpinnings for it. Now Bismarck instituted a policy of "Blood and Iron." Two wars were the key. In 1866, Bismarck defeated Austria and formed the North German Confederation, leaving Austria out. In 1871, he defeated France, annexing Alsace and Lorraine. In light of these victories the southern states of Germany—Bavaria, Baden, and Württemberg—also joined the newly formed nation.

The Rise of Zionism in Europe

One of the last of the nationalist movements to arise in nineteenth-century Europe was Zionism, the movement to recreate a Jewish homeland. Jews had been dispersed into Europe even during the time of the Roman Empire. By the beginning of the twentieth century, their principal European locations were in Poland, Russia, and Ukraine. Through the centuries Jews had prayed for a return to Zion, their ancestral homeland in modern Israel. In the second half of the nineteenth century, under the influence of various European nationalist movements, some philosophers proposed going beyond prayer. They looked forward to the establishment of a political state.

The move from prayer to political organization took concrete form at the very end of the nineteenth century. Suffering from pogroms in the Russian Empire and discrimination in much of the Austro-Hungarian Empire, Jews felt increasingly persecuted. On assignment in Paris to report on the trial of Alfred Dreyfus, a Jewish officer in the French army unjustly accused of treason, the Viennese Jewish journalist Theodor Herzl (1860–1904) encountered fierce anti-Semitism. Shocked to find such ethnic and religious hatred in the capital of the liberal world, where Jews had gained citizenship during the French Revolution, Herzl concluded that Jews could be free, independent, and safe only in a country of their own. In 1897, he founded the Zionist movement. Because Palestine, the goal of most of the early Zionists, was already the home of 600,000 Arabs, Jewish nationalism simultaneously, if unintentionally, took the form of a colonizing movement originating in Europe. Not all Jews embraced Zionism, although as discrimination and persecution increased in the twentieth century, the Zionist dream became an increasingly desirable alternative to remaining in Europe. The consequences of this nationalistic/colonizing effort are traced in Chapter 24.

THE QUEST FOR EMPIRE

The triumph of nationalism, the rise of the modern nation state, was accompanied by fierce and violent competition for power among the new states, especially during, and as a result of, the wars of the French Revolution and the Napoleonic Wars (Chapter 16). Similarly, the emergence of a global capitalist marketplace (Chapter 14) was also based on sharp competition—much of it between joint stock companies backed by their home governments. The industrial revolution (Chapter 17) also led to sharp competition, first between industrialized and non-industrialized countries—such as Britain and India—and later among the new industrialists and their newly industrializing nations. The very first triumph of British cotton textile manufacture over the traditional handicraft spinning industry of India illustrated this competition between industrialized and non-industrialized nations. The British government made sure that the field of competition between its new industrialists and the Indians was inclined in favor of its own nationals. The very first triumph of British cotton textile manufacture over the traditional handicraft spinning industry of India illustrated this unequal competition between industrialized and non-industrialized nations. The British government assisted its industrialists by protecting their infant industries with high tariffs that made the import of Indian textiles very costly. It also allowed the British East India Company to take over large parts of India as a colony and to fix low tariffs there, thus aiding and encouraging the import of British textiles to India. In these colonized regions the British also gained the power to collect taxes. These taxes enriched the British; a portion of the taxes were sent back to Britain thus draining India of a part of its wealth. Similar policies were common between colonizing and colonized countries throughout the world. As a result of their industrial ingenuity and their

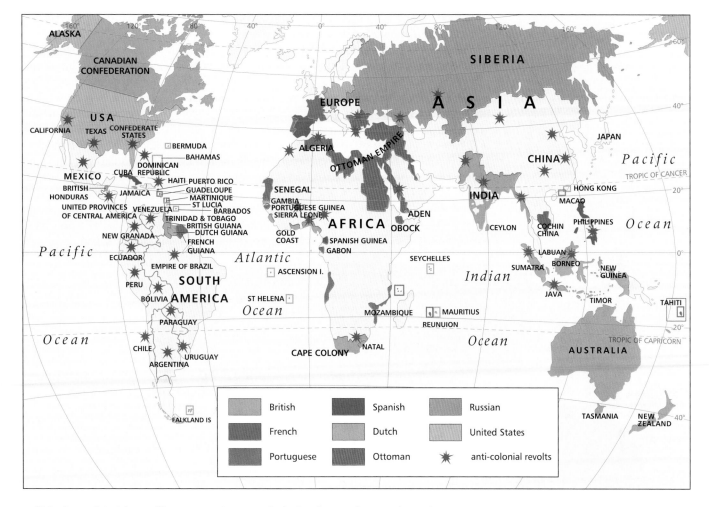

European imperialism 1815–70. By the middle of the nineteenth century, revolutions had brought independence to most of the Americas. With Africa largely impenetrable, European imperialists now focused on Asia. Russia had spread across Siberia to the Pacific, and the United States extended from the Atlantic to the Pacific, while Britain controlled India, South Africa, Australia, and New Zealand. In 1867 Canada achieved "dominion" status, virtual political independence.

political machinations, Europeans increased their share of manufacturing output from 23 percent of the global share in 1750 to 63 percent in 1900. India's, by contrast, plummeted in those same years from 24.5 percent to 1.7; China's from 32.8 percent to 6.2.

As newly industrializing nations began to compete with the British for markets for their finished products and for sources of raw materials another competition opened. At first, Britain stood pre-eminent among the newly industrializing nations, but by the mid-nineteenth century rivals had begun to appear. By the late 1800s, several of them were engaged in this industrial and commercial competition. Mostly the competition was economic, but the wealth of the nation depended in part on the success of the new industrialists, so governments regularly intervened to aid them. It seemed natural that national pride also entered into people's thinking.

Three countries provided the fiercest competition. The United States emerged from its Civil War in 1865 with a powerful industrial base and a rapidly growing immigrant population. In a quest for new land and resources to develop, Americans moved westward by railway across a continent that was abundant in both, removing Indians who blocked their way. By 1900, the US had an industrial base of production that surpassed Britain's. Germany unified its constituent states into a single country under King William I and his chief minister Otto von Bismarck in 1871, and also surpassed Britain in the early years of the twentieth century. In addition, Germany's population at 67 million was almost 50 percent greater than Britain's and was growing faster. France produced only half the industrial output of Britain or Germany, but nevertheless ranked third among European powers.

The greatest competition took place overseas, beyond the borders of Europe, in the quest for imperial power. Empires were not new, of course, but the use of advanced technology and new strategies of financial and economic dominance gave them more power than ever before. By 1914, peoples of Europe and of European ancestry had settled and were ruling, directly or indirectly, 85 percent of the earth's land surface: Canada, the United States, most of Latin America, Siberia, Australia, New Zealand, and substantial parts of South Africa by invasion, settlement, and conquest; most of India, Southeast Asia, and Africa by direct rule over indigenous populations; China by indirect rule. The map below indicates the holdings of each major imperial power in the eastern hemisphere. The British held the most overseas land, and the most people, with their dominant concentration in India, East Africa almost from north to south, large segments of West Africa, and the British settler colonies of Australia and New Zealand. British holdings were so widespread that it was said that "the sun never sets

European empires in 1914. By the beginning of World War I, European imperialism had reached its zenith, with four-fifths of the globe under the direct political control of Europeans or people of European ancestry. Only Antarctica remained unclaimed. Although this power was sustained by technological, naval, and military superiority, insurrections were widespread and increasingly well organized. Imperial trade established a global economic system and spread European cultural values.

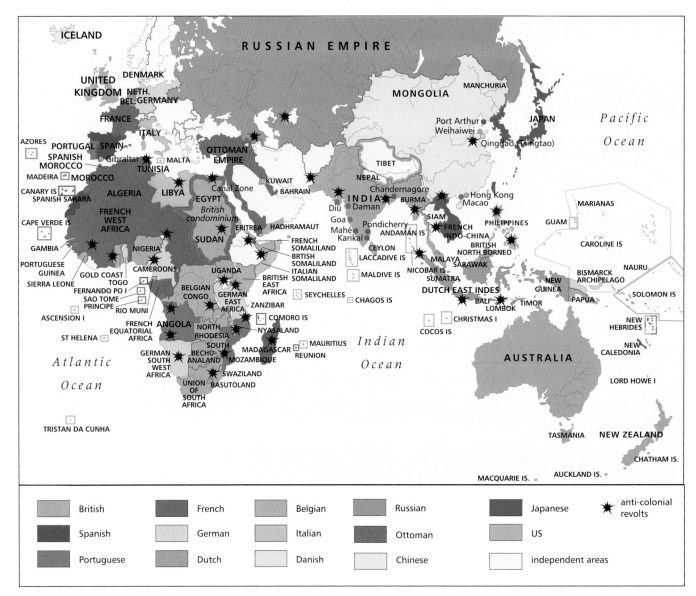

on the British Empire." The French dominated West Africa, beginning with regions directly across the Mediterranean from France itself, and important parts of Southeast Asia.

Many regions of the world were nominally independent, but in fact their economies were controlled by others. Much of Latin America, although politically independent, was dominated internally by elites of European ancestry and externally by European financial investors and their governments, especially by the British. Some states, like Russia and the Ottoman Empire, were dominated in large part by capital from north-western Europe but also, in turn, held their own colonial areas. Northwest Europe and the United States had become the *core* regions in this emerging world system, domin-ating world economic and political power, while most of the rest of the world, except-ing Japan, was incorporated and subordinated into their *periphery*, where economic and political power was subordinated to the core.

The leading states of western Europe had achieved their power through their "dual revolutions," political and industrial. Politically and socially they had achieved, or seemed to be in the process of achieving:

- consolidated nation-states;
- parliamentary democracies;
- bureaucratic administrations;
- freedom of the press, assembly, and religion;
- freedom from wrongful arrest and torture;
- increased levels of literacy and general, public education.

Economically and industrially, they had achieved or seemed to be in the process of achieving:

- high levels of productivity;
- competence in new methods of science and technology;
- relatively high levels of health and of medical care;
- an integrated world economy;
- powerful weaponry;
- high levels of trade and international exchange;
- high levels of economic entrepreneurship and legal protection of property.

Western Europeans, especially Britons, began to define themselves as people who had mastered these qualities, in contrast to the peoples whom they were colonizing and dominating, who lacked them. Charles Darwin (1809–82) shook much of the Christian world when he published *On the Origin of Species* in 1859. In this work he suggested that life developed through chance mechanisms over millions of years that allowed some species to survive over others. Soon after Darwin published *On The Origin of Species*, the philosopher Herbert Spencer (1820–1903) (mis)represented the concept of "survival of the fittest" as a doctrine explaining and justifying the rule by the strong over the weak. Spencer's "social Darwinism" argued that those who were strong deserved their superiority, while those who were weak deserved their inferiority. Spencer also believed that the European races were more advanced than those of other regions. The social-political order that confirmed wealthy, powerful, white, male Euro-peans in positions of dominance was as it ought to be. Rudyard Kipling's "The White Man's Burden" expressed these beliefs in poetic form.

> Take up the White Man's burden—
> Send forth the best ye breed—
> Go bind your sons to exile
> To serve your captives' need;

To wait in heavy harness,
On fluttered folk and wild—
Your new-caught, sullen peoples,
Half-devil and half-child.

Kipling argued in racial terms that because Europeans were more advanced than others they had an obligation to bring their civilization to those they conquered, although he saw this civilizing mission as a thankless task. Kipling's poem, perhaps naively, perhaps self-righteously, perhaps sarcastically, cites only the moral burdens of colonization without any references to its economic and political profits for the colonizer.

The Ottoman Empire: The "Sick Man of Europe," 1829–76

As the industrializing and colonizing powers of the world built their empires, they cast predatory gazes on the weaknesses of many of the formerly powerful empires around them. The closest geographically, the Ottoman Empire, had been in continuous decline since it lost control of Hungary in 1699. In 1829, the British, French, and Russians gave their support to Greece as it won its independence from the Ottomans, and aided three Balkan states—Serbia, Wallachia, and Moldavia—in gaining recognition as autonomous provinces with limited self-government, although still formally under the Ottoman Empire. In the aftermath of these imperial defeats, Muhammad (Mehemet) Ali seized his opportunity to make Egypt effectively independent of the Ottomans in 1832; the Saud family had already won similar autonomy for parts of Arabia in the early nineteenth century; and the French began their occupation of Algeria in 1830. The Ottoman Empire was unable to hold on to its territories. It had become the "sick man of Europe."

Traditionally the Ottomans had organized people by the millet system, which differentiated subjects by religious communities. Each millet had a religious leader responsible for enforcing its religion's laws and customs and for collecting taxes on behalf of the imperial government. Asserting that sometimes the influence of religion in the empire's organization created religious antagonisms, the Western, industrializing powers, used religious affiliations as an entering wedge in their move to further weaken and dismember the Ottoman Empire. Under these circumstances, different religious groups within the empire looked outward to their co-religionists in other countries for protection, if necessary. The Greek Orthodox community, in particular, looked toward Russia; the Roman Catholics looked to France, and Protestants to Britain. Religious missions from these countries received special privileges within the Ottoman Empire, and often served as bases for trade and intelligence-gathering as well. Foreigners trading within the empire were permitted the right to trial by judges of their own nation. The Ottoman theory and practice of government were quite different from those of western Europe, where the unified nation-state was becoming the norm. In addition, the Ottomans had not kept up with the industrial development of the rest of Europe. In the 1840s Sultan Abdul Mejid enacted the *Tanzimat* (Restructuring) reforms to bring the Ottoman legal code and its social and educational standards into closer conformity with those of western European states, but with very limited success because of internal opposition. The reforms created a new Western-oriented elite that threatened traditional government and its administrative and military officials.

The Crimean War of 1854–6 further revealed the weakness of the Ottoman system. On the north shore of the Black Sea, the major powers of Europe confronted one another in a conflict that tested their abilities both to fight wars and to negotiate diplomatic settlements. The war began as Russia, seeking a warm-water port, probed

Ottoman strength by attacking it in the Crimean peninsula. France and Britain came to the aid of the Ottomans, pushing back the Russian assault and restoring Crimea to the Ottomans. Austria seized this opportunity to occupy Wallachia and Moldavia, and the final peace treaty ending the war recognized both Romania and Serbia as self-governing principalities, free of Ottoman control, and under the protection of other European powers.

In an attempt to remedy its weaknesses, the Ottoman government issued the Hatt-i Humayun edict in 1856. This once again ushered in numerous changes to conform to western European standards, including equality under a common law for all citizens, tax reform, security of property, the end of torture, more honest administration, and greater freedom of the press. The Young Turks, a group of modernizing intellectuals, were delighted, and nationalistic Armenians, Bulgars, Macedonians, and Cretans hoped for greater autonomy. A change of sultan in 1876, however, brought a reverse of all these policies and aspirations. The Young Turks went into exile, and Bulgarian and Armenian nationalists were massacred.

Florence Nightingale, Turkey, c. 1854. During the Crimean War "the Lady of the Lamp" established and supervised efficient nursing departments at Scutari and Balaklava. Her unflagging efforts ensured that the mortality rate among the injured was greatly reduced. The effect of her reforms would transform nursing from the realm of menial drudgery into a skilled medical profession with high standards of education.

A weak Ottoman Empire left a power vacuum in southeast Europe, which invited continuing foreign intervention and competition. A new Russian attack through the Balkans reached Istanbul itself in 1877. Britain threatened to go to war with Russia, but Bismarck convened an international conference in Berlin in 1878 to resolve the conflict through diplomacy. War was averted for the moment, but tensions ran high. The mixture of Ottoman weakness, aggressive expansionism on the part of other European countries, assertive nationalism in the Balkans, and increasing militarization with increasingly powerful weapons threatened a later, larger war. It arrived in 1914.

Southeast Asia and Indonesia, 1795–1880

In Southeast Asia, the colonial competition that had marked the period from 1500 to 1750 continued. The British established a settlement at Penang, Malaya; took Malacca from the Dutch in 1795; and, under Sir Stamford Raffles, established Singapore in 1819 as their major port in the region. In a series of wars, the British took control of Burma and turned it into a major exporter of rice, timber, teak, and oil, and developed the port of Rangoon to handle the trade. Tin was discovered in Malaya, and its rubber plantations became the world's largest producers.

France began its conquest of Indochina in 1859, completing the takeover by 1893, ostensibly to protect French Catholic missionaries. In dislodging Vietnam from China's tributary sphere, the French interrupted a centuries-old relationship. Vietnam's leading products for export were rice and rubber. Germany, entering late into the colonial competition, annexed eastern New Guinea and the Marshall and Solomon Islands in the 1880s.

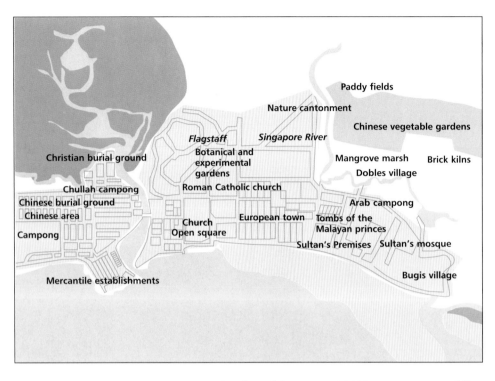

Sharing in the expansionist spirit of the times, the Netherlands decided to annex the entire Indonesian archipelago, building on its administrative center at Batavia (Jakarta) in Java and the trading posts it already occupied. The Dutch wished to dissuade other European powers from intruding and to add the profits from rubber, oil, tin, and tobacco from the other islands to those from sugar, coffee, tea, and tobacco from Java. The Dutch ruled through especially high levels of violence and cruelty. The Java War, 1825–30, had many background provocations and finally erupted when the Dutch built a highway through property housing the tomb of a Muslim saint. In five years of brutal combat between the Dutch and Javanese, 15,000 government soldiers were killed, including 8000 Dutch. Some 200,000 Javanese died in the war and in the famine and disease that followed.

A map of the town and environs of Singapore, from an actual survey by G.D. Coleman, 1839. Singapore was not an indigenous town that gradually grew up around a bustling port; it was purposely founded in 1819 on the site of a fishing village by Sir Stamford Raffles, who saw its potential as a trading center. The British actively encouraged immigration to the new port, and divided the thriving city into separate areas for the different ethnic groups that lived and worked there. The divisions can be seen clearly on the map.

In 1830 the Dutch introduced a new, particularly exploitative economic policy called "the cultivation system," *Kulturstelsel*. The Indonesian peasants were forced to devote one-fifth of their land to the production of cash crops, especially coffee, sugar, and indigo, to be turned over to the Dutch for export to the Netherlands as a kind of taxation. From 1840 to 1880 the estimated profits repatriated, or sent back, to the imperial country equaled one-fourth of the total budget of the Netherlands.

India, 1858–1914

The English East India Company had come to India in the seventeenth century to buy spices and hand-made cotton textiles in exchange for bullion, wool, and metals. The Mughal government of India granted the Company permission to trade, and through the seventeenth century it established trading posts, called factories, first at Surat on India's west coast, and then at Madras (1639), Bombay (1661), and Calcutta (1690). During the eighteenth century, the Mughal imperial government began to weaken. Imperial policies of overexpansion in the south drained the empire of funds and manpower, and alienated rural landlords whose taxes were raised to pay the costs. In addition, Emperor Aurangzeb (r. 1659–1707) imposed additional taxes on non-Muslims, which his predecessors had not done, provoking rebellions in several regions of his Hindu-majority country. As the empire weakened, various regional contestants for power sought alliances with the British traders in their by-now well-fortified trading outposts.

The British were not the only European power active in India. The French, too, controlled fortified trading posts and had entered into alliances with regional Indian powers. The French Governor, Joseph Francis Dupleix, had drilled Indian troops under his command to fight in regular formations, armed with muskets that they were trained to shoot accurately and effectively. On the British side, Robert Clive, in the service of the East India Company, similarly trained his soldiers. The British and the French in India seemed poised to reach a truce between themselves, but the general warfare that engulfed the British and French elsewhere (1744–48) pulled them into conflict. Each side won significant victories, but the French East India Company saw the cost to its trade as too great and it sharply cut back its troops and its trading enterprises. When warfare resumed, as a result of the Seven Years' War (1755–63), a global struggle between Britain and France, the British in India easily defeated the French. This victory left the British as the principal European power in India, and their services were much in demand by several emerging regional powers. In exchange for their financial and military support, the British were offered a share in the taxes and the governmental authority of these break-away regions. Beginning in Bengal with the battles of Plassey (1757) and Buxar (1765), the British began to gain control of large areas of India. The British East India Company was the instrument of rule, since it was the actual British representation in India. The British Parliament established a Board of Control in London to oversee the activities of the Company, but in large measure a joint stock trading company had become master of large, and increasing, regions of Indian territory.

The Company's principal motive was the acquisition of profits, and, now as rulers, they adopted two policies to maximize them. First, they increased tax collection, both by raising rates and by increasing the efficiency of collection. Second, they manipulated tariffs, lowering them in India so that British manufactures would have easy access to Indian markets, and lobbying to raise them in Britain in order to block the import of Indian textiles. The beginning of Britain's industrial revolution and of the Company's establishment of control over large regions of India occurred at more or less the same time, in the middle of the eighteenth century. Colonial control thus immediately protected and facilitated the development of British industry, while effectively blocking Indian competition.

British machine-made cotton textiles flooded India's markets. India was transformed into the model colony, importing manufactured goods from Britain's industries and exporting raw materials to its factories and distribution centers: raw cotton, which the British manufactured into cloth; jute for making sacks; leather; and enormous quantities of tea, as India displaced China as the leading provider of tea to Europe. Throughout the second half of the nineteenth century and the first years of the twentieth, two-thirds of India's imports from Britain were machine-manufactured textiles. Iron and steel goods came second. India became a lucrative destination for overseas investment, and about one-fifth of all overseas British investment in the late nineteenth century was in India.

India's own taxes, however, paid for the building and maintenance of the Indian railway system, one of the most extensive in the world with some 35,000 miles of track by 1914. Demonstrating the power of colonial rule, the British manufactured all of the components of the system—engines, cars, tracks—in Britain. Thus, even though the financing was drawn from India, the profits of the manufacture, the expertise in engineering, and the industrial plant that built the railway industry went to Britain rather than to India. The railway system in India made possible a wide range of diverse activities: the widespread deployment of colonial troops, increased commerce that benefited both Indians and British businessmen, the relief of famine through the shipping of food from areas of surplus harvests to areas of shortfall, the geographical spread of political dissidence, and pilgrimage visits to religious shrines throughout the country.

Under British colonial rule, India began its own industrial revolution with cotton textiles, primarily in Bombay. This textile industry was started by local Gujaratis, inhabitants of the western Indian region of Gujarat, who had long family histories of

SOURCE

"The Attack of King Industry"

Communities in India that were already active in business provided many of the new industrialists. Indian financiers became industrialists by importing the new industrial machinery ready-made from Europe. In Ahmedabad, the capital of Gujarat, local businessmen, led by an administrator with close ties to British entrepreneurs, followed Mumbai (Bombay) in establishing a local cotton textile industry in 1861. A few years earlier Dalpatram Kavi, a local poet and intellectual leader, had called on his fellow countrymen to recognize the importance of industry to their future. His Gujarati poem, "Hunnarkhan-ni Chadayi" ("The Attack of King Industry"), presents a far-reaching agenda for reform centering on industrial change and proposes social restructuring as well. It suggests that the British had brought much of value to India and that Indians were prepared to absorb and implement some of this legacy, but without the British imperial presence and its costs.

Fellow countrymen, let us remove all the miseries of our
    country,
Do work, for the new kingdom has come. Its king is industry.

Our wealth has gone into the hands of foreigners. The great
    blunder is yours
For you did not unite yourselves—fellow countrymen.

Consider the time, see for yourselves. All our people have
    become poor,
Many men of business have fallen—fellow countrymen.

Put away idleness. Fill the treasuries with knowledge.
Now awake and work new wonders—fellow countrymen.

With kith and kin keep harmony. Do not enter into debt.
Limit the dinners for your caste—fellow countrymen.

Introduce industry from countries abroad and master the
    modern machinery.
Please attend to this plea from the Poet Dalpat—fellow
    countrymen.

(trans. by Chimanbhai Trivedi and Howard Spodek)

involvement in business. The need to found new industries found expression even in local poetry, as "The Attack of King Industry" makes clear. (In Calcutta, where jute textiles were produced, industry was largely pioneered by British investors.) Mining began in the coal fields of Bengal, Bihar, Orissa, and Assam, and in 1911 the Tata family of Bombay—a Parsi family, descendants of immigrants from Persia who had come to India in the eighth century—built India's first steel mill at Jamshedpur, Bihar. At the start of World War I, factory employment in all of India had reached about 1 million (out of a total population of about 300 million). While employment in large, mechanized factories was increasing, many hand craftsmen were being displaced, so the actual percentage of people earning their living by manufacturing of all sorts stayed approximately the same, at about 10 percent of the workforce (and has continued about the same till today).

In 1857 Indians revolted against rule by the British East India Company. The British called this a "Mutiny" of army troops, but later scholars have shown it to be a more geographically widespread and more general opposition to British rule. Some nationalist historians have called it "India's First War for National Independence," but the revolt lacked unified leadership and direction. The British crushed the revolt, and from then onward they ruled India directly, imposing their influence throughout the administrative and educational systems of the country. Concepts based on European political revolutions were introduced directly and indirectly through the formal secondary and post-secondary education system, the law courts, the press, and even through very limited elections. English was designated the official language of government. As a result, imperialism confronted its internal contradiction: How could an imperial power preach and teach the values of self-rule and democracy while maintaining its own foreign rule?

When more organized movements for independence began in India in the late nineteenth century, their leaders first had to evaluate the effects of British rule and to find a balance between acceptance and rejection of its political, economic, social, and cultural models. By the early twentieth century, most politically conscious Indians had come to believe that whatever benefits British rule might have conferred, the time had come for the British to go home. It was time for India to control its own economy and to choose its own political, social, and cultural directions.

China, 1800–1914

We began Chapter 17, on the industrial revolution, with a flashback to the Song dynasty (960–1279) when China—with its sailing expertise and equipment, iron manufacturing, gunpowder, waterwheels, and canal systems—was the most technologically advanced country in the world. We also know from our survey of Zheng He's fifteenth-century seafaring expeditions under the Ming dynasty that China's astonishing maritime capabilities continued to be the most outstanding in the world. On the other hand, we also know that China fell to Chinggis Khan's onslaughts in the thirteenth century and was ruled by these foreigners until the Ming dynasty recaptured power for the Han Chinese (1368–1644). But the Ming also fell to "barbarians," Manchu invaders from north of the Great Wall, who established the Qing dynasty (1644–1911). The Ming invited Manchu warriors to help suppress a band of rebels that had seized Beijing, but after the task was complete, the Manchu refused to leave. They pushed onward to capture all of China for themselves.

The Manchus were enthusiastic colonizers. Even before they invaded and ruled China, they had established a state in their homeland of Manchuria, made Korea a vassal state, and controlled Inner Mongolia as a dependency. After establishing their rule in China, the Qing expanded westward. In the eighteenth century they annexed new lands equal to the size of China itself in Outer Mongolia, Dzungaria, the Tarim Basin, Eastern Turkestan, Tsinghai, and Tibet. They also conquered Taiwan and subordinated the peoples of Southeast Asia into tributary relationships. Revolts broke out against Manchu rule, but until 1800 they occurred mostly at the periphery of the empire and posed no serious threat to the dynasty.

Some scholars believe that the very size and power of China created a sense of invulnerability among its leaders that sometimes led the country to ignore threats from the outside until it was too late. (Of course, the court was often divided within itself, also weakening the government.) As an example, a letter from the Chinese emperor Qianlong (1736–95) to the king of Britain in 1793, is frequently cited. Britain's King George III had dispatched a mission under Lord George Macartney to open trade and diplomatic negotiations with China. For the Chinese emperor, nearing the end of his long reign, the concept of permanent representation by a European power at the Chinese court was inconceivable. The emperor replied to the British monarch in a letter that was, perhaps unintentionally, condescending. It expressed the emperor's continuing belief in China's central position in the world, and his lack of appreciation and understanding of the changes that were taking place in the West in the early stages of the industrial revolution:

> As to the request made in your memorial, O King, to send one of your nationals to stay at the Celestial Court to take care of your country's trade with China, this is not in harmony with the state system of our dynasty and will definitely not be permitted.
>
> The various articles presented by you, O King, this time are accepted by my special order to the office in charge of such functions in consideration of the offerings having come from a long distance with sincere good wishes . . . [but] there is nothing we lack, as your principal envoy and others have themselves observed. We have never set much store on strange or ingenious objects, nor do we need any more of your country's manufactures. (Teng and Fairbank, p. 19)

extraterritoriality Legal immunities enjoyed by the citizens of a sovereign state or international organization within a host country.

The steamer *Nemesis* destroying eleven Chinese junks at Cherpez Canton, China, by E. Duncan, 1843. The two separate wars fought between Britain and China in the 1840s and 1850s began when the Chinese government tried to prevent British merchants from illegally importing opium. The British responded militarily precipitating The Opium Wars (1839–42). (*National Maritime Museum, Canada*)

Although some scholars at the court warned against this policy of isolation and complacency, their opinions were disregarded.

By the early 1800s, however, China faced a range of internal problems that demanded attention. A continuously rising population put pressure on resources and government administrative capacity. The 100 million people of 1650 tripled to 300 million by 1800 and reached 420 million by 1850. More land was needed. Allowing the settlement of Manchuria seemed a suitable reply to the problem, but the Manchus would not permit Chinese settlement in their homeland. Nor did the Manchus increase the size of their bureaucracy to service the rising population, preferring to delegate administrative responsibilities to local authorities, a response that was inadequate.

One strength of the Chinese economy was the sale of tea, silk, and porcelains to the West in exchange for silver and gold. The Europeans trading with China, however, wished to staunch this flow of bullion. Finally, the Europeans trading with China, especially the British, discovered that China would accept opium in place of precious metals. Taking advantage of its multinational commercial connections, the British encouraged the growth of opium in their Indian colony and carried it from the ports of Bombay, Calcutta, and Madras to Canton in China. The centuries of paying for Chinese exports with silver and gold came to an end. By the 1820s China was purchasing so much opium that it began to export silver!

The Opium Wars, 1839–42 and 1856–60. Seeking to staunch the drain of silver and to stop the importation of opium, the Chinese attempted to ban and resist its import in 1839. It was too late. By now the British proclaimed the ideology of "free trade." When the incorruptible Imperial Commissioner Lin Zexu tried to confiscate and destroy the opium, British shipboard cannon destroyed Chinese ships and port installations in the harbor at Guangzhou (Canton). This Opium War of 1839–42 was no contest because the Chinese emperors' lack of interest in Western science and technology meant that China lacked both modern cannons and steamships. China ceded to Britain the island of Hong Kong as a colony and opened five treaty ports in which foreigners could live and conduct business under their own laws rather than under the laws of China—a condition known as **extraterritoriality**. France and the United States soon gained similar concessions. Foreign settlements were established in the new treaty ports and became the centers of new industry, education, and publishing. The focus of international trade began to relocate from Guangzhou to Shanghai, at the mouth of the Yangzi River, a more central location along the Chinese coast.

The decline of the Qing dynasty. During the course of the nineteenth century, the authority of the Qing (Manchu) dynasty in China was undermined. Beset by the aggressive actions of European colonial powers, the Qing granted extensive trade and territorial concessions. Internally, a series of increasingly violent rebellions, both within the Chinese heartland and in the western (often Muslim) regions, brought the dynasty to the verge of collapse by the turn of the century.

Qing (Manchu) Empire in 1850			other 19th-century revolts		Russian
British attacks during Opium War 1839-42			treaty ports		Japanese
area of Taiping rebellion 1850-64					French
area of Nien rebellion 1853-68					British
area of Boxer uprising 1900-01					German

areas of influence

Marble boat in the gardens of the Summer Palace, Beijing. In the last years of the nineteenth century Chinese reformers clamored for industrial, military, and administrative reform. They were incensed when the dowager empress of China built not a navy but a marble boat for entertainment in her Summer Palace.

comprador (Portuguese: "buyer") A Chinese merchant hired by Western traders to assist with their dealings in China.

Still China did not establish the formal diplomatic recognition and exchange that European powers had demanded. A second set of wars followed in 1856–60, and these led to the occupation of Beijing by 17,000 French and British soldiers and the sacking of the imperial Summer Palace. More treaty ports were opened, including inland centers along the Yangzi River, now patrolled by British gunboats. Europeans gained control over the administration of China's foreign trade and tariffs. The opium trade continued to expand. Christian missionaries were given freedom to travel throughout China. Some Chinese worked with the foreigners as **compradors**, or intermediaries in business and administration.

As the Manchu government weakened in the last decades of the nineteenth century, revolts broke out, foreign powers continued to seize parts of the country and its tributaries, and there were more calls for internal reform. (The Chinese situation showed similarities with events in the Ottoman Empire at about the same time.) The greatest of the internal revolts, the Taiping Rebellion, began in 1850 and was led by Hong Xiuquan, a frustrated scholar who claimed visions of himself as the younger brother of Jesus Christ. The main demands of the Taiping leaders, however, were quite concrete: an end to the corrupt and inefficient Manchu imperial rule, an end to extortionate landlord demands, and the alleviation of poverty. Beginning in the southwest, the Taiping came to dominate the Yangzi valley and established their capital in Nanjing in 1853. The imperial government was unable to respond effectively, but regional military leaders, equipped with more modern weapons, finally defeated the revolt with the help of the "Ever Victorious Army," a mercenary force composed of American and European soldiers, winning more power for themselves. Throughout the struggle, American officers recognized Chinese authority over military operations, while most British and French generals did not. By the time the Taiping Rebellion was suppressed in 1864, some 20 million people had been killed. At about the same time, additional rebellions broke out among tribal peoples near Guangzhou, among the Miao tribals in Guizhou, and among Muslims in Yunnan and Gansu. The largest of all the rebel groups, the Nien, controlled much of the territory between Nanjing and Kaifeng. Collectively, these rebellions cost another 10 million lives.

With the central government fully occupied with these internal revolts, foreign imperialists began to establish their territorial claims as well. Russians seized border areas in the Amur River region (1858), the Maritime Provinces (1860), and, for ten years, the Ili valley in Turkestan (1871–81). France defeated Chinese forces in a local war and seized all of Indochina (1883–4). Most humiliating of all, Japan, having embraced Western technology and imperialist ambitions, defeated China in warfare in 1894–5. China ceded Taiwan to Japan, granted it the right to operate factories in the treaty ports, and paid a huge indemnity. Korea also passed to Japanese control, although formal colonial rule did not follow until 1910. The historic relationship of China as teacher and Japan as disciple, which dated back at least to 600 C.E., had been abruptly reversed. The new industrial age had introduced new values and new power relationships.

The Boxer Rebellion, 1898–1900. In the last years of the nineteenth century, China was in turmoil. In Beijing, a group of nationalists, called "Boxers" by the Europeans, because of their belief that martial arts rendered them invincible in struggle, were enraged by foreign arrogance in China. They burned Christian missions, killed missionaries, and laid siege to the foreign legations for two months. The imperial powers of Europe and the United States put down this revolt and exacted yet another exorbitant indemnity. The Europeans and Americans did not, however, wish to take over the government of China directly. They wanted to have a Chinese government responsible for China. They wanted to preserve China as a quasi-colony, and they therefore supported the Manchus in the formalities of power, even as they steadily hollowed out the content of that power.

A group of Chinese modernizers began to organize new industries, beginning with textiles, later developing Western weapons and steamships, but the government, now in the hands of the aging dowager Empress Cixi, who controlled the heir apparent until she died in 1908, blocked their reforms. Frustrated nationalists called for revolution. Their leading organizer was Sun Yat-sen, a Cantonese educated in Honolulu, where he became a Christian, and in Hong Kong, where he became a doctor. Sun called for a twofold anti-colonial revolution: first against the Manchus and then against the European, American, and Japanese powers. Only after the first revolution was successful in overthrowing Manchu rule in 1911 did Sun begin to push against the Western powers and Japan. The story of that struggle is told in Chapter 22.

AFRICA, 1652–1912

When European traders arrived in India and China they found huge countries governed by powerful empires. Africa was quite different. Africa was an entire continent, second only to Asia in size, with many states and with even more areas under the control of local families, clans, and ethnicities. Each area had its own history, and the experience of each different European group varied in each different region.

In sub-Saharan Africa, for the most part the early European experience was limited to the

Boxers on the march. The mostly poor peasants who formed the Boxer Rebellion of 1898–1900 blamed hard times on foreign interference and Christian missionaries. Renowned for the ferocity of their attacks, the rebels terrified Western residents as they marched into Tianjin (pictured). A 20,000-strong force, comprising soldiers from different colonial powers, finally crushed the revolt in Beijing.

shoreline of the west coast. The Europeans came in search of a shipping route to Asia, and this required only coastal contact in Africa. They found that they could buy the slaves they wanted in port towns that they established also along the coast. Africans would capture, collect, and bring the slaves to them for sale. The Europeans for the most part accepted this commercial arrangement as economically efficient. It saved them from conflict with local African rulers, who resisted the entrance of Europeans into their territories and opposed them by force. It also did not endanger their health with diseases against which the Europeans had no immunity. Even from their coastal enclaves the Europeans were able to make a considerable mark on Africa, purchasing and transporting more than 10 million slaves to the New World over a period of four centuries.

South Africa, 1652–1910

The first substantial European colony in sub-Saharan Africa was established at the Cape of Good Hope on the southern tip of the continent, not for the purchase of slaves, but for fostering ocean shipping. The Dutch established a colony at the Cape of Good Hope in South Africa in 1652 as a way station en route to and from India and the Spice Islands. The settlement grew steadily, and immigrants from other European countries—especially Britain—also joined it.

European expansion at the Cape had disruptive effects on local populations. As the Dutch and the British set out to the rural areas to farm, they displaced the Khoikhoi people who had been resident in the area. The Khoikhoi chiefdoms dissolved in the face of warfare, displacement, and catastrophic smallpox epidemics that decimated their numbers. Some of the Khoikhoi, along with other African peoples, were taken as slaves to fill the labor needs of the Europeans. In 1708 the population of the Cape was about 1700 free citizens and 1700 slaves. By about 1800 it totaled about 75,000, of whom about one-third were free and two-thirds were slaves, mostly African but some of mixed race.

As a result of their victories in the Napoleonic Wars, military and legal control of the Cape Colony passed to the British. British laws and social practices were instituted, including freedom of the press and of assembly, the development of representative government, the abolition of the slave trade, and, in 1834, with the abolition of slavery throughout the British Empire, the emancipation of slaves. Nevertheless, Europeans controlled the best land of the region, leaving their former slaves to be wage workers rather than land-owners and farmers. Property restrictions on voting effectively kept Africans out of power, and the Masters and Servants Act limited the freedom of movement of black workers.

Some 8000 people of Dutch descent, unhappy with the increasingly British customs of the colony, especially the abolition of slavery went in search of new land for farming. They departed on a great march, or trek, northward in the years between 1834 and 1841. These people, usually called Boers (meaning farmers in Dutch), or Afrikaners (for the African dialect of Dutch they spoke), ultimately founded two new republics, the Orange Free State and the Transvaal. Meanwhile, the Cape Colony expanded eastward, annexing Natal in 1843, partly to keep out the Boers. As they migrated, the Boers fought, conquered, displaced, and restricted to reservations the African peoples they encountered. Seeking labor to work the land, they often captured and virtually enslaved Africans living around them.

The expansion of the European Cape Colony further destabilized a region already passing through a *mfecane*, or time of troubles. In 1816, Shaka (*c*. 1787–1828) seized the leadership of his small Zulu kingdom just to the north and east of the Cape Colony. He organized a standing army of 40,000 soldiers, rigorously trained and disciplined them,

European expansion in Africa. Steamboats, machine-guns, and quinine (to combat malaria) all gave Europeans new access to the interior of Africa in the later nineteenth century, and they intensified their nationalistic competition. The British pursued the dream of linking their possessions from Cape Town to Cairo, while France seized much of North and Central Africa. Bismarck's Berlin Conference of 1884 tried to apportion the spoils among all the competing powers.

THE RHODES COLOSSUS
STRIDING FROM CAPE TOWN TO CAIRO.

The Rhodes Colossus. Cecil John Rhodes became one of the main champions of British rule in southern Africa, promoting colonization "from Cape Town to Cairo." The statesman and financier divided his time between diamond mining and annexing territories to British imperial rule. Rhodesia (now Zimbabwe and Zambia) was named for him in 1894.

housed them in stockades separate from the rest of the population, and armed them with newly designed short, stabbing spears, which gave them enormous power over their enemies in hand-to-hand combat. He instituted new battle formations, similar to those used by the ancient Greeks, with a massed center and flanks that could encircle the enemy and cut off its rear. By 1828, when Shaka was assassinated by two half-brothers, his kingdom had expanded, forcing the Soshagane, Nguni, Ndebele, Sotho, Ngwane, and Mfengu peoples to flee their lands. Some moved into the Cape Colony, but the vast majority turned north and east, traveling hundreds of miles into what is today Mozambique, Zimbabwe, Zambia, and even Tanzania, and displacing other peoples in turn. All of these movements combined—the Boer trek, Shaka's Zulu expansion, and the migration of peoples fleeing before both of these advances—created the *mfecane* in southern and eastern Africa. Cape Colony itself, however, remained relatively tranquil, continuing to serve as a port in transoceanic trade.

When the Suez Canal restructured the shipping routes between Asia and Europe in 1869, ending the need for the long voyage around Africa, South Africa might have become a quiet colonial backwater. But in the 1870s diamonds were discovered at Kimberley, and in the 1880s the world's largest known deposit of gold was found at Witwatersrand. Competition for this new wealth intensified the general hostility between the Boers and the British into full-scale warfare. The British army of 450,000 men finally defeated the Boer army of 88,000 in the three-year-long South African War (which the British called the Boer War), 1899–1902. In 1910, the British consolidated their own two colonies (Cape and Natal) with the two Boer republics into the Union of South Africa, which became a self-governing country. After 1913 whites in South Africa had the same sorts of political institutions and rights as in the British Dominions of Australia and Canada. Because of the European domination of the life of the colony, South Africa was considered a white settler colony despite its black majority.

Egypt, 1798–1882

The European invasion of Egypt in 1798 turned out to be very brief and yet very influential. Napoleon's forces invaded Egypt in 1798 and held it until British forces drove them out in 1801. During the fighting, the Ottoman sultan called in a troop of Albanian cavalry to lead the Ottoman resistance. The commander of the troops, Muhammad (Mehemet) Ali (1769–1849), remained after both French and British troops left and took over the effective rule of Egypt in 1807, although he served nominally as a viceroy of the Ottoman Empire. He introduced some new industries and then decided to concentrate on the cultivation of cotton as a cash crop for Europe's booming textile industry. To enable year-round cultivation, he built extensive new irrigation works. He also encouraged the development of Egypt's own textile mills. For the most part, he kept this economic modernization in the hands of the state rather than of private entrepreneurs. He streamlined the administration and built a system of secular state schools to train administrators and officers, especially by training students in Western scholarship. He introduced a government printing press, which in turn encouraged translations of European books into Arabic.

A professional soldier, Muhammad Ali modernized the army and marched his newly equipped forces up the Nile, captured the Sudan, and built the city of Khartoum to serve as its capital in 1830. He also gained control of the holy cities of Mecca and Medina in Arabia to counter the power of the militantly Islamic Wahabi movement there. Threatened by trends toward Westernization and Europeanization in the Middle East, the Wahabis taught that the Quran and the traditions of Muhammad (the Hadith) contained all of the fundamental beliefs of Islam. Further, they believed that governments should be based on strict interpretations of Islamic law. (This conflict between fundamentalist Muslims and Western-oriented leadership remains a central tension in the Middle Eastern world today.) Fundamentally secular in outlook, Muhammad Ali attempted to reach accommodation with the moderate Islamic forces in Egypt rather than attempting either to attack them or to bring them around to his own perspectives. He occupied Syria and Palestine and threatened Istanbul itself until Britain and France blocked his path, offering him, instead, recognition as the hereditary ruler of Egypt. Muhammad Ali's son, Ishmail, succeeded him and commissioned a French firm to build the Suez Canal, which was opened in 1869. His grandson expanded Egyptian territorial holdings both along the coast of the Red Sea and inland toward the headwaters of the Nile.

Muhammad Ali's modernization program brought mixed results. Egypt entered the international economy based in Europe, but soon was spending more on imports, military modernization, and beautification projects in Cairo than it was earning in exports. In addition, it made commitments to cash cropping of cotton as the principal export item and thus left the country vulnerable to the instability of international price fluctuations on this single crop. As Egyptian debts rose, European creditors pressured their governments to force the khedive (the title given to Muhammad Ali and his successors) to appoint European experts as Commissioners of the Debt in 1876. In 1878 the khedive was forced to add a French and a British representative to his cabinet. Even so, in 1881 the European powers had the Ottoman sultan dismiss the khedive, Muhammad Ali's grandson. When an Egyptian military revolt then seized power, Britain sent in its forces, primarily to protect the Suez Canal, and stayed on as the power behind the throne until the 1950s. For Egypt, entanglement with Europe proved a two-edged sword.

Algeria, 1830–71

The rule of the Ottoman Empire weakened not only in Egypt, but all across North Africa. By the late seventeenth and early eighteenth century, the regions of both Tunis and Algiers were only nominally under Ottoman rule. Both regions profited from piracy and were finally invaded by seafaring nations that sought to suppress the pirates, Tunis by the Americans (from which expedition comes the phrase "to the shores of Tripoli" in the American marine corps hymn) and Algeria by the French. The French attack on Algeria in 1830 began as a campaign against piracy, but relations between the ruler of Algiers and the French government spun out of control, and ultimately the French demanded and got his surrender and control over his possessions. Political control over Algiers was fragmented, however, and the French found themselves at war with other regional leaders, especially Abd al-Qadir, son of the head of one of the most important Muslim brotherhoods, or religious/political organizations, in the Middle East. Resistance swelled under al-Qadir, and he began to build a small state with its own administration and a modernized army of 10,000 men trained by

European advisers. At first, the French avoided confrontation with al-Qadir, who stayed south of their holdings, but in 1841 bitter warfare broke out. Before the French won, they had committed 110,000 troops (a third of their army) to the war and had attacked neighboring Morocco to block reinforcements to their enemy. Revolts continued to simmer, with the last and largest repressed in 1871, with 3000 French soldiers reported killed. Since the French resorted to a policy of destroying the crops of al-Qadir's army, Algerian casualties were almost certainly much greater. French armies took over rural areas, opening them for French military occupation and settlement.

During the years of fighting and thereafter, tens of thousands of Europeans came to settle in Algiers, some in connection with the military, some in search of economic opportunity. About half were French, but all began to adopt French language and culture and to think of themselves as French people living in Algeria. By the 1850s there were 130,000 of them and by 1900 more than a half-million, about 13 percent of the population. Christians (and Jews after 1870) were deemed to be citizens of France, Muslims were legally subjects. After a change of government in France in 1870, Algeria was formally annexed to France and French citizens—but not subjects—in Algeria received the right to vote for members of the French National Assembly in Paris. Through official land transfers and sales, the best land came into French hands and was developed into commercial agriculture, while Algerian farmers were generally left with small, under-capitalized holdings. This unequal pattern of representation and development continued until the end of the very bitter and costly Algerian war for independence in 1962. Following the war, almost all of the one million descendants of the French settlers fled to France.

Islamic Religious Revival

In the western and eastern *sahel*, the dry, semi-desert area immediately south of the Sahara, stretching almost from the Atlantic Ocean to the Red Sea, political and religious movements of Islamic revival flourished. Although in some places Islamic forces engaged European Christian forces in armed conflict, these Islamic movements were not directly related to European activities in Africa. Most of them were directed at keeping Muslims loyal to the faith and at bringing polytheistic Africans under Muslim rule rather than at opposing Christians. Some historians do believe, however, that the movements drew some of their inspiration from the knowledge among the Muslims that the balance of power was shifting from an increasingly weak Muslim Middle East and Africa to an increasingly powerful Christian Europe.

In West Africa three movements stand out for special attention. They began in states founded in the eighteenth century by the Fulani peoples. In Hausaland, modern northern Nigeria, Uthman dan Fodio (1754–1817), a prominent *sufi* teacher, began to condemn the rulers of Hausaland for corruption, sacrilege, persecution of true Muslims, and polytheistic practices. After years of this opposition, of gathering supporters from nearby groups, and of receiving inconsistent responses from the Hausaland rulers, Uthman urged his followers to arm themselves for coming conflict. The outbreak of hostilities began when a new sultan attacked a group of Uthman's followers in 1804. In response, Uthman called on his son and brother to lead the military campaigns that ultimately brought all of Hausaland under his control from his new capital at Sokoto. The new empire continued until the 1890s. Under its Islamic umbrella, the Sokoto empire tended to favor Fulani people over Hausa, even though not all of the Fulani were Muslims. For the most part, however, it encouraged both Fulani and Hausa to unite in a single Islamic empire.

Other jihads, or African holy wars, were smaller in geographical and military scale. They were usually concerned with purifying the Islamic faith and practices of rulers and subjects. These included jihads in western Africa in the small states of Futa Toro, Futa Jallon, and the somewhat larger Massina. In Massina, al-Hajj Umar (*c*. 1794–1864), having returned from a pilgrimage to Mecca, and having visited Sokoto, gathered followers and armed them. He captured the kingdom of Massina and made it the center of his empire. Umar attempted to gain support from the French on the coast of West Africa, but they were uneasy with his proposal. When he attacked French river traders, perhaps seeking to capture their guns, the French-controlled armed forces repulsed his attack.

Another leader who built an empire in the name of Islam, Samori Toure (*c*. 1830–1900), organized Mandinka and Diola ethnic groups under his military leadership. Although at one point he declared himself *almami*, or leader of the faithful, his devotion to Islam was sometimes compromised by battles against fellow Muslims and his murder of Muslim scholars in his capture of the town of Kong.

Aloysius O'Kelly, *African Musician*, c. 1880. Oil on canvas. As European artists painted African scenes they often portrayed people of striking beauty and strength against exotic backgrounds. The musician may have been a *griot*, a bard whose songs and chants preserved the history of his people. (*Taylor Gallery, London*)

Toure's empire, just south of the bend of the Niger River, as well as the empire founded by al-Hajj Umar, were situated in the path of French imperial conquest eastward from the Atlantic. In 1893–4, both were defeated and brought under French control. Although Toure's record is marred by his raiding for slaves (in order to barter them for guns), by his scorched earth policy of retreat before the French, and by his destruction of Kong, the town to which he moved his capital as he retreated, he is nevertheless viewed by most historians as a guerrilla leader who could hold off the French for two years in his original empire and for two more in his second empire. In 1898 the French captured him and exiled him to Gabon, where he died in 1900.

In East Africa, near Khartoum, the city founded by Muhammad Ali, a man named Muhammad Ahmed declared that he was the Mahdi, a messiah figure who would bring a new age that would restore the true religion. In 1881, he began to build a state in the Sudan. The Mahdi began his movement in opposition to the Egyptian government, but in 1882 the British re-entered Egypt, seized Cairo and claimed the Nile valley as effective rulers of the region. The British and the Mahdi were on a collision course. At first the Mahdi was victorious. In 1885, he defeated an Egyptian force commanded by British General Charles Gordon at Khartoum. Later that year the Mahdi died, leaving his state to a successor who, though Muslim, was far less militant than the founder. For some time Britain did not respond to this new state and its successes. A decade later, however, it sent another force under General Horatio Herbert Kitchener to retake the Sudan for Egypt and to revenge Gordon's defeat and death. At Omdurman, Kitchener's army destroyed the Mahdists, killing 11,000 men and wounding 16,000 in a single battle on September 2, 1898, while losing just forty of its own soldiers. They then proceeded to reclaim Khartoum. The British forces had machine guns while the Mahdists believed they were impervious to bullets. The total imbalance of military force and strategy between the British and the Muslim forces could not have been more clear, and neither could the willingness of the African Muslims to fight and die for their cause.

A Western Orientation in West Africa. Europeans and Africans, working together, created two new responses to the abolition of the slave trade and slavery: They established two colonies as refuges for freed slaves, and they began to found businesses, mostly based on tropical agricultural products, to replace slave trading in the export economy. European port towns along the coast were always more Afro-European than European, since the Europeans stayed only briefly while their mixed-race descendants remained along with a much larger number of slaves. Saint Louis, for example, in modern Senegal, was home in 1810 to about ten Europeans, 500 Afro-Europeans, 500 free Africans who had absorbed European culture, and about 2200 slaves.

The most significant of the west coast settlements was Sierra Leone. Its capital, Freetown, was founded in 1787 and, as the name suggests, it was to serve as a haven for freed slaves. At first these were mostly black Americans who had been freed by the British in their struggle against the American revolutionaries and rebels from Jamaican slavery. After the abolition of the slave trade in 1807, increasing numbers were slaves recaptured at sea by the British navy. In 1808 the British reorganized Sierra Leone as a formal British colony and promoted Christianity and Western culture among its residents. The numbers of recaptured slaves continued to add to the size of the colony, and an important institution for training African clergy, Fourah Bay College, opened in 1827. One of its first graduates, Samuel Crowther, became the first African bishop of the Anglican Church. The overwhelming majority of the population, however, were Africans who joined the colony on their own. Some of the former slaves, especially the Yoruba, used Sierra Leone as a staging point from which to return inland to the societies from which they had been taken.

Following the example of Sierra Leone, the American Colonization Society received a charter from the United States government in 1816 to found a site on the west African coast for the repatriation of freed American slaves. In 1822, the first settlers arrived at the site that later became Monrovia, named for American President James Monroe. In 1847, at a time when Monrovia held about 5000 settlers, it formally declared its independence from the United States government. Nine years later it joined with its surrounding settlements to form the country of Liberia as an independent state, although it was still heavily reliant on American assistance. Americans supported Liberia for diverse reasons: Some saw it as a haven for former slaves; others saw it as a dumping ground in which America could rid itself of ex-slaves. As in Sierra Leone, the population of freed slaves always formed a small minority of the total population. Even today, descendants of repatriated slaves, known as Americo-Liberians, form only 2.5 percent of the total population of about 3.2 million.

As the overseas slave trade ended in the north Atlantic, Europeans and Africans sought new export communities. British schemes to develop cotton plantations on the Niger River failed disastrously as the European personnel fell sick and succumbed to tropical illnesses against which they had no resistance. French schemes for plantations in the Ivory Coast and Gabon similarly failed. Foreigners did establish some economic enterprises inland—and often the same person served as the representative of government and the representative of European business interests. Most of the basic agricultural and animal commodities, however, were produced and transported by Africans. Ivory—much in demand in the West for piano keys and billiard balls—continued as a staple throughout much of the continent. New market crops included palm nuts and kernels, peanuts, timber, dyes, wax, honey, and redwood. As steamships started to ply Africa's rivers, bulkier crops were added: cotton, coffee, sugarcane, and sugar products. Rubber came in the 1870s. In the area around the Congo River, cassava, citrus fruits, tobacco, and maize were introduced. Despite the abolition of the slave trade in the British Empire and the areas it controlled, the slave trade flourished throughout most of the nineteenth century in the south Atlantic and throughout Africa. The increase in commercial cropping, ivory harvesting, and copper and metal mining and production required labor, and slavery provided much of it. Often "freed" slaves were forced into labor on the new plantations and in the expanding caravan trade, especially in East Africa. Arab caravan leaders impressed slaves into the ivory trade in great numbers and with high mortality rates.

The transport networks within Africa were for the most part traditional ones run by groups such as the Hausa, Yoruba, and Asante in West Africa, and by the Yao, the Kamba, and especially the Nyamwezi in East Africa, with their caravans of up to several thousands of people carrying ivory from far inland to the coast. In the east, Arab traders sometimes also conducted caravans from the coast to the Lake District, especially Lake Tanganyika. The Arab traders were backed financially and militarily by the Arab planters of Zanzibar with their rich harvests of cloves. The profit to be made in Zanzibar from cloves and from coordinating caravan transportation in East Africa was so great that the Arab ruler of the Oman empire, Sayyid Said, moved his capital from Muscat in Oman to Zanzibar in 1840. Said was "pulled" to Zanzibar by its promise of profits; he was also "pushed" from Oman by increasing British naval control of the Arabian coast and sea.

River transport by ship developed along with relatively short stretches of railroads to connect the river systems or to stretch short distances from the ports to nearby inland production centers. As steamboat transportation penetrated more deeply into the continent, many of the indigenous transport groups were displaced from their jobs, and some European commercial and administrative systems were positioned inland. Some great industries were owned and run by Europeans: rubber in the Congo, coffee plantations in East Africa, and diamonds and copper in the Congo and South Africa.

During most of the nineteenth century, the Afro-Europeans did well in business, education, and local public affairs in a relatively open environment. Commercial profit became more important than political power. Beginning with the 1880s, however, Europeans in larger numbers came directly from Europe, taking over direct political and economic power and imposing increasingly racist polices. Joseph Conrad's great novel, *Heart of Darkness*, captures the mood and setting of that transformation.

European Explorers and the Scramble for Africa

To extend their commercial ventures, their political power, and their missionary activities, Europeans wanted more knowledge of Africa. Exploration of the interior attracted many adventurers: In the late eighteenth and early nineteenth centuries West Africa and the Niger River were the main attractions for men such as Mungo Park, René Caillié, Hugh Clapperton, the Lander brothers Richard and John, and Heinrich Barth. By the middle of the nineteenth century the mystery and potential of central and East Africa attracted some of the most daring explorers. David Livingstone (1813–73), a Scottish missionary and able scientist, began his career in Africa intent upon establishing a missionary station and providing medical assistance. He began in South Africa in 1841, establishing stations, providing assistance, and exploring. In 1852 he returned home briefly. In 1853 he returned to Africa, landing at Luanda along the Angola Coast. For three years he continued to explore, crossing and re-crossing the continent. Livingstone was distinguished for learning African languages, treating Africans with respect, and constantly campaigning against the slave trade that was endemic in the African interior. In his popular writings on his explorations, he included pleas to the British government to extend its power in Africa to combat this trade. Two subsequent, grueling adventures of exploration in equatorial Africa lasted a total of thirteen years. Livingstone died in the course of his explorations in what is

HOW DO WE KNOW?

Why did Europeans Colonize the World?

The industrial revolution in western Europe and the United States ushered in an era of imperialism that brought most of the world's land under European political control. Why did the industrializing nations assert their powers in this way? To some extent, the answer seems obvious: They relished the power, wealth, and prestige that apparently came with imperial possessions. They also claimed to welcome the opportunity to serve others. Further, the industrial system that they were building took on a life of its own, requiring ever-increasing sources of raw materials and more markets in which to sell. But why was trade alone not enough? Why did the industrialists feel it was necessary to take political control as well? Were there additional motives behind imperialism? And did the results of imperialism match the aspirations of the imperial rulers?

We cannot answer all these questions fully, but a review article by Patrick Wolfe in The American Historical Review, "History and Imperialism: A Century of Theory, from Marx to Postcolonialism," helps us to review and sort out some of the most prominent explanations.

Karl Marx deplored the exploitation of colonialism, but, as a European, he valued some of its contributions. Britain, he emphasized, brought to India a new economic dynamism, with railroads, industrial infrastructure, and communication networks. Ultimately this transformation would lead to capitalism and then socialism. Marx wrote in 1853: "Whatever may have been the crimes of England, she was the unconscious tool of history in bringing about that revolution" (Marx and Engels, First Indian War, p. 21).

J.A. Hobson, a British economist writing in 1902, and V.I. Lenin, the leader of the communist revolution in Russia (see Chapter 19), writing in 1916, agreed that the desire to control raw materials and markets drove imperialism.

Hobson pointed out that the profits of the imperial system went mostly to the rich. He believed that if imperialism were ended overseas, a concentration on investment and industry at home would provide greater opportunities to the working classes in Europe. M.N. Roy, a founder of the Communist Party of India, disagreed with Hobson, arguing that the profits of imperialism did provide economic gains to European workers and that they would therefore support the system. The revolt against the imperial, and capitalist, system would have to begin among the workers in the colonies who were more exploited.

Several analysts have tried to grasp the imperial system as a whole, understanding the impact of colonizer and colonized upon one another. Some, like Marx, above, saw the system introducing valuable modernization into the colonies. Most, like Immanuel Wallerstein and the American economists Paul Baran and Paul Sweezy, argued that the imperial power would always seek to keep the colonies in a position of dependency and underdevelopment. The imperial rulers might introduce some technological innovations, such as railways that were necessary for their trade, but they had no interest in enabling the colonies to become economic and technological rivals. Indeed, one reason for imposing imperial domination was to prevent the colony from taking control of its own economic policies.

Ronald Robinson and John Gallagher, British historians writing in the 1960s, and French philosopher Louis Althusser, writing in the 1970s and 1980s, stressed the need to evaluate imperialism on a case-by-case basis. British imperialism in Egypt, for example, was quite sophisticated and benign compared with the raw cruelty of Belgian imperialism in the Congo. Even within individual colonies, imperialists treated different regions and groups differently, for example incorporating educated urban groups into the administration while treating plantation workers almost like

slave labor. Imperial rule also varied considerably depending on the administration in power in the imperial country and also on the local imperial representatives on the scene. All three scholars eschewed generalizations and emphasized the complexity of the imperial enterprise.

Finally, some of the most recent scholarly analyses of imperialism—often referred to as postcolonial analyses—have stressed the cultural impact of imperialism on both colonized and colonizer. Imperial rulers usually drew a sense of pride from their conquest and exalted their own culture for possessing colonies. Colonized peoples, on the other hand, often suffered a sense of inferiority. They had to re-examine their historic cultural traditions and identities in light of the fact that they had been conquered by foreigners. The postcolonial literature that analyzes this cultural confrontation has expanded rapidly, with contributions by literary critics such as Edward Said, Homi Bhabha, and Gayatri Chakravorty Spivak. Indeed, as industrialization has brought peoples of the world into ever closer contact, and political philosophies have collided with one another, questions of personal and group identity have increased everywhere. We will explore these questions of identity in Chapters 23 and 24.

- Among the scholars who argue that economics is the main force behind imperialism, there are differences of opinion. What are these differences? Which point of view seems most persuasive to you?
- Some scholars have argued that political gain has been the main force behind imperialism. What evidence do you see to support this viewpoint?
- Many contemporary scholars argue that the colonizing countries have been influenced by colonialism culturally just as much as the colonized have been. What examples of this influence can you cite?

today Zambia in 1873. In accordance with his wishes, his heart was buried in Africa, under a tree near the place where he died. His body was returned to England and buried in Westminster Abbey.

In 1871, when premature rumors of Livingstone's death reached Europe, the *New York Herald* dispatched Henry Morton Stanley (1841–1904) to try to find him in the course of his third expedition. Not only did Stanley locate Livingstone, he also carried out expeditions of his own—traveling with an armed retinue that resembled a military expedition or a slave caravan—through the Lake District of East Africa and along the Congo River. On Stanley's return through Europe, King Leopold II of Belgium (r. 1865–1909) engaged him to establish trading stations along the Congo River. Unlike Livingstone, Stanley treated the Africans who worked for him harshly and sought personal profit. He accepted the king's proposal. The colonization of central Africa was beginning.

Stanley, representing the king and his International Association for the Exploration and Civilization of Africa, negotiated treaties with hundreds of local chiefs. The treaties gave him, personally, the power to establish a Confederation of Free Negro Republics, an estate of some 900,000 square miles, which functioned as a kind of slave plantation within Africa for the personal economic benefit of King Leopold. The brutality of his treatment of Africans was perhaps the worst in the annals of European colonialism in Africa.

As European powers explored and colonized central Africa, they came into direct competition with each other. Fearing the consequences of this competition, Germany's Bismarck employed diplomacy to defuse European conflict, as he had done a few years earlier in the Balkans. He convened a conference in Berlin in 1884–5 to determine the allocation of Congo lands and to establish ground rules for fixing borders among European colonies in Africa. The Berlin Conference assigned the administration of the Congo, an area one-third the size of the continental United States, to Leopold II personally as a kind of company government. The Congo became, in effect, his private estate, eighty times larger than Belgium itself. Its economic purpose was, first, the harvesting of natural rubber from vines in the jungles and, later, the exploitation of the area's rich mineral reserves, especially copper. Laborers were forced to work as slaves at the point of a gun. Workers could be killed or have their hands cut off for failing to make quotas. Company agents killed and maimed workers who offered resistance. During the years of the king's rule, ten million Congolese died as a result of his policies. In 1908, recognizing both the cruelty and the economic losses of the Congo administration, the Belgian parliament took over control of the colony from the king, but the Congo remained one of the most harshly administered of all the African colonies.

The Berlin Conference also divided up the lands of Africa on paper, generally apportioning inland areas to the European nations already settled on the adjacent coast. These nations were then charged with establishing actual inland settlements in those regions, and they quickly did so, dispatching settlers in a "scramble for Africa." Portugal added to its domains in Angola and Mozambique. Italy captured a piece of Somaliland at the horn of Africa and Eritrea on the Red Sea. It also attempted to conquer proud Ethiopia, but King Menelik II (r. 1889–1913) had purchased sufficient guns and trained his forces well enough to defeat Italy at the Battle of Adowa in 1896. Italy did succeed, however, in taking Libya from the weakened Ottoman Empire in 1911. Germany established colonies in German East Africa (Tanganyika), the Cameroons, Togo, and German Southwest Africa (Namibia). The Germans, like the British and French before them, established treaties with African chiefs who often did not understand the significance of the documents they ratified but nevertheless found their power over their people strengthened. The chiefs frequently became, in effect, the agents of Europeans for recruiting labor and collecting taxes. In exchange, the Europeans protected the chiefs from resistance and rebellion.

On the occasions when Africans resisted these one-sided agreements, Europeans responded with force. Between 1884 and 1898, the French put down the rebellion of the Mande peoples under the Muslim Samori Toure. The British finally quelled a series of Asante revolts in the Gold Coast in 1900. The Germans crushed perhaps the greatest of the unsuccessful rebellions, the Maji-Maji revolt of 1905–7 in Tanganyika. Led by Kinjikitile Ngwele, who claimed to have magic water (*maji*), which would make his followers invulnerable to wounds, the rebels had refused to perform forced labor on the cotton plantations. The uprising ended with 70,000 rebels dead, including those who succumbed to disease and malnutrition. Other less spectacular revolts were similarly suppressed with violence.

As British forces began to connect the north–south route through East Africa, French forces were proceeding from their huge holdings in West Africa to link up with their small toehold in the east at French Somaliland. In 1898 General Kitchener confronted French Captain Jean-Baptiste Marchand at Fashoda. War threatened, as provocative correspondence and news accounts were issued on both sides. In the end, the heavily outnumbered French backed down, and France retreated to its substantial holdings in Algeria, and to Morocco, which it later divided with Spain in 1912.

Labor Issues: Coercion and Unionization. Throughout Africa, Europeans confronted the problem of finding labor for their new farms and enterprises. By confiscating African land and redistributing it among themselves, Europeans took farms away from Africans and produced a new wage-labor force. The 1913 Natives Land Act of South Africa closed 87 percent of South African land to African ownership; the remaining 13 percent was the most marginal land. The newly displaced labor force was especially vital for the new coffee plantations in the highlands of East Africa. In the farming areas of Kenya, Northern Rhodesia, Nyasaland, and Angola a system of tenancy without wages developed, a kind of share-cropping system. Within their colonies in Angola and Mozambique, the Portuguese used intimidation to coerce labor, but the Africans often fled or otherwise subverted the plans of their colonizers. The British colonies, which used the carrot of (low) wages, seemed more successful in eliciting production. Along the coast, indentured laborers from India, China, and Southeast Asia were imported by the thousands to work in the sugar plantations.

The greatest problem was finding labor for the South African diamond and gold mines (and later for the great copper mines in the Congo as well). Taxation was introduced that had to be paid in cash, forcing all Africans to find some way of raising the money. Jobs in the mines were one alternative. Because the Europeans feared the revolutionary potential of a stable African labor force in the mines, they usually recruited workers on contracts for only one or two years at a time. They split up families, housing the male workers in barracks-like accommodations near the mines while exiling their families to distant reservations, where the women and children carried on limited farming and craft production. The mine owners did not pay the workers enough to support their families so the farming and handicrafts of the women in effect subsidized the workers' salaries.

Trade unions in the mines organized only the white skilled workers and kept Africans out of these jobs. In 1906, when the mines employed 18,000 whites, 94,000 Africans, and 51,000 Chinese indentured laborers, the white skilled workers went on strike to protest their being squeezed out by the Chinese and Blacks. Owners broke this strike through the use of Afrikaner strike breakers, but ultimately the Chinese miners were repatriated and the skilled jobs were reserved for whites. Race thus trumped both the free markets of capitalism and the solidarity of labor unions.

GENDER RELATIONSHIPS IN COLONIZATION

The Europeans who traveled overseas to trade beginning in the sixteenth century were almost invariably males, and they frequently entered into sexual liaisons with local women. As the men stayed longer, these relationships became increasingly important for business and administration as well as for social and sexual pleasure. One example was the **signares**, concubines or mistresses, of French traders in the Senegambia, present-day Senegal and Gambia. As the Senegal Company forbade its traders to marry locally, the men found concubines among the local Wolof and Lebou peoples. These women helped the men to negotiate local languages, customs, and health conditions.

signares African concubines of French traders in the Senegambia.

In India, the **nabobs**, the successful traders who often became wealthy, frequently took local women in much the same way. Not forbidden to marry, they fathered Anglo-Indian children who came to form a small but important community of their own, especially in the large port cities of Bombay, Madras, and Calcutta.

nabob A British employee of the East India Company who made a huge fortune in India, often through corruption, in the eighteenth century.

As Europeans began to establish colonies, and as women began to travel to these colonies, usually with husbands, or in search of husbands, European women discouraged relationships between the colonizing men and the colonized women. More rigid boundaries were established. In both India and Africa observers saw increasing distance and racism enter into sexual and gender relationships between colonizer and colonized. The new guidelines for inter-racial behavior restricted not only sexual but also social relationships. As these relationships between men and women became less free, so, too, did the informality among the men.

Earlier historians had attributed this increasing distance to the restrictive attitudes of the European women, who wished to prevent their husbands' mixing with the local women. More recent, feminist scholarship has attributed the responsibility for the increased distance to both husband and wife. Both exhibited racism. Whatever may have been the differences of opinion between European men and women concerning the relationships between European men and the colonized women, both usually wished to restrict local men from intimate contact with European women. As colonial settlements increased in size and stability, each family tended to view itself, somewhat pompously, as a representative of the rulers, a colonial outpost in miniature.

Christmas in India, a sketch by E.K. Johnson, *The Graphic*, 1881. Just as, for the most part, European men did not socialize or form a solidarity with the men whose country they had colonized, so, too, the women kept themselves apart and their lives centered on their families and their European friends. The wife would oversee the running of the household as she was accustomed to doing at home. Here the *ayah* looks after the youngest child in much the same way that Nanny would have back in England.

Did the colonizing women form a solidarity with their colonized sisters? Most contemporary historians think not. The colonizers tended to fasten on flaws in the gender relations among the colonized peoples, and then set out to introduce reforms. In India the British outlawed *sati*, the practice of widows burning themselves to death on their deceased husbands' funeral pyres; they introduced a minimum age of marriage; they urged widow remarriage despite upper-caste Hindu resistance. In Africa they sought to end polygamy. In each case, the colonial government emphasized the superiority of its own practices, and the good fortune of the colonized to have the Europeans there to save them from themselves. The European colonizers pointed to their

Sati **ceremony, Allahabad, India, 1946.** A widow on a funeral pyre, prepared to commit *sati* (suttee), ritual suicide, in order to accompany her husband in his death. *Sati* had been practiced for centuries by a very small number of upper caste Hindu women. The British outlawed *sati* in 1829, with the support of some Indians and against the opposition of others. Although illegal and very rare, the practice occasionally continues.

interventions in gender relations to justify and praise their own colonial rule. The colonizing women did the same.

The colonial presence did, however, introduce new patterns of gender relations into the colonies, based on the European models. At least some of the colonized peoples chose to move toward a more European style of gender relations. They wanted more education for women, more freedom of choice in marriage, more companionate marriages, and an end to *sati* in India, to polygamy in parts of Africa, and to footbinding in China. Sometimes people adopted new customs because they seemed better, sometimes because the new behavior won favor for the colonized peoples with the colonizing masters.

Later, as nationalism took root, people began to reject at least some of the foreign practices because of their colonial associations. Some women who had begun by welcoming the aspirations of Western feminist freedoms, such as equal educational opportunity, the right to work outside the home, setting limits on family size, owning property, and equal rights under law, later began to feel that these "freedoms" contradicted traditional family values in their own society, and came to reject them. They also analyzed the relationships between European men and women more closely, and often found them fraught with tension and anxiety. They caricatured at least some of the colonial intrusions into their family and gender relationships as "white men saving brown women from brown men."

ANTI-COLONIAL REVOLTS, 1857–1914

To be conquered by European colonial powers generally evoked anxiety and resentment. Not everyone, of course, shared these emotions. Some of the conquered people found new opportunities in working with or for the conquering powers. Personally, they might find jobs, education, business opportunities, and new professions. For their countries, they might find the imperial powers imposing peace among otherwise warring factions and a rule of law that might displace the arbitrary rule of local officials. New medical and technological systems might raise the standard of living.

For the most part, however, the conquered peoples usually were resentful. Or they became resentful. They might see some benefits to early colonial rule, but after a time they were usually irritated by the "glass ceilings" that kept local people out of higher level jobs in the administration, even when they were qualified. Even if new colonial businesses offered new opportunities, the bulk of the profits was sent back to the colonizing country. The new educational, legal, and administrative systems undermined local traditions, culture, and religion. The use of a foreign language in public life—the norm in colonial situations—also inhibited the development of indigenous cultures. At least as significant as any of these more tangible frustrations were the racism and disrespect that colonized peoples experienced from most of the colonizers, and that they deeply resented. Sooner or later, most colonized people wanted their independence. In region after region they rose in revolt against colonial rule.

Many of these, however, looked backward, to restoring the institutions that had preceded colonialism. This was a common early reaction to colonialism. The 1857–8 revolt in India took this position; as did the Mahdist revolt on the upper Nile (1881–98); so, too, did Shamil, "ruler of the righteous and destroyer of the unbeliever," inspired by an Islamic mystical brotherhood against Russia in the Caucasus (between 1834 and 1859); Emilio Aguinaldo against the United States in the Philippines (1898–1902); and peasant warfare against the Dutch in Bali and Lombok, Indonesia (1881–94), and in Sumatra (1881–1908).

Later, armed revolts and nonviolent political movements against colonial rule became more forward-looking. Their leaders sought not a simple return to the past but a newly restructured nation, usually incorporating significant elements of the past with new goals based in part on innovations introduced by colonial powers. In India, the Indian National Congress, founded in 1885, proposed a pattern of parliamentary democracy for India, often (but not always) with an admixture of Hindu reformism. In 1907, in Egypt, Saad Zaghlul (1857–1927) founded the Hizb al-Umma or People's Party, a reformist party which, in turn, became the core of the nationalist Wafd party after 1919. By 1911, the authors of the Chinese revolution looked forward to modernizing their country. The Young Turk party, formed in 1878 in patriotic anger against the Ottoman defeats in the Balkans, grew into a revolutionary party by 1908. The Young Turks, like the Chinese nationalists, saw as their first task the removal of the ruling government, the Ottomans, before going on to further reforms. Indonesia's first nationalist association, the Budi Utomo, was formed in 1908; South Africa's National Congress in 1912; and Viet Nam's Viet Nam Quang Phuc Hoi in 1913.

Each of these organizations had a conception of the future nation it was constructing, modeled in part on European military, economic, political, and administrative forms, but also incorporating its own cultural, religious, and social dimensions. Perhaps the most interesting of all these responses was that of Japan. By the mid-1850s, Japan had witnessed the partial colonization and humbling of China before the Western powers. When American warships entered Japanese waters in 1853, the Japanese feared that a similar fate awaited them. They took dramatic action to insure that they would not fall victim to colonial rule.

JAPAN: FROM ISOLATION TO EQUALITY, 1867–1914

In terms of nationalism, Japan was unified by race, with accepted legends of its national history and with a single dynasty of emperors that related back to the founding of the nation in the seventh century B.C.E., a single national language, an integrated national political structure, and an island-based geography. Japan's insular nature was intensified in the early 1600s when the government closed the country to foreign, especially European, contact. Rather than accept the European model of competitive nation-states, Japan at this point chose relative isolation. Faced with a challenge from Western nations in 1853, however, Japan recognized the need to transform itself militarily, economically, diplomatically, politically, and culturally. The history of Japan after 1853 charts its move from isolation to full, prominent participation in the world of nation-states.

The End of the Shogunate

By 1639, Japan had shut down commerce and contact with the European world, except for a Dutch outpost, virtually quarantined on Deshima Island in Nagasaki harbor, which was allowed to receive one ship each year. The Japanese also permitted the Chinese to trade at Nagasaki, but only under severe restrictions. Some trade could also pass through the Ryukyu Islands to China, under the guise of "tribute," and Korea could trade through the islands of Tsushima. Otherwise, Japan was isolated. In the late 1700s and early 1800s, European ships would occasionally attempt to establish contact, but the Japanese turned them away.

In 1853, however, the United States dispatched Commodore Matthew Perry (1794–1858) with a small squadron, including three steam frigates, to force Japan to open to trade as China had been opened in the Opium War a decade before. Japan lacked the means to resist the Americans and the European powers that soon followed, and over the next few years the country opened more ports, at first on the periphery, but then at Nagasaki, Kobe, and Yokohama. Japan opened Edo (Tokyo) and Osaka to foreign residents, and then granted the foreigners extraterritorial legal rights. Foreigners were permitted to stipulate Japan's tariff policies. In 1863 and 1864, in the face of firing on their ships, British, French, Dutch, and American naval forces demolished Japanese coastal forts and supplies and forced Japan to pay an indemnity. Like China, Japan seemed headed toward control by foreigners.

Unlike China, however, young, vigorous leaders seized control of the government of Japan, forcing a dramatic restructuring of the nation's politics, administration, class structure, economy, technology, and culture. These leaders, for the most part young samurai warriors in the **han** (feudal estates) of Choshu and Satsuma at the southern extreme of Japan, decided that Japan's current government was not capable of coping with the European threat. Great diversity of opinion flourished among the approximately 250 different *han* in Japan, but the most powerful regional leaders felt that the **shogun** or military governor, who ruled Japan in the name of the emperor, should be removed and the emperor himself should be restored as the direct ruler of Japan. The young samurai, members of Japan's hereditary military elite, should formulate the policies of the new administration.

The samurai were able to employ some of the technological information introduced by the Dutch from their station in Nagasaki harbor. Indeed, in 1811 the shogunate had established an office for translating Dutch material, and it was expanded into a school for European languages and science in 1857. Some of the *han*, including Satsuma, Choshu, and Mito, did the same. By 1840, some Japanese were already casting Western guns and artillery. Sakuma Zozan (1811–64), one of the advocates of adopting Western military methods, coined the motto of the movement: "Eastern Ethics; Western Science." Japan could adopt Western technology, he counseled, especially military technology, while still maintaining its own culture.

Sakuma believed that opening the country was both necessary and beneficial. Not everyone agreed, however, and in 1860 a group of samurai from the conservative

han In Japan, a territory or feudal estate controlled by a **daimyo** under the Tokugawa shogunate (1603–1868). They were abolished in 1871.

shogun The military leader who ruled Japan in the name of the emperor.

han of Mito argued a contrary position: "Revere the Emperor; Expel the Barbarian." The lines of conflict were sharpening. Political violence increased as exponents of the opposing positions attacked each other. Mito loyalists assassinated Sakuma and another reform leader in 1864 and then committed ritual suicide. Attacks on foreigners taking up residence and conducting business in Japan also increased.

In 1865, a group of young samurai in Choshu attacked and defeated their **daimyo**, the ruler of their *han*, establishing control of the government of Choshu. Next year, the armed forces of Choshu confronted and defeated those of the shogun, while the other *daimyo* sat out the contest. In 1868, the forces of Choshu and Satsuma, joining with those of several other more remote *han*, seized control of the emperor's palace in Kyoto and declared the shogunate ended, the lands of the shogun confiscated, and the emperor restored to imperial power. Most of the fighting was over by November, although naval battles continued into early 1869. The **Meiji restoration** ended the power of the shogunate forever and brought the *daimyo* and their young samurai to power in the name of the Emperor Meiji (r. 1867–1912). The emperor assumed the throne at the age of fourteen and reigned over a national transformation of astonishing scope and speed.

Policies of the Meiji Government

On April 8, 1868, the revolutionary leaders issued a Charter Oath in the name of the Emperor Meiji. The fifth and last article proved the most important: "Knowledge shall be sought throughout the world so as to strengthen the foundations of imperial rule." The new goal was "a rich country and a strong military." The new leaders had already begun to search the world for new political, economic, and military models that might be adapted to Japan's needs.

After treaty agreements had been signed in 1858, the shogun had already dispatched embassies to the United States in 1860 and to Europe in 1862, beginning official exchanges of information. Now a two-year overseas goodwill mission, headed by Prince Iwakura Tonomi (1825–83), set out in 1871 to deepen relationships with the heads of state of the treaty powers, to discuss future treaty revisions, and to enable Japanese leaders to experience the West at first hand. Fifty-four students accompanied the mission. A ministry of education was established in 1871, and its first budget (1873) included funds for sending 250 students abroad to study. Many of these students became leaders in the new Japan. Foreign instructors were also brought to Japan. The late shogun's government had employed some foreigners in industrial enterprises, but the Meiji rulers imported far more. They set out to develop Hokkaido, the northern island, and brought in American experts,

daimyo The feudal lords of Japan, who by the sixteenth century controlled almost the entire country.

Meiji restoration The reforms effected in Japan in the name of the emperor Mutsuhito (r. 1867–1912), who was known as the Meiji emperor. During his reign constitutional changes restored the emperor to full power, displacing the militarily powerful shogun, and Japan adopted many Western innovations as it became a modern industrial state.

THE MEIJI RESTORATION AND INDUSTRIALIZATION IN JAPAN

1853	Commander Perry sails into Edo Bay, ending 250 years' isolation
1854	Treaty of Kanagawa gives US trading rights with Japan
1860s	Series of "unequal treaties" gives US, Britain, France, Russia, and Netherlands commercial and territorial privileges
1868	Tokugawa shogun forced to abdicate. Executive power vested with emperor in Meiji restoration
1871	Administration is overhauled; Western-style changes introduced
1872	National education system introduced, providing teaching for 90 per cent of children by 1900 First railway opened
1873	Old order changed by removal of privileges of samurai class
1876	Koreans, under threat, agree to open three of their ports to the Japanese and exchange diplomats
1877	Satsuma rebellion represented last great (unsuccessful) challenge of conservative forces
1879	Representative system of local government introduced
1884	Western-style peerage (upper house) is created
1885	Cabinet government introduced
1889	Adoption of constitution based on Bismarck's Germany
1889	Number of cotton mills has risen from 3 (1877) to 83
1894–5	War with China ends in Japanese victory
1895	Japan annexes Taiwan and Pescadores Islands
1902	Britain and Japan sign military pact
1904–5	War with Russia ends in Japanese victory
1910	Japan annexes Korea
1914	Japan joins World War I on side of Allies

who introduced large-scale farming practices. By 1879 the ministry of industry employed 130 foreigners. Doctors were brought from Germany to teach medicine, and from America to teach natural and social sciences. After a few years, however, the cost of importing foreign experts outweighed the benefits, and fewer were employed. Missionaries, who came at their own expense, were an important exception.

Restructuring Government. The emperor was brought from his home in Kyoto to Edo, the former capital of the shogun, which was renamed Tokyo ("Eastern Capital") in 1868. In 1869, the *daimyo* of four of the most important *han*—Choshu, Satsuma, Tosa, and Hizen—turned over their estates to the emperor, setting the pattern for other *daimyo*. At first the *daimyo* were appointed governors, but two years later their domains were abolished and reorganized among the other prefectures of Japan. The *daimyo* retained certain rights of tax collection, which kept them financially well off, and stipends were paid to the samurai to avoid outright revolt. Nevertheless, a decade of samurai revolts in Choshu, Kyushu, Hizen, and, by far the largest, in Satsuma did challenge the new government. In Satsuma 40,000 troops, under the reluctant leadership of Saigo Takamori, confronted the government and were crushed. Japan's national government held firm.

The core of the central government's new army, 10,000 men drawn from Satsuma, Choshu, and Tosa, was established in 1871. In 1878, the army was reorganized and money was invested in modern equipment, much of it manufactured in Japan. An army staff college began to train an officer corps following a German model, while the navy adapted a British model, often purchasing its ships from Britain. Service in the armed forces introduced Japanese conscripts to new ways of life, some travel, reading and writing, Western-style uniforms and shoes, nationalism, and reverence for the emperor. Japan was becoming the most powerful nation in East Asia.

SOURCE

Fukuzawa Yukichi: Cultural Interpreter

Born into the lower levels of the feudal aristocracy in Kyushu, Fukuzawa Yukichi (1834–1901) had a thirst for knowledge that took him to Osaka, Nagasaki (for Dutch learning), to the United States in 1860 with the very first Japanese official mission (and again in 1867), and to Europe in 1862. Fukuzawa rejected government office, the usual alternative, in favor of private life as a journalist and teacher. He earned a reputation as the foremost interpreter of the West to Japan and his books describing the West as he understood it sold in the hundreds of thousands to a nation hungry for such observation and interpretation. He founded a school in Tokyo that later became Keio University, the training ground of many of Japan's business

leaders. The following excerpts are from Fukuzawa's Autobiography, *published in 1899. He states his goal of interpreting the West fairly, even though he knows that he will face opposition.*

The final purpose of all my work was to create in Japan a civilized nation, as well equipped in both the arts of war and peace as those of the Western world. I acted as if I had become the sole functioning agent for the introduction of Western culture. It was natural then that I would be disliked by the older type of Japanese, and suspected of working for the benefit of foreigners. ... I regard the human being as the most sacred and responsible of all orders, unable in reason to do anything base. ... In short, my creed is that a man should find his faith in independence and self-respect. (p. 214)

He investigates the style of Western institutions:

For instance, when I saw a hospital, I wanted to know how it was run—who paid the running expenses; when I visited a bank, I wished to learn how the money was deposited and paid out. By similar first-hand queries, I learned something of the postal system and the military conscription then in force in France but not in England. A perplexing institution was representative government. ... For some time it was beyond my comprehension to understand what they [political parties] were "fighting" for, and what was meant, anyway, by "fighting" in peace time. "This man and that man are 'enemies' in the House," they would tell me. But these "enemies" were to be seen at the same table, eating and drinking with each other. (p. 134)

Restructuring the Economy. Recognizing an economic principle that underlay the industrial revolution in Britain, Japan first built up its agriculture. It needed the profits, and it needed the food and manpower that an effective agriculture would make available for urban industry. New seeds, fertilizer, and methods were introduced throughout the islands, and Hokkaido was opened to farming. Agricultural colleges spread the new techniques and information. In the 1880s, agricultural production went up by about 30 percent, and from 1890 to 1915 by 100 percent. This production included not only food crops but also tea, cotton, and silk, mostly for the export market. The profits from increased agricultural production did not go to the peasants but to the landlord, who invested them in commerce or industry. Poorer peasants were squeezed off the land by high rents, and all peasants were heavily taxed to fund the large expenses of industrialization and militarization.

In large-scale industrialization, the government was the entrepreneur. It built the first railway line, between Tokyo and Yokohama, in 1872. In two decades about 2000 miles of track followed. Within the cities, trolleys and *rikishas* (rickshaws) supplemented the train lines. Telegraph lines linked all the major cities by 1880. The government financed coal mines, iron mines, a machine-tool factory, cement works, glass and tile factories, wool and cotton textile mills, shipyards, mines, and weapons manufacture. In 1873 it established the Imperial College of Engineering. But the industry that contributed the most, silk, which accounted for more than 40 percent of all of Japan's exports, was developed largely by private entrepreneurs.

Urbanization. Under the Tokugawa shogunate, 1603–1867, each *daimyo* had his own capital. As a result, Japan had a rich array of administrative towns and cities spread throughout the country. During the Meiji restoration, they provided the network for the diffusion of new cultural patterns. Some cities stood out: Kyoto, the home of the emperor, was the center of traditional culture; Osaka was the most important business center; and Edo (Tokyo) was, by the mid-1800s, the largest and most flourishing of the major cities, with a population of a half million to a million people.

Tokugawa urban culture had mixed strains. At the center of business life were merchants dedicated to making money. Yet they liked entertainment and found it outside their homes. Homes were for wives, children, and household duties. The amusement quarters of the city were for restaurants, theater, artistic culture, the female companionship of *geisha* personal entertainers, and prostitutes.

Social networks based on neighborhoods, shrines, guilds, and civic needs, such as firefighting, provided a sense of community, and cities grew relatively slowly in the first generation of the restoration. By 1895 only 12 percent of Japan's population of 42 million lived in cities. Industrialization in large factories had barely begun. In 1897 only 400,000 workers in all of Japan were working in factories employing more than five workers. By the turn of the century, however, the institutional and economic changes of the restoration were taking effect, and urban populations multiplied, so that by the mid-1930s 45 percent of the 69 million people of Japan were living in cities. The industrial labor force reached 1.7 million in 1920 (and 6 million by 1936).

The culture of the cities changed dramatically. Japanese cities, crowded and subject to fire and earthquake, changed not only with cultural and technological innovations,

East wears West. The Japanese troops pictured on the front of this French magazine are a perfect example of the detail to which the government of Japan was willing to go in their efforts to fit into the modern world of early twentieth-century politics and fashions.

Advertisement throwaway from the Mitsui dry-goods store (later Mitsuoki Department Store), Tokyo, c. 1895. Retail outlets were obvious signs of the drive to embrace industrialized Western culture, as this "before" and "after" picture aptly demonstrates. The traditional first floor (bottom), with its legions of clerks haggling over material, has been augmented by the new-fangled second floor (top), where a more serene atmosphere and slick glass display cases proclaim a new style of consumerism.

but also with the necessity to rebuild from time to time. Edward Seidensticker's remarkable study of Tokyo between 1867 and 1923, *Low City, High City*, describes a double transformation. The old heart of Tokyo, the low city, developed bigger businesses, more raucous entertainment, and newer fashions, but it remained rooted in the plebeian culture of the Tokugawa period of Edo. The high city, built literally on somewhat higher ground, was developed later, with modern buildings, more refinement of a Western sort, and a more modernist culture.

Cultural and Educational Change. Western cultural styles, superficial and profound, proliferated in Meiji Japan. The Gregorian calendar and the seven-day week, with Sunday as a holiday, were adopted in 1882, and the metric system in 1886. Samurai men began to prefer Western haircuts to the traditional shaved head and topknot. The military dressed in Western-style uniforms, and in 1872 Western dress became mandatory at all official ceremonies. Meat eating was encouraged, despite Buddhist ethics, and *sukiyaki*, a meat and vegetable dish especially cooked at the table, was developed as part of Japanese cuisine.

Japanese readers turned avidly to Western texts. Philosophers of the Enlightenment drew attention to individual rights, and Utilitarians, such as John Stuart Mill, were read and appreciated. The more combative social Darwinism of Herbert Spencer proved attractive as a justification for Japan's sense of its growing power and coming imperialism, and Samuel Smiles' emphasis on *Self Help* also found a receptive readership.

Tokugawa Japan had valued formal education. Samurai had attended Confucian-based schools run by the *han*; commoners had studied in schools located in Buddhist temples. At the time of the Meiji restoration, an estimated 45 percent of adult males and 15 percent of adult females could read and write, about the same proportions as

The expansion and modernization of Japan. Responding to the threats of foreign gunboats, Japanese samurai leaders overthrew the long-established Tokugawa shogunate and restored imperial power under the Emperor Meiji in 1868. Within fifty years, industrial development, growing international trade, and territorial expansion made Japan a world power. Initially asserting its control of neighboring islands, and then taking advantage of Manchu decline, its victories over China (1894–95) and Russia (1904–05) established Japanese control over Taiwan, Korea, and Karafuto (southern Sakhalin), and its dominant influence over Manchuria and even parts of mainland China.

in advanced European countries. Building on this base, the government introduced a highly centralized system of education and then mandated compulsory attendance. By 1905, over 90 percent of both boys and girls of primary school age were attending school. The schools were recognized for high quality, for providing public education superior to private schools, and for helping move Japan from the feudal, hierarchical society of Tokugawa Japan to a more egalitarian system than that of most European

Meiji classroom scene c. 1900. The Meiji rulers saw education as critical to Japan's modernization. The Charter Oath declared that, "Knowledge shall be sought throughout the world." Even before the Meiji, educational standards had been high; under the Meiji they approached 100 percent literacy.

countries. At the university level, a series of excellent institutions was established throughout Japan, beginning with Tokyo University in 1886.

Gender Relations. The Meiji restoration opened up entirely new arenas of public life and achievement for Japanese men, and, for a few years before marriage, some women also found new opportunities in education, factory employment, and a handful of new cultural opportunities. For the most part, however, women's public options were restricted. As the emperor's position was restored, so was male dominance in the home reinforced. Police Security Regulations of 1890, Article 5, prohibited women and minors from joining political organizations and from holding or attending meetings in which political speeches or lectures were given. (The vote was granted to women only after World War II.) The 1898 Civil Code reinforced patriarchy within the family, granting the male head of the family unquestioned authority. Women had few legal rights. At marriage, control over a woman's property passed to her husband. Fathers held exclusive right to custody over children. Concubinage was abolished in 1880, but society sanctioned prostitution and the discreet keeping of mistresses. As high school education was extended to women, the Girls' High School Law of 1899 declared its goal to create "good wives and wise mothers." Within the home, women held great authority and respect, but they were allowed virtually no place in the public life of Japan.

War, Colonialism, and Equality in the Family of Nations. From the beginning of the Meiji restoration, Japan sought to end the demeaning provisions of extraterritoriality, which required that foreigners charged with legal crimes in Japan be tried by foreign courts rather than by Japanese courts. Japan also sought to regain control of its own tariffs. These goals provided the rationales for introducing new legal systems that were more consistent with those of Western countries. If Japan's laws were in accord with those of Europe, there would be no justification for continuing extraterritoriality. The British relinquished extraterritoriality in 1899 when the new legal codes took effect. Other nations followed suit, and Japan reciprocated by allowing foreigners to establish residences outside the treaty ports. Additional treaties returned full control over tariffs to Japan in 1911.

War and colonization also seemed important to full membership in the European community of nations. Yamagata Aritomo (1838–1922), the chief proponent of the law of universal conscription in 1873 and the chief architect of Japan's new army, argued this position, and turned his attention to the conquest of Korea. Japan had forced the establishment of a legation in Korea in 1876. As political leaders in that country divided over policy issues, some sought support from more conservative China, others from more progressive Japan. When fighting between the groups broke out in 1894, both China and Japan sent in troops, and war began between the two powers. On land, Japanese armies seized all of Korea and pushed on into Manchuria. At sea, they defeated the Chinese fleet, captured Port Arthur, the naval base in southern Manchuria, and the port of Weihaiwei on the Shandong peninsula. Peace negotiations gave Japan Taiwan and the Pescadores Islands, and Japan supplanted China as the dominant nation of East Asia. Korea was formally recognized as independent, but Japan held sway there nonetheless. Japan was also to receive control over the Liaotung Peninsula, but an international diplomatic consortium led by Russia forced it to withdraw, despite Japan's resentment.

In the first years of the twentieth century, two further engagements with the West ratified Japan's arrival among the powers of the world. First, in 1902, Britain and Japan signed an alliance, the first military pact on equal terms between a European and a non-Western country. It brought together the most powerful navies of Europe and of East Asia. The treaty blocked Russian aspirations and further secured Japan's semicolonial control over China. Second, in response to continuing Russian penetration of Manchuria and increasingly hostile diplomacy, Japan attacked the Russian fleet in Port Arthur in 1904 and declared war. Fighting far from the center of their country, the Russian army was defeated. A Russian fleet dispatched from the Baltic was intercepted and annihilated by the Japanese in 1905 as it crossed the Straits of Tsushima.

An Asian power had defeated a European power for the first time since the victories of the Ottomans in eastern Europe in the seventeenth century. (In Russia, the defeat precipitated a revolution against the government in 1905.) In the peace conference convened by American President Theodore Roosevelt, Japan was given a protectorate over Korea, predominant rights over southern Manchuria (including the Liaotung Peninsula), and control of southern Sakhalin Island. In 1910, with no European power protesting, Japan formally annexed Korea. Japan had reached the international status it had desired—less than a half-century after embarking on its quest. The values of nationalism, technological innovation, and imperialism had become as supreme in Japan as they were in Europe.

NATIONALISM AND IMPERIALISM WHAT DIFFERENCE DO THEY MAKE?

Nationalism often inspired existing nations with pride in their past and aspirations for their future. It gave them a sense of their potential strength and power. It often united people together in mutual endeavors and encouraged a greater sense of equality and common purpose among them. This was part of the message of the English, American, and French revolutions. For regional groups that were not political nations, like Italy and Germany, the spirit of nationalism often inspired action toward unifying the regions into nations. For groups that felt themselves denied their national identity by a larger power that had colonized them—like the Greeks, Romanians, and Bulgarians under the Ottoman Empire, and much of the world under European colonialism—nationalism offered the promise of autonomy and control over their own affairs. At its best, nationalism encouraged nations to learn from one another, as each had something unique to contribute.

Nationalism has also inspired competition among nations that has sometimes evoked greatness, but has also frequently led to warfare, conquest, and colonialism. It has led to disputes among groups claiming national identity and national geographic borders that are difficult, if not impossible, to resolve. It has accompanied, and

RUSSO-JAPANESE WAR 1904–5: KEY EVENTS	
The war arose from conflicting ambitions in Manchuria and Korea, in particular the Russian occupation of Port Arthur (1896) and Amur province (1900).	
May 1904	Battle of Yalu River: the Russians are defeated by the Japanese in the vicinity of Antung (now Dandong), Manchuria. The river forms the border with Korea, and the Japanese army forces a crossing against light opposition. Quickly overcoming the Russians, who retreat north, the Japanese move to besiege Port Arthur (Lushun).
May 1904– January 1905	Siege of Port Arthur: the Japanese fleet blockades the harbor, keeping the Russian fleet bottled up, while the army launches a series of minor attacks. Japanese eventually overcome garrison, which surrenders, after heavy losses. Japanese lose some 58,000 men.
February– May 1905	Battle of Mukden (Shenyang): Japanese defeat Russians outside the capital city of Manchuria, in the last major engagement of the war, in which 41,000 Japanese were killed and wounded and the Russian dead and wounded totaled more than 32,000. The czar is finally persuaded to accept US mediation. Russia's Baltic Fleet is annihilated in the Tsushima Straits.
August 1905	Peace agreement: Russia surrendered its lease on Port Arthur, ceded South Sakhalin to Japan, evacuated Manchuria, and recognized Japanese interests in Korea. For the first time in more than two centuries an Asian power had defeated a European power. US president Theodore Roosevelt mediated the agreement and was awarded the Nobel Prize for peace (1906).

sometimes encouraged, racism and arrogance. It has created and perpetuated economic systems of great inequality in which the terms of trade are set by the powerful for their own benefit, often causing great suffering to the weak. All these aspects of nationalism—positive and negative—continued into the twentieth century—in ways that we shall explore in the next Part—and remain powerful today.

The political and industrial revolutions of the eighteenth and nineteenth centuries bound nations and peoples together more tightly than ever before. Historically great nations like China and Japan, which had lived mostly within their own regions, were pulled into greater participation in the global economy, politics, and culture. New political and industrial relations raised questions about the goals and the proper functions of the international economy: Is it to create profits or to provide for overall human welfare? Can it do both? How? Can the benefits of international competition be encouraged and its powers of destruction limited?

In this chapter we have seen European nations, and later Japan and the United States, backed by the power of their industrial revolutions, assert their control over much of the globe. Imperialists usually claimed that they were benefiting the peoples they ruled and cited statistics on new transport lines, new health clinics, new schools, and new political institutions. The conquered peoples usually pointed to evidence to the contrary: economies devastated, politics suppressed, and cultural traditions undermined. These legacies continued into the twentieth century, and they continue today as former colonizers and former colonies adjust their economies, cultures, and foreign relations to one another. Consciously and unconsciously the world proceeds against a background in which some nations conquered and lorded it over others. The sensitivities of those relationships are still quite raw as we see today when powerful nations attempt to exert their will politically, economically, and culturally, over weaker ones—and as the weaker choose to accept these conditions, to modify them, or to resist.

Review Questions

- How do you define nationalism? Would a strong nation and a weak nation use the same definition?
- Give examples of nations that formed by bringing together groups and regions, and give other examples of nations that formed by breaking apart from larger powers.
- In what ways were the colonization of India and China similar to each other? In what ways were they different?
- What benefits did colonialism bring to late-nineteenth-century colonies? Please cite specific examples. What benefits did it bring to colonizers? Please consider economic, political, and cultural aspects of colonialism. What were its negative effects on both colonizer and colonized?
- What do you believe to be the most important results of the coming of large numbers of European women to the colonies?
- What were the principal steps in Japan's actions to stave off colonial control?

Suggested Readings

PRINCIPAL SOURCES
Abernethy, David. *The Dynamics of Global Dominance: European Overseas Empires, 1415–1980* (New Haven: Yale University Press, 2000). Presents European expansion through a series of phases, notes its extraordinary power in reshaping the world, but sees it as ultimately self-liquidating. Comprehensive.

Bayly, C.A. *The Birth of the Modern World 1780–1914* (Malden, MA:Blackwell, 2004). A masterpiece of synthesis, combining political, economic, social, and cultural history in a global, interactive framework, by a master historian.

Cooper, Frederick and Ann Laura Stoler, eds. *Tensions of Empire* (Berkeley: University of California Press, 1997). Excellent anthology of recent writings on the social conditions in colonial life, including several essays on feminist perspectives.

Curtin, Philip, *et al. African History from Earliest Times to Independence*, 2nd ed. (New York: Longman, 1995). Masterly study especially good on the combination of history and anthropology. Four authors bring specialization across regions, disciplines, and styles of understanding. The narrative sometimes wanders among them.

Davis, Mike. *Late Victorian Holocausts: El Nino Famines and the Making of the Third World* (New York: Verso, 2001). Brings together many classic arguments about imperial exploitation of colonies, and emphasizes the cruelty of this exploitation at the time when major famines were also devastating colonial economies.

de Bary, William Theodore and Richard Lufrano, eds. *Sources of Chinese Tradition*, Vol. 2, 2nd ed. (New York: Columbia University Press, 2000). Outstanding source book, especially on cultural issues, from the Qing dynasty, to the present. Vol. 1 carries the earlier history.

Hay, Stephen, ed. *Sources of Indian Tradition*, Vol. 2, 2nd ed. (New York: Columbia University Press, 1988). Superb anthology of primary sources, especially strong on the religious and cultural bases of modern India, and their influence on its politics, about 1500 to the present. Vol. 1 carries earlier periods.

Hobsbawm, Eric. *The Age of Capital 1848–1875* (New York: Vintage Books, 1975). This series of Hobsbawm's books provide a well-written narrative sweep of world history through this period, from a leftist perspective. Often uses examples from popular culture, especially music.

——. *The Age of Empire 1875–1914* (New York: Vintage, 1987).

——. *The Age of Revolution 1789–1848* (New York: New American Library, 1962).

Hochschild, Adam. *King Leopold's Ghost* (New York: Houghton Mifflin, 1998). Narrates the horrifying story of the king's rule of the Congo, and the shipping agent who discovered and exposed it.

July, Robert J. *A History of the African People*, 4th ed. (Prospect Heights, IL: Waveland Press, 1992). Clearly written survey, especially good on political history.

Morris-Suzuki, Tessa. *The Technological Transformation of Japan* (Cambridge: Cambridge University Press, 1994). Follows the technical and managerial decisions that brought Japan to parity and even superiority in economic and technological modernization.

Said, Edward W. *Culture and Imperialism* (New York: Vintage Books, 1993). Said's various books emphasize the ways in which imperial powers used their own interpretations of culture to assert their supremacy over the countries they dominated and, often, to get the colonized people to believe it.

Tsunoda, Ryusaku, William Theodore de Bary, and Donald Keene, comps. *Sources of Japanese Tradition* (New York: Columbia University Press, 1958). Outstanding collection of primary sources, especially on the cultural leaders and philosophies of Japan, from earliest to modern times.

ADDITIONAL SOURCES

Adas, Michael, ed. *Islamic and European Expansion* (Philadelphia: Temple University Press, 1993). Still the best collection of introductory historiographic essays on the period 1000 to 1914 in world history.

Anderson, Benedict. *Imagined Communities* (London: Verso, 1983). Stresses the importance of the vision of nationalists in creating new nations, and the critical role of commercial publishing (print capitalism) in popularizing these visions.

Andrea, Alfred and James Overfield, eds., *The Human Record*, Vol. 2 (Boston: Houghton Mifflin, 3rd ed., 1998). Superb collection of primary documents on modern history.

Bayly, C.A. *Origins of Nationality in South Asia* (New York: Oxford University Press, 1998). Seeks to discover how Indians developed the concept of a modern nation from their own cultural materials as well as from new conceptions brought from the West.

Braudel, Fernand. *The Identity of France*, trans. by Sian Reynolds (New York; Harper and Row, 1988). Fascinating discussion of the process by which the various, disparate regions of France were unified into a single nation.

Briggs, Asa. *A Social History of England* (New York: Viking Press, 1983). Standard, well-written, well-illustrated history, stressing social conditions and change more than politics or economics.

Burns, E. Bradford. *Latin America: A Concise Interpretive History* (Englewood Cliffs: Prentice Hall, 6th ed., 1993). Excellent survey from a slightly leftist and critical perspective.

Burton, Antoinette. *Burdens of History* (Chapel Hill: University of North Carolina Press, 1994). Sees European women adopting positions sympathetic to imperialism as a means of showing that they deserved the same rights as men because they shared the same political perspectives.

Cheng, Pei-kai and Michael Lestz with Jonathan Spence, eds. *The Search for Modern China: A Documentary Collection* (New York: W.W. Norton, 1999). Excellent selection, very well annotated. Designed to accompany Spence's textbook of the same name, but also stands alone.

Chatterjee, Partha. *The Nation and Its Fragments* (Princeton: Princeton University Press, 1993). Analyzes some of the movements by which India began to come together as a nation. Thematically notes the importance of religion. Geographically stresses the Bengal region.

Collcutt, Martin, Marius Jansen, and Isao Kumakura. *Cultural Atlas of Japan* (New York: Facts on File, 1988). Superb introduction with fine text, maps, and illustrations that all work well together.

Columbia College, Columbia University. *Introduction to Contemporary Civilization in the West*, Vol. 2 (New York: Columbia University Press, 3rd ed. 1960). Outstanding sourcebook with lengthy excerpts from highly influential thinkers and actors.

Conrad, Joseph. *Heart of Darkness* (Mineola: New York: Dover Publications, 1990). A classic, brief novel on the cruelty and corruption of the "ruler" of a European outpost in the Congo interior.

Dalpat-Kavya Navnit (Selections from Dalpat the Poet), in Gujarati, ed. Deshavram Kashiram Shastri (Ahmedabad: Gujarat Vidyasabha, 1949). Dalpat's poetry expressed his beliefs that Indians in the mid-nineteenth century had much to learn from the British, including the methods of industrialization.

Davis, Lance E. and Robert A. Huttenback. *Mammon and the Pursuit of Empire* (New York: Cambridge University Press, 1989). Argues that imperialism did not pay, at least not financially, at least not after the beginning phases. A careful economic analysis.

Eley, Geoff and Ronald Grigor Suny, eds. *Becoming National* (New York: Oxford University Press, 1996). Excellent analysis of several major Western theories on the meaning of nationalism.

Engels, Friedrich. *The Origins of the Family, Private Property and the State*, ed. by Eleanor Burke Leacock (New York: International Publishers, 1973). Engels saw the exploitation of women as the first kind of economic exploitation that ultimately led to its fullest expression in the capitalist system.

Fujimura-Fanselow, Kumiko and Atsuko Kameda, eds. *Japanese Women* (New York: Feminist Press, 1995). Twenty-seven essays on many aspects of women in public and private life, their changing status, including men's views of the change.

Gluck, Carol. *Japan's Modern Myths: Ideology in the Late Meiji Period* (Princeton: Princeton University Press, 1985). Analyzes not only the formal ideologies, but also how they were received and perceived by the Japanese public.

Haldane, Charlotte. *The Last Great Empress of China* (Indianapolis: Bobbs-Merrill, 1965). A portrait of the powerful woman who effectively ruled China at the end of the nineteenth century and opposed reform.

Hanke, Lewis and Jane M. Rausch, eds. *People and Issues in Latin American History* (New York: Markus Wiener Publishing, 1990). Standard historical survey often presented through biography.

Headrick, Daniel R. *The Tools of Empire* (New York: Oxford University Press, 1981). Steamships, guns, and quinine were among the prerequisites of the European conquest of Africa.

Hertzberg, Arthur, ed. *The Zionist Idea* (Philadelpia: Jewish Publication Society, 1997). Still the best primary source introduction to early Zionist thought and its evolution, with a 100-page introduction.

Hirschmeier, Johannes. *The Origins of Entrepreneurship in Meiji Japan* (Cambridge, MA: Harvard University Press, 1964). Sees the economic transformation of Japan as the key to its development and demonstrates how it developed under government guidance.

Hutchinson, John and Anthony D. Smith, eds. *Nationalism* (New York: Oxford University Press, 1994). Survey of source materials on the meaning and significance of nationalism by nationalist leaders from around the world.

Kennedy, Paul. *The Rise and Fall of the Great Powers* (New York: Random House, 1987). Kennedy's discussion of what makes empires powerful, and what weakens them is engaging and provocative.

Lenin, V.I. *Imperialism, the Highest Stage of Capitalism* (Peking: Foreign Languages Press, 1965). Perhaps the strongest argument ever for the importance of the capitalist competition for markets, both for raw materials and for finished goods, as the basis for imperialism.

Magraw, Roger. *France 1815–1914: The Bourgeois Century* (Oxford: Oxford University Press, 1983). Useful survey stressing the importance of the middle classes.

Marx, Karl. *The First Indian War of Independence 1857–1859* (Moscow: Foreign Languages Press, n.d., *c.* 1960). As a journalist covering this war, Marx took a pro-European, imperialist position, that British rule in India was a benefit that would bring the colony into the modern world. Surprising?

Moore, Barrington, Jr. *The Social Origins of Dictatorship and Democracy* (Boston: Beacon Press, 1966). A classic of comparative history analyzing especially the role of the peasantry in revolutions from England to China.

Murphey, Rhoads. *A History of Asia* (New York: Addison Wesley Longman, 3rd ed., 1999). Useful survey.

Oliver, Roland. *The African Experience* (New York: Harper Collins, 1991). Sensitive, thoughtful brief survey of African history by a master of the field.

Renan, Ernest, "What is a Nation?" in Eley and Suny, pp. 42–55. A classic essay.

Restoring Women to History (Bloomington, IN: Organization of American Historians, 1988). Set of historiographic essays covering what we know of women's history around the world. Dated. Still useful.

SarDesai, D.R. *Southeast Asia Past and Present* (Boulder, CO: Westview Press, 3rd ed., 1994). Useful survey text.

Schirokauer, Conrad. *A Brief History of Chinese and Japanese Civilizations* (Fort Worth: Harcourt Brace Jovanovich, 2nd ed., 1989). Useful survey text.

Seagrave, Sterling, with Peggy Seagrave. *Dragon Lady: The Life and Legend of the Last Empress of China* (New York: Knopf, 1992). Biography of the woman who ran China's politics for her young son, and actively opposed modernization.

Spivak, Gayatri Chakravorty, "Subaltern Studies: Deconstructing Historiography," in Ranajit Guha and Gayatri Chakravorty Spivak, eds., *Selected Subaltern Studies* (New York: Oxford University Press, 1988), pp. 3–32. The subaltern scholars set out to reveal the importance of the little guy who had been left out; Spivak notes that the scholars left out women.

Strobel, Margaret, "Gender, Sex, and Empire," in Adas, pp. 345–75. Excellent introduction to issues of gender relations in imperial settings.

Teng, Ssu-yu and John K. Fairbank. *China's Response to the West: A Documentary Survey, 1839–1923* (New York: Atheneum, 1963). A superb, standard source book.

Wallerstein, Immanuel. *The Modern World-system 1: Capitalist Agriculture and the Origins of the European World-economy in the Sixteenth Century* (San Diego: Academic Press, 1974). Wallerstein's perspective on the core countries' dominance over the periphery is classic, but Eurocentric, problematic, and densely argued.

Wilentz, Sean. *Chants Democratic: New York City and the Rise of the American Working Class, 1788–1850* (New York: Oxford University Press, 1984). What was special about the American working class? Why did it not form a working-class political party? Wilentz' answers are cogent and lucid.

Wolf, Eric R. *Europe and the People without History* (Berkeley: University of California Press, 1982). Historical anthropologist Wolf looks at the systems of domination in modern history from the viewpoint of the colonized and the worker.

Wolfe, Patrick, "Imperialism and History: A Century of Theory, from Marx to Postcolonialism," *American Historical Review* CII, No. 2 (April 1997), 388–420. Enormously useful survey.

Yukichi, Fukuzawa. *The Autobiography of Yukichi Fukuzawa*, trans. by Eiichi Kiyooka (New York: Columbia University Press, 1966). Yukichi's nineteenth-century views of the West are insightful.

◉ World History Documents CD-ROM

The Olympics and International Politics

Sports such as organized, competitive athletics reflect the world around them. When, where, by whom, in front of what audiences, and for what stakes sports are to be "played" are questions decided through political, economic, and cultural negotiations. In the most famous of all competitions, the modern Olympics, these external forces appear clearly and repeatedly. The ups-and-downs of the Olympics reflect the ups-and-downs of the world outside the arena.

For example, the reopening of the Olympic Games in Athens in 1896 was due to the enthusiastic promotions of a Frenchman, Baron Pierre de Coubertin. As a founding member of the International Olympic Committee, Coubertin struggled for many years to revive the Olympic Games of ancient Greece since their last staging some fifteen hundred years ago. Although Coubertin stressed his love of athletics, he succeeded in part because of the rampant nationalism of his age. Nations were eager to compete against one another, and sports provided a welcome, non-violent forum. The competition among athletes also became a competition among nations. In 1896, thirteen nations of Western Europe and the United States participated; by 2004, some two hundred nations from all over the world took part.

The decision to hold this first revived Olympic Games in Greece was in part to reconnect with the home of

Above **The Olympic Games, Athens, 1896.**

Right **Women racing in the 100 meters, Olympic Games, Amsterdam, 1928.**

the original Olympics, but it was designed also to deliver a political message to the Ottoman Empire, Greece's former colonial ruler and hostile neighbor: that Greece had revived as an independent nation, and that other regions of the Balkans were also seeking their independence.

Women competed in track-and-field events for the first time in the 1928 Amsterdam Olympics. This breakthrough in gender relations mirrored more wide-ranging victories for feminism in society at large, most especially the right to vote, which was accorded to women in several European countries and the United States in the decade just after World War I.

Germany staged the 1936 Berlin Olympics as a showcase for Hitler and his National Socialist (Nazi) Party. Leni Riefenstahl's documentary film, *Triumph of the Will*, produced for the government, captured the intensely nationalistic spirit that was proclaimed in parades and demonstrations for the occasion. Many nations hesitated to participate since they were quite aware of the dictatorship and racism of Hitler's government; nevertheless, forty-nine did. In the end they witnessed the African-American athlete Jesse Owens deliver a great slap in the face to Hitler's racial theories of Aryan supremacy by winning the gold medal in both the 100 and 200 meter races, the long jump, and as part of the 400 meter relay race. Altogether, American track-and-field teams, including several African-American athletes, won twelve gold medals.

There were no Olympic Games in 1940 and 1944 because of World War II.

The right to host the Olympics has been a mark of national accomplishment. All of the first thirteen summer Games were hosted by cities in Western Europe and the United States. The fourteenth Games, held in Melbourne, Australia, in 1956, were the first departure from that pattern. From that time onward hosting of the Games became far more international. By according Japan the right to host the sixteenth Games in 1964, the International Olympic Committee recognized Japan's re-entry into the community of nations after World War II, and Japan went all-out in demonstrating its return to economic and political health. The new Olympic stadium designed by architect Kenzo Tange, along with the new *shinkansen*, or "bullet train" line (the fastest in the world), made clear Japan's renewed status as a world leader. In subsequent years, additional nations outside Western Europe, the United States, and Canada sought and

Above left Jesse Owens signals his acceptance of the gold medal in the long jump, and his defiance, with an American salute at Hitler's Berlin Olympics, 1936.

Above right The Tokyo Stadium (now the Yoyogi National Stadium) built by Kenzo Tange for the Tokyo Olympics, 1964.

Right A member of the International Olympic Committee talks with a masked PLO terrorist, Munich Olympics, 1972.

received the right to host the Olympics as a badge of their significance in international affairs: Mexico in 1968, Moscow in 1980, Korea in 1988. Beijing is scheduled to host the Games in 2008.

The dark as well as the bright side of international politics has spilled over into the Olympic Games. During the 1972 Munich Games, eight Palestinian terrorists brought the warfare of the Middle East to the Olympics. They invaded the Olympic Village, where athletes live during the Games, murdered two Israeli athletes, and seized nine more as hostages. Negotiations between Olympics officials and the terrorists failed. All

the Israeli hostages, one West German policeman, and five of the Palestinians were killed.

In 1979, the USSR invaded Afghanistan in support of a pro-Soviet faction in the ongoing civil war there. President Jimmy Carter responded symbolically by refusing to allow America to compete in the 1980 Olympics in Moscow. In retaliation, the USSR refused to participate in the 1984 Olympics in Los Angeles. Despite the high aspirations of Baron Coubertin in 1896, Olympic competition could not be sealed off from international political competition; on the contrary, they have always been tightly intertwined.

QUESTIONS

1. Can you imagine an Olympic Games in which athletes compete as individuals rather than as part of national teams? How would this be different?
2. Do you agree that sports as public competition mirror world events? Give examples.
3. In 1936 most eligible nations attended Hitler's Munich Olympics. In 1976, the United States boycotted the Moscow Olympics because of Russia's invasion of Afghanistan. Do you think either of these decisions was appropriate? Why?

PART 7

Exploding Technologies 1914–91

CONTESTED VISIONS OF A NEW INTERNATIONAL ORDER

The twentieth century began with great promise. The political and industrial revolutions of the previous two centuries encouraged western Europeans to believe that they were mastering the secrets of securing a long, productive, comfortable, and meaningful life for the individual and the community. They believed that they were transmitting these benefits around the globe through their colonial policies, and that their colonial possessions would continue long into the foreseeable future. Polish poet Wislawa Szymborska captured the optimism:

> Our twentieth century was going to improve on others . . .
> A couple of problems weren't going to come up anymore:
> Hunger, for example, and war, and so forth.

World War I, global economic depression, World War II, the Cold War, and revolts throughout the colonial world shattered many of these European illusions. "Anyone who planned to enjoy the world is now faced with a hopeless task," Szymborska wrote. (For the complete poem, "How Should We Live," see p. 681.)

What had gone wrong? Technology can produce catastrophe as well as creativity. Optimists at the beginning of the century overemphasized its positive potentials. They underestimated the problems of deciding its purposes, uses, and controls in a world of competition among nations, religions, ethnic groups, and ideologies.

The first half of the century saw technology put to use more in warfare than in peace (Chapters 19 and 20), but the second half brought a resurgence of optimism (Chapter 21): the United Nations emerged as a potential venue for conflict resolution and international bargaining, and the Cold War was contained as an armed truce and then came to an end virtually without bloodshed (although many

Atomic weapons test in the Marshall Islands, 1950.

proxy wars had been fought in its name). Technology—especially information and communication technology and biotechnology—was once again promising beneficial revolutions globally and in everyday life.

The world had heard such promises before, and once again the voices of caution were loud and clear: prosperity and opportunity were not trickling down to billions of impoverished people, neither in rich nor in poor countries; identity conflicts remained powerful and unresolved, and ethnic and religious violence broke out repeatedly around the globe; issues of gender identity, growing increasingly sensitive throughout the twentieth century, continued to expose tensions in family and public life; and technologies of destruction continued to multiply side by side with technologies of productivity.

LINE FOR
1¢ RESTAURANT
20 MEALS FOR $1
DONATIONS INVITED
HELP FEED THE HUNGRY
1¢ WILL FEED 20
1¢ RESTAURANT
107 W. 43rd ST.

METHODS OF MASS PRODUCTION AND DESTRUCTION

TECHNOLOGICAL SYSTEMS, 1914–37

KEY TOPICS
- Scientific and Technological Creativity
- Gender Relations
- Urbanization and Migration
- The Downside of Progress
- Outside Europe
- World War I, 1914–18
- The Russian Revolution
- Post-War America
- Methods of Production and Destruction: What Difference Do They Make?

"Technology" includes not only inventions but also the systems that produce and sustain them. Thomas Hughes, a historian of science and technology, explains this comprehensive definition:

> In popular accounts of technology, inventions of the late nineteenth century, such as the incandescent light, the radio, the airplane, and the gasoline-driven automobile, occupy center stage, but these inventions were embedded within technological systems. Such systems involve far more than the so-called hardware, devices, machines and processes, and the transportation, communication, and information networks that interconnect them. Such systems consist also of people and organizations. An electric light-and-power system, for instance, may involve generators, motors, transmission lines, utility companies, manufacturing enterprises, and banks. Even a regulatory body may be co-opted into the system. (Hughes, p. 3)

The technological enterprise grew into the most pervasive characteristic of the twentieth century and continues to grow. It has dramatically altered:

- the number, longevity, and health of the people who inhabit the globe;
- the size and organization of families;
- the location, design, and equipment of homes, neighborhoods, and workplaces;
- the nature and organization of work and the training necessary to do it;
- the quantities and varieties of food people eat as well as the regions of the globe from which they come;
- clothing;
- travel for business and pleasure;
- recreation;
- the strategies and destructive potentials of wars;
- the complexity and structure of economic, social, and governmental organizations; and
- the ecology—that is, the interaction of the life systems—of the earth.

Opposite **The Great Depression, 1929.** This photograph captures one of the many bread lines that wove their way through New York City during the Great Depression, this one being at Sixth Avenue and 42nd Street.

New farm technology. The American Burger tractor, invented in 1889, was the first to install an internal-combustion engine. With the introduction of automated farm machinery huge tracts of land around the world were brought under cultivation and food productivity soared. Here, in 1917, a woman from Vassar College in Poughkeepsie, New York, plows a field as part of the war effort.

SCIENTIFIC AND TECHNOLOGICAL CREATIVITY

The twentieth century continued to build on the inventions of the nineteenth and demonstrated an array of scientific and technological creativity never before known. As more people began to prosper, as business grew, and as new manufacturing processes spurred the development of new industries, demand led to an increasingly rapid pace of production. The ability to transmit electricity over long distances through the use of alternating current made widespread commercial grids possible. In 1886, a hydroelectric generating system was established at Niagara Falls, and by 1900, the basis of the modern electrical supply industry was in place. The first widespread application of the new energy was in lighting, with the creation of the incandescent lightbulb. Cities were eager to construct or buy into electrical grids to light up the night. In addition to street lighting and domestic lighting, workshops and factories could now operate round the clock. "Labor-saving" electrical appliances entered the home as well. The electric washing machine was patented in 1901, the vacuum cleaner in 1907. Both dramatically simplified women's domestic work. Electricity made possible the widespread use of the telegraph, telephone, and radio transmission. The phonograph had been invented by Thomas Alva Edison in 1877; by 1902, it had become a household product, with recordings of popular opera stars like Enrico Caruso and current vogues like ragtime music becoming increasingly widely available. Motion pictures had been created technologically in the 1890s, and by the early 1900s, they had become a popular entertainment. In 1909, newsreels appeared. Until 1927, the movies were silent, relying mostly on visual effects like slapstick comedy, as in the early films of Charlie Chaplin, perhaps the first great star of film. Not only was electricity functional for industry and the home, it also brought a world of fantasy to life. It encouraged people to dream.

Home life was enriched not only by the new electronic marvels, but new sources of heat made homes more comfortable and safer. Gas was beginning to displace open-fire heating, and kerosene heaters, utilizing the new by-products of the petroleum industry, were also popular. Oil lamps were used where electric lighting was not yet available, and both gas and electric cooking ranges were introduced.

In the mid-nineteenth century, the invention of the internal combustion engine, at first powered by coal gas, provided the motive force for a new industry that revolutionized transportation. The first automobiles to use these engines were produced in Germany in 1885 by Gottlieb Daimler and Karl Benz, working independently of one another. In 1908, Henry Ford produced 10,607 model T cars. In 1913, he created and shifted to assembly-line production, turning out a car every 93 minutes and making the automobile practical and cheap enough to be available for a mass market. In that year his factory produced 300,000 cars. Trucks were marketed at first in the hundreds and, by 1918, in the hundreds of thousands. Commercial bus operations began in Birmingham, England, in 1904 and in New York, Paris, and London in the next year. As automobiles, trucks, and buses multiplied, pressure mounted for road construction, and vast industries developed around the new vehicles: rubber for tires, glass for windows, steel for bodies and engines, and electrical systems for lights, starters, and, later, luxury equipment. Like the electrical industry, automobiles provided both workhorses for industry and fantasies for private consumption, opening up new vistas of personal mobility and, for courting couples, new possibilities of privacy.

Airplanes were still in their infancy. In 1903, the Wright brothers proved that heavier-than-air flight was possible, and by 1914, airplanes could fly at 60 to 70 miles per hour. Ships were certainly not new, and even steamships had existed for decades, but their design was improved. In 1907, the *Lusitania* crossed the Atlantic in five days.

Communication as well as transportation took on new speed and reach. Telegraphy had been invented by Samuel B. Morse in 1844; underwater cables connected Europe and Asia in 1866, and virtually instantaneous radio telegraphy was in place across the Atlantic in 1901 and across the Pacific in 1902. In 1904, telegraphic communication of photographs became possible. The telephone was invented in 1876. By 1907, there were 6 million phone users in the United States alone.

Chemical industries were especially creative. Industrial chemists developed new filaments that made incandescent lighting commercially viable. They created purer and stronger steel. Organic chemists working with coal and coal tar developed a wide array of new synthetic products, beginning with dyes, like indigo. The German chemist Adolf von Baeyer first determined the chemical structure of the dye in 1883, and in 1897 his company made synthetic indigo available commercially. Similar processes of chemical analysis and synthesis were applied to a wide range of consumer products. Most notably, in 1912, Fritz Haber and his colleagues in Germany invented a process for making ammonia (NH_3) directly from nitrogen and hydrogen found in the air, paving the way to the production of artificial fertilizers as well as explosives.

In medicine, antiseptic surgery had already been demonstrated in 1867. The twentieth century saw the development of the new science of bacteriology and its early success in 1909 in finding a drug with some effectiveness in curing syphilis in humans. In 1895, W.K. Roentgen discovered X-rays, and in 1898, Marie and Pierre Curie discovered radium and coined the term radioactivity, providing medicine with important new diagnostic and curative tools. In 1903, the first electrocardiograph was built.

The most significant improvements in health, however, resulted from improvements in basic cleanliness and sanitation. Public health services, and the provision of a clean water supply and adequate facilities for the sanitary disposal of waste, sharply reduced gastro-intestinal diseases and the death rates due to cholera and typhoid. Fine-sand filtration was replaced or joined by coarse-sand filters and, often, aluminum sulphate. By 1896, chlorine gas was used in the United States to purify water; in France ozone was preferred. By 1910, average life expectancy at birth in the United States reached 50 years.

Marie Curie and Pierre Curie.
Nineteenth- and early twentieth-century women increasingly carved out places for themselves at the forefront of intellectual, scientific, and political life. The Polish-born French scientist Marie Curie, seen here in a scene from 1895 relaxing with her husband-collaborator Pierre, pioneered the study of radiation.

Industrial power rose steadily and could be measured quantitatively. Between 1900 and 1913 alone, the production of steel by the world's six largest producing countries—the United States, Britain, Germany, France, Austria-Hungary, and Russia—rose from 26.4 million tons to 69.1 million tons. The energy consumption of these same six nations increased during the same 13 years from the equivalent of 638 million metric tons of coal to 1,089 million metric tons (Kennedy, pp. 200–1).

As science and technology produced one new marvel after another, the creation of large-scale facilities for research and development was both an effect and a cause. Germany and German-speaking regions of the Austrian Empire and Switzerland led the way in creating educational institutions appropriate to the needs of science and technology. In the early 1800s, they created polytechnic institutions at the high school level. Some were later upgraded as technical universities. By 1870, they began to link teaching and experimental research. Based on these models, German chemical firms created the in-house research and development laboratory in the 1870s. Bayer, Hoechst, and Badische Anilin und Soda Fabrik (BASF), the developers of synthetic indigo and other dyes, were the first. The electrical industries followed shortly afterwards. In America, Edison established his research laboratory at Menlo Park, New Jersey, in 1876. Many others followed: Standard Oil (1880), General Electric (1901), DuPont (1902), Parke-Davis (1902), Corning Glass (1908), Bell Labs (1911), Eastman Kodak (1913), and General Motors (1919).

Whereas discoveries and inventions in chemistry and biology had immediate commercial effects, in physics the major discoveries in the early years of the twentieth century were in theory and could be accomplished by individual thinkers, who were in touch with the society of scientists but worked mostly alone. The most revolutionary of the theoretical physicists was Albert Einstein (1879–1955), whose theory of special relativity was published in 1905, when he was twenty-six years old. Practical applications implicit in this theory came—explosively, in the form of the atomic bomb—decades later, but the philosophical significance (for those who could understand it) was immediate and revolutionary.

Einstein changed the way we look at the world. In an earlier paper, also published in 1905, he had helped to found the field of quantum physics by resolving the long-standing debate over the essential nature of light: was light essentially a wave-like flow, or did it take the form of small packets—quanta—of material? Einstein argued that light had both qualities. This explained, for example, the photoelectric effect, the escape of electrons from some solids when they are struck by ultraviolet light. Later in the same year, Einstein's special theory of relativity started from the postulate that the speed of light is constant and unchanging. If that is so, he argued, neither time nor motion is fixed. Both appear relative to the observer. For example, light from two stars may appear to arrive at the same time on earth, but the light has actually left each star at different times relative to earth because each star is a different distance from earth. In yet a third paper published later in the same year, Einstein set forth the principle that mass and energy are interchangeable, a relationship he expressed in the equation $E = mc^2$, energy equals matter times the speed of light squared. (The search for the atomic bomb was later undertaken on the basis of this formula, for the bomb represented the transformation of matter into enormous quantities of energy.) Throughout his life, Einstein sought a unified field theory that would explain the relationship among all the important force fields in nature. He never found this theory, but in 1916, he did publish his general theory of relativity which explored the nature of gravity and gave a new explanation for it. Physical masses do not attract other masses, rather they actually bend space toward themselves, so that objects roll toward them. Einstein thus overturned the basis of Newtonian physics, the intellectual structure on which physics had rested for two centuries, a structure with fixed space, time, matter, and light waves that appealed to "common sense." Instead, only the speed of light remained fixed. Space, time, motion, matter, energy—all were relative to one another. None was stable and predictable in itself. The time for a process to unfold and the weight and size of a material object depended on the speed and position of the observer. This indeterminacy in physics unsettled centuries of scientific thought and helped usher in a period of great indeterminacy in the affairs of the world in general.

GENDER RELATIONS

Changes in technology precipitated profound changes in gender relationships. The invention of new household appliances facilitated women's domestic work, though some historians have also argued that by making such work easier, they created a culture in which women did more of it. For example, instead of one annual "spring cleaning," women began to use their vacuum cleaners to clean the house more frequently. The invention of the telephone and the typewriter in the late nineteenth century led to the creation of the "female" occupations of telephone operator and secretary. Other women became department store clerks, selling to their customers the newest fashions produced with sewing machines. For many women, the invention of the bicycle was even more important than the car because it provided them with increased mobility, which also allowed them more flexibility in seeking work. Some women began to see themselves as professionals. Women's colleges were founded at the end of the nineteenth century, opening up still more possible careers, especially in health care, to them.

Out of the sight of parents, adolescents began exploring their sexuality. Before film censorship exploded in the 1920s, Hollywood films began to explore risqué themes and to feature the best of American technology as props. Many individuals believed that films sold a culture of sex that needed to be combated, hence the censorship of the Hays Code that emerged in the 1920s. Technology made birth control easier. Family size declined from 6.16 children in England and Wales in the 1860s to 2.82 children in 1910–14. But not everyone was pleased with the changes. Many people continued to believe that a woman's traditional role was to raise children. Margaret Sanger in the United States, Marie Stopes in Britain, and Theodore van de Velde in the Netherlands published manuals emphasizing the enjoyment of sex by both men and women in marriage and, at the same time, advocating family planning. Sanger was arrested for sending her magazines through the mail, then for opening the first "family planning" clinic in New York in 1916. Police booked her as a "public nuisance." Only in 1936 did courts in the United States decide that information on birth control was not pornographic and gave doctors the right to discuss it with their patients.

Scholars began to debate the nature of sexuality and the differences between men and women. The father of modern psychiatry, Sigmund Freud (1856–1939), believed that innate drives, especially sex, governed the behaviour of individuals. Another psychoanalyst, Karen Horney (1885–1952), who had initially studied with one of Freud's followers, began to question Freud's theories later in her life, coming to the conclusion that social and cultural factors were far more important than innate drives.

Anthropology added its insights as Margaret Mead brought back observations from New Guinea in the 1920s of aggressive women and passive men, reversing the conventional stereotypes of the West. Mead argued that sex traits were cultural and malleable, not biological and fixed. The debate continues today.

URBANIZATION AND MIGRATION

The world's growing population moved steadily into cities as the mechanization of agriculture drove people out of farming. Jobs in manufacture, bureaucracy, and service industries drew them to the cities. At the beginning of the century, urbanization was still linked to industrial growth, although many newcomers also found the cities exciting and full of attractions. Movie theaters screened sound entertainment. Department stores offered fashionable displays to entice buyers. City streets themselves provided spectacle, where men and women could see and be seen.

THE DOWNSIDE OF PROGRESS

In the early years of the twentieth century, technology and science offered seemingly endless improvements in health, wealth, invention, and the ability of humans to manufacture power and resolve problems. Progress continued in the ascendant as it had since the days of the *philosophes*. But many thoughtful people asked if this progress was only a veneer that covered more persistent problems. Even worse, perhaps the problems were multiplying even faster than "progress" was solving them.

Militarized Competition among the Great Powers

Not all scientific and industrial progress was directed toward peaceful uses. The chemical, metallurgical, and electrical marvels of the early twentieth century were devoted to military as well as to civilian goals, and the peaceful competition in invention and production was matched by military competition. The competition between Britain and Germany was especially sharp. From 1880 to 1913, Britain's share of world manufacturing output dropped from 22.9 percent to 13.6 percent, while Germany's rose from 8.5 percent to 14.8 percent. The greatest gains were actually made by the United States, which more than doubled its share, from 14.7 percent to 32 percent, but America was far away and was perceived by itself and by Europeans as relatively uninvolved. The British–German competition compelled attention. This was evident in the size of their armed forces. In 1914, on the eve of World War I, Germany's lead over Britain in terms of army and navy personnel stood at 891,000 against 532,000. In fact, both Russia, with 1,352,000, and France, with 910,000, had more men under arms. (The United States had only 164,000 in its armed forces.) In naval tonnage, however, Britain held the lead with 2,714,000 warship tons to Germany's 1,305,000 tons. The United States—bordered by two oceans—was third at 985,000 tons.

Most observers did not expect the competition to lead to war because the great powers were careful to build up systems of alliances that were expected to preserve the peace. The **balance of power** between the Triple Alliance of Germany, Austria-Hungary, and Italy and the Triple Entente of France, Russia, and Britain was expected to keep each side aware of the potential costs of war and the benefits of peace. People understood that a miscalculation could embroil all these nations and empires in catastrophic war, and the images of rationality and progress led them to discount such fears.

balance of power In international relations, a policy that aims to secure peace by preventing any one state or alignment of states from becoming too dominant.

In a very different kind of enterprise, the founder of modern psychiatry, Sigmund Freud, was developing at just this time his own concept of a balance of forces within each human being. Freud saw the primal force of the **libido** or **id** driving toward unrestrained aggression; the force of the super ego, representing the caution of parents and society, advocating almost saintly restraint; and the ego, the force for rational action, mediating between them. Freud argued that the balance was not always maintained, and when it failed individual breakdown resulted. An analogy to the military balance of forces among the European powers—and its potential for breakdown—was clear, at least to those who looked.

libido, id In Freudian psychology, the aggressive force in humans largely representing the drive for sex and power.

OUTSIDE EUROPE

Since the industrial revolution began, inventions in Europe had challenged, displaced, and even destroyed hand manufacture in the vast areas of the world that did not experience this revolution. As the pace of scientific invention and technological application increased, this displacement of traditional ways of production intensified, causing immense turmoil. In several cases, foreign colonial rule compounded the economic and technological disparities. Four examples—from India, China, Latin America, and the Ottoman Empire—reveal the process. Before the industrial revolution, India had the largest textile industry in the world, and China manufactured fine silks, porcelain, and iron. When the Spaniards first entered Mexico City, they were awed by its advanced urban structures. The Ottoman Empire preserved and exchanged with Europeans much of the knowledge of the ancient world during the late medieval and early modern periods. Yet for complex geopolitical and cultural reasons, these societies did not easily embrace the European industrial revolution, and soon the Europeans surpassed them in Science and Technology.

India

In the nineteenth century the hand spinners and weavers of India had been superseded and impoverished by the mechanized spindles and looms of Britain (see Chapter 18). Now, in the late nineteenth and early twentieth century, continuing invention in Europe destroyed still more of India's industries. In 1897, the Bayer Company of Germany succeeded in synthesizing indigo as a laboratory-produced dye. At that time, Indian farmers were producing about 9,000 tons of indigo per year. By 1913, India produced only 1,000 tons and was importing indigo from Germany. Later developments—in plastics, for example—would similarly displace hand-manufactured goods and the jobs that went with them. Technological progress in one region caused economic dislocation and suffering in other regions, a process that continues to this day.

In 1911, Britain asserted its supremacy over India through the majestic symbolism of the 1911 *darbar*—royal convocation—in Delhi, presided over by the King Emperor George V, who traveled to India to make the first-ever appearance of a British monarch in the colony, and attended by the princes and the elites of India in subordinate positions. The British proclaimed their power and enumerated their contributions to Indian progress, but in their pride and hubris the British willfully overlooked the disruptions that their rule was causing and the rising resentment against them on the part of the masses and of the elites who represented them.

The *darbar* was held in Delhi because Calcutta, the city that had served as the capital of British India for a century and a half, was seething with discontent against British rule. Indians were protesting not only Britain's economic and technological policies

The importance of prestige. European nations saw their empires—in Asia and elsewhere—as sources of both prestige and economic benefit. The benefit of prestige is well illustrated by A.E. Harris's illustration of the British King George V as he receives a group of maharajahs and other dignitaries, who are clothed in their finest garments for the honor, in 1910. (*Roy Miles Gallery, London*)

but also their political policies of control and their religious policies of "divide and rule," which were designed to turn Hindus and Muslims against each other. The combined outcry against all of these policies forced the government to transfer the capital itself. Indian leaders increasingly called for self-rule. Bal Gangadhar Tilak (1856–1920) summed up their growing demand: "Freedom is my birthright and I shall have it." Their struggle was yet in its early stages. It would take another decade, and new leadership, to consolidate the anti-colonial political alliance between leaders and masses.

China

We have already seen the struggles that occurred in China in the last years of the nineteenth century over the proper policies for confronting Western domination. For the most part, the traditionalists gathered around the dowager empress Cixi defeated the reformers at the imperial court. China chose the "self-strengthening" of its industrial capacities and a restructuring of the official civil service examinations to put greater emphasis on science and technology, but the attempted reforms were too little and too late. In 1911, out of a population of 400 million, China had only one million industrial workers. Most industry was on a small scale, much of it in textiles. Faith in the viability of the Confucian traditions and in the government that was to implement them was dying out. After seventy years of military defeat, colonial subordination, peasant revolt, and intellectual contentiousness, China was ripe for revolution. The Mandate of Heaven was passing from the Manchu dynasty.

Revolution began in China in October 1911 with a bomb explosion in the Wuhan area that triggered a series of army mutinies and civilian revolts. Within a month, the Manchu government promulgated a civil constitution and convened a provisional national assembly. Yuan Shihkai (1859–1916), the most powerful military official in China, was elected premier. In January 1912, the boy emperor Puyi (r. 1908–12) abdicated, ending 2,000 years of China's imperial tradition, and Yuan received full powers to organize a provisional republican government. But he exceeded his mandate. In January 1916, Yuan took the title of emperor, provoking widespread revolt. Under severe military attack and critically ill, Yuan died in June. With no effective governing center, China entered a decade of rule by warlords, regional strongmen who had their own independent militias.

Some of the warlords controlled whole provinces, others only a few towns or segments of railway line; some had formal military training, others were simply local strongmen; some sought to play a role in forming a powerful national government, others to continue China's division. Many were rapacious. In many parts of China, old, painful proverbs took on new reality: "In an age of chaos, don't miss the chance to loot during the fire" and "In the official's house, wine and meat are allowed to rot, but on the roads are the bones of those who starved to death".

The leading revolutionaries looked to Sun Yat-sen (1866–1925) as their mentor. Although raised in a peasant household, Sun received his secondary education in a missionary school in Hawaii and his medical training in Hong Kong. He spent most of his adult life in China's port cities or abroad.

In 1895, Sun attempted a coup in Guangzhou. It failed and he was exiled. He was in the United States organizing for revolution when the 1911 uprising began. He returned to help found the Guomindang (GMD), the leading revolutionary party. He was elected first president of the United Provinces of China, but then a jealous and fearful Yuan exiled him in 1913. He returned to Guangzhou in the early 1920s and led his movement from that port city, but he never regained power.

Sun's "Three People's Principles" included a heavy admixture of Western thought. The first, nationalism, called for revolution against foreign political control, beginning with the ousting of the Manchus from China, and against foreign economic control, which had rendered China:

Founder of the GMD. Sun Yat-sen (Yixian), photographed here in Western dress according to his custom, is considered the "father of the nation" even though he spent much of his life abroad and never achieved his own political ambitions. He was a revolutionary and helped to found the Guomindang. Although unable to stay in power himself, he influenced China's most important figures of the next generation: Chiang Kai-shek and Mao Zedong.

> the colony of every nation with which it has concluded treaties; each of them is China's master. China is not just the colony of one country, but the colony of many countries. We are not just the slaves of one country, but the slaves of many countries ... Today we are the poorest and weakest nation in the world, and occupy the lowest position in international affairs ... other men are the carving knife and serving dish; we are the fish and the meat ... we must espouse nationalism and bring this national spirit to the salvation of the country.

His second principle, democracy, emphasized a predominantly Western political model: "Since we have had only ideas about popular rights, and no democratic system has evolved, we have to go to Europe and America for a republican form of government" (Andrea and Overfield, p. 350). He did, however, claim the separation of powers as an ancient Chinese tradition.

The third principle, under the heading "People's Livelihood," revealed Sun's ambivalence toward Western technology and organization. He proclaimed the need for new technology:

> First we must build means of communication, railroads and waterways, on a large scale. Second we must open up mines. Third we must hasten to develop manufacturing. Although China has a multitude of workers, she has no machinery and so cannot compete with other countries. Goods used throughout China have to be manufactured and imported from other countries, with the result that our rights and interests are simply leaking away.

But Western-style industrialization was not his chosen model:

> With the invention of modern machines, the phenomenon of uneven distribution of wealth in the West has become all the more marked ... On my tour of Europe and America, I saw with my own eyes the instability of their economic structure and the deep concern of their leaders in groping for a solution. (Andrea and Overfield, p. 351)

Fearing "the expansion of private capital and the emergence of a great wealthy class with the consequent inequalities" in China, Sun called for a different path: state ownership and "state power to build up these enterprises." But he thought Marxism irrelevant for China: "In China, where industry is not yet developed, Marx's class war and dictatorship of the proletariat are impracticable". China's economic problem was not unequal distribution but lack of production.

Chinese of all political parties revered Sun, but they could not implement his plans. Sun, however, inspired the two leaders—Chiang Kai-shek and Mao Zedong—who contested for dominance in China for a quarter century following his death in 1925. We shall read about their struggles in Chapter 22.

Latin America

Through the late nineteenth and early twentieth centuries, Latin America began to industrialize, largely with investments from overseas. At first, Britain was the principal investor, but after World War I the United States assumed that role. For the most part, economic and technological innovations were initiated by foreigners in search of profits. Most of the investments were concentrated in primary production—that is, farming and mining—rather than in industrial manufacturing. At the time of World War I (1914–18), for example, the United States was buying about one-third of Brazil's exports, mostly coffee, rubber, and cocoa. (Half of Brazil's exports consisted of coffee.) Members of the creole elites, who saw that they too could share in the new earnings and win some acceptability among Europeans, joined in the new commerce. But for the most part the initiatives came from outside.

Most of the creole elites were content to treat their nations as private estates. Control and patronage mattered—money and profits were means to an end, not ends in themselves. In an essay, *Ariel*, written in 1898, the Uruguayan philosopher José Enrique Rodó (1872–1917) analyzed Latin America's move in the direction of an industrial democracy on the United States model and rejected it. He saw that path as barbaric and inconsistent with the more leisurely, elitist, cultured world of the creole rulers of Latin America. In the absence of democratic systems, most governments in Latin America were still in the hands of *caudillos*, strongmen who governed on their own authority.

Not everyone was content with a system of control by *haciendado* and *caudillo* elites. Businessmen who were participating in the new commerce and industry began to think of new goals: more education, more industrialization, more independence from foreign investors, and more consistent government, with a larger, formal voice in politics for themselves. Toward the end of the nineteenth century, a huge influx of immigrants from Europe, especially Italy, brought with it ideas of industrial development and union representation, and by the early twentieth century, important labor unions were in place in the larger nations of Latin America. Another group advocating reform and national pride was the army, especially its junior officers. Often drawn from middle-class urban families and aware of modern technology through their knowledge of weaponry, army officers were more used to the importance of education, industrialization, business, and stable government.

In some countries these groups worked together and achieved their goals, but even the most progressive states, like Argentina and Uruguay, failed to undertake what might have been the most influential reform of all. They did not restructure the land-holding patterns that left wealthy landlords in charge of impoverished peasants. The reformers were urban people, and they were frequently related to the landlords; they had little practical sympathy for the agricultural laborers and no intention of sharing power or profits with them.

The Mexican Revolution, 1910–20 In 1910, in Mexico, urban and rural leaders rose up against the dictatorship of Porfirio Díaz (1830–1915), who had been ruling the country since 1876. At the age of eighty, Díaz seemed poised to retire from the presidency. Under his leadership Mexico had seen the development of mining, oil drilling, and railways, in addition to increasing exports of raw agricultural products, especially henequen fibers used in making rope. The middle-class urban creole elite had prospered, but the salaries of the urban workers had declined, and rural peasants had fared even worse. Ninety-five percent of the rural peasantry owned no land, while fewer than 200 Mexican families owned 25 percent of all of the land of Mexico, and foreign investors owned another 20–25 percent. One single hacienda spread over 13 million acres and another over 11 million acres. Huge tracts of land lay fallow and unused while peasants went hungry. Finally, on a political level, no system of orderly succession had been worked out for Mexico. The reins of power rested in the hands of Díaz and his allies alone.

Democratic voting existed for a limited electorate, but when Díaz changed his mind and ran again for president, he imprisoned his principal challenger, Francisco Madero (1873–1913). Díaz won, but rebellions against his continuing rule broke out across Mexico, and he soon resigned and went into exile in Paris. Regional leaders then asserted their influence as Mexico erupted into civil war. The warfare was both personal and factional. It concerned differences in policy among the factions and the appropriate division of power between the central government and the states.

Many of the leaders who contested for power were mestizos, people of mixed race and culture (see Chapter 15), who demanded a dramatic break with the past control by the creole elite. The two most radical, Francisco "Pancho" Villa (1878–1923) from the northern border region and Emiliano Zapata (1879–1919) from the state of Morelos, just south of Mexico City, advocated significant land reform, and implemented it in the areas they captured during the civil war. They attracted mixed groups of followers, including farm workers, agricultural colonists, former soldiers, unemployed laborers, cowboys, and delinquents. In November 1911, Zapata declared the revolutionary Plan of Ayala, which called for the return of land to Indian pueblos (villages). Tens of thousands of impoverished peasants followed him, heeding his cry of "Tierra y Libertad" ("Land and Liberty") and accepting his view that it was "Better to die on one's feet than to live on one's knees." Zapata's supporters seized large sugar estates, haciendas with which they had been in conflict for years. By including previously scorned groups and attending to their agendas, the revolution became more radical and agrarian.

Mexican revolutionaries. General Francisco "Pancho" Villa and Emiliano Zapata (*right*), sporting his flamboyant moustache, sit together with their Mexican revolutionary army, men who had come from many different occupations and walks of life to join the ranks. The radical leaders hailed from different parts of the country, Zapata from south of Mexico City and Villa from the northern border, but they shared common goals.

**Diego Rivera, *The Conquest of Mexico*
(detail), 1929–30.** Rivera transformed the
tradition of painting in Mexico by
creating huge murals that tell the history
of Mexico in often brutal scenes.

With Díaz in exile, Madero became president, but he was
removed by a coup and then assassinated in 1913. General Vícto-
riano Huerta (1854–1916) attempted to take over and to reestablish
a repressive government like that of Díaz. Opposed by all the
other major leaders, and also by President Woodrow Wilson of the
United States, who sent American troops into Veracruz to express
his displeasure with Huerta, the general was forced from power in
March 1914. Alvaro Obregón (1880–1928), another general, who
made free use of the machine gun, won out militarily, but he
agreed to serve under Venustiano Carranza (1859–1920), who had
himself installed as provisional president.

The civil war continued, and control of Mexico City changed
hands several times, but ultimately the more conservative leaders,
Carranza and Obregón, forced out Villa and Zapata. Carranza
became president in 1916 and convened a constituent assembly
that produced the Mexican Constitution of 1917, promising land
reform and imposing restrictions on foreign economic control. It
protected Mexican workers by passing a labor code including
minimum salaries and maximum hours, accident insurance, pensions, social benefits, and the right to unionize and strike. It placed
severe restrictions on the church and clergy, denying them the
rights to own property and to provide primary education. (Most
of the revolutionaries were anti-clerical. Zapata was an exception
in this, as the peasantry who followed him were extremely
devoted to the church.) The constitution also decreed that no foreigner could be a minister or priest, vote, hold office, or criticize
the government.

Enacting the new laws was easier than implementing them, but
having the new constitution in place set a standard of accountability for government and served as a beacon for the continuing
revolution. On the material level, not much changed at first. In 1920, Obregón deposed
Carranza and became president. He distributed
3 million acres of land to peasants, 10 percent of
whom benefited. This redistribution helped to
establish the principles of the revolution,
demonstrating good faith on the part of the state
and putting new land into production, although
the state did not provide the technical assistance
needed to improve productivity. Politically,
Obregón began to include new constituencies in
his government, including the labor movement,
represented by a Labor Party, and the peasants,
represented by a National Agrarian Party. The
institutionalization of their presence in government promised new stability through wider

Diego Rivera, *Man at the Crossroads* (detail), 1934.
Rivera's fame spread and he was invited to create a mural
for the Rockefeller Center in New York. When John D.
Rockefeller saw Rivera's tribute to Karl Marx and
communism, he had the mural destroyed. Rivera recreated
it at the Palace of Fine Arts in Mexico City.

representation. The representation, everyone recognized, was not only by social class but also by ethnicity and culture. Mestizos and even indigenous Indians achieved a place in government. Mexico's struggle against the threefold problems of racial discrimination against Indians, economic discrimination against the poor, and the denial of both problems behind a façade of political rhetoric was an inspiration throughout Latin America. It had come at a high price: one million killed out of a total population of about 15 million.

The Ottoman Empire

Unlike Mexico, which was generally dependent on European powers for its economic investment capital and initiatives, the Ottoman Empire retained its economic autonomy, although French capital was used to construct its major technological achievement, the Suez Canal. Unlike India, the empire did not lose its sovereignty, but like China, it lost many of the attributes of self-rule, while remaining formally independent. The Ottoman Empire fell behind the industrial and political developments in western Europe and America, and it slowly disintegrated. The process by which the Ottoman Empire became "the Sick Man of Europe" took more than a century. We have already reviewed the first stages.

In 1798, Napoleon successfully invaded Ottoman Egypt. He was expelled not by the Ottomans but by his European enemy, the British. Then the Albanian general dispatched by the Ottomans in 1805 to control Egypt, Muhammad Ali, established Egypt's virtual independence of the Ottomans. In 1830, after an eight-year civil war, in which it gained the military support of Britain, France, and, especially, Russia, Greece won its independence from the Ottomans. One year earlier, as a result of the same struggles, three Balkan states—Serbia, Wallachia, and Moldavia—had also gained their autonomy from the Ottomans. Despite the *Tanzimat* (reorganization) reforms of its administration and army, leading to a parliamentary constitution in 1876, Turkey was defeated by Russia in war the next year, and the year after that, Serbia, Montenegro, and Romania became independent. In 1881, European bankers declared that the Ottoman Empire was not properly managing its finances and was defaulting on its debts. The Europeans demanded and got official representation in the offices of the Ottoman treasury. European powers also claimed rights to intervene in internal Ottoman affairs in order to defend the rights of Christian communities living in the Islamic Ottoman Empire. They stationed representatives of various Christian denominations in Constantinople to assert and represent those rights. Nevertheless, fearing continuing revolt from the restless community of Armenian Christians in Anatolia, the Ottoman government supported a series of attacks on them, killing about 200,000 in 1895.

In 1908, a group of progressive army officers and liberal professionals—collectively called "Young Turks"—seized control of the government under the sultan. During these years, however, the dismemberment of the empire continued. Almost all of its remaining European and North African holdings were stripped away. Bulgaria declared its independence (1908) and Bosnia was annexed by Austria-Hungary (1908). Italy seized the North African territories of Libya and the offshore Dodecanese Islands. Bulgaria, Serbia, and Greece aided Albania in gaining its independence in 1912.

A second Balkan war in the next year concerned the appropriate size of Bulgaria and control over Albania. Serbians, Greeks, Austrians, and even Italians were involved. The decision, favored by Austria, to make Albania an independent kingdom infuriated the Serbians, who wanted to control the region for its access to the sea, and agitated the Russians, who had backed the Serbians as brother Slavs. The economic and military competition among the great powers was embedded in these still larger

The end of the Ottoman Empire. The last decades of the nineteenth century saw the Ottoman presence in Europe decline as Austria–Hungary, Russia, and several aspiring new nations challenged its power. Arab revolt and internal dissent, combined with the Turkish defeat in World War I, brought to an end 600 years of Ottoman domination. Turkey was the core residual state, while several other regions were mandated to British and French control.

issues of nationalism, a very powerful force in early twentieth-century Europe (see Chapter 18).

People's reverence for their nation-states, and for their shared language, history, ethnicity, and aspirations within those states, had grown so passionate that they were willing to fight and die for them. Cynics argued that the masses of the population were being manipulated into battle by industrialists in each country who stood to profit from war production, but the national feelings were powerful in themselves. Nationalism evoked just as much emotional commitment among the citizens of smaller, newer states with little economic base in military production—like the states in the Balkans—as it did among the great empires.

By 1914, the dismemberment of the Ottoman Empire, the power struggle in the Balkans created by this collapse, and the constant warfare over control of this area created one of the most dangerous regions of the world. Having fallen behind the industrial and military advances of its European rivals, the Ottoman Empire could no longer keep the peace in its region. Without effective Ottoman rule, the multitude of rival ethnic and religious groups encouraged strife and invited the intervention of the major powers of Europe. These powers were already deeply involved in competition for arms, markets, and prestige, and they were committed to mutually antagonistic military alliances, which, for decades, had preserved the peace through a balance of power.

On the one hand, peace and progress appeared to be the hallmarks of the era. On the other hand, international relations were tense and in a state of flux. Peripheral areas had become central. Historically great powers had become colonies and pawns in the hands of relative newcomers. Ethnic tensions and nationalisms of various sorts seemed to appear everywhere, especially in the Balkans. From one point of view, the status of world politics and economics appeared rosy and optimistic; from another, it was tense and potentially explosive.

WORLD WAR I, 1914–18

On June 28, 1914, a Serbian nationalist assassinated Archduke Franz Ferdinand, heir to the Austro-Hungarian throne, and his wife. The assassin was outraged because the Austro-Hungarian Empire had seized Balkan territories with heavily Serbian populations. His bullets were the matches that lit the spark of World War I (called the Great War until World War II surpassed it in magnitude). One month after the murder, at the end of July, Austria-Hungary declared war on Serbia, triggering a domino effect. Under the system of alliances that had been built up over the preceding three decades, countries now came to the aid of one another. Russia mobilized its armies to defend Serbia and to take up positions on the borders of Germany. Fearing attack, Germany declared war on Russia and its ally, France. Intending to strike France quickly and decisively, Germany took the most direct route, invading and crossing Belgium, thus violating an international treaty guaranteeing Belgian neutrality. Britain declared war on Germany on August 4, as did Britain's geographically remote ally, Japan. The alliance system, which had been expected to prevent war among the highly competitive and nationalistic states of Europe, had instead drawn all the major powers into what had begun as a regional conflict in the Balkans. The lack of any organized system for preserving international order was clearly exposed. Within one week, all the major powers of Europe were at war. In November, the Ottoman Empire joined Germany and the Austro-Hungarian Empire in an alliance called the Central Powers. On the other side the British, French, and Russians, joined by the Italians in 1915, formed an alliance called the Allied Powers (the Allies).

Europe had not faced continent-wide warfare since the end of the Napoleonic wars a century earlier. Despite all their armaments, neither side was prepared militarily or psychologically for the years of devastating trench warfare of the Western Front. Germany, attacking France through Belgium, expected a quick victory, but the French response was powerful, and meanwhile the Russians opened an Eastern Front with unexpected speed, forcing the Germans to divide their troop strengths. Military leaders seemed to lack an understanding of how new technology had changed the face of war. The Battle of the Marne River, in northeastern France, fought to a draw between September 5 and 12, set the pattern for the next four years. Each side continuously extended its battle lines outward until the enemies faced each other over a 400-mile front that extended from the North Sea to Switzerland. Each side hunkered down in trenches for a kind of siege warfare, armed with machine guns and artillery, and protected by barbed wire. Attacks by either side, going "over the top" of the trenches,

World War I. European rivalries for political and economic superiority, within Europe and throughout its imperial holdings, erupted in 1914. A fragile system of alliances designed to contain the ambitions of Germany and Austria-Hungary (the Central Powers) collapsed, resulting in a conflict of horrific proportions. Turkey joined the Central Powers. In France and Belgium a stalemate war of attrition developed. In the east a war of thrust and counter-thrust caused enormous popular dissent and exhaustion, eventually bringing the collapse of the Turkish, Russian, and Austrian empires alike. In all, 20 million people died.

were met by withering machine-gun fire. In addition, Germany later introduced poison gas, leading to subsequent international bans against its use (although many nations still continue to store poison gas in their armories). In the first month alone, each side suffered more than a quarter-million casualties and used up ammunition that they thought would last for any future war. Erich Maria Remarque captured the horrors of this trench warfare in his 1929 novel *All Quiet on the Western Front.* Soldiers lived in mud and knew that it could be deadly to leave their trenches. Disease killed many. Altogether millions were killed and millions more were wounded, often with horrendous injuries. An entirely new industry developed to replace absent faces and lost limbs. Generals grasped any new weapon they thought might change the course of war, but the results of experiments generally involved more loss of life.

Major campaigns to overwhelm the opponent by sheer numbers in direct infantry charges resulted in catastrophic losses. In February 1916, the Germans attacked at Verdun, near the confluence of the borders of France, Belgium, and Germany. The battle ground on for six months, with casualties of about 350,000 on each side, before the Germans gave up their attack. In July 1916, the French opened their own attack at

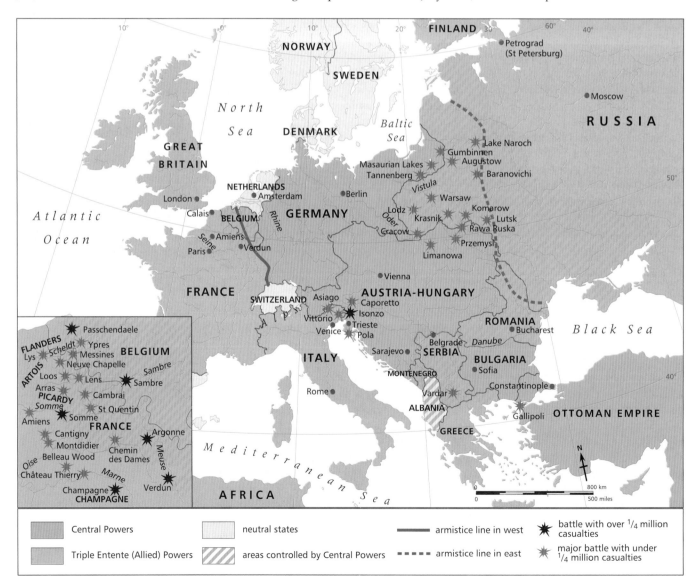

the Somme River, some 50 miles to the north. By this time the British had joined the French in force, bringing in heavy artillery and even some of their new tanks, which could penetrate the barbed wire and the trenches to knock out enemy machine guns. There were, however, few tanks, and the main strategy of the generals on both sides was simply to throw waves of attacking men at one another, directly into the machine-gun fire of the enemy. The costs in lives were almost unbelievable. In four months, the Germans lost a half-million men, the British 400,000, and the French 200,000. On the Western Front the war was essentially a stalemate from this time until the end.

In the east, the Germans defeated the Russians repeatedly, yet the ill-equipped, ill-fed, ill-commanded Russians continued to fight. In 1914, in the first months of the war, 225,000 Russian troops were captured by the Germans at the Battles of Tannenberg and the Masurian Lakes. In 1915, the Germans and Austro-Hungarians launched major offensives against Russia, killing, wounding, or taking captive 2 million Russians, many of whom fought with their bare hands. To send relief to Russia through the Black Sea, the British and French landed some 450,000 troops on the Gallipoli peninsula, at the entrance to the Dardanelles and the Black Sea. In the course of almost a year of fighting, 145,000 of these men were killed or wounded, and the operation was terminated.

In June 1916, Russia launched its own counteroffensive, but by 1917 the war had alienated the Russian people almost entirely. In March 1917, troops in St. Petersburg mutinied. The Russian **Duma** (Parliament) pushed for reforms and the tsar abdicated. The new provisional Russian government attempted to continue the war, but the armies collapsed. In November a Bolshevik communist revolutionary government, headed by V.I. Lenin—whom the Germans had helped to return to Russia—captured power and sued for peace, withdrawing Russia from the war. (The Russian Revolution, one of the most significant events connected with the war, is discussed below.)

Life in the trenches. World War I became notorious for its trench warfare, in which combatants dug themselves into positions but made few territorial gains. The horrifying drudgery, the cold, the wet, the shelling, the machine gun fire, the nervous tension, the smell of corpses and mustard gas lasted for years. By 1918, the end of the conflict, around 8.5 million soldiers had lost their lives.

The British opened another front against the Ottoman Empire by siding with the Arabs of Arabia and Palestine in their struggles against Ottoman imperial rule. British Colonel T.E. Lawrence, "Lawrence of Arabia," took charge of this insurrection and, with his support, the emir Husayn of Hejaz (the west coast of Arabia, including Mecca) declared himself king of the Arabs. Thanks to this pressure of Arabs against Turks, General Edmund Allenby was able to push through Turkish lines and capture Jerusalem, Baghdad, and, finally, Damascus, in October 1918, in a series of battles remembered for their tactical brilliance and for their use of armed cavalry and air support. Faced with this combination of Arab revolt and British military victories, the Ottomans sued for peace in October 1918.

Farther away, in the colonies, British and French forces seized the German colonies in Africa—in Togo, Cameroon, South West Africa, and Tanganyika (now Tanzania)—vowing that the Germans should never come back. Similarly, in East Asia and the Pacific, Japan, an ally of Britain, declared war on Germany in 1914 and quickly took over the German concessions in China and the German-held Marshall and Caroline Islands. In 1915 it presented China with a list of "Twenty-One Demands" to which the

Duma The Russian parliament established by Nicholas II in response to the Revolution of 1905. Its powers were largely restricted to the judicial and administrative areas; the tsar retained control over the franchise.

Chinese had to accede, against their wishes. China felt it was being turned into a colony of Japan.

In the Atlantic, both Britain and Germany disregarded the accepted law of the sea permitting the shipment of cargo not related to military equipment and supplies. The British, whose navy was by far the most powerful, regularly stopped all ships bound for Germany and other enemy states, and confiscated their cargo. The Germans, with a smaller navy, were less able to carry out such a policy. Instead, they directly attacked shipping headed for England and France, torpedoing and sinking ships, especially in the waters surrounding the British Isles. The biggest of these ships, the *Lusitania*, was torpedoed off the Irish coast in May 1915, and 1,200 passengers, including 118 Americans, drowned as the ship sank. America had been slow to enter the war, both because it preferred the peace of neutrality and because it saw no overriding virtue in one side over the other in this war of contending imperial powers. The sinking of the *Lusitania* inclined the Americans to the side of the Allies—reaffirming also a basic preference for more democratic Britain and France over more autocratic Germany and Austria-Hungary—but America joined in the conflict only after another two years and additional provocations.

In January 1917, Arthur Zimmerman, Germany's foreign minister, sent a secret telegram instructing the German ambassador in Mexico City to offer the president of Mexico "an understanding on our part that Mexico is to reconquer her lost territory in Texas, New Mexico, and Arizona," if Mexico joined in an alliance with Germany against the United States. The telegram was intercepted, translated, and published in the United States, astonishing and inflaming public opinion against Germany. At about the same time, at the end of January 1917, Germany announced to the Americans that they would begin unrestricted submarine warfare, sinking on sight all merchant ships around the British Isles or in the Mediterranean.

The United States, which had remained neutral, declared war against Germany and the Central Powers in April 1917. This decision sealed the fate of the combatants, all of whom were thoroughly exhausted by four years of relentless, enervating, disastrous warfare. The American contribution was smaller, and much briefer—only about four months of actual combat—than that of the major European countries, but it came at a decisive time when the Europeans were exhausted. By the end of the war, a year and

HOW DO WE KNOW?

War Experiences Subvert Colonialism

Colonial powers employed their colonial armies in fighting both world wars, transporting them from one battle front to another. Military service overseas often transformed the soldiers, making them skeptical of the advantages of European civilization. Some European soldiers came to realize that at least some of the people they colonized did not respect them but rather feared and hated them. A young journalist from India, Indulal Yagnik, serving briefly as a World War I correspondent in Iraq, wrote of his growing realization of the resentment

Arabs felt for British colonization. He saw Arab women in particular transmitting their resentment by asserting their religious and cultural conventions. He began to understand more fully the opposition to colonialism shared by Indians and Arabs:

> We understood ... that in the entire region Arabs regarded the English as their enemies. Bitter antagonism dripped from their eyes. They moved about like lost undertakers, joking among themselves but stopping the moment they saw the British. They talked with the foreigners mechanically, speaking only when it was completely unavoidable. They took their few cents in pay, and otherwise behaved like defeated and dependent enemies. Their dignified women

hid themselves in burkhas, which covered them from head to foot. The white soldiers must have sensed their independent temper, however, and therefore their military superiors issued strict orders not to talk with the local women. (Yagnik, p. 262, translated from the Gujarati by Devavrat Pathak and Howard Spodek.)

- How did Yagnik's experiences in Arabia strengthen his anti-colonial viewpoint?
- How important was Arab women's behavior in convincing Yagnik and the British that the Arabs were anti-colonial?
- Does the evidence suggest that Arab women were more anti-colonial than the men?

a half later, the United States had 4 million soldiers and sailors under arms—two million of them in France and another million on the way—had lent $10 billion in military and civilian assistance, and had set its farms and factories to producing record amounts of food and supplies. Shipping capacity multiplied from one million tons before the war to 10 million by the end. Consumer production facilities in the United States were restructured to provide military equipment and supplies. Sugar and other consumer commodities were rationed. Eight thousand tons of steel were saved in the manufacture of women's corsets.

Once the United States began providing its abundant supplies and fresh troops, the Allied victory was secure. In the spring and summer of 1918, the German high command made a last attempt at an offensive, but they could not withstand the Allied counterattack. Germany sought an armistice. It took effect at 11 a.m. on November 11—11/11/11. As Austria-Hungary, Turkey, and Bulgaria had already withdrawn from battle, the war was over.

The cost in life defied imagining. Some 70 million armed forces were mobilized. Most, of course, were European, but there were also 1.4 million from India who served in the Middle East, East Africa, and France; 1.3 million from the "white" dominions; and 134,000 from other British colonies. The French recruited 600,000 men from their colonies as soldiers and another 200,000 to work in factories in France. Almost 10 million soldiers had been killed and 20 million wounded. England lost one million; France one and one-half, Germany almost two million, Russia one and three-quarters, the Austro-Hungarian Empire somewhat more than one million, Italy half a million, the Ottoman Empire 325,000, and the United States 115,000.

Post-war Expectations and Results

After the bloodshed, destruction, and chaos of the war, it was clear that the world was in for major changes. Defeat in the war forced the end of three historic empires: the Ottoman, the Austro-Hungarian, and the Russian. The British Empire survived, but it had made wartime promises to India of increasing self-government that might limit Britain's imperial power. Internal revolution had brought the 2,000-year-old Chinese Empire to an end shortly before the war began, and Japanese wartime conquests in China suggested that Chinese sovereignty might also be in danger.

In addition, promises had been made during wartime that raised aspirations around the globe. Perhaps the most utopian and most celebrated of all these promises issued from Woodrow Wilson. The American president had declared that the goal of the Allies was to "make the world safe for democracy." Allied war aims, as expressed by Wilson in his Fourteen Points, called for:

> A free, open-minded, and absolutely impartial adjustment of all colonial claims, based upon a strict observance of the principle that in determining all such questions of sovereignty the interests of the population concerned must have equal weight with the equitable claims of the Government whose title is to be determined. (cited in Hofstadter, pp. 224–5)

As leader of the country that had swayed the balance of victory, and as an intellectual in politics, Wilson commanded attention. Minority groups within many different nations, and colonized peoples responded to his apparent message that all peoples should have a voice in their own governments. In addition, millions of people in the colonies had contributed to the war effort of their colonizers. They expected—and sometimes they were explicitly promised—political rewards after the war.

The Arab regions of the Ottoman Empire, for example, understood Wilson's agenda to include independent states for them. They had fought alongside the British against

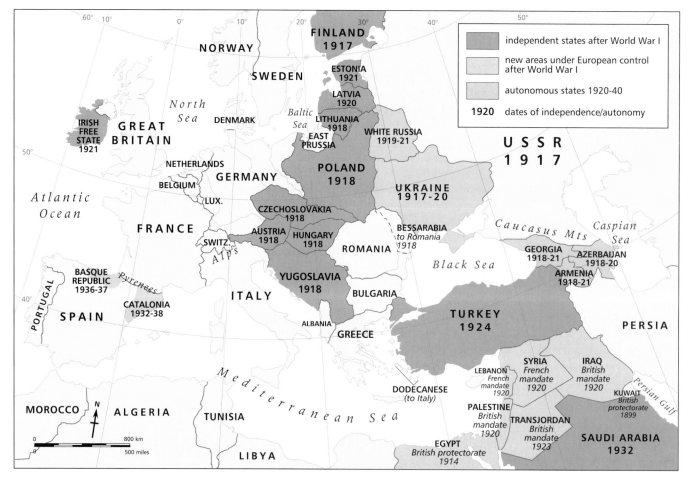

The new post-war nations. In the wake of World War I, old empires fell and new states and colonies (euphemistically called mandates and protectorates) were created. The Austro-Hungarian and Ottoman Empires were eradicated. A belt of nation-states was established throughout Central and Eastern Europe; some had brief lives and were soon annexed by Russia. The core of the Ottoman Empire became Turkey, while other segments were mandated to Britain and France as quasi-colonies.

the Ottoman Empire, and they expected that this wartime contribution would be rewarded. Moreover, in 1915, the British high commissioner (ambassador) in Egypt had privately told Mecca's leading official, Sharif Husayn, that Arabs would receive some kind of independence if they fought against the Ottoman Turks. In addition, and just before the Armistice was signed in 1918, Britain and France declared as their goal: "the complete and definitive liberation of the peoples so long oppressed by the Turks and the establishment of national governments and administrations drawing their authority from the initiative and free choice of indigenous populations."

Jews also looked forward to important changes. Had not the British government promised them "the establishment in Palestine of a national home for the Jewish people" if the Ottoman Empire was conquered? This declaration, issued by Britain's foreign secretary, Lord Balfour, in 1917, may have been issued primarily to enlist Jewish support for Britain against the Ottoman Empire, which held Palestine at the time. It captured the imagination of Jews around the world, especially those who had already emigrated from eastern Europe to settle in Palestine and those left behind in conditions of discrimination and persecution. The Arabs, however, noted that the same Balfour Declaration promised that "nothing shall be done which may prejudice the civil and religious rights of existing non-Jewish communities in Palestine." They believed these two promises to be incompatible.

India, which had contributed not only 1.4 million men, but had also paid £100 million in 1917 and some £20–30 million each year towards Britain's wartime debts, had also received a promise in 1917. The secretary of state for India, Edwin Montagu, declared

Britain's goal to be "the increasing association of Indians in every branch of government, and the gradual development of self-governing institutions, with a view to the progressive realization of responsible government in India as an integral part of the Empire."

Many linguistic and ethnic minorities scattered among the nations of eastern and central Europe, in particular Czechs, Slavs, Estonians, Latvians, and Lithuanians, also looked forward to gaining independent states of their own. The Chinese looked forward to the return of some colonial territories to them, at least those of Germany, which had been seized during the war by the Japanese. Africans in Africa, almost entirely under colonial rule, and in the diaspora, often suffering from crippling discrimination, also took heart. Wilson's pledges appealed, for example, to the brilliant African-American scholar and activist, W.E.B. DuBois, and the Pan-African movement that he headed. DuBois and his movement demanded equality for all people, an end to a kind of internal colonization of blacks in the United States and the colonization of Africa by European powers.

Before the war, only a few nations and regions had granted women the right to vote: Norway, New Zealand, and some of the states in Australia and in the western United States. The suffrage movements elsewhere had not won their objectives. With the end of the war, however, populations and their legislatures, grateful for the contributions of women to the war effort—in the armed services, in factories, and at home—reconsidered. In 1918, Britain granted the vote to women over the age of thirty and, in 1928 extended the right to women over the age of twenty-one. Germany granted women's suffrage in 1918, and the United States in 1920.

The Paris Peace Settlements, 1919

The peace conference convened in Paris in 1919 amid optimistic hopes and high expectations. Thirty-two states were invited, but not the defeated powers nor Russia. Many of their agendas, however, were in conflict with one another. In the redrawing of postwar national borders and the settling of financial accounts, each major power sought its own benefit. Japan, for example, sought to maintain control over the East Asian possessions of Germany that it had captured during the war. Since some of these colonial possessions were in China, the Chinese naturally protested. Prince Faisal represented the Arabs who had contributed to victory over the Ottoman Empire and now sought the creation of new, independent states. Representatives of colonies and of subnational ethnic groups, encouraged by Wilson's doctrine of self-determination of nationalities, sought recognition and some measure of independence and sovereignty. W.E.B. DuBois called for racial justice on behalf of the Pan-African Congress, a group of fifty-eight delegates from Africa and the African diaspora who convened in Paris at the time of the conference. In the end, despite all of the participants who attended—whether officially or unofficially—the American, British, and French delegations were most critical to the negotiations.

Political borders across Europe and the Middle East were redrawn, punishing the states that had lost the war or, in the case of Russia, had withdrawn from it. The Austro-Hungarian and Ottoman Empires were dissolved. Austria-Hungary was reduced and divided into two separate states. Czechoslovakia and Yugoslavia were created from its former territories. The Ottoman Empire disappeared; its core region in Anatolia and the city of Istanbul became the new nation of Turkey. Romania and Greece were expanded from the remainder of the empire's European territories. From its Middle Eastern regions, four new nations were created and then mandated for tutelage to European powers until they would be considered ready for independence. Although the term "mandate" was used, most observers understood these nations to be colonies under a new name. Syria and Lebanon were mandated to France, Palestine

The signing of the Treaty of Versailles, 1919. The French Premier Georges Clemenceau speaks at the signing of the Treaty of Versailles. Woodrow Wilson, the American president, is seated to his right.

and Iraq to Britain. During the war, the Russian Empire had also collapsed and withdrawn from the fighting. A communist government, which seemed threatening to the Allies, had replaced its ruling Romanov dynasty. From territories of the former empire, the new states of Poland, Finland, Estonia, Latvia, and Lithuania were created.

All three of these great empires had held vastly diverse ethnic, religious, and cultural minorities within their borders. The Paris negotiators intended that the new states and new borders that they carved out would give some of the larger minorities their own states and protect hostile ethnic groups from each other and from external domination. Minority rights and legal safeguards were also legislated into the constitutions of the new states and the remaining cores of the old empires.

Germany lost Alsace-Lorraine to France, large areas in the east to Poland, and small areas to Lithuania, Belgium, and Denmark. Germany was ordered to pay heavy reparations for the cost of the war, although in practice not much was paid. Most gallingly for Germany, it was forced officially to accept total responsibility for causing the loss and damage of the war. Germany signed the Treaty of Versailles, which concluded the war, and left Paris humiliated, resentful, but, despite the loss of lands and the financial reparations, potentially still powerful.

The League of Nations

The negotiators in Paris generally agreed on the need for some form of organization to provide for international cooperation, to adjudicate disputes among nations, and, it was hoped, to prevent future warfare. To this end they created the League of Nations in 1920, but disillusionment soon followed. The league was crippled by three congenital defects. First, its principal sponsor, the United States, refused to join because of congressional opposition. The world's most powerful technological, industrial, financial, and military power, the United States withdrew back into the isolation of its ocean defenses. Germany was admitted to membership in 1926; the USSR joined in 1934.

Second, the League failed to resolve the complex issues of national identities and increasing anti-colonialism. In accord with the principle of national self-determination, ten new states were born, or reborn, as a result of the Paris accords, and fourteen states were specifically charged with protecting racial, religious, and linguistic minorities within their borders, assuring those minorities of equal rights with all citizens, including the right to primary school instruction in their mother tongue. In central Europe, however, nationality groups were widely dispersed, and many minorities continued to feel aggrieved.

The antagonism of colonized peoples towards their colonial rulers also intensified as the powerful nations of the world soon returned to business-as-usual. Despite their many wartime promises of self-rule, the League had neither the will nor the power to intervene. For example, even as France and Britain had been promising independence to Arab regions of the Middle East during the war, they had actually signed the Sykes–Picot Agreement in 1916 to divide these regions among themselves. The grant of mandatory powers to Britain over Iraq and Palestine and to France over Syria and Lebanon broke the promise while carrying out the agreement.

Turkey itself was marked for further dismemberment into spheres controlled by France, Italy, and, most provocatively, by Greece, the centuries-old Christian enemy of the Muslim Turks. An independent Armenian state was to be established in eastern Turkey on the shores of the Black Sea, and an independent Kurdistan just to the south of it. Only the armed resistance of Turkish forces led by General Mustafa Kemal (1881–1938) prevented implementation. Musafa Kemal, later called Atatürk, Father of the Turks, drove out the foreign troops stationed in Turkey and preserved the geographical and political independence of his state until Turkey's full sovereignty was recognized by the 1923 Treaty of Lausanne.

In East Asia, the peace treaties assigned Germany's holdings in the Shandong Peninsula of north China to Japan rather than returning them to China. In Paris, Chinese protestors physically blocked the nation's delegates from attending the signing ceremonies, and thus China never did sign the peace agreements. Within China, protests against the treaties by students and others began on May 4, 1919, engendering a continuing critique of China's international humiliation, the apparent bankruptcy of its historical traditions, and the value of its cultural links to the West. This "May Fourth Movement" also helped to sow the seeds of the Chinese Communist Party (CCP), which came to fruition in 1921 following discussions between Chinese revolutionaries and representatives of the newly formed Comintern (Communist International) of the USSR.

In India, Britain fell short of its wartime promise to expand the institutions of self-government; on the contrary, it passed the Rowlatt Acts, which restricted freedoms of the press and assembly. In addition, India faced an inflation that doubled the prices of basic commodities between 1914 and 1920, and an influenza epidemic that killed 12 million people in India alone (of a world total of about 20 million), twice as many people as had been killed in the war. Going into the war, most Indians seem to have trusted that Britain would bring self-government back to India, even if the process seemed very slow. Mohandas Karamchand Gandhi (1869–1948), who was becoming the leader of the Indian national movement, had even recruited troops, unsuccessfully, for the British war effort. All this changed after the war as the British cracked down and the Indians protested. In Amritsar, Punjab, a British general, Reginald Dyer, ordered his troops to fire on an unarmed protest rally. Blocking the only exit, the soldiers turned the outdoor meeting-place of Jalianwala Bagh into a gruesome shooting gallery, killing 379 people and wounding 1,100. The government forced the general to resign, but a popular outpouring of support for him in Britain thoroughly alienated Indian moderates. World War I had already exposed a murderous brutality within European civilization; now it appeared in India as well, thoroughly laced with racism. From this point onward in the eyes of even moderate Indians, British colonial rule had forfeited its legitimacy.

In 1919, Gandhi began to reorganize the Congress around India's peasantry, broadening and deepening a movement that had been based on urban and upper middle classes. In 1920, he began the first of his non-cooperation campaigns, and in 1930 he led the Salt March, a protest movement that mobilized the country and reached media attention throughout the world.

In Africa, Europeans continued to administer the colonies they had seized in the late nineteenth century. British settlers began to move into new settlements, especially in the highlands of Kenya and in Southern Rhodesia (today's Zimbabwe). Especially in the British colonies, African tribal leaders were incorporated into the ruling structures, following some of the policies of indirect rule first evolved in India.

The existence of the League of Nations and its mandate system did, however, begin to suggest that colonialism might be limited over time. In Egypt, the Wafd Party began demonstrations and riots that persuaded the British to grant Egypt nominal independence while still controlling its foreign policy and defense, and the Suez Canal. In 1921, Britain granted dominion status to a new state in southern Ireland, ending centuries of colonial oppression (but leaving Northern Ireland still a part of Great Britain). It granted Iraq nominal independence in 1932.

The League itself, however, had no armed forces. This limited its willingness to intervene in disputes, and made it impossible to back up even the decisions that it was willing to take. The great powers signed the Kellogg–Briand Pact in 1928, agreeing to settle their disputes without warfare, but the pact proved meaningless. The League effectively died when it failed to counter Japan's invasion of China in 1931; Italy's invasion of Ethiopia in 1935, which turned one of only two independent countries in Africa (Liberia was the other) into a colony; Germany's rearmament through the 1930s; and the outbreak of the Spanish Civil War in 1936 (see Chapter 20).

Poster commemorating "The Internationale," the rallying anthem of the Communist movement. Karl Marx (*left*) and Friedrich Engels (*right*), who appear at the top of this poster, collaborated in developing the theoretical principles underlying "scientific socialism" and in organizing a working-class movement dedicated to revolting against capitalism.

THE RUSSIAN REVOLUTION

The war broke the back of the Russian government and brought to power a new form of government that most western European nations and the United States found dangerous and threatening. Others, including some Americans, found it an interesting alternative to the decadence of the West. They saw it as a dream for a better world. The Russian Revolution of 1917 challenged the capitalist order by instituting communism. As we noted in Chapter 17, communism advocated the abolition of private property and the control of a country's economic resources by the state, at least temporarily. It argued that the Communist Party should spearhead this system, by the use of violence if necessary. Leaders of the party believed that Russia could telescope the development process and catapult itself quickly into the ranks of the wealthy and powerful nations. The Bolshevik Party, renamed the Communist Party in 1918, asserted its own dominance over the politics, economy, and society of Russia. Through the worldwide organization of the Communist International, it proposed itself as a model for, and leader of, colonized and backward countries in overthrowing foreign control and capitalist economic development. It argued that poor nations had been intentionally "underdeveloped" by, and for, the rich. The new communist system established by the Russian Revolution endured through years of hardship and of war, both civil and international.

The Build-up to Revolution, 1914–17

Geographically and politically Russia has one foot in Europe, another in Asia. As we have seen, Peter the Great (r. 1682–1725) turned westward, founding St. Petersburg as his capital, port, and window on the west. Catherine II, the Great (r. 1762–96), further nurtured the European Enlightenment at the Russian court. Stunned by his defeat in the Crimean War (1853–6) at the hands of Britain and France in alliance with Turkey, Tsar Alexander II (r. 1855–81) adopted a more liberal policy. He freed Russia's serfs in 1861, instituted the **zemstvo** system of local self-government in 1864, reduced censorship of the press, reformed the legal system, encouraged industrialization, and promoted the construction of a nationwide railway system. Tsar Nicholas II (r. 1894–1917) furthered heavy industrialization under two progressive ministers, Count Sergei Witte (1849–1915) and Peter Stolypin (1862–1911), and allowed the birth of some representative political institutions, but he rejected the democratic reforms demanded by intellectuals, workers, and political organizers.

zemstvo A rural council in the Russian Empire, established by Tsar Alexander II in 1864 and abolished in 1917.

Despite the industrialization introduced under Nicholas II, on the eve of World War I Russia lagged far behind the western European countries economically and industrially. Its population of 175 million was about 75 percent more than that of the United States, more than two and a half times that of Germany, and four times that of Britain; its energy consumption was one-tenth that of the United States, 30 percent that of Germany, and one-fourth that of Britain. Its share of world manufacturing was 8 percent compared with the United States' 32 percent, Germany's 15 percent, and Britain's 14 percent.

Nicholas II had made great strides in increasing industrial production. Energy consumption had increased from 4.6 metric tons equivalent in 1890 to 23 million in 1913; railway mileage from about 22,000 miles in 1890 to 31,000 miles in 1900 to 46,000 miles in 1913; and the per capita level of industrialization doubled from 1880 to 1913. But during that same period, 1880–1913, the United States's per capita level of industrialization quadrupled, Germany's rose three and one-half times, and France's, Italy's, Austria's, and Japan's all slightly more than doubled. In a rapidly industrializing world, Russia had to race much faster just to keep up. To obtain the capital to build its industries Russia invited foreign investment, but this opened the nation to foreign control. In 1917 foreigners held nearly 50 percent of the Russian national debt. Russia was Europe's largest debtor.

Russia's agriculture was unproductive and its technology was primitive. A wealthy elite held enormous power over the land and the peasants who worked it. An exploited peasantry living in **mirs** (village collectives) had neither the economic incentive nor the technical training to produce more. The small parcels of land they farmed privately were subdivided into tiny plots, as sons in each generation shared equally in the inheritance of their fathers. Finally, the government forbade the sale of village land to outsiders. This prevented exploitation by absentee landlords, but it blocked the investment from outside the village that might have funded agricultural improvement through new technology. Productivity stagnated. The sharp class divisions between the peasants and the gentry persisted, marked by differences not only in wealth and education, but also in dress and manners. Moreover, the costs of industrialization and the repayment of foreign loans had to be squeezed out of the agricultural sector. The result was a mass of peasants impoverished, technologically backward, despised by the wealthy elite, and suffering under the weight of a national program of industrialization for which they were made to pay.

mir A self-governing community of peasants in pre-revolutionary Russia having control over local forests, fisheries, and hunting grounds; land was allocated to each family according to size, in return for a fixed sum.

Lenin and the Bolshevik Revolution

Several revolutionary groups protested these conditions, each offering a different plan. The Social Democrats followed George Plekhanov (1857–1918), who saw the need for more capitalist development in Russia to create new urban working and middle classes, which Plekhanov's party would then organize to overthrow the bourgeoisie.

Plekhanov was actually an orthodox Marxist thinker who believed that before a communist revolution could emerge, capitalism would first have to lay the foundations of industry and industrial laborers. A lawyer, Vladimir Ilyich Ulyanov (1870–1924), later calling himself Lenin, advocated a far more immediate and abrupt communist revolution, and he stressed the need for the communist party to provide its leadership.

> Not a single class in history has reached power without thrusting forward its political leaders, without advancing leading representatives capable of directing and organizing the movement. We must train people who will dedicate to the revolution, not a spare evening but the whole of their lives. (Kochan and Abraham, p. 240)

In 1902, in a pamphlet entitled *What Is to Be Done?* Lenin again underlined the need for an absolutely dedicated core of leaders to carry out the revolution: "Give us an organization of revolutionaries and we will overturn Russia!" In January 1905, with revolutionary feelings running high, some 200,000 factory workers and others in St. Petersburg, led by a priest, Father Gapon, assembled peacefully and respectfully to deliver to the tsar a petition for better working conditions, higher pay, and representative government. On that "Bloody Sunday," January 22, the tsar was not actually in the city but his troops fired on the demonstrators, killing several hundred and wounding perhaps a thousand. The government's lack of moral authority was unmasked. By the end of the month almost 500,000 workers were on strike, joined by peasant revolts, mutinies of soldiers, and protests by the intelligentsia of doctors, lawyers, professors, teachers, and engineers.

Before this domestic turmoil erupted, the tsar had committed Russia to war with Japan, but defeats at sea and on land further revealed Russia's inadequacies in both technology and government organization. The defeat in the Russo-Japanese War, domestic tax revolts in the countryside, and strikes in the industrializing cities forced the tsar to respond. Yielding as little as possible, he established the first Duma, or Parliament, representing peasants and landlords, but allowing workers only scant representation. The tsar limited the powers of the dumas, frequently dismissed them, sometimes jailed their members, and chose their class composition selectively to divide the principal revolutionary constituencies, workers and bourgeoisie. The dumas endured as a focus for democratic organization and aspiration, but they were unable to work cooperatively, and the tsar was able to stave off revolution for a decade.

Unable to match the new technological warfare of other European countries, Russia suffered 2 million casualties in World War I. These losses finally united the many forces of opposition and brought down the monarchy. In the midst of revolutionary ferment, in February 1917, 10,000 women in St. Petersburg marched to protest the rationing of bread and demanded the tsar's abdication. Despite government orders, the army refused to fire on them.

In the first revolution of March 1917, the duma forced the tsar to abdicate and established a new provisional government under Aleksandr Kerensky (1881–1970). But the war persisted. The turmoil of mutiny and desertion in the army, food shortages, farm revolts, and factory strikes ground on. More radical groups sought to seize control. Lenin, with the assistance of the German government, which wished to sow discord in Russia, returned from exile in Switzerland. With the

Looters, St. Petersburg, 1905. Small pockets of revolutionary fervor flared up prior to 1917. In 1905, the year these peasants are depicted looting bosses' houses, twenty officers and 230 guards were arrested in St. Petersburg when a plot to assassinate the tsar was uncovered.

motto "Peace, Land, Bread," he called for an immediate withdrawal from the war, land for the peasants, and a government-run food distribution system. Lenin organized an armed takeover of the government headquarters, the railway stations, power plants, post offices, and telephone exchanges. On November 7 (October 25 on the old, Julian calendar), this revolutionary coup succeeded, and the communists seized power. Confounding Marxist doctrine, the revolution had occurred not in one of Europe's most capitalistic and industrialized countries, but in one of the most industrially backward. In March 1918, by signing the Treaty of Brest–Litovsk with Germany the communist government took Russia out of the war.

Civil war between communist revolutionary "Red" and anti-revolutionary "White" forces enveloped the country. Contingents of troops from fourteen countries (including a small number of Americans in the Baltic and 8,000 at Vladivostok on the Pacific) joined the Whites. The Bolshevik government took over ownership of land, banks, the merchant marine, and all industrial enterprises. It confiscated all holdings of the church and forbade religious teaching in the schools. It established the **Cheka** (security police) and instituted a reign of "Red Terror" against its opponents' "White Terror." In Yekaterinburg, the local soviet executed the tsar, his wife, and their children. By 1920, the communists, as the Bolsheviks now called themselves, were victorious in the civil war. In 1921, they banned all opposition, even dissenting voices within the party, and made the central committee, now under Lenin's control, the binding authority in the government. Lenin began the pattern of imprisoning his opponents in labor camps—a policy that was later expanded under his successors into a huge network of camps for political opponents of the government. Millions of citizens were ultimately imprisoned in this **gulag** or prison system.

World war and civil war, which were followed by even more devastating drought, famine, and economic dislocation, convinced Lenin of the need for economic stability and an incentive to produce. In 1921, he implemented the New Economic Policy (NEP), which allowed peasants to sell their products on the open market and middlemen to buy and sell consumer goods at a profit. The central government, however, controlled the "commanding heights" of the economy: finance, banking, international trade, power generation, and heavy industry.

State Planning in Soviet Russia

Lenin sought the industrial transformation of Russia. In 1920, as he established the State Commission for Electrification, he declared: "Communism is Soviet power, plus electrification of the whole country." Lenin invited German and American technicians to Russia to improve productivity by harnessing capitalist means to communist goals. He took special interest in the system of scientific management and time studies in the workplace that had been introduced in America by Frederick Taylor.

Lenin's death in 1924 ushered in a bitter power struggle from which Joseph Stalin (1879–1953) emerged triumphant over Leon Trotsky (1879–1940). Trotsky, a brilliant, ruthless man, who had organized the Red Army, had argued that through careful but

Lenin and Joseph Stalin at Gorki, Russia, 1922. After Lenin's premature death two years after this photograph was taken, Stalin battled to eliminate his rivals (Leon Trotsky was banished abroad and eventually assassinated in Mexico) before emerging as supreme dictator of the Communist Party in 1929. He soon abandoned Lenin's New Economic Policy in favor of a series of brutal five-year plans to enforce the collectivization of agriculture and industry.

Cheka The secret police of early Soviet Russia, established by the Bolsheviks after the revolution of 1917 to defend the regime against dissidents. Criticized for its severe brutality, the agency was reorganized in 1922.

gulag The acronym of Glavnoye, Upravleniye Ispravitelno Trudovykh Lagerey, the "Chief Administration of Corrective Labor Camps," a department of the Soviet secret police founded in 1934 . It ran a vast network of forced labor camps throughout the USSR to which millions of citizens accused of "crimes against the state" were sent for punishment.

bold planning a technologically backward country could leapfrog stages of growth and, through the "law of combined development," quickly catch up to the more advanced. Having defeated Trotsky, Stalin now implemented Trotsky's program. He declared his driving nationalist passion that Russia must no longer lag behind the more developed nations.

> those who fall behind get beaten. But we do not want to be beaten. No, we refuse to be beaten! One feature of the history of old Russia was the continual beatings she suffered for falling behind, for her backwardness. She was beaten by the Mongol Khans. She was beaten by the Turkish beys. She was beaten by the Swedish feudal lords. She was beaten by the Polish and Lithuanian gentry. She was beaten by the British and French capitalists. She was beaten by the Japanese barons. All beat her—for her backwardness: for military backwardness, for cultural backwardness, for political backwardness, for industrial backwardness, for agricultural backwardness. She was beaten because to do so was profitable and could be done with impunity. …
>
> That is why we must no longer lag behind. (Andrea and Overfield, p. 398)

Stalin's rhetoric appealed not only to his immediate audience in Russia, but also to a more global audience of poorer states and colonies beginning to protest against their subordination and to seek independence and development.

To achieve "combined development," in 1928 Stalin instituted nationwide, state-directed five-year plans that covered the basic economic structure of the whole country. In place of capitalism, in which market forces of supply and demand determine production goals, wages, profits, and the flow of capital, labor, and resources, Stalin instituted government planning to make those decisions, from the large-scale national macro-level to the small-scale local micro-level.

Where could Russia find capital to invest in industrial development, especially with most world capital markets closed to the communist state? Stalin turned to his own agricultural sector and peasantry. By artificially lowering the prices for agricultural products and raising the prices for agricultural tools and materials, Stalin used his planning apparatus to squeeze capital and labor out of agriculture into industry. But he squeezed so hard that agricultural productivity fell and peasants withheld their crops from the artificially deflated market. State planning was not working.

Nevertheless, in 1929 Stalin increased the role of the state still further. He collectivized agriculture. More than half of all Soviet farmers were compelled to give up their individual fields and to live and work instead on newly formed collective farms of 1,000 acres or more. The communist government increased the use of heavy machinery and large-scale farming operations, stipulated the goods to be produced and their sales prices, encouraged millions of peasants to leave the farms for work on the state's new industrial enterprises, and eliminated wealthier peasants and middlemen.

Although some farmers were living better in 1939 than 1929, many others were not. The most industrious and talented farmers were killed or imprisoned. Hundreds of thousands of better-off peasants, **kulaks**, who refused collectivization were murdered; millions were transported to labor camps in Siberia. Peasants who owned animals preferred to slaughter them rather than turn them over to collectives. There had been over 60 million head of cattle in the USSR in 1928; by 1933, there were fewer than 35 million. Initiative shriveled as the more entrepreneurial farmers were turned into a kind of rural proletariat. The government continued to collect high proportions of the agricultural production to pay for the imports of foreign technology and machinery for its industrial programs. Although few developing countries today are willing to reduce private consumption below 80 percent of the national product, Russia reduced it to little over 50 percent. Much of the difference went to industrial development. The government chose guns over butter. The political coercion and chaos introduced by these

kulak A prosperous peasant in late tsarist and early Soviet Russia. The leaders of local agricultural communities, kulaks owned sizeable farms and could afford to hire labor.

policies, combined with bad harvests in southeast Russia, led to the tragic and wasteful deaths of between 2 and 3 million peasants by 1932.

While the peasants suffered enormous hardship, industry flourished as never before. At first, Russia hired foreign technology and imported foreign machinery. Despite ideological differences with the United States, Stalin, like Lenin before him, saw the necessity of importing American materials, machinery, and even some organizational programming. In 1924 Stalin declared:

> American efficiency is that indomitable force which neither knows nor recognizes obstacles; which continues on a task once started until it is finished, even if it is a minor task; and without which serious constructive work is inconceivable. ... The combination of Russian revolutionary sweep with American efficiency is the essence of Leninism. (Hughes, p. 251)

Meanwhile, the Russian government was training its own personnel and learning to construct its own massive industrial plants. At the falls of the Dnieper River, the communist state constructed Dnieprostroy, which, when it opened in 1932, was the largest hydroelectric power station in the world. In the early 1920s, the USSR had imported tens of thousands of tractors, most of them Fords and International Harvesters from the United States. By the 1930s, however, Russia constructed a giant plant at Stalingrad to manufacture its own tractors. At Gorki (Nizhny Novgorod) the government built a plant based on the American Ford model at River Rouge, Michigan. At Magnitogorsk, in Siberia, they constructed a steel complex based on US Steel's plant in Gary, Indiana.

From 1928 to 1938, the per capita level of industrialization nearly doubled. From 1928 to 1940, the production of coal increased from 36 to 166 million tons, that of electricity from 5 to 48 billion kilowatt hours, and that of steel from 4 to 18 million tons. Stalin explained: "The independence of our country cannot be upheld unless we have an adequate industrial basis for defense" (Kochan and Abraham, p. 368). The planners began to convert a nation of peasants into a nation of industrial workers, as the urban population of the country increased three and one-half times from 10.7 million in 1928 to 36.5 million in 1938, from 7 percent of the country's population to 20 percent.

Most dramatically, the Soviet increases came when western Europe and North America were reeling under world depression (see Chapter 20). The communist system won new admirers in the West. The American political comedian Will Rogers commented: "Those rascals in Russia, along with their cuckoo stuff have got some mighty good ideas. ... Just think of everybody in a country going to work." Journalist Lincoln Steffens wrote: "All roads in our day lead to Moscow." British political critic and historian John Strachey exclaimed: "To travel from the capitalist world into Soviet territory is to pass from death to birth."

Women in the Soviet Union

For women, too, the Soviet system led to great change, but perhaps less than promised. As elsewhere, World War I brought women into factories, fields, and even the armed forces, and the civil war continued the pattern. Over 70,000 women served in the Red Army. In 1921, 65 percent of Petrograd's factory workers were women. In 1917, the first Soviet marriage law constituted marriage as a civil contract and provided for relatively easy divorce and child maintenance procedures.

The government ordered equal pay for equal work, but the provision was not enforced. To bring law into line with practice, and recognizing the lack of availability of effective birth-control methods, abortion on demand was granted as a right; so was maternity leave with full pay. When the men returned from the war, they wanted their

Russian poster for women textile workers, 1930. Despite the government's difficulties in enforcing "equal pay for equal work," women's rights improved markedly under the communist system. This poster appears to idealize full-time employment combined with raising a family.

jobs back and their women at home, but Russian women retained most of the benefits they had won and "legally speaking, Russian women were better off than women anywhere in the world" (Kochan and Abraham, p. 337). Over the next decades women entered professions so rapidly that they became the majority in medicine and teaching—care-giving occupations—and a substantial minority in engineering, technical occupations, and law.

In practice, however, women bore the "double burden" of continuing the major responsibility for running their homes and caring for their families while working full time. With the introduction of state-planned heavy industrialization after 1929, the double burden on women increased. The factories invited their labor, while shortages of foodstuffs forced them to spend more time and energy in ration lines and in the search for food. Abortion became so common that it was once again outlawed for a time after 1936. The struggle to balance the new legal equality and protection with older social and family traditions continued (and continues today).

Many political leaders of countries under European colonial control saw the Russian example—telescoped development, state planning, rapid industrialization, the transformation of the peasantry into an urban labor force, emphasis on education and health services, national enthusiasm in rebuilding a nation along scientific lines—as just what they needed. As a political prisoner in British India in July 1933, Jawaharlal Nehru, future first prime minister of independent India, wrote to his daughter:

People often argue about the Five Year Plan. ... It is easy enough to point out where it has failed. ... [but] One thing is clear: that the Five Year Plan has completely changed the face of Russia. From a feudal country it has suddenly become an advanced industrial country. There has been an amazing cultural advance; and the social services, the system of social, health, and accident insurance, are the most inclusive and advanced in the world. In spite of privation and want, the terrible fear of unemployment and starvation which hangs over workers in other countries has gone. There is a new sense of economic security among the people ... further ... this Plan has impressed itself on the imagination of the world. Everybody talks of "planning" now, and of Five-Year and Ten-Year and Three-Year plans. The Soviets have put magic into the word. (*Glimpses of World History*, pp. 856–7)

POST-WAR AMERICA

America left World War I as the technological and financial leader of the world. The factories that had supplied war goods returned to producing domestic, consumer products that made the American middle and upper classes the envy of many around the world. Automobile registration rose from about a half million in 1910 to over 8 million in 1920 and 23 million in 1930. In addition, in 1930, American farms employed some 920,000 tractors and 900,000 trucks. Even Stalin in Russia invited American technical assistance in establishing some of the gigantic industrial complexes of the Soviet Union.

In 1910, there were 82 phones per thousand Americans; in 1930, 163. Only in the early 1900s did wealthier people begin to introduce indoor flush toilets and cast-iron bathtubs. By 1925, America was producing 5 million enameled bathroom fixtures annually. Thanks to the efforts of labor unions, the work week was being reduced from 60 hours per week to 45. Paid vacations were becoming common, with 40 percent of large companies giving at least one week of paid vacation per year. Diet improved; sales of fresh vegetables increased 45 percent in the decade after World War I. Life expectancy increased by more than a dozen years between 1900 and 1930, from 47 years to 60 years.

Electricity replaced steam as the major source of power. In 1929, 80 percent of all industrial power was produced by electrical generators, and two-thirds of America's homes were electrified. Washing machines, electric irons, vacuum cleaners, electric toasters, and sewing machines became common in urban homes, and standards of household cleanliness were raised. Commercial radio began broadcasting in 1920 and millions of homes soon had receivers. Many people built their own. Movies became the main mass entertainment, with the first "talkie," *The Jazz Singer*, released in 1927. In 1929, 100 million people attended the movies each week. Watching film stars such as Charlie Chaplin, Gloria Swanson, Mae West, Greta Garbo, and Rudolph Valentino gave viewers new ideas—and new fantasies—about what their lives might be. The films gave audiences around the world their own peculiar version of American life.

Women's lives changed, too, in this decade. Although the sale and prescription of the means of birth control was illegal in most states, Margaret Sanger convened the first birth control conference in 1921 and traveled around the world spreading her message. The size of American families dropped from 3.6 children in 1900 to 2.5 in 1930. About one-fourth of all women of working age actually worked outside the home, especially in office jobs, teaching, and nursing. In 1920, American women were constitutionally granted the right to vote, as they were at about the same time in Britain and Germany.

Much of the image of post-war America is of flappers, speakeasies (after prohibition was introduced by the Eighteenth Amendment to the Constitution in 1919), increased recognition of sexuality of women as well as men, and a general flamboyance. This image may have been true for an urban, upper middle class, white population, a small—if conspicuous—minority of the total population. For most of working class and rural America, life was still quite difficult.

Also, fear permeated some corners of America. The United States engaged in international commerce with its great industrial, agricultural, and administrative power. But it refused to join the League of Nations and generally withdrew from participation in international politics outside of Latin America, where it had substantial financial investments and repeatedly intervened with military force. It seemed to fear involvement outside its own hemisphere.

Internally, in the immediate post-war years, many strikes hit industries in the United States. A third of

Civil aviation. A steward serves passengers on board a KLM Fokker F18 in 1932. In the 1920s, the popularity of aerial circuses and flying clubs, run by former World War I pilots, combined with rapid improvements in technology, heralded a new age of civil aviation. By the 1930s a worldwide network of commercial routes had developed. In these early years the high cost of air travel created an aura of glamor and exclusivity.

a million workers struck against US Steel in 1919. In the same year the Boston police force went on strike. The home of the attorney general, A. Mitchell Palmer, was bombed. Coming as they did just after the Communist Party took over the government of Russia, these events gave many Americans a "Red Scare," and Palmer began rounding up, jailing, and deporting thousands of people accused of being communists, anarchists, and radicals. Hundreds of aliens were deported. The Ku Klux Klan was revived to terrorize Catholics, Jews, and African-Americans, especially the black soldiers returning from war who might no longer know their "place." At its height in the early 1920s the Klan enrolled several million members. By the end of the decade, the fears and frenzies had abated, but new, perhaps greater fears were in store, as the stock market crash of October 29, 1929, following years of economic difficulties on America's farms, ushered in the Great Depression.

The Depression

Worldwide economic depression destabilized domestic and international politics worldwide, but especially in Europe. Depression is a severe economic downturn in production and consumption that continues for at least several months. Periods of depression were considered normal in a free-market economy as the forces of supply and demand periodically fell out of step and then came back into line. But the Great Depression was far more extreme in its extent and duration. On October 29, 1929— "Black Tuesday"—the New York stock exchange crashed. The decline continued for years. By 1933, stocks were worth 15 percent of their value in 1929, ending five years of relative prosperity and marking the beginning of a worldwide economic Depression, which would continue until the outbreak of World War II in 1939.

The United States had emerged from World War I as a creditor nation. To pay the reparations from the war, Germany depended on loans from several nations, especially the United States. With the stock market crash of 1929, however, American financiers called in these loans, undercutting the European economy. In addition, farmers who had produced at record levels during the war had difficulty cutting back production, resulting in huge, unsold surpluses and a depression in agriculture. Faced with such economic difficulties, countries closed their borders to imports so that they could sell their own products internally without competition. But as each country raised its barriers, international markets contracted, increasing the Depression.

Mass unemployment swept Britain, America, and Germany; the unemployment rate among industrial workers in Germany was 30 percent in 1932. Latin American countries, notably Argentina, which had been approaching a European standard of living, found their economies devastated, turned away from European markets, and sought to salvage what they could through domestic development. The value of world trade in 1938 was 60 percent below what it was in 1929.

Communist Russia, standing somewhat apart from the world economy, had introduced centralized national planning in 1928, emphasizing heavy industrialization. Its factories flourished, but agriculture was devastated and levels of private consumption plummeted.

In 1921 there were 2 million unemployed in Britain. They collected unemployment insurance in accord with an act that had been passed a decade earlier. The government also implemented an old-age pension system, medical aids, and subsidized housing. But the world Depression increased this unemployment to almost 3 million. Unemployment payments multiplied while tax collections dropped. The welfare state expanded and government remained stable, but the Depression ground on.

America, the country most dedicated to private enterprise and "rugged individualism," and therefore most reluctant to expand government social welfare programs,

SOURCE

How Should We Live?

The Polish poet Wislawa Szymborska, winner of the Nobel Prize for Literature in 1996, reflects upon the disillusionment of the twentieth century and assumes that life should and must go on nevertheless. "How should we live?" she asks at the close of one of her most poignant poems, written in the 1970s. In this poem, however, she offers no answers:

Our twentieth century was going to
  improve on the others.
It will never prove it now,
now that its years are numbered,
its gait is shaky,
its breath is short.

Too many things have happened
that weren't supposed to happen,
and what was supposed to come about
has not.

Happiness and spring, among other things,
were supposed to be getting closer.

Fear was expected to leave the mountains
  and the valleys.
Truth was supposed to hit home
before a lie.

A couple of problems weren't going
to come up anymore:
hunger, for example,
and war, and so forth.

There was going to be respect
for helpless people's helplessness,
trust, that kind of stuff.

Anyone who planned to enjoy the world
is now faced
with a hopeless task.

Stupidity isn't funny.
Wisdom isn't gay.
Hope
isn't that young girl anymore,
et cetera, alas.

God was finally going to believe
in a man both good and strong,
but good and strong
are still two different men.

"How should we live?" someone asked me
  in a letter.
I had meant to ask him
the same question.

Again, and as ever,
as may be seen above,
the most pressing questions
are naive ones.

saw national income drop by half between 1929 and 1932. Almost 14 million people were unemployed. Elected in 1932, in the midst of national despair, Democratic President Franklin Delano Roosevelt rallied the nation with charismatic optimism. Declaring that "The only thing we have to fear is fear itself," he instituted social welfare programs as a means of preserving the capitalist foundation. He provided financial relief for the unemployed; public works projects to create construction jobs; subsidies to farmers to reduce production and eliminate surpluses; and federal support for low-cost housing and slum clearance. A Civilian Conservation Corps was established, ostensibly to promote conservation and reforestation, but mostly to provide some 3 million jobs to the young. The Tennessee Valley Authority created an immense hydroelectric program, combining flood control with rural electrification and regional economic development.

Roosevelt increased the regulation of business and promoted unions. The Securities and Exchange Commission, created in 1929, regulated the stock exchange. The National Recovery Administration encouraged regulation of prices and production until it was judged unconstitutional in 1935. The Social Security Act of 1935 introduced unemployment, old age, and disability insurance—policies already in place in parts of Western Europe well before World War I. Child labor was abolished. Forty hours of work was set as the weekly norm. Minimum hourly wages were fixed. Union organization was encouraged and union membership grew from 4 million in 1929 to 9 million in 1940. The most capitalist of the major powers thus accepted the welfare state. Throughout the century, the scope of welfare expanded and contracted with different governments, philosophies of government, and budgetary conditions, but the principle that the state had a major role in protecting and advancing the welfare of its people persisted.

In Germany, the Depression followed on the heels of catastrophic inflation. In the 1920s the Government induced hyperinflation to pay the resented war reparations, thus wiping out the savings of the middle classes and amplifying further resentment over the punitive Versailles Treaty, including its emphasis on German war guilt and insistence on Germany's disarmament. By 1924 industrial production had recovered but then the Depression wiped out the gains. The new government, called the Weimar Republic, was perceived by many as a weak and precarious experiment in constitutional democracy in a nation accustomed to a military monarchy. Exciting new movements in art and architecture that were responsive to a new technological potential for creativity, notably the Bauhaus school of architecture, were threatened and ultimately driven out of the country. Anti-democratic forces and political ideologies, backed by thugs on the streets, triumphed over aesthetic and cultural creativity.

METHODS OF PRODUCTION AND DESTRUCTION WHAT DIFFERENCE DO THEY MAKE?

The early twentieth century taught us skepticism. The greatest triumphs of science and technology could be transformed into instruments of death. Principles of physics that had been accepted as laws for two centuries and more, were found to be only fragments of larger principles. Public health measures and medicine extended lifespans; world warfare cut them down. Nationalism inspired people to work for the betterment of their country and its people, but at the same time to compete with, and make war against, those in neighboring countries, and often to limit freedoms of minorities even at home. Revolutions continued for a decade and more, benefiting many people, but not fulfilling their promises to the masses. Great empires, some of them hundreds of years old, one of them 2,000 years old, toppled and dissolved in civil warfare. World warfare ended, but left clear indications that it would soon resume because the issues that had caused it remained unresolved. Perhaps most frightening of all, totalitarian governments came to power in parts of the world that had been considered among the most civilized, only to challenge and subvert the whole basis of modern civilization, as we shall see in Chapter 20. This chapter ends with stories of warfare, imperialism, economics, science, and technology that were clearly unfinished. Many of them are still unfolding.

Review Questions

- What did the poet Wislawa Szymborska have in mind when she wrote that in the twentieth century, "A couple of problems weren't going to come up anymore: hunger, for example, and war, and so forth"?
- In what way does the Mexican Revolution appear to be a product of the technological developments of the early twentieth century? What other conditions promoted this revolution?
- What were the chief causes of World War I, and why were the Balkans so important in its origins?
- What promises were made by colonial powers during the war that were not kept afterward?
- What were the most important actions of the Soviet Union in the first decade after the Communist Revolution?
- In what ways was the United States a world leader in the decade following World War I? In what ways was it not?

Suggested Readings

Adas, Michael. *Machines as the Measure of Man* (Ithaca, NY: Cornell University Press, 1989).

Andrea, Alfred and James H. Overfield, eds. *The Human Record*, Vol. 2 (Boston: Houghton Mifflin, 3rd ed., 1998).

Bulliet, Richard W., ed. *The Columbia History of the 20th Century* (New York: Columbia University Press, 1998).

Camus, Albert. *The Myth of Sisyphus* (New York: Vintage Books, 1959).

Chafe, William H. and Harvard Sitkoff, eds. *A History of Our Time* (New York: Oxford University Press, 3rd ed., 1991).

Crossley, Pamela Kyle, Lynn Hollen Lees, John W. Servos. *Global Society. The World since 1900* (Boston: Houghton Mifflin, 2004).

Fox, Richard G., ed. *Urban India: Society, Space and Image* (Durham, NC: Duke University Program in Comparative Studies on Southern Asia, 1970).

Freeman, Christopher. "Technology and Invention," in Bulliet, pp. 314–44.

Freud, Sigmund. *Civilization and its Discontents* (New York: W.W. Norton and Co., 1961).

——. *A General Introduction to Psychoanalysis* (New York: Pocket Books, 1952).

Gandhi, Mohandas Karamchand. *Hind Swaraj or Indian Home Rule* (Ahmedabad: Navajivan Press, 1938).

Hemingway, Ernest. *For Whom the Bell Tolls* (New York: Scribner, 1940).

Hofstadter, Richard, ed. *Great Issues in American History: A Documentary Record* (New York: Vintage Books, 1959).

Howard, Michael and William Roger Louis, eds. *The Oxford History of the Twentieth Century* (New York: Oxford University Press, 1998).

Hughes, Thomas. *American Genesis* (New York: Viking, 1989).

Inkster, Ian. *Science and Technology in History. An Approach to Industrialization* (London: Macmillan, 1991).

Johnson, Paul. *Modern Times* (New York: Harper and Row, 1983).

Keegan, John. *A History of Warfare* (New York: Knopf, 1994). Compares and explicates the history of warfare through styles of war rather than strict chronology. Themes are stone, flesh, iron, and fire.

Kennedy, Paul. *The Rise and Fall of the Great Powers* (New York: Random House, 1987).

Kochan, Lionel and Richard Abraham. *The Making of Modern Russia* (London: Penguin Books, 1983).

Kragh, Helge. *Quantum Generations. A History of Physics in the Twentieth Century* (Princeton: Princeton University Press, 1999).

Landes, David S. *The Wealth and Poverty of Nations* (New York: W.W. Norton, 1999).

Lewis, David Levering. *W.E.B. Du Bois: Biography of a Race 1868–1919* (New York: Henry Holt, 1993).

Pacey, Arnold. *Technology in World Civilization* (Cambridge: MIT Press, 1990).

Pickering, Kevin T. and Lewis A. Owen. *An Introduction to Global Environmental Issues* (New York: Routledge, 1994).

Ramanujan, A.K. "Towards an Anthology of City Images," in Fox, pp. 224–42.

Remarque, Erich Maria. *All Quiet on the Western Front*, trans. by A.W. Wheen (Boston: Little, Brown, 1958).

Rosenberg, Rosalind, "The 'Woman' Question," in Bulliet, pp. 53–80.

Szymborska, Wislawa. *View with a Grain of Sand* (San Diego: Harcourt Brace, 1995).

Wilkie, Brian and James Hurt, eds. *Literature of the Western World*, Vol. 2 (New York: Macmillan, 1984).

Williams, Trevor I.A. *Short History of Twentieth-Century Technology c. 1900–c. 1950* (Oxford: Oxford University Press, 1982)

Yagnik, Indulal. *Autobiography*, Vol. 1 (in Gujarati) (Ahmedabad: Ravaani Publishing House, 1955).

◉ World History Documents CD-ROM

22.1 The Horror of Battle

22.2 Slaughter on the Somme

22.3 "World War I: A Frenchman's Recollections"

22.4 The Perversion of Technology: War in "No Man's Land"

22.5 Sir Henry McMahon: *Letter to Ali Ibn Husain*

22.6 The Balfour Declaration

22.7 Woodrow Wilson: *Speech on the Fourteen Points*

22.8 *The Covenant of the League of Nations*

23.1 The Bolshevik Seizure of Power (November–December 1917)

23.2 Nadezhda K. Krupskaya: *What a Communist Ought to Be Like*

23.3 John Scott: *Behind the Urals*

WORLD WAR II AND THE COLD WAR

THE WORLD IN PERIL, 1937–49

KEY TOPICS
- Portents of Disaster
- The Contest of the "isms": Fascism and Communism
- The Descent Toward World War
- World War II
- The Image of Humanity
- The United Nations, Postwar Recovery, and the Origins of the Cold War
- Entering the Second Half of the Twentieth Century:
  What Difference Does it Make?

PORTENTS OF DISASTER

No sooner had the Paris peace treaties been signed than leading economists predicted disaster. In *The Economic Consequences of the Peace*, published in 1920, John Maynard Keynes argued that the treaties would push Germany and Austria into starvation. Like all of Europe, these countries would suffer from the crippling disruption of coal and iron supplies, transport, and imports of food and raw materials. In addition, the treaties stripped Germany of her overseas colonies and investments and her merchant fleet. It imposed on her crushing financial reparations to be paid to the victor nations. Keynes blamed the leaders of Britain, France, Italy, and the United States for their short-sightedness in making these demands, and he warned that starving people "in their distress may overturn the remnants of organization, and submerge civilization itself in their attempts to satisfy desperately the overwhelming needs of the individual."

In the next year, from a very different perspective, the poet William Butler Yeats added his own fears concerning a profound cultural sickness that he saw infecting all of Europe in the wake of the war and the Russian Revolution:

> Things fall apart; the center cannot hold;
> Mere anarchy is loosed upon the world,
> The blood-dimmed tide is loosed, and everywhere
> The ceremony of innocence is drowned;
> The best lack all conviction, while the worst
> Are full of passionate intensity.

Yeats held out no hope in rationality, nor in technological progress, although he professed belief in some mystical religious experience that was yet to come:

> Surely some revelation is at hand;
> Surely the Second Coming is at hand. (cited in Wilkie and Hurt, p. 1655)

A decade later, as worldwide depression confirmed the fears and pessimism of the economist Keynes and the poet Yeats, the psychoanalyst Sigmund Freud, who had pioneered depth studies of the human mind and spirit, wrote of even deeper anxieties. Freud questioned the direction of all civilized, technologically advanced societies and feared that they might all be destroyed:

Opposite **Nazi rally at Nuremberg, 1937.** Nazi Party members fill a stadium at a party meeting in Nuremberg, 1937.

Men have gained control over the forces of nature to such an extent that with their help they would have no difficulty in exterminating one another to the last man. They know this, and hence comes a large part of their current unrest, their unhappiness and their mood of anxiety. (Freud, pp. 34–5)

The events of the next decade, 1930–39, continued to feed the worst fears of the economist, the poet, and the psychoanalyst. The outbreak of World War II at the end of the decade confirmed their bitter and tragic predictions.

THE CONTEST OF THE "ISMS": FASCISM AND COMMUNISM

Desperate times evoke desperate responses. We have already seen in Chapter 19 one of these desperate responses: the triumph of communism in the Soviet Union. In this chapter we shall see its further development. First, however, we analyze the rise of **fascism** in Italy in the 1920s under Benito Mussolini (1883–1945), in Germany after 1933 under Adolf Hitler (1889–1945), and, to a lesser degree, in Japan, building throughout the 1930s. The term fascism was coined to describe the ideology of Mussolini's movement, party, and government. Fascism exalted the nation over the individual. It called for centralized autocratic government with tight control of the economy and social life of the nation. It demanded the suppression of all opposition through unofficial paramilitary organizations, which often took to the streets and whose members appeared to be thugs. If and when fascists took office, they used the armed forces of the government to suppress opposition. They glorified warfare as a positive virtue. Why people supported fascism is unclear. Some followers must have been attracted by the promise that violence could solve the nation's problems, many more by the promise of a better government and a more prosperous economy than the weak parliamentary governments could deliver. Fascism vested the power of the nation in a supreme leader. In Italy Mussolini, who had himself referred to as *Duce* (pronounced doo-chay), or supreme leader, filled that function.

fascism A political philosophy, movement, or government that exalts the nation over the individual, the antithesis of liberal democracy. It advocates a centralized, autocratic government led by a disciplined party and headed by a dictatorial, charismatic leader.

Italy

Although it had been on the side of the victors, Italy was beset by wartime losses of people and property, economic depression, and the social unrest that beset much of Europe. Labor strikes and peasant unrest in the form of non-payment of rents and occasional seizures of land spread throughout the country. Governments elected in 1919 and again in 1921 were not able to deal with them effectively. Mussolini organized groups of men—mostly thugs—from among the ex-soldiers of the war, calling them *fascio di combattimento*, groups of combatants—derived from the Latin word *fasces* (the bundle of sticks carried by *lectors* of ancient Rome as symbols of power)—and dressed them in uniforms of black shirts. These were his core supporters. When his attempts at winning power through elections in 1921 brought him only about 7 percent of the vote, he turned his men loose on the streets to beat up labor organizers, communists, socialists, and local officials belonging to communist and socialist parties. The fascists claimed that they killed 3,000 opponents in Italy from 1920 to 1922.

Announcing that the nation had descended into chaos, Mussolini declared a "March on Rome" in 1922 and threatened to take over the government. The government capitulated to his threat and asked him to take over for a year as prime minister with full emergency powers. In the next elections, in 1924, Mussolini's party—through the use of violence, intimidation, and fraud—took more than 60 percent of the vote. Seizing control of the state, Mussolini abolished all other parties, took away the right to strike, destroyed labor unions, and sharply censored the press. He instituted his own propaganda wing within the government to indoctrinate Italy into endorsing his programs. He organized the country according to twenty-two major economic categories. For each category he had fascist representatives of labor, employers, and government meet together to decide wages, prices, working conditions, and industrial policies. All of them were assigned to a government minister and brought into the parliament. In fear of Mussolini's power, organised labor toed the line. Mussolini built roads, drained several hundred thousand acres of swamp lands for wheat production and malaria control, and "made the trains run on time". While communists, socialists, liberals, and labor union leaders had little appreciation for either the man or his methods, businessmen and others wanting a society that functioned with little public turmoil gave their approval. They also took patriotic pride in the new colonial war that he led. In 1935, Mussolini attacked Ethiopia, completing his conquest there in 1936. When the League of Nations demanded Italian withdrawal, Mussolini scoffed. The League did nothing of substance to push him, and Mussolini withdrew Italy from the League.

Benito Mussolini (*center*) during the Fascist march on Rome, 1922. Mussolini glorified violence and employed armed thugs against his opponents. His methods worked. Even his threat to march his troops into Rome was enough to force the feckless Italian government to hand power over to him.

Germany

Mussolini's fascism drew the admiration of the young Adolf Hitler in Germany. Born in Austria, Hitler dropped out of high school at sixteen and went to the national capital, Vienna, at nineteen, supporting himself at odd jobs, especially painting pictures. Much in pre-war Vienna offended him: the wealthy royalty and aristocrats of the court; the prosperous businessmen; the socialist workers; the easy internationalism of the artists and the intellectuals; and, most of all the Jews, who had assimilated into Austrian society and often held high positions in business and the professions. Like many in Vienna, Hitler became a virulent racist, exalting the "pure" German "race" and disparaging all others in a hierarchy that stretched downward from northern Europeans to southern Europeans, to Africans, to Jews at the very bottom.

Moving to Munich in south Germany in 1913, Hitler felt himself more at home. When war broke out, he volunteered for military service—serving as a dispatch runner—and came to value warfare as a blood-stirring and liberating experience. After the war, he began to work against the communist influences that were spreading among workers. In 1919 he joined the anti-communist German Workers' party and became its head. He transformed the party into the National Socialist German Workers' party—abbreviated as "Nazi"—thus launching his political career. Following Mussolini's model, the Nazis built up a group of storm troopers (the SA)—a paramilitary organization that often carried out violence in the streets—and gave them a uniform of brown shirts. The organization of these thugs was just one sign of Hitler's disdain for the democratic German government of his day, usually called the Weimar

Republic for the city in which it met. As in Italy, many people in Germany preferred the order imposed by these paramilitary groups to what they perceived as the weakness of parliament and the street demonstrations of communists and socialists.

The Weimar Republic, an elected government of both working- and middle-class membership, had succeeded the German monarchy which withdrew from power at the end of the war. Both the militant right wing, who wanted a more centralized and powerful government under more autocratic leadership—like the Nazis—and the militant left wing, who wanted a socialist or even communist government and hoped for a revolution like that in Russia, had little respect for Weimar. Both saw the centrist government as too weak.

1923 was an especially difficult year. Germany could not keep up with its payments of war reparations. In response, France seized the highly industrialized Ruhr valley, provoking national outrage in Germany, a good part of it directed against the weakness of the Weimar government itself. In addition, extraordinary inflation completely eroded the value of the German mark, making it hardly worth the paper it was printed on, wiping out the savings of the middle class, impoverishing the lives of workers, and endangering the stability of the government. Among those who further inflamed public opinion against the government, Hitler attempted a *putsch*, a revolt, to overthrow it, in Munich in 1923. Some army officers had already attempted a *putsch* in 1920 but failed. Hitler also failed, and was imprisoned for nine months. But he gained greater popular attention and during his months in jail he wrote *Mein Kampf* (*My Struggle*), his political manifesto, filled with his denunciation of the government, strident nationalism, plans for a Germany restored to—and beyond—her former greatness, the subordination of eastern Europe to Germany, and bitter, all-consuming anti-Semitism. He blamed Jews for being on the left with the communists, on the right with the capitalists, too foreign and exotic, and too assimilated into modern German life. For Hitler, Jews had become the scapegoat whom he could blame for all of Germany's woes.

Recognizing, and frightened by, the dangers of an unstable Germany, the French withdrew from the Ruhr, and the former wartime Allies (excluding the Soviet Union) rescheduled the reparation debts to make them less onerous. For a few years, prosperity returned, but then the international depression of 1929 swept the country back into poverty and renewed humiliation. Germany seethed in anguish. From communists on the left to Hitler on the right, German democracy was held responsible for the nations troubles. Hitler's became the strongest voice. In a series of national elections from 1928 to 1932, his Nazi party's proportion of seats in the German parliament, the Reichstag, went from about 2 percent to about 46 percent, although in the next election, later in 1932, it fell to just below 40 percent. He gained support not only from backers who approved his entire program, but also from many conservatives, including army officers and influential business people, who differed on many points from Hitler's crude nationalism and racism, but who saw him as their chief defense against communism, which they feared even more. In 1933, German political leaders turned to Hitler—the head of the largest single party in the Reichstag—to head a coalition government. Hitler became chancellor of Germany by entirely legal processes. In order to rule without the constraints of a coalition, Hitler called for another election later in the year. In a contest marked by the violence of the SA, suspension of freedoms of speech and press, and a fire in the Reichstag building that Hitler blamed on the communists, the Nazis gained 44 percent of the vote. This was not enough, so Hitler announced a national emergency and, again using his SA thugs to intimidate the opposition, got the votes of a majority of the Reichstag to rule as dictator.

Once in power, Hitler moved swiftly to establish the kind of state that is often called totalitarian—that is, a state in which the individual is subordinated to a centralized administration that controls the national economy, politics, media, and culture, usually under a single dictator or a small council. As Mussolini had himself called *Duce*, so Hitler had himself called *Führer*, leader. In 1925, Hitler had created the SS, another paramilitary organization, dressed in black uniforms. Though initially subordinated to the SA, they rose in prominence. All political parties apart from the Nazis were abolished, and leading Nazis who were viewed as opponents of Hitler were murdered on 30 June, 1934 in an operation carried out by the SS. A secret police force, the *Gestapo*, was established in 1936. Opposition leaders proposing anti-Hitler ideologies were killed or dispatched to concentration camps. Churches were forbidden to criticize the government, and they were encouraged

Nazi Party rally. Over 750,000 Nazi Party workers, soldiers, and civilians greeted Adolf Hitler at the 1934 Nuremberg conference. Against the backdrop of a giant swastika, the German chancellor proclaimed that the Third Reich would last for the next thousand years. Ironically, the trial of Nazi war criminals by the victorious Allied powers would take place in the same city eleven years later.

to cut their ties with overseas branches of their denominations. By contrast, the government encouraged the worship of pre-Christian Teutonic gods. Strikes were forbidden and employers were granted new powers in dealing with workers. Policies were based on "racial science," with Aryans declared to be the most elevated of races, Jews the lowest. Jews were dismissed from public office, including university service and the civil service. In 1935 they were stripped of citizenship.

Why did people tolerate this new order? Some, of course, accepted the new, totalitarian order as appropriate. Others, frightened by the prospect of chaos, impoverishment, and communism, saw it as a severely flawed, but better, alternative. Also, Hitler commanded the use of force in the country, now not only through the SS, but through the legitimate use of the army, police, and secret police. Citizens could protest only at risk to their life and safety. Finally, Hitler's program for rebuilding the country economically and militarily had great appeal. So, too, did his emphasis on the need for *lebensraum*, space for living, an expansion of Germany's territory first into Austria and Czechoslovakia and then through Poland, the Ukraine, and Russia. The Nazi propaganda machine, orchestrated by Joseph Goebbels, indoctrinated the nation, often spreading "the big lie," because, as Hitler said, "in the big lie there is always a certain force of credibility."

Hitler set the nation to work on programs of public works, building housing and superhighways, draining swamps, and reforesting rural areas. In 1936, following the Soviet model, he introduced state planning, although unlike the Russian case, he worked within the framework of private property. He urged Germany to become economically self-sufficient, and its skilled scientists developed many artificial products—such as rubber, plastics, and synthetic fibers—that enabled it to reduce its imports. Germans went back to work. Germany escaped the severe unemployment suffered in most European countries during the Great Depression. The most remarkable dimension of his rebuilding program, however, was the most dangerous and

Führer German for "leader", the title taken by Hitler to assert his total control over Germany.

most threatening: In violation of the Paris peace accords, Hitler began rebuilding Germany's military, and soon he deployed these forces in missions that precipitated world war.

Hitler's Germany shared many characteristics with Mussolini's Italy. Both had developed strong governments that brooked no opposition. Both followed policies of militarism and glorified war. The leaders in both set themselves up as the unchallenged and unchallengeable center of their states. In October 1936, the two governments proclaimed an "axis" that bound them together in international affairs. In the next month, Germany signed an Anti-Comintern Pact with Japan, pledging mutual support against possible attacks from the USSR. The next few years brought these three countries—Germany, Italy, and Japan—together as the axis powers in World War II.

Japan

During the Meiji restoration, Japan had achieved an astonishingly rapid reorganization of government, administration, economy, industry, and finances.

As we saw in Chapter 18, Japan followed Western examples in asserting a sphere of influence in China and seized colonies for itself. It defeated China in Korea in 1895 and became the dominant nation of east Asia, reversing its previous student–teacher relationship with China. Japan made Korea and the island of Taiwan into colonies and defeated Russia by land and sea in East Asia, in 1904–5, after signing a military alliance with Britain in 1902. For the first time in modern history, an Asian country had defeated a European one.

World War I also touched East Asia and profoundly affected its postwar politics. Japan was seated as one of the victorious Five Great Powers at the 1919 peace conference in Paris—the only non-Western nation accepted as an equal at the proceedings. It was assigned control over Germany's Pacific colonies, including the Liaotung Peninsula in north China, which Japan had seized in 1914. This led to the "May Fourth" movement of Chinese students in China, originally a student demonstration that metamorphosed into a broader intellectual movement for Chinese reforms (see Chapter 19). In the end, the Chinese refused to sign the Versailles Treaty.

World War I presented Japan with an unprecedented economic opportunity. While other industrialized countries were occupied with war in Europe, Japan developed its industries relatively free from competition. Between 1914 and 1918 Japan's gross national income rose by 40 percent, and for the first time Japan began to export more than she imported. Heavy industry showed particularly impressive growth. Manufacturing increased by 72 percent while the labor force expanded by only 42 percent, indicating the growing use of machinery to increase productivity. Transport increased by 60 percent. Between 1914 and 1919 Japan's merchant marine almost doubled, to 2.8 million tons. The production and export of consumer goods also advanced. In the first decades of the twentieth century, Japan's most important exports were textiles, primarily silk, 80 percent of which was produced by women.

As a latecomer, Japan could take advantage of technology already developed in the West (the "leapfrogging" path that Trotsky preached in Russia). Japanese industries practiced three different patterns in importing that technology. Some signed agreements with foreign firms to establish branches in Japan; some negotiated for licenses to use the new technologies; and some practiced "reverse engineering," analyzing foreign machinery and reproducing it with adaptations appropriate to Japanese needs. Adaptation produced innovations—for example, in applying chemical research to agricultural and even ceramics production. Private firms imported most of the foreign technology, but the government also encouraged research by funding state universities, laboratories, and the development of military technology.

Japan bridged the "dual economy," the separation between large-scale and cottage industries that has inhibited growth in many countries. In a "dual economy," one sector consists of large, highly capitalized, technically advanced factories employing thousands of workers producing modern products; the other sector includes small-scale workshops, with relatively low capitalization and less up-to-date equipment, often employing fewer than thirty workers, producing traditional goods. In most countries, the small-scale sector tends to shrivel as larger firms achieve economies of scale and put it out of business. Governments, too, often invest their resources in large industries, neglecting the small sector. But in Japan, the smaller factories adopted appropriate scale, new technologies, and began to produce new goods needed by the larger industries. From the early years of the century, Japan evolved systems of sub-contracting between the large and small sectors, which made them interdependent and complementary.

Because of poor harvests in 1918 the price of rice, Japan's staple food, rose sharply. In response, massive riots broke out in hundreds of cities and towns, involving some 700,000 people, lasting fifty days, and resulting in 25,000 arrests and 1000 deaths. The government responded by importing rice and other staples from its colonial territories in Korea and Taiwan. The riots represented the growth of Japan's urban voice as the urban proportion of the population rose from just over 10 percent in 1890 to close to 50 percent in the 1920s (to 78 percent in the 1990s). Labor was increasingly organized and the citizenry politicized. In 1925 all male subjects over the age of twenty-five, 12.5 million people, were given the vote.

The riots also reminded Japan of its increasing dependence on its colonies for daily commodities. In the later 1920s, Taiwan and Korea provided four-fifths of Japan's rice imports and two-thirds of its sugar. For industrial raw materials, such as minerals, metals, petroleum, fertilizers, and lumber, Japan had to look farther afield, and this would lead it into fatal colonial adventures.

In the 1920s, industrial production increased by two-thirds, and the **zaibatsu** (huge holding companies or conglomerates) came to control much of the Japanese economy and were very influential in politics. The four largest—Mitsui, Mitsubishi, Sumitomo, and Yasuda—were controlled by individual families, and each operated a bank and numerous enterprises in a variety of industries, ranging from textiles to shipping and machinery. A Mitsubishi mining company, for example, would extract minerals, which would then be made into a product by one of the Mitsubishi manufacturing companies. Next, this product would be marketed abroad by a Mitsubishi trading firm and transported in ships of another Mitsubishi affiliate. The whole process would be financed through the Mitsubishi bank.

The *zaibatsu* combined large size with an ability to shift production to meet demands. The *zaibatsu* families also held

zaibatsu (Japanese: "wealthy clique") A large Japanese business conglomerate holding many different companies, usually under the control of a single family.

Workers winding induction regulator coils in a Shibaura Engineering Works plant, Tsurumi, Honshu, Japan, 1930. In the 1920s–1930s the Japanese often borrowed from Western models by inviting foreign firms to establish Japanese branches; by obtaining licenses to produce foreign technologies; and by adapting those technologies to Japanese conditions. Their industries consequently "leapfrogged" ahead very rapidly.

Samurai warrior. The ancient and proud warrior class of the samurai worshiped athletic prowess, swordsmanship, and fierce loyalty to the emperor. In 1877 the last 400,000 samurai were pensioned off to become *shizoku,* Japanese gentry, but their virtues lived on in the country's psyche. In times of crisis, the warriors' values turned Japanese nationalism into a potent force.

considerable influence in government, both through the money they controlled and their close family links with prominent politicians. The Major Industries Control Law of 1931, for example, encouraged large companies in key industries to join in cartels to regulate production and prices.

International respect, growing wealth, rising urbanization, increasing industrialization, high rates of literacy, universal male suffrage (1925), and the institutionalization of political parties suggested that Japan was embracing liberal democracy. But the political power of the *zaibatsu* undermined people's faith in democratic practice, and the military held extraordinary power, both under law and in popular opinion. In contrast to most democratic countries, in which the civilian government controls the military, Japanese law specified that the ministers of war and of the navy had to be active generals or admirals. Conversely, the formal powers of the diet were restricted. In theory, the Japanese emperor held the ultimate political authority for the country, and, although he never did govern actively, political leaders speaking in his name dominated public policy at home and abroad. Japan's traditional Shinto religion (see Chapter 9) emphasized the emperor's divinity and asserted the leading role of Japan's samurai warrior ethic.

Many of these military elites began to claim expanded powers for the armed forces. They wished to protect Japan, a resource-poor island nation, especially vulnerable to shifts in international trade and its regulation. The world depression of 1929 shocked the Japanese economy as the value of exports dropped 50 percent between 1929 and 1931. Unemployment rose to 3 million, with rural areas hardest hit. Many civilians seemed to agree with the military: the future would look brighter if Japan could reorganize and control the economy of East Asia for its own benefit. Although the civilian government continued to criticize the military, generals increasingly gained control of the state and turned it toward military goals.

THE DESCENT TOWARD WORLD WAR

The 1920s appeared to usher in a time of peace. The League of Nations had been founded in 1920. The league was not entrusted with peace-keeping missions, but it was expected to be a forum in which international conflicts could be managed through negotiations. It also carried out valuable humanitarian work in fighting epidemic disease in eastern Europe and in resettling political refugees—Russians fleeing the communism of the Soviet Union and Greeks and Armenians expelled from Turkey, for example. The league's Intellectual Cooperation Organization sponsored cultural activities that brought together people from around the world. The organization's annual meetings in Geneva, Switzerland, attracted representatives not only from western European countries and the United States, but also from Mexico, Venezuela, Brazil,

Japan, China, India, Egypt, Poland, Czechoslovakia, and Hungary. They highlighted the increasingly global interaction of the arts and the desire for a free flow of artistic expression.

Individual nations took various steps to prevent war and promote peace. In 1921, a conference was convened in Washington to set limits on competition in naval forces. It achieved agreement on a 5:5:3 ratio in the total tonnage of large ships among Britain, the United States, and Japan, with other World War allies accepting lower limits. In 1925, the major powers, meeting in Locarno, Switzerland, signed a number of agreements designed to relieve some of the burden of guilt that Germany had been forced to accept for World War I and to reintegrate Germany into the European diplomatic world. Germany accepted its western borders with France and Belgium unconditionally and agreed that it would use only diplomacy, and not force, in any attempt to alter its eastern borders with Poland and Czechoslovakia. To reinforce this agreement, France agreed to defend Poland and Czechoslovakia in case of any future attack. (Britain did not sign, arguing that its interests were not involved.) In 1928, sixty-five nations signed the Pact of Paris, known as the Kellogg–Briand Pact for the American secretary of state Frank Kellogg and the French foreign minister Aristide Briand who prepared the groundwork. The signatories to this pact agreed to renounce war as a means of settling international conflicts. By 1928, optimism—and prosperity—had returned to the European world. By 1925, the index of manufacturing in western and central Europe surpassed that of pre-war 1913. (Russia, the worst-hit of all world powers by the war, had returned only to 70 percent, from a low of 13 percent in 1920.) Lasting peace, too, seemed to have been achieved.

And then came the Great Depression and its economic and political pressures. Most remarkably, as the democratic, capitalistic countries of western Europe, the United States, and Latin America struggled with the world depression of the 1930s, the USSR (see Chapter 19), Germany, Italy, and Japan were thriving. Each of the four had adopted dictatorship, national planning, and militarization. Indeed three of them—Germany, Italy, and Japan—launched military campaigns that ultimately resulted in World War II, and the fourth, the USSR, built up a massive military force in anticipation of having to fight them off. The build-up of the militaries and the war campaigns fed on one another. The cost of maintaining the armed forces became so exorbitant that only war victories could pay for them, and to achieve war victories ever-increasing militarization was necessary.

The steps to war unfolded in the 1930s. In 1931, strongly influenced by its wealthy business conglomerates, the *zaibatsu*, and by hyper-nationalist officers in the armed forces, Japan seized Chinese arsenals in Manchuria and began to take over the entire province. Japanese troops had been in place in Manchuria since their victory over the Russians in 1905. As justification for the takeover, they blamed China for the murder of a Japanese officer in Mukden, Manchuria, and for economic boycotts of Japanese goods. In 1932, Japan declared Manchuria an independent state, which it then ruled by establishing the last Chinese emperor, Pu Yi, who had been deposed in 1911, as a puppet head of government. The government was nominally Chinese but the Japanese pulled the strings. China, joined by several small nations, protested to the League of Nations. Japan quit the league, and, in any case, the league took no serious action. None of the other powers felt threatened. They did not want to commit troops, and the western Europeans did not want to alienate Japan at a time when they felt the need for Japan as a partner in a quiet alliance against the Soviet Union. As noted above, many in Japan opposed Japanese militarism, but, as in Germany, violent attacks stifled the opposition. Between 1930 and 1936, two prime ministers, one finance minister, and one important banker were assassinated. Speaking out against militarism in Japan was dangerous.

In 1935, Italy invaded Ethiopia. Once again, the League of Nations imposed no serious response when Ethiopia, a member nation of the league, lodged a protest to the international body.

In 1936, civil war broke out in Spain. The country had been in turmoil as a relatively bloodless revolution deposed the king of Spain in 1931 and established a democratic Spanish republic. For five years, power oscillated between conservative rightists—including members of the clergy, the military, and business elites—and the liberal leftists—including workers, socialists, communists, and anarchists. In elections in 1936, the leftists won, and the rightists, led by General Francisco Franco, began an insurrection that turned into a civil war. Many observers called this a dress rehearsal for World War II because Germany and Italy sent men (Italy sent 50,000 soldiers), money, and weapons to aid Franco and the rightists, while the Soviet Union sent technicians, political advisers, and equipment to bolster the republican government. The major democratic governments of western Europe—including Britain and France—condemned Franco, but sent no support and prohibited the shipment of weapons. The United States declared its neutrality and declared an embargo on the export of arms to Spain. Privately, thousands of volunteers from the democratic nations went to Spain as volunteers to serve with the republican forces. Ernest Hemingway immortalized this International Brigade in his novel *For Whom the Bell Tolls.* Hitler used the war as an opportunity to test the utility of the air force that he was building. Mostly he used them to transport Franco's troops, but on April 28, 1937, German air force squadrons supporting Franco bombed and destroyed the unprotected civilian town of Guernica, the capital of the Basque region of northern Spain. Pablo Picasso, a Spaniard, and probably the most famous painter of his time, immediately painted *Guernica*, perhaps the most famous anti-war painting in history, depicting the anguish, pain, and suffering of men, women, children, and animals. The Spanish Civil War continued on for three years; 600,000 people died. Franco's victory established a right-wing dictatorship that lasted four decades until he died in 1975. The League was not able to resolve the conflicting claims peacefully, and it commanded no armed forces of its own. Armed nationalism triumphed over unarmed internationalism.

Pablo Picasso, *Guernica,* **1937.** Painted as a protest over the German bombing of the little village of Guernica during the Spanish Civil War, this became one of the most famous of all anti-war paintings. Picasso refused to allow it to be moved to Spain from France until after Franco's death in 1975.

On July 7, 1937, Japan invaded China. The pretext was an assault on Japanese troops near Beijing; the goal was the takeover of China. Within months, Japan gained control of most of the densely populated eastern half of the country, although the Chinese withdrew ever deeper into the interior and continued to fight until the very end of World War II. The League of Nations condemned Japan, but took no substantive action. The Japanese refer to this war as the "Pacific War." In global terms, the Japanese invasion of China is usually considered the beginning of World War II, although the war in Europe did not begin until September 1939.

In Europe, after his appointment as chancellor in 1933, Hitler began almost immediately to expand Germany's military position despite the restrictions of the Paris peace treaties. In 1933 he took Germany out of the League of Nations and out of a disarmament conference that was taking place at the time. In 1934, Nazis in neighboring Austria assassinated the prime minister and demanded union with Germany. Hitler's takeover of Austria at this time was prevented only by Mussolini, who declared his opposition to German troops occupying a neighboring country and stationed Italian troops at the Austrian border. In 1935, Nazi intimidation influenced voters in the rich, industrialized Saar region, on the border with France, to vote for annexation to Germany. Most provocatively, in 1935, Hitler began to re-arm Germany. In 1936 he sent his new troops into the Rhineland, German territory just west of the Rhine river, that had been designated a demilitarized zone. No one acted to oppose him. In March 1938, now with Mussolini's consent, German troops moved into Austria, declaring an Anschluss, or union, of the two countries.

Next Hitler focused on Czechoslovakia, and in particular the Sudeten area of that country where some 3 million Germans lived as a minority in the larger Slavic state. He threatened to invade the Sudetenland to annex it to Germany. As fears of war spread, the British prime minister, Neville Chamberlain, and the French premier, Edouard Daladier, flew to Munich to negotiate the fate of Czechoslovakia. They persuaded the Czechs to cede the Sudetenland to Germany, which left the rest of the country open to further German unilateral action. They had persuaded Czechoslovakia to sign its death warrant. They had bought off Hitler by offering up Czechoslovakia, not allowing themselves to realize that they had only delayed the war that was to come. The image of Chamberlain returning from Munich to London proclaiming that he had won "peace for our time" has, ever since, served as a symbol of the folly of appeasing aggressors. The Germans invaded and took over the remainder of Czechoslovakia in March 1939. In the next month, Italy took over Albania.

Russia had agreed to fight against Germany over the issue of Czechoslovakia, if only the French or British would join in, but they would not. Indeed, the British seemed to give more diplomatic attention to Germany, their potential enemy, than to Russia, their potential ally. On August 23, 1939, Russia stunned the

THE MARCH TO WAR	
1935–36	Italy conquers Ethiopia
1936–39	Spanish Civil War
July 7, 1937	Japanese troops invade China
Sept 1938	Appeasement in Munich; Germany annexes Sudetenland
Sept 1939	Nazi-Soviet Pact: Germany invades Poland; Britain and France declare war; Poland partitioned between Germany and Russia
Mar–Apr 1940	*Blitzkrieg*: German forces conquer Denmark and Norway
May–June 1940	Italy declares war on Britain and France; German forces conquer France, the Netherlands, and Belgium
June 1940 –June 1941	Battle of Britain; Britain holds firm against German bombing attacks
June 21, 1941	German forces invade USSR
Dec 7, 1941	Japanese bomb US Navy, Pearl Harbor
Jan–Mar 1942	Japan conquers Indonesia, Malaya, Burma and the Philippines
June 1942	US Navy defeats Japanese at the Battle of Midway
1942–43	End of Axis resistance in North Africa; Soviet victory in Battle of Stalingrad
1943–44	Red Army slowly pushes Wehrmacht back to Germany
June 6, 1944	Allies land in Normandy (D-Day)
Feb 1945	Yalta conference: Churchill, Roosevelt, and Stalin discuss post-war settlement
March 1945	US planes bomb Tokyo
May 7, 1945	Germany surrenders
August 6, 9, 1945	US drops atom bomb on Hiroshima, and then on Nagasaki
August 14, 1945	Japan surrenders

world by signing a non-aggression pact with Germany, its geopolitical archenemy and ideological rival. A secret protocol of the treaty was an agreement to divide up Poland between them if Poland's territory would ever be conquered. For Hitler, the way was now clear. On September 1, German forces invaded Poland. On September 3, Britain and France finally declared war on Germany. The European theater of World War II had opened.

The early results were ominous. Implementing its strategy of *Blitzkrieg*, lightning war, Germany sent one million troops into Poland, with armored forces in the front and air support above. Poland was not equipped to defend itself, and within a month organized resistance had ended. Germany incorporated western Poland into its new empire. Meanwhile Russia invaded and seized eastern Poland, in accord with its non-aggression pact with Germany. Russia also stationed troops in the Baltic countries of Lithuania, Latvia, and Estonia and attacked Finland militarily to seize part of its land. The League of Nations expelled Russia, but the Russians got the land they wanted from the Finns.

The Early Cost of War Technology

The figures on the military build-up demonstrate the shift from technologies of peace to technologies of war that had occurred throughout the 1930s. The military expenses of the USSR, high even at the outset, multiplied almost eight times; Japan's also multiplied eight times; Germany's, highly restricted by postwar agreements, 46 times.

Defense Expenditures of the Great Powers, 1930–38
(millions of current dollars)

	Japan	Italy	Germany	USSR	UK	France	USA
1930	218	266	162	722	512	498	699
1938	1,740	746	7,415	5,429	1,863	919	1,131

Germany, Japan, and the USSR were all spending about one-fourth of their total national income on defense in 1937, Japan and the USSR slightly more, Germany slightly less. By 1938, Japan's military expenses took up 70 percent of the government's national budget; Germany's 52 percent; Russia's in 1940 reached 33 percent (Kennedy, pp. 300–332). Figures on aircraft production mark the shift to military spending in very specific terms:

Aircraft Production of the Powers, 1932–39

	Japan	Italy	Germany	USSR	UK	France	USA
1932	691	*c*. 500	36	2,595	445	*c*. 600	593
1939	4,467	*c*. 2,000	8,295	10,382	7,940	3,163	2,195

Preparations for war had been going on for a decade.

WORLD WAR II

The War in Europe, 1939–45

After their declaration of war, France and Britain took no immediate military action against Germany and the lull through the winter of 1939–40 is often called the "phony war." In April 1940, however, Hitler resumed his strategy of *blitzkrieg*. Germany invaded Denmark and Norway. On May 10, Germany invaded Belgium, Luxemburg, the Netherlands, and France. Nothing could stop them. The French had prepared an elaborate "Maginot Line" of defended trenches, underground bunkers, minefields, and barbed wire that they thought impregnable. The Germans went around the line to the northwest and penetrated France. German tanks also entered France through Luxemburg and the Ardennes forest, which the French had thought impassable by tanks. Everywhere the Germans scored victories. With Rotterdam under air attack, the Netherlands surrendered. Belgium sued for peace. British, and some French, troops retreated to the French seaport of Dunkirk, and on June 4, leaving their armor behind them, they were hastily evacuated to England. On June 10, Mussolini joined in the attack on France, and soon invaded Greece as well. On June 13, the Germans occupied Paris, and on June 22, France surrendered. The country had been conquered in only one month of fighting. Germany chose to administer the northern two-thirds of France directly. The southern third was administered from the town of Vichy by French officials who collaborated with the Germans. Some French joined General Charles de Gaulle with French forces in exile; some began guerrilla warfare against the Germans. Most acquiesced in the conquest and went about their daily life under German occupation.

World War II in Europe. Fighting began in 1939 with a "blitzkrieg," or lightning war, by Germany and her Italian ally. By late 1942 they controlled most of Europe. But Germany's invasion of Russia in 1941 brought the power of that huge state into opposition and enmeshed Germany into exhausting land war. Britain held out defensively and then began to fight back, especially after the United States entered the war, bringing in air power and material support. By early 1944, the tide had turned.

For an interactive version of this map, go to: http://www.prenhall.com/spodek/map20.1

Britain now stood alone against Germany, and Hitler attacked. He launched heavy bombing of London and other strategic cities in Britain throughout the summer and autumn. Prime minister Winston Churchill, who, at the age of sixty-six, had replaced Chamberlain in May 1940, confronted directly the desperation of the situation and addressed his nation in rhetoric that stirred the blood and strengthened the backbone. Within a few days of assuming office, he announced in Parliament: "I have nothing to offer but blood, toil, tears, and sweat!" And a month later:

> We shall go on to the end, we shall fight in France, we shall fight on the seas and oceans, we shall fight with growing confidence and growing strength in the air, we shall defend our island, whatever the cost may be, we shall fight on the beaches, we shall fight on the landing grounds, we shall fight in the fields and in the streets, we shall fight in the hills; we shall never surrender.

Despite heavy losses, including 20,000 dead in London alone, the British held firm, thanks to the Royal Air Force, the invention of radar, and success in cracking German secret codes. By the end of 1940, Germany abandoned the "Battle of Britain" in the air, and gave up plans to invade the island by sea.

To the east, the USSR, operating under cover of the non-aggression pact, had not only seized the eastern half of Poland, and parts of Finland, and incorporated the Baltic States into its empire, it had also seized and incorporated parts of Romania that it had lost in World War I and began to move toward the Balkan states. Hitler moved first. He brought Romania, Bulgaria, and Hungary into the Axis, and occupied Yugoslavia and Greece. Then, in an unexpected, fierce attack, he turned his forces eastward, broke the non-aggression treaty, and invaded Russia on June 22, 1941, a date thereafter viewed in Russia as its Pearl Harbor. A German army of 3 million men and some 3,500 armored vehicles, covered by the air support of the *Luftwaffe* (the Nazi air force), invaded a 2,000-mile front in Russia. The Russians retreated from the central European lands they had taken, and hundreds of miles into the interior of their own country. They transported whole industrial plants deep into the interior. Finally, Stalin, who had been taken completely by surprise by the attack despite his years of preparation for warfare, counter-attacked. The Russian army, under General Georgi Zhukov, pushed the Germans back from their positions around Moscow, relieving that capital city. The Germans, like Napoleon a century and a half earlier, retreated from Moscow in the face of the counter-offensive and the severe winter.

The European war had another front in North Africa. In September 1940, the Italians, who held Libya, invaded Egypt, heading for the Suez Canal. To protect the canal, Churchill diverted troops and supplies from the Battle of Britain to North Africa. The British forces defeated the Italians in Egypt and Libya and even forced them out of Ethiopia. The Germans, however, under General Rommel, entered North Africa and

German soldiers on the Eastern Front, Russia, October 1941. The men moving this field gun into position for the Russian front were Hitler's most elite soldiers, SS Troops of the Police Division. The man in the foreground (*right*) is a "runner" from the cycling troops.

battles raged back and forth between them and the British in 1941 and 1942. British lines, however, held at El Alamein, west of Alexandria, and the Suez Canal remained in British hands. Nevertheless, German submarines in the Mediterranean closed down transportation across the sea, and took a heavy toll on shipping across the Atlantic.

Hitler re-organized his Russian campaign in 1942, directing his troops to the south, in the direction of the rich oil fields of the Caucasus Mountains and the Caspian Sea. By the summer of 1942, Germany had taken all of the western possessions of Russia—the Baltic States, Byelorussia, Poland, and the Ukraine—and stood at the gateway to Leningrad. It held its lines not very far from Moscow, and besieged Stalingrad. Historians sometimes compare Hitler's position to that of Napoleon. Each man held approximately the same areas of Western Europe and each launched an assault into Russia that would devastate the country and force it into deep retreat, but would also leave Germany itself exhausted. To the west, each faced a determined Britain that responded to attacks with unexpected, and ultimately victorious tenacity. The presence of the United States in World War II, however, added a new and additional ingredient into the balance.

From the beginning of the war in Europe, in September 1939, President Roosevelt had supported Britain and the Allies, but his support was limited by the isolationist feelings of many Americans. Roosevelt was able to lift the ban on arms sales in 1939. In 1940, he sent a shipment of arms to England, and later in the same year he added fifty destroyers in exchange for the right to establish military bases in some British possessions in the New World. In 1941, the Congress introduced the Lend–Lease program to provide weapons and supplies to the Allied forces. In 1940 the United States began military conscription, increased the size of its armed forces, and secured bases in Greenland and Iceland in order to protect American and Allied shipping. Still, however, Roosevelt could not commit his country to war—until Japan attacked at Pearl Harbor. To understand this attack, we return to the Pacific theater of warfare.

The War in the Pacific, 1937–42

In 1937, a clash between Chinese and Japanese troops at the Marco Polo Bridge near Beijing triggered a full-scale war with China, which marked the beginning of the Pacific War. The Japanese had not expected the fierce resistance of the Chinese. Planning to end the "China problem" with a single quick victory that would terrify the enemy into suing for peace, the Japanese army launched a full-scale attack on Nanjing, capturing the city in December. Japanese troops murdered, raped, and pillaged in what is now generally known as "the Rape of Nanjing." Twelve thousand noncombatant Chinese were killed in the first two or three days after Nanjing was captured, and about 20,000 cases of rape were reported in the first month. In the first six weeks some 200,000 civilians and prisoners of war were killed in and around the city. The atrocities set an ugly precedent for later Japanese cruelty toward many of the peoples they defeated throughout Asia during the war.

In the face of repeated Japanese advances, the Chinese government retreated to Chongqing, on the upper Yangzi River deep in the interior of the country. The Chinese, like the Russians retreating before the Germans, followed a **scorched-earth** strategy, leaving little in their wake that the enemy could use. The war in China became a stalemate. (Even in 1945, when Japan itself was under attack, about a million Japanese soldiers were still fighting in China, and another 750,000 in Manchuria. China's sheer persistence helped wear out the Japanese.)

In September 1940, Japan signed the Tripartite Pact, formally aligning itself with Germany and Italy as the "Axis Powers." Axis plans, however, were not well coordinated. Japan could have joined in the war against the USSR, opening a second front

scorched earth A strategy of defensive warfare, in which everything that might be of use to an invading army is destroyed by the defending army as it retreats.

from Manchuria, as Germany wished. Instead, it signed a neutrality pact with the Soviet Union in April 1941 and turned southward to capture French Indochina, putting it on a collision course with the USA.

Isolationist pressure in America had thus far kept the USA out of armed warfare, but America did respond to Japanese aggression in China and Southeast Asia by placing an embargo on trade with Japan and by freezing its assets in July 1941. Resource-poor Japan, fearing for its supplies of oil and other raw materials, now had to choose between pulling back from China or confronting the United States in open warfare. Many Japanese resented American resistance to Japan's growing power as just another example of white man's colonialism. On December 7, Japan bombed the American Pacific fleet at Pearl Harbor, Hawaii, with over 300 planes. The Japanese destroyed several battleships and inflicted serious damage on three cruisers, three destroyers, and other ships of various kinds. They also destroyed at least 180 airplanes. Altogether, more than 2,000 people were killed in the attack and over a thousand more were wounded. The attack severely crippled American seapower in the Pacific, though the Navy was able to repair some of the ships. The United States was also extremely fortunate that the three aircraft carriers attached to the Pacific fleet were training elsewhere at the time. America declared war the next day. In Britain, Winston Churchill immediately understood the consequences:

> Hitler's fate was sealed. Mussolini's fate was sealed. As for the Japanese, they would be ground to powder. All the rest was merely the proper application of overwhelming force. (Kennedy, p. 347)

The Japanese leaders who advocated the attacks—and many opposed them—believed that they could defeat America if they struck before American industrial power and troop mobilization could move into high gear. So, on the same day as the attack on Pearl Harbor, Japan also attacked the Philippines, Hong Kong, Malaya, and other bases in Southeast Asia and the Pacific. By the middle of 1942, Japan had conquered the Philippines, the Malay peninsula and Singapore, Indonesia, parts of New Guinea, Indochina, Thailand, and Burma. In the Pacific, it reached almost to Australia. Designating the conquests as the "Greater East Asia Co-Prosperity Sphere," Japan attempted to build an imperial system that would provide raw materials for its industries and markets for its finished products and that would willingly adopt Japanese cultural practices as well.

The plan did not work. The colonial economies could not produce and deliver the supplies that Japan wanted, and, more crucially, Japan could not absorb the agricultural products they could produce. Market structures based on the existing integration of world trade systems were not easily re-organized. Instead of implanting its culture, Japan's occupations generally evoked nationalistic opposition. Japan's treatment of conquered

US servicemen in the Pacific. Landing in Higgins boats from a base in Australia, American troops of the 163rd Infantry Regiment, 41st Division, hit the beach running during the invasion of Wake Island, May 18, 1944. Two months earlier, the United States had begun firebombing Japanese cities.

peoples and prisoners of war was notably harsh and earned it a reputation for cruelty. The brutalizing of thousands of Korean, Chinese, and Filipina women to serve as "sex slaves" for Japanese soldiers came to international attention half a century after the war was over.

Turning the Tide, 1942–5

By the end of 1942 the Allied counter-offensive began. The alliance of Britain, the Free French (an exile government based in London under the leadership of General Charles de Gaulle), the Soviet Union, the United States, and some twenty allied countries slowly evolved. Roosevelt already called them the United Nations. Roosevelt and Churchill, establishing a Combined Chiefs of Staff, decided to concentrate on the western and African fronts, leaving the main fighting against Japan for later.

In the Battle of the Atlantic, British and American navies successfully fought German U-boat (submarine) warfare and opened the ocean to much safer shipping. American troops could now be transported to Europe in relative safety. Under General Eisenhower, Allied forces launched a huge, surprise, amphibious invasion of Algeria and Morocco in November 1942 and pushed eastward. By the spring of 1943 they were met by British forces moving westward from Egypt under General Montgomery, and by May 1943, north Africa was completely recaptured and the sealanes of the Mediter-ranean were again safe for shipping.

The Russians called on its allies to open a massive, land-based western front that would relieve the German pressure on Russia. The Americans and the British deferred such an attack until they had made more thorough preparations, leaving the Russians to rely on their own resources (and to doubt the commitment of the British and Amer-icans to their Russian allies). Nevertheless, in the winter of 1942–3, the Russians held out successfully against German troops at the Battle of Stalingrad, but at the cost of up to a half-million Russian soldiers killed. More Russians died in the Battle of Stalingrad, between September 1942 and February 1943, than Americans died in the entire war. The Axis powers lost fewer, about 150,000 killed and 90,000 captured. Stalingrad was the turning point in the eastern front. Once the siege was lifted, General Zhukov—already a hero for lifting the siege of Moscow in 1941—opened a Russian counter-attack that began to push the Germans steadily westward. By now, also, food, supplies, and material were reaching the Soviet troops under the American Lend–Lease program for the Allies. The millions of Russian troops deployed in these waves of assault tied down millions of Axis troops, as in Operation Bagration, Russia's massive offensive in the summer of 1944. In that year, the Russians recaptured the Ukraine, Byelorussia, the Baltic states, eastern Poland, Romania, and Bulgaria. In early 1945 they entered Germany. These battles on the eastern front also allowed the Allies to open fronts in western Europe with greater safety.

In contrast to the large-scale warfare of the massed armies of the major belligerents, in many countries, partisan, underground resistance also developed—sometimes against the Allies, especially the Russians in eastern Europe, more frequently against the Axis powers. Because warfare had become so mechanized and so overwhelming in its size and scope, the partisans usually had more social and psychological importance than military. In some cases, however, they were quite significant, even militarily.

Yugoslavia presented the most extreme case. It was captured by the Axis powers in April 1941, and partitioned among them, with Germany and Italy taking the largest shares. From one part of the country an independent state of Croatia was created and placed in the charge of the Ustasa party, run by fanatical anti-Serbs. Even the Nazis were shocked at their virulence. Ustasa murdered hundreds of thousands—estimates run as high as 2 million—Serbs and other "undesirables" in 1941. Two groups of

Bombers on a raid. By World War II aircraft of all kinds were poised for aerial combat. Here an SAAF/BAF Beaufighter fires 3-inch RPs during an attack on German positions in the Yugoslavian town of Zuzemberg in 1945. The astronomical cost of bombs and aircraft contributed to the Allies' wartime expenditure of $1,150,000,000,000.

Serbian resistance fighters formed, one led by a Serbian officer in the Yugoslav army, the other by a communist named Josip Broz (1892–1981), who took the name Tito. Tito himself was not a Serb—he had a Croat father and a Slovene mother—but he was willing to work with the Serbs. The two leaders and their groups could not cooperate, so they fought separately against the Axis troops, and sometimes they fought against each other. Tito proved the more effective, and in 1943, after Italy withdrew from the Axis, Britain and America gave him direct support. By the end of the war, Tito commanded some 250,000 men and women and had emerged as the undisputed leader of Yugoslavia.

In the spring of 1943, the American and British air forces, from their bases in Britain, began bombing German cities. Unable to target military positions with accuracy, the air assaults became, in effect, attacks on civilians as well as military objectives. Some officers debated the morality of these attacks, but they continued and increased. Some cities, like Hamburg, were mostly destroyed in fire bombings with far more civilian than military casualties.

On July 10, 1943, the Allies invaded Sicily to begin their Italian campaign, and on July 23, Mussolini's government fell. In September, Italy surrendered and switched sides in the war, joining the Allies. German armies, however, continued to hold Rome. The city was liberated only in June 1944. Finally, the long-awaited land invasion of western Europe began. D-Day, June 6, 1944, brought the largest amphibious military operation in history as Allied forces, American, British, and Canadian troops, under Eisenhower, invaded Normandy and began the push eastward. More than 4,000 ships carried the men; some 10,000 aircraft provided support. On the first day, 130,000 men landed by ship and parachute, one million within a month. Although there were some disagreements over strategy among the Allied generals—the American Eisenhower and the British Montgomery—and some setbacks –as in the Battle of the Bulge in the Ardennes forest of Belgium—the new offensive steadily pushed the Germans back. Paris was liberated in August. Allied troops entered Germany in September.

In the last few months of the war, however, new technologies of destruction were introduced. In September 1944, Germany launched V-2 missiles for the first time against Britain, ushering in an age of missile warfare. In February 1943, the Allies began fire bombing the German city of Dresden, leveling most of it and killing some 50,000 civilians. Since the city had no military or strategic value, the raids were widely condemned as purely punitive. As the Allies finally conquered Germany in bitter combat, the war in Europe finally ended on May 7, 1945 with Germany's surrender. The war in the Pacific continued for another three months.

War in Asia and the Pacific, 1942–5

Even though the War in the Pacific received less Allied attention than the war in Europe, once America committed its industrial and technological strength to fighting Japan, the tide turned. Despite the losses of most of its Pacific fleet, in June 1942 American naval forces won their first battle at Midway Island. Then, from bases in Australia, they moved northwestward, "island hopping," taking Guadalcanal and New Guinea, recapturing the Philippines and the Pacific island chains. During the spring of 1945 they captured Okinawa after three months of brutal fighting. As early as March

1944, the Americans had begun fire bombing Japanese cities. Japan had expected Americans to become tired of the war and negotiate a peace, but instead America demanded unconditional surrender.

The fire bombing intensified. On March 9, 1945, 83,793 people were killed, 40,918 injured, and 267,000 buildings were destroyed in Tokyo alone. Burning and starving—caloric intake had dropped from a daily standard of 2,200 to 1,405 by 1944—Japan fought on. Finally, America dropped the atomic bomb on Hiroshima on August 6, 1945. With the European war won, the USSR invaded Manchuria and Korea on August 8. On August 9, America dropped a second atomic bomb, this time on Nagasaki. On August 15, 1945, Japan offered its unconditional surrender.

Japan lay in ruins. Some 3 million Japanese had died in the war, a fourth of Japan's national assets were destroyed, industrial production was at barely 10 percent of

Summary executions in the Pacific. Japanese soldiers were notoriously brutal in their treatment of prisoners during World War II. British servicemen captured in the Pacific theater were forced to construct the Burma Railway and many died of starvation and disease in the process. Some were murdered in cold blood, as here, the imminent execution of three Allied fighters before open graves.

A-bomb devastation. On August 6, 1945, the "Enola Gay" Super-Fortress aircraft released the first atom bomb ever used in warfare over Hiroshima, an important Japanese military base and seaport. Over 130,000 people were killed or injured and the city was largely flattened. The USA took the action—and again, three days later at Nagasaki—in a (successful) bid to end the Pacific War.

World War II in the Pacific. Japan mounted combined operations in 1941 in East Asia, Southeast Asia, and across the Pacific, opening a war front from the borders of India to Hawaii. This supremely aggressive move was meant to secure the resources and markets needed to sustain the "Greater East Asia Co-Prosperity Sphere." It proved impossible to defend: Chinese resistance, a daring US island-hopping campaign in the Pacific—culminating in the explosion of atomic bombs over Hiroshima and Nagasaki—and Soviet assaults on Manchuria defeated Japan completely.

pre-war levels, millions of homes had been destroyed, and Japan had lost all its colonial holdings. Mass starvation was prevented only by food imported by the occupation authorities.

Assessing the Results of the War

World War II is often called a "total war" because it involved the entire populations and economies of the nations that fought it. The distinction between military and civilian disappeared. Non-combatants were bombed and killed on both sides. It is estimated that about 50 million people died—30 million of them civilians. The heaviest fighting was in the Soviet Union, which lost more people than any other country—about 20 million. Japan lost about 2 million people and Germany just over 4 million. Though there are no reliable statistics, China lost at least a million people. Britain and the United States each lost about 400,000. Six million Jews died in Nazi concentration camps along with hundreds of thousands of Poles, gypsies, homosexuals, and handicapped persons.

Japan's early victories over European colonizers provided a double shock. Asians were able to defeat—at least for some time—the most advanced European countries and the United States. As these victories enhanced the image of Japanese power, they undermined the image of the Europeans in Asia. After the war, when the European colonizers attempted to return—the British to Burma and Malaya, the French to Indochina, the Dutch to Indonesia—local nationalist groups rose in protest, sometimes armed, and eventually achieved independence. In this sense, the Japanese victories were responsible for ending European colonialism in the Pacific region.

Technology in the War

World War II witnessed a dramatic increase in the use of technology—tanks, submarines, and aircraft—as well as the number of troops. The sheer costs were staggering, and the forces that could spend more on armaments won the war. The productivity and availability of aircraft on each side represent their overall technological capacity.

Armaments Production of the Powers, 1940–43 (billions of 1944 dollars)		
	1940	1943
Allied combatants		
USA	(1.5)	37.5
USSR	(5.0)	13.9
Britain	3.5	11.1
Axis combatants		
Germany	6.0	13.8
Japan	(1.0)	4.5
Italy	0.75	—
(Source: Kennedy, p. 355)		

Aircraft Production of the Powers, 1939 and 1944		
	1939	1944
Allied combatants		
USA	5,856	96,318
USSR	10,382	40,300
Britain	7,940	26,461
Axis combatants		
Germany	8,295	39,807
Japan	4,467	28,180
Italy	1,800	—
(Source: Kennedy, p. 354)		

Tanks, too, were vital weapons. In 1944, Germany produced 17,800; Russia, 29,000; Britain, 5,000; and the USA, 17,500 (Kennedy, p. 353). In addition to quantitative superiority, the planes, tanks, and other material produced by the Allies were generally qualitatively more modern and sophisticated than those of the Axis powers. No wonder that after the initial shock and advantage of their first attacks, the Axis powers began steadily to fall behind the Allies. The technological and industrial capacity of the Axis powers simply could not keep up.

Women and the War

The military and industrial needs of World War II put new demands on the labor force and women's lives were deeply affected. The demands of keeping factories running at full blast during the war while putting millions of soldiers onto the battlefields required an unprecedented commitment of labor. Even during World War I, millions of women began to work outside the home for pay, and the stereotypes of "men's work" and "women's work" began to erode. This experience contributed to the achievement of women's suffrage in the United States (1920) and in western Europe. Although South American countries were not much involved in World War I, many of them—Brazil, Cuba, Ecuador, El Salvador, and Uruguay—also granted female suffrage between 1929 and 1939 (Rosenberg, p. 67). After World War I, the majority of women did not remain in the workforce, but after World War II, women continued in unprecedented numbers to work in industrial and unconventional jobs.

The mobilization of women was, however, culturally specific. Different combatant countries followed different family and gender policies. German and Japanese women were encouraged to continue to stay at home, despite the exigencies of war. Women served actively in Russian factories. Britain conscripted some women in World War II.

The Allies—the United States, Britain, and the USSR—generally encouraged women to join the wartime workforce. The image of Rosie the Riveter became the recognized symbol of women's contribution to factory work in the Allied countries. The Axis powers, on the other hand, did their best to keep women at home despite the needs of the war. Hitler offered women "emancipation from emancipation." He offered marriage loans to married women who left their jobs, and then cancelled one-fourth of the loan for the birth of each child. The Nazis banned abortion and closed sexual counseling clinics. Mussolini excluded women from government office, doubled the fees of female students in secondary schools and universities, and tried to prevent rural women from relocating in cities. In China, the communists encouraged women to join in the struggle directly; the nationalists kept them at home.

As the troops returned from war to their old jobs, the tendency was for women to return from factory and military service to the home, both by choice and because of social pressure. However, gender relations could not remain unaffected by wartime experience. After the war, feminism found new voices. Simone de Beauvoir published *The Second Sex* in France in 1949, advancing the argument that while sex is biological, gender, the behavioral traits associated with each sex, is learned. As she wrote: "One is not born, but rather becomes, a woman." In the United States, Betty Friedan's *The Feminine Mystique* (1963) challenged women to ask if life as homemaker in suburbia was fulfilling, to consider working outside the home, and to advocate for equal conditions in that work.

In Europe and the United States the new feminism became a powerful, if controversial force. In other parts of the world, the concept of new roles for women outside the home and community was more disputed. Often the very fact that new concepts of gender relations came from the West, from colonial powers, influenced their reception, making them more attractive to some, more suspect to others.

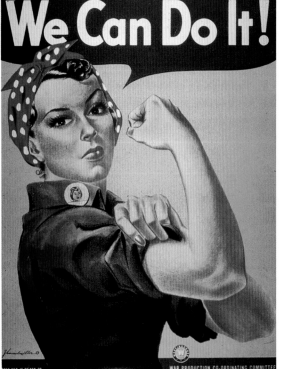

"Rosie the Riveter," symbol of World War II American women workers, on a poster from the War Production Coordinating Committee.

SOURCE

Women as Spoils of War: Japan's Comfort Women

From earliest recorded history, stories of warfare include accounts of soldiers abusing women and of victors seizing women as their reward for victory. The story of Japan's "comfort women" during World War II carries these stories to an unusually cruel extreme. From 1932 to 1945, thousands of women—estimates vary from a few thousand to 200,000—were rounded up and forced into sexual slavery by the Japanese military as "comfort women" serving in "comfort stations"—that is as captive sexual slaves in brothels administered by the Japanese armed forces. Although the situation was widely known in the military and was the subject of a Japanese novel in 1947, later made into a movie, the facts were generally swept under the rug. In 1990, the Korean Council for the Women Drafted for Military Sexual Slavery by Japan began to collect and publish the stories of many Korean women who had been taken by the Japanese and who were willing to talk publicly, forty years after the events.

The Korean women were especially badly treated since the Japanese historically have looked down on Koreans. Subsequently, the Japanese government was called upon to apologize and pay reparations to the women. It has officially refused, although it has encouraged private Japanese donations to the women and it has given some payments without acknowledging official responsibility. The government of Japan has frequently argued that the women were simply sex workers who sold their services to soldiers.

The testimony of Kim Young-shil, interviewed in North Korea in 1992, tells not only of sexual slavery but also of racial cruelty:

There was a girl next to my cubicle. She was younger than I, and her Japanese name was Tokiko. One day an officer overheard her speaking to me and accused her of speaking Korean [which had been forbidden]. He dragged her out to a field and ordered all of us to come out there. We all obeyed. He said, "This girl spoke Korean. So she must die. You will be killed if you do too. Now, watch how she dies." He drew his sword. Horrified, I closed my eyes and turned my face away. When I opened my eyes, I saw her severed head on the ground.

On Sundays we were made especially busy. Soldiers stood in line in front of our cubicles. They got ready for their turn by undoing their puttees from their legs, rolling them up and holding them in their hands. They shamelessly exhibited their lust like animals in heat. Many of them could not control themselves and shouted, "Madaka? Hayaku! Hayaku! [Not finished yet? Hurry! Hurry!] Some even came into my cubicle even before the act was finished.

I was totally exhausted. I could keep neither my sense of humiliation nor my dignity. I felt like a living corpse. When soldiers came to my room and did it to me one after another, it was done to a lifeless body. Again. And again. And again.
(Schellstede, pp. 50–51)

Horrors of the War

Two horrors distinguished World War II from all others that came before. Massive warfare had been known before. So too had leaders bent on world conquest, from Alexander the Great and Chingghis Khan to Napoleon. But the decision by the Nazis to obliterate an entire people—the Jews—from the world, without any ostensible economic or territorial goal, and mobilizing the full resources of the state against an unarmed opponent to carry out the task, constituted a new goal, executed by new technology. It was later given a new name, genocide, the extermination of an entire people.

Anti-Semitism was not new in Europe, but the Nazi program was unprecedented. First, it reversed the trend of acceptance and civic equality for Jews advanced a century and a half earlier by the French Revolution. Second, it targeted Jews as an ethnic or racial group rather than as a religious community. This was not a policy for conversion or even for exile. Anyone with a Jewish grandparent was considered Jewish under Nazi laws and marked for death. Third, it put the entire weight of a nation into the task of wiping a people off the face of the earth, using all the technological and organizational skills at its disposal to carry out the mission, and continuing with it even when it was clear that the larger war was lost.

Hitler had made clear his beliefs in racial hierarchy—with Jews at the bottom. Once in power he set out to enslave and later to exterminate these "lesser peoples." He built concentration camps where prisoners were used as slave labor before being gassed and cremated. Millions of Jews were brought to the camps by a railway network

The liberation of Belsen. Shocked British soldiers liberating Belsen concentration camp in 1945 found 40,000 Jews and other victims of the Holocaust dying of starvation, typhus, and tuberculosis. Many prisoners had been used for medical experiments. Framed by an open grave, a Dr Klein is shown speaking to Movietone News. His experiments included injecting benzine into his victims to harden their arteries. He was responsible for thousands of deaths.

specially constructed for this purpose. Even in the closing days of the war, when Germany clearly had been defeated, Hitler ordered the trains and the crematoria to continue operations. By 1945, some 6 million Jews, accompanied by millions from other "inferior" races, especially gypsies and Poles, joined also by homosexuals and handicapped people, had been murdered. The Holocaust, as this butchery was named, made World War II into a conflict of good versus evil even in the eyes of many Germans after the war. The moral crisis and the appalling devastation of the Holocaust are impossible to fully comprehend, but the writing of survivors such as Elie Wiesel helps us to understand them.

The atomic bombs dropped by the United States on Hiroshima and Nagasaki, Japan, introduced a new weapon ultimately capable of destroying all life on earth, changing both the nature of war and peace as well as humanity's conception of itself. At the first test of the bomb, as the fireball rose over the testing grounds at Alamogordo, New Mexico, J. Robert Oppenheimer, architect of the bomb and director of the $2 billion Manhattan Project that produced it, quoted from the Hindu *Bhagavad Gita*: "I am become as death, the destroyer of worlds." Of the 245,000 people living in Hiroshima on August 6, 75,000 died that day, perhaps another 100,000 thereafter, while still others suffered radiation poisoning, cancer, and genetic deformation. Three days later, a second bomb was dropped on Nagasaki, and on August 14, Japan surrendered unconditionally. Today, despite years of continuing efforts toward arms control, there are tens of thousands of nuclear bombs and warheads on missiles,

Atom bomb test in the Marshall Islands, 1950. The bomb has enormous destruction capability through its sheer explosive power, its radiation, and its ability to plunge the earth's ecology into a "global winter." On the one hand, fear of its power has prevented its use in warfare since 1945. On the other hand, more and more nations have access to the bomb.

submarines, and airplanes capable of destroying human life many times over. Most recently, fears have increased that terrorist individuals or groups might gain access to small nuclear devices.

In retrospect, debate has raged over the wisdom and purpose of using the atomic bomb to end the War in the Pacific. Critics see the act as racist, pointing out that this weapon was not used in Europe (although the bomb had not yet been prepared at the time Germany surrendered in May 1945). Cynics suggest that its real purpose had less to do with defeating Japan than with demonstrating United States power to the USSR on the eve of the Cold War. Those who justify the use of the bomb suggest that losses of life on both sides would have been higher had the Allies invaded Japan's home islands. The use of the bomb certainly saved Allied lives, and may even have saved Japanese lives. The casualties in the battles for Pacific islands had been in the hundreds of thousands, and war in Japan itself might have cost a million Allied troops and even more Japanese. Finally, the advocates argue, in a war of such scope and brutality, combatants inevitably use the weapons that are available.

Some of the war technology, however, had by-products of use to civilians. Radar, which Britain developed to protect itself from Germany in the Battle of Britain in 1940, was valuable in commercial aviation. Nuclear energy could be employed under careful supervision for peaceful uses in power generation and medicine. Drugs, such as sulfa

---

HOW DO WE KNOW?

The Milgram Experiment and The "Final Solution"

How could people carry out acts of such inhumanity as the genocide against the Jews? Perhaps the leaders of Nazi Germany were insane, unrepresentative of normal people. But what about the ordinary Germans who said that they were simply following orders? To what extent do people just follow orders more or less blindly even if they know they are inflicting pain? In 1961, Yale psychologist Stanley Milgram set up an experiment to find out. He solicited volunteers from in and around Yale University. He brought them to a laboratory and explained that the experiment would test the effects of punishment on learning. The volunteer, who was to play the role of "Teacher," was briefly introduced to the "Learner," who was to learn pairs of words read aloud by the Teacher. Each time the Learner failed to learn properly, the experimenter would instruct the Teacher to inflict punishment by delivering an electric shock. The first time, the shock was 15 volts. The second 30, and each successive shock would add 15 additional volts up to a maximum, on the thirtieth failed attempt, of 450 volts.

The Teacher was told that the experiment would test the efficacy of the shocks in promoting learning. In fact, the experiment was to test how much voltage the Teacher would apply to the Learner. Teacher and Learner were sent to separate rooms, but the Teacher could see the Learner through a window. As the Learner made mistakes the experimenter told the Teacher to apply the voltage shocks. At the tenth shock, 150 volts, the Learner—who was an actor playing the role—demanded to be let out of the experiment. But this was not permitted. At this point only ten of the Teachers refused to give any more shocks. Seventy continued applying greater voltage for each wrong answer, in accordance with the experimenter's orders. The Learner continued moaning, shrieking, and demanding to be let out of the experiment. By the time the twentieth shock—300 volts—was administered, the Learner said that he refused to give any more answers. By this point, twenty-one of the volunteers stopped administering shocks despite the commands of the experimenter. At the twenty-first level, the Learner screamed out in sheer pain and gave no answer. Five more volunteers stopped their participation. From the

twenty-third shock onward, the Learner remained silent, perhaps unconscious, perhaps dead. Nevertheless, most Teachers continued applying the shocks on command. Of the eighty volunteers, fifty-one continued to administer the shocks all the way to the top level—450 volts—long after the Learner appeared to be unconscious, if not dead. Milgram concluded that, at least within the confines of this narrowly bounded experiment, "normal" people follow orders in inflicting pain, even to the point of murder, so long as they believe that the person in charge, the experimenter, has the authority and the expertise to give the orders.

- Do you think Milgram's experiment is a valid way to research the question of why apparently normal people followed orders in wartime and the Holocaust? Why or why not?
- If you were the Teacher in the experiment, at what level do you think you would quit? Do you think you are different from the majority here? Why or why not?
- Were you surprised at the results of Milgram's experiment? Why or why not?

and penicillin, entered the civilian pharmacopoeia. But the technology of warfare drew the lion's share of the scientific and technological budgets of many nations, including the largest industrial powers, the United States and the USSR, and of many developing countries, as well.

THE IMAGE OF HUMANITY

Until the eve of World War I, the Western idea of human progress through rationalism, science, and technological progress had been widely accepted. There had been no war between the great European powers since the 1871 conflict between France and Germany, and even that had been relatively small and contained (although 250,000 people died). Democracy seemed both progressive and in the ascendant. Life expectancy and quality seemed to be improving steadily.

The colonial dominance of Europe over ancient Asian and African civilizations had the effect of reaffirming Europeans' belief in the supremacy of their technology and political systems. Students from all over the world were coming to Europe's universities to study Western sciences and arts. If machines were "the measure of man," European civilization measured best of all, and was steadily gaining ground.

Some contrary voices, however, were already breaking through the self-congratulation. Mohandas Gandhi (1869–1948) of India, writing in 1906 in *Hind Swaraj or Indian Home Rule*, caricatured and reevaluated Western accomplishments from a different perspective.

> Formerly when people wanted to fight with one another, they measured between them their bodily strength; now it is possible to take away thousands of lives by one man working behind a gun from a hill. This is civilization. Formerly, men worked in the open air only as much as they liked. Now thousands of workmen meet together and for the sake of maintenance work in factories or mines. Their condition is worse than that of beasts. They are obliged to work, at the risk of their lives, at most dangerous occupations, for the sake of millionaires. Formerly, men were made slaves under physical compulsion. Now they are enslaved by temptations of money and of the luxuries that money can buy. ... This civilization takes note neither of morality nor of religion. Its votaries calmly state that their business is not to teach religion. Some even consider it to be a superstitious growth. Others put on the cloak of religion, and prate about morality. ... Civilization seeks to increase bodily comforts, and it fails miserably even in doing so. (Gandhi, p.36)

Gandhi concluded: "This civilization is such that one has only to be patient and it will be self-destroyed."

At about the same time in Vienna, in the heart of central Europe, Sigmund Freud's (1856–1939) new art of psychoanalysis ascribed humanity's most profound moving force not to rationality, the pride of European science and technology, but to sexuality. He argued that people did not understand their own deepest drives; these were hidden in the unconscious. He, too, questioned the ability of European civilization to survive:

> There are two tenets of psychoanalysis which offend the whole world and excite its resentment. ... The first of these displeasing propositions of psychoanalysis is this: that mental processes are essentially unconscious ... [the] next proposition consists in the assertion that ... sexual impulses have contributed invaluably to the highest cultural, artistic, and social achievements of the human mind. ... Society can conceive of no more powerful menace to its culture than would arise from the liberation of the sexual impulses and a return of them to their original goal. (Freud, pp. 25–7)

New, non-representational, or abstract, art also seemed to question the significance of rationality. The most innovative and honored of its creators, Pablo Picasso, drew from African "primitive" art to create new forms of his own. Through these African-inspired innovations, he demonstrated that the West had much to learn from the naturalism and spirituality of cultures that it dominated politically, economically, and militarily.

Voices of despair multiplied. Even the end of war did not bring renewal. T.S. Eliot's "The Waste Land" (1922) depicts, among its many gloomy scenes, the impending reunion of a wife with her husband, a soldier returning from war. The anticipation is grating and crude, even foreboding, rather than romantic, as the poet tells the wife to prepare:

> Now Albert's coming back, make yourself a bit smart.
> He'll want to know what you done with the money he gave you
> To get yourself some teeth. He did, I was there.
> You have them all out, Lil, and get a nice set.
> He said, I swear, I can't bear to look at you.
> And no more can't I, I said, and think of poor Albert,
> He's been in the army four years, he wants a good time,
> And if you don't give it to him, there's others will, I said.
> Oh is there, she said. Something o' that, I said.
> Then I'll know who to thank, she said, and gave me a straight look.

Eliot (1888–1965), perhaps the most influential English language poet of his generation, captures an arid, spiteful, loveless individual relationship and suggests that the same empty bitterness pervaded the entire society.

With the far greater destruction of World War II and its atomic bombs and genocide, literature reflected humanity at rock bottom, estranged from itself and from the universe. In 1941, at the age of twelve, Elie Wiesel had immersed himself in the practices of Hasidic, orthodox, devotional Judaism in Sighet, Hungary. In reply to the question, "Why do you pray?" he had said, "Why did I pray? A strange question. Why did I live? Why did I breathe?" But in 1944, after three years in a Nazi ghetto, he arrived in Birkenau, the gateway to Auschwitz, the hungriest of the concentration camps.

> Not far from us, flames were leaping up from a ditch, gigantic flames. They were burning something. A lorry drew up at the pit and delivered its load—little children. Babies! Yes, I saw it—saw it with my own eyes … those children in the flames. (Is it surprising that I could not sleep after that? Sleep had fled my eyes.)
>
> So this was where we were going. A little farther on was another and larger ditch for adults. I pinched my face. Was I still alive? Was I awake? I could not believe it. How could it be possible for them to burn people, children, and for the world to keep silent? No, none of this could be true. It was a nightmare. (Wiesel, p. 16)

Wiesel soon becomes aware of someone reciting the Kaddish, the Jewish prayer for the dead.

> For the first time, I felt revolt rise up in me. Why should I bless His name? The Eternal, Lord of the Universe, the All-Powerful and Terrible, was silent. What had I to thank Him for? (Wiesel, p. 22)

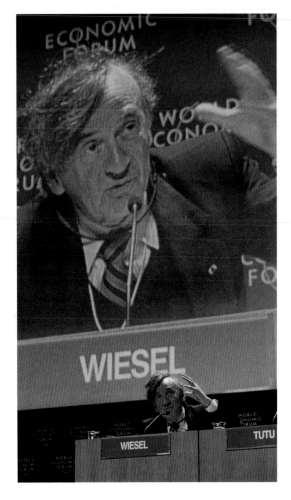

The Nobel prize winner Elie Wiesel at the World Economic Forum, 1998. Wiesel survived the Holocaust and devoted his life to alerting the world to its horrors, so that it might never happen again. Unfortunately, other "smaller" Holocausts continue to occur without external intervention.

HOW DO WE KNOW?

The Decision to Drop the Atom Bomb

Because nuclear weapons have so thoroughly changed the nature of war, peace, and diplomacy, and have even changed the way we think about the future of life on earth, attitudes toward them continue to change over time. Since Hiroshima and Nagasaki remain the only wartime deployment of the bomb, the decision to use it has received intense scrutiny. Even as the Manhattan Project was developing the bomb, at least one of the scientists central to its development counseled against using it. Leo Szilard wrote, "A nation which sets the precedent of using these newly liberated forces of nature for purposes of destruction may have to bear the responsibility of opening the door to an era of devastation on an unimaginable scale" (Rhodes, p. 749). President Truman nevertheless chose to drop the bomb, not just once, but twice. In the immediate aftermath of the explosions and Japan's surrender, an overwhelming proportion of Americans approved the decision. Even then, however, "Pacifist groups, a number of atomic scientists, some religious leaders and organizations, and a scattering of political commentators, both liberal and conservative, condemned the atomic attacks because of their indiscriminate killing of civilians and/or the failure of the United States to give Japan an explicit warning about the bomb before Hiroshima (Walker, p. 98).

The United States Strategic Bombing Survey, published in July 1946, concluded that "certainly prior to 31 December 1945, and in all probability prior to 1 November 1945, Japan would have surrendered even if the Atomic bombs had not been dropped" (Walker, p.100). Such a "counterfactual" judgment, however, cannot be proved or disproved.

In 1961, former State Department official Herbert Feis, in his book Japan Subdued, agreed that the Japanese would have surrendered by the end of the year, even without the bomb and even without

an invasion, nevertheless "the impelling reason for the decision to use [the bomb] was military—to end the war victoriously as soon as possible (Walker, p. 104). He also noted that had there been an invasion, American casualties would probably have been in the thousands rather than the hundreds of thousands.

Gar Alperovitz, first in his dissertation and then in his book, Atomic Diplomacy, concluded on the basis of diplomatic sources, and especially the diary of Henry Stimson, Secretary of War, that Truman used the bomb more to impress the Russians and improve his bargaining position with them than to subdue the Japanese. Secretary of State James Byrnes, for example, told the American ambassador to the Soviet Union, Joseph E. Davies, that American possession of the bomb "would have some effect [on the Soviets] and induce them to yield and agree to our position" (Walker, p. 64). Through the 1970s and 1980s scholarship responding to new documents tended to confirm a composite account: the bomb had been used both to end the war quickly—although the Japanese would have surrendered even without the bomb and without an invasion—and to intimidate the Russians.

J. Samuel Walker, who summarizes these debates in his book, Prompt and Utter Destruction, adds three more arguments that have been suggested as reasons for the use of the bomb. "Justifying the costs of the Manhattan Project" was one. How could the government spend $2 billion, and employ the efforts of 600,000 workers, and then not employ and demonstrate the results? As Truman's Secretary of War Henry Stimson put it when he heard that the first test bomb had been successful: "I have been responsible for spending two billions of dollars on this atomic venture. Now that it is successful I shall not be sent to prison in Fort Leavenworth" (Rhodes, p. 686). Also, there was a "lack of incentives not to use the bomb." As Stimson wrote, "I believe that no man, in our position and subject to our responsibilities, holding in his hands a

weapon of such possibilities for accomplishing this purpose and saving those lives, could have failed to use it and afterwards looked his countrymen in the face." Finally, Truman believed he was dealing with an enemy that was "a beast." Loathing of Japan as a cruel and bitter enemy enabled Truman to use the bomb with a clear conscience. In questioning charges of racism, Walker adds that Truman might have used the bomb against Germany as well, but Germany had surrendered by the time the bomb was ready.

All these arguments came bubbling to the surface in 1995 when the Smithsonian Institution prepared a major display at the National Air and Space Museum in Washington of the Enola Gay, the plane that dropped the bomb on Hiroshima, in commemoration of the fiftieth anniversary. The display was to suggest some of the criticism of the decision that had surfaced since the bombing, but many groups across the United States protested, and the entire exhibit was scaled back and introduced differently. The Enola Gay protest underlined the gap that persisted through a half century between the views of scholars and those of the general public as to the necessity and the morality of the use of the bomb. These questions concerning necessity and morality r emain with us. They surround not only the use of the bomb in the past, but also its potential use in the future. Indeed they surround all decisions concerning the use of massive force in warfare.

- In light of these assessments, would you have chosen to use the bomb on August 6, 1945? Would you have used it again on August 9? Why or why not?
- Which reasons would you consider appropriate for using the bomb? Which would you consider inappropriate?
- What have been the bases for different scholars arriving at different conclusions about the reasons for the decision to drop the bomb?

Long-cherished images of humanity and of the gods it had held sacred perished in the Holocaust. Yet Wiesel found the courage to make of his experiences in the death camps the stuff of literature and the basis of a new morality:

> Never shall I forget that night, the first night in camp, which has turned my life into one long night, seven times cursed and seven times sealed. Never shall I forget that smoke. Never shall I forget the little faces of the children, whose bodies I saw turned into wreaths of smoke beneath a silent blue sky.
>
> Never shall I forget those flames which consumed my faith forever.
>
> Never shall I forget that nocturnal silence which deprived me, for all eternity, of the desire to live. Never shall I forget those moments which murdered my God and my soul and turned my dreams to dust. Never shall I forget these things, even if I am condemned to live as long as God Himself. Never. (Wiesel, pp. 41–3)

To transmit this horrible personal history, to warn humanity of its own destructiveness, and to proclaim the need to preserve life became Wiesel's consuming passion. The award of the Nobel Peace Prize in 1986 recognized his mission.

From Japan, which suffered the world's first and only nuclear explosions in warfare, came similar meditations of anguish and despair, followed later by a commitment to prevent such catastrophe in the future. A student in Hiroshima Women's Junior College, Artsuko Tsujioka, remembered the atomic attack on her city in which 75,000 people were killed instantaneously and tens of thousands lingered on to die later or to be misshapen and genetically damaged from the persistent radiation:

> It happened instantaneously. I felt as if my back had been struck with a big hammer, and then as if I had been thrown into boiling oil. … That first night ended. … My friends and the other people were no longer able to move. The skin had peeled off of their burned arms, legs and backs. I wanted to move them, but there was no place on their bodies that I could touch. … I still have the scars from that day; on my head, face, arms, legs and chest. There are reddish black scars on my arms and the face that I see in the mirror does not look as if it belongs to me. It always saddens me to think that I will never look the way I used to. I lost all hope at first. I was obsessed with the idea that I had become a freak and did not want to be seen by anyone. I cried constantly for my good friends and kind teachers who had died in such a terrible way.
>
> My way of thinking became warped and pessimistic. Even my beautiful voice, that my friends had envied, had turned weak and hoarse. When I think of the way it was then, I feel as if I were being strangled. But I have been able to take comfort in the thought that physical beauty is not everything, that a beautiful spirit can do away with physical ugliness. This has given me new hope for the future. (Andrea and Overfield, pp. 417–19)

On a national scale, Japan's peace parks at both Hiroshima and Nagasaki record the nuclear destruction as well as subsequent commitments to seeking international peace. Since World War II, Japan has been committed to keeping nuclear arms out of Japan and has been intensely involved in the efforts of the United Nations to work for peace. Its increased wealth and potential military power in the Pacific, however, put stresses on Japan's anti-militaristic patterns at the turn of the twenty-first century.

The French existentialist author Albert Camus (1913–60), perhaps the most influential voice in European literature in his time, wrote in 1940, the year France fell to Germany: "There is but one truly serious philosophical problem, and that is suicide. Judging whether life is or is not worth living amounts to answering the fundamental question of philosophy." Perhaps, however, rock bottom had been reached, or perhaps hope is part of the human condition, even in conditions of apparent hopelessness, for

Camus answered his own question in *The Myth of Sisyphus* (1942) with an affirmation, which he repeated in 1955:

> This book declares that even within the limits of nihilism it is possible to find the means to proceed beyond nihilism … Although *The Myth of Sisyphus* poses mortal problems, it sums itself up for me as a lucid invitation to live and to create, in the very midst of the desert. (p. 3)

THE UNITED NATIONS, POSTWAR RECOVERY, AND THE ORIGINS OF THE COLD WAR

Out of the rubble of the war, both victors and losers had to restructure new relationships. The creation of the United Nations, "to save the world from the future scourge of war," represented one of their most hopeful responses.

The United Nations

President Roosevelt first used the term "United Nations" publicly in issuing a joint declaration of war aims with Britain, the USSR, China, and twenty-two other countries on New Year's Day, 1942. Planning for a permanent organization began in 1944,

Post-war Europe. Western and eastern bloc competition, following their alliance in crushing Nazi Germany, crystallized in the Cold War. The Soviet Union annexed territories in the Baltic states and eastern Poland and set up a string of puppet communist states later known as the Warsaw Pact alliance, from East Germany to Bulgaria. The Western Allies formed the countervailing NATO alliance. The stalemate continued for forty years.

SOURCE

Preamble to the Charter of the United Nations

We the peoples of the United Nations determined

- to save succeeding generations from the scourge of war. . .
- to reaffirm faith in fundamental human rights, in the dignity and worth of the human person, in the equal rights of men and women and of nations large and small. . .
- to establish conditions under which justice and respect for the obligations arising from treaties and other sources of international law can be maintained. . .
- to promote social progress and better standards of life in larger freedom.

And for these ends

- to practice tolerance and live together in peace with one another as good neighbors . . .
- to unite our strength to maintain international peace and security . . .
- to ensure, by the acceptance of principles and the institution of methods, that armed force shall not be used, save in the common interest . . .
- to employ international machinery for the promotion of the economic and social advancement of all peoples.

Have resolved to combine our efforts to accomplish these aims.

culminating in the Charter of the United Nations, which was signed in San Francisco by fifty countries on June 26, 1945 (and by Poland, also considered a founding member, in October). The main purpose of the organization was "to save succeeding generations from the scourge of war," and its major institutions were designed to respond to threats to the peace. The United Nations' General Assembly, in which every member country was represented and had a vote, provided a forum for the discussion of the major issues threatening world peace. The Security Council, with five permanent members (the United States, the USSR, Britain, France, and China), and several others elected for fixed terms by the General Assembly, could dispatch peace-keeping forces. An International Court of Justice was created to decide disputes among member states. In 1946, the League of Nations was formally dissolved and the United Nations (UN) took on many of its missions, such as promoting public health through the World Health Organization (WHO), and educational, economic, and cultural activities through the United Nations Economic, Scientific, and Cultural Organization (UNESCO). In its early years, the peace-keeping function of the UN was stymied by the mutual hostility of the United States and the Soviet Union. As permanent members of the Security Council, each had the right to veto major policy decisions of the UN, leaving the organization mostly powerless to resolve the key Cold War conflicts between these two postwar superpowers. Nevertheless, its service as a forum for discussions, and its humanitarian activities ensured the place of the UN in the new, emerging international order. Its role increased in significance through the years.

Resettlement

Almost 100 million soldiers served under arms during the war, many of them in foreign lands. Some 15 million of them were killed. Millions more were captured as prisoners of war and required repatriation, resettlement to the areas from which they came. Millions of civilians had also been resettled or imprisoned by conquering armies that feared revolt among their newly subject populations. In addition, Germany and Japan had fought, in part, for *lebensraum*, or more "living space." They had dispatched millions of their civilians to new homes in newly conquered territories. These civilians, too, had to return to their original homes—or, at least, to new homes. Additional millions had been displaced by the warfare, fleeing as best they could from approaching armies. National borders changed as a result of the war, especially in central and eastern Europe, and nationals of various countries often chose, or were forced, to move in accord with the new national geographies. Finally, millions also traveled in the hope of finding lost family members and in search of food.

During the war, for example, millions of Germans had moved, as soldiers or civilians, into eastern Europe and the Baltic countries. The Russians had also exiled about a half million Germans to Siberia. They had similarly deported some 2 million Poles and 180,000 Balts to Siberia, and replaced them with about equal numbers of Russians and Ukranians.

In the years immediately following the war, some 15 million Germans who had been living or fighting in eastern Europe returned to Germany. Four and a half million Poles, most of whom had fled the Nazis or the Communists, or both, returned to Poland. The Russians continued to enforce population exchanges, exiling almost 2 million Ukrainians and central Asian peoples to Siberia, along with some 300,000 Balts to eastern Russia and Siberia. Here, too, they replaced them with about equal numbers of Russians and Ukrainians regarded as loyal to the new communist administration. Some 300,000 Balts fled westward to escape their new Russian masters. Hundreds of thousands of other, smaller groups—Hungarians, Slavs, and Finns—also moved. Also some 320,000 Jews, survivors of the Holocaust in eastern Europe, emigrated to join the effort to create a new Jewish homeland in Palestine.

Similar migrations occurred in East Asia as some 5.5 million Japanese returned home. Most were demobilized soldiers, but hundreds of thousands were civilians who had established homes in Korea and Taiwan over several decades of Japanese colonization. In Manchuria, the Soviet troops, who had entered the war in Asia only in its last few days, seized thousands of Japanese to labor in Siberian labor camps. Other thousands were murdered by Chinese taking revenge.

All these movements were quite different from the return home by millions of victorious American troops. (Some 400,000 had been killed.) The American mainland had been essentially untouched by the war, and the soldiers were repatriated back in more-or-less orderly fashion to their own homes. Moreover, in gratitude for their service and in eagerness to reintegrate the troops peacefully and productively into civilian life, the United States government instituted new programs such as the G.I. Bill of Rights, which enabled millions of the veterans to go to college, an aspiration that otherwise might have been beyond their means. The booming wartime and postwar economy of the United States made these veterans' benefits financially possible, and soon the addition of millions of more highly educated veterans increased the productivity of the country's workforce still further. The postwar period here —and elsewhere—saw a very rapid rise in the birthrate as the country and much of the world recovered from a decade and a half of economic depression and world war. The postwar years brought a baby boom.

Political Reconstruction in Japan and Germany

Following the explosion of atomic bombs on Hiroshima and Nagasaki, Japan signed an unconditional surrender agreement to end the war and came under American occupation and guidance. Germany also surrendered unconditionally to the Allies and was divided into two states that remained separate for forty-five years.

Japan. Japan awaited an uncertain future under American occupation headed by the Supreme Commander for the Allied Powers, General Douglas MacArthur. The occupation lasted until 1952 and focused on four goals: punishing some Japanese leaders as war criminals; establishing democratic institutions and practices; reviving the devastated Japanese economy; and enlisting Japan as an ally in the new Cold War against the USSR. All four goals were achieved.

Some 200,000 wartime leaders were barred from office. Twenty-five of the top leaders were tried for starting the war, and seven were hanged. The emperor was no longer to be regarded as sacred, nor would he wield political power. He would now serve as a constitutional monarch. The preservation of the emperor as a symbol probably made Japanese acceptance of the occupation less difficult.

The colonial empire was dissolved completely, and 5.5 million expatriate Japanese were returned to Japan. The military was completely demobilized. State support for Shinto was ended. Police authority was reduced. Freedom of speech was reintroduced. Political prisoners were freed. A new constitution, issued in 1947, granted universal adult suffrage to everyone over the age of twenty, including women for the first time. The diet became an elected, British-style parliament, with two houses. The judiciary was independent, headed by a supreme court. Guarantees of freedom of assembly, the press, "life, liberty, and the pursuit of happiness," and the "right to maintain the minimum standards of wholesome and cultural living" were also written into the constitution.

Economically, the Occupation Authority pushed ahead on four fronts. First, it redistributed agricultural land. Land held by absentee landlords and land in excess of 10 acres per family had to be sold to the government at low rates. The government, in turn, sold it to small farmers who prospered and felt strong allegiance to the government.

Second, the largest *zaibatsu* were dissolved into their constituent companies and anti-monopoly legislation was passed. Over the next decades, new conglomerates, called **keiretsu**, grew up with many qualities of the *zaibatsu*, but they were less restrictive, and they allowed more scope for the start-up of new companies.

Third, the Occupation Authority encouraged the formation of labor unions, legalizing the right to organize, bargain, and strike. Within three years the unions had grown to several million members and had begun to turn communist. The Occupation Authority then passed new laws to restrict the unions and purge their communist leaders. Unionization and strikes declined, but labor unions, which work closely with management, remained important in Japan's socio-economic life.

Finally, the Occupation Authority restructured the educational system. The contents of school textbooks were dramatically revised to remove much of the emperor-centered, nationalistic wartime ideology. The number of middle school students increased from 2.4 to 4.3 million; high school students from 380,000 to 1.2 million by 1952 to 4.3 million by 1975. By 1995, 90 percent of the appropriate age group graduated from high school. University students increased from 84,000 to 2.5 million in 1995, one-third of the university-age group.

Ironically, within five years of the end of World War II, the United States enlisted Japan as its ally in the Cold War against China and Russia. Japan's postwar

The first meeting of General MacArthur and Emperor Hirohito, September 27, 1945. The seemingly simple news photograph upset Japanese viewers, who thought that General MacArthur insulted the emperor by dressing too casually. The picture reputedly marked the moment when the Japanese recognized that they had been defeated and that the Americans were in charge. Yet the picture also showed that the Americans would support some form of continuing monarchy.

keiretsu Alliances of independent Japanese firms, joining either large corporations in different industries or a large corporation and sub-contractors. They are successors of the pre-war **zaibatsu**.

constitution limited its military commitments, but a United States–Japanese Security Treaty did allow the United States to maintain military bases throughout Japan and to retain Okinawa until 1972. Under this treaty Japan was protected militarily by the United States.

Meanwhile, Japan became a principal supplier of materials and support services to the Americans fighting in neighboring Korea. The Korean War (1950–53) was an economic boon to Japan, providing a jump-start to the new growth. During the war, America bought $4 billion worth of military manufactures and tens of thousands of American troops were stationed in Japan. Between 1950 and 1973, Japan's economy grew at a phenomenal average rate of 10.5 percent a year. The gross national product grew from $24 billion in 1955, to $484 billion in 1975, to $4.3 trillion in 1994.

The American occupation introduced to Japan many management training experts. The most influential was W. Edwards Deming, who brought the concept of quality control systems, or "TQM," Total Quality Management, involving all workers throughout the entire process of production. Japanese businessmen adopted this concept more fully than Americans did. Japanese workers were encouraged to feel themselves a valued part of the production process, their suggestions solicited and taken seriously, their job security ensured to the extent possible, their pay and benefits kept at high levels. Japanese consumer goods, produced through this system of personal dedication combined with the highest technological efficiency, earned a reputation for excellent quality and began to take over large shares of the world market, challenging more established producers, including the Americans.

Germany. At the end of the war, Germany lay devastated. One-fourth of the housing stock was destroyed as was about half of the economic infrastructure. Food supplies, although rationed, left many Germans malnourished, even as millions of refugees were returning. The German state had ceased to exist, and the country was divided by its conquerors into four parts: American, British, French, and Russian. In addition, segments of eastern Germany—East Prussia, Pomerania, and Silesia—were transferred to the Soviet Union and almost 10 million German inhabitants of these lands were forced back into the remainder of Germany.

At first, the Russians, which had suffered horribly during the war, also demanded reparations to be collected from all four zones of Germany, but, beginning in 1946, the Western allies refused to cooperate. The four regions were developing separately and differently. Even on subjects on which they agreed, such as punishing people who had been active officials in the Nazi government, the Russians punished them more severely. All four nations, however, participated in the trial at Nuremberg of twenty-two of the most powerful surviving Nazi leaders for crimes against humanity: mass murder and genocide. Twelve were sentenced to death, seven to lengthy prison terms, and three were acquitted. The Nuremberg Trials have been criticized as "victor's judgment," finding people guilty of crimes that had not been classified at the time they were committed; but other observers hailed them for setting an example of establishing standards of accountability among the highest authorities of government.

The Nuremberg Trials, Nuremberg, October 1945. After the war, the Allies put on trial twenty-two of the most notorious Nazis for crimes against humanity. Some critics called this "victor's judgment", but others thought it established new and better standards of international accountability.

During the first two years of occupation, fundamental differences developed between the zones administered by the Russians and the rest. Free democratic elections took place in the western zones, a free market was restored, and the economy was linked with that of western Europe. Prosperity returned. In the areas controlled by the Russians, elections were rigged, the economy was controlled by the state and it did not quickly recover. In 1948, seeking to gain control of the entire city of Berlin, the Russians instituted a blockade of the city. Although Berlin was also shared by the four powers, it lay deep inside the territory controlled by the Russians. The **Berlin Blockade** was one of the clear opening salvos in the Cold War. President Truman responded with an airlift of supplies that continued for almost a year until the Soviets lifted the blockade.

Berlin Blockade In 1948 the Russians barred the entrance and exit of people and supplies to and from Berlin in an attempt to gain control of the city.

Economic Reconstruction and the Cold War

Europe lay in ruins after six years of the most destructive warfare. Fifty million people were dead, about 20 million of them soldiers in the prime of life. Much of the physical plant was destroyed, including industries and homes. National treasuries were bankrupt. Transportation and communication systems did not work. International trade, which had been disrupted for years, would not revive immediately both because of Europe's inability to pay for imports, and because other nations, both colonies and independent countries like those of Latin America, had developed greater self-sufficiency during the war. They would be in much less need of European exports, even if the exports were available. John Maynard Keynes, the British economist, warned that his nation was facing a "financial Dunkirk."

On the other hand, some of the industrial plant remained operative, and Europeans had not forgotten their skills in managing a flourishing economy. They also received billions of dollars in aid from the United States. The lesson of Germany's retaliation for its feeling of humiliation and impoverishment at the end of World War I would not be repeated. All European nations were eligible for assistance in recovery, and by 1947 recovery had begun, especially in western Europe, but it was fragile.

Communist labor unions, which had at first cooperated with national recovery efforts, began strikes, and communist political parties began winning substantial minorities in national elections. In Greece a civil war that had begun in 1946 pitted communist guerrilla forces against a British-supported government. Tito, in neighboring Yugoslavia, aided the guerrillas. Russian troops on the borders of Turkey threatened to upset the political stability of that country. The United States, fearing that communist Russia would take advantage of European economic weakness and political uncertainty, formulated three new policies. In March 1947, the American President Harry Truman laid down the doctrine that carried his name, describing a polarization that he saw dividing the world between countries with democratic freedoms and majority rule and those based on minority regimes relying upon "terror and oppression, a controlled press, framed elections, and the suppression of personal freedom." The Truman Doctrine offered "to help free people to maintain their institutions and their integrity against aggressive movements that seek to impose upon them totalitarian regimes."

In the same year, the United States began the Marshall Plan, named for the US secretary of state, which offered a total of about $12 billion in financial assistance and equipment to all European nations that wanted it and had appropriate plans for using it. The Marshall Plan expedited Europe's recovery, created new markets for American goods, and reduced the threat of communist takeover. Europe's economic growth reached spectacular levels. By 1950, West Germany's economic production was greater than that of pre-war Germany. By 1958, it outpaced in its national economic product all other European countries, including those that had defeated it in war just a few years before. All western European countries did well, however, in an "economic miracle" that lasted until 1974.

Third, politically and diplomatically the United States implemented a policy of "containment" in regard to the USSR. Formulated by State Department official George Kennan, the containment policy argued that Russia would constantly probe western European and American weakness, but sometime in the future Russia would moderate its aggressiveness. Meanwhile, it could be restrained peacefully. The West should keep up its own economic strength and help others to build theirs; it should use all diplomatic means to limit Russian threats; and it should maintain its military forces at high levels of preparedness.

Both sides feared one another. The Americans saw Russia take over the governments of the countries of eastern Europe, using its armies of post-war occupation to impose communism, in contravention of treaties agreed upon at a wartime conference in Yalta in February 1945. They saw communists attempting to take over the government of Greece in a civil war that lasted from 1946 to 1949. They saw the communists in China under Mao Zedong defeat their opposition and take over that country. They felt that communism might take over the world politically and economically, by fair means or foul. The USSR, on the other hand, as leader of the communist world, feared American capitalist hegemony and military power, especially its sole possession of the A-bomb. It feared the military and economic power that America might bring to bear in any confrontation. It feared encirclement by American allies in Europe and the Pacific.

Russia dominated a wall of allied states in central and eastern Europe and claimed it as a defensive buffer. It moved as quickly as possible to build its own atomic bomb, with nuclear secrets stolen from America. It kept its armed forces extremely strong. In reply, the United States created the North Atlantic Treaty Organization (NATO) in 1949. NATO included democratic countries with capitalist, socialist, and mixed economies: Britain, France (until 1966), Italy, Canada, Denmark, Norway, Iceland, Belgium, the Netherlands, and Luxemburg. Portugal, though not a democracy at first, was also a charter member. In 1952 both Greece and Turkey joined, as did West Germany in 1955. The USSR then formally established the Warsaw Pact among the nations of Bulgaria, Czechoslovakia, East Germany, Hungary, Poland, and Romania, which were communist in their politics and economics. Forty years of Cold War competition had begun.

The wariness of the two sides toward one another led to a polarization of much of the world and a massive arms race. Other American-led pacts included the Organization of American States (1948) and the Southeast Asia Treaty Organization (1954). Defense expenditures of the United States and the Soviet Union mushroomed in an arms race unprecedented in peacetime. In 1948, the United States spent about $10 billion on its military; the USSR about 13. By 1950 these figures had reached 14.5 and 15.5, respectively, and by 1960, 45.3 and 36.9, and they continued to rise. Pessimists lamented these expenditures as wasteful; optimists pointed out that the USA and the USSR actually avoided direct warfare, although some of their allies did not. In the next two decades, from 1945 to 1965, most of the major colonies of the European powers would become independent, and both the USA and USSR would try to win them over to their separate camps. The joining together of these two great movements, the Cold War and decolonization, is a central issue in the next chapter.

ENTERING THE SECOND HALF OF THE 20TH CENTURY WHAT DIFFERENCE DOES IT MAKE?

The first half of the twentieth century ended in horror and hope. Two world wars, holocaust, and nuclear weapons killed some 75 million people. Between the wars economic depression also afflicted most parts of the world, and at their end a new kind of Cold War, waged by two newly risen superpowers, threatened to plunge the world into nuclear destruction that might threaten all human life on earth. These were the greatest horrors.

On the other hand, people around the world joined with Roosevelt in his 1941 statement looking forward "to a world founded upon four essential human freedoms": freedom of speech and expression, freedom to worship God as one chooses, freedom from want, and freedom from fear. They applauded the Atlantic Charter issued by Roosevelt and Churchill, which stated that the two leaders and their countries "respect the right of all peoples to choose the form of government under which they will live; and they wish to see sovereign rights and self-government restored to those who have been forcibly deprived of them." Churchill took this to mean freedom for the countries that had suffered under Axis rule; Roosevelt said that it meant an end to colonialism. People living under colonial rule accepted Roosevelt's reading. Indeed, colonized nations were already gaining independence: Jordan, Lebanon, and Syria in 1946; India and Pakistan in 1947; Ceylon (Sri Lanka), Burma (Myanmar), and Israel in 1948; Indonesia in 1949; and China, completing its communist revolution in 1949, expelled foreign powers from its territories. Racism, especially after the Holocaust, came under attack as never before. Aimé Césaire, the poet and politician from Martinique, wrote caustically:

> At bottom, what . . . the very distinguished, very humanistic, very Christian
> bourgeois of the twentieth century . . . cannot forgive Hitler is not crime in itself,
> the crime against man, it is not the humiliation of man as such, it is the crime
> against the white man, the humiliation of the white man, and the fact that [Hitler]
> applied to Europe colonialist procedures which until then had been reserved
> exclusively for the Arabs of Algeria, the coolies of India, and the blacks of Africa. (Lee,
> p. 145)

Many Europeans agreed with Césaire, although with a different emphasis, that Hitler's racism had shocked them into a new understanding of its viciousness, and to a struggle against it.

The Senegalese poet/statesman Léopold Sédar Senghor held out the promise that Africa, finding its freedom and voice anew, could help Europe to return to health after a generation of destruction:

> The Africa of the empires is dying, see, the agony of a pitiful princess
> And Europe too where we are joined at the navel.
> Fix your unchanging eyes upon your children, who are given orders
> Who give away their lives like the poor their last clothes.
> Let us report present at the rebirth of the World
> Like the yeast which white flour needs.
> For who would teach rhythm to a dead world of machines and guns?
> Who would give the cry of joy to wake the dead and the bereaved at dawn?
> Say, who would give back the memory of life to the man whose hopes are
> smashed?
> They call us men of coffee cotton oil
> They call us men of death.
> We are the men of the dance, whose feet draw new strength pounding the
> hardened earth. (Okpewho, p. 134)

Finally, the formal creation of the United Nations in 1945 offered hope that the peoples of the world could resolve their disputes peacefully and work also for better public health, more fulfilling cultural life, and more fully developed international law.

Review Questions

- How did the depression of 1929–39 affect the recovery from World War I? Please discuss the effects on different countries, such as, Germany, the USA, the USSR, Japan.
- How important were thugs in the rise of fascism in Italy and Germany? What roles did they play? Why did people decide in large numbers to follow them?
- Compare fascism and communism in terms of: (1) power of the state; (2) power of the leader; (3) role of private property; (4) value put on warfare; (5) willingness to enter international, diplomatic relations with other nations as an equal; and (6) individual human rights?
- Warfare had an effect on the role of women, but the effect was different in different countries. Discuss these differences and similarities in the USA, the USSR, Germany, and Japan.
- Elie Wiesel reports losing his faith not only in his fellow humans but also in God as a result of his experiences in the Holocaust. How does this compare with other responses to this disaster and to the atomic bombing of Japan?
- What are the reasons given for the Cold War between the USA and the USSR? Which reason do you think was most significant?

Suggested Readings

PRINCIPAL SOURCES

Dower, John. *Embracing Defeat*. Superb account of Japan under American occupation, 1945–52.

Freud, Sigmund. *Civilization and its Discontents* (New York: W.W. Norton and Co., 1961). Freud explains the battle between love and war. He is not sure which will win out.

Kennedy, Paul. *The Rise and Fall of the Great Powers* (New York: Vintage Books, 1989). Very good on the human and economic costs of war.

Rhodes, Richard. *The Making of the Atomic Bomb* (New York: Simon and Schuster, 1986). A comprehensive study of the Manhattan Project, including the science, administration, and politics of the production of the first nuclear weapon.

Weinberg, Gerhard. *A World at Arms: A Global History of World War II* (Cambridge: Cambridge University Press, 1994). Massive, one-volume history of the war, in all theaters, examining the use of both force and diplomacy.

Wiesel, Elie. *Night* (New York: Bantam Books, 1962). Terrifying personal account of Wiesel's youth in the concentration camps.

Yoshimi, Yoshiaki. *Sexual Slavery in the Japanese Military During World War II*. trans. by Suzanne O'Brien (New York: Columbia University Press, 1995). A comprehensive, academic account of the sexual slavery of the "comfort women" and their relatively recent demands for reparations from the Japanese government.

ADDITIONAL SOURCES

Alperovitz, Gar. *The Decision to Use the Atomic Bomb* (New York: Knopf, 1996). Examines the entire range of debate by both decision makers and later commentators.

Andrea, Alfred and James H. Overfield, eds. *The Human Record*, Vol. 2 (Boston: Houghton Mifflin, 3rd ed., 1998). Excellent collection of primary documents.

Bosworth, R.J.B. *Mussolini* (London: Oxford University Press, 2002). The most recent and important biography of Mussolini.

Browning, Christopher. *Ordinary Men: Reserve Police Battalion 101 and the Final Solution in Poland* (Harper Collins, 1992). An excellent analysis of ordinary people involved in the Holocaust.

———. *The Path to Genocide: Essays on Launching the Final Solution* (Cambridge, England: Cambridge University Press, 1992). An analysis of Nazi Jewish policy.

Bulliet, Richard W., ed. *The Columbia History of the 20th Century* (New York: Columbia University Press, 1998). Excellent selection of academic articles tracing the key themes of the twentieth century.

Cook, Haruko Taya and Theodore F. Cook. *Japan at War: An Oral History* (New York: New Press, 1992). Japanese civilians and soldiers recall their own experiences.

De Grazia, Victoria. *How Fascism Ruled Women: Italy, 1922–1945* (Berkeley, CA: University of California Press, 1992). An examination of the ideas of womanhood under fascism in Italy.

Eliot, T.S. *Collected Poems 1909–1962* (New York: Harcourt, Brace Jovanovich, 1936). Includes "The Waste Land." Eliot's poetry, with its startling imagery, irony, and often despairing search for meaning in the midst of a barren culture, defined modernism in literature.

Friedan, Betty. *The Feminine Mystique* (New York: Dell, 1963).

Gandhi, Mohandas Karamchand. *Hind Swaraj or Indian Home Rule* (Ahmedabad: Navajivan Press, 1938). The Mahatma's classic denunciation of the materialism of Western civilization.

Hilberg, Raul. *The Destruction of the European Jews* 3 Vols. (New York: Holmes and Meier, 1984). Comprehensive analysis of the Holocaust.

Keegan, John, ed. *The Times Atlas of the Second World War* (New York: Harper, 1989). Indispensable for following and understanding the unfolding of the war.

Kershaw, Ian. *The 'Hitler Myth': Image and Reality in the Third Reich* (London: Oxford University Press, 2001). A collection of essays attempting to explain why people followed Hitler.

Keynes, John Maynard. *The Economic Consequences of the Peace* (New York: Harcourt Brace Jovanovich, 1920), pp. 211–16. Highly influential critique of the terms of the peace agreements as setting the stage for renewed warfare.

Lee, Lloyd E. *World War II* (Westport, CN: Greenwood Press, 1999). Somewhat sketchy coverage of major issues and campaigns of the war, useful chronology, primary documents, biographies, and bibliography, especially of films and electronic sources.

Marrus, Michael. *The Holocaust in History* (London: Plume Books, 1988). An assessment of literature on the Holocaust.

Morris-Suzuki, Tessa. *The Technological Transformation of Japan*. (Cambridge: Cambridge University Press, 1994).

Okpewho, Isidore, ed. *The Heritage of African Poetry* (Harlow, Essex: Longman Group, 1985). Remarkable anthology with interesting discussions.

Overy, Richard *Why the Allies Won* (New York: W.W. Norton, 1995). An assessment of the economic, strategic, political, and moral balance between the combatants.

Peukert, Detlev, J.K. *The Weimar Republic* (Hill and Wang, 1993). An excellent social and political history of the Weimar Republic and the conditions that led to the rise of Hitler.

Rosenberg, Rosalind, "The 'Woman' Question," in Bulliet, pp. 53–80. Superb, brief survey of the major issues.

Schellstede, Sangmie Choi, ed. *Comfort Women Speak: Testimony by Sex Slaves of the Japanese Military* (New York: Holmes and Meier, 2000). The "comfort women" tell their own stories. Includes photographs of the women today, and a United Nations report on the situation.

Slater, Laura. *Opening Skinner's Box: Great Psychological Experiments of the Twentieth Century* (New York: W.W. Norton, 2004). One of the experiments presented and discussed is Stanley Milgram's.

Speer, Albert. *Inside the Third Reich: Memoirs* (New York: Macmillan, 1970). An insider's account of Nazi administration and wartime operations.

Walker, J. Samuel. *Prompt and Utter Destruction: Truman and the Use of Atomic Bombs against Japan* (Chapel Hill: University of North Carolina Press, 1997) Discusses the pros and cons of the decision to bomb, in light of the knowledge that policy makers had at the time.

Wilkie, Brian and James Hurt, eds. *Literature of the Western World*, Vol. 2 (New York: Macmillan, 1984). Excellent anthology. Gives complete works.

Young, Louise. *Japan's Total Empire: Manchuria and the Culture of Wartime Imperialism* (Berkeley, CA, 1998). An outstanding analysis of Japan's imperial ambitions.

◉ World History Documents CD-ROM

23.4 Nadezhda Mandelstam: *Hope Against Hope*
23.5 The Rise of Benito Mussolini
23.6 Adolf Hitler
24.1 Kita Ikki: *Outline for the Reconstruction of Japan*
24.2 Japanese Imperialism
25.1 Adolf Hitler: *The Obersalzberg Speech*
25.2 *The Atlantic Charter*
25.3 The Rape of Nanjing
25.4 Hiroshima and Nagasaki
25.5 Lindsey Parrot: *Tojo Makes Plea of Self Defense*
25.6 *The Charter of the United Nations*

COLD WAR AND NEW NATIONS

REMAKING THE POST-WORLD WAR II WORLD 1945–89

KEY TOPICS
- The Cold War, 1945–89: USA vs. USSR
- The Cold War and the Emergence of New Nations
- The Emergence of the Third World
- Terrorism
- In Pursuit of Peace
- NGOs and Transnationals
- Legacies of the Cold War, Decolonization, Economic and Social Development: What Difference Do They Make?

Three issues dominated the first two generations following World War II. The first was the Cold War. Two powers, previously at the periphery of Europe's dominance of global economics and arms, now surpassed Europe, challenging and threatening each other, and insisting that the rest of the peoples of earth choose sides between them. Few political, economic, or cultural events of this period escaped the intense competition of the USSR and the United States. Second, in the twenty years following the war, more than fifty European colonies gained their independence. Each sought its own road to development, many sought to cooperate with like-minded, friendly nations for their mutual support, and almost all were solicited by the two new superpowers to take sides in their global competition. Finally, a variety of strategies and technologies of development resulted from the new competition and the new freedom.

THE COLD WAR, 1945–89: USA VS. USSR

From the middle of the nineteenth century, many leaders of the United States held a belief in its "manifest destiny," a faith that the nation would spread westward from its Atlantic origins, first across the Appalachian mountains, later to the Pacific, and finally overseas. They believed that America had a message to spread about proper governance in the world, first by setting an example, a modern example of the biblical "City upon a Hill," and, second, by actively taking its message to other nations, as Woodrow Wilson had done in his Fourteen Points during World War I and Franklin Roosevelt had done in his "Four Freedoms" address and the Atlantic Charter (with Winston Churchill) during World War II. These extroverted missions often alternated with introverted periods when a policy of isolationism was pursued, but after World War II the extrovert United States prevailed. It emerged from the war victorious and by far the richest, most powerful, and most industrially productive country in the world, and it acted with a vigorous sense of optimism.

In the first years after the war, the United States replaced the Pax Britannica with a **Pax Americana**, a worldwide peace enforced by American arms and wealth. Through its $12 billion investment in the Marshall Plan it encouraged the reconstruction of western Europe along democratic and mixed capitalistic–socialistic patterns. It paid special attention to Germany, attempting to restore its briefly held democracy and to

Pax Americana Literally "American peace," a Latin phrase derived by analogy from Pax Romana (the peace enforced within the boundaries of the Roman Empire by Roman rule) to designate the relative tranquility established within the American sphere of influence after World War II.

Opposite **Zhou Enlai, Bandung Conference, Indonesia, 1955.** Zhou Enlai (center) arrives at the Bandung Conference along with many Third World leaders to articulate a post-colonial world order.

rebuild its economy. It paid even more attention to Japan, which it occupied militarily and politically for seven years. America outlawed the divine status attributed to the emperor, promulgated a democratic constitution and educational system, and introduced new concepts of business management. In part as a result of America's actions, western Europe and Japan became once again two powerhouses of the global economy.

The Soviet Union had a similar sense of mission for extending its power territorially and ideologically. In 1919, just two years after the success of their own revolution, Soviet leaders had established the Third Socialist International, or Comintern (Communist International), to encourage communist parties and revolutionaries throughout the world. Under Stalin, the Comintern continued to dispatch agents around the world to promote communist revolution. To some nations that had been devastated by World War II and to others just emerging from colonialism and seeking a model for rapid modernization, the Soviet Union's government-sponsored industrial successes (see Chapters 19 and 20) appeared attractive. The USSR's ability to survive ferocious punishment in World War II, to fight back, and to triumph, despite untold material damage and the deaths of some 20 million people, earned its people and its government great respect in the world community.

In the closing months of the war, agreements among the Allies signed at Yalta, on the Black Sea, and at Potsdam, Germany, provided some hope that the United States and the USSR would find a way to accommodate their different philosophies and compromise on their aspirations. Unfortunately, this did not happen. Americans interpreted the somewhat vague Yalta agreements as allowing the USSR some dominance among the nations of central and eastern Europe, in its own backyard, but leaving those countries generally independent and free to choose their own governments. Instead, they saw the Soviet Union using armed force to build a central and eastern European empire of its own. Between 1945 and 1948 the USSR imposed communist governments, controlled from Moscow and backed by Soviet troops, on Czechoslovakia, Romania, Bulgaria, Poland, Hungary, and Eastern Germany—adding them to its European empire along with the northern nations of Lithuania, Latvia, and Estonia, which it had annexed in 1940. The USSR then organized the economies of these satellite nations to serve its own, having them produce goods needed by the USSR at artificially low prices. Despite its anti-imperial rhetoric, the Soviet Union had kept control of the tsar's empire and was now adding to it. Observing the Soviet takeover of central Europe, Britain's Winston Churchill observed ruefully, "An iron curtain has descended across the continent." In several western European states, especially Italy, France, and Greece, communist parties were making major inroads in electoral politics.

The Russians interpreted the global political scene quite differently. They saw America's assistance to western Europe and Japan, and its additional support to Turkey and Greece, as an attempt to encircle them. Most of all, the Soviet Union knew that America alone had the atomic bomb, and this made it the most dangerous power on earth.

The Yalta Conference, 1945. At Yalta in February 1945 Stalin (far left), Roosevelt (center), and Churchill (far right) planned their post-war positions in Europe. Misunderstandings between them led later to Cold War tensions and recriminations.

Each side provoked the other, sometimes to the brink of war. The first open test of will came in Germany. Following World War II, the allied victors divided Germany into east and west. The United States, Britain, and France held the western sector, and the USSR held the east. The former capital, Berlin, was divided in the same way, but geographically the city lay deep inside the Russian-held eastern sector, about one hundred miles from the western sectors. In March 1948, the USSR blockaded land access to West Berlin, challenging the ability of the western powers to maintain control over their sectors. Recognizing that Soviet land forces commanded overwhelming power in central Europe, President Truman used the immense air power at his command to airlift supplies and personnel into West Berlin until, almost a year and a half later, in September 1949, Russia lifted the blockade. Nevertheless, Germany remained a divided country, and Berlin a divided city.

Nuclear weapons were the most terrifying arena of competition. Just as the Soviet Union had trembled when the United States exploded the world's first atomic bomb in 1945, so America reverberated in shock when the USSR followed with a bomb of its own in 1949. The American monopoly on nuclear weapons had lasted only four years. (Britain followed in 1952, France in 1960, China in 1964, Israel, unacknowledged, in the 1960s, India in 1974, Pakistan in 1998, and North Korea in 2004). How had Russia managed to crack the monopoly? Spies were suspected—and found—in the government and the scientific community in the United States. In response, Senator Joseph McCarthy unleashed a hunt for spies, communists, and "fellow travelers"—people sympathizing with communist perspectives—in a mixture of serious investigation and paranoia that threatened freedom of expression in the United States for several years. Public proclamations at this time also emphasized the importance of participation in organized religion in American life and contrasted it to the official atheism of the Soviet Union.

In 1952, the USA thought it was once again gaining nuclear supremacy as it exploded the world's first hydrogen bomb, but, to America's consternation, the USSR matched this accomplishment in the very next year. Atomic bombs gain their explosive power when a heavy nucleus splits or fissions into two lighter nuclei. Hydrogen bombs, on the other hand, explode when two lighter nuclei fuse into a heavier nucleus. Hydrogen bombs can be hundreds or thousands of times more powerful than atomic bombs and produce even more deadly radioactive fallout. The "Red scare" and McCarthyism gained renewed strength. Many government bureaucrats, artists, film producers, writers, and university professors suspected of present or past membership in the Communist Party of the United States, or of expressing views considered overly critical of the United States, lost their jobs and were blacklisted. Investigations of such people were carried out by a committee of Congress called the "House Unamerican Activities Committee." This nibbling away at freedom of speech in America was not comparable to the almost complete suppression of it in the Soviet Union, but it did reflect a fear that pervaded America and threatened some of its core values.

The heavens, too, became a field of contest, and here the Russians took an early lead, putting the first space satellite, the *Sputnik*, into orbit in 1957, followed by the first manned satellite in 1961. Embarrassed, President Kennedy vowed that America would be the first to land a man on the moon, within a decade, and in 1969 that mission was accomplished.

The second unnerving shock to the United States was the victory of Mao Zedong's communist People's Liberation Army in China and the expulsion of the nationalist forces to the offshore island of Taiwan. We have touched on the communist revolution in China in Chapter 19, and in the next chapter, Chapter 22, we will give more detail on that revolution and its consequences. Here we note that the communist victory in China—the most populous country in the world, one of its great historic civilizations,

"A great step for mankind ..." Edwin ("Buzz") Aldrin, the second man on the moon, clambers down the ladder of the Apollo II lunar module "Eagle" in July 1969. Neil Armstrong had set foot on the moon moments earlier. The race for supremacy in space between the superpowers was fueled by the Cold War.

and a nation that the United States had helped with military, technical, and food aid for more than a decade—undermined many American beliefs and hopes. Debate raged in the United States about "How We Lost China," revealing the (false) belief that somehow China had once been America's. In any case, the communist camp, with significant help from Russia, now controlled it.

The Korean War, 1950–53

On June 25, 1950, the armed forces of communist North Korea invaded South Korea. The Korean peninsula had been a colony of Japan from 1910 until 1945. At the end of the war, control over the peninsula was divided at the 38th parallel between the Soviets to the north and the USA to the south. The prospect of independence and unification was left for future negotiation. The North Koreans apparently attacked on their own, without Russian or Chinese support. They drove all the way to the southernmost part of the peninsula before American troops, sent as part of a United Nations force, drove them back to North Korea by September, and then kept pushing them farther north toward the border with China. In response, China entered the war, sending in hundreds of thousands of troops in wave after wave of assaults. China crossed the border into the south, capturing the South Korean capital of Seoul for a second time, until additional US and UN forces pushed them back to the 38th parallel, and brought the military and political situation to a stalemate. By war's end in 1953, 115,000 soldiers, including 37,000 Americans, and a million civilians had died in the south. (North Korea did not release statistics.) At least a million Chinese were also killed in the struggle.

The Korean War reconfirmed America's armed opposition to communism but actually increased the American feeling of threat, since now China was also involved. The war strengthened the reputation of the Chinese since they had held the mighty Americans to a military stand-off. Mao had called America a "paper tiger" despite its nuclear weapons. He believed that, after Hiroshima and Nagasaki, America could never again use the arsenal of nuclear weapons that it possessed, and Korea seemed to confirm his view. Ironically, the war poisoned the atmosphere between China and Russia as well, because Stalin had at first offered to support China if it went to war with America, and then withdrew the pledge. Mao made the agonizing decision to proceed alone. In the end, the USSR did lend some support, but Stalin's equivocation left the Chinese leadership feeling betrayed.

The war brought some prosperity to Japan. It made the island nation a manufacturing base for United States war supplies and a prime location for rest-and-relaxation by US troops. It increased the personal contact between Americans and Japanese, especially between GIs and Japanese women. It also led the United States to see Japan as its new ally in the Pacific. The United States terminated its occupation of Japan in 1952, and, reversing its earlier wish that Japan remain unarmed, encouraged that country to create some armed defense forces.

The Korean War tended to drive a wedge between the United States and many of its European allies who had supported the early war effort to repulse the North Korean attack but who felt that the continuing drive into North Korea was unnecessarily belligerent and costly, and provoked the Chinese response. Also in light of this war, America encouraged Germany to grow once again into a major ally with significant armed forces. European nations who had so recently been at war with Germany were apprehensive about a rearmed Germany.

Technologically, helicopters played a major role in the war. US forces in Korea employed them in unprecedented numbers to convoy troops, to stage aerial attacks, and to ferry wounded soldiers to mobile army surgical hospitals (MASH) units. The Chinese threw waves of soldiers into their attacks, compensating with numbers for what they lacked in equipment.

Driven by their mutual hostility, the two superpowers carried "brinksmanship" farther and created militarized organizations of their allies. With its western European allies and Canada, the United States created the North Atlantic Treaty Organization (NATO) in 1949. NATO included democratic countries with capitalist, socialist, and mixed economies: Britain, France, Italy, Canada, Denmark, Norway, Iceland, Belgium, the Netherlands, and Luxembourg. Portugal, though not a democracy at the time, was also a charter member. In 1952, both Greece and Turkey joined, as did West Germany in 1955, only a decade after its defeat in World War II. In response, the USSR formally established the Warsaw Pact in 1955 among the nations of Albania, Bulgaria, Czechoslovakia, East Germany, Hungary, Poland, and Romania, which were communist in their politics and economics, and under the control of the USSR. Four decades of Cold War standoff in Europe had begun. When the USSR crushed democratic revolts in East Germany (1953), Hungary (1956), Czechoslovakia (1968), and Poland (1981), NATO protested but did not intervene.

The Soviet Union after Stalin

Nikita Khrushchev, 1953–64 The USSR itself was changing. After Stalin's death in 1953, Party General Secretary Nikita Khrushchev (1894–1971) began to reveal and reject some of the coercive powers of the communist state. At the Twentieth Party Congress in 1956, Khrushchev exposed the extent of Stalin's tyranny, declaring that:

> Arbitrary behavior by one person encouraged and permitted arbitrariness in others. Mass arrests and deportations of many thousands of people, executions without trial and without normal investigation created conditions of insecurity, fear, and even desperation. (Kochan and Abraham, p. 447)

In 1961, at the Twenty-second Party Congress, Khrushchev denounced Stalin more fully and had his body removed from Lenin's Mausoleum. Khrushchev released a number of political prisoners of conscience, permitted the publication of many politically banned works, and moderated Stalin's plans for heavy industrialization in favor of greater production of consumer goods. The Soviet government itself gradually began to portray Stalin as a political monster, as Khrushchev also began to open more of the record, publicly revealing Stalin's atrocities.

In the new climate of openness, Russian novelist Alexander Solzhenitsyn (b. 1918) was able to publish *A Day in the Life of Ivan Denisovich* (1962), a realistic novel depicting conditions in one of the Soviet prison labor camps. Khrushchev fell from power in 1964, however, and Solzhenitsyn could publish his next two novels—*The First Circle* (1968), set in a prison, and *Cancer Ward* (1968), set in a hospital—only in editions smuggled out of Russia. Internally his writings circulated illegally in **samizdat** ("self-published"), privately copied, formats. In 1970, the novelist was awarded the Nobel

samizdat From the Russian *sam-*, "self-", and *izdatel'stvo*, "publishing house." Literature printed (often in typescript) and circulated secretly to evade official suppression and punishment by the government; also this illegal, underground system of private publication.

gulag The acronym of Glavnoye, Upravleniye Ispravitelno Trudovykh Lagerey, the "Chief Administration of Corrective Labor Camps," a department of the Soviet secret police founded in 1934 under Stalin. It ran a vast network of forced labor camps throughout the USSR to which millions of citizens accused of "crimes against the state" were sent for punishment. The system was exposed by Alexander Solzhenitsyn in *The Gulag Archipelago* (1973).

Prize for Literature. He did not travel to Stockholm to receive the award, however, fearing that he would be denied re-entry to the Russia he loved despite its political problems.

Solzhenitsyn courageously took it upon himself to go beyond *Ivan Denisovich*. In the three volumes of his *Gulag Archipelago* (1973–8), he revealed fully the extent of the **gulag**, the nationwide archipelago of prison labor camps spread throughout the country, most of them in cold, vast, remote Siberia.

> This Archipelago crisscrossed and patterned that other country within which it was located, like a gigantic patchwork, cutting into its cities, hovering over its streets. Yet there were many who did not even guess at its presence and many, many others who had heard something vague. And only those who had been there knew the whole truth. (Solzhenitsyn, p. X)

As many as 8 million citizens were imprisoned at any given time, and some 20 million may have died in the camps. After the publication of the *Gulag Archipelago* in 1973, Solzhenitsyn was stripped of his Russian citizenship and exiled. For about fifteen years he lived in Vermont, USA, until in 1990 a new government in Russia restored his citizenship and he returned in 1994.

Under Khrushchev, the Soviet Union continued to attempt to catch up to the West militarily and economically—and in some competitions even to surpass it, as it did with the *Sputnik* space satellite in 1957. Khrushchev tried, unsuccessfully, to develop agriculturally more of the "virgin lands" of Kazakhstan and Siberia. Agriculture continued to lag and consumer goods continued to be limited, but the USSR seemed on a par with the United States militarily and industrially. But for how long could its relatively backward economy continue to support its investment in heavy military industries? The Soviet government saw no alternative. It felt surrounded and threatened by the United States and its allies, and saw no choice but to continue preparing its defenses—mirroring Stalin's defensive policies in regard to Germany in the 1930s.

In foreign affairs, Khrushchev was as aggressive as Stalin. He maintained Russia's domination of eastern Europe. He crushed the Hungarian uprising of 1956. He stationed nuclear-tipped missiles in Cuba. He allowed the East Germans to build a wall through the heart of divided Berlin in 1961 to close escape routes to the West. The Soviet Party leadership considered Khrushchev reckless and removed him from power in 1964. He was followed by almost two decades of bureaucratic stagnation under Leonid Brezhnev (1906–82).

Leonid Brezhnev, 1964–82 Brezhnev ruled the Soviet Union from 1964 to 1982 as head of the government and general secretary of the Communist Party. In the spring of 1968 Czechoslovakia tried to escape Russian control and establish an independent government. Brezhnev ended the hopes of this "Prague Spring" by declaring that the Soviet Union would intervene in the affairs of its satellites to prevent counter-revolution, a policy later named the "Brezhnev Doctrine." Soviet troops crushed the Czech revolt. In the first years of his administration, Brezhnev built up the armed forces of the USSR, although later he made cutbacks.

Despite the Brezhnev Doctrine, unrest simmered in eastern Europe, most strongly in Poland. Here the Roman Catholic Church remained a powerful voice critical of communist rule, and when Karol Wojtyla, the Polish archbishop of Krakow, was elected pope in 1978, dissidents throughout Poland took heart. Although their country, under communism, was officially atheistic, they now had a symbolic leader at the pinnacle of religious authority in Rome who could address their spiritual longings and provide a beacon of hope for independence from Soviet control. Lech Walesa, a shipyard worker in Gdansk, began to organize what ultimately became Solidarity, an independent trade union federation with a membership of more than 10 million industrial and agricultural workers. Solidarity demanded not only lower prices and higher wages, but also the right to strike, freedom for political prisoners, an end to censorship, and free elections. At Moscow's bidding, the Polish government jailed Walesa and other Solidarity leaders and declared martial law. The pope, however, supported Solidarity, and the United States imposed economic sanctions. In 1982 Brezhnev died, martial law ended, and Walesa was freed. In 1983 he received the Nobel Peace Prize. Demands for more freedom continued to build in Poland and throughout the Soviet Union.

Moscow power parade. At the height of the Cold War, the arms race against the West saw Russian leaders Khrushchev and Brezhnev pouring colossal sums of money into military hardware. This parade shows tanks moving through Red Square, Moscow, to mark the sixty-sixth anniversary of the 1917 October Revolution. Lenin keeps watch.

The USSR suffered its Vietnam in Afghanistan. In 1978, a pro-Soviet coup took over that country. The USSR sent in troops and supplies to put down anti-communist, Islamic revolts against the new government, and sponsored a second coup in favor of an even more pro-Soviet government. More than 100,000 troops helped the new government secure the cities, especially the capital, Kabul, but the Muslim rebels, supported by assistance from the United States, controlled the rural areas. Among the rebels receiving aid from the USA was a group of militant Muslims called the Taliban, and among them was a young Saudi guerrilla fighter named Osama bin Laden. The USSR lost some 15,000 soldiers in eight years of fighting, leading to intense criticism of the Russian government back home. The United Nations brokered a peace agreement in 1988 that called for the withdrawal of all foreign troops, and the Russians went home discredited and in disarray. Afghanistan itself was thoroughly destabilized and descended into continuing civil war, with the Taliban generally taking command, but with no group firmly in control of the entire country.

The American Military-Industrial Complex

The costs of the military-technological competition of the Cold War were astronomical. In 1960, in peacetime, the governments of the world spent nearly $100 billion on military expenses.

In his 1961 farewell address as president of the United States, Dwight Eisenhower, a five-star general who had served as supreme commander of Allied Forces in Europe during World War II, now warned his nation against the dangers of the "military-industrial complex," the combination of military and industrial leaders who might find it in their mutual interests to promote warfare:

> We must never let the weight of this combination endanger our liberties or democratic processes. We should take nothing for granted. Only an alert and knowledgeable citizenry can compel the proper meshing of the huge industrial and military machinery of defense with our peaceful methods and goals, so that security and liberty may prosper together.

Defense expenditure. Fueled by the conflict and the Cold War, massive expenditure by the US and USSR on military hardware kept them neck and neck. After 1960, the rapid militarization of the developing nations increased expenditures. After the fall of the Soviet Union, 1989–91, they decreased. Sources: Paul Kennedy, *The Rise and Fall of The Great Powers* and *New York Times 2000 Almanac.*

DEFENSE EXPENDITURE (in billions of current dollars)

	USA	USSR	China	Germany	UK	Japan
1930	.699	.722	–	.162	.512	.218
1938	1.13	5.43	–	7.41	1.86	1.74
1950	14.5	15.5	2.5	–	2.3	–
1970	77.8	72	23.7	6.1	5.8	1.3
1987	293.2	274.7	13.4	34.1	31.5	24.2
1997	273.0	64 (Russia)	36.6	33.4	35.7	40.9

Eisenhower's warning went unheeded. The military build-up continued. So did the direct confrontations with the Soviet Union and its allies. President Kennedy confronted Cuba at the Bay of Pigs and the USSR in the Cuban Missile Crisis. He also committed American advisers to South Vietnam in its conflict with communist North Vietnam. Under President Lyndon Baines Johnson, this assistance mushroomed into a commitment to full-scale warfare with more than a half million US troops fighting in Vietnam.

Most of the armed confrontations were not directly between the Soviet Union and the United States. Despite, or perhaps because of, the destructive power of their arsenals, the European and North American powers exercised restraint. The Cold War never turned hot within their borders. As colonized countries escaped colonialism and became independent—like Korea, Vietnam, and, in a way, China—each of the two superpowers sought to enlist them on its side. In their **client states** (states reliant on them for aid and assistance) in the Middle East, Africa, Asia, and Latin America warfare did break out repeatedly. As a result, many of the wars of the 1950s, 1960s, 1970s, and 1980s were **proxy wars**, wars fought between allies of the US and USSR, as the superpowers usually stood in the background and let others fight and kill on their behalf. In these localized wars the great powers could sell or give away their older weapons systems and test the newer ones in countries whose leaders were only too eager to get them. Many of these proxy wars were fought in Africa—in Congo (Zaire), Nigeria, Ethiopia, Angola, and Mozambique—sometimes with Cuban troops fighting very far from home. In Central American guerrilla wars in Guatemala, Nicaragua, and El Salvador, the United States and the USSR supported opposing parties. In the Middle East, Israel was widely viewed as a client state of the USA, and, in response, many Arab states turned to the USSR for economic aid and military assistance. Some, however, played both sides diplomatically to get whatever benefits they could from the Cold War competition.

client state A state that is economically, politically, or militarily dependent on another state.

proxy war A war waged between dependent, **client states** of larger, more powerful states that do not become directly involved in the fighting.

The Cuban Missile Crisis

The most frightening moment of the Cold War took place in 1962 in a confrontation over nuclear-tipped missiles deployed in Cuba. Following a revolution in 1959, led by Fidel Castro, Cuba had become a communist country only 90 miles off the coast of Florida, threatening America's self-confidence and its hold over Latin America. Castro, a lawyer who had taken himself into the hills of eastern Cuba to lead a guerrilla war against American-backed dictator Fulgencio Batista, declared a six–point program:

- extensive land redistribution and collectivization, with common use of expensive equipment;
- limits on foreign investment and mobilization of Cuba's own capital through the national bank for investment in industrialization;
- housing policies that would enable each Cuban family to own its own home;
- full employment;
- full literacy in an educational system appropriate to an agrarian country;
- health care facilities for all.

Contrary to promises made before the revolution, Castro did not hold elections, declaring that "the intimate union and identification of the government with the people," made elections unnecessary. Although Castro denied that he was a communist and did, for a time, try to negotiate agreements with the United States, he soon established close military and economic ties with the Soviet bloc. In the Cold War environment of the time, the United States viewed Castro as a communist. When three multinational oil refineries refused to process oil brought to Cuba from the USSR, Castro expropriated the refineries. In response, the United States ended the special quota of sugar that it had guaranteed to purchase from Cuba since the 1930s. In December 1961, Castro openly announced his allegiance to Marxism-Leninism. From that time, Cuba became dependent on the Soviet Union, reversing Batista's earlier dependence on the United States.

Castro then proceeded to carry out his announced program. He expropriated or confiscated foreign assets, including $1 billion in North American property and investments in Cuba. He collectivized farms, which took land away from peasants, and centralized control of the economy in the hands of the government. He took human development issues seriously, and devoted money and energies to health, education, and cultural activities. Education and all medical services were free.

The living standards of most Cubans improved sharply. Most of the elites—hundreds of thousands of people—fled, however, with the acquiescence of the government, which was pleased to have them gone. These exiles were received with open arms in the United States, where they formed a new large community, centered in Miami, which lobbied heavily for the United States to take action against Castro. Meanwhile Castro and his close associate Ernesto "Che" Guevara dispatched advisers throughout Latin America and Africa to promote guerrilla war.

Two confrontations between Cuba and the United States followed. The American government agreed to arm and support a group of about 1,500 Cuban exiles who wanted to invade the island on the assumption that Cuba's people would welcome the opportunity to overthrow Castro. When the exiles did invade, on April 17, 1961, at the Bay of Pigs, they were met not by a popular uprising, but by Cuban armed forces who immediately defeated them. In the next year, Cuba was the focus of the most direct confrontation of the Cold War between the United States and the Soviet Union. The Soviet Union had positioned nuclear missiles in Cuba. They denied the existence of these missiles, but American reconnaissance aircraft obtained photographic evidence. President Kennedy demanded that the missiles be withdrawn, even threatening nuclear war over the

Castro, victorious, en route to Havana. Fidel Castro embraces a child amongst a crowd of well-wishers shortly after taking power. In January 1959, Cuban dictator Fulgencio Batista was ousted by Castro and his popular revolutionary army. The revolutionaries had been hiding in the mountains since December 1956, fighting against Batista's regime. Their fight to overthrow the dictator was called the "26th July Movement," after the date of their first insurrection against Batista.

SOURCE

Guerrilla Warfare

With the success of Mao's communist, agrarian revolution in China and Castro's in Cuba, and continuing peasant uprisings around the world, including Vietnam, the 1960s were especially alive with rural guerrilla warfare. Usually led by young, vigorous, brave, and single-minded revolutionaries, the guerrilla movements had a powerful mystique, and a number of successes. They demonstrated the potential of very simple conflict techniques against the most sophisticated modern weapons. One of the most charismatic of the guerrilla warriors was Ernesto "Che" Guevara, who was born in Argentina in 1928 and who was captured and killed while organizing a guerrilla movement in Bolivia in 1967. He participated in Castro's revolution in Cuba and was later appointed head of the national bank. But Guevara chose life as a full-time revolutionary, helping to establish guerrilla focos, revolutionary outposts, in many locations. His speeches and writings, like Mao's, were a bible to guerrilla warriors.

Nuclei of relatively few persons choose places favorable for guerrilla warfare, sometimes with the intention of launching a counterattack or to weather a storm, and there they begin to take action. But the following must be made clear: At the beginning, the relative weakness of the guerrilla fighters is such that they should endeavor to pay attention only to the terrain, in order to become acquainted with the surroundings, establish connections with the population, and fortify the places that eventually will be converted into bases. The guerrilla unit can survive only if it starts by basing its development on the three following conditions: constant mobility, constant vigilance, constant wariness …

We must carry the war into every corner the enemy happens to carry it—to his home, to his centers of entertainment: a total war. It is necessary to prevent him from having a moment of peace, a quiet moment outside his barracks or even inside; we must attack him wherever he may move …

Our every action is a battle cry against imperialism, and a battle hymn to the people's unity against the great enemy of mankind: the United States of America. Wherever death may surprise us, let it be welcome, provided that this, our battle cry, may have reached some receptive ear and another hand may be extended to wield our weapons and other men be ready to intone the funeral dirge with the staccato singing of the machine gun and new battle cries of war and victory.

(Sigmund, pp. 370, 381)

issue. As the world watched, terrified, in fear of imminent Armageddon, Russian leader Nikita Khrushchev announced that the USSR would remove the missiles in exchange for American promises not to invade Cuba again and to remove its own missiles from Turkey. According to the most recent scholarship, Khrushchev acted here against the wishes of Castro, who was willing to push the nuclear challenge to the Americans even further to the brink. From this point onward, however, the two superpowers pulled back from such direct confrontation.

THE COLD WAR AND THE EMERGENCE OF NEW NATIONS

The Cold War was one of the great postwar reconfigurations. The collapse of colonialism and the emergence of more than eighty new nations from colonial control to independence was another. This process of decolonization was in large part a legacy of the world wars and the global depression, 1914 to 1945. These cataclysms depleted the colonizing powers of manpower, financial resources, and moral status. They no longer had the power to hold on to their colonies, especially as many of the colonies began to assert their right to independence. The colonized peoples, and many of the colonizers themselves, no longer believed in the "White Man's Burden" of civilizing the non-Western world. The almost unimaginable devastation of the wars exploded the myth of the superiority of the civilization of the colonizers.

The allies in World War I had proclaimed the mission of making the world safe for democracy and had promised increased self-government after the war to many of their colonies. Britain had made such promises to its European colony, Ireland, in 1914, and to India in 1917. It promised a new homeland for Jews in Palestine and at the same time promised to do no harm to the existing Arab population of Palestine. At war's end, the smaller ethnic groups in southern and eastern Europe had hoped for new states. Middle Eastern regions, like Lebanon, Syria, Jordan, and Palestine, had looked forward to self-government. Most of these aspirations were quashed. Ireland was given independence, but only after an armed uprising. The Protestant north remained a colony of England. India continued in colonial status. Much of the Middle East was mandated to Britain and France.

As independence movements intensified, Kwame Nkrumah of Ghana wrote:

> I saw that the whole solution to this problem lay in political freedom for our people; for it is only when a people are politically free that other races can give them the respect that is due them. It is impossible to talk of equality of races in any other terms. No people without a government of their own can expect to be treated on the same level as peoples of independent sovereign states. It is far better to be free to govern or misgovern yourself than to be governed by anybody else. (Nkrumah, p.9)

The anti-colonial nationalists gained important new allies as the United States and the Soviet Union both added their voices. The Soviet Union had from its inception under Lenin declared its opposition to overseas colonialism, although its post-World War II holdings in central and eastern Europe and central Asia looked like its own form of colonialism close to home. The United States, too, especially under Franklin Delano Roosevelt and Truman, spoke out for an end of colonialism. These anti-colonial stands had some effect. Churchill, for example, moderated his pro-colonial positions, especially in regard to India, in deference to his wartime colleagues.

In the long run, Churchill's increased moderation wasn't enough. The British voted his party out of office at the end of the war. The people felt that Churchill was the right man for the war, but his was not the right party for the peace. They wanted new directions at home and abroad, including an end to their imperial holdings, which they began to see as economically and militarily costly in the face of renewed colonial resistance, and perhaps as morally inappropriate as well. The combination of increasingly resistant colonized nations and colonizing powers no longer able to repress them led to the conferring of independence.

Ghana's independence. Prime minister (later president) Kwame Nkrumah waves to a celebrating crowd as the Gold Coast colony becomes the newly independent country of Ghana on March 6, 1957. Nkrumah formed a one-party state in 1964. His regime was ended by a military coup in 1966 during his absence on a trip to China.

The British- and French-mandated territories in the Middle East were the first to gain their freedom. Iraq had been granted formal independence from Britain in 1932 as a kingdom. British troops were called in, however, when coups were attempted to overthrow the monarchy. In 1958, a leftist coup did succeed in overthrowing the king, breaking the ties to Britain, and reorienting the country's foreign policy toward the USSR. Jordan gained independence from Britain in 1946, as did Lebanon in 1943 and Syria in 1946 from France.

India, the largest of all the colonies, had begun to organize a modern nationalist political movement from 1885 and finally won its independence from Britain in 1947, although the subcontinent was partitioned on religious grounds into two nations, India and Pakistan. Because of its size and importance, India will be discussed at greater length in the next chapter (Chapter 22).

In the same year the United Nations passed a resolution agreeing to partition the British-mandated land of Palestine between its bitterly antagonistic Jewish and Arab populations. In 1920, only about 60,000 Jews were living in Palestine, about one-tenth the number of Arabs. Jewish immigration and settlement increased between the two world wars, driven in part by the increasing persecution of Jews under the Nazis in Germany and its conquered territories. Arab resistance to this new stream of immigration from Europe led to repeated armed clashes between the two groups. To reduce the tensions, the British severely restricted Jewish immigration. In the face of the Holocaust, however, the Jewish people felt a desperate need for a safe haven under their own national sovereignty, and they continued to immigrate illegally.

In 1947, as the UN declared its partition plan, the British prepared to leave. Arabs and Jews armed for battle. David Ben-Gurion's declaration of statehood for Israel in 1948 triggered an immediate armed attack by its neighbors. The new state survived the war, even expanding its borders slightly, but no peace treaties were signed, only agreements to cease fire. Since no new government had yet arisen to claim sovereignty over the remaining parts of Palestine, the king of Jordan asserted his country's control of that territory. The area was generally referred to as "the West Bank" of the Jordan River. The entire situation remained volatile.

In China, the communist revolutionaries led by Mao Zedong captured the government in 1949, closed down the foreign holdings in the treaty ports, and asserted China's control over its own destiny. The anti-communist, nationalist Chinese armies fled to the island of Taiwan, leaving China divided as well, although Taiwan was only one third of 1 percent of the size of the mainland in area, and held only about 2 percent of its population. Again, because of China's size and importance, its history of revolution and reconstruction as a communist state will be told in the next chapter.

In Southeast Asia, the Japanese had driven out the European colonial powers during World War II. At the end of the war, the Europeans tried to return but they faced nationalist opponents who wanted no more of colonialism. In Indonesia, the largest of these countries, Achmed Sukarno (1901–70), who had been imprisoned by the Dutch and freed by the Japanese, declared Indonesia's independence in 1945, before the Dutch tried to return. The Dutch did return in 1946 and, with the help of the British, attempted to reestablish their rule through force of arms. In 1949, however, after four years of fighting, and after the United States threatened to cut off Marshall Plan aid to the Dutch, they withdrew, recognizing Indonesian independence.

The Japanese had also seized Vietnam. After World War II, the French attempted to reestablish colonial rule but met armed opposition and guerrilla warfare led by Ho Chi Minh, the leader of the communist Vietminh or Independence League. The Vietminh had established themselves in 1939 to fight against French colonialism. Then they had fought against the Japanese occupation. Now they were once again fighting the French. After the French lost the decisive battle of Dienbienphu in May 1954, they signed an armistice agreement with the Vietminh that partitioned the country at the 17th parallel. The Vietminh governed the north. In the south, the French transferred full sovereignty to a new anti-communist government and withdrew their troops. Civil war engulfed the south. The north, under a communist government, called repeatedly for the reunification of the country and supported communist insurgents, the Vietcong, against the government of the south. America, tragically misreading an

Children fleeing from Trang Bang, South Vietnam, June 8, 1972. The children were fleeing from an American napalm attack.

essentially nationalist civil war as a Cold War battle, and unskilled in fighting guerrilla warfare, committed increasing numbers of its own troops to supporting the government of the south in an ultimately doomed cause. It finally signed a peace agreement in 1973 and evacuated its last troops in ignominious defeat in 1975. More than 58,000 US armed forces died in Vietnam during the war: 200,000 South Vietnamese, 5,000 other allied forces, and more than a million Vietnamese civilians also died. The war displaced more than six and a half million people in South Vietnam alone. The country was reunified in 1976 under the rule and administration of the North Vietnamese.

America evacuating its last personnel from Saigon in defeat, April 30, 1975. More than a decade of warfare in Vietnam convulsed America in bitter disagreements at home, and exposed its inability to understand nationalist guerrilla warfare overseas.

The Vietnam War intruded deeply and divisively into US domestic life. In the 1960s and early 1970s, the civil rights and feminist movements coalesced with the nationwide protest against the war in Vietnam, creating a vibrant, creative, colorful, shrill, and sometimes violent culture conflict that convulsed the country with its excesses on both sides. Publicly and privately, within millions of families, citizens struggled with questions concerning the legitimacy of draft-dodging, the use of drugs, sexual freedom, and the appropriate length of hair. President Johnson (1963–8), buffeted by the anti-Vietnam War movement, declined to run for a second term. The war ended only under President Richard Nixon in 1973. Nixon's opening to communist China marked a turning point in US relations with communist countries as he visited China in 1972, recognized it diplomatically, and finally allowed it to take China's seat on the UN Security Council, replacing the government of Taiwan on that body.

Africa

Although nominally independent since 1922, Egypt gained full sovereignty over the Suez Canal only in 1956. In 1957, Ghana became the first black African country to win its independence, from Britain. Most of the French colonies gained their independence in 1960. Dozens more followed these precedents in the next decade.

Egypt

In 1952, a group of Egyptian army officers, among them Gamal Abdel Nasser (1918–70), overthrew the government of their country, forced King Farouk to abdicate, and asserted their independence from Britain's influence over the country. In 1956, the British withdrew their troops from the Suez Canal and Egypt nationalized the waterway. Israel, which had been suffering from guerrilla attacks across its border from Egypt, reached an agreement with Britain and France jointly to retake the canal, put an end to cross-border attacks, and change the governing policies of Egypt. At the end of

Dismantling of the blockade of the Suez Canal, set up during the Suez Crisis, 1956. The Egyptian frigate *Abukir*, loaded with explosives to form part of an effective blockade of the Suez Canal, is raised between two German salvage ships, the *Energie* and the *Ausdauer*. The *Abukir* was the last of a series of obstructions in the canal, and once it was raised and disposed of, the waterway could be reopened to navigation.

October, Israeli forces attacked Egypt, and a few days later Britain and France bombed Egypt and air-dropped troops to join in the fighting. President Eisenhower, blind-sided and infuriated by this neo-colonial act by his own allies, put pressure on them to withdraw from Egypt and the canal. As a result, Nasser's reputation reached heroic heights throughout the Arab world as a man who had confronted the Western powers, divided them, and got rid of them. In 1967, Nasser concluded an agreement with the Soviet Union accepting its assistance in building the Aswan High Dam on the Nile River, one of the most significant engineering and hydro-electric projects of the day, which went out of its way to preserve ancient Egypt's architectural wonders, despite the problems for the ecology of the region. Nasser died in 1970, and his successor, Anwar Sadat (1918–81), expelled all Soviet advisers, once again demonstrating that third-world politics were mercurial, and could cause problems for both first and second world countries. In 1981, Sadat was assassinated, but his successor, Hosni Mubarak (b. 1928), continued his policies of keeping the Soviets at a distance, and maintaining collegial diplomatic relations with the United States.

Congo

The "Congo crisis" of 1960 demonstrated again the cross-cutting interests of the Cold War superpowers, other international interest groups, and the complex and diverse sub-national units within a newly created nation. The Congo is rich in diamonds, copper, coffee, and crude oil. It has 70 percent of the world's known reserves of cobalt. In earlier days it was also known for its natural rubber, before the general use of its synthetic alternative. For the profits of these products, Leopold II, king of the Belgians, had first taken the Congo as his personal colony in 1885. Because of the extraordinary cruelty of his rule, the Belgian government itself took control in 1908, but violence and autocracy remained characteristic of Belgian rule. Political devolution to limited self-rule began only in 1957. A small group of educated Congolese, who saw the preparations for independence in other African colonies, began to assert national political demands, and the Belgians allowed elections for local self-government. Among the leading contestants, Joseph Kasavubu (*c.* 1910–69) was an early advocate of independence, but his focus was primarily on his own ethnic Bakongo people. Patrice Lumumba (1925–61) provided a more national and more militant leadership. Anti-government rioting began in January 1959. Belgium began reconsidering its options. In January 1960, it convened a Round Table Conference in Brussels and, with breakneck, unrealistic speed, declared that the Congo would be independent on June 30, 1960.

At the independence celebrations, Lumumba, the newly elected prime minister, delivered a bitter speech revealing his deep-seated, festering rage toward the Belgians:

> We are no longer your monkeys … We have known the back-breaking works exacted from us in exchange for salaries which permit us neither to eat enough to satisfy our hunger, nor to dress and lodge ourselves decently, nor to raise our children as the beloved creatures they are.

HOW DO WE KNOW?

Evaluating the Legacies of Colonialism

As the colonial era ended, historians divided sharply in assessing the impact of colonial rule. Leften Stavrianos, who spent most of his career at the University of California, San Diego, presented a Marxist, primarily economic, critical perspective. Colonial rule created "an unprecedented increase in productivity" in commerce and industry, but no corresponding increase in pay for the workers nor in distribution of wealth to the colony. In many colonies, white settlers and plantation owners seized the best lands. Rural communities were disrupted as

> private property arrangements displaced the former communal ownership and cultivation of land ... Land now became a mere possession, food a mere commodity of exchange, neighbor a mere common property owner and labor a mere means of survival. (Stavrianos, p.9)

As the industrial revolution matured into industrial capitalism, exploitation became more severe. The results were unfortunate and long lasting:

> All these global economic trends combined to produce the present division of the world into the developed West as against the underdeveloped Third World. But underdevelopment did not mean nondevelopment; rather it meant distorted development—development designed to produce only one or two commodities needed by the Western markets rather than overall development to meet local needs. In short, it was the familiar Third World curse of economic growth without economic development. (Stavrianos, p.11)

Theodore Von Laue, who studied Westernization, on the other hand, said very little about economic inequalities. Deeply influenced by Judeo-Christian perspectives, he emphasized the cultural upheavals of colonialism and the paradoxical introduction by force of Western values of freedom:

> The world revolution of Westernization, in short, carried a double thrust. It was freedom, justice, and peace—the best of the European tradition—on the one hand; on the other hand (and rather unconsciously) raw power to reshape the world in one's own image.

The transformation to Western values was not complete, however:

> Underneath the global universals of power and its most visible supporting skills— literacy, science and technology, large-scale organization—the former diversities persist. The traditional cultures, though in mortal peril, linger under the ground floors of life. Rival political ideologies and ambitions clash head on. The world's major religions vie with each other as keenly as ever. Attitudes, values, life-styles from all continents mingle freely in the global marketplace, reducing in the intensified invidious comparison all former absolute truths to questionable hypotheses.

Von Laue looked forward to the day when all people

> Will be ready to fuse their personal egos with the egos of billions of other human beings, even in intimate matters like procreation and family size.

It would appear that the common values on that day would be the Western values of the Enlightenment.

Dipesh Chakrabarty questioned this assumption that Western values would be the governing ones. Born in India after independence, trained in Australia and the United States, and later teaching there as well, Chakrabarty argued that the greatest (self-)deception of the colonizers was to project European values as the appropriate goals for the entire world, and to see history moving in that direction: "First in Europe, then elsewhere." He rejected the idea that the rest of the world exists in Europe's "waiting room." He did appreciate European, Enlightenment values, but he did not think that they were the only valid ones, nor that they ought to or necessarily will become universal. Chakrabarty did not address economic issues. On cultural transformations brought by colonialism, however, he was not prepared to accept Von Laue's celebration of exclusively Western values, nor to look forward to the day when they alone would triumph.

- Which effects of colonialism do you think were more important, the economic and technological effects, or the cultural effects? Please be specific in the effects you are discussing.
- To the extent that the Cold War that lasted from the mid-1940s to the mid-1980s represents in part the values of the West, what values do you think colonized countries learned from the West?
- Do you think it is a good idea that some day the peoples of the world may share a similar set of values? Why or why not? If it is a good idea, then what should those values be? To what extent are they technological values?

We have known the mockery, the insults, the blows submitted to morning, noon, and night because we were *nègres* [blacks]. We have known that our lands were despoiled in the name of supposedly legal text which in reality recognized only the right of the stronger ... And, finally, who will forget the hangings or the firing squads where so many of our brothers perished, or the cells into which were brutally thrown those who escaped the soldiers' bullets—the soldiers whom the colonialists made the instruments of their domination? (Andrea and Overfield, pp. 507–8)

Aerial view of rioting in Leopoldville, Belgian Congo, January 6, 1959. The shot shows Congolese streaming through the streets, pillaging and burning the Belgian shops in the village. Riots raged for two days in the Congolese capital, leaving thirty-five dead.

Within days of independence, the army mutinied; Kasavubu, the new president, dismissed Lumumba, the prime minister; Lumumba, in turn, dismissed Kasavubu; Moise Tshombe (1919–69) declared Katanga, the Congo's richest region, independent under his leadership; the Belgians supported Tshombe's move; both Kasavubu and Lumumba appealed to the United Nations for assistance. Lumumba wanted the UN peacekeeping force that arrived to act with force to bring Katanga, with its rich mineral wealth, back into the Congo, but Kasavubu did not, and ultimately the UN forces did not act. Lumumba called on the USSR for assistance, placing the Congo in the middle of the Cold War struggles. Lumumba was captured by Kasavubu, escaped, was recaptured, turned over to the Katanga secessionists, and murdered, apparently with the complicity of the Belgian government and the assistance of the American Central Intelligence Agency (CIA). UN forces defeated Katanga and its mercenary armed forces only in 1963. By this time, however, other provinces of Congo also revolted against the central government and were subdued with the help of European mercenary troops. Most surprisingly, in the movement to restore the authority of the central government, Moise Tshombe—who had been the leader of secessionist Katanga—became prime minister.

Continuing disputes between Tshombe and President Kasavubu opened the way for a military coup led by Joseph Mobutu (1930–97; later Mobutu Sese Seko). With help from Morocco, France, and the United States, Mobutu held out against invasions and continuing attempts at secession. Mobutu ruled with dictatorial powers, changed the name of the country and of its principal river from Congo to Zaire, and transferred much of the wealth earned by Congo's exports to his own overseas accounts—knowledgeable observers guessed $4 to 5 billion—until he was forced from office and into exile in 1997.

Congo is an especially stark example of the confluence of a weak, poor, new nation, deeply divided among the various ethnic groups within its population, caught in the politics of both the Cold War and the international marketplace, and captured by a kleptomaniac, tyrannical dictator for his own purposes.

Algeria

Algeria, which held a million French settlers, won independence in 1962 after a long and bitter struggle that threatened to plunge France itself into civil war. France had been the colonizing power in Morocco, Algeria, and Tunisia. Independence for Morocco and Tunisia came relatively easily and peacefully in 1956 through negotiations with France. Algeria won its independence, however, only through violence and civil war.

Algeria had the largest European settler community in North Africa. The French in Algeria numbered one million, about 12 percent of the total population, but they held one-third of all the cultivable land. These settlers had become prosperous and comfortable. For them, Algeria was home. By the early 1950s, 80 percent of them had been born in Algeria. Officially, Algeria was not a colony, but an integral part of France with constitutional representation in the French National Assembly. In addition, through the 1930s, the Algerian elite were French-educated and saw themselves as more French than Algerian. By the 1940s, however, reformists were moving to create a more powerful Arab-Islamic nationalism, fostering social unity, a distinct national consciousness, and solidarity with other Arabs against foreign rule.

Charles de Gaulle visits Algiers in June, 1958. Algeria had been agitating for independence since 1954, and in 1956, Ben Bella, one of the main Algerian leaders, was arrested. Two years later a political crisis in France, precipitated by continuing Algerian frustration and pressure for independence, put de Gaulle into office as the new president of the Republic. De Gaulle maintained French rule in Algeria as long as possible, while he prepared the French people for the inevitable shift in power. Finally, in 1962, Algerians achieved independence and the French withdrew.

By the mid-1950s, an Algerian revolution against French rule led by the National Liberation Front (FLN) was met by French repression. The two sides became increasingly entrenched. The violence ratcheted upward and spread not only throughout Algeria, but to France as well. The governmental system of France, the Fourth Republic, was weak, and it fell as civil war seemed to threaten. The hero and leader of the French resistance in World War II, General Charles de Gaulle, was asked to take over as president of France under a new constitution. Despite an apparent mandate to continue the war, de Gaulle chose to negotiate a settlement and finally granted independence in 1962, but only after 300,000 Algerians and 20,000 Frenchmen had been killed. Virtually all the one million European residents, many of whom had lived in the country for generations, left Algeria.

Of the Algerians, only 7,000 were in secondary school, and as of 1954, only seventy living, native Algerians had had a university education. The leaders of the new nation, hardened by their years of guerrilla warfare, and ideologically committed to centralized control, took over the tasks of development. They instituted a four-year plan in 1969, and nationalized the petroleum and natural gas resources that had been discovered in 1956. They devoted much of the new oil revenues to industrialization. They increased education's share of the national budget from 2.2 percent of the gross national product to 10 percent. The birth rate, however, remained very high. Rural migrants streamed toward the cities, and hundreds of thousands of Algerians emigrated to France in search of jobs.

Mozambique, Angola, and Guinea

Portugal held on in Africa longer than any other major colonial power, giving up Mozambique and Angola, and some smaller holdings as well, only after lengthy colonial wars as well as a government coup at home in 1974. Ruled by a dictator, Antonio Salazar, from 1932 to 1968, and then by Marcelo Caetano, Portugal was not about to

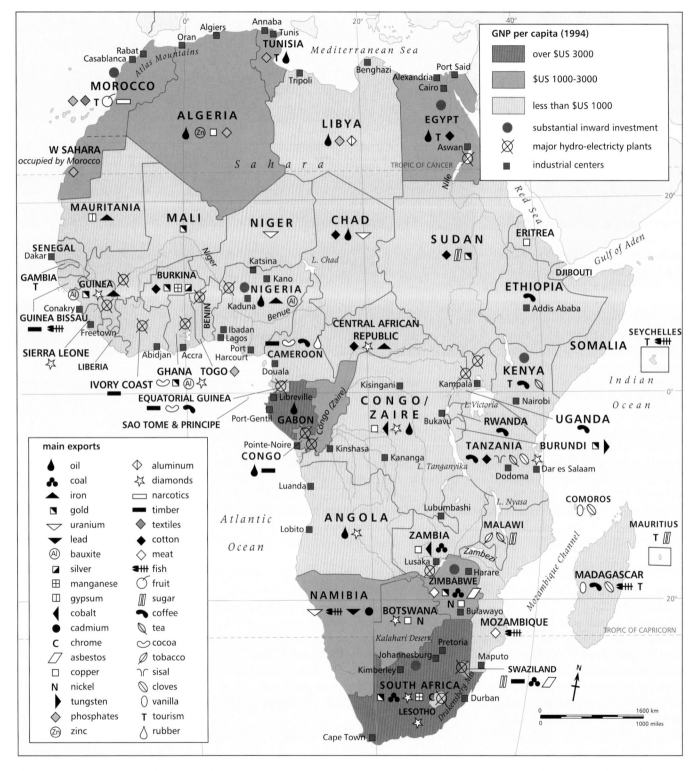

The economic development of Africa. The legacy of European colonialism has determined Africa's economic development, with a persistent reliance upon primary products, mainly mineral wealth and cash crops. Both are widely exploited by multinational franchises, bringing little real economic benefit to local economies. Political instability, corruption, disease, and natural disaster combine with low investment in education and health to create a general condition of underdevelopment. The northern tier of Arab states and South Africa stand out with greater wealth compared with the central part of the continent.

give up control of its large African colonies of Angola and Mozambique, where many Portuguese had settled, and the much smaller colony of Guinea. It governed harshly, with repressive labor policies that forced some 65,000 to 100,000 Mozambiquans to travel each year to work in the mines of South Africa. Each person had to keep an identification passbook at all times. The press was rigidly censored. The police were ruthless. Most of all, alone among the European colonizers Portugal, believed that its own future greatness depended on continuing to control its African colonies. (Portugal was not willing to cede its historic, but tiny, possession of Goa to India until, in 1961, the Indian government dispatched armed forces to seize the enclave.)

In the face of mounting international pressure against colonialism, Portugal maintained that Angola, Mozambique, and Guinea were not colonies, but "overseas provinces." In 1961, revolts broke out in all three colonies. Supported by white-dominated South Africa, Portugal fought fiercely against guerrilla freedom fighters, but the warfare placed great strains on Portugal's economy and armed forces. Moreover, the three colonies were drawn into the Cold War as the USSR and Cuba dispatched troops to aid the guerrillas. Finally, in 1974, a military coup captured the government of Portugal and granted independence to all three colonies. Once again, third-world resistance movements had triumphed over European colonial powers and, in the process, had forced changes in the home government.

In claiming their national independence, individual countries stressed such diverse ideologies as bourgeois democracy, workers' socialism, Islamic resurgence, and indigenous nationalism, often in various combinations. Most African countries obtained independence from 1945 to the 1970s, yet many became unstable countries, in part because when Europeans colonized the countries they drew boundaries for their own convenience regardless of tribal and ethnic differences. These issues of identity will be explored in more depth in Chapters 23 and 24.

Even among the colonizers, colonialism was no longer considered an appropriate form of government, except in rare cases of geographically tiny dependencies, Caribbean or South Pacific islands, for example. As new countries became independent, however, the two contesting blocs of the Cold War tried to win them over and often involved them in proxy wars, as we have seen, and will see further below. One reaction against such interference from the USA and the USSR was the formation of a third bloc, of **non-aligned nations**.

non-aligned nation A newly independent nation that chose not to align itself with either the USA or the USSR in the Cold War.

THE EMERGENCE OF THE THIRD WORLD

As decolonization created new nations in Africa and Asia at the same time that the Cold War divided Europe, many commentators spoke of the emergence of three worlds, or styles of development. The first world consisted of the wealthy, capitalist, democratic countries of western Europe and the United States; the second world was composed of the Communist Party-dominated, middle-income countries of the Soviet Union and its eastern European allies; the third world included the poorer nations, just emerging from colonization and now seeking their appropriate place in the world.

Today the term "third world" is frequently used with a negative, and much resented, connotation to designate poor, technologically backward, inefficiently organized nations. When the term first came to be used in the 1950s, however, it carried more inspirational connotations. In the first wave of decolonization following World War II, newly independent nations faced a world bitterly and expensively polarized into two hostile, belligerent, heavily armed blocs: the North Atlantic Treaty Organization (NATO), led by the United States, and the Warsaw Pact, led by the USSR.

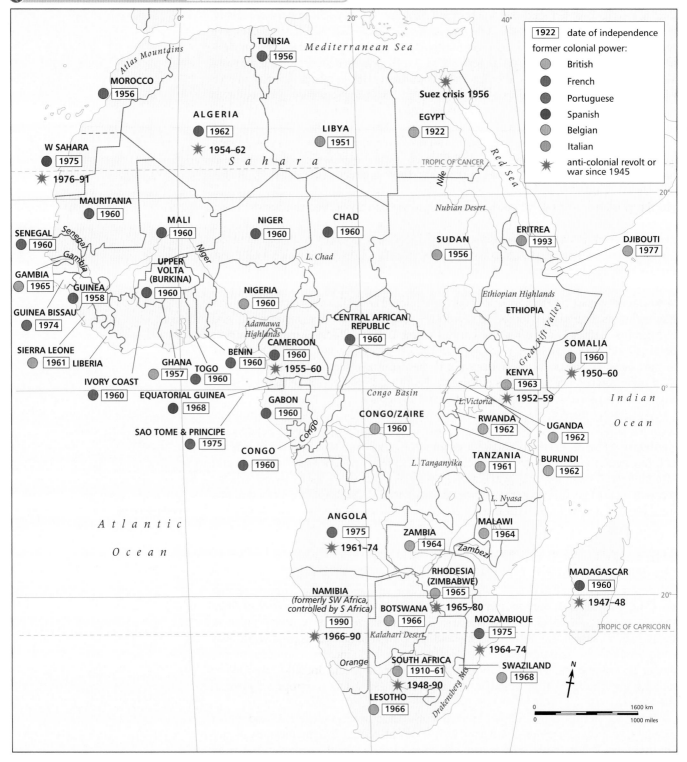

For an interactive version of this map, go to: http://www.prenhall.com/spodek/map21.2

The decolonization of Africa. Ethiopia had been colonized only briefly by Italy, Liberia had been established as an independent state, and Egypt had nominal independence from 1922, but most African states gained their independence after World War II, first those in North Africa, and then, following Ghana in 1957, those of sub-Saharan Africa. Each colonial power had its own pattern for granting independence. The British and French hoped to establish amicable relations, generally, while the Portuguese and Belgians left in more bitter circumstances.

Many of the newly independent nations, advocated a third alternative, a "third world." Many wished to be non-aligned, to avoid taking sides. They felt that Europe and the United States regarded human life as cheap—as two world wars had demonstrated. These new nations urged disarmament, especially nuclear disarmament, at a time when the first two worlds were locked in an arms race to build, first, the atomic bomb, then the hydrogen bomb, and ever more powerful rockets to launch them. They advocated state investment in such basic human needs as food, clothing, shelter, medical care, and small, appropriate-scale technology, often through international assistance, rather than in the purchase of weapons. They reminded the rest of the world that although they were "new nations" politically, many of them, such as India, Egypt, and Ethiopia, were ancient civilizations that took pride in centuries of traditional wisdom.

As they gained independence, these former colonies entered the United Nations, changing the size and complexion of that organization. Although race was not usually mentioned overtly in third-world advocacy, almost all members of the "third world" were peoples of color, while the overwhelming majority of both first and second world groups were white. In 1955, third world representatives convened by Jawaharlal Nehru (1889–1964) of India, Gamal Abdel Nasser (1918–70) of Egypt, and Marshal Tito (1892–1980) of Yugoslavia—who had struggled to set his communist nation free from Soviet control—met at Bandung, Indonesia, to launch their collective entry into international politics. At the Bandung Conference leaders of twenty nations of Africa and Asia articulated a post-colonial agenda. They called for a global reduction in military expenditure and ideological confrontation, and an increase in expenditure for economic development, health, education, welfare, and housing.

The representatives at Bandung were not all from Africa and Asia—Tito, for example, represented Yugoslavia, a European, communist country, that he had set free from Soviet control. Nor were they all non-aligned—Zhou Enlai represented China. Nor did any permanent organization emerge. But for the first time, non-Western leaders assembled to articulate their own vision of a new world order. Many of them also formed regional groups to resolve regional problems and to present a united front in confronting other international organizations, including NATO and the Warsaw Pact. The new regional organizations included the League of Arab States (1945); the Organization of American States (1948), although this organization included the United States and was heavily influenced by it; the Organization of African Unity (1963); the Association of Southeast Asian Nations (1967); the Caribbean Community and Common Market (1973); and the South Asian Association for Regional Cooperation (1983). In 1960, the Organization of Oil Exporting Countries (OPEC) was created primarily by the oil-rich states of the Middle East, but it also came to include oil-producing states in Africa, Indonesia in Southeast Asia, and Venezuela in South America. OPEC's original goals were economic, but in the 1970s it began also to support actively the political goals of its member states in confrontations with Western countries, especially on issues involving Israel and the Arab states. Further meetings of the non-aligned nations took place in Belgrade, Yugoslavia, in 1961; Cairo, Egypt, in 1964; and Lusaka, Zambia, in 1970.

Client States and Proxy Wars

At independence, many of the third world states were unstable politically, impoverished economically, and challenged by their social diversity. Many of them were, nevertheless, rich in natural resources. To prevent instability, to preserve access to natural resources, and for reasons of national and ideological pride, both the Soviet Union and the United States sought these new nations as their allies and clients. The superpowers were often willing to instigate coups to overthrow hostile governments in these new nations and sometimes to involve them in wars against one another.

The internal and external warfare that resulted from this bitter competition was devastating. The warfare usually did not involve the two superpowers directly—although the bloodiest struggles did—but were fought by their proxies. Between 1945 and 1983, perhaps 19 or 20 million people were killed in over one hundred wars and military conflicts, almost all of them in the third world, including: 9 million in East Asia—mostly in the wars in Korea and Vietnam; 3.5 million in Africa; 2.5 million in south Asia; more than a half million in the Middle East, and perhaps another million in the Iran–Iraq war, which lasted from 1980 to 1988 (Hobsbawm, p. 434). Military expansion and the resulting expansion of the state proceeded, proportionately, even more rapidly in the third world than in the first and second. While military expenditures doubled in the developed world of North America and Europe, from $385 billion in 1960 to $789 billion in 1988, in the same period in the developing world they multiplied almost five times, from $28 billion to $134 billion. Between 1960 and 1988, the number of soldiers in the developing nations doubled from 8 million to 16.5 million, in the developed nations it remained stationary at about 10 million. About a third to a half of the wars fought in the third world were, however, guerrilla wars, as peasants and urban workers fought armed struggles in small groups—usually under the leadership of young intellectuals—against their exploitation by the rulers of their country, and against the superpower that backed them.

Despite their poverty and political weakness, third world countries began to have powerful influences in the world, with effects that seriously unsettled the superpowers. In 1948, for example, Marshal Tito of Yugoslavia, who had led his guerrilla forces against the Nazis during World War II, rejected Soviet assistance, even though his country was communist in its politics and economics. He expelled Russian advisers and, in turn, Yugoslavia was expelled from the Comintern.

In 1949, Chinese communist revolutionaries, who had been fighting guerrilla warfare for a generation, successfully took possession of the government of China and forced Chiang Kai-shek and his forces to evacuate to the island of Taiwan. The Chinese communists signed a thirty-year treaty of "friendship, alliance, and mutual assistance" with the Soviet Union. The United States officially chose not to recognize the new government, and within a year China and the US were at war in Korea. China's relations with the USSR also deteriorated. In 1958, the Chinese leader Mao Zedong expressed his frustration with the Russians who seemed far too conservative in spreading communism and who had refused to share their nuclear technology with him. He expelled all his Soviet advisers, accusing them of arrogance. By 1960, the two communist titans were fighting in armed skirmishes over their mutual borders. Russia cancelled its assistance to China, and China began to spread propaganda against the USSR.

Latin America

At about the same time that Congo gained its independence from Belgium, Fidel Castro was completing the revolution in Cuba that overthrew the dictator Fulgencio Batista and soon put Castro on a collision course with the United States. As noted earlier in this chapter, Castro became closely allied with and dependent on the USSR, infuriating the Americans, and especially those new Americans who emigrated from Cuba to escape Castro's revolution. The Americans feared also that Castro's revolutionary rhetoric and example would spread throughout Latin America. It worked actively to isolate the Cuban government from participating in markets, organization, and diplomacy with other governments in the hemisphere.

During the 1960s and the next decades, however, Latin America in general, and especially Central America, was another area of the third world that brought headaches to American policy makers, and embarrassment especially to President Ronald Reagan. Nicaragua, Guatemala, Panama, and Chile were not "new nations." They had become formally independent a century and a half earlier, but they remained poor, divided by social and ethnic differnces, and economically dependent on wealthy, external countries, especially the United States. They identified with the developmental issues of the third world.

Nicaragua Strains in the relationship between the USA and Nicaragua had deep roots. To overthrow a Nicaraguan government, which had begun to grant economic concessions to governments other than the United States, the United States encouraged a revolt in 1909 and dispatched marines to support it. The troops remained, with very few breaks, until 1933, training a Nicaraguan National Guard to join them in defense of US interests. One Nicaraguan army officer, Augusto Cesar Sandino (1893–1934) rejected American hegemony and for seven years fought a guerrilla war against the US marines and the Nicaraguan National Guard until he was deceived during peace negotiations, arrested, and murdered by officers of the guard under Anastasio Somoza Garcia (1896–1956). Somoza subsequently seized control of the national government and, with the support of the United States, turned the presidency into a family dynasty for his two sons after him.

Disgusted with the wretched conditions of the common people at a time when Somoza and his allies were prospering, the editor of *La Prensa* turned his newspaper against the regime in the 1950s. In the 1960s, a revolutionary movement largely composed of students, and naming itself the Sandinista Front for National Liberation in memory of Sandino, initiated an armed guerrilla revolt. As the Somoza government became more rapacious, the resistance expanded and intensified, finally driving the government into exile. By the time the Sandinistas came to power in 1979, however, some 50,000 people had been killed in guerrilla warfare.

United States President Jimmy Carter (1977–80), a liberal in foreign policy, attempted an accommodation with the new Sandinista government, but his successor, Ronald Reagan, pursued a policy of destabilization with almost fanatic zeal. He froze loans that Carter had negotiated. He authorized the creation of a paramilitary force—often referred to as Somocistas or, more commonly, *contras*—to be based in neighboring Honduras for raids across the border into Nicaragua. The US Central Intelligence Agency (CIA) trained and supplied the contras, instructed them in terrorism, and also mined Nicaraguan harbors. These activities violated United States laws and treaties, and were condemned by the World Court, which ordered the United States to end its military and paramilitary actions against Nicaragua. The Reagan administration rejected the authority of the court. When Congress would not sanction further funding for this clandestine war, the Reagan administration arranged for some of the profits of a secret arms sale to Iran—a country generally considered hostile to the United States—to be secretly diverted to financing the contras. The double scandal of the arms sale to Iran and the transfer of funds to the contras embarrassed the Reagan administration and provided a window of opportunity for several Central American

An anti-American poster from the time of the Sandinista revolution, Nicaragua, 1979. Note the various drawings on the figure: military helicopters on the hat; a peace sign ("paz") among the little egghead representations of people massed together demonstrating; an ironic dollar bill with "In God we trust" on the leg. The final touch is the cowboy boot resting firmly on Uncle Sam's hat to keep him in check. Uncle Sam is even a sickly gray color in contrast with the brightly colored cowboy.

governments to negotiate a settlement of the civil war in Nicaragua, including an end to foreign military involvement and a call for honest elections. For his initiative in this effort to negotiate an end to the Nicaraguan conflict, Costa Rican President Oscar Arias was awarded the Nobel Prize for Peace. The nine years of warfare, 1981 to 1990, had cost approximately 60,000 deaths and another 28,000 casualties. Since 1990, Nicaragua has been ruled by democratically elected governments and relationships with the United States have normalized.

Guatemala As we have seen, Latin American critics of United States economic power were often branded communists, and the United States often condemned as communist Latin American attempts to make their societies more egalitarian. In Guatemala, the world's second largest producer of bananas, Colonel Jacobo Arbenz (1913–71) won election as president in an open, free election in 1951. Arbenz proceeded to seize some 400,000 acres of fallow land held by the United Fruit Company, a private company owned mostly by United States citizens. He offered compensation according to the value of the land declared for tax purposes by the Company, but the Company found this insufficient. Arbenz also wanted to build a highway from his capital to the Atlantic Ocean, which would have broken the Company's transportation monopoly. He proposed building a hydroelectric power plant, which would free Guatemala from its dependence on a foreign supply. Finally, fearing an attack by exiles training in neighboring countries, Arbenz sought to buy arms from the United States. When the US turned him down, he bought from Poland, which was then a communist country. Almost immediately a small Guatemalan army-in-exile of some 150 soldiers, equipped by the United States, attacked from Honduras. The Arbenz government fell, virtually without defenders.

Arbenz's successor, Carlos Castillo Armas (1914–57), returned the lands taken from the United Fruit Company, abolished several political parties, disenfranchised all illiterates, about half the adult population, and had those who opposed him jailed, tortured, exiled, or executed. (The term "banana republic" evolved to describe countries like Guatemala that were economically dependent on a single crop that they sold primarily to a superpower, and were helpless in the face of superpower political and military intervention.) Castillo Armas was assassinated in mid-1957, and soon Guatemala plunged into a civil war in which 100,000 people died before a negotiated resolution was achieved in the 1990s. In 1999, President Bill Clinton, speaking in Guatemala, "apologized for US support of right-wing governments that killed tens of thousands of rebels and Mayan Indians in a thirty-six year civil war" (*New York Times Almanac, 2000*, p. 16).

Panama In 1878, a French company, with the permission of the government of Colombia, began to build a canal across Panama, then the most northern region of that nation. The project failed and was put up for sale. The US Congress agreed to pay $40 million for the rights, but the Colombian Congress refused to ratify the new agreement. In 1903, President Theodore Roosevelt encouraged the revolt of a small Panamanian independence movement and ordered American warships to block the arrival of Colombian troops. Three days after the revolt began, he recognized Panama as an independent country. Twelve days later the USA had its treaty, including powerful rights of interference in

Rigoberta Menchu. Menchu, a Guatemalan Indian, won the Nobel Peace Prize in 1992. Her book, *I, Rigoberta Menchu: An Indian Woman in Guatemala*, was published in 1983 and became a bestseller. Although later challenged as exaggerated and "borrowed," this autobiography presents an accurate account of Indian oppression and suffering.

Panama's affairs for the protection of the canal and a 6-mile wide buffer zone along its sides. Panama began its national life as a protectorate of the United States. In 1977 Panama's military government reached an agreement with President Jimmy Carter for the return of the Canal Zone to full Panamanian control in 2000 and that transfer took place calmly, peacefully, and punctually on December 31, 1999.

Chile From 1964 to 1970, Eduardo Frei (1911–81) led a Christian Democratic government in Chile that began a program of agrarian reform and nationalized, with compensation, copper mines owned by United States' private companies. Considered moderate, Frei had good relations with the United States government. In 1970, seeking more radical reform, the voters in Chile elected the socialist Salvador Allende (1908–73). The United States government and major transnational corporations opposed his election and once in office, President Allende confirmed their fears. He increased agrarian reform, purchased control of most banks, and continued the nationalization of the foreign-owned copper industry, which produced three-fourths of Chile's exports. Allende increased the salaries of government workers and expanded medical and housing programs. The usual conflict arose between the desire to improve economic and social benefits, on the one hand, and the problem of finding resources to pay, on the other. Shortages and inflation resulted. The United States government sharply reduced loans and aid to Allende's socialist government, and international banks also cut back on loans. The CIA, with a mandate to overthrow Allende, covertly financed opposition parties and labor strikes. Finally, the middle class, and especially women, who found the resulting chaos and economic instability intolerable, persuaded the military to act. In September 1973, they attacked and bombed the presidential palace, killing Allende.

General Augusto Pinochet (b. 1915), who headed the new government, immediately killed or detained hundreds of thousands of Allende supporters, men and women. He ruled until 1988, feared and hated for his violence toward the opposition, but effective in restoring the economy, with the aid of advisers from the United States. In a plebiscite in 1988, Pinochet was rejected by Chile's voters, and the government passed to the opposition. Chile had returned to democracy.

Iran

In contrast to their apparent victories in Latin America, in Iran, the Americans were humbled. During World War II, the British forced the abdication of Iran's Shah Reza Khan in favor of his son, the pro-British Muhammad Reza Pahlavi. Meanwhile, the increased exploitation of Iran's oil resources had begun to bring new wealth to the kingdom. In 1951, Prime Minister Muhammad Mussadeq (1880–1967) nationalized the Iranian oil industry against the wishes of the shah. In response, Britain and the US conspired with the Iranian army in a coup that supported the shah and overthrew Mussadeq.

Deeply indebted to the West, the shah joined the American-inspired Baghdad Pact, a military alliance directed against the Soviet Union. He invited additional Western oil investment, and proceeded to use Iran's oil wealth to fund deep and massive—but convulsive, erratic, and uneven—Westernization of the country. By the mid-1970s, about 150,000 foreigners had come to Iran to run the new high-technology industries and to live a luxurious lifestyle in secluded "colonies." Rural people were also flooding into the cities, putting great strains on the urban infrastructure. Shortages of foodstuffs and other basic necessities resulted and corruption was everywhere: in the shah's court, the government, the bureaucracy, and within the business community. Opponents of the shah's system of forced modernization—including much of the student community—were pursued, jailed, and often tortured by SAVAK, the shah's secret police.

Opposition to the shah's forced modernization included *ulama*—religious scholars—on the right, who lamented the suppression of traditional religion; students and intellectuals on the left, who were deprived of freedoms of expression; and farmers, who had become urban immigrants, squeezed by inflation, recession, unemployment, and a loosening of what they felt to be the moral foundations of the society. In 1963, a Shiite Muslim religious leader, the Ayatollah Ruhollah Khomeini (1902–89), led an abortive uprising against the shah. The army killed 15,000 rebels and exiled Khomeini. But from Paris the ayatollah kept in contact with dissidents in Iran via tape recordings and telephone, and in 1979 he returned to lead popular demonstrations of as many as 5 million people. Now the shah was forced into exile. Islamic law, the *sharia*, became the law of the land and Islamic government was introduced. Women were ordered to return to draping themselves in the *chador*, or head scarf, and shawl as Iran became a theocracy. Khomeini declared:

> No others, no matter who they may be, have the right to legislate, nor has any person the right to govern on any basis other than the authority that has been conferred by God … It is the religious expert and no one else who should occupy himself with the affairs of the government. (Robinson, p. 171)

The religious fervor of the revolution—especially in the wake of the modernization that had been introduced by the shah—astonished many Western observers.

Strategically located, rich in oil, religiously militant, and internally secure, Khomeini's revolutionary government terrified its neighbors and wreaked havoc on many others more distant. In its first two years, it executed 800 people and exiled thousands. When America offered humanitarian refuge to the exiled shah, who was suffering from cancer, Khomeini seized the American embassy in Tehran and held fifty-two of its staff hostage. President Carter failed to secure their release through negotiations. He then attempted a guerrilla air rescue, which was aborted in humiliating failure. Carter's defeat in the 1980 election was due in part to these failures to cope with Iran. The third world again had powerful effects on Western, superpower politics.

Khomeini's militancy also introduced additional instability into the Middle East. It inspired religious dissidents in Saudi Arabia to attempt to trigger a revolt against the government by attacking the Great Mosque in Mecca during the *hajj* or pilgrimage period in 1979. Three hundred people were killed, and the Saudi government drew closer to the Americans. In Egypt, in 1981, Islamic militants, linked to Iran, assassinated President Anwar Sadat. In 1989, following the publication of the novel *The Satanic Verses*, Iranian clerics proclaimed the Indian-born British author Salman Rushdie a heretic and marked him for execution. A bounty of $5 million was placed on his head, and he was forced into hiding under the protection of the British government. In Beirut and other Middle Eastern centers, Western hostages were seized. Fearing that Iran's Shiite religious revolution would spill across the border, Iraq under Saddam Hussein, with the quiet support of the United States, attacked Iran, precipitating eight years of warfare and hundreds of thousands of deaths.

Legal restrictions on women based on interpretations of religious principles continued, calling for Islamic dress codes and Islamic legal authority over marriage, divorce, child custody, and the right to work. Most Iranian women accepted these restrictions willingly as a stand against Western culture and imperialism. Women's literacy rose to 59 percent, with 95 percent of girls of primary school age attending classes. Birth rates dropped from forty-nine per thousand under the shah to thirty-nine per thousand under Khomeini. The percentage of families using contraception rose from 3 to 23 in

1987 (*World Resources*, 1987, p. 257). Feminism, nationalism, and religion in Iran were intertwined in a unique configuration that did not fit any stereotype.

With Khomeini's death in 1989, more moderate leaders came to power in Iran, seeking more peaceful international relations and limited political moderation at home.

TERRORISM

In addition to the inter-state warfare of the first part of the twentieth century, and the guerrilla warfare of the second half, a third style of warfare became more evident in the 1960s and 1970s: terrorism. Like conventional and guerrilla warfare, terrorism is a style of fighting that can be used by any group. It usually employs violence aimed at civilian non-combatants as a means of creating fear and undermining the enemy's will to fight so that the terrorists may gain aims that they could not otherwise achieve. It is thus normally a weapon of the weak. Nevertheless terrorism can also be used by national governments to force their citizens, or their enemies, to submit to the will of the state. In order to generate the maximum fear, and therefore the greatest gains, terrorist attacks must be high-profile and dramatic. Within recent years they have included airplane hijackings, hostage takings, kidnaps, car bombings, and suicide bombings. They have often targeted geographical locations that will draw the greatest attention. To some degree terrorism and guerrilla warfare may be indistinguishable from one another. The Red Brigades in Italy, the Baader-Meinhof gang or Red Army Faction in Germany, the Sendero Luminoso, or Shining Path in Peru, and the ETA, a Basque separatist group in Spain, were among the most notorious terrorist groups of the 1960s, 1970s, and 1980s. Each of these groups attempted to overthrow a government or, at least, to force major changes in state policy.

The twentieth century has many examples of terrorism. Both Nazi Germany and Communist Russia employed state terrorism—extra-legal detention, imprisonment, torture, and execution—to control their populations. Many of the anti-colonial conflicts included the use of terror, including that of the Irish Republican Army against British rule in Northern Ireland; the FLN revolutionary force against the French in Algiers; the Vietcong against the American presence in Vietnam; the Tamil Tigers, seeking a separate territory under their own control for south Indian Tamils in the predominantly Sinhalese, Buddhist nation of Sri Lanka. Some of the most spectacular acts of terrorism were directed against the government and people of Israel for their occupation of Palestinian land. These included numerous airline hijackings and an assault on the Israeli team at the 1972 Munich Olympic games that left most of the Israeli team dead, and left the Olympic ideal of universal peace in tatters. Palestinians, in turn, asserted that Israel used "state terror" in suppressing them in the West Bank and Gaza Strip.

While the goal of terrorism is to frighten citizens and governments into submission, frequently its effects are the opposite. The public may be inflamed against the terrorists and choose to hunt them down and capture or kill them. Nevertheless, terrorism remains a strategy commonly used by those without substantial armies. Because terrorism has been, and can be, used for a wide variety of causes, the commonly used phrase evolved: "One person's terrorist is another person's freedom fighter."

IN PURSUIT OF PEACE

Perhaps the most amazing outcome of the Cold War was that, for the superpowers, it remained mostly cold. Despite all the saber-rattling, all the expense of weaponry, all

UNITED NATIONS AGENCIES

The primary focus of attention in the United Nations has been on peace and war, but its various programs and agencies, many concerned with technology, have provided forums for the resolution of other issues and the promotion of international welfare. The United Nations' key agencies include:

- International Court of Justice (World Court), has dealt with issues such as territorial rights, territorial waters, rights of individuals to asylum, and territorial sovereignty

- Food and Agricultural Organization (FAO), monitors information for improving food supply and distribution

- World Trade Organization (WTO), oversees international trade, settles trade disputes, and negotiates trade liberalization

- World Bank, provides financial assistance to developing nations

- United Nations Educational, Scientific, and Cultural Organization (UNESCO), sponsors research and publication

- United Nations Children's (Emergency) Fund (UNICEF), establishes programs for family welfare

- World Health Organization (WHO), monitors and researches health conditions

- International Labor Organization (ILO), promotes employment and seeks to improve labor conditions and living standards

- World Intellectual Property Organization, protects the interests of the producers of literary, industrial, scientific, and artistic works

- Commission on Human Rights, gathers information and formulates policy on the rights of persons belonging to national, ethnic, religious, and linguistic minorities, including indigenous peoples

the conniving with client states, despite even the Cuban Missile Crisis, the United States and the Soviet Union pulled back from nuclear war. Although they fought proxy wars, they did not confront each other in direct warfare at all. Some observers speculated that the investment in the threat of nuclear war—in Mutually Assured Destruction, MAD—provided a ritualized pose of macho strength on both sides that allowed the superpowers to avoid actual warfare.

Meanwhile, the United Nations was demonstrating some success as an arena for defusing international tensions, for providing peacekeeping missions to global trouble-spots, and for developing programs for international cooperation.

The United Nations: Growth and New Missions

The membership of the United Nations expanded to 159 sovereign states by the end of 1984, the overwhelming majority of the world's nations. It provided a home in which the newly emerging nations could gain political recognition and representation. The diversity of states brought a diversity of ideologies, and UN decisions and activities were subjected to a constant stream of criticism from one point or another on the political spectrum. Yet within that highly politicized framework the organization went on with its work, providing a forum where nations could meet, discuss common goals, and negotiate agreements. It did not always succeed, but such a forum was invaluable. In the mid-1980s, Soviet leader Gorbachev called the United Nations a "unique instrument without which world politics would be inconceivable today," even though it lacked the sovereignty of a government and commanded only such powers as its members chose to vest in it.

The United Nations began dispatching "peacekeeping" armed forces, with military personnel drawn from many different countries, to police zones of potential conflict. These missions were not designed to fight wars, but to maintain the peace in cases in which antagonistic nations agreed that they did want peace, but feared that without an honest "police force" to maintain that peace war would break out (again). United Nations peacekeeping forces were first sent to the Middle East in 1948 to monitor the ceasefire between Israel and its Arab neighbors. They continue in place even today, with separate but related forces on the Lebanese border and on the Golan Heights in Israeli-occupied Syria. A small force was sent to Cyprus in 1964 to maintain a buffer between the Greek Cypriots and the Turkish Cypriots who had been fighting for control of the entire island. They were also sent to Kashmir in 1972 to monitor the Line of Control between the two countries after peace agreements were signed between India and Pakistan to end their 1971 warfare.

On a third level, asserting its global reach, the United Nations undertook many initiatives in organizing for the general welfare of the globe. These included: coordinating the first global census in 1953; sponsoring the first of a series of meetings of criminologists to establish international principles and standards of criminal justice (1955); helping to negotiate a resolution of the Cuban Missile Crisis (1962), the

A girl vaccinated against smallpox, Nigeria, 1969. By 1979, the World Health Organization declared that smallpox had been eradicated. Every human being on earth had been inoculated against it.

Arab–Israeli war of 1967, and the Iraq–Iran war of 1988. The United Nations also called for the first arms embargo against South Africa (1963) and made it mandatory in 1972. It set up the first rules regulating the laws of the sea, including laws regulating ocean fishing (1970). In 1975, the United Nations sponsored a "Decade for Women," opening with a huge international conference in Mexico City. Later women's conferences followed in Cairo, focusing on reproductive issues, in 1985, and in Beijing in 1995.

In 1979, the World Health Organization (WHO) declared that smallpox had been eradicated by ensuring that every human being on earth had been inoculated against the disease. The WHO was only one of numerous international organizations working officially with the United Nations, many of them created by the UN. Others included: the Food and Agriculture Organization (FAO), which works to increase the productivity of farms, forests, and fisheries; the International Atomic Energy Agency, which monitors the non-proliferation of nuclear weapons and promotes the peaceful use of atomic energy; the International Labor Organization (ILO), which creates labor standards and promotes the

SOURCE

Rachel Carson's Silent Spring

American biologist Rachel Carson's Silent Spring (1962) exposed the devastating effects on humans, wildlife, and plants caused by the use of toxic chemicals—pesticides, fungicides, and herbicides—in everyday farming and insect control throughout the world. By virtue of its combination of scientific rigor and journalistic vividness, Silent Spring is frequently credited as the founding statement of the ecological movement in the twentieth century.

The most alarming of all man's assaults on the environment is the contamination of air, earth, rivers, and sea with dangerous and even lethal materials. This pollution is for the most part irrecoverable; the chain of evil it initiates not only in the world that must support life but in living tissues is for the most part irreversible. In this now universal contamination of the environment, chemicals are the sinister and little recognized partners of radiation in changing the very nature of the world—the very nature of its life … Chemicals sprayed on croplands or forests or gardens lie long in the soil, entering into living organisms, passing from one to another in a chain of poisoning and death. Or they pass mysteriously by underground streams until they emerge, and through the alchemy of air and sunlight, combine into new forms that kill vegetation, sicken cattle, and work unknown harm on those who drink from once-pure wells. (Carson, pp. 23–4)

Carson's powerful voice evoked responses. For example, after she revealed that DDT, one of the most powerful chemicals used to combat mosquitoes and, thus, malaria, was also poisonous to humans, governments throughout the world generally banned its use. "Green" parties, with strong platforms on ecological issues, began to organize in many countries, especially in western Europe, and more mainstream parties began to adopt some of their programs. Citizens founded organizations such as the World Wildlife Fund and Greenpeace in order to protect the environment. Some farmers began to use natural means of pest control in place of chemicals, and consumers began to seek out "natural" or "organic" foods raised without the use of chemical fertilizers and pesticides.

As Carson pointed out, the political issues, and their implications for the standard of living in each country, were thornier than the technological:

The Earth is one but the world is not. We all depend on one biosphere for sustaining our lives. Yet each community, each country strives for survival and prosperity with little regard for its impact on others. Some consume the Earth's resources at a rate that would leave little for future generations. Others, many more in number, consume far too little and live with the prospect of hunger, squalor, disease, and early death. (Carson, p. 28) welfare of international workers everywhere; UNESCO, the UN Educational, Scientific, and Cultural Organization, which promotes research and publication; and the World Bank, which extends loans to help poor countries in their development tasks.

Finally, in recognition of the global interdependence of all people in terms of the quality and quantity of air, water, and other basic human necessities found in nature, the UN began its struggle against global ecological destruction with the United Nations Conference on the Human Environment meeting in Stockholm in 1972. Many concerns dominated the agenda, but the main ones were:

- the depletion of the ozone layer through the introduction into the environment of chlorofluorocarbons, formerly a principal chemical in aerosol sprays and in most coolants, such as refrigeration and air-conditioning units;
- global warming, or the greenhouse effect, caused primarily by the introduction into the environment of carbon dioxide, which traps heat in the earth's lower atmosphere, raising temperatures around the globe;
- the destruction of the marine environment through ocean dumping, ship pollution, and the absorption of chemicals into the water table;
- acid rain, the pollution of the atmosphere with chemical pollutants that descend with rainfall;
- deforestation, especially in the tropics, where at least 25 million acres of trees are cut down yearly;
- at a more local level, polluted air, contaminated water, and cigarette smoke are now clearly associated with carcinogens.

In general, more developed countries tended to place the blame for ecological problems on the increase in global population, an increase most marked in the less developed countries. The less developed countries, in response, blamed the more developed as the source of the industries that created the pollution. On the issue of world hunger, the developed countries again pointed to population pressures on food supplies in the less developed countries, while the less developed blamed flaws in the world economy and the food distribution mechanisms, both controlled by the wealthier countries. Agreement was emerging on the need for international cooperation in a stronger UN Environment Program, but the United Nations lacked sovereign power. It could gather information, carry out research, make recommendations, hold conferences, and provide counsel, but it had no powers of enforcement. Implementation depended on the decision of member nations.

Demographics: Health, Migration, Urbanization, and the Green Revolution

Among the first activities of the United Nations was coordinating a global census in 1953. One of the very first specialized agencies that it created was the Food and Agriculture Organization (1945). Soon after came the World Health Organization (1948). The Centre for Human Settlements (Habitat) followed in 1978. All these organizations reflect the importance of the demographic change of the late twentieth century.

The world experienced a population explosion in this period, more than doubling from about 2.5 billion people in 1950 to about 6 billion in 2000. This global population had been only 1.6 billion in 1900, so the growth rate was extraordinary, with the world's population quadrupling in a single century. Alarmed observers spoke of a "population bomb," of a world unable to cope with the population growth, unable to feed the rising population, unable to provide the services needed to sustain them— water, sewerage, public health measures, outdoor resources. The alarm bells clanged even louder as people noted that the population in the less developed, poorer parts of the world was growing much more rapidly than in the wealthier areas, expanding from 1.7 billion in 1950 to 4 billion in 1990. The least developed countries grew fastest of all.

On the other hand, toward the end of the century, birth rates began to decline. Parents exercised family planning. The invention of the birth control pill in 1954 helped in this decision. Among teenagers and young adults the pill was instrumental in altering sexual practices as well as birth rates. In many of the richer countries, especially in Europe, birth rates dropped below replacement levels, that is, more people died than were born.

In the less developed areas birth rates were also decreasing, but much more slowly. China was an exception with a very rapid drop in birth rates as the central government, fearing the results of continuing population growth in their country that already had more than one billion people, implemented a one-family-one-child policy, especially in urban areas. Death rates also decreased almost everywhere, providing for population growth and an increasingly aging population as people lived longer. Japan reached an average expected life span of 80—77 for males, 84 for females.

The surprise, however, was that the world's food supply more than kept pace with the population growth. Per capita food production grew substantially for thirty years from the 1960s, especially as the "green revolution" took root. Under the auspices of the Rockefeller Foundation, agricultural scientists discovered and disseminated new strains of wheat and other grains that increased food productivity by as much as five times. This green revolution saved the world from mass starvation despite continuing population growth. Norman Borlaugh, who directed these efforts, won the Nobel Peace Prize in 1970 for his work.

Many political observers feared, however, that the green revolution would ultimately make the rich richer and the poor poorer, because the new seeds also required

AT A GLANCE : EUROPE AND THE UNITED STATES

DATE	POLITICAL	SOCIAL AND CULTURAL
1950	■ Korean War (1950–53) ■ Egypt nationalizes Suez Canal, establishing independence from Great Britain (1956) ■ Treaties of Rome (1957) lead to establishment of European Community ■ Ghana wins independence from Great Britain (1957)	■ Contraceptive pill becomes available in the late 1950s
1960	■ Cuban Missile Crisis (1962) ■ Algeria wins independence from France (1962) ■ Group of 77 reforms (1964) ■ America involved in Vietnam War (1964–73) ■ Lyndon Johnson sponsors Voting Rights Act (1965) ■ US Defense Department creates internet (1969)	■ Rachel Carson, *Silent Spring* (1962) ■ Betty Friedan, *The Feminine Mystique* (1963) ■ Martin Luther King delivers "I Have a Dream" speech in Washington Mall (1963) ■ Stanley Kubrick, *Dr Strangelove* (1964) ■ Malcolm X assassinated (1965) ■ Apollo II lands on moon (1969)
1970	■ Formation of OPEC (1973) ■ Watergate affair forces resignation of President Nixon (1974)	■ United Nations conference on the Human Environment (1972) ■ Near meltdown of nuclear reactor at Three Mile Island, Penn. (1979)
1980	■ "Star Wars" Strategic Defense Initiative, proposed by President Reagan (1981–8)	■ World Wide Web created (1989)
1990	■ Maastricht Treaty (1991) ■ Bosnian War (1991–5) ■ Russia joins the Group of Seven, forming the G-8 (1997) ■ War in Kosovo (1998–9)	■ United Nations "Earth Summit" in Rio (1992) ■ Around 10 percent of the US population are foreign-born (1997) ■ Internet connection worldwide rises from 3 million people in 1993 to 200 million in 1999 ■ Protests in Seattle, Washington, against the World Trade Organization (1999)

Indian squatter settlement. In the huge cities of the underdeveloped world, shanty towns have sprung up—a makeshift solution to endemic poverty and overcrowding. This squatter settlement in Bombay (population: 11.5 million) might be unsightly, but represents one answer to the acute housing shortage in urban India.

new fertilizers and an abundance of irrigation water and pesticides. Richer farmers could afford to use them, while poorer farmers often lost their land. In addition, over time the chemical fertilizers reduced the fertility of the soil. Finally, because the new seeds were so much more productive than older varieties, farmers began to abandon the multitudes of older seed varieties for the few new ones. Agricultural experts feared that a plant blight affecting even one of these few new seed strains could have catastrophic results. To hold off these frightening prospects, they kept samples of old as well as new crop strains in scientific laboratories where they could be retrieved if necessary.

Population growth was not uniform everywhere. People moved steadily from rural to urban areas and urban growth rates shot up. Estimates suggest that in 1950 about 30 percent of the world's 2.5 billion people, about 750 million people, lived in cities. By 1990, about 45 percent of the world's 6 billion people, about 2.7 billion people, lived in cities. In other words, by 1990, more people lived in the cities of the world than had lived in the entire world in 1900. At the beginning of the century, urbanization was still linked to industrial growth; toward the end of the century, however, the most rapidly growing cities, and, increasingly, the largest of them, were in the poorer, less industrialized areas of the world—for example, São Paulo in Brazil, and Mexico City each with about 15 million in 1990; Mumbai (Bombay) and Kolkata (Calcutta) in India; Buenos Aires in Argentina; Seoul in South Korea; Shanghai and Beijing in China; Lagos in Nigeria; and Rio de Janeiro in Brazil, each with between 10 and 15 million.

Cities strained to provide adequate water, sewerage, electricity, transportation, and public health systems for the newcomers. Many of them lived in slums, and the contrast of slums at the foot of luxury high-rise apartments became a common sight in these third world cities. The images of the slums were sometimes somewhat misleading. Some of the slums were dead-end residential areas. But some were temporary homes of urban immigrants who were trying their best to find a way into jobs that would enable them to improve their conditions. Urban analysts drew a contrast between "slums of despair" and "slums of hope."

Economic Growth

The green revolution helped lead the way to increased economic growth in some of the less developed areas. The great surprise, however, was the extraordinary growth in the "first world," in countries that had been devastated by World War II. The war's biggest losers became the biggest winners in the postwar period.

Western Europe In 1947, Winston Churchill had described Europe as "a rubble heap, a charnel house, a breeding ground for pestilence and hate." But out of the wreckage came several "economic miracles," many of them the result of cooperation between recent enemies. In 1950, French and West German offi-cials agreed to form the European Coal and Steel Community and to place these key economic ele-ments under an independent international authority. The ECSC was born in 1952 with the addition of Italy and the Benelux countries (Belgium, the Netherlands, Luxembourg). Its success led to the Treaties of Rome in 1957 that established the European Economic Com-munity (EEC), or Common Market, to lower, and ulti-mately remove tariffs among member countries; to foster the free movement of goods, labor, and capital; and to establish a single external tariff. The treaties also established Euratom to create common policies for the peaceful development of atomic energy. Agreement on agricultural policy was more difficult because it involved issues of national self-reliance in food, the mystique of family farms, and the need to accommodate rural and urban interests. Never-theless, in 1962, a Common Agricultural Policy was also negotiated.

In 1965, the Brussels treaty merged the ECSC, the EEC, and Euratom, and created the basis of a unified West European economic administration. Additional nations were admitted, including Britain, Ireland, and Denmark in 1973, Greece in 1981, and Spain and Por-tugal in 1986. Western Europe was moving toward a "Europe without frontiers," and its economy flour-ished. Per capita income multiplied. In Germany it went from $320 in 1949 to over $9,000 in 1978; in Italy it rose from $638 in 1960 to over $5,000 in 1979. In West Germany the number of automobiles per 1,000 population rose from 6 in 1948 to 227 in 1970; in France it rose from 37 to 252.

The recovery of West Germany outpaced the rest of Europe. Before the war, West Germany had possessed the most developed infrastructure and a highly trained professional and technical workforce. With the war over, the country refocused on peace-ful production and, with the help of Marshall Plan assistance, rebuilt quickly. By 1960, it had the highest per capita income in Europe. By the late 1970s, its per capita income surpassed that of the United States. In tribute to German skills and hard work, the rise of East Germany, the segment of the country that was incorporated into the Soviet bloc, was similar. It was the fastest growing economy in eastern and central Europe.

Japan Equally startling was the recovery of Japan. Like Germany, it had an industrial infrastructure and a highly skilled work force that could shift into production for peace. The US occupation, 1945–52, improved Japan's competitive position by redis-tributing land, breaking up the *zaibatsu* holding companies that had controlled the economy, encouraging the growth of labor unions (until some of them began to become communist), and restructuring the educational system, opening up high school and college education for the first time to millions of Japanese students. The United States also encouraged Japan, as it had Germany, to join it in the Cold War struggle against the Soviet Union, and Japan benefited both from US investment and

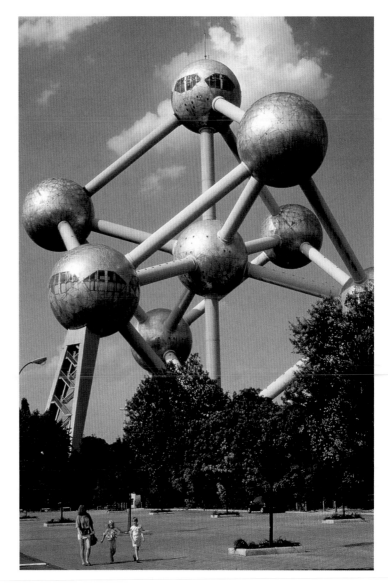

The Atomium, Euratom headquarters, Brussels. As European countries that had fought each other for centuries began to forge institutions of cooperation after 1945, collaboration in the peaceful development of atomic energy took on both practical and symbolic importance. The 1957 Treaty of Rome that established the European Economic Community (EEC) also created Euratom to create joint policies. The Atomium at Euratom headquarters in Brussels symbolized this new commitment.

from US reliance on the Japanese economy for supplies during the Korean War—and later during the Vietnam War—and for bases for American troops and for their rest-and-relaxation during these wars. Finally, Japan took seriously—more seriously than the United States did at first—the business management advice of the American W. Edwards Deming. Deming called for Total Quality Management (TQM), the highest standards of quality in production, and for including workers from the factory work floor as well as the administrative offices in the planning and evaluation processes for industrial production.

Three events in 1964 symbolized Japan's political reentry into the family of nations and of its resurgent economic power. It was admitted to the Organization for Economic Cooperation and Development (OECD), which until then had included only European and North American nations. The *shinkansen*, or "bullet train," began carrying passengers between Tokyo and Osaka at speeds of 125 miles per hour, the fastest in the world. Tokyo played host to the summer Olympics, winning universal praise for its new architecture, stadiums, hotels, and ability to accommodate and please both the participants and the throngs of spectators. Between 1950 and 1973, Japan's gross domestic product grew at 10.5 percent per year.

In 1973, when the OPEC nations restricted their exports of petroleum and increased the price, creating havoc for most energy reliant countries, Japan replied with the most effective programs for conservation and increased industrial efficiency. It reduced its dependence on oil by 25 percent, it sought oil imports from new sources, and it began to shift into even more knowledge-intensive industries, such as electronics and computers, which are much less energy-dependent. By 1980, Japan's per capita income, at almost $10,000 per year, rivaled America's at $11,400. Economists were beginning to speak of "Japan as Number 1" for the efficiency and quality of its consumer products,

AT A GLANCE : THE SOVIET UNION AND JAPAN

DATE	SOVIET UNION	JAPAN
1950	■ At the 20th Party Congress Nikita Khrushchev officially exposes Stalin's tyranny (1956) ■ Khrushchev crushes Hungarian uprising (1956) ■ Soviet space program puts first rocket, Sputnik, into space (1957)	■ Economic benefits from American participation in the Korean War (1950–53)
1960	■ Alexander Solzhenitsyn, *A Day in the Life of Ivan Denisovich* (1962) ■ Cuban missile crisis (1962) ■ Leonid Brezhnev puts down Czech revolt, or "Prague Spring" (1968)	■ Admitted to Organization for Economic Cooperation and Development (OECD) (1964) ■ Bullet train inaugurated (1964) ■ Hosts Olympics (1964)
1970	■ Lech Walensa begins to organize independent trade union federation, or Solidarity, in Poland (1978) ■ Pope John Paul II visits Poland (1979)	■ Economy hit badly by "oil shocks" (1973)
1980	■ Mikhail Gorbachev institutes policies of glasnost and perestroika on coming to power (1985) ■ Partial meltdown of Chernobyl nuclear power plant (1986)	■ Trade frictions with United States and Europe ■ Equal Employment Opportunity Act (1986) ■ Death of Emperor Hirohito (1989) ■ Hit by recession (1989)
1990	■ Coup attempt against Gorbachev by die-hard communists fails (1991) ■ USSR dissolves into fifteen independent states of which Russia is largest (1991) ■ Boris Yeltsin convenes Constitutional Assembly that produces new constitution for Russia (1993) ■ Russia accorded associate status in NATO (1997) ■ Yeltsin resigns as president (1999)	■ Becomes world's largest donor of foreign aid—$14 billion (1994) ■ East Asian financial collapse (1997)

especially its automobiles, skill in overseas marketing, and prospects for soon sur-passing even the United States as the world's leading economy.

Japan's economic success also turned on its ability to bring together government advice and guidance with freely operating private enterprises. Its Ministry for International Trade and Industry (MITI) successfully guided Japanese industries away from "sunset" industries, like steel production, into "sunrise" industries, like automo-biles and computers, and helped them find financial investments and marketing opportunities. Several countries of east and Southeast Asia—especially Korea and Taiwan, Japan's former colonies—adopted this model of state guidance and private enterprise with great success. These two nations, along with the city-states of Hong Kong and Singapore, were often referred to as the "Asian tigers" for their aggressive and successful economic development along the Japanese model.

A new model of economic growth was developing, an amalgam of the Russian com-mitment to planning, the US emphasis on unbridled competition, the wartime experi-ence of national and even international cooperation, and full, guaranteed employment. In the period from the 1950s to the 1980s, the Japanese and their Asian imitators had perhaps gotten it most precisely right, combining free enterprise, state planning and guidance, concern for worker welfare, and a welfare state to provide security. But Japan was not alone in moving toward this model. With different emphases it charac-terized most of the nations of the industrialized world in these years, often referred to as the "golden years." Even in the face of the "oil shocks" imposed by OPEC in 1973 and again in 1979, these nations could go on building their economies, although some-what more slowly.

The organization of the economy was not the only change during these years. The goods produced also were new: Private cars and trucks—already very common in America—now became more universal. Plastics and synthetic materials based on poly-mers replaced conventional materials from cotton and wool in clothing to steel and wood in construction. Television, tape recording, jet engines, radar, transistors and the computers that came from them, nuclear energy—some invented just before World War II, some during the war, some just after—were the new products that helped entice the citizens of wealthier nations, and to some degree even of poorer ones, into a consumer society. Minor differences in product design and quality were the result, and sometimes the goal, of the new competition for the consumer dollar, yen, mark, pound, franc, and lira.

This competition also required that producers—enormous international corpora-tions—invest in research and development in unprecedented volume. Every impor-tant company had a division devoted to "R&D" as the value of education and scientific and technological research increased. In conditions of full employment, which became the norm in the wealthier countries in these times, producers also sought labor-saving inventions. Industrial production became more automated everywhere, with Japan leading the way in robotics, the replacement of humans with machines that did rela-tively detailed and specialized work. More than most countries Japan was driven to robotics by an aging population. As Japan's population had the longest life spans of any nation in the world, its proportion of working age population to the very young and the very old decreased. Robots were part of the answer to this problem.

International Organization

The successes of the "golden years" rested on international cooperation. Part of the institutional base was prepared in 1944 in Bretton Woods, New Hampshire. Represen-tatives of forty nations gathered there to plan a new global economy for the postwar period that would escape the catastrophic depression that had followed World War I.

HOW DO WE KNOW?

The Social Setting of Technology

Even as the developed world created new products, established ever more efficient means for producing them, and designed advertising to convince people that these new products were necessary, a few people raised their voices to ask if this form of economic and technological development was "progress." One of the most prominent of these critics, E.F. Schumacher, declared as the title of his 1973 book: Small Is Beautiful. Schumacher, a British economist, served for twenty years as head of planning at the British Coal Board, but his economic philosophy stressed the small scale rather than the large. He wanted an economics based in nature rather than in the subjugation of nature:

> In the excitement over the unfolding of his scientific and technical powers, modern man has built a system of production that ravishes nature and a type of society that mutilates man ... The development of production and the acquisition of wealth have thus become the highest goals of the modern world in relation to which all other goals, no matter how much lip-service may still be paid to them have come to take second place ... This is the philosophy of materialism, and it is this philosophy—or metaphysic—which is being challenged by events ... It is of little use trying to suppress terrorism if the production of deadly devices continues to be deemed a legitimate employment of man's creative powers ... Equally, the chance of mitigating the rate of resource depletion or of bringing harmony into the relationships between those in possession of wealth and power and those without is non-existent as long as there is no idea anywhere of enough being good and more-than-enough being evil.

Schumacher briefly explored the history of the economics profession to chart its transformation. The first professorship in political economy was endowed at Oxford in 1825, and from the beginning philanthropists and economists alike asked what should be its scope; many, including Schumacher, argued that economics should be subservient to ethics. In 1969, the Nobel Prize for "economic science" was established, suggesting that this discipline would not rank second to any other. Schumacher, however, argued that the earlier evaluation was more appropriate.

Arnold Pacey, a British physicist who became an historian, also argued that technological developments were most effective when they fit the society that was adopting them. Pacey was not directly arguing ethics, as Schumacher was, but his idea that inventions should fit the needs of society, and the society's ability to absorb them, agreed with Schumacher that technological "development" should not proceed for its own sake, but rather for the sake of society. In an era of rapid technological development, when third world nations frequently wanted the same technology for war and for peace as the first world had, the moral principles expressed directly by Schumacher and indirectly by Pacey set up a challenge: What would be the appropriate scale for the technology to be adopted? The argument for appropriate scale technology was made forcefully, in practical terms, by Mahatma Gandhi of India, as we shall see in the next chapter.

- Was Schumacher correct that technological "progress" is pursued, at least some of the time, simply for the purpose of making a profit, whether or not new technology is needed? Please explain with examples.
- Have you examples of technologies that seem appropriate for the people and societies that use them and examples of technologies that seem inappropriate?
- How important do you think it is to ask about the appropriate scale of technology? Can you give an example of such a question in your own life?

They created three new institutions: the International Monetary Fund (IMF), the International Bank for Reconstruction and Development (World Bank), and the General Agreement on Tariffs and Trade (GATT). The IMF provided short-term loans for countries that were having difficulty meeting their balance of payment obligations. These were designed for moments of extreme, but short-term, crisis. The first goal of the World Bank was to provide capital for rebuilding war torn nations. By the late 1960s and 1970s, as European nations had recovered from the economic devastation of the war, the bank increasingly turned to the developmental needs of the third world, although not to their short-term needs for relief. The GATT was designed to promote world trade by bringing down tariffs among all member nations. Until the 1980s all of these organizations were generally praised for their achievements among the capitalist nations of the world. The communist bloc—both the European nations in the Soviet sphere and China after the communist revolution—refused to participate because they did not trust the open market as a means of economic decision making. They rejected the capitalist laws of supply and demand in favor of state planning and therefore could not accept the Bretton Woods principles. In this sense, Bretton Woods helped to divide the world into opposing blocs, even as it proved successful for the West.

Third world nations were not at first much affected by the new international financial agreements, but as they entered more fully into the global economy in the 1980s and 1990s they would raise new issues, as we shall see in Chapter 23. A preview of some of the issues to be raised, however, came with the "oil shocks" created by OPEC in 1973. The Organization of Petroleum Exporting Countries had been formed in 1960, but it first used its economic muscle in international politics during the 1973 Yom Kippur War between Israel and its Arab neighbors. In order to force the West, and especially the United States, to abandon its support for Israel, OPEC embargoed its oil exports to the United States and any other countries that supported Israel. Americans felt the effects personally as they waited in long lines at the pumps for available gasoline. American industry, lacking energy, cut production and laid off workers. Globally the cost of oil quadrupled, forcing similar cutbacks elsewhere. Most third world nations are not oil producers and they were actually hurt most of all, since they could least afford the higher prices and shorter supplies.

To some degree OPEC achieved its political aims. Some companies stopped doing business with Israel, and France agreed to sell advanced weapons to some Arab countries in order to gain assured access to oil supplies. Over time, the industrialized nations learned to cope. Through conservation and the creation and use of more energy-efficient machinery they reduced their oil dependency. To some degree they switched to other fuels. They also found that the Arab oil-rich countries, seeking investment opportunities for their newfound profits, often invested them in first world countries, including the United States. The "oil shocks" demonstrated, however, that at least some third world countries were positioned to demand greater voice in the world economy, and the first world nations would have to listen.

NGOs AND TRANSNATIONALS

Thus far we have mostly discussed governments—making war, making peace, intervening in economies and technologies. The second half of the twentieth century also saw an enormous growth in the number and power of non-governmental organizations (NGOs). They changed the way nations and economies carried out their work.

Normally, the term NGO does not include private businesses, but they too are NGOs, and they created in the later years of the twentieth century not only multinational corporations but even transnational corporations. Multinationals were companies headquartered in one nation but operating in several. By the late twentieth century, America alone had tens of thousands of such corporations. Transnational corporations also operated in many countries, but had no clear headquarters. Sometimes, for financial purposes, often to evade taxes, they placed much of their financial structure in small, relatively unregulated nations, like the Cayman Islands or Curaçao. Regulating and policing the transnationals was not easy. Also, while multinational corporations might finally have to balance their desire for bottom-line profits against the need to live within the laws and values of their home country, transnationals had no other allegiances than profit. Transnational business became more competitive, but less responsive to values other than profit.

At the same time, more conventional non-governmental organizations, much smaller to be sure, also took shape. The World Wildlife Fund, for example, founded in the 1950s, now has more than 5 million members and works in more than one hundred countries. It became the world's largest privately financed conservation organization working to conserve the world's biological diversity, advocate for the use of renewable natural resources in sustainable fashion, and promote the reduction of pollution and wasteful consumption.

Amnesty International grew into a worldwide movement of people with close to 2 million supporters dedicated to the protection and promotion of human rights. Amnesty took as its model the Universal Declaration of Human Rights. It acted to stop grave abuses of the rights of physical and mental integrity, freedom of conscience and expression, and freedom from discrimination. It campaigned to free prisoners of conscience, ensure fair trials for political prisoners, protect refugees, abolish the death penalty, end political killings, and torture. It sought to bring to justice those responsible for human rights violations. It publicized its findings in order to bring public pressure on governments, armed political groups, companies, and others in order to stop the abuses. It worked "within a global community of organizations to ensure broad support and respect for all human rights." In order to maintain its independence of action, Amnesty International accepted no government funding.

Oxfam, originally the Oxford Committee for Famine Relief, traces its origins to a group of Quaker intellectuals, social activists, and Oxford University academics who founded an organization to provide famine relief to Greece during World War II. In the immediate postwar years it directed its attention to European needs, but as early as 1951 it extended famine relief to people in India, and in 1953 to the homeless, hungry, and orphaned at the end of the Korean War. In the 1960s, Oxfam turned primarily to third-world needs. It focused less on famine relief and more on supplying the tools by which people could improve their living standards. Self-help programs emphasized communities improving their own water supplies, farming practices, and health provisions. Oxfam also began to prepare educational materials to explain in the first world the root causes of poverty and suffering, the connections between the first and third worlds, and the role that first world people could play in improving the physical conditions of life in the third world. It began its public lobbying for government and private assistance in development programs throughout the third world and began establishing field offices in the third world to help implement these self-help programs. In 1963, Oxfam Canada was established, the first of several affiliated national Oxfam committees. Oxfam America was established in 1970. Like the other Oxfams, it is a grassroots, broad-based organization that accepts no government funding.

These three well-known organizations are only a few of the thousands of multinational and transnational NGOs. Many of the larger ones are organizations of trade unionists, religious groups, sports enthusiasts, and artists. The Soviet Union dissolved, for example, in part because of international labor support for Lech Walesa's Solidarity Movement and because Cardinal Wojtyla was elevated to the position of pope in the Roman Catholic Church. Many of the same interests that created international governmental and business organizations, and much of the same technology that made them possible, also led to the creation of vast numbers of non-governmental organizations, through which common people created the networks for international contact, cooperation, and action.

Voluntary organizations testified to the importance of grassroots participation in public life and to the ability of small groups of people to affect even the largest of governments and corporations. Through the steady work of NGOs and through the occasional outbursts of public demonstrations, common people expressed their wishes.

LEGACIES OF THE COLD WAR, DECOLONIZATION, ECONOMIC AND SOCIAL DEVELOPMENT WHAT DIFFERENCE DO THEY MAKE?

A healthy skepticism colors the transformations of the twentieth century. "Winners" gained more wealth, power, and convenience than had ever been known. Hundreds of millions of people, long colonized, won their political independence. Yet even the most fortunate often felt insecure, for the wars of the century were the bloodiest ever, the weaponry the most powerful and frightening, carrying the potential to destroy all human life. Governments had shown the power not only to fight wartime enemies but also to attack, imprison, exile, and destroy masses of their own citizens. Transportation and communication meant that almost no area of the world was unaffected by others. Serious questions arose as to the ability of the earth and the seas to withstand the pressures of the new technologies on planetary resources. Even for "winners," this was an age of anxiety.

For those less fortunate, poverty, servitude, ill-health, and hunger remained the common fate. Even though experts declared that new technologies provided the capacity to feed the entire, growing population of the earth, governmental policies, national and international, did not provide the necessary legal and technological means of distribution.

The postwar years, however, seemed to favor the optimists over the pessimists. Global wars stopped. Despite proxy wars, the nuclear weapons of the Cold War remained unused. Almost all colonies gained their independence. The United Nations organization offered a global forum in which the peoples of the world could come together to address their common needs. The purview of the UN was continually extended to include not only conflict resolution, peace keeping, and international law, but also issues of education, child welfare, the condition of women, labor relations, human rights, ecology, settlements patterns, and appropriate technologies. The world's economy—its production of food as well as of consumer goods—expanded more rapidly than its population. Some observers called the postwar years of reconstruction, decolonization, and economic expansion a golden era.

Review Questions

- What were the reasons for the Cold War competition between the USA and the USSR?
- Why did decolonization take place so quickly once the process had begun?
- How did the superpowers and the new nations attempt to use one another for their own benefit? Please give examples.
- What function do voluntary organizations serve in a society? Give examples of how a voluntary organization has changed the policies of a country.
- Why did ecological issues rise to such great importance in the period 1945–85? Give some examples of the issues.

- Many observers have termed the period 1945–73 in western Europe especially a "golden age." Why? Would the same term hold for Africa, Asia, or Latin America in that period? Why or why not?

Suggested Readings

PRINCIPAL SOURCES

Applebaum, Anne. *Gulag. A History* (New York: Doubleday Books, 2003). A comprehensive scholarly account, stressing the economic importance of the Gulag and humman relations inside it. Complements Solzhenitsyn's first-person, fictionalized account.

Bulliet, Richard W., ed. *The Columbia History of the 20th Century* (New York: Columbia University Press, 1998). Comprehensive and thoughtful collection of articles by theme rather than chronology.

Burns, E. Bradford. *Latin America: A Concise Interpretive History* (Englewood Cliffs, NJ, 7th ed., 2001). A standard comprehensive, thematic approach, examines social and political relationships. Especially strong on Brazil.

Carson, Rachel. *Silent Spring* (New York: Penguin Books, 1965). An attack on the chemical and pesticide industries. The most important single book in launching the modern ecological movement.,

Dower, John. *Embracing Defeat* (New York: W.W. Norton, 2000). A comprehensive, wonderfully readable story of America's occupation of Japan, 1945–52. Emphasizes the human contacts more than the institutional changes.

Fieldhouse, D.K. *Black Africa 1945–1980* (London: Allen and Unwin, 1986). An attempt to understand what has gone wrong in independent Africa, and why.

Friedman, Thomas. *From Beirut to Jerusalem* (New York: Farrar, Straus and Giroux, 1989). Presentation of the continuing Israeli-Arab hostility by a leading *New York Times* reporter.

Goncharov, Sergei N., John W. Lewis, and Xue Litai. *Uncertain Partners: Stalin, Mao, and the Korean War* (Stanford: Stanford University Press, 1993). Reveals the bargaining and ultimately the hostility between the communist leaders.

Harden, Blaine. *Dispatches from a Fragile Continent* (Boston: Houghton Mifflin, 1990). *Washington Post* bureau chief in sub-Saharan Africa calls it the way he sees it, and not much is very pleasant or elevating.

Keen, Benjamin. *A History of Latin America*, 2 vols. (Boston: Houghton Mifflin, 7th ed., 2004). Good, standard comprehensive coverage. Now expanded into two volumes.

Kenez, Peter. *A History of the Soviet Union from the Beginning to the End* (Cambridge: Cambridge University Press, 1999). A study and evaluation of principal institutions and their impact. Thoughtful analyses and evaluations.

Kennedy, Paul. *The Rise and Fall of the Great Powers* (New York: Random House, 1987). Kennedy's focus on the balance between economic health and military preparedness among the great powers provides a fascinating theme and an abundance of useful data.

Morris, Benny. *The Birth of the Palestinian Refugee Problem 1947–1949* (Cambridge: Cambridge University Press, 1988). A major revisionist historian indicts the Israelis for driving many Palestinians out of their homes.

Morris, Benny. *Righteous Victims: A History of the Zionist-Arab Conflict, 1881–1999* (New York; Knopf, 1999). Revisionist historian finds plenty of blame to go around for the continuing Arab-Israeli struggle and the inability to resolve it.

Service, Robert. *A History of Twentieth Century Russia* (Cambridge: Harvard University Press, 1997). The story told largely through the actions and statements of Russia's leaders.

Sigmund, Paul, ed. *The Ideologies of the Developing Nations* (New York: Praeger Publishers, 2nd rev. ed., 1972). Excellent selection of observations, analyses, and manifestos by leaders from throughout the third world in its heyday.

Solzhenitsyn, Alexander. *The Gulag Archipelago*, 3 vols. (New York: Harper and Row, 1974–8). The terrifying revelations of the prison system at the base of Soviet government control of its citizens.

Stavrianos, Leften. *Global Rift* (New York: Morrow, 1981). A left-wing interpretation of the divisions between the rich and poor nations of the world, and what caused it.

Vogel, Ezra. *The Four Little Dragons: The Spread of Industrialization in East Asia* (Cambridge: MA: Harvard University Press, 1991). Korea, Taiwan, Singapore, and Hong Kong demonstrated that countries could leap from the third world to the first. Vogel shows how they did it.

ADDITIONAL SOURCES

Andrea, Alfred and James H. Overfield, eds. *The Human Record*, Vol. 2 (Boston: Houghton Mifflin, 3rd ed., 1998).

Avishai, Bernard. *The Tragedy of Zionism* (New York: Farrar Straus and Giroux, 1985). Covers the impact on the Arab world as well as the Jewish.

Black, Maggie. *A Cause for Our Time: Oxfam, the First Fifty Years* (Oxford: Oxford University Press, 1992). Recounts the history of the organization, the tough decisions it has made, and its increasing influence in development planning.

Duus, Peter. *Modern Japan* (Boston: Houghton Mifflin, 2nd ed., 1998). Excellent, comprehensive text.

Fanon, Frantz. *The Wretched of the Earth*, trans. by Constance Farrington (New York: Grove Press, 1963). Classic statement of the psychological wounds of colonialism. Calls for anti-colonial violence as a means of healing.

Gibney, Frank. *Japan: The Fragile Superpower* (Tokyo: Charles E. Tuttle, 3rd rev. ed., 1996). Captures both the strengths, and the surprising weaknesses, of Japan near the end of the twentieth century.

Hobsbawm, Eric. *The Age of Extremes: A History of the World, 1914–1991* (New York: Pantheon Books, 1994). The dean of living historians surveys the scene politically, economically, and culturally. Engagingly written.

International Institute for Environment and Development and the World Resources Institute. *World Resources 1987* (New York: Basic Books, 1987). Basic report with abundant quantitative information.

Johnson, Hazel and Henry Bernstein, eds. *Third World Lives of Struggle* (London: Heinemann Educational Books, 1982). Marvelous and touching selection of biographical and autobiographical sketches of people's lives with some poetry and interpretive articles as well.

Kaufman, Burton I. *The Korean Conflict* (Westport, CN: Greenwood Press, 1999). Brief history and analysis of the war supported by primary documents and biographical sketches.

Kochan, Lionel and Richard Abraham. *The Making of Modern Russia* (London: Penguin Books, 1983). Useful on the Khrushchev and Brezhnev years.

Nkrumah, Kwame. *Ghana: The Autobiography of Kwame Nkrumah* (New York: Thomas Nelson and Sons, 1957). Leader of the first black African country to achieve independence from British rule tells his story, up to 1957.

Nugent, Neill. *The Government and Politics of the European Union* (Durham, NC: Duke University Press, 5th ed., 2003). Dry but comprehensive, thorough examination of the major institutions and their significance.

Power, Jonathan. *Like Water on Stone: The Story of Amnesty International* (Boston: Northeastern University Press, 2001). Recounts the struggles of this pre-eminent international human rights organization.

Robinson, Francis. *Atlas of the Islamic World since 1500* (New York: Facts on File, 1982). Basic reference guide to history as well as geography, with excellent text, maps, and selected topics.

World History Documents CD-ROM

26.1 Joseph Stalin: *The Soviet Victory: Capitalism versus Communism* (February 1946)
26.2 Sir Winston Churchill: *An Iron Curtain Has Descended Across the Continent* (March 1946)
26.3 Harry S. Truman: *The Truman Doctrine* (March 1947)
26.4 George C. Marshall: *The Marshall Plan* (June 1947)
26.5 Korea: The Thirty-eighth Parallel
26.6 General Douglas MacArthur: Report to Congress, April 19, 1951: *Old Soldiers Never Die*
26.7 Henry A. Myers: *East Berliners Rise Up Against Soviet Oppression*, A Personal Account
26.8 Nikita Khrushchev: *The Victory of Communism Is Inevitable!*: Speech to the 22nd Communist Party Congress (1962)
27.1 Mohandas K. Gandhi
27.2 Jawaharlal Nehru: Gandhi and Nehru: *Two Utterly Different Standpoints*
27.3 Frantz Fanon: *The Wretched of the Earth*
27.4 Kwame Nkrumah: *I Speak of Freedom: A Statement of African Ideology*
27.5 Israel's Proclamation of Independence
27.6 Palestinian Declaration of Independence
27.7 Views of a Viet Cong Official
27.8 An American Prisoner of War

CHINA AND INDIA

POSTWAR DEVELOPMENTS, 1914–91

KEY TOPICS
- China, 1925–89
- India, 1914–91
- Comparing China and India: What Difference Does It Make?

Home to some of the world's most ancient and influential civilizations, China and India are almost worlds in themselves. Both are vast and densely populated countries containing, together, some 40 percent of the world's population. Both were subject to European colonial domination in the nineteenth and early twentieth centuries. Both gained full political independence in the middle of the twentieth century and both were, and remain, predominantly agrarian countries. Nevertheless they followed very different paths of development. Because of their sheer size, the similarity of many of their circumstances, and the contrast in their decisions on development, we devote a full chapter to them.

At the turn of the twentieth century China, with 400 million people, contained about one-fourth of the world's population. The India of the British Empire—which included today's Pakistan and Bangladesh—contained about one-sixth, about 285 million people. Both countries were overwhelmingly agricultural, with populations about 80 to 85 percent rural. Both were vast in territory and densely populated.

Politically, India was ruled as a colony of Britain until 1947. China was not administered directly by foreign powers, but Britain, France, Russia, Germany, and Japan had great economic and cultural control over the huge nation and directly ruled small portions of it. Under British rule, India had a single central administration, despite its diverse ethnicities, languages, religions, castes, and local princes. China, on the other hand, was without an effective central government through most of the first half of the century, suffering both civil war and invasion from Japan.

Both countries sought independence from foreign control. Both began these struggles as protest movements from within their modern sectors, envisioning an industrialized, bureaucratized future, led by professional men trained in modern administrative, educational, journalistic, legal, and military skills. As they began to gain success, however, leaders of the struggle for independence in both countries found this urban- and professional-based organization inadequate. They turned instead to mass movements of the peasantry and common people, who were the overwhelming majority of the population.

India and China attained independent statehood at about the same time. India won independence from Britain in 1947. After Japan was defeated in World War II, China continued its nationwide communist revolution that drove out foreign powers and unified almost the entire country in 1949 (except for Taiwan, Hong Kong, and Macao). Then the two countries chose different strategies of development. Influenced by British colonial legacies and by its own heterogeneity, India chose democratic electoral politics and a mixed socialist–capitalist economy, with strong cultural ties to the Western democracies and some military links to the Soviet Union. In China, on the other hand, a victorious communist army asserted strong central control after years of warfare. At first China looked to the Soviet Union for advice and assistance, but soon came into conflict with these mentors on issues of ideology, policy, and national self-interest. Despite the central role of the peasantry in attaining independence, both countries quickly turned toward developing their cities and industries.

Opposite **Jawaharlal Nehru and Zhou Enlai, 1954.** Prime Minister Nehru (right) is cheered by crowds as he arrives on a State Visit to Red China.

For an interactive version of this map, go to: http://www.prenhall.com/spodek/map22.1

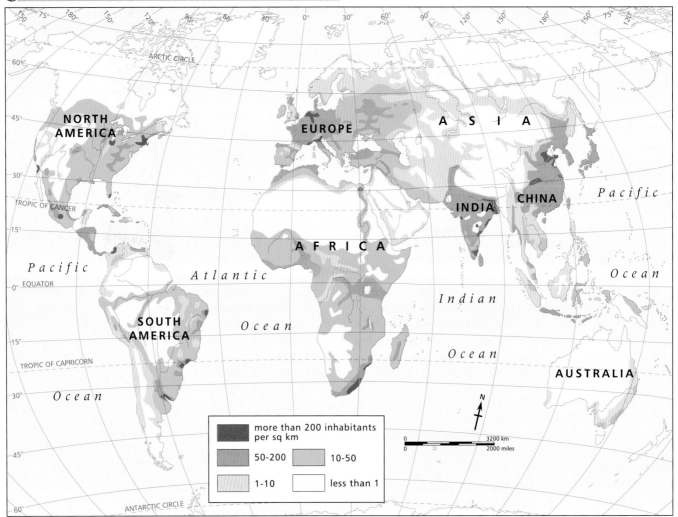

World population distribution today. While the bulk of the world's population lives, as always, in coastal regions or along river valleys, the rapid rise in urbanism over the last century has created enormous imbalances as cities attract economic migrants from their hinterlands and from abroad. Some areas, like Europe, are so urbanized that their entire surface has high densities; others, like China and India, are so packed that even rural areas house urban densities. The only areas with low densities are those ecologically difficult for human life—deserts, mountains, frozen regions.

Both countries also had large rural populations that made industrialization along Western lines, based on smaller populations and urban settings, difficult. They turned to models of technology that were appropriate for their populations and the rural conditions. Often relying on models of development that were different from those used in the West, both countries have become formidable competitors with Europe and the United States in the twenty-first century in spite of their alternate strategies of development.

CHINA, 1925–89

Prelude to Revolution

We have already discussed in Chapter 19 the 1911 revolution that ended China's 2,000-year-old empire, and China's subsequent descent into political and military chaos as local warlords seized control of various regions of the country. We have seen two groups emerging from these divisions as the most powerful and the most likely to subdue the warlords and consolidate a national government: the Guomindang (GMD, National People's Party), led by Chiang Kai-shek (Jiang Jieshi, 1887–1975), and the communists commanded by Mao Zedong (1893–1976). Chiang began as a military commander and later sought to build a government based on his GMD party. Mao began as a Communist Party organizer and later built an army. Both leaders revered Sun Yat-sen (1866–1925) and accepted his "Three People's Principles" as guidelines for their political and economic programs, but they interpreted Sun's teachings quite differently. Where Chiang emphasized the role of businessmen, international alliances, and individual initiative, Mao stressed the peasant farmer, community organization, and indigenous institutions. The two men and their parties fought for control in a bitter civil war that festered for a quarter century following Sun's death in 1925. Both learned that "in a country ruled and plundered by marauding warlord armies, it was naked military power that was crucial in determining the direction of political events" (Meisner, p. 21). In Mao's blunt words: "political power grows out of the barrel of a gun."

Power Struggles, 1925–37

Chiang Kai-shek and the Guomindang Chiang had studied in a Japanese military academy, fought in the 1911 revolution to overthrow the Manchu government, and rose to command China's own new military academy near Guangzhou, established with Soviet financing. After Sun's death, he succeeded to the leadership of the GMD. A staunch advocate of the neo-Confucian New Life movement in the 1930s, Chiang wrote *China's Destiny* in 1943 to reaffirm the conservative virtues of China's indigenous, hierarchical, genteel culture. Yet he also became a Methodist, as Sun had. Also like Sun, Chiang married a Chinese Christian woman (who, also like Sun's wife, was a sister of a wealthy Chinese industrialist), and valued contributions of foreign Christians in China's economic modernization.

Chiang maintained a wide and diverse array of close personal, professional, and financial connections with Shanghai underworld figures, Soviet Comintern agents, Western businessmen, and Christian missionaries. As China dissolved into warlordism, Chiang was named commander-in-chief of the GMD's National Revolutionary Army, and for a quarter of a century he fought to unify China under his own control against three powerful enemies: the warlords; the Japanese, who had invaded Manchuria in 1931 and China itself in 1937; and the communists.

Foreign powers in the treaty ports monitored China's shifting fortunes with considerable self-interest. By 1931, foreigners had invested US$3.25 billion in China, slightly more than double the amount in 1914; which was, in turn, slightly more than double that in 1902. Foreign loans financed Chinese railways and heavy industry, and foreigners held three-fourths of all investments in shipping, almost half of the cotton spindles, and 80–90 percent of the coal mines. Through the early 1920s, the politicization and unionization of industrial workers encouraged many strikes, to which the employers, many of them foreigners, often responded with violence. The employers wanted a compliant government that would help them break the strikes. Most of these employers and foreign investors aided Chiang, hoping to manipulate him as the leader closest to their interests. During the period 1929 to 1937, they lent him much of the money needed to cover the GMD government's annual deficits.

Foreign-based Christian missionaries and educational institutions also supported the GMD, attracted partly by Chiang's own Christian affiliation. The YMCA movement claimed 54,000 members in 1922. In the early 1920s, some 12,000 Christian

AT A GLANCE : CHINA AND INDIA

DATE	CHINA	INDIA
1900	■ Boxer Rebellion against Western influence is suppressed by foreign troops (1900)	■ Mohandas Karamchand Gandhi publishes *Hind Swaraj*, or Indian Home Rule (1909)
1910	■ 1911 Revolution ends Manchu dynasty and 2,000 years of imperial rule ■ Yuan Shihkai elected premier (1911); dies 1916 ■ Warlords battle throughout China ■ May 4th Movement (1919)	■ Gandhi returns from South Africa and establishes new ashram in Ahmedabad (1915) ■ Government of India Act creates dual British/Indian government (1919) ■ British crack down on freedom of the press and assembly in the Rowlatt Acts (1919) ■ Amritsar (Jalianwala Bagh) massacre (1919)
1920	■ Chinese Communist Party formed (1921) ■ Sun Yat-sen dies (1925) ■ Guomindang (GMD) and Communists vie for power (1925–49) ■ Chiang Kai-shek captures Beijing (1927–8); rules from Nanjing ■ Mao's Report on Hunan Peasant Movement (1927)	■ Non-cooperation campaign boycotts British interests (1920–2) ■ Gandhi fasts for twenty-one days to promote Hindu–Muslim unity (1924)
1930	■ Mao Zedong leads Communists on the Long March, from Jiangxi to Yan'an (1934) ■ Japanese seize Manchuria (1931) and go on to invade China proper (1937) ■ Communists kidnap Chiang to gain cooperation in the war against Japan (1936)	■ Salt March campaign (1930–2) ■ Gandhi outflanks socialists by persuading Jawaharlal Nehru to postpone land redistribution ■ Congress appoints National Planning Commission (1938)
1940	■ Japan surrenders; civil war resumes (1945) ■ Foundation of the Communist People's Republic of China (1949) ■ Foreigners expelled (1949)	■ "Quit India" campaign (1942) ■ Independence from Great Britain is followed by partition of the subcontinent (1947)
1950	■ China invades and colonizes Tibet (1950) ■ Korean War (1950–3) ■ "100 Flowers Campaign" briefly permits some freedom of expression (1956–7) ■ Mao initiates "Great Leap Forward" experiment (1958–60)	■ Policy of protective discrimination reserves jobs for untouchable castes (1955) ■ Hindu Marriage Act (1955) and Hindu Succession Act (1956) increase rights for women
1960	■ Diplomatic relations with Russia are severed (1961) ■ Sino-Indian border war (1962) ■ Cultural Revolution initiates party purges and reignites revolutionary zeal; formation of Red Guard (1966)	■ Death of Nehru (1964)
1970	■ China joins United Nations (1971) ■ Groundbreaking visit to China by President Nixon (1972) ■ Mao dies; "Gang of Four" arrested (1976) ■ Deng Xiaoping comes to power; economic liberalization (1979) ■ One family, one child policy (1980)	■ Civil war leads to creation of Bangladesh on land of East Pakistan (1971) ■ Prime Minister Indira Gandhi asserts dictatorial powers during "Emergency Rule" (1975–7) ■ Policy of forced sterilization (1975–7)
1980	■ China joins World Bank and the International Monetary Fund (1980) ■ Students demonstrating in Tiananmen Square are killed by soldiers (1989)	■ Indira Gandhi assassinated (1984)
1990	■ Hong Kong reverts to Chinese sovereignty after 155 years as a British colony (1997) ■ Macao returned to China by Portugal (1999) ■ China voted "most favored nation" trading status by US (2000)	■ Rajiv Gandhi assassinated (1991) ■ Prime Minister P.V. Narasimha Rao lowers tariffs and begins to welcome foreign investments (1991) ■ Pakistan and India test nuclear devices in violation of international treaties (1998) ■ Population reaches 1 billion (1999)

missionaries, slightly more Protestants than Catholics, served in China. Christian and foreign colleges enrolled 4,000 of the 35,000 students in Chinese colleges in 1922, and 9 percent of their students were women. Much Western culture and literature was incorporated in the new curricula of China's universities. Chinese students and intellectuals were eager to hear voices from the West and East, and such luminaries as

Bertrand Russell, John Dewey, Albert Einstein, and Rabindranath Tagore visited and lectured widely.

With the support of Western business and cultural leaders, and of the Soviet Comintern as well, Chiang undertook to defeat the warlords and to reestablish a viable central government. Through the great northern expedition from Guangzhou, Chiang captured Beijing in 1927–8, established his own capital in Nanjing on the lower Yangzi River, and began to consolidate GMD power over China.

Despite these early military victories, Chiang ultimately failed. His government, permeated by corruption, alienated the peasantry by forging alliances with exploitative landlords. High officials sold off provisions intended to feed and clothe China's starving armed forces. When the Japanese invasion of 1937 forced Chiang's retreat into the remote mountainous reaches of Chongqing (Chungking), the communists persuaded the Chinese peasants that they, not the GMD, could best fight off the Japanese and represent peasant interests in a free China.

Mao Zedong, Peasant Revolt, and the Communist Party The communist leader, Mao Zedong (1893–1976), Sun's other principal successor, shared his goals of a strong, united, independent China and the improvement of the people's livelihood, but his background was quite different from Sun's and from Chiang's. First, the 1911 revolution, in which he participated, was over by the time he was eighteen, and was therefore no longer an issue. Second, Mao's personal experience was limited to China. Although he read widely in Western as well as Chinese literature and philosophy, his first travel outside China, a visit to the Soviet Union, came only in 1949. Other Chinese students had traveled to Europe during World War I, and he had helped them. For himself, however, he explained, "I did not want to go to Europe. I felt that I did not know enough about my own country, and that my time could be more profitably spent in China" (Snow, p. 149).

Third, Mao had little experience of the Western business and missionary establishments in China. His own formative experiences were in the countryside and in educational institutions. Compared with both Sun and Chiang, Mao cared little for China's reputation in the West but much for the quality of life of the Chinese peasant. He had grown up on his father's farm in Hunan province, where he learned at first hand of the exploitation of the peasant, in part through the oppressive strategies of his own father, who rose from poverty to become a middle-level farmer and small-scale trader. Mao later recounted that he left this life to become an athletic, serious, politically committed student, reading widely, and consolidating a core group of similarly inclined young men: "My friends and I preferred to talk only of large matters—the nature of men, of human society, of China, the world, and the universe! ... We also became ardent physical culturists" (Snow, p. 146).

By 1919, Mao's educational quests had brought him to Beijing (Peking) University, just as China's resentment against foreign imperialism was boiling over. The peace treaties of World War I

Poster from 1960 showing Mao Zedong and supporters of the Cultural Revolution, each holding a copy of Mao's teachings, the "Little Red Book." Mao realized early on that the peasantry could carry forward the ideals of communism, even when the workers' movement was destroyed by Chiang Kai-shek. Mao was determined to eliminate "foreign dogmatism" and was against copying the Soviet blueprint for communism. His unique application of Marxism to China's needs gave rise to a mass following.

assigned Germany's holdings in the Shandong Peninsula of north China to Japan rather than returning them to China. In Paris, indignant Chinese protestors physically blocked their nation's delegates from attending the signing ceremonies, and thus China never did sign the peace agreements. Within China, protests against the treaties by students and others began on May 4, 1919, engendering a continuing critique of China's international humiliation, the apparent bankruptcy of its historical traditions, and the content of its cultural links to the West. The "May Fourth Movement" also helped to sow the seeds of the Chinese Communist Party (CCP), which came to fruition in 1921 following discussions between Chinese revolutionaries and representatives of the newly formed Comintern of the USSR. At that time, Mao was a participant in the study group of Li Dazhao, chief librarian of Beijing University and one of the founders of the CCP. In a statement quite unusual for a Chinese intellectual, Li had already proclaimed the importance of the peasantry and called on the university students to help them to mobilize:

> Our China is a rural nation and most of the laboring class is made up of peasants. If they are not liberated, then our whole nation will not be liberated ... Go out and develop them and cause them to know [that they should] demand liberation, speak out about their sufferings, throw off their ignorance and be people who will themselves plan their own lives. (Spence, p. 308)

Peasant Organization and Guerrilla Warfare When Mao joined the party he began organizing workers in the industrial plants of the Wuhan region, but in 1925 he was reassigned to peasant organization in his native Hunan. Despite the orthodox Marxist doctrines of Comintern advisers, Mao in Hunan came to see the Chinese peasantry, rather than the proletariat, as China's revolutionary vanguard. In terms of technology, he abandoned the emphasis on large-scale industrial planning and sought instead local solutions to local problems through locally developed, appropriate rural technologies. Mao's enthusiastic and influential, but polemical and doctrinaire, 1927 report on the Hunan peasant movement updated Li's rural emphasis:

> the broad peasant masses have risen to fulfill their historic mission ... the democratic forces in the rural areas have risen to overthrow the rural feudal power. The patriarchal-feudal class of local bullies, bad gentry, and lawless landlords has formed the basis of autocratic government for thousands of years, the cornerstone of imperialism, warlordism and corrupt officialdom. To overthrow this feudal power is the real objective of the national revolution ... The leadership of the poor peasants is absolutely necessary. Without the poor peasants there can be no revolution. (de Bary, p. 869)

The peasants had to use their strength to overthrow the authority of the landlords. This revolution required violence.

Mao's enemies had their own tools of violence. While Mao was organizing peasants in the 1920s, Jiang was massacring the core of the revolutionary proletariat. As Chiang completed the northern expedition and consolidated his control over the warlords, he turned, in alliance with the international business community and without excessive objection from the Comintern, to murdering thousands of communist workers in the industrialized cities of Shanghai, Wuhan, and Guangzhou in the spring of 1927. In Changsha, local military leaders joined with the GMD and local landlords to slaughter thousands of peasants who had recently expropriated the land they worked from its legal owners. By the summer of 1928, only 32,000 union members in all of China remained loyal to the Communist Party. By 1929, only 3 percent of party members were proletarians. Mao's peasant alternative was, of necessity, the communists' last resort.

When the GMD put down the Hunan Autumn Harvest Uprising in 1927, Mao's core group retreated to the border area between Hunan and Jiangzi. Other communist leaders, driven from the cities, joined them in this rural area. They built up a **soviet**, a local communist government, redistributing land, introducing improved farming methods, and instituting new educational systems to spread literacy along with political indoctrination. They recruited and trained a guerrilla army. Mao himself formulated its tactics: "The enemy advances, we retreat; the enemy camps, we harass; the enemy tires, we attack; the enemy retreats, we pursue" (Spence, p. 375).

The guerrillas could exist only with the cooperation of the peasantry whom they wished to mobilize. Appropriate, rather revolutionary rules were established to govern soldiers' behavior: "prompt obedience to orders; no confiscations whatever from the poor peasantry; and prompt delivery directly to the Government, for its disposal, of all goods confiscated from the landlords" (Snow, p. 176). These were later elaborated to include: "Be courteous and polite to the people and help them when you can … Be honest in all transactions with the peasants … Pay for all articles purchased" (Snow, p. 176).

Gender Issues under Mao Mao recognized the changes already taking place in women's rights. Feminism had begun to flourish in China by the 1920s with the formation of such organizations as the Women's Suffrage Association and the Women's Rights League. Its constituency was mostly Western-influenced urban intellectuals. *New Youth* magazine, for example, which was often critical of Confucius for his emphasis on patriarchy and obedience to authority, had translated and published Ibsen's *A Doll's House* in 1918. Ba Jinn's novel *Family*, one of the key works of China's reformist New Culture Movement, transplanted Ibsen's advocacy of women's equality and independence into a modern Chinese setting. Margaret Sanger, American feminist and advocate of contraception, toured and lectured throughout China in 1922. There were also some 1,500,000 women working outside their homes for pay in light industrial factories, mostly textiles, in China's cities. Now Mao refocused feminist attention on the countryside and the peasantry:

> the authority of the husband … has always been comparatively weak among the poor peasants, because the poor peasant women, compelled for financial reasons to take more part in manual work than women of the wealthier classes, have obtained more right to speak and more power to make decisions in family affairs. In recent years the rural economy has become even more bankrupt and the basic condition for men's domination over women has already been undermined. And now, with the rise of the peasant movement, women in many places have set out immediately to organize the rural women's association; the opportunity has come for them to lift up their heads, and the authority of the husband is tottering more and more every day. (de Bary, p. 872)

Communist policies took two complementary directions. The first, and more effective, restructured the labor and military

soviet A council, the primary unit of government in the Soviet Union at local, regional, and national levels, later adopted by other communist regimes.

Women of Shanghai with tiny, bound feet working at frames for sorting tea leaves. From the early years of the twentieth century urban women had begun to leave the confines of home to work in light industry. The move from home to workplace gave women more status, which was further strengthened by the reforms of the communist government when it came to power. The abandonment of footbinding in all but the most outlying areas of China did much to enhance the freedom of women.

forces to give more scope and power to women. Building the Chinese soviet and fighting guerrilla battles required the support of every available resource. While women did not usually participate in warfare directly, the increased need for production and personnel brought them out of the house into new jobs, effectively raising their status.

Later, after the revolution had succeeded in 1949, the communists issued a new marriage law forbidding arranged marriages, stopping all purchase and sale in marriage contracts, and encouraging free choice of marriage partners. This law met strong resistance. Men who had already bought their wives objected; so did mothers-in-law, who ruled over each household's domestic labor force. The traditional Chinese family provided for old age security, child-care, medical facilities, and the production and consumption of food, clothing, and shelter. The new communist marriage law seemed to threaten this structure without providing any alternative. The law was not widely enforced. Also, the leadership of the party remained conspicuously male.

The Long March and the Communist Triumph, 1934–49

Chiang sent five successive military expeditions against the Jiangzi soviet, beginning with 100,000 men and leading up to one million. By 1934, the communists could no longer hold out. Mao led some 80,000 men and thirty-five women out of the siege and began the Long March, a 370-day, 6,000-mile strategic retreat, by foot, under constant bombardment and attack from Chiang's forces, across rivers, mountain ranges, marshes, and grasslands, westward to Guizhou and then northward to a final new base camp in Yan'an. Some 20,000 men finally arrived in Yan'an, of whom about half had marched since the beginning, the rest having joined *en route*. The courage, comradeship, commitment, and idealism of this march, in the face of seemingly insurmountable natural obstacles and enemy harassment, were the formative experience of a generation of Chinese communist leaders. At the front, Mao now became the unquestioned leader of the movement, party, and army.

In remote, impoverished Yan'an, Mao established his capital and rebuilt his soviet structure, nurturing his army, inducting its soldiers into agricultural assistance work; redistributing land; encouraging handicrafts; and establishing newspapers and schools, an arts and literature academy, and medical programs for training paramedical "barefoot doctors." The Chinese communist program developed more fully here: a peasant-centered economy, administered and aided by guerrilla soldiers, capped by a dictatorial but comparatively benevolent communist leadership, encouraging literacy accompanied by indoctrination in communist ideology. Tension built up, however, between ideological goals and practical implementation, between being "Red" and being "expert."

Although Yan'an was remote from the main fighting, and was subject to GMD attacks, the communists launched guerrilla action against the Japanese after their invasion of China proper in 1937. By comparison, Jiang seemed less nationalistic. He appeared willing to compromise with the Japanese and more eager to pursue the Chinese communists than to fight the foreign invaders. Mao, on the other hand, wished to join forces with Jiang to unite China against the foreigner. In the "Xian incident," dissident generals arranged the bold kidnap of Jiang in 1936, threatening the life of the GMD leader if he did not join more vigorously in the fight against the Japanese; after this, Jiang moved toward temporary cooperation with the communists.

At first, the Japanese had hoped to rule China with the help of Chinese collaborators, as they had Manchuria, but their cruelty after the capture of Nanjing in December 1937 dashed those hopes. The Chinese vowed to fight back. The communists fought a rearguard guerrilla war from their northern base in Shaanxi, while Jiang led

Legend:
- occupied by Japan 1933
- area of Japanese influence 1932-37
- Communist strongholds to 1935
- Long March Oct. 1934-Oct. 1935
- Communist base 1935-45
- occupied by Japan by 1944
- Communist controlled by 1945

a scorched-earth retreat to a new headquarters far up the Yangzi River in Chongqing. Soldiers and civilians suffered catastrophically.

By the early 1940s, nationalist cooperation began to unravel as communists and GMD forces jockeyed for temporary power and future position. After a temporary respite in 1945, full-scale civil war resumed. The USA extended help to Chiang in training his troops, airlifting them to critical military locations, and turning over to them war *matériel*. The Soviet Union, fighting for its life against Germany, stayed out of the conflict against Japan until the last week of the war.

The Communist Revolution in China. Chinese communists and nationalists (GMD) united briefly to subdue the warlord factions which emerged after the collapse of the Manchu (Qing) dynasty, and to consolidate a national government. After 1927 Nationalist repression forced the communists to retreat to remote areas, focussing in the northwest after the Long March of 1934–5, where guerrilla warfare continued. With the Japanese invasion of China proper in 1937, China was torn by both international and civil war. After Japan's defeat in 1945, the communists turned to defeating the GMD as well.

Then it entered Manchuria, carrying off a great deal of that region's military and industrial equipment to the Soviet Union, while turning over some of it to the Chinese communists. As China's civil war continued after 1945, communist forces in many parts of the country, well disciplined and warmly supported by peasants, defeated the ill-disciplined and ill-provisioned GMD forces, whose rations and materials were often sold off for private profit without ever reaching them. By the fall of 1949, the communists had driven the GMD completely out of mainland China to the island of Taiwan. The GMD occupied and took over houses and businesses of Taiwanese who already lived there. They claimed that Taiwan was the true China that should be reunited with what became known as mainland China. The Communist People's Republic of China was born.

Revolutionary Policies, 1949–69

Implementing the Principles of the Long March, 1949–55 For Mao and the guerrilla veterans who dominated the new government, the principal fears were foreign domination, internal chaos, and the lingering power of the wealthy classes and the large-scale landholders. The new rulers modeled much of their new government on their experiences during the Long March and the Yan'an soviet. They returned to these experiences for inspiration in difficult times as long as they lived. Important policies included:

- redistribution of land;
- women's rights to hold land;
- appropriate technology;
- production and equal distribution of basic necessities for everyone;
- universal literacy (actually reaching about 69 percent by 1980, about 60 percent for females, 78 percent for males).

The government mobilized tight-knit, local, social networks not only to suppress such vices as opium addiction and prostitution but also to enforce rigid political indoctrination and conformity, including the informing by one family member against another and coercing personal confessions of political deviance.

Land redistribution was a top priority. During this class revolution, perhaps half the peasantry of China received at least some benefits while as a many as one million landlords were killed. Lacking experience in urban economic affairs, the communist government at first invited the cooperation of businessmen, both Chinese and foreign. But policies changed abruptly as China entered the Korean War in October 1950. Threats, expropriation, and accusations of espionage—sometimes justified—against businessmen and Christian missionaries forced almost all foreigners to leave China by the end of 1950. Numerous campaigns against counter-revolutionaries; the confiscation and redistribution of private property; hundreds and even thousands of executions; intensive public, group pressure to elicit confessions from those perceived as enemies of the revolution; and regular confrontations between workers and owners, now incorporated into the processes of labor relations, destroyed the capitalist sector in China. Pressured by the United States, many countries refused to recognize the new government. The communist Soviet government, on the other hand, maintained a strong alliance and helped to draft and implement China's first five-year plan between 1952 and 1957.

Communist policies on urbanization and industrialization were more ambivalent. The communists had come to power as an anti-urban, peasant movement. The large cities, especially Shanghai, had fostered the foreign enclaves, extraterritorial law, and colonial behavior that flagrantly insulted the Chinese in their own country, but they also housed China's industrial base, military technology, administration, and cultural life. As the communists began to capture the nation's cities, Mao began to reevaluate their potential:

> From 1927 to the present the center of gravity of our work has been in the villages—gathering strength in the villages, using the villages in order to surround the cities, and then taking the cities. The period for this method of work has now ended. The period of the city leading the village has now begun. (Spence, p. 508)

Trial of a landlord. Most such trials ended with a confession and a promise to reform; some with a bullet for the accused. In its first moves toward collectivization, the communist government instituted a number of land reforms that gave the land to the peasants who worked it and did away with the landlords—literally.

Policies and results, however, were uneven. To restrain urban growth, the government promulgated severe limitations on internal migration, but movement from the countryside continued steadily, if slowly. China's population, which had been 10.6 percent urban in 1949, reached 17.4 percent urban in 1976. In sheer numbers this was an increase from 57 million to 163 million people. As time went by, the cities again challenged communist ideological purity—Guangzhou promoted capitalism; Beijing, political protest; Shanghai, internationalism. Chinese leaders like Liu Shaoqi and Deng Xiaoping argued on behalf of urban, bureaucratic, centralized, "expert" industrialization; Mao and Lin Piao wanted rural, grassroots, "Red" populism. Some, like Zhou Enlai, sought a compromise and synthesis.

Militarily, the communists extolled the spirit of the guerrilla warrior over high-tech weaponry. They taunted America, the world's most heavily armed country, as a "paper tiger," unwilling or unable to use its vast arsenal, especially its nuclear weapons, in combat. Indeed, China itself fought the United States to a draw in Korea, 1950–3, and then saw America withdraw in defeat from Vietnam in 1975. Nevertheless, China also bought, produced, or purloined up-to-date military technology. In 1964, China exploded its first atomic bomb; in the mid-1970s it followed with hydrogen bombs; in 1980 it tested missiles with a range of 7,000 miles; and in 1981, launched three space satellites.

"Let a Hundred Flowers Bloom," 1956–7 Economically, China adopted a five-year plan based on the Soviet model. It called for multiplying the value of industrial output between 1952 and 1957 almost two and one-half times, and claimed at the end to have overachieved the target by 22 percent. By the end of the plan, even democracy seemed a possibility. In 1956–7, Mao's call, "Let a hundred flowers bloom, let a hundred schools of thought contend," opened the gates of public expression and even criticism of government. In Beijing, students and others posted their thoughts on what became known as Democracy Wall. By late 1957, however, fearing uncontrolled, growing protest, the government shifted its policies. It jailed protesters, sent them to labor camps, and exiled them to remote rural farms.

HOW DO WE KNOW?

A Journalist–Activist Responds to the "Hundred Flowers" Campaign

When Mao introduced the "Hundred Flowers" campaign, journalist Liu Binyan praised him for his democracy. As he saw the reaction of the party, however, and the subsequent use of the campaign as a means of identifying and punishing critics of the government, he came to see the entire movement as a trap. Liu Binyan became one of the most prominent and most active of the opponents of the communist government of China. Not all historians agree with this assessment of Mao's motives, although the results were clear.

This excerpt is both a primary document, as the record of a participant, and a secondary document, as a later assessment of a previous event.

I do not remember a moment in my life more exhilarating than when Mao Zedong's February 1957 speech to the State Council was released. My estimation of him soared to sublime heights. At China Youth News the response was equally enthusiastic; it seemed as if we were at the beginning of a new era in China … In that speech, Mao announced that dogmatism should not be mistaken for Marxism; he reiterated his policy of letting "a hundred flowers bloom and a hundred schools of thought contend"; he advocated open criticism and reiterated that senior party leaders should not be exempt from criticism. As for strikes by workers and students—unprecedented since the founding of the People's Republic and now taken seriously for the first time—he said the right way of dealing with them was not by force or coercion but by overcoming bureaucratism.

These issues were exactly the unspoken ones that had been weighing on me for the last few years—special privileges with party ranks, bureaucratism, and dogmatic tendencies. Now my disquiet had been dispelled as if by magic. The political climate in Beijing cleared up; the mood of intellectuals brightened, everything seemed to take on a rosy hue. Mao was virtually advocating more democracy and liberalization in matters of ideology; as a journalist and writer, I now felt I had a free hand in pursuing my vocation.

[Liu then describes meetings with local party officials that demonstrated that many did not interpret Mao's words as he did. They saw any approval of open expression to be very limited, at most.]

Thirty years later, I reread Mao's speech (the original version, not the one revised for publication) and realized that at the time I had been too preoccupied with his main drift to detect hints of other tendencies hidden between the lines. For instance, he did not mince words over Stalin's dogmatism, but then insisted that Stalin must be assessed on the "three-seven" principle—that is, seven parts merit to three parts fault. Again Mao considered "democracy" as basically a tool to mobilize the people for the Party's own ends. (Liu, pp. 69–70.)

- Which of Liu's points make his document a primary source document? Which of his points make it a secondary source document?
- Why did Liu find Mao's campaign to let a "hundred flowers bloom," surprising?
- What led Liu to change his mind in assessing the purpose of Mao's "hundred flowers bloom" campaign?

Steel furnace, Shiu Shin, China, 1958. Every thirty minutes, some 50 kilos of iron is smelted in the several hundred ovens at this steel furnace.

The "Great Leap Forward," 1957–60 Increasingly threatened by population growth in Chinese cities and an inability to feed urban populations, the government implemented the "Great Leap Forward," grouping almost all of rural China into communes, "sending down" city people to villages, virtually terminating whatever small private enterprises had survived, and attempting to downscale and disperse industry by establishing local, small-scale enterprises, referred to generically as "backyard steel mills." The Great Leap Forward, administered by powerful, distant government officials who attempted to restructure the entire economy of the nation according to communist ideology, led to economic catastrophe, including millions of deaths by starvation.

The Cultural Revolution, 1966–69 Unhappy with what he saw was going on in China, Mao began to silence resistance. The government relaxed for a few years, but then reinstated even more extreme ideological and economic policies in the Great Proletarian Cultural Revolution in 1966. Mao sought through this revolution to purge the party of time-serving bureaucrats and to reignite revolutionary fervor. Those who responded most enthusiastically were the army and students, who, with Mao's encouragement, organized themselves into the Red Guard. Teachers were denounced by their students and by party officials; professors and intellectuals were exiled to remote villages and forced to undertake hard labor.

The Long March was now thirty years in the past, yet nostalgia for its ideological zeal still motivated China's aging leaders. Mao was venerated as their last hope to restore the intensity of those early days of the revolution. Key quotations from his statements were published in millions of copies of *The Quotations of Chairman Mao*, often called the Little Red Book because of its size and the color of its cover. These were circulated and read publicly throughout the country. Economic chaos and starvation on the one hand and the total stifling and destruction of intellectual and academic life on the other brought China to a standstill. For three years, 1966–9, militant, committed anarchy reigned.

Recovery, 1970–76

As the damage became clearly visible, China reversed its policy in yet another example of *fang–zhou*, loosening up– tightening down. The People's Liberation Army was given the task of suppressing the Red Guards, the youth and student cadres who had wreaked chaos in the name of Mao. New international respectability was sought, most dramatically by the normalization of relations with the United States after President Nixon visited China in 1972. Domestically, attention refocused on the restoration of economic productivity. Imports and exports, which had held roughly flat for several years at slightly over $2 billion each through the late 1960s, rose steadily until, in 1978, each registered $10 billion. One fourth of the imports were machinery and equipment, including complete plants—6,934 of them in 1978—built entirely by foreigners (Spence, p. 641). Almost all of these new factories were in heavy industries, especially petrochemicals and iron and steel. By 1980, China was producing more steel than Britain or France.

"Between 1950 and 1977 industrial output grew at an average annual rate of 13.5 percent … the highest rate of all developing or developed major nations of the world during the time, and a more rapid pace than achieved by any country during any comparable period of rapid industrialization in modern world history" (Meisner, pp. 436–7). Meanwhile, agriculture was upended, collectivized, and relatively neglected in terms of investment. The agonizingly slow growth of agriculture at 2.3 percent a year from 1952 to 1977 could barely keep pace with population growth of 2 percent a year. By the time Mao died in 1976, China was poised for a dramatic change in leadership and policies.

International Relations

USSR In terms of international relations, also, China had already implemented a series of dramatic turnabouts. In the first decade of communist rule, its chief ally was the USSR, which helped the new communist state

Tiananmen Square, June 5, 1989. Tanks traveling down Changan Boulevard, in front of the Beijing Hotel, are confronted by a brave Chinese man who pleads for an end to the killing of demonstrating students. This photograph came to symbolize the struggle of the Chinese people to reassert their dignity and gain democracy in the face of the huge and powerful communist regime.

irredentist An individual or group that seeks to restore territory to the state that once owned it.

design its five-year plan, train and provision its armed forces, and build factories, transportation facilities, urban neighborhoods, and administrative centers. But in the mid-1950s, the USSR under Khrushchev began to moderate its own militant policies both domestically and internationally. China, however, remained more "Red," and the two countries quarreled bitterly over ideology, as they had in 1927. In the summer of 1960, the USSR recalled all of its technical advisers in China, including those working on atomic energy projects. Diplomatic relations were severed in 1961. In China's border disputes with India, which spilled over briefly into warfare in 1962, the USSR backed India's claims and entered into defense alliances with China's opponent.

Armed conflicts with the USSR arose over borders in northern Manchuria and Xinjiang province. Fighting in 1969 led to about 100 Russian and 800 Chinese casualties. At considerable expense, China then concentrated its defense forces in these border areas. Only after 1985, under Gorbachev's new policies of *glasnost* (political and cultural openness) and *perestroika* (economic restructuring) in the Soviet Union, were diplomatic relations between the two countries normalized. Still, the two powers remained wary and armed across thousands of miles of shared borders.

The United States Relations with the United States began in cold hostility. For almost two decades after 1949, America lamented and resented the "loss" of China and continued to support Chiang's **irredentist** forces on Taiwan after 1949, mostly because it wanted to combat communism. Communist policies thoroughly alienated capitalist business people and Christian religious communities, both of which had invested in China. The Chinese government's use of "brainwashing" tactics to convert their internal opponents through unremitting propaganda, group pressure, and official coercion,

President Nixon meets with Communist Party Chairman Mao Zedong in Beijing, during his groundbreaking 1972 visit to China. The Chinese government, clearly worried by aggressive Soviet policy in Czechoslovakia, took steps to improve relations with the United States. Four years after the Sino-Western rapprochement, begun in 1971, foreign trade with China had tripled, and by 1980, China had joined the International Monetary Fund and the World Bank.

China's pingpong team are invited to America by the National Pingpong Association, USA, April 1972. In this friendly match, a Chinese and an American pingpong player are on the same side, a symbol of the new friendship between China and America.

scandalized Americans. China's "liberation" of Tibet in 1950, and the ruthless suppression of the Tibetan Buddhist revolt in 1959, seemed to confirm the militaristic, brutal nature of the government, although no one moved to aid the Tibetan resistance. The Korean War, provoked by North Korea's invasion of the south in 1950, led to the three-year engagement of American and United Nations forces against those of China, ended in a deadlock. Against the advice of its closest overseas allies, the USA lobbied to keep the People's Republic of China out of the United Nations; the government of Taiwan represented the Chinese people.

In the early 1970s, however, the diplomatic scene changed dramatically. Mao and his new advisers, retreating from the economic catastrophe of the Cultural Revolution, sought assistance from abroad. President Nixon and Secretary of State Henry Kissinger also favored more pragmatic policies. In 1971, the USA did not stand in the way of China's joining the United Nations, and in the next year, Nixon visited China, advancing the normalization of relations between the two countries, but at the expense of Taiwan.

East Asia Within its own area of the world, China for 2,000 years has viewed itself as the dominant, central power, and has sought that recognition from its neighbors with mixed success. In many of these countries, China was a feared and resented neighbor, not an uncommon relationship for a regional superpower. China invaded Tibet in 1950 and forced the Dalai Lama to flee and to seek refuge in India in 1959. In Cambodia, it backed the murderous Khmer Rouge Party and its leader Pol Pot in the vicious civil wars through the 1970s, even committing troops briefly to combat.

On the other hand, the astonishing economic recovery of Japan after World War II, challenged China's leadership position and forced the country to reconsider its economic programs. Moreover, in several nearby states, Chinese minorities were viewed with suspicion as possible subversive infiltrators for the Chinese nation and the Communist Party. In anti-Chinese and anti-communist riots in Indonesia in 1965 thousands of Chinese were murdered, and hundreds of thousands more were exiled.

India Finally, China's relationship with India has been complex. When India became independent in 1947 and China completed its revolution in 1949, they chose dramatically different social, political, and economic paths, and both saw themselves as leading the third world in new patterns of development. At the Bandung Conference in 1955 both offered leadership to nations newly emerging from colonialism. China became a model for agrarian guerrilla revolt throughout Southeast Asia and beyond, while India's non-violent path inspired others, especially in Black Africa.

India did not protest China's takeover of Tibet in 1950 and consistently backed China's petition to enter the United Nations. But differences over border demarcations in the mountainous regions of Leh and Ladakh led to open warfare in 1962. The Chinese decisively defeated Indian troops, penetrated through the mountain passes to within striking distance of India's heartland, and then withdrew voluntarily to the borders they had claimed. The war undercut the concept of third world solidarity, and India's first test of nuclear devices in 1974 increased the mutual suspicion.

Post-Revolutionary China

China demonstrated the inevitability of each huge nation of the world finding its own developmental path. China might for a time take guidance from one foreign ideology or another, and it might enter into alliances with various powers at one time or another, but finally it sought a path appropriate to its own size, geography, power, technology, and historical experience. Chinese at home and abroad, including many who disapproved of current government policies, took pride in the newfound unity, power, and independence of the Central Kingdom. China might make mistakes, but they would be its own mistakes. Leaving behind a century of humiliating colonialism and devastating international and civil war, China sought to establish stability and ideological purity. Soon it would seek a larger place in the world.

INDIA, 1914–91

The Independence Struggle, 1914–47

British Policies and Practices Established in 1885 at British initiative as a vent for Indian nationalist criticism, the Indian National Congress led the resistance to British rule in the early twentieth century, usually through constitutional protest. The Congress leadership was concentrated in the hands of men who were educated in British ways, through British-run schools, sometimes in Britain itself. Somewhat more than a third of its members were trained in the legal profession. In 1835, T.B. Macaulay, legal adviser to the British government of India, had declared the intent of the government's educational policies to create a class "Indian in blood and colour, but English in taste, in opinions, in morals, and in intellect" (Hay, p. 31); the Congress leadership reflected the results. By 1906, Muslims began to fear an India under exclusive Hindu control and formed their own organization, the All-India Muslim League.

The British in India claimed to be preparing India for democratic, responsible government and in 1917, the British Secretary of State for India, Edwin Montagu, announced the goal of British policy to be "increasing association of Indians in every branch of the administration, and the gradual development of self-governing institutions, with a view to the progressive realisation of responsible government in India as an integral part of the British Empire." A series of constitutional reforms had already established official councils with substantial Indian membership,

INDIAN INDEPENDENCE—KEY FIGURES	
Rabindranath Tagore (1861–1941)	Indian poet, painter, and musician from Bengal, who translated his own verse into English. He received the Nobel prize for literature in 1913. An ardent nationalist and advocate of social reform, he resigned his knighthood (granted in 1918) in protest against British repression in India.
Mohandas Karamchand Gandhi (1869–1948)	Indian political and spiritual leader, who fought against anti-Indian discrimination in South Africa before returning to India in 1914. He became leader of the Indian National Congress in the 1920s. Gandhi maintained non-violent ideals through civil disobedience campaigns and was imprisoned in 1922, 1932, 1933, and 1942 for anti-British activities. He played a crucial part in the negotiations leading to independence.
Muhammad Ali Jinnah (1876–1948)	The founder of Pakistan. A member of the Indian National Congress, at first he advocated cooperation between Hindus and Muslims. Later, he transformed the Muslim League from a cultural to a political organization. In 1940, Jinnah demanded the partition of British India into separate Muslim and Hindu states. Jinnah achieved his goal, but he had to accept a smaller state than he had demanded. He became governor-general of Pakistan in 1947 and died in office.
Jawaharlal Nehru (1889–1964)	Indian nationalist politician and prime minister, 1947–64. Before partition, he led the socialist wing of the Congress Party and was regarded as second only to Gandhi. Between 1921 and 1945, he was imprisoned by the British nine times for political activities. As prime minister he developed the idea of non-alignment (neutrality toward the major powers), established an industrial base, and sustained a parliamentary democracy based on the rule of law.
Subhas Chandra Bose (1897–1945)	Indian nationalist leader (known as "Netaji"—"RespectedLeader"), who called for outright Indian independence. Frequently imprisoned, he became president of the All-India Congress (1938–9). He supported the Axis powers (Germany, Italy, and Japan) during World War II and became commander-in-chief of the Japanese-sponsored Indian National Army. He was reported killed in a plane crash during his military career, adding to his stature as a martyr for his nation.

elected by very limited elites, to advise the government. The Government of India Act, 1919, expanded provincial and central legislatures and created a dual government, or dyarchy, transferring powers over agriculture, public works, education, local self-government, and education to Indian elected legislators at the provincial level.

This half-way house proved unstable; Britain had trouble deciding whether it wished India to be a democracy or a colony. Each new issue revealed the contradiction. When the post-war years increased the demands for political independence, the government responded with repression. Against the advice of all of the elected Indians in the Imperial Legislative Council, in 1919, the government cracked down on freedom of the press and assembly by passing the Rowlatt Acts. When British troops shot into a protest meeting in Amritsar, Punjab, killing 379 Indians and wounding 1,100 (see Chapter 19), the British government lost its aura of legitimacy. Even Indian moderates could no longer justify British rule.

Gandhi's Innovations and Courage   At this juncture Mohandas Karamchand Gandhi—Mahatma Gandhi—emerged as a leader offering new political directions, new moral perspectives, and new programs of internal reform. Gandhi called India to find strength and courage in its own peasant roots and spiritual traditions. His success had limitations, but all political activity until well past independence, almost to the present, would revolve around the Congress, which he now reconstructed into a mass movement.

Gandhi Develops *Satyagraha* in South Africa   Gandhi's family had been advisers to local rulers in western India for several generations, and his uncle felt that if Mohandas were to maintain the family tradition under British rule, he must travel to Britain to study law. Gandhi emerged from three years of study in London with a deeply considered reaffirmation of his Indian heritage in Hinduism, in religious openness, and in an appreciation of localized, small-scale organizations. Two days after completing his legal training, one day after being admitted to the bar, Gandhi boarded a steamship returning to India. He practiced law for a year, with no special distinction, and then accepted the case of an Indian emigrant business firm in South Africa. There, apparently for the first time, Gandhi suffered racist persecution personally and repeatedly.

The Indian community in South Africa had mostly come to work as indentured laborers. The South African government wanted them to return home at the end of their service and instituted laws to make their long-term status untenable. Indians were required to carry identification cards at all times and to pay heavy head taxes. Most disturbing of all, in 1913, the government nullified all marriages not performed by Christian clergy, rendering illegitimate the children of almost all the Indian immigrants. Although he had arrived as the lawyer for a wealthy Indian Muslim client, Gandhi identified with the pain and humiliation of his less privileged countrymen and, indeed, suffered along with them. He was physically evicted from public facilities and threatened with beatings and even death for asserting his rights. Until now a rather private person, Gandhi began to organize a protest movement.

Instead of leaving at the end of his year's employment, Gandhi remained in South Africa for twenty-one years, 1893–1914, advancing methods of resistance:

- *Satyagraha*, "truth force," called for self-sacrificing, non-violent mass demonstrations, demanding that the persecutors recognize the immorality of their own position and redress the suffering of the oppressed;
- *Ahimsa*, non-violence, in the face of attack;
- Civil disobedience against unjust laws, with a willingness to suffer the legal consequences, including imprisonment, and frequently the illegal consequences, such as beatings;

SOURCE

Gandhi's First Experience with Racism in South Africa

Mahatma Gandhi published his Autobiography originally as a series of newspaper articles. Many of the episodes also carried a moral message for readers. The story of his first encounter with racism in South Africa implies that he had never experienced such severe discrimination, neither in colonial India nor during his law school days in London.

On the seventh or eighth day after my arrival, I left Durban. A first class seat was booked for me. ... The train reached Maritzburg, the capital of Natal, at about 9 p.m. ... A passenger came next, and looked me up and down. He saw that I was a "colored" man. This disturbed him. Out he went and came in again with one or two officials. They all kept quiet, when another official came to me and said, "Come along, you must go to the van compartment."

"But I have a first class ticket," said I.

"That doesn't matter," rejoined the other. "I tell you, you must go to the van compartment."

"I tell you, I was permitted to travel in this compartment at Durban, and I insist on going on in it."

"No you won't," said the official. "You must leave this compartment, or else I shall have to call a police constable to push you out."

"Yes, you may. I refuse to get out voluntarily."

The constable came. He took me by the hand and pushed me out. My luggage was also taken out. I refused to go to the other compartment and the train steamed away. I went and sat in the waiting room, keeping my hand bag with me, and leaving the other luggage where it was. ...

It was winter, and winter in the higher regions of South Africa is severely cold. Maritzburg being at a high altitude, the cold was extremely bitter. My overcoat was in my luggage, but I did not dare to ask for it lest I should be insulted again, so I sat and shivered. There was no light in the room. A passenger came in at about midnight and possibly wanted to talk to me. But I was in no mood to talk.

I began to think of my duty. Should I fight for my rights or go back to India, or should I go on to Pretoria without minding the insults, and return to India after finishing the case? It would be cowardice to run back to India without fulfilling my obligation. The hardship to which I was subjected was superficial—only a symptom of the deep disease of color prejudice. I should try, if possible, to root out the disease and suffer hardships in the process. (Jack, p. 29–30)

- the establishment of a headquarters, modeled on the Hindu religious *ashram*, providing living and working quarters for himself, his family, and the closest allies in his campaigns;
- the creation of a publishing house for spreading the principles of his movement.

Because he renounced violence, Gandhi called these methods "passive resistance," but there was nothing passive about them; they were actually systems of "militant non-violence." These techniques were later adopted by leaders of resistance movements around the world from Martin Luther King (1929–68) in the USA to Nelson Mandela (b. 1918) in South Africa itself.

In 1909, Gandhi published *Hind Swaraj or Indian Home Rule*. Banned in India, this short book championed India's own civilization, exhorted Indians to conquer the feelings of fear and inferiority inherent in their colonial situation, and forthrightly attacked British hegemony.

We have hitherto said nothing because we have been cowed down ... it is our duty now to speak out boldly. We consider your schools and law courts to be useless. We want our own ancient schools and courts to be restored. The common language of India is not English but Hindi. You should, therefore, learn it. We can hold communication with you only in our national language ...

We cannot tolerate the idea of your spending money on railways and the military. We see no occasion for either ... We do not need any European cloth. We shall manage with articles produced and manufactured at home. You have great military resources ... You may, if you like, cut us to pieces. You may shatter us at the cannon's mouth. If you act contrary to our will, we shall not help you; and without our help, we know that you cannot move one step forward. (Jack, pp. 118–19)

Gandhi's success in South Africa was limited to short-term compromises with the government, but he earned the esteem of his countrymen in both South Africa and India. When he returned home and established a new *ashram* in Ahmedabad in 1915, they eagerly awaited his political initiatives for India itself

Gandhi Returns to India and Leads the Congress Popular discontent with British rule already existed. By 1907, the extremist wing of Congress, led by Bal Gangadhar Tilak (1856–1920), called for the British to leave India immediately. Tilak and the extremists employed the idioms and festivals of Hinduism as the basis for Indian nationalism. Economically, *swadeshi* ("of one's own country") campaigns for the use of indigenous products, especially after 1905, had demonstrated that voluntary boycotts of imports could spur Indian industrial productivity and profits. How much more effective legal control over tariffs could be once the British left! Businessmen and industrialists were especially attracted by these *swadeshi* boycotts. They resented British reluctance to share industrial secrets, restrictions on industrial and infrastructural investment, removal of tax monies from India back to Britain in the form of "home charges," and limits on career advancement for Indians. Gandhi did not create the independence movement in India, rather he gave it new leadership and direction.

Gandhi soon demonstrated this organizational genius. Several peasant movements that Gandhi would come to direct began with their own local organization, as in Champaran in Bihar, 1917; in Kheda, 1917; in Bardoli, 1922; and in Gujarat 1928. Peasants from these areas asked Gandhi to provide more sophisticated and effective leadership to advance their own initial activities. Millworkers in Ahmedabad, too, had already organized themselves (against local employers, not against the British), when they asked Gandhi to take charge of their strike in 1919. As he responded to these requests from local groups, Gandhi recognized India's smoldering grass-roots anger, inflamed by postwar economic hardship and political repression. He reconstituted the Congress into a mass organization with millions of dues-paying members, a standing

swadeshi "Of one's own country," a Hindi word used as a slogan in the Indian boycott of foreign goods, part of the protest against Britain's partition of Bengal in 1905.

Gandhi and Nehru. Mahatma Gandhi, wearing his customary *dhoti*, and Jawaharlal Nehru are deep in conversation at the All-India Congress Committee Meeting in Bombay, July 6, 1946, where Nehru took office as president of the Congress. Gandhi and Nehru were the charismatic figures who led the Indian National Congress, a broad-based political organization which was the vehicle for the nationalist movement for independence.

satyagraha A Hindi expression meaning "truth force," applied to Gandhi's policy of non-violent opposition to British rule in India.

executive committee to keep the organization functioning between annual meetings, and a program of mass civil disobedience, *satyagraha* (truth force).

Gandhi mobilized India's enormous size and diversity by cultivating personal and political alliances with the major regional leaders. His most analytic and thorough biographer, Judith Brown, praises his skill in winning the allegiance of such regional giants as C. Rajagopalachari (1879–1972) in Madras; Rajendra Prasad (1884–1963) in Bihar, later the first president of independent India; Vallabhbhai Patel (*c*. 1873–1933) in Gujarat, who went on to become chairman of the entire Congress Party; and Jawaharlal Nehru (1889–1964) in Uttar Pradesh (then called United Provinces), who became the first prime minister of independent India in 1947, a post he held until his death.

Gandhi was not successful everywhere, however. He did not capture the leadership nor the rank and file of the large eastern state of Bengal. In Calcutta, Subhas Chandra Bose (1847–1945) often opposed Gandhi as too ascetic in his personal life, too narrow in his intellectual interests, too dictatorial in his political authority, and too compromising with business and landlord interests in consolidating his power. Left-wing socialists throughout India also found Gandhi too cozy with big business and landlord interests. When the Congress socialists advocated land redistribution in the 1930s, Gandhi successfully won over the highly respected, usually socialist, Nehru, and the divisive issue was deferred until after independence. Despite valiant efforts, Gandhi failed to capture the most important Muslim leadership. Mohammed Ali Jinnah (1876–1948), leader of the movement for a separate Pakistan, found Gandhi's style both too ascetic and too Hindu. As independence neared, Jinnah did not trust Gandhi's Congress to deal equitably with Muslims.

Hindu–Muslim Unity Gandhi attempted to hold Hindus and Muslims together in a secular, egalitarian India. After World War I, he supported the caliph as the chief religious authority of the Muslims of the Ottoman Empire against British designs, even after the fall of the Ottoman Empire. In 1924, Gandhi fasted for twenty-one days to promote Hindu–Muslim unity. During the partition riots in 1947, he walked through violence-torn areas to advocate peace in Calcutta, Bengal, Bihar, and Delhi. In both Calcutta and Delhi he fasted for several days on behalf of Hindu–Muslim peace. And at least temporarily the antagonists on both sides put down their weapons. The British viceroy referred to Gandhi as a "one man boundary force" and marveled that Gandhi had achieved by moral persuasion what four army divisions might not have been able to accomplish.

Nevertheless, many Muslims doubted that they would receive fair treatment in a majority Hindu country. They regarded even Gandhi's political idiom as excessively Hindu. Gandhi believed that his greatest political failure was the partition of India into two nations, secular India with its Hindu-majority and Muslim Pakistan. He refused to participate in independence celebrations and spent his time trying to bring peace to areas of Hindu–Muslim conflict. In 1948, Gandhi was assassinated by a Hindu fanatic who found him soft on Muslims. The Hindu–Muslim breach remains a problem today, both in tensions across the international border between India and Pakistan, especially in Kashmir, and in domestic conflict between Hindus and Muslims.

harijan A Hindu term meaning children of God, applied by Mahatma Gandhi to the poorest classes of Indian society, including the **untouchables**.

Abolition of Untouchability Gandhi worked to end untouchability. He was not opposed to the general concept of the caste system, seeing differences among people, even by birth, as a part of social reality, but he fought the designation of about 15 percent of India's Hindu population as outcastes, humiliated and oppressed. Declaring, "It has always been a mystery to me how men can feel themselves honored by the humiliation of their fellow beings," Gandhi coined for the untouchables a new name, *harijan*, "children of God."

Many ex-untouchables saw Gandhi as patronizing. They did not call themselves children of God, but **dalits**, "oppressed peoples". In 1932, a political issue crystallized the differences. In preparing for a new constitution, there was general agreement that a proportion of elective offices should be "reserved" for ex-untouchables. The *dalit* leaders insisted on more: that the voting for these reserved seats be limited only to *dalits*. Gandhi rejected this demand. He wanted all voters to select from among the untouchable candidates. Otherwise the untouchables would form a political nation-within-a-nation, as Muslims were beginning to do. He declared a fast-unto-death on the issue. After a week, the untouchables' leader, B.R. Ambedkar (1893–1956), a lawyer trained in part at Columbia University, acceded to Gandhi's demands. At the same time Hindu leaders, their consciences touched, began to push for an end to restrictions on untouchables and opened many Hindu temples to *dalit* participation.

dalit "oppressed person," a blunt term adopted by ex-untouchables to describe their status.

In 1955, the government began a policy of protective discrimination, reserving a limited percentage of places in government jobs, universities, and elected offices only for the "scheduled castes," those castes that were listed on an official schedule as formerly untouchable. The issue of reservations for scheduled castes has continued as a hot, sometimes violent topic since Independence. Over the years the questions of how many places should be reserved, for whom, under what categories, and for how long have not been resolved.

Cultural Policies Gandhi rejected the use of English in India's public life and schools. He urged instead the development of India's regional languages and literatures. In his first major address after returning to the subcontinent he argued:

> Suppose that we had been receiving, during the past fifty years, education through our vernaculars … we should have today a free India, we should have our educated men, not as if they were foreigners in their own land but speaking to the heart of the nation; they would be working among the poorest of the poor, and whatever they would have gained during the past fifty years would be a heritage for the nation. (Jack, p. 131)

After Independence, Indian vernaculars increasingly displaced English as the language of instruction in India's educational institutions from primary school through university level. The constitution called for two link languages for official communication: English and Hindi. English was to be phased out by 1965, but as the date approached, rioting by opponents assured that both languages would be kept. Widespread knowledge of English among India's high school and university educated classes kept the country more closely in touch with world developments. Parents with aspirations for their children's career prospects usually encouraged them to study English as skills in English continued as one of the markers separating the upper classes from the lower.

Prohibition Gandhi led a temperance movement to ban alcoholic drinks. His argument was based primarily on concern for the effects of alcohol abuse on working-class families, especially when the husband/breadwinner spent his earnings on drink. After Independence, many states of India chose to restrict the use of liquor, but only Gandhi's home state of Gujarat retained almost total prohibition—and this encouraged enormous problems of bootlegging and of collusion between politicians and bootleggers.

Appropriate Technology Because of Gandhi's concern for appropriate technology, the Congress Party made the spinning wheel its emblem; hand-spun, hand-woven cloth its dress; and the production of a daily quota of hand-spun yarn a requirement for

SOURCE

Gandhi and Labor Relations

Most famous for his advocacy of the spinning wheel and his condemnation of mechanized industry, Gandhi was actually very pragmatic in his approach to technology. He recognized that the mechanized Indian textile industry gave jobs to hundreds of thousands of workers and produced yarn and cloth that Indian consumers desperately needed. Cynics added that the millowners were among Gandhi's most generous financial supporters. Gandhi played a pivotal role in founding the Ahmedabad Textile Labour Association, one of India's most powerful labor unions, and he served as an adviser to several others. His advice to labor, and to management as well, reflected his view of the importance of harmony rather than conflict in industrial relationships, as in all human relationships.

Two paths are open before India today, either to introduce the western principle of "Might is right," or to uphold the eastern principle that truth alone conquers, that truth knows no mishap, that the strong and the weak alike have a right to secure justice. The choice is to begin with the laboring class. Should the laborers obtain an increment in their wages by violence? Even if that be possible, they cannot resort to anything like violence, howsoever legitimate may be their claims. To use violence for securing rights may seem an easy path, but it proves to be thorny in the long run. Those who live by the sword die also by the sword …

If, on the other hand, they take their stand on pure justice and suffer in their person to secure it, not only will they always succeed but they will also reform their masters, develop industries and both master and men will be as members of one and the same family. A satisfactory solution of the condition of labor must include the following:

1. The hours of labor must leave the workmen some hours of leisure.
2. They must get facilities for their own education.
3. Provision should be made for an adequate supply of milk, clothing and necessary education for their children.
4. There should be sanitary dwellings for the workmen.
5. They should be in a position to save enough to maintain themselves during their old age.

None of these conditions is satisfied today. For this both the parties are responsible. The masters care only for the service they get. What becomes of the laborer does not concern them … The laborer, on the other hand, tries to hit upon all tricks whereby he can get maximum pay with minimum work.

A third party [the union] has sprung up between these two parties. It has become the laborer's friend. (from *Young India*, June 1, 1921, reprinted in Homer Jack, pp. 157–9)

membership. Gandhi expressed his early denunciation of modern machinery in *Hind Swaraj* in a mystical, religious idiom. Later he demanded small-scale, labor-intensive, alternative technologies for economic and humanitarian reasons:

> Hunger is the argument that is driving India to the spinning wheel … We must think of millions who are today less than animals, who are almost in a dying state. The spinning wheel is the reviving draught for the millions of our dying countrymen and countrywomen … I do want growth. I do want self-determination. I do want freedom, but I want all these for the soul … A plea for the spinning wheel is a plea for recognizing the dignity of labor.

Again, not everyone agreed with Gandhi. His most powerful disciple, Jawaharlal Nehru, advocated modern machinery and technology. Nehru could see both sides of the technological debate. He had been educated in England, but Gandhi had introduced him—as he had introduced a generation of India's leaders—to the reality of India's 500,000 villages, where 85 percent of its population lived a technologically simple, generally impoverished existence:

> He sent us to the villages, and the countryside hummed with the activity of innumerable messengers of the new gospel of action. The peasant was shaken up and he began to emerge from his quiescent shell. The effect on us was different but equally far-reaching, for we saw, for the first time as it were, the villager in the intimacy of his mud-hut, and with the stark shadow of hunger always pursuing him. We learnt our Indian economics more from these visits than from books and learned discourses. (Nehru, p. 365)

In the end, however, Nehru came down unequivocally in favor of large-scale industry. Otherwise India might again become a colony:

> It can hardly be challenged that, in the context of the modern world, no country can be politically and economically independent, even within the framework of international inter-dependence, unless it is highly industrialized and has developed its power resources to the utmost … Thus an attempt to build up a country's economy largely on the basis of cottage and small-scale industries is doomed to failure. It will not solve the basic problems of the country or maintain freedom, nor will it fit in with the world framework, except as a colonial appendage. (Nehru, p. 414)

In his studies in Britain, and in a visit to the Soviet Union in the 1930s, Nehru had become a socialist and an advocate for national economic planning to guide the uses of high technology. In 1938, the Congress appointed its own National Planning Commission, the forerunner of the official planning commission established after Independence.

Congress Campaigns for Independence, 1920–22, 1930–32, 1942 Gandhi led the Congress in three massive, nationwide *satyagraha* campaigns. The non-cooperation campaign of 1920–22 boycotted British colonial schools, law courts, administrative positions, manufactures, and imports. The Congress began to provide internally for these functions, encouraging the creation of a separate school system, facilities for conflict resolution, and *swadeshi*/boycott activities that took the place of a tariff in restricting foreign imports. The Congress was not only opposing the British government, it was also constructing a parallel government. In a few localities, Indians refused to pay taxes.

A decade later, in the Salt March campaign of 1930–32, Gandhi mocked the government's monopoly on the manufacture and sale of salt by marching to the sea and manufacturing salt from seawater. This simple action initiated a nationwide campaign of civil disobedience and law breaking. It focused world attention on the colonial government's lack of authority and respect in the eyes of most Indians. Ten years later, the "Quit India" campaign of 1942 refused Indian political support to Britain's efforts in World War II unless independence was granted. (The Indian army, however, did fight loyally under British command.) Despite these three massive, nationwide campaigns, the British did not finally concede independence until 1947.

Most Indians praise Gandhi as the father of the new nation and many regard him as saintly, but India's transformation into an independent state was not only a moral victory, but also an exercise in *realpolitik*, in the reality and importance of everyday politics. In granting independence to India, Britain was responding not only to Gandhi's politics and moral message, but also to enormous losses in the global economic depression and World War II. Britain had lost both the ideological commitment to maintaining its empire in India and the economic and military power to hold India against its will.

The Salt March. Mahatma Gandhi begins the symbolic 240 mile, 27-day walk from Ahmedabad to Dandi on the coast, where he collected sea salt and thus technically broke the salt law—the government's monopoly on salt production. Civil disobedience did not win independence immediately, but it did discredit the moral and political authority of the colonial government.

Independence, 1947

Pakistan At independence, despite Gandhi's efforts to maintain unity, the subcontinent was partitioned into Hindu-majority India, governed by the officially secular Congress Party, and Muslim-majority Pakistan, under an officially Muslim government. The creation of Pakistan was a response to both cultural–religious claims and to political-economic demands. Muhammad Iqbal had turned his poetry into a persuasive plea for a nation governed according to Islamic principles, while Muhammad Ali Jinnah, Pakistan's first president, argued the political case for an equitable distribution of national positions and patronage between Hindus and Muslims.

Pakistan's peculiar geography, with two "wings," east and west, separated by some 800 miles of hostile Indian territory, reflected the distribution of Muslim majorities in the subcontinent. At partition an estimated 12 million people shifted their homes—6 million Hindus and Sikhs from east and west Pakistan moving to India, 6 million Muslims from India transferring to Pakistan. The transfer of population was bloody; between 200,000 and one million people were murdered. Few Hindus remained in Pakistan, but a sizeable Muslim minority, 10 percent of India's population, remained in India. While Hindus and Muslims mostly cohabited the land peacefully, under a

Political change in South Asia after 1947. At independence in 1947, British India was partitioned into secular, but Hindu-majority, India and Muslim Pakistan amid enormous violence and migration. Disputes over Kashmir continue until today. In 1971, the east wing of Pakistan fought, with Indian assistance, a war of independence against the west and became Bangladesh.

secular constitution, tensions between them remained and were sometimes exploited by political leaders.

Kashmir Relations between India and Pakistan remained tense after partition, and exploded into warfare in 1947 and again in 1965 over the issue of Kashmir. Under British rule, partly as a tactic of "divide and rule," about one-third of India's land, with one-fourth of its population, was governed indirectly by local "princes." At the time of independence, the rulers of these local states were officially given the option of joining India or Pakistan or remaining independent.

Mass migration. The partition of India at independence created an unprecedented transfer of population in two directions: Hindus fled Pakistan for the safety of India, and Muslims living in India struggled to get safely over the border into their new homeland. This packed train, groaning with refugees from Pakistan, arrives in Amritsar, just over the Indian border, on October 16, 1947.

Through the craft and coercion of India's home minister, Vallabhbhai Patel, every state finally opted to join India or Pakistan, according to geographical proximity—except Kashmir. The largest of all the princely states geographically, and situated between India and Pakistan, it appeared that Kashmir might choose independence. As the maharaja was considering his options, armed guerrilla fighters invaded from Pakistan. The maharaja asked India to defend him. India agreed, on condition that he bring Kashmir into the Indian union, and he agreed. The decision was contested because the ruler was a Hindu while the overwhelming majority of the population was Muslim.

The wars that broke out in 1947 and 1965 effectively divided Kashmir, with the larger, richer sector held by India, the smaller, poorer sector by Pakistan. The cease-fire line became the *de facto* border between them. Although India promised a plebiscite, it was not held and no one has ever consulted the Kashmiris formally and systematically about their wishes. Relations between India and Pakistan remained hostile and the Kashmir border remained the flashpoint of greatest tension. Sri Lanka, an island off the coast of southern India and also a British possession, gained independence in 1948.

Bangladesh Pakistan and India also fought in 1971. That war was triggered by the break-up of the two wings of Pakistan and the formation of the new nation of Bangladesh in the east. The union of Urdu-speaking, arid, West Pakistan, with Bengali-speaking, marshy, East Pakistan, despite their separation by 800 miles of hostile Indian territory, had been peculiar and unstable from its creation. India, which had officially declared itself a secular democracy, had always maintained that religion alone could not be the basis of a state. When East Pakistan challenged the dominance of West Pakistan, India saw its own philosophy validated, and its arch-rival divided in two. In 1971, East Pakistan declared its independence and India fought alongside the newly emerging nation of Bangladesh, an impoverished, densely populated country of 125 million people.

Problems of the New Government of India

Unifying and Consolidating the Nation Despite Gandhi's quixotic vision of transforming the Congress from a political lobby into a non-official, social service institution, the Congress members quickly transformed the organization into a formal political party and took over the new government of India. Swift action by the independent government quickly consolidated the country. Home Minister Vallabhbhai Patel convinced and coerced India's 562 "princes" to declare their merger with India, ending the fear of a break-up of the subcontinent into numerous, separate, small states. Dispute over the legitimacy of Kashmir's accession was the sole exception.

Other threatened fragmentation was also averted. Gandhi had organized the Congress by linguistic regions, different from the administrative units employed by the British. After independence, following several regional disputes, the Congress government drew up the new state borders in accordance with these linguistic borders.

Strong separatist movements emerged in Punjab, based on discontent within the Sikh religious community; in Muslim-majority Kashmir; and in the far distant and ethnically Mongoloid northeast Himalayan regions of Assam. Separatism also simmered in the southern state of Madras based on linguistic and cultural differences from the north. The state was later renamed Tamil Nadu, in recognition of its Tamil-speaking population. A combination of political bargaining and armed force has kept the country together.

Democracy and its Challenges Gandhi's Congress generally respected constitutional process, and the democracy proposed by British rulers became a reality in India after Independence. Except for two years of "Emergency Rule," 1975–7, during which Prime Minister Indira Gandhi (1917–84) asserted dictatorial powers, India has functioned democratically and constitutionally as a union of some thirty states and territories, with universal adult franchise and guaranteed freedoms of press, assembly, speech, religion, and an independent judiciary. Despite imperfections, India prided itself on being the world's largest democracy. Within its democratic framework, communist governments have also been freely elected in individual states, first in Kerala in 1957—the first freely elected communist government in the world—and later in West Bengal.

In the 1950s, small groups of revolutionary guerrillas, named Naxalites, for the village of Naxalbari in Bihar where they began their activities, have attacked government authorities in local areas, but Indians have not given strong support to militant communism. The reasons may be India's generally religious orientation, skepticism about a philosophy and organization tied to foreign governments, recognition of communism's origin as a proletarian rather than a peasant movement, and state repression of revolutionary organizations.

Until 1991, laissez-faire capitalism fared even less well. Only one party ever directly espoused a capitalist philosophy of development, and it had limited success and a short life. Indians, including much of the business community, seemed to view capitalism as excessively individualistic and materialistic, based on a philosophy of self-interest often seen as greed, and associated with colonialism in the past and the return of a neo-colonial economic dominance in the present. Despite a large free-enterprise sector in the economy, especially in agriculture, most major Indian parties have advocated socialism, on the grounds of its stated concern for the common good. Nehru, in particular, espoused "a socialist pattern of development." His policy continued in force for a generation after his death, despite widespread criticism that it led to excessive power—and corruption—concentrated in the state and in the bureaucrats who controlled access to business licenses and investment capital. Many of these views changed in 1991 when India was forced by regulations of the International Monetary Fund to move towards a more free-market economy (Chapters 23 and 24).

Through the first four decades of Independence, India's democracy was dominated by one party, the Congress, and the party's leadership was dominated by one family, the Nehru dynasty. Jawaharlal Nehru, prime minister from Independence until his death in 1964, was soon succeeded by his daughter, Indira Gandhi, who was prime minister in 1967–77 and from 1980 until her assassination in 1984. She was followed by her son, Rajiv, 1984–9. When Rajiv was also assassinated while seeking reelection in 1991, many Congress leaders asked his widow, Italian-born Sonia Gandhi, to take up the family political mantle. At the time, she declined.

Gender Issues The struggle for independence recruited women, and after independence India instituted universal adult suffrage. In each national election approximately 55 percent of women voted, compared with about 60 percent of men. In 1988, women held forty-six seats out of 537 in the lower house of Parliament, twenty-eight out of 245 in the upper, indicating a slowly increasing proportion from 1950. State government ratios were similar. With Mrs. Gandhi serving as prime minister (1966–77, 1980–84), a woman reached and held the pinnacle of political power. Although first nominated and elected to office on the strength of her father's reputation, later on Mrs. Gandhi was elected on her own merits.

Prime Minister Indira Gandhi Of course, not all women are feminists, including Mrs. Gandhi. Her father introduced her to politics from childhood. When he became prime minister, he asked her to preside over his official residence, since his wife, Indira's mother, had died ten years earlier. At Nehru's death in 1964, Indira was named minister of information and broadcasting, and two years later the Congress High Command named her prime minister, under the mistaken assumption that they could control her. Instead she split the party in a bitter struggle, and gained control of the majority. Declaring her motto of "Down with Poverty," she followed socialist policies, for example, nationalizing India's major banks, and ending the special annual financial allotments to India's former princely rulers. Her reputation as a tough, determined leader grew when she ordered Indian troops into East Pakistan in the 1971 civil war; her support facilitated the creation of Bangladesh. In 1974, she ordered India's first underground test of an atomic bomb.

Mrs. Gandhi's political manipulations partially undermined India's democratic system. In 1975, facing the likely loss of political power, she had the president of India declare an "Emergency." She jailed the leaders of the opposition, curtailed freedom of speech and of the press, and set quotas of people to be rounded up for forcible reproductive sterilization, largely in response to India's large population. For these dictatorial excesses she was voted out of office when she restored elections in 1977.

Voted back to power in 1980, after a brief period in jail for election irregularities, Mrs. Gandhi once again used her popularity to manipulate the Congress Party, especially at the state levels, to ensure that the major regional leaders were dependent on her. One of these leaders, a Sikh extremist who was for a time her ally, escaped her control and mobilized an armed opposition, centered in the most important Sikh shrine, the Golden Temple in Amritsar. Mrs. Gandhi finally ordered the army to capture and secure the temple. Thousands died in the confrontation and sacred shrines were

Indira Gandhi, prime minister of India (1966–77; 1980–84), inspects the guard at an Independence Day celebration, August 23, 1967. Mahatma Gandhi did much to encourage women's participation in public life during the years leading to Independence. Although many women are well-educated, overall the literacy rate among females is only 38 percent (66 percent for males).

destroyed. Four months later, in 1984, two Sikh members of her personal bodyguard assassinated her.

As prime minister, Mrs. Gandhi relied on her sons for advice, a common relationship between widows and their sons, especially in India. Sanjay, the younger, was widely regarded as unprincipled in his actions, and many of the excesses of the Emergency were a result of his advice. When Sanjay died in the crash of the stunt airplane he was flying, Indira prevailed upon his older brother Rajiv, a pilot with Indian Airlines, to fill in as her chief adviser. When Mrs. Gandhi was assassinated, Rajiv was chosen by the party as prime minister. Both of the sons counseled a greater concern with modern technology, and began to guide India in that direction.

Legal Changes The 1955 Hindu Marriage Act raised the age of marriage for Hindu women to fifteen (eighteen for men) and assured Hindu women the right of divorce. The Hindu Succession Act of 1956 gave daughters equal rights with sons in inheriting their father's property. On the other hand, parliament did not legislate new personal law for non-Hindus, so other religious communities continued under their traditional laws. The issue disturbed many feminists but they trod lightly here because many Muslims, even feminist Muslims, did not want the secular state to interfere in the religious law of their community.

Social Changes Because family structures in India, especially north India, are both **patrilineal** and **patrilocal**—that is, inheritance and residence patterns follow the family of the male—the birth of a female child is often regarded as a financial and even emotional burden. Years of childcare and expense culminate in the girl's leaving home for marriage into another family, often somewhat distant and with limited ties to the family of origin.

The sex ratio in India in 1991, about 927 women to 1,000 men, is one of the lowest in the world. It suggests the systematic neglect of females, especially young girls. As amniocentesis and sonograms become more widely available, allowing parents to know the sex of unborn children, abortion of females may result. Suicide rates for Indian women are high, and isolated cases of *sati* (*suttee*), in which a widow immolates herself on her husband's funeral pyre, continue. In 1987, the literacy rate among females was 29 percent as compared with 57 percent for males; but this was up from 8 percent and 25 percent, respectively, in 1951. South India's treatment of women is widely regarded as more egalitarian, perhaps because of different local traditions, including some influence of matrilineal systems that follow the females line in inheritance and residence.

Economic Changes Disconcerting results from a 1984 anthropological study of a village near Delhi suggest that the position of poor, rural women was actually deteriorating as a result of increasing general prosperity in the new economic system and of increasing urbanization.

There were several factors affecting women's work, all producing a marked decline in women's employment opportunities. First, women who had worked in agriculture alongside their male kin were displaced when their husbands left field work to seek jobs in the cities. Second, women who traditionally worked in caste-based occupations as servants through *jajmani* (family patronage systems) could no longer find such jobs. Third, mechanization had replaced female labor in a variety of arenas. Finally, changes in cropping patterns had made female help in the fields less necessary. These factors all contributed to the marginalization of poor women, giving them less voice in their families and ultimately devaluing them (Wadley, in Wiser and Wiser, p. 287).

patrilineal The tracing of ancestry, kinship, and inheritance through the male line.

patrilocal Residence by a couple in or near the home of the male's family or group.

sati (*suttee*) An ancient Hindu custom that requires widows to be burned on the funeral pyre of their husbands, or soon afterward.

An encouraging contrary development was the organization of working women into effective unions that provide both economic opportunity and political representation. In cities such as Mumbai (Bombay), Madras, and Ahmedabad, voluntary organizations of tens of thousands of working women have begun to gain access to capital for working-class women who carry on their own small businesses; to form cooperatives, which help them secure raw materials and market finished products; to lobby government for workers' safety, health, insurance, maternity, and job protection in non-unionized, small-scale shops; to develop new educational models for job training; and to create new systems of health delivery, especially for women. One of the most important of these organizations is the Self-Employed Women's Association (SEWA) in Ahmedabad, a daughter organization of the Textile Labour Union, which had been founded with the help of Mahatma Gandhi.

Economic and Technological Change after Independence

The Green Revolution Economically and technologically, India has accomplished the once seemingly impossible feat of producing enough food to feed its growing population. At independence, India had 361 million people; by the mid-1980s, the population had more than doubled to three-quarters of a billion people. During droughts in 1964–6 mass-starvation was averted only by the importation of 12 million tons of food grains each year, primarily from the United States. Then, in the late 1960s, the "green revolution" took root in India. New strains of wheat, developed in Mexico under the auspices of the Rockefeller Foundation, were introduced. They increased India's productivity even faster than her population. India, almost miraculously, proved able to feed itself. Between the early 1960s and the late 1970s, rice production rose by more than 50 percent; wheat production tripled. Total grain production rose from about 50 million tons per year at independence to about 150 million tons in the mid-1980s.

Meanwhile, a "white revolution" in dairy production and distribution was also taking place. Dairy cooperatives were formed throughout India, enabling village farmers to pool and ship their highly perishable products to urban markets—as fresh milk in refrigerated train cars, and as processed cheese and dairy products in conventional shipping—thus providing incentives for increasing production.

These revolutions in agriculture were not without their problems. First, ecologically, questions were raised about relying so exclusively on so few new strains of "miracle wheat." Were too many seeds coming from too few genetic baskets? Would the massive new quantities of chemical fertilizers needed to support the new seeds ultimately ruin the ecology? Second, economic growth increased disparities and tensions between haves and have-nots and between those who worked more entrepreneurially and those who did not. The new productivity benefited most those who already had the economic resources to afford the new seeds, fertilizers, pesticides, and irrigation water. The rich were getting richer—although the poor did not seem to be getting poorer—and social

New technology crosses gender lines. Power tillers provide a new technology more appropriate economically than either bullock-drawn plows or tractors in some areas of India. They are available through collaboration with Japan (Mitsubishi). In entering her new occupation, the driver has received financial and technical assistance from SEWA, the Self-Employed Women's Association in Ahmedabad.

tensions increased. Similarly, disparities between rich and poor states grew. The Punjab, in particular, progressed dramatically in transforming both its agriculture and small industries. The small northern state became the richest in India, the country's breadbasket.

Land Redistribution Control of land and its redistribution was a matter for each state in India, and different states enacted different policies. In general, redistribution was accompanied by compensation paid by the new owners, and the process has been peaceful but slow.

Family Planning, Life Expectancy, and the Condition of Children Government implementation of family planning, rejected overwhelmingly in the wake of Indira Gandhi's program of forced sterilization in 1975–7, has been soft-pedaled ever since. Nevertheless birth rates fell to about 33 per thousand in 1985, down from about 44 per thousand at independence, indicating great general interest in smaller, planned families. Life expectancy at birth rose from about 30 years at independence in 1947 to 56 in 1985. On the other hand, at the outset of the 1990s, the World Bank reported that 66 percent of India's children under age five were malnourished.

Industrialization and its Consequences Industrial productivity increased, but the structure of the workforce did not change—exactly the process Gandhi had feared. New machinery produced more goods more efficiently, but it did not provide proportionately more jobs. The business and industrial sectors contributed only 5 percent to the nation's income in 1947; slightly more than 30 percent by the mid-1980s. Industrial production multiplied almost five times between 1951 and 1980. In the 1980s it was increasing almost 8 percent a year. Urbanization increased to 27 percent, up from 17 percent at independence. On the other hand, the percentage of workers in industry essentially stagnated: about 10 percent in 1951; about 13 percent in 1980. Unemployment was reported steady at 8 percent.

Until the 1980s, industrial policy derived from Gandhi's and Nehru's conflicting philosophies. Gandhi had urged austere consumption levels, handicraft production, spinning wheels, and national self-sufficiency through import substitution. Nehru implemented socialism, central planning, industrialization, government control and development of the "commanding heights" of the economy—energy, steel, petroleum, banking—and regulation of the large-scale capitalist sector. Despite their strong differences on the importance of large-scale industry and modern technology, both Gandhi and Nehru stressed internal self-sufficiency in production.

These policies were increasingly challenged by a new international political-economic wisdom in the 1980s based on the economic successes of the East Asian countries and the political policies of President Reagan in the USA and Prime Minister Margaret Thatcher in Britain. Increased consumption spurred increased productivity, and a consumer society began to appear in India.

High-tech innovation for both home and foreign markets increased productivity, and India began to manufacture submarines, computer software (of which it had become a world center) and hardware, and machine tools, and even prepared to export nuclear power plants adapted to third world conditions. Its impressive scientific and technological establishment had the capacity to adopt and adapt the newest technological advances.

In part, these technological successes were possible because of an extraordinary imbalance in India's educational expenditures. The government strongly favored higher education while starving the primary schools. These policies, rooted in traditional hierarchical attitudes and interests, produced a skewed society in which the

HOW DO WE KNOW?

Technological Hazards and Questionable Accountability

Indian attitudes toward modern technology have fallen between the skepticism of Gandhi and the enthusiasm of Nehru. Some of the most biting critiques of India's technological policies on development came from a "modern intellectual," Ashis Nandy, who criticized the government for giving excessive power to the scientific-technological establishment. In particular he focused on India's nuclear establishment in the mid-1980s:

Nuclear scientists were freed from all financial constraints. The budget of the nuclear program ... was routinely pushed through parliament without any scrutiny whatsoever. And the expenditures ... were never publicly audited. All data on performance ... failures, unsafe technology and insufficient regard for human rights ... were protected by law from the public gaze. And all enquiries made from outside the nuclear establishment were pre-empted with the help of a special act that made it impossible to mount any informed,

focused, data-based criticism of India's nuclear programme. (Nandy, p. 5)

Further skepticism concerning winners and losers in the quest for industrial modernization resulted from a tragedy of poison gas leakage in a Union Carbide insecticide plant in Bhopal in 1984, the worst industrial accident of its kind in the world up to that date. Compounding the tragedy for the victims, the American-owned corporation resisted payment of compensation:

Dreadful tragedy struck central India's Bhopal ... in December 1984 ... Deadly invisible gas from Union Carbide's insecticide storage tanks had escaped through defective valves to be blown by ill-winds over the slumbering bodies of thousands of poor innocents outside that giant plant's walls, less than 400 miles south of New Delhi. Within hours, 2,000 people were dead and hundreds of thousands of others had been injured by the worst industrial accident of recent history. Union Carbide was still American owned, one of the few multinationals in India that had not been taken over by a majority of Indian shareholders and management ...
   Though hundreds of billions of dollars in damages were quickly claimed in

thousands of lawsuits filed both in India and America, virtually nothing was paid to any of the actual victims for seven full years after the tragedy devastated Bhopal. Legal snares and questions of jurisdiction plagued the process, serving to thwart justice instead of expediting its realization. (Wolpert, pp. 421–2)

- Why do you think that India's nuclear development program had such independence of action without public political supervision? Do you approve of such secrecy in India? In the nuclear development programs in the USA? Why or why not?
- On what basis do you think Union Carbide resisted paying compensation to most of the victims of the leak? After you have made your guesses, you may wish to check Bhopal and Union Carbide on the Web to see what answers you can find.
- In an overwhelmingly agrarian, poor, rural society such as India, what do you think is the proper place for modern industry, such as nuclear weapons? Peaceful use of atomic energy? Chemical insecticides?

highly educated elites compared with the best anywhere in the world, but overall basic literacy was only 43 percent. Again, Gandhi's fears were coming true.

International Relations

India was the first major colony to win independence after World War II, and it served as a leader to other newly emerging countries. Nehru, in particular, provided articulate, innovative direction, and after independence India remained a model of democratic political stability and gradual economic growth in a society of unparalleled heterogeneity. Its international role, however, declined. India's border war with, and defeat by, China in 1962 crippled its claim to third world harmony and leadership. In the wake of this war, India began to spend more on its armed forces. Military expenditures rose from US$ 1.7 billion in 1960 to US$ 9.8 billion in 1987 (in constant dollars).

Decolonization throughout the world was virtually complete by the 1980s, and political colonialism was no longer a major global issue. The attention of new nations shifted to economic development. Japan and the highly successful "tigers" of East and Southeast Asia, with their more open, more liberalized, and more expansive economies attracted them. In a world concerned with economic growth, the persistence of poverty and illiteracy made India a questionable model for others. Its progress seemed too slow. It remained, however, the dominant power in the South Asia region.

COMPARING CHINA AND INDIA
WHAT DIFFERENCE DOES IT MAKE?

At the end of World War I, India's demand for independence ignited a mass movement that bore many similarities to China's. With the vast majority of its population in rural areas, India, like China, was rooted in agriculture and its peasantry. Like China's Mao, India's Mahatma Gandhi mobilized this rural constituency. Both leaders created new social and economic institutions for greater equity and also emphasized the need for new, simple technologies appropriate to their agrarian, impoverished societies. Both regarded their methods and solutions as models for others to copy.

The differences between the two mammoth countries were at least equally significant. Unlike China, which had no functioning central government between 1912 and 1949 and had been carved into numerous European and Japanese spheres of influence, India had a central government, which was under British colonial control until independence in 1947. While China suffered decades of civil warfare, political disputes in India were addressed through generally peaceful, constitutional processes. India's nationalist leaders, unlike those of China, welcomed businessmen and professionals along with the peasantry in their independence struggle. Unlike China, in its independence movement India pursued an extraordinary strategy of non-violent mass civil resistance. It fought no civil war nor did the battles of World War II significantly touch its borders. When independence came, relations with colonial Britain continued harmonious, and India retained membership in the Commonwealth of Nations. Even the partition of the subcontinent into India and Pakistan in 1947 followed constitutional processes, although the subsequent transfers of population were enormously violent. The 1971 creation of the independent country of Bangladesh on the land of East Pakistan was the product of civil war, in which India aided Bangladesh against West Pakistan. Naxalite movements brought outbursts of guerrilla warfare in localized regions. Hindu–Muslim and high caste–low caste tensions sometimes also burst into violence, but the open violence of these confrontations was usually confined to local areas and short periods of time.

A generation after ending colonialism, both countries could point to significant accomplishments including: cumulative and growing economic expansion, more rapid in China, slower in India; political cohesion; and social transformation in accord with their differing agendas. Both countries had moved from concentration on rural areas, a promise of their colonial struggles, to concern also with their cities and their industries. They shared a similar challenge: How to maintain a coherent national agenda after the unifying enemy of colonialism had been defeated?

After 1949, China continued to live out its revolutionary, agrarian heritage. Soon after taking power, it expelled foreigners—capitalist, communist, and Christian—and sought to develop internally, with its own resources. With the Korean War it immediately signaled its willingness to assert leadership in third-world armed struggle. Periodically, it created development plans modeled on the experience of the Long March and the Chinese soviet in Yan'an: the Great Leap Forward, with its backyard steel furnaces, and the Great Proletarian Cultural Revolution, with its exile of urban bureaucrats and intellectuals to forced labor in rural China. The new government also turned to developing its cities and industries. Through it all, the Communist Party remained in control. When policy disputes threatened to pull the party apart, Chairman Mao reasserted his control. He rewarded the "Red" rather than the "Expert" among his colleagues, and lost power only as he neared his death in 1976.

After 1947, as an independent country, India chose a pattern of political democracy and a mixed economy, balancing a "socialist pattern of society," with considerable allowance for private ventures. India confronted enormous, persistent challenges from both its own social structure and the colonial heritage: hierarchical caste divisions, especially discrimination against ex-untouchables; conflict between religious communities, especially Hindus and Muslims, but Sikhs as well in and around the Punjab; tensions among regional and linguistic groups; renewed oppression of women; an economy of scarcity with widespread, persistent hunger and poverty; and continuing massive population growth. In these struggles, India followed policies of political stability for development, including technological policies of great diversity.

Both China and India were aware of the technological and economic progress of Japan and the Asian tigers. For China this represented a galling challenge since the Japanese powerhouse dominated the economics of east Asia, displacing China from her historic position. India did not see itself in competition with Japan, but it recognized that the smaller countries of Southeast Asia, which had previously trailed India, had now surpassed it economically and in consumer technology. India, too, saw this as a model and a challenge.

Review Questions

- Compare Mao and Gandhi in terms of both their personal experience with agrarian issues and their policies for dealing with them.
- Compare Mao and Gandhi in terms of their policies on the use of violence and non-violence in attaining their political objectives. To what extent are the differences in their philosophies a result of differences in the political context in which they lived and worked?
- Compare the status of women in the philosophies of Mao and Gandhi.
- To what degree did the experiences of the Long March and the guerrilla war of the Chinese communist revolution provide good guidelines for government policy in governing China after 1949?
- To what degree did the experiences of the Indian independence movement provide good guidelines for government policy in governing India after 1947?
- In the debate over the technology to be used in modern India, what do you think are the strong and weak points of Gandhi's position and of Nehru's position?

Suggested Readings

CHINA

Andors, Phyllis. *The Unfinished Liberation of Chinese Women 1949–1980* (Bloomington: University of Indiana Press, 1983). Feminist, anti-patriarchal ideology was central to the Chinese communist program. Andors captures the ideology and the degree of implementation.

Blunden, Caroline and Mark Elvin. *Cultural Atlas of China* (New York: Facts on File, 1983). Another in the excellent Facts on File series. More than an atlas, it is a comprehensive approach to China, scholarly yet very accessible.

de Bary, W. Theodore, *et al. Sources of Chinese Tradition*, Vol. 2 (New York: Columbia University Press, 1999). An outstanding anthology of statements by China's intellectual and political leaders. The 1999 revision doubled the number of selections.

Ebrey, Patricia Buckley, ed. *Chinese Civilization: A Sourcebook* (New York: The Free Press, 1993). A very different selection from de Bary's. Ebrey's selections capture the lives of common people. Illuminating and excellent.

Meisner, Maurice. *Mao's China and After* (New York: The Free Press, 1986). A thoughtful, rather pro-Mao account of the revolution. A scholarly, accessible standard.

Schell, Orville, ed. *The China Reader*, 4 vols. (New York: Random House, 1967–74). These volumes tell the story of China's revolution from the end of the colonial era through the end of Mao's years through an exceptional array of documents.

Snow, Edgar. *Red Star over China* (London: Victor Gollancz, 1968). Journalist Snow visited Mao in Yan'an and brought back to the West the first detailed knowledge of the man and the movement. Inspiring from a very pro-Maoist viewpoint.

Spence, Jonathan D. *The Search for Modern China* (New York: W.W. Norton & Company, 1990). Clearly written, detailed yet highly accessible, excellent as an introduction to the subject and to further scholarly investigation. Reissued in paperback in 2000.

INDIA

Bayly, Susan. *Caste, Society, and Politics in India from the Eighteenth Century to the Modern Age* (Cambridge: Cambridge University Press, 1999). Accessible, highly scholarly introduction to the phenomenon of caste, the changing meaning of caste, and the changing economic and political significance of caste.

Brown, Judith M. *Modern India: The Origins of an Asian Democracy* (New York: Oxford University Press, 1984). Stresses the constitutional processes in achieving independence, and in the negotiations between the British and the Congress. Brown sees India's post-independence democracy as a result of that process.

Chandra, Bipan. *India's Struggle for Independence, 1857–1947* (New York: Penguin Books, 1989). Chandra stresses the popular, revolutionary side of the independence struggle, and sees Gandhi as the integrative force who encouraged it to take democratic directions.

Dalton, Dennis. *Mahatma Gandhi: Non-Violent Power in Action* (New York: Columbia University Press, 1993). Remarkably lucid account of Gandhi's theory and practice of *satyagraha*, especially good on his fast in Calcutta, 1947.

Forbes, Geraldine. *Women in Modern India* (Cambridge: Cambridge University Press, 1998). Useful survey of women in education, cultural and social life, and reform, the nationalist movement, the economy, and recent political action. Especially interesting for shift from elite issues to the masses.

Hay, Stephen, ed. *Sources of Indian Tradition*, Vol. 2 (New York: Columbia University Press, 2nd ed., 1988). Excellent selection of statements by Indian political and cultural leaders. Stresses the elites.

Nehru, Jawaharlal. *The Discovery of India* (Bombay: Asia Publishing House, 1960). A personal history, Marxist in orientation, written from jail by the prime minister of India, illuminating both of the nation's history and of Nehru's understanding of that history.

Rothermund, Dietmar. *An Economic History of India: From Pre-Colonial Times to 1991* (London: Routledge, 1993). Clearly written, succinct introduction to the subject.

Rudolph, Lloyd I. and Susanne Hoeber Rudolph. *The Modernity of Tradition* (Chicago: University of Chicago Press, 1967). Still the clearest introduction to the idea that tradition and modernity are not opposites, but interact in the hands of creative leaders—like Gandhi, and like later caste leaders.

Wiser, William H. and Charlotte Viall Wiser, *Behind Mud Walls 1930–1960* (including Susan Wadley, "The Village in 1984," "The Village in 1998")

(Berkeley: University of California Press, 2000). The Wisers kept revisiting a north Indian village and writing down their observations. A fascinating, very readable review. Make sure to get the latest edition, as Susan Wadley continues to update the Wisers' work.

ADDITIONAL SOURCES

Bouton, Marshall M. and Philip Oldenburg, eds. *India Briefing: A Transformative Fifty Years* (Armonk, NY: M.E. Sharpe, 1999). Every year or two, Oldenburg and a co-editor bring together an excellent, scholarly set of interpretive essays on current events in India under the title *India Briefing*. This edition covered the entire period from independence.

Brass, Paul. *The Politics of India since Independence* (Cambridge: Cambridge University Press, 2nd ed., 1994). Another in the Cambridge series of comprehensive introductions to India. Brass is comprehensive, thoughtful, and, appropriately, quite skeptical of official rhetoric.

Drèze, Jean and Amartya Sen. *India's Economic Development and Social Opportunity* (Delhi: Oxford University Press, 1998). Sen won the 1998 Nobel prize for economics for his stress on the importance of education and health in development economics. Here he and Drèze bring that perspective to an analysis of India's record.

Fairbank, John King. *The Great Chinese Revolution: 1800–1985* (New York: Harper & Row, 1986). Until his death, Fairbank was one of the masters of Chinese history. This book is now dated, but very useful and interesting.

Frankel, Francine. *India's Political Economy, 1947–1977* (Princeton: Princeton University Press, 1978). To know how India said it was doing, and how it was actually doing in economic and political development after independence, this is a good place to begin.

Goldman, Merle and Roderick MacFarquhar, eds. *The Paradox of China's Post-Mao Reforms* (Cambridge: Harvard University Press, 1999). Although focused on China after Mao, the contrast is illuminating.

Hardgrave, Robert L. and Stanley Kochanek. *India: Government and Politics in a Developing Nation* (Stamford, CT: Harcourt College Publishers, 1999). A standard, introductory text, continuously revised for three decades.

Jack, Homer, ed. *The Gandhi Reader* (New York: Grove Press, 1956). A comprehensive source book covering Gandhi's philosophies and activities in politics, economics, and moral life, mostly by Gandhi, some about him.

Jayakar, Pupul. *Indira Gandhi* (New York: Viking, 1992). A friendly, but critical biography by a friend and colleague.

Karlekar, Hiranmay, ed. *Independent India: The First Fifty Years* (Delhi: Oxford University Press and the Indian Council for Cultural Relations, 1998). A set of assessments of uneven quality, but many quite fascinating of many aspects of India since independence. Written in India for Indians, may be somewhat dense for foreign readers.

Kennedy, Paul. *The Rise and Fall of the Great Powers* (New York: Random House, 1987). Kennedy looks at the great powers since 1500. He introduces China only in recent times. India doesn't make it. Interesting for his view of what counts in national greatness.

Liang, Heng and Judith Shapiro. *Son of the Revolution* (New York: Vintage Books, 1983). Liang's biography as a young man who survived the Cultural Revolution, but saw it destroy his parents, their marriage, his schooling, and his earlier belief that the revolution was benign.

Liu Binyan. *A Higher Kind of Loyalty* (New York: Pantheon, 1990). Exiled from China, journalist Liu Binyan writes from America incisive, angry criticism of the actions of the government of the country that he loves.

MacFarquhar, Roderick Timothy Cheek, and Eugene Wu, eds. *The Secret Speeches of Chairman Mao* (Cambridge, MA: Council on East Asian Studies, 1989).

Nandy, Ashis, ed. *Science, Hegemony and Violence* (Delhi: Oxford University Press, 1988). Nandy is an oddity, a prominent, Western-educated intellectual who is quite skeptical of Western influences in India, including scientific and technological influences.

Pa Chin. *Family* (Garden City, N.Y.: Doubleday & Company, 1972). This novel of the 1910s and 1920s presented a new, feminist vision of what a family might be in modern China.

Ramusack, Barbara, *et al. Women in Asia: Restoring Women to History* (Bloomington: Indiana University Press, 1999). Product of a decade-long project of the Organization of American Historians to provide perspectives and bibliographies on the study of women in the non-Western world. Other volumes treat sub-Saharan Africa, the Middle East, and Latin America.

Schell, Orville and David Shambaugh, eds. *The China Reader: The Reform Era* (New York: Vintage Books, 1999). An excellent selection of essays and observations on the changes in China after Mao's death. Updates the earlier four volumes of *China Reader* noted above.

Weiner, Myron. *The Child and the State in India* (Princeton: Princeton University Press, 1991). In a very critical, down-to-earth assessment, Weiner asks why literacy rates and school attendance are so low, and child labor so extensive. Hierarchical values are a major culprit.

Wolf, Eric R. *Peasant Wars of the Twentieth Century* (New York: Harper & Row, 1969). A classic comparative study of the philosophies and strategies of modern guerrilla warfare. China figures prominently.

Wolpert, Stanley. *A New History of India* (New York: Oxford University Press, 7th ed., 2004). A useful, standard, sometimes rambling, highly readable text.

Wu, Harry. *Bitter Winds* (New York: John Wiley, 1994). One of the most bitter attacks on political repression in contemporary China.

World History Documents CD-ROM

Into a New Century

During the last decades of the twentieth century many people felt that they were living through the end of an old era and the birth of a new one. The Cold War ended, the process of decolonization was complete, free-market economics gained ground, the computer revolution was underway, feminism continued to make great strides. All of these transformations forced people to rethink their identities. Where did they stand on the great issues of the day? How were their lives changed by them? To what degree could they live lives of their own choosing?

The women's movement now reached out to include global constituencies and concerns. In Mexico City in 1975 the United Nations sponsored the first World Conference on women's issues. Here and in subsequent related meetings in Copenhagen (1980), Cairo (1994), and Beijing (1995) women learned about the concerns of one another across national borders and political systems. Often they came away surprised at the differences in their perspectives. Westerners stressed access to better jobs, for example, while women from poorer countries sought changes in the power structures of international politics and economics that left them impoverished. Despite these glaring differences, participants also came away with new strategies and renewed appreciation for women's power in collective action.

The ecological devastation of the earth also evoked international action, also not always successfully. The logging of the Brazilian rainforest continued, and some of the activists working to preserve the forest were shot to death. Scientific evidence of global warming continued to accumulate, and progress was made in assembling a global response to cut back on the production of toxic chemicals and gases. The United States, however, refused to sign the Kyoto Agreement on global warming, nor did it offer feasible alternatives. Since the USA was the largest producer of toxic substances, the refusal partially undermined the movement. Many nations and localities did introduce effective conservation and anti-pollution programs locally, within their own borders.

In the face of hunger and starvation in Africa, a number of internationally renowned popular musicians banded together to give a series of concerts (Live Aid) in 1985 in London and around the world, raising awareness of global poverty and contributing the proceeds to alleviate the hunger in Africa.

The 2001 strikes on the World Trade Center in New York City and the Pentagon outside of Washington shocked America, and the rest of the

Above Leah Rabin, wife of the Israeli Prime Minister Yitzhak Rabin (later assassinated), at the World Conference on International Women, Mexico City, 1975.

Right The Brazilian rainforest after logging and burning, 1985.

Live Aid concert finale, London, 1985. From left are George Michael, Paul McCartney, Andrew Ridgeley, Freddie Mercury, David Bowie, and Bob Geldof.

world, by demonstrating the worldwide reach of the militant Islamic organization al-Qaeda. Unlike other terrorist organizations, which usually had specific, negotiable goals, al-Qaeda seemed to target US power and interests in an attempt to frighten America out of its involvement in the Middle East or even to undermine the entire capitalist-military structure of the Western world. American President Bush declared war on terrorism, identifying militant, terrorist elements in the Islamic world as America's new chief enemy.

The attack on the World Trade Center, New York, September 11, 2001.

The 2004 meeting of the World Social Forum in Mumbai (Bombay), India, brought together some 100,000 people, representing many of the identities contesting for recognition in the early twenty-first century. The Forum began as an alternative to the

meetings of the G-8, the leading industrialized powers of the world. It has continued to grow as it has added to its agenda concerns for gender relations—including not only women but also gays, lesbians, bisexuals, and transgendered people; global ecology; and the dramatically unequal distribution of political and economic power. The contrast between the elite G-8 and the populist Forum made clear some of the alternative identities that clamored for recognition in the first years of the new century.

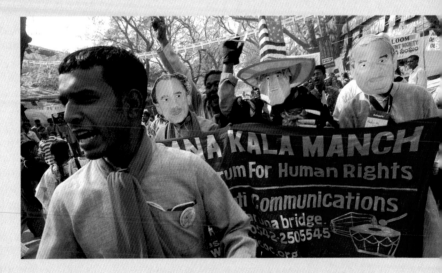

More than 100,000 demonstrators take to the streets to protest at the World Social Forum, Bombay, 2004.

QUESTIONS

1. In what ways were the issues of Western middle-class women different from the issues of the women of the Third World?
2. Why has it been difficult to create an international consensus on a program to preserve the ecology of the globe?
3. Do you think that the musicians who performed in the Live Aid concerts would have been comfortable attending the World Social Forum? Why or why not?

PART

Evolving Identities

1979–Present

We have chosen "identities" as the theme for this Part. Everyone acts out of a sense of identity, our understanding of who or what we are, have been, and wish to become. Beyond the individual, a sense of identity is important also to groups, institutions, and nations. In large part identities are based on historical experiences. Through them the past has a strong influence on the future. At the same time, identities are flexible. To some degree they change as we change and as circumstances change. Some parts of our identities change with our changing age and status.

Nations, too, have complex identities. Consider the United States. It is a relatively new nation, born in 1776, yet it is one of the very oldest of the world's constitutional democracies. It has protected private property, yet it has enacted important laws restricting the freedom of businesses in favor of a larger public good. It proclaims democracy and freedom for all, yet it held slavery as legal until 1865, practiced Jim Crow policies formally and informally for another century, and it continues to show significant levels of racial discrimination in practice even today.

Religions, as well, have diverse aspects to their identities. Sometimes they emphasize the literal, historic teachings of their founders and sometimes they emphasize the need for flexibility in interpreting those teachings. Sometimes they seek greater centralization and conformity, at other times they may promote greater individual freedom of conscience and action. Economic systems also undergo changes in their identity, from an emphasis on private enterprise to an emphasis on government control— to one on cooperative enterprise.

The formation of identity in recent years has been subject to more diverse and more intense influences than ever before. Transportation, travel, communication, and, most especially the World Wide Web have multiplied the influences on our sense of individual and collective identity.

In this Part we shall be examining the end of the Cold War; the collapse of the Soviet Union; the realignment of Third-World countries; the renewed infusion of religion into politics; the rise of global terrorism; the expansion of illegal trafficking—of drugs most of all, but also of weapons, women and children, and human organs; women's issues; the spread of new, fearsome, formerly unknown epidemic diseases such as AIDS; the rise of East Asian economic power; the emergence of the United States as the unrivalled master of large-scale military power; the damage being done to the world's ecology. In Chapter 23 we shall consider some of the major challenges to established identities that have arisen in the recent past. In Chapter 24 we shall examine several case studies of responses to those challenges.

UN World Conference on Women, Great Hall of the People, Beijing, China, 1995.

NEW PUBLIC IDENTITIES

1979–PRESENT

KEY TOPICS
- Political Identities
- Religious and Cultural Identities
- Globalization: New Economic and Cultural Identities
- Ecological Issues
- Public Identities: What Difference Do They Make?

This chapter explores four central elements of individual, group, national, and global identities. It begins with political identities, addressing especially the disintegration of the Soviet Union and the end of the Cold War. It continues with a discussion of the increasing importance of religion in public life in many different ways and in many different parts of the world. It next considers the phenomenon of economic and cultural globalization—that is, the increased importance of global markets and the international exchange of commodities and culture. Finally, it will examine the changes in global ecology over the past two to three decades.

POLITICAL IDENTITIES

The Soviet Union Dissolves

The collapse and disintegration of the Soviet Union, and of the Communist Party that created and administered it, shocked the political and cultural world of the late twentieth century. The entire process unfolded in just two years, 1989–91, and transformed identities around the globe. From the time of its establishment in 1917, the Soviet Union had offered alternative models to the capitalism and individualism of western Europe and the United States. Through the global depression, it had demonstrated that state planning could keep an economy—at least its industrial sectors—humming. It alone had responded vigorously to the dangers posed by the rise of Nazism by building up a strong military defense, and throughout World War II it held the Eastern Front at enormous cost in lives and specie. During the Cold War, the Soviet Union alone provided a balance against the overwhelming military power of the United States, and offered support and an alternative path for newly independent nations emerging from colonialism. At the same time, the totalitarian power of the communist government and the gulag of prison camps through which it enforced that power were crucial ingredients in Soviet identity. Its occupation of central and eastern Europe from 1945 made it an imperial, and dreaded, neighbor.

Individuals, institutions, states, and governments had looked to the Soviet Union as a model for seven decades—some with hope, others with fear and apprehension. With its collapse they lost a pole star in their map of the political universe. Political identities everywhere were reshuffled. Two men guided the process that brought the Soviet Union to its end, Mikhail Gorbachev and Boris Yeltsin.

Mikhail Gorbachev, 1985–91 Mikhail Gorbachev (b. 1931) came to power in the USSR in 1985. He assessed the problems of the Soviet Union directly and bluntly. Its

Opposite **Protest against global warming, Pontianak, Indonesia, 2000.** Due to forest fires that rage on unchecked, and to urban congestion, Indonesia is one of the most polluted places on earth.

economy was neither producing nor distributing goods effectively. Its bureaucracy was bloated with Party officials, while the growing professional classes protested restrictions on freedom. The Churches continued to seek greater freedom of expression. In the satellite countries of eastern Europe and in the non-Russian states of the USSR itself—especially the Baltic states and in the states of Central Asia, which were culturally, linguistically, and religiously different from Russia—nationalist groups sought greater independence. In its haste to industrialize, the USSR had allowed technology to get out of control, as evident in the massive pollution of air and sea, most frighteningly in the Aral Sea, which was drying up. In addition, the ongoing war in Afghanistan was bleeding the country of lives, treasure, and spirit. Finally, the Soviet Union was engaged in an arms race with the United States that it could no longer afford.

glasnost A Russian word meaning "openness," adopted as a political slogan by the Soviet leader Mikhail Gorbachev in 1986. It encouraged greater freedom of expression and genuine debate in social, political, and cultural affairs; with **perestroika**, it heralded greater democracy and improved relations with the West.

perestroika A Russian word meaning "restructuring," used, like **glasnost**, to describe the reforms introduced by the Soviet leader Mikhail Gorbachev after 1985. It marked the development of a more flexible socio-economic system, distinguished by a move to a market-oriented economy, increased private ownership, and decentralization.

In response to these problems, Gorbachev introduced his policies of **glasnost** (political and cultural openness) and **perestroika** (economic restructuring). Glasnost meant, first of all, telling the truth about communist Russia, and this included the truth about the past. Khrushchev had already revealed many of Stalin's atrocities. Under Gorbachev historians revealed even more: some 20 million people killed under Stalin and a similar number oppressed. Glasnost also extended to the present. Russians, who would have agreed with novelist Alexander Solzhenitsyn's 1973 statement, "It has always been impossible to learn the truth about anything in our country," now heard directly about the depth of their nation's problems.

Glasnost revealed the problems. Perestroika looked for solutions. Gorbachev tried to reduce the size of the bureaucracy, to increase the efficiency of agriculture and industry, and to trim the military budget. He appointed reformers like himself to important government offices. He planned and began a more competitive economic system, but still under the general direction of state planning. The competition was among state-owned firms rather than among private companies, which did not exist. Gorbachev was somewhat trapped by his own promises, for soon the reformers were criticizing him for moving too slowly and for an unwillingness to cut free of discredited communist economics. Neither the bureaucracy nor the economy responded adequately to his reforms. The nuclear explosion at Chernobyl in the Ukraine in 1986, the worst industrial accident in history in terms of short- and long-term damage, and a gas pipeline fire that killed hundreds in 1989 exemplified and added to his woes.

In terms of political reforms, Gorbachev moved more boldly, and this paradoxically proved his downfall. Under glasnost, ethnic groups throughout the length and breadth of the highly diverse Soviet Union began to voice their grievances. Riots between ethnic groups broke out in Kazakhstan, Tajikistan, Kyrgyzstan, and Uzbekistan. Gorbachev could restore order only with difficulty. He was unable to stop the fighting in Nagorno-Karabakh, an enclave within Muslim Azerbaijan but with a majority of Christian Armenians. Full-scale independence movements began in the Baltic states of Lithuania, Latvia, and Estonia, as well as in Georgia. Others soon followed.

Meanwhile, the war in Afghanistan that Brezhnev had initiated in 1979 ground on, with about 2000 Russian soldiers dying every year and no evidence of Soviet gains. In 1988, Gorbachev allowed multi-candidate elections and began to give the Supreme Soviet increased powers. In February 1990, he announced that non-Party candidates could stand for office. The monopoly of the Communist Party over the government ended. Gorbachev was willing to see the Soviet empire and the Communist Party disintegrate, and they did. His spokesman announced that he was replacing the Brezhnev Doctrine of massive intervention in rebellious satellite countries with the (Frank) Sinatra Doctrine of "My way," allowing them to break free of the Soviet Union however they chose. The fervor of their response was most clearly demonstrated when Germans tore down the Berlin Wall on November 9, 1989. Gorbachev continued his

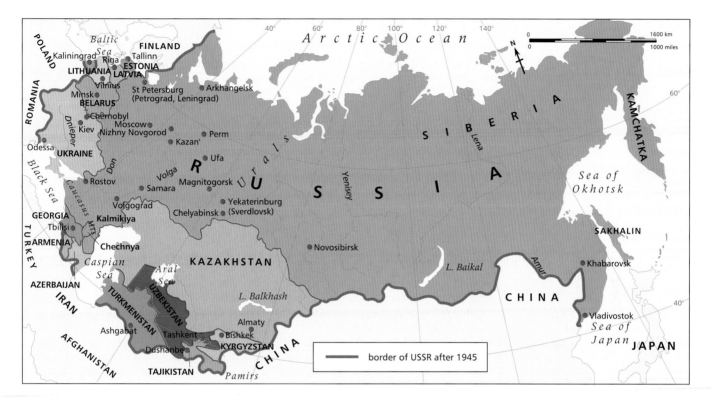

The map labels include:

Arctic Ocean, Baltic Sea, POLAND, FINLAND, Kaliningrad, Riga, Tallinn, ESTONIA, LITHUANIA, LATVIA, Vilnius, Minsk, BELARUS, St Petersburg (Petrograd, Leningrad), Arkhangelsk, ROMANIA, Chernobyl, Moscow, Nizhny Novgorod, Kiev, Dnieper, Perm, Kazan', SIBERIA, KAMCHATKA, Odessa, UKRAINE, Ufa, Urals, RUSSIA, Don, Volga, Rostov, Samara, Magnitogorsk, Black Sea, Caucasus Mts, GEORGIA, Volgograd, Yekaterinburg (Sverdlovsk), Chelyabinsk, Lena, Yenisey, Sea of Okhotsk, Tbilisi, Kalmikiya, TURKEY, ARMENIA, Chechnya, SAKHALIN, Caspian Sea, Aral Sea, Novosibirsk, L. Baikal, Amur, Khabarovsk, AZERBAIJAN, IRAN, TURKMENISTAN, UZBEKISTAN, KAZAKHSTAN, L. Balkhash, CHINA, Vladivostok, Sea of Japan, JAPAN, Ashgabat, Tashkent, Almaty, Bishkek, KYRGYZSTAN, AFGHANISTAN, Dushanbe, CHINA, TAJIKISTAN, Pamirs

border of USSR after 1945

negotiations for arms reductions with US Presidents Reagan and Bush, and in December 1989, Gorbachev and Bush formally announced the end of the Cold War.

With the removal of Soviet armies, all six satellite nations in eastern and central Europe became independent: East Germany, Poland, Hungary, Czechoslovakia (which, in 1993, divided into the Czech and Slovak Republics), Bulgaria, and Romania. Divided at the end of World War II, East and West Germany re-united after tearing down the Berlin Wall that had most conspicuously marked their division. Gorbachev at first resisted the right of constituent republics of the USSR to declare their independence and leave the union, but many now defied his wishes: the Baltic states of Estonia, Latvia, and Lithuania; the eastern European Slavic states of Belarus, Ukraine, and Moldova; the Caspian Sea states of Armenia, Georgia, and Azerbaijan; and the Muslim majority states in Central Asia: Turkmenistan, Uzbekistan, Tajikistan, Kyrgyzstan, and Kazakhstan. With government control uncertain, historic national and ethnic identities re-emerged within and between these states. These identities were sometimes hostile to one another, and violent clashes, as well as celebration, marked the end of the Soviet empire.

Reformers criticized Gorbachev for moving too slowly, but in August 1991 diehard communists mounted a coup against him because they felt he had moved too quickly. While Gorbachev was vacationing in the Crimea, a group of anti-reform members of his government, with the support of a number of military officers, placed Gorbachev under house arrest and assumed control of his Kremlin offices. The coup failed largely because Boris Yeltsin, one of the reformers and the elected president of the Russian Federation, opposed it. He turned his headquarters in the Russian parliament building into the center of public resistance to the coup, contacted political leaders across Russia and around the world to gain support, and courageously went out to the streets and climbed atop an armored troop carrier to make his position clear. When the army refused to attack Yeltsin and his headquarters, the coup was finished. Gorbachev returned from the Crimea, but Yeltsin was the hero of the moment.

The break-up of the Soviet Union. The Soviet experiment with Marxist ideology crumbled, after seventy years, at the end of the 1980s. President Gorbachev's policy of *glasnost* (1985) allowed the nations of eastern Europe to move, largely bloodlessly, toward independence and economic reform, but in the Caucasus mountains and Central Asia reform was often accompanied by an insurgence of nationalism, organized crime, and power struggles. In 1991 these nations also became independent—except for Chechnya, where fighting continued for years.

SOURCE

Gorbachev at the United Nations, December 7, 1988

Gorbachev left two contrasting legacies. At home, he failed in his practical attempts to bring perestroika, the restructuring of the Russian economy, politics, and society. On the other hand, his vision of the future for the world inspired people everywhere. It underpinned his dismantling of the Soviet Union, its Communist Party, and its control over the satellite countries of central and eastern Europe. The vision seemed utopian yet, somehow, perhaps, achievable. Gorbachev's speech at the United Nations General Assembly in New York City on December 7, 1988, summarized his goals and aspirations. It called for global cooperation, tolerance for diverse social and political systems, protection for the globe's ecology, assistance for development in the poorer nations, and disarmament, which he pledged to begin immediately in the Soviet Union on his own initiative. This was quite a new agenda for the Soviet Union, and for the world. The speech drew enthusiastic, even ecstatic praise from statesmen and common people around the world.

Further world progress is now possible only through the search for a consensus of all mankind, in movement toward a new world order . . . It is a question of cooperation that could be more accurately called "co-creation" and "co-development." The formula of development "at another's expense" is becoming outdated. In light of present realities, genuine progress by infringing upon the rights and liberties of man and peoples, or at the expense of nature, is impossible . . .

It is evident, for example, that force and the threat of force can no longer be, and should not be instruments of foreign policy . . .

The variety of sociopolitical structures which has grown over the last decades from national liberation movements also demonstrates this. This objective fact presupposes respect for other people's views and stands, tolerance, a preparedness to see phenomena that are different as not necessarily bad or hostile, and an ability to learn to live side by side while remaining different and not agreeing with one another on every issue . . .

In the course of such sharing, each should prove the advantages of his own system, his own way of life and values, but not through words or propaganda alone, but through real deeds as well . . . Otherwise we simply will not be able to solve a single world problem; arrange broad, mutually advantageous and equitable cooperation between peoples; manage rationally the achievements of the scientific and technical revolution; transform world economic relations; protect the environment; overcome underdevelopment; or put an end to hunger, disease, illiteracy, and other mass ills. Finally, in that case, we will not manage to eliminate the nuclear threat and militarism.

Now about the most important topic, without which no problem of the coming century can be resolved: disarmament . . .

Today I can inform you of the following: The Soviet Union has made a decision on reducing its armed forces. In the next two years, their numerical strength will be reduced by 500,000 persons . . . The Soviet forces situated in those countries [of central and eastern Europe] will be cut by 50,000 persons, and their arms by 5000 tanks.

We would also like to draw the attention of the world community to another topical problem, the problem of changing over from an economy of armament to an economy of disarmament. Is the conversion of military production realistic? . . . We believe that it is, indeed, realistic . . . It is desirable that all states, primarily the major military powers, submit their national plans on this issue to the United Nations.

We are talking first and foremost about consistent progress toward concluding a treaty [with the United States] on a 50 percent reduction in strategic offensive weapons . . . about elaborating a convention on the elimination of chemical weapons—here, it seems to us, we have the preconditions for making 1989 the decisive year; and about talks on reducing conventional weapons and armed forces in Europe. We are also talking about economic, ecological and humanitarian problems in the widest possible sense . . .

One would like to believe that our joint efforts to put an end to the era of wars, confrontation and regional conflicts, aggression against nature, the terror of hunger and poverty, as well as political terrorism, will be comparable with our hopes. This is our common goal, and it is only by acting together that we may attain it. Thank you.

http://www.cnn.com/SPECIALS/cold.war/episodes/23/documents/gorbachev

Since most of the leaders of the coup attempt were diehard members of the Communist Party, Yeltsin outlawed the activities of the Party in Russia. A few days later Gorbachev resigned as general secretary of the Party and moved to dissolve it altogether. On December 24, 1991, the USSR recognized the legitimacy of the claims to independent national identity of its constituent states and formally dissolved itself into fifteen independent states. The new states joined in a loose Commonwealth of

Independent States (CIS) as a mechanism for continuing cooperation. The USSR was no more; the Communist Party was reduced to a shell; the global political landscape was transformed. The nation that Gorbachev had ruled no longer existed. Yeltsin's Russia was by far its largest surviving state.

Boris Yeltsin, 1991–9 One of the first problems facing Boris Yeltsin (b. 1931) was disposing of the nuclear arsenal of the former USSR. Eighty percent of these weapons were on Russian soil and under Russian control. Yeltsin reopened discussions with the USA concerning arms reductions and signed treaties to carry them out. He achieved an agreement with Belarus to control its weapons, but others of the new states kept at least limited control over the weapons on their soil. The rest of the world worried about the final disposal of the enormous nuclear arsenals that remained in the states of the CIS, including Russia, which were poor and of questionable stability. The fear was not so much that the weapons would be used by these states but that they might be sold off, in whole or in parts, to other nations eager to gain access to nuclear weapons and technology.

Mikhail Gorbachev, 1991. President Gorbachev speaks at a press conference during a peace summit in Moscow.

Yeltsin convened a constitutional assembly, which produced a new constitution in 1993. The Russian economy continued to lag, however, and Yeltsin and the parliament came into direct, violent conflict. Following armed battles in which about 150 people were killed, Yeltsin reasserted his power as president. He was re-elected in nationwide multiparty elections in 1996 that reaffirmed Russia's commitment to democracy.

In its first post-communist years, Russia suffered grievously. In the decade 1991 to 2000, the gross domestic product dropped by 50 percent, the lifespan of citizens fell by two and a half years, the birthrate dropped by a third, and the mortality rate rose by a quarter, while a small class of entrepreneurs made great profits. The government privatized its economic holdings, selling them off at bargain rates to its supporters, who became very wealthy overnight. In a face-off with government, "robber capitalists," wielding huge economic power, refused to pay taxes, bringing the nation to near bankruptcy. Petty crime also became commonplace, and organized criminal gangs flourished.

Internationally, Yeltsin's greatest success may have been winning the confidence and support of foreign financial institutions and governments, which kept Russia's floundering economy afloat through investments, loans, and debt rescheduling. In 1997, Russia was accorded associate status in NATO, its former arch-enemy, while the Czech Republic, Poland, and Hungary were invited as full members, an astonishing turnaround after four decades of cold war.

Yeltsin's greatest embarrassment was the continuing war in the breakaway province of Chechnya, an Islamic-majority region near the Caspian Sea. Chechnya was not given its independence from Russia along with the other states of the former USSR. It therefore declared its independence and secession from Russia in 1994 and began a

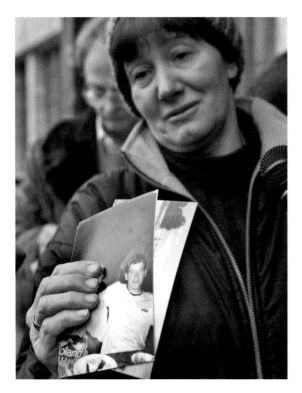

A Russian woman with a photo of her son killed during the assault by Russian special forces on the Moscow Theater, Moscow, 2002. Russian special forces stormed the Moscow Theater after Chechen rebels had taken hundreds of hostages in their demands for the release from captivity of leading Chechen separatists.

guerrilla war. All the technology of the once proud Russian army could not permanently defeat the nationalist rebels, although there were periods of relative calm, nor could the Russian government negotiate a graceful retreat. On December 31, 1999, in the face of continuing economic difficulties, charges of corruption, war in Chechnya, and concerns about his health and drinking problems, Yeltsin resigned as president of Russia, naming Vladimir Putin acting president.

Vladimir Putin, from 2000 Vladimir Putin (b. 1952) was subsequently elected Yeltsin's successor. He continued the war in Chechnya and it drags on, with occasional terrorist attacks in Moscow, as probably the greatest drain on his presidency. Under Yeltsin, and continuing under Putin, the economy has been on a roller-coaster, which at present seems to be moving stably, if slowly, upward. Putin has not, however, moved toward political and economic liberalization. Formerly head of Russia's secret police, he has brought into his government people of similar background. He has jailed prominent leaders who seemed to threaten to expand freedom of the press, to build personal economic fortunes, and to challenge him politically. Putin's methods appear popular and his government stable. He was reelected president in March 2004, with 72 percent of the vote, although most observers questioned the fairness of the election, citing manipulation of the state media and stuffing of ballot boxes. Russia has moved from its former identity as a totalitarian state, but it has not (yet) become a liberal democracy. The highly respected *Economist* magazine of London remarked that, despite its new orientation, "Russia has a corrupt legal system, a monstrous bureaucracy, and laws like thick mud" (*Economist*, 22 May 2004).

European Identity

While nationalism was growing among the states and satellites of the former Soviet Union—many of them in Europe—so too was a new sense of European identity. The definition of Europe has always been contested. Sometimes it has referred to the entire continent—a geographical peninsula, really—from the Ural mountains in the east to the Atlantic Ocean in the west; sometimes it has been used as a shorthand for the industrialized, mostly democratic nations of western Europe; sometimes it has designated the areas of the peninsula where Christianity, and especially Roman Catholicism and Protestantism, have flourished. The rise of the Soviet Union and the Cold War had introduced an East–West political–military division into Europe. The breakdown of the USSR also began to break down that division and identity. In 1990, East and West Germany were reunited amid great jubilation. In 2004, Hungary, the Czech Republic, Slovakia, Poland, Lithuania, Latvia, and Estonia—along with Malta, Cyprus, and Slovenia—joined the European Union, an economic and political union that already included 15 nations of western Europe. Other nations waited in the wings, having already submitted, or beginning to prepare, their applications for membership: Romania, Bulgaria, Croatia, Serbia, Macedonia, and, largest of all, Islamic Turkey.

The USA as the Lone Superpower

The disintegration of the Soviet Union left the United States as the only country in the world able to project massive military, economic, and cultural power everywhere on the globe. The USA had become the only "superpower." This level of unparalleled political, military, and economic power created a new identity for the USA and for the world. For centuries, world politics had turned on a balance of power among the major nations. This was true even during the Cold War, when the two superpowers balanced one another.

In the 1990s, however, America's position was confirmed economically as well as politically, as Japan, America's number one economic competitor globally, sank into a recession from which it has still not fully recovered. Until the end of the 1980s, Japan's economy continued to outperform that of any other major nation (see Chapter 19), but in 1989 an economic "bubble" burst in Japan and the country slipped into an unexpected recession. Land values plummeted by two-thirds. (The total land of Japan had been valued at four times the total value of land in the United States.) The Nikkei stock market index followed, dropping by 60 percent from 1989 to 1992. Billions of dollars in paper wealth were wiped out, and Japan fell into a long-term depression. The Japanese government that had been credited with masterminding forty years of continuous growth was now blamed for economic recession. By contrast, in the early 1990s, the American economy entered into a new phase of growth, one of the longest and steepest in the history of the country, led by innovations in communications technology.

In 1992 Francis Fukuyama published *The End of History*, building on over a decade and a half of research and argumentation. He argued, triumphally, that the fall of Russian communism had left just one viable political-economic system in the world, the capitalist-democratic system of the United States, western Europe, and a few other countries. This system had won, he argued, because it was the best.

There were some outstanding examples that seemed to support his point. In 1991, India, which was already democratic, began a set of policy changes crafted to reduce the role of the state in the national economy and to convert to greater reliance on free markets both at home and in international trade and investment. In addition, without the Soviet Union as an alternative, many nations turned toward America for assistance or advice. Almost all the former satellites of the USSR chose to move toward free-market economic policies, and the Czech Republic, Hungary, and Poland joined NATO, with Russia's full consent. Middle Eastern nations had no alternative to aligning their foreign policies toward America and to relying on America to mediate the Arab–Israeli dispute. In the Caribbean, Cuba's economy, which was already weak, virtually collapsed as the Soviet Union could no longer buy its sugar crop nor supply subsidies. Economically crippled, the Caribbean island no longer had the strength to send guerrilla troops to other parts of Latin America nor to parts of Africa where it had been deeply enmeshed: Angola, Mozambique, and Ethiopia.

Despite the examples that seemed to support Fukuyama's thesis, there were more examples that contradicted it. Triumphalism, it turned out, was not justified. Nationalism remained a powerful force, often without regard for economic or even military consequences. For example, going from west to east across Afro-Eurasia:

Osama bin Laden appears on Al-Jazeera television, October 17, 2001. Bin Laden here praises the attacks of September 11 and defies the US in its threats to attack Afghanistan's Taliban government. The US overthrew the Taliban some days later.

Northern Ireland continued to gain in its struggle against Britain for self-government, but periodic armed guerrilla attacks by the Irish Republican Army impeded the process. Yugoslavia, as we shall see in Chapter 24, shattered into separate states that went to war against each other for reasons of ethnicity and religion more than economics. Fighting to determine the borders between Ethiopia and Somalia and Ethiopia and Eritrea continued for years, long after Soviet intervention in the area ended. Tens of thousands of people in each of the three countries died in the warfare. North Korea pursued a policy of isolation from the rest of the world under the rigid dictatorship of Kim Il Sung (r. 1972–94) followed by his son Kim Jong Il (r. 1994–). Since 1993, North Korea has been working on a program for developing nuclear weapons and is now believed to have such weapons, adding an element of instability in East Asia and beyond. North Korea pursued its program of nuclear development despite poverty to the point of starvation among its people.

Most dramatically, terrorist attacks on the United States and its interests at home and overseas exploded any illusions that American values were prevailing globally or that there was a single unified American identity. One attack was from within as Timothy McVeigh blew up the federal building in Oklahoma City in 1995, in retaliation for the government's 1993 armed assault on the Branch Davidians, a small religious sect based in Waco, Texas. More typically these attacks occurred overseas and were part of a violent dialogue with Islamic militancy. In 1983, a suicide car-bomb destroyed the US embassy in Beirut, Lebanon, killing 63. Later in the same year suicide bombers exploded a truck-bomb at US Marine headquarters at the international airport in Beirut, killing 241 US Marines and sailors. (Minutes later another bomb killed 58 French paratroopers in their barracks also in Beirut.) In 1993, a bomb delivered by Muslim terrorists exploded in the garage under the World Trade Center in New York, killing six. In Saudi Arabia, a bomb killed seven Americans at a military training installation in 1995, and another exploded at an American air force barracks in 1996, killing 19. In 1998 almost simultaneous explosions at US embassies in Kenya and Tanzania killed 220 people. In 2000 a small boat sailed alongside the USS *Cole*, a US Navy destroyer, in the harbor at Aden, Yemen, and bombed the ship, killing seventeen sailors. Most spectacularly, on September 11, 2001, representatives of the Islamic militant group al-Qaeda hijacked four American commercial jet airliners and used them as suicide bombers in exploding and destroying the two buildings of the World Trade Center in New York, killing some 2800 people, a wing of the Pentagon outside of Washington, D.C., and crashing one, apparently targeted for a major government installation in Washington, in western Pennsylvania.

Shocked out of a sense of its own invulnerability, America declared war on terrorism. Terrorism is usually defined as a form of guerrilla warfare. It is a strategy employed by the weak against the strong. It attacks civilian non-combatants, in civilian locations, to terrify a general population into conceding political benefits. Although the strike on September 11, 2001 against America was extraordinary in its daring, scale, and spectacle, and in not having a specific political goal, in principle, terrorism was not a new method of fighting. According to statistics compiled by the US Department of State, there had been hundreds of terrorist attacks around the world annually. From 1981 to 1991, counting all attacks against all victims in all places, they averaged more than 500 a year. From 1991 to 2001 there were never fewer than the 274 in 1998. When America proclaimed a "war on terrorism," many wondered what form would such a war take, how would it be fought, and how would one know when victory was achieved?

In addition to terrorist attacks by enemies of US interests, American actions on the international stage were isolating the superpower from its allies. America's penchant for acting unilaterally frequently appeared arrogant and alienated friends as well as enemies. America imposed sanctions on Iran and Cuba and forced others to comply. It

SOURCE

Osama bin Laden, leader of al-Qaeda

Osama bin Laden was born in Saudi Arabia in 1957, the seventeenth child and seventh son of a devout Sunni Muslim family that had become extremely wealthy in the construction business. He grew up in an atmosphere of militant Wahabi puritan interpretations of Sunni Islam, at a time when Islamic nationalism was growing, and earned a degree in public administration in Jeddah in 1981. He went to Afghanistan to join in the struggle against Soviet occupation and created al-Qaeda ("the base") to obtain and organize war supplies and to lead troops in the field. When the Soviets withdrew, bin Laden returned to Saudi Arabia committed to a militant, politicized vision of Islam. When the USA invaded Iraq in 1991, he offered to help the Saudi government in case of attack. Bin Laden was enraged as the government turned to the Americans for their defense, invited US troops onto Saudi lands, and put him under government surveillance. He returned to Afghanistan, only to find that it had collapsed into civil war. He went to Sudan, then led by a militant Islamic government. In 1994, the government of Saudi Arabia revoked his citizenship and froze his assets in Saudi Arabia. Under pressure from Saudi Arabia and the United States, Sudan expelled bin Laden in 1996 and he returned to Afghanistan, which had come under the government of the Taliban, a group of seminary students with military experience who had unified the country after eighteen years of warfare. Here bin Laden established the World Islamic Front for the Jihad against Jews and Crusaders, a headquarters for radical Muslim movements. He issued a fatwa *stating that it was the duty of Muslims to kill US citizens and their allies. In his camps he trained jihadis for these tasks.*

Shortly after the attacks on the United States on September 11, 2001, bin Laden broadcast the following message on the Arabic news channel al-Jazeera:

What the United States tastes today is a very small thing compared to what we have tasted for tens of years. Our nation has been tasting this humiliation and contempt for more than 80 years. Its sons are being killed, its blood is being shed, its holy places are being attacked, and it is not being ruled according to what God has decreed. Despite this, nobody cares.

When Almighty God rendered successful a convoy of Muslims, the vanguards of Islam, He allowed them to destroy the United States.

I ask God Almighty to elevate their status and grant them Paradise. He is the one who is capable to do so.

When these defended their oppressed sons, brothers, and sisters in Palestine and in many Islamic countries, the world at large shouted. The infidels shouted, followed by the hypocrites. One million Iraqi children have thus far died in Iraq although they did not do anything wrong. Despite this, we heard no denunciation by anyone in the world or a *fatwa* by the rulers' *ulema* [body of Muslim scholars].

Israeli tanks and tracked vehicles also enter to wreak havoc in Palestine, in Jenin, Ramallah, Rafah, Beit Jala, and other Islamic areas and we hear no voices raised or moves made. But if the sword falls on the United States after 80 years, hypocrisy raises its head lamenting the deaths of these killers who tampered with the blood, honor, and holy places of the Muslims.

The least that one can describe these people is that they are morally depraved. They champion falsehood, support the butcher against the victim, the oppressor against the innocent child. May God mete them the punishment they deserve.

They came out in arrogance with their men and horses and instigated even those countries that belong to Islam against us. They came out to fight this group of people who declared their faith in God and refused to abandon their religion. They came out to fight Islam in the name of terrorism.

Hundreds of thousands of people, young and old, were killed in the farthest point on earth in Japan. [For them] this is not a crime, but rather a debatable issue. They bombed Iraq and considered that a debatable issue.

But when a dozen people of them were killed in Nairobi and Dar es Salaam, Afghanistan and Iraq were bombed and all hypocrite ones stood behind the head of the world's infidelity—behind the Hubal [an idol worshipped by pagans before the advent of Islam] of the age—namely, America and its supporters. These incidents divided the entire world into two regions—one of faith where there is no hypocrisy and another of infidelity, from which we hope God will protect us . . .

As for the United States, I tell it and its people these few words: I swear by Almighty God who raised the heavens without pillars that neither the United States nor he who lives in the United States will enjoy security before we can see it as a reality in Palestine and before all the infidel armies leave the land of Mohammed, may God's peace and blessing be upon him.

God is great and glory to Islam. May God's peace, mercy, and blessings be upon you.

http://news.bbc.co.uk/1/hi/world/south_asia/1585636.stm

refused to ratify international treaties, cut foreign aid, withheld dues to the United Nations and other international agencies, cut State Department funding, and abolished the United States Information Agency. In declining to sign the Kyoto Protocol on

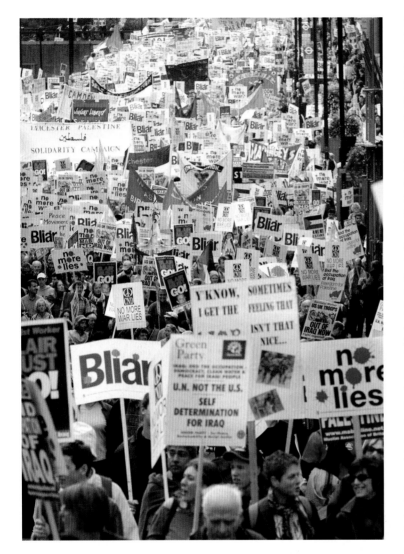

Anti-war protesters march through the streets of Piccadilly, central London, 2004. Up to 100,000 people from across the UK attended the march and rally, calling for troops to be removed from Iraq. The Campaign for Nuclear Disarmament, Stop The War Coalition, and the Muslim Association of Britain organized the event. Hundreds of thousands also marched in Rome, New York, and other major cities worldwide.

the reduction of greenhouse gases, a bill signed by 178 nations and recommended by all the major advocates of a healthy global ecology, and by offering no alternative vision, America was perceived as flouting world opinion. In supporting Israel's assassination attacks on Palestinian guerrilla leaders, which often also killed innocent civilians, America differed from most of the rest of the world.

Most of all, in going to war against Iraq in March, 2003, America stood blatantly—advocates would say boldly—against most of world opinion. On February 15, 2003, as American leaders threatened to attack Iraq, street demonstrations were held in cities in the United States (again demonstrating the lack of a homogeneous "American identity) and around the world, many of them attracting hundreds of thousands of participants. In both London and Rome up to a million demonstrated against the coming war. Most of the rest of the world wished to investigate America's claims that Iraq might have weapons of mass destruction, but they were willing to trust United Nations weapons inspectors to find them and to allow international sanctions to keep Iraq under control. If further military action was necessary, they wished it to be under UN auspices. They called America's actions unilateral and arrogant, and America found itself isolated in many of its foreign policy decisions.

In the form of its fight against terrorism, America also evoked some criticism. At the time of the September 11 attacks, America had received the sympathy of the world, but questions arose as it responded by attacking Afghanistan unilaterally, killing thousands of civilians as well as some Taliban members, and then withdrawing before a new government capable of administering the entire country had been established. Questions increased as America attacked Iraq in 2003, without any credible proof that Iraq had been involved in the earlier attacks.

Defending free and open societies from terrorism presents enormous challenges: to maintain the openness of the society, to track down and prosecute the terrorists, and not to provoke others into joining them. Would America be able to do it? Was America's response appropriate to and commensurate with the attacks? Would America's responses not actually provoke more terrorists to attack? Was America losing perspective both at home and abroad in this war against terrorism? These were questions echoing around the world and in the 2004 presidential election in the United States itself.

RELIGIOUS AND CULTURAL IDENTITIES

The past twenty to thirty years have provided abundant evidence of the power of religious faith to motivate public as well as private action, in all major religions and regions. The 1979 revolution in Iran provides a good example and is a good place to begin a global survey. That revolution, led by the Ayatollah Khomeini, not only over-threw the shah of Iran, but also successfully challenged the power of the United States that stood behind the throne. The resistance of the Islamic militant Taliban in Afghanistan, successfully repelling the Soviet invasion of its country through the 1980s, further extended that message. Organized religious groups were capable of inflicting great punishment on even the most powerful nations. In Iran and Afghanistan resurgent Islam had confronted and repelled both of the world's super-powers.

Islamic identity was not, however, easy to define. Among the 1.3 billion Muslim faithful and the dozens of Islamic-majority nations, there are many different group-ings, sects, and perspectives. As we saw in Chapter 22, Iraq felt threatened by its neigh-bor Iran. The new Iranian leadership aggressively proclaimed its Shi'a identity, while Iraq was ruled by a more-or-less secular dictator who nevertheless identified with his own Sunni sect, which dominated over a 60 percent Shia majority. In addition, both nations claimed control over the Shatt al-Arab waterway at the entrance to the Persian Gulf. Scattered fighting between them escalated into full-scale warfare that dragged on for eight years at the cost of up to a million lives. Saudi Arabia, also Sunni, felt threat-ened by potential Iranian subversion, especially after Iranians set off a bomb in Mecca, near the sacred Ka'aba, in 1987. The Saudis, at least briefly, drew closer to the United States.

In several countries with overwhelmingly Muslim populations, struggles broke out between forces that wished to keep the country secular and those that wanted Islamic principles and practices to be institutionalized as official public policy. In Turkey and Algeria secular armed forces intervened in elections throughout the 1990s to keep Islamic political parties from coming to power. In 1981, in Egypt, members of the Islamic Brotherhood assassinated the relatively secular President Anwar Sadat, who had jailed many of their members and had made peace with Israel. They also attempted to assassinate his successor, Hosni Mubarak, who followed similar policies.

In Africa, south of the Sahara, where Islam, Christianity, and indigenous African religions had usually coexisted peacefully, armed struggle broke out among them. In Chad, which is about 50 percent Muslim, mostly in the north, and 25 percent each Christian and followers of indigenous religions, mostly in the south, civil war broke out in 1966 and has continued on-and-off, with the occasional intervention of French troops, at the request of the government, and of Libyan troops, sometimes at the request of the government of Chad and sometimes in order to claim parts of the war-torn country for themselves.

Neighboring Sudan has experienced similar instability in government, with ineffec-tive parliaments and unstable military governments alternating in power through a series of coups. In addition, the people of the north, home to the 70 percent of the pop-ulation that is Sunni and mostly Arab, have repeatedly attempted to impose Islamic law on the south, which is mostly black and mostly practices indigenous religions. The result has been a series of civil wars in a country that is overwhelmingly poor and prone to famine. As many as 2 million people died in wars and famines—mostly southerners—and millions more, mostly southerners, have been displaced from their homes. In 1993, Amnesty International charged that the government was carrying out ethnic cleansing against the southerners. In 2004, forces in the north and south appeared poised to reach accommodations that might allow peace and stability, but forces in the Darfur region of the western part of the country, claiming oppression, were still at war with the central government and with local armed groups, the Jan-jaweed, which were backed by the government. In Darfur, however, the issue seemed to be ethnic rather than religious, northern Arabs against western black Africans. Both groups were Muslim by religion. The United Nations and several individual nations extended relief aid and considered military intervention to protect the inhabitants of Darfur and impose peace on the region.

Nigeria, by far the most populous African country, with 130 million people, has been beset by many cross-cutting struggles, of which the attempt to impose Islamic law has been only one. But in this country whose population is about 45 percent Muslim, 45 percent Christian, and 10 percent followers of indigenous religions, this issue has led to rioting. In early 2000, some 2000 people were killed in northern Nigeria when Shari'a law was instituted in Kaduna State. In retaliation, several hundred Muslims were killed in the east and south, and many more began to migrate to areas where their religious group was dominant. In May 2004, in the central Nigerian Plateau State, Christians attacked the Muslim market town of Yelwa, leaving an estimated 67 to 670 people dead. Muslims and Christians fled areas in which they were minorities and resettled in areas of their own majorities. In the north around the town of Jos, Muslims retaliated, leaving 20,000 Christians homeless. President Obasanjo put the area under military command, bringing, on the one hand, relief from the violence but, on the other, fear for Nigeria's fragile democracy. Despite the hostility it engendered among non-Muslims, several additional northern states instituted Islamic law as the basis of their official legal codes.

Although perhaps not significant in internal politics, issues of Islam and women have brought unwanted international attention to Nigeria. In 2002, a young woman accused of adultery was to be stoned to death, but she appealed the case, and its disposition is not yet clear. In 2002, the Miss World Pageant was scheduled for Nigeria until Muslim leaders decried the spectacle as incompatible with Islam. Riots broke out killing one hundred people, and the Pageant was moved to London, where such exhibitions of attractive young women in competition are considered acceptable.

One of the worst examples of religious strife occurred in eastern Europe, in the Balkans, where civil war raged from 1992 to 1995 and continued to sputter afterward as well. Hundreds of thousands of people died and many more were made at least temporarily homeless in the worst warfare in Europe since World War II. The Balkans are a region of divisive nationalisms, and although religion was not the only issue in the war, it was important. The ethnic diversity of the Balkans was most clear in the multi-ethnic new state of Yugoslavia that was created after World War I. After World War II, ethnic hostilities were suppressed by the nation's leader Marshal Tito, and even after his death the communist government of the country continued his policies.

After communism collapsed along with the Soviet Union in 1989, however, Yugoslavia splintered into three major regions, and religion was one of the key elements in the division. Serbia's population was about 65 percent Orthodox Christian, 19 percent Muslim; Croatia's was 77 percent Roman Catholic, 11 percent Orthodox; and Bosnia-Herzegovina's was 40 percent Muslim, 31 percent Orthodox, and 15 percent Catholic. The country was divided into three, and war broke out among the three new states, as well as within them. As fighting intensified, many observers noted that religious identity became increasingly important. People who had not identified strongly with any religious group found that they had to choose sides. Religious identity seemed to inspire the worst violence, murder, rape, and torture. In Chapter 24 we shall look more closely at the case of the breakdown of Yugoslavia into these constituent units in 1991–2, noting here only that religion was one of the key factors.

Hinduism and Islam in South Asia

As India approached independence in 1947, many Muslim leaders held out for a Muslim homeland, and finally this demand led to the partition of India into India and Pakistan (see Chapter 22). As these events unfolded, most attention focused on Muslim religious identity. The Congress Party asserted that it was not a Hindu organization, but a secular political party. This was the basis for its claim that there was no need for a separate Muslim country; everyone could live under a secular government in a secular state. This was Gandhi's claim, and Jawaharlal Nehru, first prime minister of India, 1947–64, sustained India's official secularism. He governed India as a "composite," or multicultural, society. If anything, he tended to favor Muslims as a minority in need of protection.

Even during the Independence struggle, however, there was a strong Hindu movement that did not welcome secularism nor the equality of non-Hindus, and especially Muslims, in India. The Hindu Mahasabha (Great Assembly) was largely eclipsed by the Congress, but it represented a powerful group within India. The Mahasabha's cultural organization, the RSS (Rashtriya Swayamsevak Sangh, National Volunteer Organization) was temporarily banished from public life in India because one of its members assassinated Gandhi for being too accommodating toward Muslim demands.

In the 1980s Hindu militants resurfaced as a significant political voice in India, reconstituted as the Bharatiya Janata Parishad (Indian People's Party), or BJP. At first the BJP drew little attention and few votes, but then its leadership began to stress its Hindu nature. They scorned Muslims as not being true Indians, but rather descendants of military invaders, or converts to their foreign religion, and more loyal to the world community of Muslims, and in particular to Pakistan, than to India.

L.K. Advani, the chief organizer of the BJP, organized a tour across north India in 1990, riding in a van decorated as a war chariot of Lord Rama. To add to the religious symbolism, Advani began his tour from the west coast town of Dwarka, the home of the Somnath Temple, destroyed by Muslim, Mughal invaders when they entered India in 1296, and rebuilt immediately after India became independent. To complete the symbolism, Advani ended his tour at the north Indian town of Ayodhaya, the home of a mosque built by the first Mughal emperor allegedly on the grounds of a Hindu temple that he destroyed and that was said to mark the earthly birthplace of the Hindu Lord Rama. Actually Advani himself did not complete the pilgrimage. He was arrested by the chief minister of the state in which Ayodhaya is located on the grounds of inciting to riot. The pilgrimage had instigated rioting between Hindus and Muslims throughout its journey.

Two years later, in defiance of the government of India and in violation of a pledge that he had made, Advani instigated the destruction of the Ayodhaya mosque. In response, riots broke out throughout India. In Mumbai (Bombay) 2000 people were killed and bombs exploded in the city's stock exchange. Nevertheless, the BJP's electoral totals continued to climb from one election to the next. By the end of the decade, the BJP won enough votes to achieve a governing coalition.

In office, the BJP leadership stressed "Hindutva," or "Hinduness" as the basis of their political identity. "Hindutva" was to some degree a call for greater piety in religion, but it was far more a political rallying call to make Hindu identity the basis of national identity, and thus to exclude non-Hindus from full membership in the Indian nation. In 2002, a group of militant Hindus were returning from a pilgrimage to Ayodhaya. They apparently heckled some Muslim vendors on a train platform in one of the towns of Gujarat State,. In response, Muslims burned part of the train, killing 59 pilgrims. Across Gujarat State, attacks against Muslims followed, killing at least 1000 people and leaving some 100,000 homeless, in refugee camps. The attacks seemed organized, and the state police did little to stop them, bringing charges against the state government of complicity in the killing.

This called attention to one of the most important elements in civil riots. Riots and attacks may break out at any time, but the key question is: What does the government

Militant Hindus atop and around Babri Mosque, Ayodhaya, India, 1992. In December 1992 many thousands of Hindu extremists destroyed the 430-year-old Muslim mosque, claiming that it had been built on ground originally sacred to Hindus as the birthplace of the Lord Rama.

do about them? If the police and government act immediately to stop them, the damage is minimal; if they do not, the damage increases; if the police and government actually help in the attacks, the situation is called a pogrom, an attack on a specific ethnic, racial, or religious group, that has the backing, or a least the complicity, of the state.

In the next state elections, the ruling BJP party won a landslide victory, gaining its biggest majorities in areas where the attacks had been most deadly, and suggesting that the call of Hindutva and the attacks on Muslims were politically effective. Meanwhile, throughout India, wherever the BJP held power, school textbooks were being rewritten to give prominence to stories of Hindu power and to show Muslims as foreigners and unpatriotic. Muslims seemed to be under siege.

On the other hand, in the national elections of 2004, the BJP was badly defeated. Mostly the vote seemed to be, once again, an anti-incumbency response of the lower middle classes and the poor, based at least as much on opposition to economic policies that favored the wealthy, as it was a vote against Hindutva. To complicate the analysis of the election, the BJP party had actually reduced its emphasis on Hindutva and had begun attempting some rapprochement with Muslim Pakistan. Some more militant members of the party argued that the BJP had not emphasized Hindutva enough to win the election!

To add to the complication that is Indian identity, the head of the triumphant Congress Party was Sonia Gandhi, the widow of the assassinated former prime minister, Rajiv Gandhi, and the daughter-in-law of his mother, the assassinated former prime minister Indira Gandhi. Sonia was Italian by birth, and the BJP had derided her Indian political credentials throughout the election. As it came time for the Congress to select a new prime minister, she voluntarily stepped aside, apparently to allow a native-born Indian to take the position, perhaps also to reduce the threat of further assassinations in her family. Manmohan Singh became the new prime minister. For the first time a Sikh rather than a Hindu was prime minister. And the president of India, filling a largely ceremonial position, was a Muslim! Despite the emotional appeal of Hindutva, most Indians seemed to appreciate the virtues of a composite identity.

Confucianism

As the "Asian tiger" nations in East and Southeast Asia—especially Taiwan, Korea, Singapore, and Hong Kong—began to improve their economies, a reassessment of the virtues of Confucian philosophy took place. Economists and sociologists who had earlier argued that an emphasis on family solidarity and social integration were inhibiting growth, now began to argue that these were among the most significant cultural characteristics promoting growth! (We have discussed in Chapter 22 some of these attempts by academics to evaluate the significance of cultural identity in economic and political development.)

In China, the communist government had forbidden the teaching and practice of Confucianism for decades, rejecting its elitism and hierarchy. In the 1990s the government began to change course, allowing some degree of cultural liberalization along with economic liberalization. Confucianism has had a limited rebirth in China that may also facilitate better relationships with overseas Chinese who also accept

Confucianism. In 1999, the government celebrated lavishly the 2550th anniversary of the birth of Confucius, praising him for his exemplary humanity and benevolence.

Judaism

Religious identities in Judaism also underwent enormous change. After almost 2000 years of living as minorities in diaspora communities, Jews gained a (small) state of their own in Israel. They were, however, surrounded by hostile neighbors. With some, Egypt and Jordan, they could achieve political settlements and peace treaties. But with others, like Syria and Lebanon, they could not. The greatest hostility appeared between them and the Palestinians whom they had conquered in warfare. As a result of their changed status, Jewish political philosophy seemed to change. Previously, as weak and dependent people, they emphasized the biblical concept that they would live "not by might and not by power," but by God's spirit. Now, surrounded by hostility, many of them came to believe that only might and power would enable them to survive. In control of their own state, they built the most powerful armed force in the Middle East, and used it in ways that appeared necessary to the Israeli government but excessively brutal to many others.

Through immigration, the United States had become the home of about 5 to 6 million Jews, about 40 percent of the world's total (about a million more than in Israel). Here unprecedented freedom for this minority group served to loosen the bonds of group solidarity. Many chose not to affiliate. Slightly more than 50 percent of American Jews intermarried with their Christian neighbors, and various studies arrived at different predictions as to what might be the religious identity, if any, of their children. On the other hand, a new, very liberal, branch of Judaism, Reconstructionism, joined the Orthodox, Conservative, and Reform movements, and all four labored intensely to ensure that their sense of Jewish identity would continue.

Christianity

Christianity, by far the world's largest religion, with two billion people professing the faith, found itself no longer predominantly European. By the year 2000, somewhat more than one half billion Christians lived in Europe, somewhat less than a half billion in Latin America, somewhat more than a third of a billion in Africa, somewhat less than a third of a billion in Asia, somewhat more than a quarter of a billion in North America, and about 25 million in Oceania. All the years of missionary proselytizing throughout the colonies of Europe reaped an abundant harvest.

Half of this Christian population were Roman Catholics, and half of these lived in Latin America. The election of Polish Cardinal Karol Josef Wojtyla as Pope John Paul II (b. 1920) in 1978 reflected the international diversity of the Roman Church, for he was the first non-Italian Pope since 1523. His career highlighted some of the identity issues in the Catholic Church at the turn of the twenty-first century. First, by selecting a cardinal from behind the "Iron Curtain" the Church was directly giving moral support to the people under the control of the Soviet Union. The communist government was officially atheistic and suppressed religious freedom both in Russia, where Orthodox Christianity had been dominant for a thousand years, and in the eastern and central European countries where Roman Catholicism had been more prominent. The Church, and many others, saw the Cold War not only as a struggle between economic and political systems, but also as a struggle between atheism and religious faith. In his first overseas trip, to Mexico in 1978, John Paul II stressed this theme to a crowd that some estimated at 5 million people, the largest crowd in human history. (In 1995, in Manila, 4 million are estimated to have attended the pope's mass.) In the year after his elevation to the papacy, John Paul II visited Poland to the enthusiastic welcome of millions of his countrymen who saw him as a beacon of hope for greater freedom. Throughout the 1980s, as Lech Walesa organized the Solidarity labor movement in Poland against the government, the pope offered moral support. He began his many travels abroad stressing human rights and the importance of religious and national freedom everywhere. As communism collapsed by the end of the decade, many felt that John Paul II was giving a belated reply to Stalin's sarcastic question about the power of the pope, "How many divisions has *he* got?"

Poland itself had suffered grievously during his lifetime. During World War II the young Karol Wojtyla had been forced to work as a manual laborer, interrupting his university education, and developing a lifelong concern for the welfare of the laboring poor. In his 1987 encyclical *Sollicitudo rei socialis* (On Social Concern) John Paul II pointed to the danger of the ever-widening gap between the rich and poor in all countries. He preached "the right of every individual to the full use of the benefits offered by science and technology" for the good of all people. (In a belated rapprochement with science, in 1984 the Vatican announced that the Church had erred in prosecuting Galileo.) "The voice of the Church, echoing the voice of human conscience . . . deserves and needs to be heard in our time when the growing wealth of a few parallels the growing poverty of the masses" (Lernoux, p. 409). While he was an enemy of atheism and communism, he was no friend of capitalism, which he saw as exploitative of workers. In 1979, at Yankee Stadium in New York City, he denounced the rich of the United States, and of other wealthy countries, for neglecting their poor.

In terms of ecumenical relationships, John Paul II demonstrated his openness to the world by his remarkable record of world travels—to Mexico, the United States, Turkey, India, China, Cuba, Africa, the Philippines, Haiti, Egypt, Israel, and many others—about 100 overseas trips in all, traveling a greater distance than all previous popes combined. He reached out to non-Catholics and non-Christians, especially Jews and Muslims in his trip to the Holy Land in March 2000, and in his meeting with the chief Sunni cleric, the Sheikh al-Azhar in Cairo. He called anti-Semitism a sin and referred to Jews as "our older brothers in faith." He visited Canterbury Cathedral in England, the most important cathedral in the Anglican faith, and Lutheran churches in Germany and Sweden.

The pope's positions were, however, quite complex. His conservative orientation of the Church had already appeared in his rulings on personal, family, and sexual issues. During the meetings of the Second Vatican Council, convened in Rome in 1962 by the much beloved Pope John XXIII (r. 1958–63) to update several of the Church's teachings, the future John Paul II articulated his more conservative positions: opposition to abortion, birth control, the ordination of women as priests, and homosexual practices, and in favor of clerical celibacy. Nevertheless, Catholics around the world practiced birth control to about the same extent as their non-Catholic neighbors, ignoring the Church's teachings on this issue. Meanwhile many other Christian groups were liberalizing their attitudes toward gender differences. For example, the Church of England, founded in part because of King Henry VIII's wish to divorce his first wife, voted to ordain women as priests in 1994. The Episcopalian Church in the United States ordained a female bishop for the first time in 1988 and the first openly gay male bishop in 2003.

John Paul II also took a conservative position on the means of combating poverty. In the late 1960s and 1970s a new school of thought, called liberation theology, was taking shape in Latin America. Identifying with Jesus' ministry to the poor, it began to establish grassroots organizations in poor neighborhoods of cities and in rural pockets of poverty. These *communidades de base* combined study, prayer, and active efforts to identify, define, and solve the problems of their localities by directly confronting them. They challenged local leaders to effect needed change. By the late 1970s, some observers estimated 80,000 *comunidades de base* in Brazil alone.

As liberation theology threatened the state and the wealthy, it confronted powerful opposition forces that were willing to engage in violence if necessary. In March 1980, Archbishop Oscar Romero of El Salvador was assassinated as he was officiating at mass in a San Salvador chapel. The right-wing assassin had opposed the archbishop's message: "When all peaceful means have been exhausted, the church considers insurrection moral and justified" (Keen, p. 595). Romero, who had also advised soldiers that it was morally just to refuse to follow unjust orders, was only one of about 850 Church leaders who had been assassinated since the assassination of Camilo Torres, a priest and sociologist in Colombia. An outstanding scholar and teacher, Torres gave up on peaceful reform and joined Colombia's communist-led guerrillas. He was killed in a battle with government forces in February 1966. In December 1980, three American nuns and a lay missionary who had gone to work with poor refugees in El Salvador were also murdered by security officers of the state.

Radical religion. A priest holds hands with members of the Base Christian Community in Panama. Proponents of liberation theology, which originated in Latin America in the 1960s, typically aligned themselves with left-wing, revolutionary movements, such as the Sandinistas in Nicaragua. When influential priests and bishops espoused a Marxist view of society and argued that the Church's role was to assist the oppressed, they came into conflict with established Catholic authorities as well as political leaders.

The advocates of liberation theology claimed to combine Christian ethics with Marxist politics, and Pope John Paul II, raised in communist Poland, rejected this confrontational Marxist orientation toward class struggle. As new posts opened, he appointed mostly conservative clergy, and as a result the clergy in Latin America were deeply split. About 20 percent aligned themselves with liberation theology, but the overwhelming majority, especially in Brazil, aligned themselves with the new orientation of Rome and rejected this level of activism. Some critics claim that the pope's opposition to liberation theology helped open the door to the rapid growth of Protestant evangelical Christianity in Latin America.

Evangelical Christianity

Evangelical Christianity was giving a new face to the world's largest religion especially in the Americas. In 1940 there were barely a million Protestants in all of Latin America; by 2004 there were some 50 million, one-tenth of the total population. About half of them live in Brazil. About 80 to 90 percent of the Protestants are Pentecostals, appealing usually to the very poorest groups in society, and often to those who have been uprooted from rural areas to the growing cities of the continent. Pentecostals differ from more mainstream Protestants in their emphasis on direct, personal experience of God and revelation, rather than on the authority of scripture or of the Church hierarchy. Many of these Pentecostal groups are allied with North American churches and often receive assistance from them. Pentecostal religion seems to appeal most to women in Latin America. It often refers to Jesus as Divine Husband and Father, emphasizes male responsibility and chastity, and calls for a "reformation of machismo" in family relationships. Poor women see Pentecostalism improving their lives and the lives of their family.

The Church of Jesus Christ of Latter Day Saints, the Mormon Church, is another North American denomination—although not an evangelical denomination—with growing representation in Latin America. Today, somewhat fewer than half of all Mormons live in the United States, about 5.2 million people, where the faith was founded in the nineteenth century. About a third live in Latin America.

The new Protestant religious groups provide the same kind of support in Latin America that early Christianity did in the Roman Empire: community, cooperation, material assistance, along with spiritual fulfillment, emotional spontaneity, enthusiasm, and even ecstasy. The God of the Pentecostals, like the God of the born-again Christians in the United States, is very near and very personal.

Religion in the United States

Throughout our period, America has been the most formally religious of all industrialized countries, as measured by the proportion of the population who are members of churches and attend them regularly. In the years of the Cold War, Americans proclaimed their religious belief as one of the characteristics that set them in opposition to "godless Communism." By 1960, 95 percent of Americans identified with some religious denomination. In 1954, Congress added the words "under God" to the pledge of allegiance to the flag, and in 1955 required the words "In God we trust" to be included on all American currency. President Eisenhower declared, "our government makes no sense unless it is founded in a deeply felt religious faith—and I don't care what it is." The center of gravity of American religion rested with the "mainline" Churches—Baptists, Episcopalians, Lutherans, Methodists, Presbyterians—each with membership numbering in the millions, and established, formal organizational structures and forms of prayer. That center was expanding to include Roman Catholics, symbolized by the election of John Kennedy as President in 1960. Although generally associated with conservative, status quo politics, much of the American "mainline" religious community was also open enough to support the Reverend Martin Luther King, the African-American Baptist minister, who led the fight for equal rights for blacks and minorities in the 1950s and 1960s.

As American culture began to move in new directions in the 1960s and 1970s, the mainline religious groups were often willing to modify their conservative positions, to become more relativistic, and embrace, accept, or at least tolerate these changes: the anti-Vietnam War protests, the Civil Rights movement, the women's movement, the increased immigration of Latin Americans and Asians, the revolution in sexual mores, the public expression of gay and lesbian lifestyles, and the development of a "counterculture," which embraced drugs, folk and protest music, provocative styles of dress and self-presentation, and freer sexual expression.

Many believing Christians, however, saw the social and cultural habits of America changing beyond recognition. They (re)turned to their Bibles to rediscover the fundamentals of their faith, and decided that America was moving in the wrong direction. These **fundamentalists** began creating more of their own organizations and institutions.

fundamentalist a person who believes in the literal truth of the bible as a revelation from God. Sometimes, more loosely, people of any religion who express intense devotion to their faith.

They certainly had the numbers to do it. A Gallup poll in 1979 showed that one out of three American adults reported a "born-again" conversion, an experience of being touched and changed by a personal encounter with Jesus. 50 percent believed that the Bible was an accurate account of history. 130 million people reported listening to and watching 1300 evangelical Christian radio and television stations.

American demographics enhanced the power of the fundamentalists. Northerners and Midwesterners were moving to the south and southwest. These migrants brought more liberal views into these areas, but at the same time they also absorbed more conservative values. The south began once again to provide Presidents: Carter of Georgia in 1976, Clinton of Arkansas in 1992 and 1996, and Bush of Texas (although he had been born and raised in New England) in 2000. For Carter and Bush, "born-again" experiences figured prominently in their understanding of the world. Bush stated that Jesus Christ was the philosopher most important in formulating his own thinking. A gap of incomprehension was growing between northeastern and west coast religious and cultural liberals on the one hand and southern, southwestern, and midwestern religious fundamentalists and cultural conservatives on the other.

With incomprehension came fear and some confrontation on both sides. The US government besieged for 51 days and finally assaulted the small Branch Davidian religious enclave, an illegally-armed splinter group of the Seventh Day Adventists, directed by David Koresh in Waco, Texas, in 1993, leading to the deaths of four federal agents and more than seventy people inside the compound. Some more violent vigilante groups, including white supremacist groups, began to see the US government as the enemy of individualism and freedom of religion. In Oklahoma City, Timothy McVeigh bombed the federal building in April 1995, killing 168 people.

Islamic Cultural Center, New York City. Religions from around the world were finding new homes in America, often transplanted by new groups of immigrants and supplemented by native-born American converts.

Sexuality and family relations resurfaced as bitterly contested religious issues. The Supreme Court's Roe vs. Wade decision (1973) legalized abortion, but abortion clinics were attacked and burned by people who viewed abortion as murder. Some doctors who performed abortions were murdered, and across the country Planned Parenthood offices and clinics hired armed security personnel for their safety. Feminists like Congresswoman Patricia Schroeder pushed for legal rights through the Equal Rights Amendment. They were opposed, successfully, by anti-feminists like Phyllis Schlafly, who organized within the "Moral Majority" movement of the Reverend Jerry Falwell. Falwell had become the most famous of the evangelists of the 1970s and 1980s. His home congregation in Lynchburg, Virginia, grew to 18,000 members with sixty associate pastors. Its religious services were broadcast on 392 television channels and 600 radio stations.

A few of the leading televangelists were disgraced in public sex scandals involving adultery, consorting with a prostitute without regard to public scrutiny, and accusations of participating in homosexual relationships that they themselves had condemned as sinful. In the early 2000s, the Roman Catholic Church was severely embarrassed by public revelations of the sexual exploitation of children by priests. In dioceses throughout the country, the Church attempted to resolve these issues through increased training, monitoring, and disciplining of its clergy, by public apologies, and by cash payments of restitution to past victims. Sex scandals enveloped President Clinton, who carried on a sexual affair with a young White House intern but publicly denied it for several months. Clinton survived an impeachment trial for perjury, but the serious business of governing the country was neglected during these long proceedings. Clinton's defenders charged that conservatives in the opposition party had fastened on his private behavior in order to cripple him politically.

Pornography became a multi-billion dollar industry involving some of the nation's most reputable companies, distributors like Time Warner and Comcast for home video, and major chains like Marriott and Hilton for hotel distribution. For many Americans, viewing pornography was simply a form of recreation, but to counter the perceived exploitation and degradation of sex, Tim LaHaye, co-founder of the Moral Majority, published *How to Be Happy Though Married* (1968), *Understanding the Male Temperment* (1977), *The Battle for the Family* (1982), and *Sex Education in the Family* (1985). His wife Beverley published *The Spirit-Controlled Woman* (1976), *I Am a Woman by*

HOW DO WE KNOW?

Perspectives on Religious Identity in the United States

Two recent studies of religious identity in the United States have painted contrasting pictures. Diana Eck celebrates an ever-increasing array of new and different religious communities. After noting the increasing diversity of their congregations and services in her Cambridge neighborhood, Eck sent her Harvard students to explore more systematically, first around Boston and then in their hometowns across America. In her book, A New Religious America, she reports the results of this Pluralism Project, exploring the extent to which "new" religions—especially Hinduism, Buddhism, and Islam, are appearing in America. She links her findings directly to the recent global migrations that are bringing about a million new immigrants to America every year:

> The immigrants of the last three decades . . . have expanded the diversity of our religious life dramatically, exponentially. Buddhists have come from Thailand, Vietnam, Cambodia, China, and Korea; Hindus from India, East Africa, and Trinidad; Muslims from Indonesia, Bangladesh, Pakistan, the Middle East, and Nigeria, Sikhs and Jains from India; and Zoroastrians from both India and Iran. Immigrants from Haiti and Cuba have brought Afro-Caribbean traditions, blending both African and Catholic symbols and images. New Jewish immigrants have come from Russia and the Ukraine, and the internal diversity of American Judaism is greater than ever before. The face of American Christianity has also changed with large Latino, Filipino, and Vietnamese Catholic communities; Chinese, Haitian, and Brazilian Pentecostal communities; Korean Presbyterians, Indian Mar Thomas, and Egyptian Copts. In every city in the land church signboards display the meeting times of Korean or Latino congregations that nest within the walls of old urban Protestant and Catholic churches.

Karen Armstrong's cross-cultural study of militant fundamentalist movements in Islam in Egypt and Iran, in Judaism in Israel, and in Christianity in the United States, paints a very different picture. Armstrong spent seven years as a nun, then became a college professor, and during the past two decades has become one of the most respected writers on religious history, especially on Christianity, Islam, and Judaism and their relations to one another. Her reflections on fundamentalist Christianity in the United States suggest very little flexibility, compromise, or openness to new religious groups:

> Fundamentalism is not going to disappear. In America, religion has long shaped opposition to government. Its rise and fall has always been cyclical, and events of the last few years indicate that there is still a state of incipient warfare between conservatives and liberals which has occasionally become frighteningly explicit. In 1992, Jerry Falwell, who still adheres to the old-style fundamentalism, announced that with the election of Bill Clinton to the presidency, Satan had been let loose in the United States. Clinton, Falwell thundered, was about to destroy the military and the nation by letting "the gays" take over. Executive orders permitting abortion in federally funded clinics, research on fetal tissue, the official endorsement of homosexual rights, were all signs that America "had declared war on God."

How can we reconcile these very different perspectives on religious identity in contemporary America? Philip Jenkins, in his study of the global expansion of Christianity suggests that we consider the demographics:

> The number of adherents of non-Christian religions in the United States is strikingly small. If we combine the plausible estimates for the numbers of American Jews, Buddhists, Muslims, and Hindus, then we are speaking of about 4 or 5 percent of the total population.

This proportion is not so different from western Europe where non-Christians form about 10 percent of the population of France, 4 percent of Britain, and 5 percent of Germany and the Netherlands. In many African and Asian nations, religious minorities make up 10 to 20 percent of the population, and in some cases even more. The same questions that attend religious diversity in many other countries of the world appear also in the USA.

So Eck's celebratory report is restricted to a very small, and perhaps not quite so remarkable, proportion of the population. On the other hand, Armstrong's fundamentalists also do not make up an American majority. In a 1984 poll, only 9, percent of Americans identified themselves as "fundamentalists," although "44 percent believed that salvation comes only through Jesus Christ."

Religious identity is important to most people in America. Both new immigration and "old time religion" are having their effects on shaping it. The results of this amalgam are not yet clear. As Eck remarks, "diversity alone does not constitute pluralism . . . whether we are able to work together across the lines of religious difference to create a society in which we actually know one another remains to be seen."

- What other historical examples can you give of national religious identity changing under the influence of new immigrant groups?
- What other historical examples can you give of new religious identities clashing with older established ones?
- Do you think that demographics is the main reason for the differences in perception about American religious life as represented by Eck and Armstrong? What other reasons can you suggest?

God's Design (1980), and The Restless Woman (1984). Together they published The Act of Marriage: The Beauty of Sexual Love (1976). For these fundamentalist religious authors, same-sex marriage, approved in Massachusetts in 2004 (and legal in the Netherlands since 2000), was unthinkable.

Fundamentalist books and films captured huge audiences. From 1995 to 2004, Tim LaHaye and Jerry B. Jenkins published twelve volumes in the "Left Behind" series, which describes the last days on earth before the second coming of Jesus Christ. According to *Newsweek Magazine*, the books sold a total of 62 million copies. Mel Gibson's film *The Passion of the Christ* (2004) touched a chord among believers, grossing $368 million in the first three months following its release in February 2004, although no major studio had been willing to distribute it and most major film reviewers criticized the film for excessive violence in depicting Jesus' crucifixion.

Despite the continuing power of the mainline Churches and of the rising visibility of the "born-again" fundamentalists, secularism and non-affiliation also increased in the period 1990 to 2001. The percentage of adults who reported their religious identity as Christian dropped from 86 to 76. The number of adults who did not subscribe to any religion doubled from 14.3 million to 29.4 million, from 8 percent to 14 percent of the total population. Another 5 percent were unwilling to answer survey questions about their religious identity posed by the American Religious Identification Survey of the Graduate Center of the City University of New York, in 2001, up from 2 percent in 1990. While 80 percent of the population did claim some religious identity, only 54 percent reported that they lived in a household where at least one member belonged to a formal religious institution of worship. This quiet decline in religious affiliation, quite different from the very public pronouncements of the religious evangelists, suggested that perhaps, beneath the surface, America was moving in the direction of European countries, with their much lower proportions of religious affiliation.

New immigrants brought yet another, international, dimension to American religious identity, increasing its diversity and cosmopolitanism. As Hindus and Sikhs immigrated from India; Muslims from the Middle East and Pakistan; Buddhists from Southeast Asia; and other religious groups from elsewhere, American religious identity broadened. The new immigrants and their native born children sometimes encountered xenophobia, but they enriched and extended religious identity and ethnic identity in the United States. They made up only about 7 to 8 percent of the total population, but with their mosques, temples, sanctuaries, and church announcement boards in non-European languages, they added an extremely visible new dimension to American religious identity. That identity continues in flux.

GLOBALIZATION: NEW ECONOMIC AND CULTURAL IDENTITIES

Increasing communication technology, free market capitalism, and decreasing government regulation made "globalization" the buzzword of the turn of the twenty-first century. Technologies, markets, and nations were being brought together:

> in a way that is enabling individuals, corporations and nation-states to reach around the world farther, faster, deeper and cheaper than ever before, and in a way that is also producing a powerful backlash from those brutalized or left behind by this new system. (Friedman, 1999, pp. 7–8)

Economically, globalization thrives on inexpensive transportation and communication. Politically, it requires freedom of movement of goods, services, capital, knowledge, and people across borders, although the freedom of people to move is more restricted than the other categories. It functions with little regard to international borders, rules, and regulations; it creates new institutions for working independently of them. It increases the level of interaction of peoples, producing new and different social and cultural forms. It brings increased travel and tourism, brings more world music and literature, as well as new dimensions of international economic investment. It allows billions of dollars of investment capital to move across the globe at the stroke of a computer keypad. The sums are staggering, and increasing. In 1990, total private capital for investment going from the United States, Japan, and the European Union totaled $43.9 billion; in 1997, $299 billion. In 2001, the US alone invested a total of $114 billion overseas. According to the World Trade Organization, total exports of merchandise and commercial services worldwide reached $6.5 trillion in 1997. US trade alone in 2000 reached $2.7 trillion.

Globalization evokes passionate responses both pro and con. Under its umbrella, local and global identities meet and interact with one another and both identities are modified in the process. Usually both become more flexible, but sometimes, people and groups resist modification and change. They insist on keeping their identity as "pure" as possible. We have seen examples of both of these reactions at the beginning of this chapter. Pessimists argue that globalization threatens to homogenize the world's cultures into a single "McDonald's" culture and to replace its many languages with a single, dominant global language, English. Optimists assert that globalization provides communication networks that allow small, niche cultures, languages, and organizations to flourish. At the international level, globalization may appear uniform and corporate, but at the local level it may encourage the evolution of enriched economic and cultural patterns.

Although many advocates of globalization claim that its home is the entire world and its benefits are equally accessible to everyone, more critical observers see it headquartered in the United States, and spread not only by America's businesses but also by its effective control over the World Bank and related global financial institutions. They see globalization as just one more measure of the superpower status of the United States.

The Internet and the World Wide Web

The technologies of globalization are computerization, satellite communication, the internet, and the world wide web. The growth of these communication networks is astounding. The first modern, practical computers were created during and immediately after World War II, at first based on vacuum tubes and then in the late 1950s on transistors. The first integrated-circuit based computer was marketed by IBM in 1965. The internet was created by the United States Defense Department in 1969 as an intricate web of tens of thousands of computer networks linked by telephone lines to expedite communication within the government and related agencies, and to provide emergency backup in case other communication means failed. Commercial service began in the 1980s when the US National Science Foundation created facilities for connecting private computer networks to government networks. The first computer virus was created by a Cornell University graduate student in 1988. In 1989 Tim Berners-Lee, a British scientist working in a nuclear energy laboratory in Geneva, posted a message to an internet newsgroup announcing the "World Wide Web (www) Project," a kind of electronic public access bulletin board. In 1993 an American, Marc Andreeson, developed a new form of browser that made the WWW accessible to the general public. Both of these inventors allowed their inventions to be used without charge, making the WWW essentially a free service.

In 1994, some 3 million people were connected to the internet worldwide; by mid-1999, 200 million. By 2002, the number of users had risen to 650 million worldwide, including 166 million Americans. About 35 percent of the users claimed English as their native tongue; about 12 percent Chinese. The internet became "the fastest growing form of media in history" (*New York Times Almanac*, 2000, p. 816).

HOW DO WE KNOW?

Evaluating Globalization

Globalization—in the sense of global networks of economic, political, and cultural exchange—is not new. We have seen examples throughout this text going back thousands of years. The increasing sophistication of transportation and communication, especially the computer, the internet, and the world wide web, however, have given globalization far greater scope in the last two decades than ever before. As the power of globalization has increased over the past fifteen years, its evaluations have become more careful and more nuanced.

Thomas Friedman, chief foreign political correspondent for the New York Times, introduced his highly influential The Lexus and the Olive Tree with a sense of the inevitability of globalization:

> I feel about globalization a lot like I feel about the dawn. Generally speaking, I think it's a good thing that the sun comes up every morning. It does more good than harm. But even if I didn't much care for the dawn there isn't much I could do about it. I didn't start globalization. I can't stop it—except at a huge cost to human development—and I'm not going to waste time trying. All I want to think about is how I can get the best out of this new system, and cushion the worst, for the most people. (p. xviii)

Joseph Stiglitz, Nobel Prize winner in Economics, served for a number of years as vice president and chief economist of the World Bank. Stiglitz came away from the experience appalled by the failures of globalization and the hardships it often inflicted, especially on the poor. His powerful critique, Globalization and its Discontents, differs sharply from Friedman's general acceptance of the system:

> I have written this book because while I was at the World Bank, I saw firsthand the devastating effect that globalization can have on developing countries, and especially the poor within those countries. I believe that globalization—the removal of the barriers to free trade and the closer integration of national economies—can be a force for good and that it has the potential to enrich everyone in the world, particularly the poor. But I also believe that if this is to be the case, the way globalization has been managed, including the international trade agreements that have played such a large role in removing those barriers and the policies that have been imposed on developing countries in the process of globalization, need to be radically rethought. (pp. ix–x)
>
> Today, few—apart from those with vested interests who benefit from keeping out the goods produced by the poor countries—defend the hypocrisy of pretending to help developing countries by forcing them to open up their markets to the goods of the advanced industrial countries while keeping their own markets protected, policies that make the rich richer and the poor more impoverished—and increasingly angry. (p. xv)

Professor of politics Manfred Steger introduces Rethinking Globalism by denying the inevitability of globalization—despite Friedman's assertions—and arguing for his own vision of an egalitarian, peaceful world order as a guideline for world economic planning:

> The contributors to this volume are united in their conviction that globalization is an incipient process, slowly giving rise to new forms of globality whose eventual qualities and properties are far from being determined. Globalization is neither inevitable nor irreversible; it does not necessarily have to mean or to be what globalists say it means or is . . . The central task for scholars committed to a study of the ideological dimensions of globalization lies in offering both the general public and the academic community thoughtful analyses and critiques of globalism, the dominant ideology of our time . . . Hence, a "critical theory of globalization" is explicitly guided by a normative vision—the ideal of a more egalitarian and less violent global order. (pp. 10–11)

- What experience has each author had in defining, evaluating, and implementing globalization?
- To what degree is each author dogmatic in his evaluation of globalization? What dogmas does he seem to accept or to reject?
- To what extent can you begin, on the bases of these authors' suggestions, to formulate your own values in evaluating globalization? On the bases of these introductions, which of the three books do you think you would find most interesting? Most useful?
- How do the ideas of George Soros, discussed in our text above, compare with those of these authors?

In 1999, the file-sharing service Napster became available, allowing users to exchange files, including music, without need of copyright. Millions used this service until a court ruled Napster illegal in 2001. Users shifted to other file-sharing services, but the courts continued to investigate them for breach of copyright. Within the computer and the music industries fierce battles were underway to determine how copyrights would or would not be implemented when technology had created such new means of access to materials virtually without cost. By April 2002, one billion personal computers had been manufactured since the first one in 1975. Among the ten wealthiest Americans in 2003, according to *Forbes Magazine*, four had amassed their fortunes in the computer industry, led by Bill Gates with $46 billion. (Four others were heirs of Sam Walton of Walmart.) With the internet and world wide web, shopping, research, and accessing documents could all be done while sitting in front of a computer at home or in an

Before the silicon chip. Immediately after World War II, when the first practical computers were constructed, advances in information theory and the invention of the transistor gave birth to such hulking monsters as ENIAC, developed at the University of Pennsylvania in 1946. It weighed 50 tons and occupied 2000 square feet of floor space.

office, or even from a portable computer while traveling. E-mail, another facility of the internet, made instantaneous global communication available at nominal cost.

Many people lost their jobs to more efficient and cost-effective technology-based organizations, and many with less education were threatened by economic organizations that required ever more training. In the United States and globally, the new technologies increased the gap between rich and poor, as those who access and guide the technological transformation did well, but many others were left behind. Poor nations are also left farther behind as the rich nations, notably the United States, were richer. Moreover, because the new technologies were dependent on research laboratories, these facilities, especially in the United States, continued to attract talented, skilled persons, draining them from less technologically sophisticated nations. To some degree this was offset by new employment opportunities. New, communications-related jobs are foot-loose, and many highly skilled jobs were being outsourced to third-world countries, where salaries were lower. For example, Bangalore and Hyderabad, cities in India, became miniature "Silicon Valleys" through the investments of multinational companies like IBM, Texas Instruments, and Microsoft, and through the entrepreneurship of local information technology experts. Here, highly skilled personnel earned salaries far higher than most local salaries, yet substantially below those of the US, the European Union, and Japan. These salary differentials helped drive the constant flow of investment capital, goods, and labor around the globe.

Disparities, Disruptions, and Crises: A Cautionary Tale from Asia

Average living standards around the world have been improving. During the 1990s the proportion of people suffering from extreme poverty fell from 30 to 23 percent (*Human Development Report*, p. 5), in large part thanks to the improvements in China's economy. The disparities between rich and poor are increasing, however, as often happens when new sources of wealth become available for private development. In 1996, the poorest 20 percent of the world's population received only 1.4 percent of the world's income, down from 2.3 percent in 1966; the richest 20 percent received 85 percent, up from 70 percent (statistics from *United Nations Development Report*, p. 80). Poverty can increase even in conditions that are improving overall. "Over the past two decades [1983–2003] income inequality worsened in 33 of 66 developing countries with data" (*Human Development Report*, p. 5).

Whole regions of the world could rise and fall economically by abrupt shifts in global investment patterns as the countries of East and Southeast Asia discovered at the turn of the twenty-first century. Following Japan's model of development (see Chapter 21), the countries of East and Southeast Asia experienced extraordinary growth. Between 1965 and 1996, the average annual growth of the GNP for the world as a whole was 3.1 percent. For South Korea it was 8.9 percent; Singapore, 8.3; Hong Kong, 7.5; Thailand, 7.3; Indonesia, 6.7; Malaysia, 6.8; the Philippines, 3.5. Japan's growth had slowed after its 1989 recession, but still averaged 4.5 percent. China, although it followed different models, grew at 8.5 percent. "Before July 2, 1997 the Asian Pacific was considered, rightly, to be the world's success story of economic development and technological modernization of the past half-century" (Castells, Vol. 3, p. 206).

Then the currency of Thailand fell sharply, as investors recognized that the national economy was not expanding as rapidly as incoming investment and loans, and the country had a mounting trade deficit. The values of land and industry on which the loans and investments had been based were artificially inflated, and they collapsed, as did the value of Thai currency. Investments stopped abruptly and loans were recalled, first from Thailand and then from neighboring countries with similar financial problems. South Korea, Thailand, Indonesia, Malaysia, and the Philippines, which had seen $93 billion in net investments enter their countries in 1996, saw $12 billion leave in 1997. In the space of a few months entire national economies collapsed and others went into a deep recession. Japan, the world's second largest economy, suffered financial bankruptcies and the devaluation of its stocks and bonds.

What had happened? The Asian economies had been doing many things right. They had budget surpluses, low inflation, high rates of savings, and substantial exports. But they had taken on more loans, especially short-term loans, than their productivity justified, and as collateral they had presented real estate, which was dramatically and unrealistically overpriced. Beyond this, their internal financial systems were not "transparent"—that is, not open to external analysis and evaluation. Presumably they were hiding some important information. (Similar problems had surfaced in Japan after the 1989 "bubble" burst.) Corrupt politicians, bureaucrats, bankers, and organized crime leaders were guiding investments inappropriately, for their own benefit, and covering up their actions. Meanwhile investment money and loans poured in from overseas. The monies were misused, pocketed, or poorly invested in speculation, until finally the economies collapsed.

The governments, which had been so helpful as their economies had grown, were now not strong enough to bail out the failing banks and industries. (In the United States, in the 1980s, the government had spent $250 billion bailing out savings and loans associations that had made bad investments.) The system of government direction, which had produced economic miracles, now left a wake of recession and depression. Those that had relied less on international funds and that had paid more attention to basic business fundamentals—like Taiwan and Singapore—had fewer troubles; those that had taken in the most foreign loans and investments and had invested least prudently—like South Korea, Indonesia, and Thailand—were most affected.

The International Monetary Fund came to the rescue in some of these countries with massive loans, but the very arrival of the IMF frightened off other investors, who saw this as a sign of economic insolvency. Also the IMF was more concerned with recovering its loans and investments than with the economic health of the defaulting country. It implemented the "Washington consensus": opening the borders to international investment (although this was already in place and had caused some of the problems), lowering or removing tariffs against imports, privatizing (selling off) government businesses, reducing government welfare programs, laying off government employees, and devaluing local currency. All these measures are the instruments of classical, conservative economic theory, although many economists argued that these measures had never been rigidly enforced in the economies of wealthy countries. The IMF virtually took over control of the economy of the defaulting country. It demanded a regimen of economic austerity so severe that it jeopardized the health and welfare of the citizens of the country. This was the experience in South Korea in 1997, which accepted a bail-out loan of $58 billion, the largest ever in the history of the IMF.

Some international bankers, like billionaire George Soros, saw the need for countries to be more honest and more transparent. They argued that state guidance and regulations should be cut back as national economies grew and that private enterprise should be given more scope. But they also argued that some regulation was needed at the international level. Trillions of dollars in investment funds were swirling around the globe without guidance or tracking or common purpose, battering the economies of all but the largest states. As Soros argued:

> The world has entered a period of profound imbalance in which no individual state can resist the power of global financial markets and there are practically no institutions for rule-making on an international scale. Collective decision-making mechanisms for the global economy simply do not exist . . . In short we need a global society to support our global economy. A global society does not mean a global state. To abolish the existence of states is neither feasible nor desirable; but insofar as there are collective interests that transcend state boundaries, the sovereignty of states must be subordinated to international law and international institutions.

Capital markets had become global, but the national and international institutions for keeping them honest and transparent had not. This was the great institutional deficiency now exposed by the experience of East and Southeast Asia. After several years of suffering and of economic restructuring, these countries have mostly recovered their former economic health, and some like Korea and Singapore have pushed far ahead. Their experience, however, highlights the dangers of global capital movements and of wishful thinking.

Opposition to Globalization

In December 1999, the World Trade Organization (WTO), the United Nations' agency for setting the terms of international trade, met in Seattle, Washington. Protestors blocked the streets of this normally tranquil city and demonstrated dramatically their apprehensions at the increasing tempo of world trade and their demands for more regulation by national governments and by the United Nations. Many of the protestors argued that they favored world trade, but with some regulations to provide protection for the environment, human rights, labor, and children's welfare. They feared that the demands for profits would overrun these humanitarian concerns. Similarly, many national and religious groups feared that the spread of powerful global communications systems would overwhelm their unique cultures. Few such groups wished to stop globalization entirely, but they sought limits and restraints that would protect their cherished identities and interests.

Similar protests have stalked subsequent meetings of the WTO and of other groups promoting globalization in Davos, Switzerland, Salzburg, Austria, Bangkok, Thailand, Melbourne, Australia, Quebec City, Canada, Gothenburg, Sweden, and elsewhere. In August 2001, over 100,000 gathered in Genoa, Italy, to protest at the meeting of the G-8, the leaders of the eight most prominent economically advanced countries. The meeting was protected by 16,000 police and military police. In a tense confrontation, one of the protestors was shot to death.

In 2001, a new umbrella organization of protestors took form as the World Social Forum. They held their first meeting in Porto Alegre, Brazil, in January 2001, attracting thousands of delegates. The 2002 meeting took place in Florence, Italy; 2003 in Paris, France; 2004 in Mumbai (Bombay), India. At first, many of the costs of the meetings were underwritten by major international foundations, but both the foundations and the participants came to believe that this funding undercut the populist nature of the sessions. Although many groups gathered to protest a wide array of perceived injustices, the main goal of the Forum was to find alternative political and economic models to those that dominate the world today. The Forum seeks new paradigms, new policies, and new identities for world development.

At the dawn of the twenty-first century, we are witnessing a global balancing act between rapidly expanding technological capabilities, the desire for economic profits, the need to protect human rights, a passion to preserve group identities, and the uncertain power of the state to intervene on behalf of those contentious interests. The balancing act in itself is not new, but its global pervasiveness is.

The Global Criminal Economy

Just as the global economy is part of our reality and identity, so transnational, organized crime is also part of that reality and identity. For transnational organized crime is big business. Although carried out against the law, and therefore requiring special under-the-table arrangements with law officers and government officials, transnational crime employs many of the same information networks as does legal business.

The scale and scope of the illegal economy is staggering. Drugs are the largest segment, nuclear weapons perhaps the newest and most frightening. Because these activities are illegal, estimates of their size varies. "The 1994 United Nations Conference on Global Organized Crime estimated that global trade in drugs amounted to about $500 billion a year; that is, it was larger than the global trade in oil" (Castells, Vol. 3, p. 172). The leader of the Medellin drug cartel in Colombia, Pablo Escobar, was a billionaire, listed in *Forbes Magazine* as the world's seventh richest man (although he was killed by Colombian security forces in 1993). Overall profits from all kinds of organized international criminal activities were estimated at between $750 billion and $1 trillion a year. Sociologist Manuel Castells lists some of the leading participants in this vast global market place:

> Crime is as old as humankind. But global crime, the networking of powerful criminal organizations, and their associates, in shared activities throughout the planet, is a new phenomenon that profoundly affects international and national economies, politics, security, and ultimately, societies at large. The Sicilian Cosa Nostra (and its associates, La Camorra, Ndrangheta, and Sacra Corona Unita), the American Mafia, the Colombian cartels, the Mexican cartels, the Nigerian criminal networks, the Japanese Mafiyas, the Turkish heroin traffickers, the Jamaican Posses, and a myriad of regional and local criminal groupings in all countries [including the Chinese Triads and the Japanese Yakuza whom he discusses later], have come together in a global, diversified network that permeates boundaries and links up ventures of all sorts. While drugs traffic is the most important segment of this worldwide industry, arms deals also represent a high-value market. (Castells, Vol. 3, pp. 166–7)

The 1994 United Nations Conference cited seven major forms of international organized crime.

Drugs The most widespread and the largest of all illicit international businesses in terms of volume of business and profits are drugs of various kinds. Their major sources include Colombia and Mexico in Latin America, Thailand and Myanmar in Southeast Asia, and Afghanistan in Central Asia. In some of these countries, notably Colombia and Afghanistan, control of the drug trade has given regional warlords the power to challenge and sometimes to control the central government. Synthetic drugs,

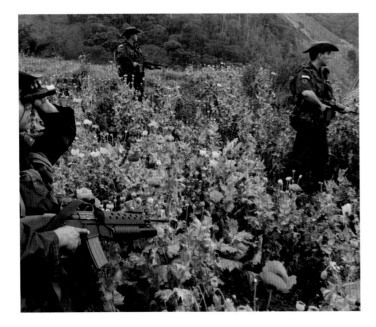

Colombian anti-narcotics police in a poppy field, El Silencio, Colombia, 2002. This area was once the safe haven of rebels from the Revolutionary Armed Forces of Columbia (FARC). They controlled the area from 1998 until 2002 during failed attempts to find a peaceful settlement between them and the government.

such as LSD and Ecstasy, are more commonly made in the United States and Europe.

Smuggling of Illegal Immigrants In 2000, this "human cargo" was estimated at 4 million people per year, and its profits at $5 to $7 billion. It represents a new form of slavery. Estimates of illegal migrants from Latin America—especially Mexico—into the United States are about one million each year. Through the 1990s, illegal immigration into the European Union rose to an estimated half-million persons per year.

Trafficking in Women and Children Most of this illegal commerce is for sexual slavery, mostly from Southeast Asia, but with an increasing number of women coming from Russia and eastern Europe after the fall of the Soviet Union. Some of the women travel voluntarily, but many are abducted or deceived or deeply in debt and are then sold. Because they are watched closely so that they cannot escape their condition and their debts, their position is different from that of a sex worker who works voluntarily for payment. A report in the *New York Times Magazine* in early 2004 asserts the existence of a very significant trade in women being brought either by force or through false promises from Russia and eastern Europe via Mexico into the United States. A growing traffic in children for adoption has also arisen, especially from Latin America to the United States. The babies and children are often sold with the consent of their parents, but sometimes they are kidnapped.

Trafficking in Body Parts The modern medical miracle of organ transplants has also inspired a new criminal industry: trafficking in body parts. Sometimes these parts are taken from corpses, without permission from the family. Some of these may be unclaimed bodies in morgues. Particularly extensive practices have been reported from Russia. The Chinese government apparently routinely harvests the organs of criminals who have been executed and keeps the profits for the government. In Japan, loan sharks are reported to have demanded body organs in repayment of overdue debts. Less commonly, and more clearly criminal, the organs may be stolen in surgical operations performed without consent—as the recent film *Dirty Pretty Things* portrayed graphically.

The greatest problem has been the harvesting of the organs—kidneys, for example—of the living poor for the benefit of transplant recipients who can afford to pay for them. In this "organ bazaar," the "donors" may sell their organs to pay their way out of debt. "Transplant tourism" has emerged. "Affluent transplant tourists can travel to select medical sites in Turkey, eastern Europe, Cuba, Germany and the United States in search of transplants that they cannot arrange quickly or safely enough at home" (Scheper-Hughes, p. 3). To "explore the social and economic context of organ transplantation, focusing on the human rights implications of the desperate, world-wide search for organs," a team of anthropologists, human rights activists, physicians, and social medicine specialists has founded "Organs Watch" at the University of California, Berkeley. Its reports chart recent developments.

Money Laundering In 1999, the International Monetary Fund estimated global money laundering between $.5 trillion and $1.5 trillion. The range, as well as the amount, give some sense of the size of the business. "Laundering" is the process by which illegal profits are disguised as legal. The first step is to deposit them in banks or other financial institutions that do not inquire as to their source. Such banks are located in small countries—for example, Panama, Aruba, the Cayman Islands, and the Bahamas—that do little to control banking procedures. Once in these banks, the funds can be transferred electronically to other financial institutions and invested in legitimate businesses. This network link between the worlds of illegal and legal business gives the world of illegal business its power and viability. Launderers may earn up to 25 percent of the total value of the transaction.

Weapons Trafficking Most weapons sales are legal, but sales to nations under international embargo—for example, Iran, Iraq, and Libya—are not. Nor are sales to guerrilla groups, partisans in civil wars, and terrorist groups. Some of the weapons for sale are remnants of Cold War stocks first supplied to their clients by the United States and Russia. Others are newly produced weapons. As in illegal transactions generally, these illicit arms sales earn great profits because of the need for secrecy and pay-offs.

Trafficking in Nuclear Materials From the early 1990s this threat was especially severe from the stocks of nuclear materials in the Soviet Union and its eastern European allies. Enormous stockpiles were in storage. Security was light. Demand was great. And some one hundred thousand workers connected with nuclear production and storage were receiving very inadequate pay, and sometimes were not paid at all, as the economies of eastern Europe collapsed. As disarmament continued, more material was likely to be available and the risks have probably increased. After the 9/11 terror attack in the United States, fears also increased that nuclear materials might pass not only to the hands of states, but also to the hands of terrorist organizations.

As additional nations have entered into the "nuclear club," illegal sales of weapons-grade nuclear materials are increasing. In February 2004, Dr. Abdul Qadeer Khan, the "father" of Pakistan's nuclear bomb, announced publicly that he had personally been operating an international black market in weapons-grade nuclear materials. This confession made public what had been an open secret for almost two decades, that Pakistan had been involved in such nuclear transfers. Although both Khan and Pakistan's president, Pervez Musharraf, denied that the government of Pakistan was involved in the nuclear materials sales, no serious observer believed that such operations could be carried out by a single individual.

The illegal trafficking of women, Xiamen, China, 2003. A Chinese man is here detained in a police van with women whom he has been accused of trying to smuggle to Taiwan.

Pakistan's activities in the nuclear market place suggested that countries like Libya and Iran would be able to acquire and assemble nuclear weapons— although Libya offered to give up its quest for nuclear weaponry in early 2004. Perhaps Islamic nations—and perhaps private armies—would benefit most from Pakistan's technology and sales, but more comprehensively, the entire network of nuclear transactions around the world would be encouraged. A Pakistani weapons expert, disturbed by his country's entry into the international bazaar, described the nuclear marketplace: "Once they had the bomb, they had a shopping list of what to buy and where. A.Q. Khan can bring a plain piece of paper and show me how to get it done—the countries, people, and telephone numbers. 'This is the guy in Russia who can get you small quantities of enriched uranium. You in Malaysia will manufacture the stuff. Here's who will miniaturize the warhead. And then go to North Korea and get the damn missile.' ... This is not a few scientists pocketing money and getting rich. It's a state policy."

International networks played an increasingly important role in the global criminal economy. Through the 1960s, 1970s, and 1980s, and even into the 1990s, specific criminal groups worked through their own localized networks. The most famous perhaps were the two drug cartels based in Colombia—one in Cali, the other in Medellin, each with its own leaders and policies—and the Russian mafia, much of it Jewish, seizing new opportunities offered by the breakdown of Communist Party control over the Russian economy. By 1997, Russian and Colombian criminal organizations were forging alliances in the Caribbean. The Russians offered access to new drug markets in eastern Europe to the Colombians, who sought, in exchange, heavy equipment that would enable them to protect and deliver their drugs, including a submarine, armored helicopters, surface-to-air missiles that would let them attack government helicopters, and small arms. The Russians also opened banks in the Caribbean and strip clubs in south Florida that would facilitate money laundering. Each of the groups retained a high degree of internal secrecy and cohesion, but networked to take advantage of the opportunities offered by the other.

In 2000 the United Nations adopted a "Convention against Transnational Organized Crime," the first legally binding UN instrument in the field of crime. The convention suggests ways of improving international cooperation against crime that crosses national borders and legal systems. It considers the laws of extradition, provides for witness protection and for shielding legal businesses from investments by illegal businesses. Signatories to the convention are required to establish domestic criminal laws against: participating in an organized criminal group; money laundering; corruption; and obstruction of justice. Additional protocols were adopted to combat the smuggling of migrants, and the buying and selling of women and children for sexual exploitation or sweatshop labor. Another protocol under consideration would address the illicit manufacture of and traffic in firearms that supported civilian, terrorism, and organized crime. The battles between the forces of law and order and the organizations of internationally organized crime were, however, far from over. As a senior American enforcement official told a *Washington Post* reporter, "American law enforcement is not organized to fight this threat. We are in for a long, long battle, and we are sort of outnumbered at this point." The law enforcement agencies of other nations were no better equipped for the international battleground.

Medicine, Science, and Global Ecology

People are living longer. Many factors contribute: more and better food for many (but not all); better public sanitation and health; cleaner cities and streets; more focused and effective medicines; more thorough medical care. Globally, the average life expectancy for females rose from 52 in 1960 to 65 in 1980, to 68.5 in 2000. Male life expectancy also rose steadily, although it lagged behind female: 49 in 1960 to 61 in 1980 to 65 in 2000. In this forty-year period, people in low-income countries gained about sixteen years of life expectancy, those in high-income countries gained about nine years, because they started from a higher base. In 1960, people in low-income countries had lived about twenty-six years less than those in high-income countries; in 2000, only about eighteen years less. In 2003, Japan had reached the highest average longevity rates in the world: 77.6 for males; 84.4 for females. These increasingly high rates of longevity, combined with declining birth rates, especially in wealthy countries, meant that as people reached old age, they would constitute a large proportion of the population, and they would require care from the decreasing proportion of younger people. The way in which younger and older people estimated their mutual rights and obligations was undergoing a change, although no one knew how it would work out.

In countries where parents had a preference of one sex over another in their children—usually preferring males over females—new medical procedures such as amniocentesis and sonograms were used to determine the sex of fetuses, and females were often aborted. In addition, boy children received better care—more and better quality food, medical care, and education—than girls. As a result, sex ratios in such countries as China and India began to shift. No one knew what would be the ultimate effect of having an adult population that had substantially more men than women nor how this would affect men's and women's identities.

Access to medicine and medical care was also becoming an issue, especially in the struggle to bring the global AIDS epidemic under control. When AIDS first appeared as a health threat in the late 1970s, no drugs were available for treatment, and the disease was deemed to be fatal. By the end of 2002, approximately 28 million people had died of the disease and 42 million more were infected. By 1996, various drugs were found to be effective in inhibiting the development of the disease, but the drugs were very expensive. In the third world, where 95 percent of the cases occur—70 percent in sub-Saharan Africa—the drugs are prohibitively expensive.

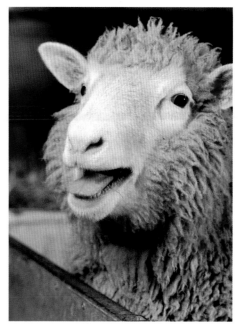

Dolly, the cloned sheep, 1997. Genetic engineering offered great hopes for increasing longevity, health, and food supplies, but it enters a new, unknown world of biological transformation that cannot be reversed.

Several issues are emerging from this situation. First, from a humanitarian point of view, AIDS is a dreadful killer, and the search is on for more effective ways of preventing, inhibiting, and curing it. Second, in the face of such pervasive death, especially concentrated in sub-Saharan Africa, where as much as 25 percent of the population is infected in some states, fear is increasing that the social fabric of the society will unravel. Third, negotiations have been taking place between political and humanitarian leaders and drug companies to manufacture the appropriate antiretroviral drugs and make them available at low cost in low-income countries.

Finally, some nations of the world have begun to see the political as well as humanitarian implications of the widespread AIDS epidemic and have pledged their support to fighting it. For example, in May 2003 the United States Congress voted to spend $15 billion to fight AIDS globally, and especially in Africa, although actual allocation of the money has been slow. The question of the cost of drugs will continue to surface in a wide array of contexts—in addition to AIDS—as drug companies discover and create ever newer and more effective drugs, and people live longer and become more reliant on the drugs. How can prices be set high enough to satisfy the needs of drug companies to carry on their business and research with a reasonable profit, and yet low enough so that people can afford the drugs they need? How will the drug companies, drug users, and governments view their obligations to one another?

The biology of human identity came to the center of world attention in 1997 when scientists in Scotland succeeded in cloning a sheep and were experimenting with producing blood in the bodies of animals that could be used for human transfusions. The long-term consequences of such genetic engineering are as yet unknown, but they are permanent, transmitted to every subsequent generation of their recipients, so the procedures are the subject of intense scrutiny and debate. In 1990 the United States government initiated the Human Genome Project to identify all the approximately 100,000 genes in human DNA, and to "map" the sequences of the 3 billion chemical bases that make it up. In June 2000, it announced success, as did a private research laboratory. The next task was to understand the functioning of each component. Here, too, private laboratories were also working aggressively on these puzzles for the new technology promises great wealth to its masters, although the costs to consumers are not yet known. In 2003 the government announced completion of the project as they had found up to 99 percent of the structure of the human genome. The project had taken thirteen years and cost $2.7 billion.

Biologists and biochemists have learned how to substitute one gene for another, yielding astonishing new hybrids of grains that have multiplied food productivity and of animals that are more productive of meat, milk, and even certain chemicals useful in medicine. Genetic engineering in humans promises to cure certain genetically based illnesses like cystic fibrosis, muscular dystrophy, and Huntington's chorea—although this has not yet been accomplished. The science carries the promise, and the threat, of creating humans who are taller or shorter, heavier or lighter, blue eyed or brown. The ethical issues involved in genetic manipulation are as significant as the scientific ones.

ECOLOGICAL ISSUES

In 1990, the United Nations became involved in organizing against global ecological destruction. Many concerns filled the agenda. The main ones were:

- The depletion of the ozone layer through the introduction into the environment of chlorofluorocarbons, a principal chemical in aerosol sprays and in most coolants, such as refrigeration and air-conditioning units;
- Global warming, or the greenhouse effect, caused primarily by the introduction into the environment of carbon dioxide, which traps heat in the earth's lower atmosphere, raising temperatures around the globe;
- The destruction of the marine environment through ocean dumping, ship pollution, and the absorption of chemicals into the water table;
- Acid rain, the pollution of the atmosphere with industrial chemicals that descend with rainfall;
- Deforestation, especially in the tropics, where at least 25 million acres of trees are cut down yearly;
- At a more local level, polluted air, contaminated water, and cigarette smoke that were clearly associated with carcinogens.

Trees destroyed by acid rain, Sebestiana, Czech Republic, 1997. Acid rain is one of several pollutants produced by industry that threaten life and health on our planet.

In general, more developed countries tended to place the blame for ecological problems on the increase in global population, an increase most marked in the less developed countries. The less developed countries, in response, blamed the more developed as the source of the industries that create the pollution. On the issue of world hunger, the developed countries again pointed to population pressures on food supplies in the less developed countries, while the less developed blamed flaws in the world economy and food distribution mechanisms, both controlled by the wealthier countries. Agreement is emerging on the need for international cooperation in a stronger UN environment program, but for the present the United Nations lacks sovereign power. It can gather information, carry out research, make recommendations, hold conferences, and provide counsel, but it has no powers of enforcement. Implementation depends upon the decision of member nations. Local and global identities have not yet merged. Nor have the peoples of the earth yet accepted their obligations to future generations.

PUBLIC IDENTITIES
WHAT DIFFERENCE DO THEY MAKE?

With this chapter we can no longer assess the messages that may be deciphered from the past for the future, for here we are studying contemporary history. We do not have closure. We do not know how events will unfold. We do not know their consequences. As we assess the significance of changing human identities in regard to politics, religion, economics, culture, and the natural world, we use the tools that the study of history has taught us. We learn to weigh evidence, evaluate sources, find appropriate contexts, reckon what seems to us believable on the basis of our understanding of how people and systems work. We use our own identities as touchstones to understand the identities of others. Not that ours and theirs are alike. They are not. But the better we understand our own identities and how they have been formed, the better able we are to understand others. With self-knowledge, with historical tools, with the best evidence we can assemble, we do our best to understand current trends in order to make our way into the future.

Review Questions

- To what extent would you classify the broadcast of the Olympics or World Cup soccer or a Cricket Test Match series or the Baseball World Series as an example of globalization? You may wish to consider political, economic, social, and cultural issues concerning the broadcast.
- What is the nature of religious beliefs that lead some people to claim that their religious belief is their principal identity?
- What is the nature of nationalism that leads some people to claim that their national identity is their principal identity?
- What is the nature of economic systems that leads some people to claim that their economic identity is their principal identity? Please give an example from this text of a person or a group that has proclaimed such an economic identity. How does the economic identity interact with the global identity?
- How do ecological concerns build a global identity? How do they interfere with a global identity?
- In your own life, what do you see as the relationship between local identities and global identities?

Suggested Readings

Appadurai, Arjun. *Modernity at Large* (Minneapolis: University of Minnesota Press, 1996). Global thinking on the cultural implications of modernization, especially on the impact from lesser developed countries to more developed.

Arab Human Development Report 2003: Building a Knowledge Society (New York: United Nations Press, 2003). In this volume, in an annual series, 26 Arab scholars examine the development and dissemination of knowledge in the Arab world and find it lagging. Makes suggestions for improvement. Abundant statistical tables along with qualitative assessments.

Armstrong, Karen. *The Battle for God* (New York: Knopf, 2000). A thoughtful, thorough assessment of religious militancy in Egyptian and Iranian Islam, Israeli Judaism, and American Christian fundamentalism.

Bulliet, Richard W., ed. *The Columbia History of the 20th Century* (New York: Columbia University Press, 1998).

Castells, Manuel. *The Information Age: Economy, Society and Culture*, 3 vols. (Malden, MA: Blackwell, 1996–2000). An amazingly comprehensive assessment of the contemporary global scene, including universal perspectives and local case studies from a wide range of locations.

Chomsky, Noam. *Hegemony or Survival: America's Quest for Global Dominance* (New York: Henry Holt, 2003). A blistering attack on US foreign policy as excessively violent and self-interested, by a foremost American critic.

Duus, Peter. *Modern Japan* (Boston: Houghton Mifflin, 2nd ed., 1998). Summary narrative and interpretation, highly accessible, by a scholarly expert.

Enwezor, Okwui. *The Short Century. Independence and Liberation Movements in Africa 1945–1994* (Munich: Prestel, 2001). History told through art, cloth, posters, photography, architecture, music, theater, literature, and film—as well as a relevant selection of primary documents in politics, ideology, and ethics. The lavish catalogue of a blockbuster museum show. Emphasizes the interweaving of African and Western forms.

Esposito, John. *Unholy War: Terror in the Name of Islam* (New York: Oxford University Press, 2002). Masterful explanation of the role of jihad in Islam historically, and most of all, today. Sees the issue in context, and explains what is and is not Islamic about holy war.

Farah, Douglas, "Russian Mob, Drug Cartels Joining Forces," *Washington Post*, September 29, 1997, A-1. Reports their alliance for mutual business profits and protection. http://www.washingtonpost.com/wp-srv/inatl/longterm/russiagov/stoiries/mafia0902997.html

Freeman, Christopher. "Technology and Invention," in Bulliet, pp. 314–44.

French, Howard. *A Continent for the Taking. The Tragedy and Hope of Africa* (New York: Knopf, 2004). Outstanding journalistic account primarily of west and central Africa. Tragic in its perspective, with lots of responsibility placed on outsiders—Europeans, Americans—as well as on Africans.

Friedman, Robert I. "Land of the Stupid: When You Need a Used Russian Submarine," *New Yorker*. Recounts the career in crime of Ludwig Fainberg, key member of the Russian mafia.

Friedman, Thomas L. *The Lexus and the Olive Tree* (New York: Farrar, Straus, Giroux, 1999). Highly influential, generally favorable, assessment of globalization by the principal foreign affairs correspondent of the *New York Times*.

——. *Longitudes and Attitudes* (New York: Anchor Books, 2003). Selection of articles, mostly on global terrorism and its effects after 9/11, still optimistic, but much more cautious about the direction of globalization.

Fukuyama, Francis. "The End of History?" *National Interest*, Summer 1989, pp. 3–18. An early, highly influential, presentation of the thesis later developed in his book of the same name.

Fukuyama, Francis. *The End of History and the Last Man* (New York: Free Press, 1992). Argues that the combination of democracy and capitalism is proving to be the best system ever devised. Very self-congratulatory concerning the system.

Gibney, Frank. *Japan: The Fragile Superpower* (Tokyo: Charles E. Tuttle, 3rd rev. ed., 1996). Widely read, highly controversial prediction of future armed clashes between religions and ideologies, especially between Christianity and Islam unless increased cross-cultural dialogue takes place. Sees hostility prevailing over accommodation.

Hersh, Seymour M. "Annals of National Security," *The New Yorker*, March 8, 2004. http://newyorker.com/fact/content/?040308fa_fact. Analysis of the nuclear sales conducted by Pakistani nuclear scientist A.Q. Khan and the role of his government and the US government in the process.

Human Development Report 2003: Millennium Development Goals: A Compact among Nations to End Poverty (New York: Oxford University Press, 2003). Published for the United Nations Development Program, looks especially at issues of reducing poverty. Excellent qualitative essays and useful array of statistical tables.

Jenkins, Philip. *The Next Christendom: The Coming of Global Christianity* (New York: Oxford, 2002). Charts the transformation of Christianity from a European to a global religion and speculates on its future.

Keen, Benjamin. *A History of Latin America* (Boston: Houghton Mifflin, 6th ed., 2000).

Khalidi, Rashid. *Resurrecting Empire* (Boston: Beacon Press, 2004). Head of Columbia University's Middle Eastern Institute examines new suggestions that an American imperial policy would be good for the world, and argues that they are incorrect.

Kosmin, Barry and Egon Mayer, "American Religion Identification Survey," Graduate Center of the City University of New York, 2001. http://www.gc.cuny.edu/studies/aris_index.htm

Landesman, Peter, "The Girls Next Door," *New York Times Magazine*, January 5, 2004. Exposes trafficking in women bought and sold as sex slaves, some of them from Russia and eastern Europe, coming via Mexico and ending up in the United States.

Lernoux, Penny. *Cry of the People* (New York: Penguin, 1982). A personal and scholarly account of liberation theology and its effects in Latin America.

Maalouf, Amin. *In the Name of Identity: Violence and the Need to Belong*, trans. from the French by Barbara Bray (New York: Arcade Publishing, 2001). An essay both scholarly and personal on identities that divide and separate people and other identities that provide solidarities, with many historical examples.

McGrath. Alister. *The Future of Christianity* (Oxford: Blackwell, 2002). A personal overview of Christian religious trends worldwide. Emphasizes the increasingly non-European nature of Christianity.

Nash, Gary, *et al. The American People* (New York: Harper Collins, 3rd ed. 1994).

Newsweek Magazine. May 24, 2004, "Religion: The Pop Prophets."

Nye, Joseph S., Jr. *The Paradox of American Power* (New York: Oxford University Press, 2002). International power can be manifest in military, economic, and cultural terms. America at the turn of the century is emphasizing the first two, but losing out in the third.

Scheper-Hughes, Nancy, "The Organ of Last Resort," *The UNESCO Courier* (July/August) 2001.

Soros, George. *The Crisis of Global Capitalism* (New York: Public Affairs, 1998). Soros is a billionaire capitalist who had great respect for the potentials of the system, but also sees the dangers of unregulated behavior. He surveys the system and proposes rules and regulations.

Speth, Gustave. *Red Sky at Morning: America and the Crisis of the Global Environment* (New Haven: Yale University Press, 2004). A sobering assessment of the state of the world's ecology, and of our responsibilities, by a former environmental adviser to Presidents Carter and Clinton.

Steger, Manfred. *Rethinking Globalism* (Lanham, MD: Rowman & Littlefield, 2004). A collection of academic essays generally critical of globalization because of its social and cultural effects as well as its economic effects. Several articles bring third-world perspectives.

Stiglitz, Joseph. *Globalization and its Discontents* (New York: W.W. Norton, 2002). A devastating attack on the IMF and World Bank by a Nobel Prize winner who has served as a high official in them.

Watson, William E. *The Collapse of Communism in the Soviet Union* (Westport, CN: Greenwood Press, 1998). Brief introduction with narrative and analysis of key events, chronology, biographies, and primary source documents, from the 1950s to 1991.

World Development Report 2003: Sustainable Development in a Dynamic World: Transforming Institutions, Growth, and Quality of Life (New York: World Bank and Oxford University Press, 2003). Annual World Bank assessment of the condition of economic and social development worldwide. This volume reflects the Bank's greater concern with issues of poverty and sustainability.

DOCUMENTS

United Nations Office on Drugs and Crime. "The United Nations Convention against Transnational Organized Crime and its Protocols." http://www.unodc.org/unodc/crime_cicp_convention.html http://www.unodc.org/adhoc/palermo/theconvention.html

"Organs Watch" http://sunsite.berkeley.edu/biotech/organswatch/pages/about.html

JOURNALS

The Journal of Contemporary Criminal Justice contains frequent articles on international crime.

FILMS

Dirty Pretty Things produced by Stephen Frears, 2003. Focuses on immigrants, many of them illegal, struggling to get by in London, evading the police, exploited by employers, and some of them involved in trafficking in human organs. Shocking, moving, and believable.

Maria Full of Grace, written and directed by Joshua Marston, 2004. Maria rejects her dead-end life in Colombia to sign on as a "mule," carrying cocaine illegally to the United States. Suggests the contrast between the legitimate and illegitimate opportunities in a drug-based economy that includes Colombia and the USA.

World History Documents CD-ROM

REGIONAL IDENTITIES AND THE TWENTY-FIRST CENTURY

KEY TOPICS

- Europe
- Africa
- Latin America
- China and India
- Israel and Palestine: Jews and Arabs

In Chapter 23 we examined the development of new identities around the globe. We explored these new identities in politics, religion, economics, culture, and ecology. In this final chapter, we examine a series of case studies of new identities being formed, encouraged, and sometimes resisted. In two regions of the world—Europe and Africa—we will look at contrasting uses of identity. Western and central Europe have made great progress toward forging a common European identity among nations that had been enemies and had fought to exhaustion in long and bitter warfare. In south-eastern Europe, in sharp contrast, nationalist-ethnic-religious divisions—manipulated by ruthless political leaders—carved up Yugoslavia into warring states. In Africa, South Africa broke out of its apartheid past and forged a new multiracial identity, while Rwanda and Congo collapsed into ethnic warfare that killed millions. The two largest nations of Latin America, Brazil and Mexico, moved toward achieving identities as democratic countries in which the voices of the poor would be taken seriously. Powerful, wealthy interests at home and abroad introduced challenges to these goals, but promising negotiations moved ahead. China and India, the world's two most populous countries, were each moving toward new identities as capitalistic economies, although at different tempos. China moved aggressively to leave behind its recent history of economic communism and embrace capitalism. India moved more tentatively from a less doctrinaire socialism to a less fervent capitalism. Finally, the conflict in the Middle East between Israel and the Palestinians demonstrated the enormous, continuing influence of identity on religious, ethnic, and international relations.

EUROPE

Western and Central Europe

In the aftermath of the devastation of the world wars, western Europe turned itself around and set an example of regional cooperation and even unification. After the end of the Cold War, the countries of central Europe also joined in. The resulting European Union (EU) brought to the region a half-century of peace, rapid economic reconstruction and growth, a more prominent voice in international affairs, and restored cultural creativity.

In 1947, Britain's wartime leader Winston Churchill described Europe as "a rubble heap, a charnel house, a breeding ground for pestilence and hate." Many of Europe's leading statesmen agreed with this brooding assessment and sought to create new institutions that would transform the continent from a killing field into a zone of

Opposite **Israeli-Palestinian relations on the West Bank, 2000.** An Israeli soldier is seen in discussion with two Palestinian women.

peace. Many of them, including Germans, believed that, after the wars, they had to reintegrate and restrain Germany within the framework of European civilization. They saw economic cooperation as a means of achieving these goals. In 1950, the French foreign minister, Robert Schuman, and the West German Chancellor, Konrad Adenauer, agreed to form the European Coal and Steel Community (ECSC) to place these key industries under an independent international authority. Its first president was the French administrator Jean Monnet (1888–1979), who is often called "The Father of Europe." The ECSC expanded as a multinational organization in 1952 with the addition of Italy and the Benelux countries (Belgium, the Netherlands, and Luxembourg).

The political and economic success of the ECSC encouraged further moves toward west European integration. The Treaties of Rome in 1957 established a customs union, the European Economic Community (EEC), or Common Market, to lower and, ultimately, remove tariffs among member countries; to foster the free movement of goods, labor, and capital; and to establish a single external tariff. The treaties also established Euratom to create common policies for the peaceful development of atomic energy. Agreement on agricultural policy was more difficult because it involved issues of national self-reliance on food, the mystique of family farms, and the need to accommodate rural and urban interests. Nevertheless, in 1962, a Common Agricultural Policy was also negotiated, although it remains one of the most contested and controversial of European policies. European nations often accuse one another of seeking special privileges for their own agriculture, and third-world countries charge, correctly, that Europe's subsidies to its own agriculture give it special and unfair advantages in global, competitive markets. Until the early 1980s, "agriculture took up 80 percent of the Community's budget and the rows provoked by the costs of agricultural policy absorbed (it sometimes seemed) 99 percent of its energies" (Gilbert, p. 7).

In 1965, the Brussels Treaty merged the ECSC, the EEC, and Euratom, and created the basis of a west European economic administration with a commission, council, parliament, and court. From 1972, the heads of the governments of the EEC nations began to meet on a regular basis in an assembly soon known as the European Council. Additional nations were admitted: Britain, the Republic of Ireland, and Denmark in 1973, Greece in 1981, and Spain and Portugal in 1986.

In 1986, the leaders of the twelve members of the EEC of that date signed the Single European Act, committing themselves to the creation by the end of 1992 of "an area without internal frontiers in which the free movement of goods, persons and capital is ensured" (Gilbert, p. 175). Also in 1986, the flag of the European Community, twelve gold stars arranged in a circle on a light blue background, was flown for the first time. The EEC adopted Beethoven's Ninth Symphony, with its chorus of Schiller's *Ode to Joy*, as its anthem. Western Europe was moving well beyond a free-trade common market toward a "Europe without frontiers."

In 1991, the Treaty of Maastricht proposed a monetary union and paved the way to the creation of a European Central Bank (ECB) and a single European currency, the Euro, introduced in 1999 and fully operational in 2002. Maastricht also called for the creation of common policies in foreign and security matters, and cooperation in issues of justice and internal affairs, but these initiatives have not yet been implemented. When ratified in 1993, the treaty converted the EEC into the European Union (EU). In 1995, Austria, Finland, and Sweden joined, creating in western Europe the world's largest integrated market with over 370 million people in fifteen nations.

Following the collapse of the USSR in 1991, many of the nations of central Europe, freed from Soviet control, began to submit their applications for membership of the EU. In 2004, seven of them were admitted as new members—Lithuania, Latvia, Estonia, the Czech Republic, Slovakia, Hungary, and Poland—along with the two island nations of Cyprus and Malta, and Slovenia, newly independent from the former

SOURCE

The Continuing Rationale for European Integration

In 1995, François Mitterrand (1916–96), past president of France and an elder statesman both of his own country and of the European Union, spoke passionately to the parliament of the EU, summarizing its great accomplishments in binding up the physical, emotional, and economic wounds of war-devastated Europe. He looked forward to even greater achievements in formulating and enhancing its collective cultural identity. Mitterrand asserted that the success of the EU as a whole would also enhance the cultural identity and creativity of each of its member states, just as the collective success of its economic policies had benefited the economies of the individual member nations.

Our Europe must be embodied in something more than simply balance sheets and freight tonnages. I would go as far as to say ... that it needs a soul, so that it can give expression ... to its culture, its ways of thinking, the intellectual make-up of its peoples, the fruits of the centuries of civilization of which we are the heirs. The expressions of Europe's many forms of genius are rich and diverse; and, as in the past, we must share with the whole world—while not seeking to impose them, somewhat differently from in the past—our ideas, our dreams, and, to the extent that they are of the right kind, our passions. ...

The cultural identity of nations is reinforced by the process of European integration. The Europe of cultures, ladies and gentlemen, is a Europe of nations as opposed to a Europe of nationalism. ...

I was born during the First World War and fought in the Second. I therefore spent my childhood in the surroundings of families torn apart, all of them mourning loved ones and feeling great

bitterness, if not hatred, towards the recent enemy, the traditional enemy. ...

My generation has almost completed its work; it is carrying out its last public acts, and this will be one of my last. It is therefore vital for us to pass on our experience. Many of you will remember the teaching of your parents ... will have felt the suffering of your countries, will have experienced the grief, the pain of separation, the presence of death—all as a result of the mutual enmity of the peoples of Europe. It is vital to pass on not this hatred but, on the contrary, the opportunity for reconciliation which we have, thanks—it must be said—to those who, after 1944–1945, themselves bloodstained and with their personal lives destroyed, had the courage to envisage a more radiant future which would be based on peace and reconciliation. That is what we have done.

(*Official Journal of the European Communities: Debates of the European Parliament*, 1994–5 Session No 4–456, pp. 45–51, excerpted in Hunt, p. 343)

Yugoslavia. These states added another 75 million people to the EU. The dream of a unified, peaceful, prosperous, democratic Europe seemed in large part fulfilled in most of the territory from the Atlantic to the borders of Russia. Europeans shared a common market, without internal tariffs, and a common currency regulated by the ECB. They could travel throughout the EU with only a basic identity card, for the most part encountering no customs formalities, and they could live wherever they chose within the EU. Although the EU recognizes twenty official languages, English has become the most common language for commercial, political, and cultural exchange throughout the continent, as it has throughout the world.

The increased regional and economic diversity of the EU, however, raised new challenges. In 2004, the text of a new constitution for the organization was under consideration, and the members jockeyed for power as between larger states and smaller, richer and poorer, those with long-standing membership and the newcomers, and those more friendly toward the foreign policies of the United States and those less. As always, some nations were more jealous of their national culture and identity and more resistant to entering more deeply into the EU and to giving it more powers. Others were more willing to see the EU play a larger role in their national lives and in setting international foreign policy. The European Union has become far more than a loose association but is less than a unified state. It provides neither welfare nor basic educational functions to its inhabitants. It does, however, finance programs in science and technology, culture, and the environment, and it supports efforts to raise the economic status of its poorer member states to that of the wealthier. It sets standards for health and safety regulations, social security and working conditions, and agriculture.

Many questions about the further significance of the EU remain. Elections to the European parliament in 2004, the fifth of the every-five-year elections, saw the lowest turnout of voters ever. Only about 45 percent of eligible voters turned out, suggesting that the EU is of greater significance to its political and economic elites, who generally promote it, than to its rank-and-file, whose voting has been unenthusiastic.

One of the most significant sets of questions still facing the EU concerns its reception of new applicants. Several new nations in the Balkans wished to enter, and the EU continues to consider—and to postpone—the application of Turkey to join. What would be the geographic and cultural limits of the new integrated Europe? Should the EU add a nation that is geographically mostly not in Europe, and religiously and culturally Islamic, although constitutionally secular? How far is the EU willing to push the envelope of "European" identity?

Euro-pessimists also note the inability of the EU to respond effectively to warfare and genocide in the former Yugoslavia. The European Union was slow to react during the initial warfare, 1992–5, and again in 1998 during the warfare and "ethnic cleansing" in Kosovo.

Yugoslavia

While western and central Europe were creating a new, integrated identity, Yugoslavia, in the Balkan region of southeastern Europe, moved in the opposite direction. The Balkans are home to diverse religions and nationalisms, although the peoples of the region are ethnically similar to one another, mostly descendants of groups that immigrated some 1400 years ago. Throughout most of their history, these peoples have lived together in relative harmony, but external political pressures and internal political leaders have sometimes inflamed fault lines among the population to create bitter warfare. The last century has seen examples of both harmony and lethal conflict.

The new state of Yugoslavia ("land of the South Slavs") that was created after World War I contained a wide variety of national groups, somewhat uneasily. During World War II, the different groups fought against one another, some siding with Germany, others with Russia. Marshal Josip Broz Tito led the pro-Russian guerrilla forces. After the war, Tito became leader of the devastated country. He suppressed ethnic hostilities and enforced policies of Yugoslavian national integration and identity, maintaining political control through the Communist Party. However, he allowed individual ownership of most of the agricultural economy and decentralization of industry. Remarkably, he was able to break free from Russia's control to chart a separate Yugoslav path. The economy grew at an average pace of 7 percent per year, and Yugoslavia seemed to be developing an integrated nationalism that subsumed all of its diverse groups. This integration continued for another decade after Tito's death in 1980.

After communism collapsed in the Soviet Union in 1989, and the Soviet Union itself dissolved in 1991, Yugoslavs, too, voted to break up their union. Four of the six political regions declared their independence, leaving Serbia and Montenegro as the rump Yugoslavia. Three of the regions found separation especially difficult because they were composed of different national groupings internally. To some degree these national identities were also religious

Josip Broz Tito with troops, 1951. Tito salutes as he reviews troops of the Yugoslav army.

identities, although Yugoslavs were not especially zealous in their religious observance, especially after a half-century of communist rule. Serbians were generally Orthodox, while most Croatians were Roman Catholic. Bosnians were the most mixed, but with a plurality Muslim. Intermarriage between religious and national groups was not uncommon.

Serbia's president, Slobodan Milosevic, and the head of his military, Radovan Karadzic, rejected the new national divisions of Yugoslavia. They attempted to keep Croatia and Bosnia-Herzegovina (the complete name of the state including all its regions), and especially their regions with large Serbian populations, under Serbia's control. Civil war raged for three years, 1992–5, during which Serbia undertook a policy of "ethnic cleansing," a euphemism for genocide, attempting to kill or drive out the Muslim and Croat populations, especially from Bosnia. Milosevic employed rape and torture as instruments of policy. Hundreds of thousands of people died and many more were made homeless in the most devastating warfare in Europe since World War II. The United Nations attempted repeatedly to broker a peace agreement, but each attempt was rejected or broken. Many observers faulted the European Union, the United States, and the United Nations for indifference to the warfare, in part because they were unwilling or unable to commit the military forces necessary to impose peace. In 1995, however, US diplomat Richard Holbrooke succeeded in brokering a peace agreement that was initiated in Dayton, Ohio, in November 1995 and signed in Paris in December by the presidents of Bosnia-Herzegovina, Croatia, and Serbia. To oversee the agreements, the United Nations dispatched 60,000 peacekeeping troops.

None of the three new states was, however, internally homogeneous. Within the newly created nation of Serbia, one province, Kosovo, had a majority of people who were Albanian by ethnicity and Muslim by religion. Kosovo also had enormous historical significance. In 1389, the conquest of Kosovo by the Muslim Ottoman Turks marked their triumph over Serbia and the destruction of the Serbian state for 600 years. Political leaders of both Bosnians and Serbs could stoke lingering historical memories of this battle in order to inflame current-day antagonisms, if they chose. For example, on June 28, 1989, the 600th anniversary of the Battle of Kosovo, one million Serbs assembled to hear Milosevic recall the glories of Serbia's past.

In 1998, when the Albanian Muslims of Kosovo declared their intention to secede from Serbia and launched a guerrilla war, Milosevic responded with fury, driving some 700,000 ethnic Albanians from their homes in Kosovo and resuming his policies of ethnic cleansing. As Kosovars were murdered, tortured, and raped, the UN and NATO debated whether they should intervene in the internal affairs of a sovereign state. Many observers saw this debate as a legalistic evasion of humanitarian responsibility. Finally, NATO began a seventy-two-day campaign of bombing that led Serbia to surrender and give up its claims. Milosevic accepted 50,000 UN troops as peacekeepers. Before the UN soldiers arrived, however, the remaining Albanian Muslim Kosovars and the returning refugees drove out the Serbian residents of Kosovo, implementing reverse ethnic cleansing. Hatreds and revenge flowed in both directions. As peace was established and enforced, the Serbs were also invited to return.

In 1993, the UN Security Council established an ad hoc International War Crimes Tribunal at The Hague to rule on the atrocities that emerged during the warfare. In

Former Yugoslavian president Slobodan Milosevic talks to the judges at the UN Tribunal in The Hague, 2001. With a guard at his side, and as seen on a video screen at the press center, this is the second court appearance of Milosevic, accused of war crimes in the former Yugoslavia.

2000, Milosevic was defeated in Serbian elections and the new government turned him over to this tribunal for trial as a war criminal for his actions in Kosovo, the first European invocation of such a trial since World War II. Nevertheless, even from his position under trial in The Hague, Milosevic continues to be influential in Serbian politics. Many consider him an ardent patriot and his party remains powerful. When the Serbian prime minister, Zoran Djindjic, was assassinated in 2003, Milosevic, in The Hague, was suspected as one of the planners, although Serbian drug dealers were also under suspicion. Also in 2003, a Bosnian Serb leader, Biljana Plavsic, was sentenced to eleven years in prison by the International War Crimes Tribunal in The Hague. Known as "the Iron Lady," she surrendered voluntarily and pleaded guilty to war crimes during the 1992–5 civil war, the first high-ranking official actually to be punished by the tribunal.

The tribunal also indicted eight men for sexual assault, the first time that the systematic practice of rape had been condemned and prosecuted as a weapon of war and a "crime against humanity," and not just overlooked as "something that happens" during the stress of warfare. Thus another identity—sexual identity—was partly redefined, and legally protected, as a result of the 1992–5 warfare.

AFRICA

The Nigerian Nobel Laureate author Wole Soyinka said in the 1990s, "South Africa is our dream, Rwanda our nightmare." South Africa became the model of a nation forsaking an apartheid identity of racial separation for a new identity as a multiracial, multi-ethnic democracy. At the same time Congo, Rwanda, and Burundi broke down into internal civil warfare and international conflict as well.

South Africa

Wole Soyinka at UNESCO, Paris, October 16, 1986. Soyinka is here seen celebrating his Nobel Prize for Literature.

The first major group of European settlers in Africa came from the Netherlands in 1652 and established themselves around the Cape of Good Hope. A century and a half later, during the Napoleonic wars, British settlers arrived and took possession of this colony. As the British Anglicized the government and freed the slaves, the Dutch settlers, called Afrikaners or Boers, felt alienated and left in a "great trek" that took them north of the Orange River. The discovery of diamonds in 1867 and of gold in 1876 increased the value of South African land and brought the two groups into conflict. The South Africans of British descent defeated the Boers in three years of warfare, 1899–1902, but the two groups finally came together to form the Union of South Africa (USA) in 1910.

The new Union adopted the Afrikaners' harsh policies toward the black majority. Wages and conditions in the European mines were so abysmal that Africans would not work them, and Chinese contract laborers were imported. The 1913 Native Land Acts restricted African residence and purchase of land to only 13 percent of the surface of the country, effectively forcing black Africans into service as landless laborers in white-controlled farming and industry. The labor market had two impermeable tiers, the top with better conditions and pay for whites, the bottom for blacks. Non-whites had no political rights.

Still more restrictive laws after 1948 established apartheid (segregation of the races). Blacks working in the cities could not legally establish residence but had to commute long distances each day from black residential areas or to stay in dormitory settings, leaving their families behind in the village areas.

Black African frustration, resentment, and anger at first expressed itself principally through independent Ethiopian Churches as early as the 1870s and 1880s. The African

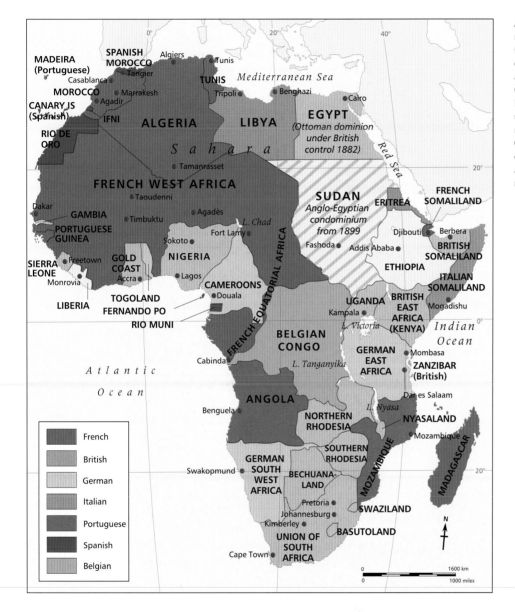

Africa in 1914. By the end of the nineteenth century, Africa presented European imperialists with their last chance to claim a "place in the sun." In a scramble for territory, Belgium, Germany, and Italy joined Spain, Portugal, Britain, and France in carving up the continent, riding roughshod over native concerns with brutal insensitivity. Conflict between the colonists was common, the war between the British and Dutch in South Africa being the most bloody.

National Congress (ANC) formed in 1913 as a constitutional party of protest and grew steadily over several decades. In the 1950s, as other African nations began to win independence, Europeans urged South Africa to liberalize its racial policies, but the government of South Africa stubbornly resisted. It confronted unarmed political protest in March 1960 at Sharpeville with a massacre in which sixty-nine black Africans were killed and many were wounded. The ANC shifted to strikes and armed protest, renouncing attacks on people and limiting itself to sabotage of property. The South African government continued to crack down, maintaining its apartheid policies and sentencing ANC leader Nelson Mandela (b. 1918), a brilliant and charismatic forty-six-year-old lawyer, to life imprisonment. At his trial in 1964, Mandela expressed his frustration with the white government of South Africa and its apartheid rule, his own commitment to his country, and his vision for its future:

> I have fought against white domination. I have cherished the ideal of a democratic and free society in which all persons live together in harmony and with equal

Ethnic groups in Africa. The insensitivity to local conditions of many European colonial administrators created territorial boundaries which failed to match the underlying cultural map of Africa and its peoples. The results of this were seen in post-independence internecine conflicts between ethnic groups hemmed into artificial national territories: Congo (Zaire), Nigeria, Uganda, Angola, Zimbabwe, Sudan, and, more recently, Rwanda and Burundi are among those that have reaped this bitter harvest.

opportunities. It is an ideal which I hope to live for and to achieve. But if needs be, it is an ideal for which I am prepared to die. (Edelstein, p. 73)

The ANC and the general movement for racial justice were crippled but not killed off by the government's repression. As Zambia and Zimbabwe, Angola and Mozambique won independence and majority rule in the 1960s and 1970s, world attention focused on South Africa as the last remaining center of white, minority rule. In addition, the newly independent, "frontline" nations bordering South Africa sheltered members of the ANC and other movements for majority rule, including some dedicated to guerrilla warfare. Through the United Nations as well as through unilateral actions, many nations adopted sanctions against South Africa, restricting or stopping trade; "disinvesting" or withdrawing economic investments; and ending diplomatic, cultural, and sports exchanges. South Africa was to be treated as a pariah nation, cut off from intercourse with much of the rest of the world until it moved toward racial equality.

Enforcing the sanctions proved difficult. South Africa was a regional economic powerhouse, with rich resources: 85 percent of the world's platinum; two-thirds of its chromium; half its gold; half its manganese; and substantial proportions of its gem-quality diamonds. Its GNP, which had been 30 percent of all of sub-Saharan Africa's in 1960, increased to 35 percent by 1987. Geopolitically, 90 percent of Europe's oil passed by its waters. Many large and powerful nations saw sanctions as self-destructive and did not fully comply. The frontline states had tens of thousands of workers who subsisted only through jobs in the South African mines and industries; these states continued surreptitious trade and diplomatic relationships. In addition, to withstand guerrilla threats, South Africa increased its military personnel from 24,000 in 1960 to 97,000 in 1987, and its military expenditures from US$243 million to US$3,292 million, equal to about 50 percent of the military expenditures of all of black Africa combined (Sivard, p. 53).

Nevertheless, the sanctions did gradually exact their toll; isolation was painful, culturally and diplomatically as well as economically. The continuing expansion of independence among the African states brought black rule ever closer to South Africa's borders, and unrest within the country continued. In 1976 protests against government educational policies began in Soweto, a black township outside Pretoria, and led to nationwide riots in which 600 people were killed. Some liberalization was granted: black labor unions were legalized, the prohibition of interracial sex was abolished, segregation in public transportation ended. Finally, in 1990, the new government of President F.W. de Klerk (b. 1936) lifted its ban against the ANC and freed Nelson Mandela after he had spent twenty-seven years in prison. It repealed apartheid laws and began wary and difficult negotiations with the ANC for transition to majority rule. In 1993, de Klerk's National Party and the ANC under Mandela's leadership agreed on the principle of a new constitution. In 1994 elections, open equally to all races on the principle of one person-one vote, the ANC won 62 percent of the vote.

South Africans confronted the problem of establishing a new political and cultural identity for themselves after the collapse of apartheid government. For the first time in their history, the blacks of South Africa counted as political equals to the whites. But unlike many other colonial situations in which most white colonizers left the newly independent colony, in South Africa, the whites had been residents of the country for centuries. This was their home. They viewed themselves as Africans, and most of them had no intention of leaving. Even if they did, they had no other home to which to go. Thus 32 million mostly impoverished and until-recently suppressed and persecuted blacks and 8 million mostly wealthy and highly privileged whites had to find new ways of getting along together. One of their highly imaginative solutions was a Truth and Reconciliation Commission, which functioned from 1996 to 1998 in an effort to clear the air for further interracial cooperation in the future.

The commission was initiated by President Nelson Mandela and headed by Archbishop Desmond Tutu, the recently retired Archbishop of Cape Town and head of the Anglican Church in South Africa. Its goal was to bring the peoples of South Africa together by exposing the bitter and violent realities of the past and, through that exposure, enabling all of its peoples to see themselves as part of a single nation. The commission heard cases of some 20,000 people who suffered gross human rights violations from the Sharpeville massacre in 1960 until the first democratic election in 1994. They discovered horrifying documents, such as the minutes of the State Security Council directing undercover operations in the 1980s seeking "the identification and elimination of revolutionary leaders, particularly those with charisma"; "to make the rotten areas clean before they become too infected. To establish that requires a lot of violence from our side, regardless of the international reaction" (Edelstein, p. 178).

Thousands of people from all corners of the country stepped forward to testify. Thousands were granted some measure of reparations from the state treasury. Most

Seaside segregation. South African apartheid manifests itself on a beach in Durban, in 1985. The sign, written in English and Afrikaans, proclaims that the beach "is reserved for the sole use of the members of the white race group." Apartheid (Afrikaans for "apartness"), the policy of separate development and segregation of the races of South Africa, was supported and encouraged by the Nationalist Party when it came to power in 1948. With the African National Congress in power in South Africa, the country is emerging from the constraints of its racial policies and building a more united nation.

whites, unable to state publicly that they had benefited from apartheid, did not initiate the act of admitting their crimes. Some, however, did step forward, helping in the process of reconciliation. Many others came because of accusations of criminal activity brought against them. The proceedings of the commission were not equivalent to criminal trials, and amnesty could be granted to those who could demonstrate that they were carrying out the political policies of the state, rather than their own agendas, and were acting without sadism. In his concluding remarks, Archbishop Tutu proclaimed the exemplary success of the commission in healing South Africa's racial wounds and facilitating the emotional unification of the country and a new national identity:

A new and democratic dawn for South Africa. South African president Nelson Mandela and second deputy president F.W. de Klerk address a huge crowd in front of the Union Building in Pretoria, after the inauguration ceremony on May 10, 1994. Only a few years earlier it would have been inconceivable that the imprisoned Nelson Mandela could ever attain high office in a country so firmly wedded to the policies of apartheid.

> We have been privileged to help to heal a wounded people ... When we look around us at some of the conflict areas of the world, it becomes increasingly clear that there is not much of a future for them without forgiveness, without reconciliation. God has blessed us richly so that we might be a blessing to others. Quite improbably, we as South Africans have become a beacon of hope to others locked in deadly conflict that peace, that a just resolution, is possible. If it could happen in South Africa, then it can certainly happen anywhere else. Such is the exquisite divine sense of humor.
>
> Truth and Reconciliation Commission of South Africa Report
> http://www.info.gov.za/reports/2003/trc/

Rwanda and Congo

While South Africans of different ethnic origins were learning to live together, the Hutus and Tutsis were committing mutual genocide that ripped apart Rwanda and then helped accelerate Congo's descent

HOW DO WE KNOW?

South Africa's Truth and Reconciliation Commission

Many observers of the commission's proceedings raised serious criticisms. Some felt that the granting of amnesty came too easily to defendants in these non-criminal proceedings. Defendants could plead that they were simply following orders of the government and that they had not acted sadistically, and receive amnesty. Dirk Coetzee, first commander of a counter-insurgency unit, and his team, were convicted in criminal court for the murder of Griffiths Mxenge, a civil rights lawyer, but subsequently the commission granted them amnesty because they were simply carrying out their duties as policemen engaged in the government's struggle against the liberation movement. Griffiths's brother was disgusted with this decision for amnesty:

My main objection is that amnesty promotes the interests of the perpetrators, as once they are granted amnesty they are not criminally liable and no civil action can be instituted against [them], and that is totally against the interests of the victims. It is totally unjust. (Edelstein, p. 113)

On the other hand, Josephine Msweli was more forgiving of the men who killed her sons:

I want the people who killed my sons to come forward because this is a time for reconciliation. I want to forgive them and I also have a bit of my mind to tell them. I would be happy if they could come before me because I don't have [my] sons today ... I want to speak to them before I forgive them. I want them to tell me who sent them to come and kill my sons. Maybe they are

my enemies, maybe they are not. So I want to establish as to who they are and why they did what they did. (Edelstein, p. 154)

One member of the commission, Pumla Gobodo-Madikizela, a clinical psychologist, reaffirmed the healing power of public disclosure by victim and perpetrator alike: "If a memory is kept alive in order to transcend hateful emotions, to free oneself or one's society from the burden of hatred, then remembering has the power to heal" (Edelstein, p. 30). She lamented, however, the inability of most whites, despite the commission, to recognize that they had benefited from the general violence of the system of inequality imposed by apartheid.

Despite its shortcomings, the commission brought truth to light, and most commentators believed that this truth allowed purification of the body politic. It allowed the true identity of the old state to be exposed so that a new identity could be formed. Michael Ignatieff, director of the Carr Center for Human Rights Policy at the Kennedy School of Government, Harvard University, wrote:

Any society that allows its torturers to retire with medals and pensions inevitably pays the price. The price of lies is immobilized nostalgia for tyranny ... you cannot create a culture of freedom unless you eliminate a specific range of impermissible lies ... The Truth Commission had rendered some lies about the past simply impossible to repeat. (Edelstein, pp. 20–21)

Ignatieff concluded that the Truth and Reconciliation Commission made it impossible for white South Africans to deny the violence of their society. They

could no longer deflect blame by saying that any problems were caused only by

a few rotten apples, but those were the exceptions rather than the rule. What the TRC uncovered was something very different indeed: not a few bad apples, not a few bad cops ... but a system, a culture, a way of life that was organized around contempt and violence for other human beings. The truth, the cold core, of apartheid was the Sanlam building in Port Elizabeth where they threw you against radiators and beat you with wet towels. Every South African citizen was contaminated by the degradation, that deadness, that offence against the spirit. (Edelstein, p. 21)

Knowing the painful truth, however, would ultimately set the society free.

- President Mandela inspired the creation of the commission and Bishop Tutu was its chairman. Based on the concept and workings of the commission, how would you characterize the politics and ethics of these two men?
- How would you interpret the key goals of the commission? Were they realistic? Do you think they correspond to human nature as you understand it?
- Ignatieff argues that torture and violence against citizens were not an aberration caused by "a few rotten apples," but by "a system, a culture, a way of life that was organized around contempt and violence for other human beings." To what extent do you think his rhetoric and his description of consequences mirror the debate about the actions of Americans in the Abu Ghraib prison scandal in Iraq in 2004?

into civil war. The origins of the hostility between Hutus and Tutsis confounds easy understanding. On the one hand they appear to be age-old enemies, with often distinct physical and psychological attributes. On the other, they have often gotten along well together. This mixture of alternating antagonism and cordiality—so reminiscent of the Balkans—defies simple definition. In a prize-winning and influential book on the Rwandan genocide, *We Wish to Inform You that Tomorrow We will be Killed with Our Families: Stories from Rwanda*, Philip Gourevitch discusses the complexity:

First-time voters, South Africa, 1994. Residents of the Western Transvaal queue to vote for the first time in South Africa's multiracial elections in 1994. After years of apartheid and oppression, black South Africans showed a respect and devotion to their new democracy that inspired citizens of democracies around the world who often took for granted their own right to vote and to participate in governance.

> While convention holds that Hutus are a Bantu people who settled Rwanda first, coming from the south and west, and that Tutsis are a Nilotic people who migrated from the north and east, these theories draw more on legend than on documentable fact. With time, Hutus and Tutsis spoke the same language, followed the same religion, intermarried, and lived intermingled, without territorial distinctions, on the same hills, sharing the same social and political culture in small chiefdoms. The chiefs were called Mwamis, and some of them were Hutus, some Tutsis; Hutus and Tutsis fought together in the Mwamis' armies; through marriage and clientage, Hutus could become hereditary Tutsis, and Tutsis could become hereditary Hutus. Because of all this mixing, ethnographers and historians have lately come to agree that Hutus and Tutsis cannot properly be called distinct ethnic groups. (Gourevitch, pp. 47–8)

The groups, nevertheless, have developed separate identities. The Hutus were originally cultivators, the Tutsis pastoral herdsmen, in a society where possession of cattle outranked farming. Although in many cases the two groups are physically indistinguishable, in general the Tutsis are "lanky and long-faced, not so dark-skinned, flat-nosed, thick-lipped, and square-jawed," while the Hutus are "stocky and round faced, dark-skinned, flat-nosed, thick-lipped, and square-jawed" (Gourevitch, p. 50). Rwandans have no written records of their history before the appearance of Europeans, so there is no further clear explanation of the evolution of the relationships between the groups.

As in other parts of the world, however, emerging ethnic identity became the basis of power. After 1860, a Tutsi became king of a small region and expanded it to about the size of present-day Rwanda. He favored Tutsis in his government and reduced the status of Hutus. European rulers—Germans before World War I and Belgians afterward—reinforced these ethnic identities by making them official. Both favored the Tutsis. In 1933–4, the Belgians took a census of Rwanda and issued identification cards that categorized each Rwandan as either Hutu or Tutsi. (Only about 1 percent of the population was of a different group, mostly Twa, or Pygmy.) Belgians were carrying out the same sorts of policies that the British had established with the caste system in

India, in making official and formal the distinctions that until now had been unofficial and informal. They were imposing on the people of Rwanda the same sort of separate identity that divided Belgians at home between the French-speaking Walloon minority to the south and the Flemish-speaking majority in the north. Further, the Belgians forced the Hutus into work on plantations and in construction, and set up the Tutsis as their taskmasters. In the public schools they instructed students in the official hierarchy between the elevated Tutsis and the diminished Hutus. Identities that had formerly been porous took on new, powerful reality. Many Hutus left Rwanda for Congo and Uganda in order to escape this system of degradation.

As independence approached, Hutus, who made up 85 percent of the population, seized on the concept of majority rule and on their identification as the earlier arrivals in Rwanda to claim that they should rule Rwanda, publishing the *Hutu Manifesto* in 1957 to make this argument. In 1959, a Hutu activist was attacked and beaten nearly to death by Tutsi activists, and Hutus responded by attacking Tutsi homes throughout Rwanda. This was the first recorded actual physical attack by one group on the other.

In 1962, Rwanda became an independent country with the Hutu majority in control. Battles broke out regularly between Hutus and Tutsis. About a quarter-million Tutsis fled Rwanda itself, some of them conducting guerrilla attacks back across the border. The patterns of violence depended on the political leadership. Under the first president, Grégoire Kayibanda (1962–73), violence against the Tutsi increased; the second president, Juvénal Habyarimana (1973–94), otherwise a dictatorial military ruler, ordered an end to violence against the Tutsis, and it stopped.

In 1990, a Tutsi-led army, the Rwandan Patriotic Front (FPR), led by Paul Kagame, invaded from Uganda. In 1991 a ceasefire was negotiated and the constitution was amended to allow multiparty participation in the government. In 1993 the government and the FPR agreed to a broad-based transitional government that would include the FPR. Many Hutus believed that Habyarimana was too accommodating to the Tutsis, and when his plane was shot down and he was killed in April 1994, popular belief held that extremist Hutus were responsible. An immediate—and apparently planned—genocide was unleashed against the Tutsi minority. About 800,000 Tutsis were murdered in less than four months. The United Nations, the United States, and world opinion responded with horror, but no action. The genocide ended only when a Tutsi army, made up of men who had taken refuge in Uganda, returned to Rwanda, captured the capital and established a new government.

The warfare spilled over into Congo (Zaire as it was then called), where about 2 million Hutus had taken refuge. Many of the refugees were armed, and they conducted border raids back into Rwanda, attempting to destabilize the Tutsi-led government. In response, the Rwandan government attacked the Hutus in Congo, making no distinction between guerrilla fighters and

Rwandan refugees at Rusomo, Tanzania, May 1, 1994. Some 250,000 refugees from civil war in Rwanda crossed the border into Tanzania in 1994.

simple refugees. The government of Congo was in a very weakened state as its dictator for the past quarter-century, Mobutu, was dying of cancer. The Rwandans easily fought off the Congolese troops sent to protect the Hutu refugees. The Rwandans then entered into an alliance with Laurent Kabila, a rebel determined to overthrow Mobutu's government. The Hutu–Tutsi wars now expanded into the international arena. Within months, in May 1997, Kabila, with his Rwandan Tutsi allies, plus allies from Uganda, had conquered Congo, and Mobutu fled. As they marched across the country the Tutsis killed Hutus wherever they found them.

Kabila's new government was unstable, and his opponents accused him of selling out to the Rwandans and the Ugandans. So he terminated those alliances and made new ones with Angola, Zimbabwe, and the Hutu people, who had been his enemies. Congo is extremely rich in diamonds, oil, and metals, including gold, copper, cobalt, and tantalum, an important component in miniaturized electronics, and other nations were eager to enter the fighting in order to claim a part of this wealth for themselves. By 2000, soldiers from Rwanda, Uganda, Angola, Zimbabwe, Namibia, and perhaps Chad, along with many independent rebel groups, were involved in the fighting, in which about 300,000 people were killed, while another 3 million died of starvation and disease. Some called it the First African World War.

Laurent Kabila was assassinated in 2001. His son Joseph succeeded him and began to reach peace agreements among the warring parties. But Congo is both rich and weak, so fighting over its natural wealth continues, although at lower levels of intensity. Periodic attacks between Hutus and Tutsis also continue, both in Congo and in Rwanda. Major powers from outside Africa, notably the United States, have been reluctant to enter the warfare, but do act behind the scenes, backing whichever local forces seem most likely to help them gain access to Congo's resources.

LATIN AMERICA

Approaching the last quarter of the twentieth century, Latin America had to cope with fundamental demographic problems while trying to mark out its place in the global economy. In addition, as it observed cultures changing everywhere, it had to determine what its own cultures might become. The thirty-three countries of Latin America that had held 38 million people in 1900 and 166 million in 1950 had grown to just under a half billion in 2000. In that last half century, the population of the countryside had remained approximately stable, at about 100 million, but the urban population soared from 40 percent of the population to 75 percent, from about 66 million to about 375 million. The giant metropolises of Mexico City and São Paulo, Brazil, testified to the urban transformation. Each had between 15 and 20 million people and was still growing rapidly.

The older, rural-based systems of caudillo (strong-man ruler) and rural hacienda estates, worked by largely illiterate peasantry, were giving way to urban life, higher levels of education, some industrialization and an industrial labor base, and telecommunications, which kept Latin Americans up-to-date participants in the latest shifts of global economics and culture. A general movement after the 1970s away from military rule and toward democratization was part of the result. In some countries, notably Colombia and Mexico, the illegal drug trade was also a mark of Latin America's integration into the global economy (see Chapter 23). No single country in Latin America is representative of the whole, but two stand out by reason of their size, Mexico, with a population of slightly more than 100 million, and Brazil, with about 175 million. Together they represent more than half the population of the entire region. Their quests for new identities deserve special attention.

Mexico

The Mexican revolution beginning in 1910 brought Mexico more stable government, some commitment to improving the life of common people, concern for bringing together the varied population strands of this ethnically diverse country, and, in 1929, the seeds of the Institutional Revolutionary Party (PRI). This party was founded to bring democracy to Mexico, and to some degree it did. By 2000, when it was defeated in a presidential election for the first time, it had become the longest-ruling party in the world. That longevity was marked, inevitably, by corruption and a growing desire to enjoy the perquisites of office without responding to the needs of the people. The PRI hold on power began to diminish in the 1980s as it lost substantial numbers of elections for regional officials. Even in elections that it did win, its percentage of the vote declined sharply, and in 1997 it lost control of the Chamber of Deputies, Mexico's parliament. In 2000, when Vicente Fox of the National Action Party (PAN) was elected president, the PRI was finally removed from power. Political and cultural observers attributed Fox's victory in part to a general disgust with the PRI's abuses of power over a very long time, but they also wrote of a shift in Mexico's identity.

In 1968, student protests against the abuses of power of the government and its lack of support for effective economic development—similar to student movements around the world in that tumultuous year—sparked much larger demonstrations of hundreds of thousands of Mexicans. President Díaz Ordaz put down these riots with a massive show of force that led to the murder of several hundred protestors. The demonstrations and the government's use of force alerted the world to problems in Mexico that could not be covered over even by the Olympic summer games, which Mexico hosted for the first time just a few days later.

The 1970s brought improvement in Mexico's economy as the world price of oil escalated and Mexico became a major exporter. The country spent its profits and went into debt, which others were happy to fund. When oil prices fell in 1986, Mexico needed a loan from the International Monetary Fund (IMF) and was required to accept belt-tightening measures. Investment in Mexico declined, and people of means left the country. The PRI barely won the presidential election of 1988, even though it was widely thought to be rigged.

Mexico's transformation was continuing quietly behind the scenes as well as publicly. New election procedures were put in place to ensure fairer and freer elections. The Chamber of Deputies began to take on real powers to limit and counterbalance presidential powers. Various grassroots groups were growing up to protect the environment and to demand that criminal gangs be prosecuted. Journalists were increasingly active in investigating corruption. Businessmen, who once supported the PRI for its protection, began to find that its corruption weighed heavily on the national economy. With increasing urbanization, and through the years of the oil boom, these business interests became larger and better connected with world markets and thinking.

In 1994, Mexico, the United States, and Canada established the North American Free Trade Association (NAFTA), an agreement to end all tariffs and trade barriers among them. By opening the markets of Mexico and the United States to competition, NAFTA challenged Mexico to compete against the greater productivity of US industrial technology and challenged the United States to compete against the lower wages of Mexican labor. Both sides feared a loss of jobs and markets. The value of the Mexican peso dropped sharply, and once again an international consortium of lenders came to the rescue, but also imposed austerity measures that compromised Mexico's financial independence in the short run and brought cries of protest against the World Bank and the IMF.

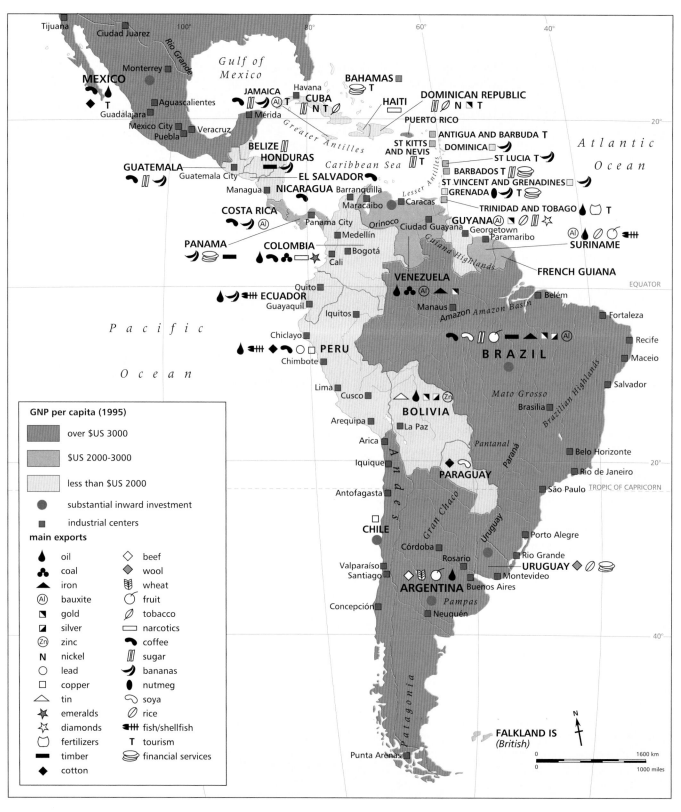

The economic development of Latin America. Following the Great Depression and World War II, the nations of Latin America sought to move beyond their dependence upon the export of primary goods—minerals, timber, and food. Investment from North America and Europe allowed some industrial development in Chile, Argentina, Brazil, and Mexico, but was often undermined by political instability. Development throughout the region is diverse as are economic policies.

On January 1, 1994, the very day NAFTA took effect, Maya Indians in the economically backward Chiapas state rose in armed confrontation against the policies of the central government, leaving forty-five dead. The incident called into question the cultural accomplishments of the Mexican revolution in uniting the people. Academic and journalistic analyses of the Chiapas uprising begin with the intense poverty of this most southern state of Mexico. The state is rich in oil, coffee plantations, and sugar, but in the mountainous regions, where most of its Maya Indians live, the soil is poor and quickly exhausted by the meager corn crop. Second, although a minority of the population of the state, the Maya dominate the mountain regions and had historically resisted the Spanish takeover of the land. As remote, mountain Indians, they were scorned and persecuted both by the Spanish and by their mestizo successors. The Maya revolt was quite complicated, for it turned not only against the government but also pitted Maya against Maya, more revolutionary groups against those seeking a negotiated solution, Catholics against Protestants, and rival families against one another seeking vengeance in ongoing feuds. The breach between mestizos and Indians, however, continued to fester as another fault line in Mexican national identity.

Vicente Fox on the campaign trail, 2000. Presidential candidate Fox greets supporters at a rally in Sinaloa City, Mexico.

In urban areas, too, culture was undergoing profound change. Two *New York Times* journalists captured the changes:

> Patterns of everyday life were changing. Businessmen were forgoing their traditional three-hour tequila lunch, and the Veracruz cigar and game of dominoes that followed it. Now young executives were gobbling a sandwich at their desks and washing it down with a diet Coke. The bittersweet November 2 Day of the Dead celebrations— when Mexicans traditionally stream into cemeteries with baskets of food for graveside picnics with the spirits of their departed—were giving way to the trick-or-treat processions of Halloween. (Preston and Dillon, p. 477)

Many Mexicans were ready for the political change that removed the PRI from power, at least temporarily, and brought in Vicente Fox, a former Coca-Cola executive, to office. Fox has had a difficult time governing this country in transition. As a man of wealth and education he did not fully identify with the majority of his nation, although he did better than many previous PRI presidents. He lived a lavish life, as did his advisers; he did not carefully supervise financial transactions of his government; the economy lost 500,000 jobs in his first year in office (including some that moved to China, where labor was even cheaper than in Mexico); he failed to solve the standoff with the Maya in Chiapas; and agreements that he hoped to reach with President Bush to legalize the status of a substantial proportion of the millions of Mexicans living illegally in the United States fell through when Bush turned his attention elsewhere after the attacks of 9/11. By 2004, Fox was a much weakened president. Nevertheless, with his victory in 2000 Mexico had turned a corner in moving toward a new identity with fuller democracy and representation of the common person. Perhaps Fox would not be the man to bring the process to fruition, but that process seemed larger than the man himself, and careful observers believed that it would continue.

Brazil

As Brazil sorts out its identity, it moves between several key contradictions created by its history. Brazil remained a slave-holding country until 1888, and for decades after emancipation Brazilian authorities attempted to "whiten" the country by barring immigration of blacks while promoting immigration from Europe and East and West Asia.

Economic inequality is more severe in Brazil than in any other major nation. The top 10 percent of the population earns 50 percent of the wealth, and the bottom 10 percent less than 1 percent. About 1.7 percent of the landowners hold nearly half the arable land. The so-called "Brazilian economic miracle," especially from 1969–74, did little to change these ratios. The country became richer, but the vast majority of the people did not. Urbanization has not helped very much. In 1950, Brazil was one-third urban, two-thirds rural. By 1980, those proportions were reversed. The cities, however, are ill-equipped to service the needs of their vast new populations.

Culturally, Brazil has preserved and extended two traditions that have earned international praise, but they are also problematic in terms of the nation's identity. One is soccer, the national sport, which virtually everyone plays and in which Brazil excels. Brazil is the only country to have won five World Cups in the sport, from their first in 1958 to their most recent in 2002. Their most outstanding players—Pele, probably the most famous ever; Ronaldo, named the world's best player in 1996 and 1997; and, more recently, Roberto Carlos—are the world's best. Many of them, however, play for Brazil only during the World Cup games. Otherwise they play for other teams in other countries that pay higher salaries. Brazilian teams cannot afford them.

Another area of excellence is the samba dance form and especially its annual representation in Rio's great pre-Lenten celebration of Carnival, the festival of dance, song, revelry, and sexual and class role-reversal for which the city is world famous. Here, too, however, contradictions abound. The samba grew up among the poor, black people of Rio's slums, or *favelas*. In the 1920s, the government attempted to outlaw this dance and other expressions of African-based culture. Then, in the 1930s and 1940s, the government reversed course and sponsored samba exhibitions and the Carnival celebration itself as a means of proclaiming Brazilian cultural authenticity and racial integration. In most recent years, however, the rich people of Rio celebrate Carnival in designated parade grounds in downtown Rio, while the poor and common people of the city continue to dance in the *favelas*. The two groups do not often meet during Carnival.

The divisions between rich and poor have also created a climate of violence in the major cities and in rural areas as well. By the end of the twentieth century, Brazil was averaging an annual homicide rate of 25 per 100,000, somewhat more than double the very high rate of the United States. Important leaders of reform have been assassinated, including leaders of the ecology movement in Brazil, such as Chico Mendes Filho (1944–88), who organized inhabitants of the rainforest into a union to gain benefits in education, health care, and to defend the forest itself against loggers and immigrants, and Ademir "Dema" Federicci (1959–2001), who struggled to stop the illegal logging on Indian reserves and to stop the construction of a dam that would help big landholders at the expense of small farmers.

From 1964 to 1988 Brazil was ruled by a military dictatorship—usually endorsed by the United States—which exercised widespread political repression and drove its enemies to exile, prison, and death. In 1979, however, political parties were allowed to form, and, after 1984, elections were permitted. In 1994, Fernando Henrique Cardoso was elected president, and he initiated some legislation to protect the rainforest and reduce disparities in wealth.

In 2002, the election of Luis Inacio Lula da Silva (Lula) promised a possible turning point in Brazilian public life. Lula had been born into extreme poverty and hunger, the seventh child of a working-class woman whose husband walked out on her shortly after Lula was born. From a teenage job as a factory worker he grew over the years to become one of the nation's most militant and effective union leaders. On the basis of the union, he helped to found the Workers' Party (PT). On his fourth attempt in 2002, he was elected president.

In office, however, Lula trimmed his rhetoric and actions as he discovered that big business interests could not easily be defied. On the one hand, he introduced a program called *bolsa familia*, which gives $25 per month to the poorest families, with the hope of expanding it to some 50 million people. He also moved to settle some 500,000 poor, landless families on land of their own, but by mid-2004 he had accommodated only one-tenth that number. In the eyes of the poor this seems a small return on their expectations. The $25 monthly dole is helpful, but jobs would be better, and they are not forthcoming. Beyond the tens of thousands who have received land, millions more still clamor for their share.

Lula has continued Brazil's policies of borrowing from the IMF and even exceeding the belt-tightening measures called for by these loans. At the end of 2003, interest payments on Brazil's debt required about 40 percent of the nation's gross domestic product. Worse, in the first year of Lula's presidency, Brazil's economy shrank slightly and the number of jobs declined. Street crime as well as white-collar corruption continued as major problems. Loggers and settlers continued to encroach on the Amazon rainforest. Brazil's bankers and capitalistic businessmen have been pleased with Lula's conservatism in office, but his constituency of the impoverished has grown disillusioned.

Lula has traveled extensively and has begun to help build a coalition of nations that are relatively poor, but whose size guarantees them a voice in world affairs, including India, South Africa, and, perhaps, China. He has argued successfully in the World Trade Organization (WTO) against the subsidies that richer nations have given their agricultural producers to give them an unfair advantage in world trade. He hopes to force the rich countries to fulfill their part of international bargains and to recognize that poverty and inequalities are unhealthy for everyone.

Lula's Brazil is searching for new identities that respond to the internal tensions between rich and poor, races and ethnicities, geographic regions, and, externally, to the power of the global economy, the possibility of forming new international coalitions, and the despair and dynamism of the poor.

Brazilian fans celebrate as their soccer team parades in triumph in Brasilia, 2002. Brazil captured their unprecedented fifth World Cup title in Japan by defeating Germany 2–0 in the final.

CHINA AND INDIA

Again, because of their enormous size, we devote a section to China and India. Each is in the process of developing a new sense of the relationship between government and civil society, between government and the economy, and the nation's place in world affairs. China's new identity represents a sharper break with its communist past. India, which was less radical to begin with, also changes more slowly.

China after Mao: An Era of Reform

On September 9, 1976 Mao died. By the end of the year, the "Gang of Four," the four leaders who claimed to be closest to Mao, including his wife Jiang Qing, were under arrest. They had been among the most militant of the high-level officials responsible for the Cultural Revolution of 1966. China was in the midst of a struggle for succession. By December 1978 it became apparent that Deng Xiaoping (1904–97) and his allies had achieved control of the party and its agenda. They remained in control for the next two decades.

Born in Sichuan Province, Deng spent his formative years, from the age of sixteen to twenty-one, studying, doing factory work, and organizing on behalf of the Communist Party among the expatriate Chinese. After a few months' visit in Moscow, he returned to China as a political and military organizer of soviets in southwest China. On the Long March he became a close companion of Mao. As an army officer, he shared the military command of as many as 300,000 troops. In 1952 Mao called him back to Beijing, and his star continued to rise until 1966 when he appeared too moderate for the leaders of the Cultural Revolution. He was stripped of his offices and exiled to a tractor repair factory in southern China. Deng was recalled to Beijing by Mao only in 1973.

Deng advocated economic liberalism, but within a state firmly controlled by the Communist Party. By the time of his death, Deng and his colleagues had sold off about half of the state's economic holdings leaving only 18 percent of the workforce in state employment, down from 90 percent in 1978. He welcomed foreign investment, which reached $42 billion in 1997, and loans, reaching a total of $130 billion in foreign debt. Exports rose to account for 25 percent of total production. Per capita income quadrupled. Deng also shifted more investment to agriculture, ended collectivization, and introduced a "private responsibility system," unleashing enormous productivity gains of 9 percent a year in the early 1980s. The growth in China's total gross domestic product (GDP) led the world, averaging 11.2 percent per year, 1986–97. Health standards improved. Life expectancy reached seventy.

As its population topped one billion, China acted aggressively, and successfully, to limit population growth. Government programs for "small family happiness," beginning in 1974, culminated in the 1980 policy of one family, one child. The party set birth quotas for each county and city, established a nationwide system for distributing contraceptive devices, enforced regulations against early marriage, provided incentives for having only one child and disincentives for having more. The bureaucracy monitored pregnancies and births carefully and abortions were frequently coerced if necessary (Rosenberg, p. 70). Fertility rates dropped to 2.3 per hundred women in the 1980s, indicating considerable success. The policy evoked massive unrest, evasion—more easily accomplished in rural areas—and, in some case, female infanticide, as couples preferred their one child to be male. The smaller families, however, led to a dramatic reduction in the responsibilities of child care and encouraged greater freedom for women in the home and greater equality and participation in work and public life outside. In a society accustomed to having large families, many observers thought it also produced spoiled only-children. By the year 2000, the birth rate had dropped so low that the government began considering relaxation of the policy. In 2004 they introduced a change: If both parents were themselves only children, products of the one-family-one-child policy, they were permitted to have two children.

HOW DO WE KNOW?

The Force behind China's Economic Growth: Capitalism or Socialism?

As Chinese productivity grew at record rates in the 1980s, and even faster in the 1990s, almost all commentators attributed the economic expansion to the capitalistic reforms promoted by Deng Xiaoping. They usually contrasted Deng's success to the failed communist policies that he discarded. See, for example, the very representative point of view presented in a fine, new history of the twentieth century:

> The Chinese state had established a Soviet-style command economy in the 1950s by nationalizing industry and foreign trade, setting prices and collectivizing agriculture; inefficiency and low growth resulted ... Living standards remained low, and most people lived in cramped, unmodernized housing ...
>
> After Mao's death in 1976, reformers gained more power and began more active restructuring of the economy. Deng Xiaoping, a masterly politician who became head of the Central Advisory Commission, slowly moved the party toward economic reform. Once they were allowed to contract out of their agricultural communes, peasants deserted them in droves, working as family units and selling their surpluses in private markets. Output and rural incomes rose, stimulating rural industry. As trading companies under local control multiplied, foreign contacts expanded and foreign investment poured into the country. Overseas Chinese returned to invest.

> ... a new private sector boomed in southern coastal areas ... Wages rose and so did demand for consumer goods. (Crossley et al., p. 476)

Nobel Prize-winning economist Amartya Sen might not disagree with the analysis of Deng's reforms, but he gives much more credit to the accomplishments of Mao's communist government in paving the way. His analysis of China's success comes as part of a discussion of the market-based economic policies that India began to adopt in 1991. Sen uses China's example to caution against the transition to capitalism before appropriate social policies have been set in place:

> While pre-reform China was deeply skeptical of markets, it was not skeptical of basic education and widely shared health care. When China turned to marketization in 1979, it already had a highly literate people, especially the young, with good schooling facilities across the bulk of the country. In this respect, China was not very far from the basic educational situation in South Korea or Taiwan, where too an educated population had played a major role in seizing the economic opportunities offered by a supportive market system. In contrast, India had a half-illiterate adult population when it turned to marketization in 1991, and the situation is not much improved today [1999].
>
> The health conditions in China were also much better than in India because of the social commitment of the pre-reform regime to health care as well as education. Oddly enough, that commitment, while totally unrelated to its helpful role in

market-oriented economic growth, created social opportunities that could be brought into dynamic use after the country moved toward marketization ... But the relevance of the radically different levels of social preparedness in China and India for widespread market-oriented development is worth noting even at this preliminary stage of the analysis. (Sen pp. 42–3)

Sen does credit Indian democracy with other advantages for development that are lacking under China's communist government. In general, however, he seems to turn upside-down Marx's view of the triumph of communism arising out of a base constructed by capitalists. In China he sees capitalism arising out of a base constructed by communists.

- Is Sen's account of the achievements of Chinese communism inaccurate, or is he simply giving credit to a human-welfare achievement that others are overlooking? Why is he giving this emphasis? Is he right to stress the importance of human welfare measures in economic development?
- According to Sen, why should Indian leaders be cautious in adopting for their own country the free-market policies that seem to work for China?
- To what degree should human welfare be considered in the assessment of the success of an economic system? Can an economic system be considered successful if education, health, and welfare standards of the general population are not rising?

After Deng's death, the transition of power occurred smoothly, with Jiang Zemin succeeding him as China's most important political leader. China moved to liberalize the economy even further, especially by selling off state-run enterprises to private ownership. By 2003, the United Nations Development Programme reported that

China has enjoyed the fastest sustained economic advance in human history, averaging real per capita growth of 8% a year over the past decade. Its per capita income is now $3,976 in purchasing power parity terms. ... According to World Bank estimates based on consumption surveys, the proportion of people living on less than $1 a day declined in China from 33% in 1990 to 16% in 2000. ... China's exceptional growth is partly explained by its market-based reforms that started in 1978 ... These reforms have enabled China to integrate with the global economy at a phenomenal pace. Today it is the largest recipient of foreign direct investment among developing countries rising from almost zero in 1978 to about $52 billion in 2002 (nearly 5% of GDP) … Manufactured exports accounted for … 90% [of all of Chinese exports] in 2001. … telecommunications equipment and computers now account for a quarter of its exports … Literacy stands at 84%. (*Human Development Report 2003*, p. 73)

After fifteen years of debate, China was admitted to the World Trade Organization in November 2001, recognizing its full participation in the world of global trade on capitalist principles.

The evident successes of China's combination of communist government with capitalist economics nevertheless left the country with many problems. Despite the rise in overall national wealth, distribution of the wealth was a problem. There are still some 220 million people living in abject poverty on less than $1 per day. Although even the poor are becoming richer, the divisions between rich and poor are growing. These divisions are largely regional. The economy of the coastal and southern regions of China, with their manufacturing industries and export trade, grew through the 1990s at 13 percent per year, five times the rate of the inland and northern regions.

China's "floating population," rural people who shifted to China's cities, and from inland areas to the coast, in search of jobs, grew to more than 100 million. Previously, government regulations had forbidden such internal migration. Now these new urbanites, still without legal permits for long-time residence, formed up to one-third of the population of some of China's cities. They were blamed for increases in crime and social unrest. Of course they also provided low-cost labor for China's growing economy—when they could find jobs.

Environmental degradation, including the pollution of air and water, has increased with China's industrialization. The rise of factories and cars and the use of artificial fertilizer increased dramatically the level of pollution of land, air, and water in China. Some of the most colossal projects were the largest offenders. The Three Gorges Dam on the upper Yangzi River, the largest hydro-electric project in the world, not only displaces more than one million residents, flooded out by the reservoir that forms behind the dam, but also mixes the industrial wastes that have been emptied into the river through the years into that reservoir of water that will be drunk downstream throughout central China. The cost of the dam, to be opened in 2009, is about $30 billion. The government justifies the dam as a project befitting China's status as one of the great powers of the world, and one whose electricity generation will in fact save China's air from the pollution that would otherwise have come through coal generation of electricity.

More recently, China's use of high-sulfur gasoline as a means of fueling its ever-increasing engines is drawing enormous criticism. Sulfur levels in fuels are tightly regulated in the United States and Europe because of their high toxicity. China feels it cannot be so picky. Despite the fact that the sulfur pollutes the air, ruins the catalytic converters that have been designed to cut down on other pollutants, and burns at very low efficiency, it is cheap and available. China feels that this is a necessary alternative for a relatively poor, rapidly developing country.

At higher levels of the economy, white-collar crime and corruption became major problems. As in Russia, as the government liberalized, state assets were often sold to the Party faithful at bargain prices. Meanwhile, the lure of new profits, a relaxation in law enforcement, and a rise in bribery created a new class of privately wealthy moguls. China witnessed a rapid recrudescence of quasi-illegal night spots, gangsterism, drug dealing, secret societies, prostitution, and gambling, much of it owned and run by the police and military.

Deng's government could speak proudly of its accomplishments in the "four modernizations" of agriculture, science and technology, industry, and defense. Critics, however, called for the "fifth modernization"—democracy. In 1989, tens of thousands of demonstrators, mostly students, assembled in Tiananmen Square, demanding democracy as the antidote to a government ruled by old men, infested with corruption, and no longer in touch with the grass roots. The government called in the army to clear the square. In the process, several hundred (some say as many as 5000) demonstrators were killed, and more injured. The students' protests were tragically validated, but their proposed solution would have to wait.

Also in 1999 the government arrested thousands of members of the Falun Gong religious movement. Falun Gong combined elements of Buddhism, Taoism, and the martial arts. The group declared itself apolitical, but the government of China feared that any group of such size had potential political implications. Its membership surpassed that of the Communist Party. In 1999 after the Falun Gong staged the largest unauthorized demonstration in Beijing since 1989, the government banned the sect entirely. No potential challenge to the government would be tolerated.

The Three Gorges Dam, Hubei Province, China, 2003. By 10 a.m. each morning at the dam site, the Yangtze River rises 114 meters above sea level. Despite the criticism of the dam's impact on the ecology and residents of its region, the Chinese government views this as one of its most beneficial and spectacular technological accomplishments.

The government's public statements on the SARS health epidemic of 2002 reflected its ambiguous relationship with transparency. The epidemic of this previously unknown disease that killed some 350 people in China was, at first, not reported. The Chinese understood, correctly, that news of the epidemic would cut into its international business and travel. As news did emerge, however, the World Health Organization and others censured China for covering up news that could have enabled faster health responses throughout the world. From then on, China released news about the epidemic promptly and widely.

China also permitted and even encouraged the growth of Non-Governmental Organizations, as long as they did not appear to threaten government control. NGOs are the heartbeat of democracy, since they encourage the participation of the people in public affairs, and frequently involve foreign participation as well. NGOs work in China, for example, in rural education and development, biodiversity, drug control, family planning, environment and science, and women's and children's development. They are the backbone of civil society and are beginning to flourish, expanding in numbers of participants, areas of activity, and foreign involvement. (Americans tend to take NGOs, usually referred to as voluntary organizations in the USA, for granted since they are so widespread and so active throughout the country. In many other nations, like China, they are a relatively new phenomenon, and must constantly negotiate their status with the government, which usually regulates them lest they challenge government authority.)

In terms of international relations, also, China implemented a series of dramatic turnabouts. Within its own area of the world, China for 2000 years has viewed itself as the dominant, central power, and has sought that recognition from its neighbors with mixed success. The startling economic success of South Korea and Taiwan, not to mention that of Japan, at first challenged both China's regional supremacy and its communist path of development. As the Chinese economy grew at unprecedented rates after 1979, however, China began to regain some of its historic pre-eminence in the region. In 1997 the island of Hong Kong, and the tiny strip of adjacent territories on the mainland, which had been a British colony since 1842, reverted to Chinese sovereignty. (Two years later tiny Macao was returned to China by Portugal.) Commercial and political observers, as well as the people of Hong Kong themselves, wait and watch to see the policies that China implements in this historic outpost of capitalism. Political demonstrations in favor of continuing democratic institutions have become commonplace in Hong Kong. In July 2003, for example, an estimated 500,000 people demonstrated in Hong Kong against proposed laws that would have curtailed civil rights—and the laws were abandoned.

In many neighboring countries, China was feared and resented, not an uncommon relationship for a regional superpower. Even internally, it was viewed as an invading and conquering power. In its own Xinjiang Autonomous Region, the Central Asian Muslim Uighur population resented Chinese rule and waged low-intensity guerrilla war against it. The Tibet Autonomous Region similarly opposed Chinese rule. China invaded and colonized Tibet in 1959, driving Tibet's religious-political leader, the Dalai Lama, into exile. From his home in exile in India, and during his frequent world travels, the Lama spoke out for more freedom, especially religious freedom for Tibetans. China backed the murderous Khmer Rouge Party and its leader Pol Pot in the vicious civil wars in Cambodia in the late 1970s and 1980s, even committing troops briefly to combat.

In several nearby states, Chinese minorities were viewed with suspicion as possible fifth-column infiltrators, for both the Chinese nation and the Communist Party. In anti-Chinese and anti-communist riots in Indonesia in 1965, thousands of Chinese were murdered, and hundreds of thousands more were exiled.

After early cooperation, misunderstandings and even armed border conflicts had marked China's relations with the USSR. The two nations argued over ideology. In the 1980s, however, both countries softened their positions. With Gorbachev promoting glasnost (political and cultural openess) and perestroika (economic restructuring) in the USSR, and Deng advocating greater economic openness and diplomatic pragmatism in China, relations between the two countries normalized. In July 2002, they signed a twenty-year friendship agreement.

Relations with the United States also warmed. After decades of conflict—armed in Korea, diplomatic over issues like the fate of Tibet and its exiled leader, the Dalai Lama—in the early 1970s the diplomatic scene changed dramatically. Mao and his new advisers, retreating from the economic catastrophe of the Cultural Revolution, sought assistance from abroad. President Nixon and his Secretary of State, Henry Kissinger, also favored more pragmatic policies. In 1971, the USA did not stand in the way of China's joining the United Nations, and in the next year, Nixon visited China, advancing the normalization of relations between the two countries. In 1979 formal diplomatic relations were resumed. While the USA still formally protests the 1989 Tiananmen Square crackdown on democracy, relations are improving and top-ranking American government officials visit Beijing regularly, albeit on Chinese terms. In 1997, the United States Congress voted to continue China's permanent "most favored nation" trade status, and further bilateral trade agreements followed, despite opposition to China's persistent and extreme human rights abuses. One-fifth of all China's exports go to the USA and these form 9 percent of all US imports. In 2002, the USA imported $125 billion of goods and services from China while exporting only $22 billion, leaving a trade surplus for China of $103 billion. In 2001 China was welcomed into the WTO.

China's identity shifts over the past thirty years have been astonishing: from inward looking to full participant in global affairs, from communist economy to capitalist, from economic catastrophe to the fastest growing of all the major world economies. And while the government remains thoroughly vigilant against any direct challenge to its authority and control of power, much within this formerly closed society has opened up with more consumer goods and a rampant desire for them: fashionable clothes, more open expressions of sexuality, Western and world music, new telecommunications, including internet connections and access to the broadcasts of the BBC, the Voice of America, and CNN. How long and how deeply the economic boom can continue, how the authoritarian government can coexist with a broadening band of civic activism and consumer expression, are critical questions that will absorb China's attention, and the world's.

India after Congress Dominance: A Quiet Revolution in Caste and Politics

In the first years of India's Independence, the Congress Party under Jawaharlal Nehru represented the public face of India's identity. The government was committed politically to democratic institutions and processes; socially to a composite society that had a place for all of India's religious and ethnic groups; and economically to a mixed economy that maintained private property rights and freedom for private entrepreneurs, but with government control of major industries, financial institutions, and access to the permits and licenses needed to create or expand businesses. The Congress itself was largely an upper-middle-class institution, although its rank-and-file membership included millions of peasants and workers. The Nehru family embodied the Congress system. Two years after Nehru died in 1964, his daughter, Indira Gandhi, became prime minister and ruled for most of the years until her assassination in 1984. Then her son, Rajiv, became prime minister and governed until 1989. The Congress did not die at this point, nor did the Nehru dynasty pass away. To some degree these identities remained remarkably stable through more than a half century. In 2004, the Congress Party returned to its position as India's largest, although not so dominant as before, and Rajiv's widow, Sonia, is today its head. But new parties, some of them national, many more of them existing only within individual states, grew up to challenge Congress rule and reduce its power. Even in 2004, when it recaptured the central government, Congress did so only through alliances with other parties.

As parties have multiplied in number, India has become far less centralized than it was at Independence. Three issues have dominated public life, often referred to as the three Ms: Mosque, Mandal, and Markets. In Chapter 23 we discussed at some length the public attacks on the Muslim role in India's public life—symbolized by the destruction of the Babri Mosque at Ayodhaya and the rise of the BJP political party. Here we will discuss Mandal and Markets.

The Mandal Commission B.P. Mandal was appointed by the prime minister of India to deal with an economic and social problem that had bedeviled Indian politics for decades. Even under the British in 1935, untouchables, called scheduled castes (SCs) because they were listed on an official government schedule, were given special "reservations" or minimum quotas in public life. This affirmative action program in the fields of government jobs, elected positions, and education covered 15 percent of the population. But what of the next levels up, usually referred to as the Other Backward Classes (OBCs)? Some additional 50 percent of the population—more in some areas—had also suffered severe discrimination on the basis of caste, although perhaps not quite so extreme as the SCs. In south India, where the proportion of Brahmins and other high castes is very low—perhaps 3 percent Brahmins, for example—and where these Brahmins are often referred to as colonialists, reservations had begun a century before, in 1870, under the British. A regional party, the Justice Party, arose to represent the lower castes and oppose Brahmin control. In 1920, it won the elections for the limited government positions then available. In the south, the upper castes were already being displaced from power.

In north India, where Brahmins formed about 10 percent of the population and other higher castes another 10 to 15 percent, government had postponed confronting the issue. The Mandal Commission was the second formal attempt to address it. In

AT A GLANCE : NEW IDENTITIES

DATE	ISRAEL	E./CENTRAL AFRICA	S. AFRICA	MEXICO	BRAZIL
1970	■ Arab terrorists attack Israeli athletes at Munich Olympics (1972)	■ Uganda: Under Idi Amin's regime, 300,000 killed in ethnic war; Asians expelled from the country (1971–9) ■ Rwanda: tensions between rival Tutsi and Hutu tribes erupt in repeated warfare and massacres (from 1972)	■ Portugal's dictatorship overthrown; Mozambique and Angola (1974) ■ South Africa: Protests in Soweto against apartheid education policies lead to nationwide riots (1976)	■ Steady economic growth, 1950s–1980s, based largely on oil	■ Military dictatorship in power (1964–88) ■ Political parties form (1979)
1980	■ Palestinians begin *intifada* against Israeli control (1987)	■ Tanzania's Julius Nyerere retires (1985)	■ South Africa only white-ruled country south of the Sahara (after 1980) ■ Commonwealth and US sanctions (1986)	■ Collapse of oil price forces Mexico to turn to IMF and other international lenders (1980s)	■ Elections permitted (1984)
1990	■ Jordan signs peace treaty with Israel (1995) ■ Assassination of President Yitzhak Rabin cripples peace process (1995)	■ Somalia dissolves into severe civil warfare (1991) ■ Eritrea achieves independence from Ethiopia (1993) ■ Zaire (renamed Republic of Congo): Laurent Kabila seizes power (1997); civil war continues	■ South Africa: President F.W. de Klerk lifts ban against ANC; Mandela freed (1990) ■ National Truth Commission investigating abuses under apartheid (1995)	■ North American Free Trade Association (NAFTA) (1994) ■ Peso collapses ■ 145 Maya Indians killed in riots in Chiapas state (1994)	■ President Fernando Collor de Mello driven from power on corruption charges (1992) ■ International Monetary Fund loans give the IMF influence over Brazilian policy ■ MERCOSUR, free-trade zone (1995)
2000	■ Failed Camp David negotiations between Ehud Barak, Yasser Arafat, and Bill Clinton (2000) ■ World Court condemns Sharon's wall separating Jews and Palestinians (2004)	■ Laurent Kabila assassinated (2001) ■ Joseph Kabila takes power (2001)	■ First democratic elections in South Africa; Nelson Mandela as President (1994–2003)	■ Vicente Fox elected President of Mexico (2000)	■ Lula da Silva elected President of Brazil (2002)

1980 the commission made its report public, arguing that OBCs constituted about 52 percent of the nation's population and recommended that 27 percent of the positions in the central administration and in the public sector should be reserved for them. Although the "C" in OBC officially referred to class rather than caste, the Mandal Commission argued that caste was the most significant indicator of class and identified some 3743 castes as OBCs.

Congress Party leaders at first chose to do nothing, but by the mid-1980s other parties, some representing primarily OBC constituents, began to clamor for implementation of the commission's report. The road was rocky. The Congress government of Gujarat State, led by an OBC in 1985, attempted to implement the principles of the Mandal Commission report and was forced from office by mass protests and riots from the upper castes. (Americans, accustomed to class-based public protests coming from below and attacking elites, may be surprised that such protests may also come from above. Backlash protests against racial desegregation in the 1960s, however, were also of this nature.) New parties, however, began to form around the issue of reservations, sometimes led by OBCs themselves, particularly at the state level, and sometimes by upper-caste members committed to concepts of equality, or seeking additional votes, or both.

In 1990, the prime minister, V.P. Singh brought the issue to a head nationally by implementing the Mandal Commission recommendations. This and other of his reformist programs alienated many upper-class and upper-caste people, and he was forced from power in 1991 when new elections brought the Congress Party back to power. Nevertheless, a transformation was taking place. In the major north Indian states, from 1984 to 1999 the percentage of upper castes elected to the national parliament dropped by a third, from 47 to 31, while the percentage of OBCs doubled, from 11 to 22. India's two largest states, Uttar Pradesh and Bihar, were ruled by OBC parties headed by OBC leaders. Singh explained the overall significance of the shift that was taking place:

> Now that every party is wooing the deprived classes, with every round of elections more and more representatives of the deprived sections will be elected. This will ultimately be reflected in the social composition of the local bodies, state governments, and the central government. A silent transfer of power is taking place in social terms. (Jaffrelot, p. 139)

Many predictable problems have occurred. When caste alone was the criterion for affirmative action, the beneficiaries were often the wealthiest and best educated members within the lowest castes, the so called "creamy layer," rather than the poorest and least educated. Antagonism between castes was common as the new reservation policies were put into place, challenging old hierarchies. Upper-caste people scoffed at the SCs and OBCs in public office, claiming that standards were dropping. Lower-caste groups resented the oppression and scorn of the upper. Parties formed very odd coalitions for election purposes. SCs and OBCs, who might have made common cause against the upper castes, chose instead to form separate coalitions with them. Old hierarchies were giving way to a new fluidity in political relationships. New identities were being formed as voters began to see that they had unprecedented powers if they could take advantage of new opportunities for organization. Caste identity itself was being transformed from a ritual and economic category to a political identity that required coalition-building among groups that previously had seen each other as separate and unequal.

Attempts to redress gender discrimination arose from somewhat different motivations than the system of caste reservations. Nevertheless, the 73rd amendment to the Constitution, passed in 1992, did set aside specific reservations for women. It guaranteed to women one-third of the seats in elected bodies in both urban and rural local government. By 2003, an estimated one million women across India filled these seats. On the other hand, the powers of local government are quite limited, and attempts to extend the reservation policy for women to state-wide and national government offices have not gone beyond the talking stages. The percentage of women voting in national elections rose from 37 in 1952 to 58 in 1998. The number of women members of the Lok Sabha, the lower house of parliament, has increased from 22, about 4.5 percent, in 1952 to 45, about 9 percent, in 2004. Women have served as chief ministers in several states throughout the country, but the percentage of women voting in many state assemblies has actually gone down. Women are beginning to organize effectively as they understand the power of the vote, but they have not created the collective power that the lowest castes have managed to develop.

Markets, the IMF, and Capitalist Economics As upper-caste groups have lost some of their political powers, they have moved more actively into business careers, and the growth of private economic markets is the third area in which Indian identity is taking on new forms. In 1991, under pressure from the IMF, India began to move away from the state-guided, socialistic, and red-tape-laden economy of the early days of Independence toward a free-market economy. It was not India's choice to move in this direction, however, and the transformation has not been whole-hearted. A shortage of foreign exchange funds forced the nation to turn to the IMF for a loan. In exchange, the IMF insisted that India follow the IMF prescription of "the Washington consensus": fire excess government workers, cut subsidies to the poor, privatize government-owned businesses, devalue the currency, eliminate government controls over business, open domestic markets to international investment and trade. In short, accept a free-market economy.

To some extent, India did accept this new economic dispensation. Many politicians and economists who had been devotees of socialism and state control of the development of the country changed their minds, and for the first time since Independence, many people spoke favorably of capitalism. Not everyone, to be sure. Many believed capitalism to be rapacious, interested only in profit and not in human welfare. But others admitted that the government had become a drag on economic development. India's policy of "permit raj"—of requiring government permits to open new businesses or expand old ones, or to import capital goods—had stifled investment and promoted the corruption of government officials. They admitted that keeping India's domestic markets relatively closed to foreign imports and investments raised the price of Indian goods for consumers and enabled Indian business to operate inefficiently, and to charge high prices for shoddy products. They admitted that the government hired far too many workers where few were needed, and subsidized some poor people who were, as a result, working less hard than they might. Many industrialists feared that India could not compete in world markets once tariffs and subsidies were removed, but many others welcomed opportunity and the challenge.

India's economic growth rate rose to about 6.5 percent per year in the 1990s, and even a little higher in the early 2000s. Foreign direct investment rose to about $3 billion per year, much higher than the $200 million in the years before 1991, although this was only a small fraction of China's rate of foreign direct investment. India's holdings of foreign currency rose from a crisis level of only about $1 billion in 1991 to about $40 billion a decade later. Firms became more efficient and more profitable. Stocks sold on the Indian stock exchange multiplied in value 500 percent between 1990 and 1999.

As is common in a capitalist economy, some sectors and regions began to move ahead much faster than others, increasing inequalities. For example, the state of Gujarat, the fastest growing state in India at the time, saw its per capita gross development product increase at 7.6 percent per year from 1991 to 1997. Gujarat began to compare its growth rate with that of the East Asian tigers. In the same period, however, India's slowest growing states economically—and largest in terms of population—Bihar and Uttar Pradesh, grew by only about 1.2 percent per year. Previously, the central government had tried to compensate for these kinds of disparities by giving higher levels of assistance to poorer states. Now the richer states, embracing capitalist doctrine, protested this allocation of assistance, arguing that it rewarded economic incompetence and punished economic accomplishment.

The information technology (IT) sector has been a leader in growth domestically and internationally, while some older, declining, "sunset" industries, like jute, lag far behind. IT has become a leader not only in producing software, but in serving as a "backoffice" for international businesses, creating hundreds of thousands of jobs. The excellence of India's upper levels of education in technology has also made it possible for many Indians, skilled in IT, to find jobs elsewhere. Silicon Valley in the USA has been a prime destination. Here, too, there has been a change in Indian identity: as India becomes a recognized leader in IT research and productivity, the Indians who relocate to Silicon Valley are no longer seen as a "brain drain," depleting India's supply of trained manpower, but rather as valuable contributors to India's development. The accusation that Indians who go overseas to earn a living are deserters has changed as they obviously keep closely in touch with family and friends back in India, remit money to them, and establish new outposts of Indian culture in their new homes. Indian Americans are the first or second most wealthy ethnic community in the United States, and their influence in America, and their assistance to India in the form of remittances and investments, gives them a respected position in the eyes of most Indians. Indian enterprise appears ready for further export growth. A new area ready for expansion appears to be pharmaceuticals and perhaps the film industry, known as "Bollywood," a merger of the styles of Bombay and Hollywood, will follow.

Man Mohan Singh, 2004. Man Mohan Singh, an expert in economics, presided over the restructuring of India's economy after 1991 and became prime minister in the Congress Party-dominated government in 2004. He is here flanked by the Congress Party chief Sonia Gandhi, widow of the assassinated Prime Minister Rajiv Gandhi.

The new economic identity, based on free markets, is far from dominant in India. First, government still acts as a drag on business. It has not withdrawn completely from the processes of regulating Indian business, nor has it privatized some of the biggest state-run enterprises, nor has it removed all subsidies. Its policies of providing subsidies to economically less successful states has drawn the opposition of stronger states that believe that their hard work goes unrewarded. It is also widely viewed as corrupt in using its powers to extort money from businessmen to the extent that business suffers. Also, the benefits of the new economy have gone especially to those who are already skilled and experienced, like the IT elites, while they leave out the common, relatively poor citizens.

The 2004 national election seemed to echo the resentment of the poor for the rich, as voters defeated the incumbent BJP party and gave a surprising victory to the Congress, nowadays considered more "pro-poor" than the BJP, and to Prime Minister Man Mohan Singh. One of the most prominent advocates of the importance of information technology in India's development, Chandrababu Naidu, the chief minister of the south Indian state of Andhra Pradesh, was one of the candidates most severely routed in the election. The opposition charged that while a relative few were benefiting from IT,

The Middle East since 1945. The presence of oil and gas reserves, the establishment of a Jewish homeland state of Israel in Palestine (1948), and the intervention of outside states have dominated the the region. In addition to Arab–Israeli confrontations, an eight-year conflict between Iran and Iraq, a war over Iraq's invasion of Kuwait, the American invasion of Iraq in 2003, and civil wars and revolutions have kept the region in turmoil.

millions of simple peasants were still going hungry, and a conspicuous number were committing suicide as a result of their poverty. Naidu's defeat carried an important lesson. India was moving to open its economy to capitalism far more cautiously than China, in large part because India was a democracy and had to take popular opinion into consideration. This democracy had become firmly rooted since Independence, and it, too, was part of India's identity.

ISRAEL AND PALESTINE: JEWS AND ARABS

The relationships between Israelis and Arabs combine so many compelling issues and tell so many intertwined stories that collectively they have touched the imagination of much of the world. Of all issues in the modern Middle East, Israeli–Arab relations have been the most contentious and the most discussed by historians. At their heart are multiple, intertwined conflicts of identity: religious, political, territorial, economic, colonial, and generational. Although this case study will focus on events of the past two decades, in order to understand them, we must go back about a century in terms of politics, and two millennia in terms of religion.

The conflict of religious identities between Jew and Muslim seems, at first glance, to be the most important. Ever since 135 C.E., when the Romans exiled the Jews from Judaea (Israel), they sought to return. They believed that God had promised this land to them, as recorded in the Bible, and their prayers regularly included a reminder to God of his promise.

After the Jewish exile, other peoples occupied the land. After its conquest by Muslim empires, at the end of the seventh century, the overwhelming majority of the residents of Palestine (the generally accepted geographical name of the area through the centuries after the Romans departed) were Muslims. When Jews actually did begin to return to Palestine in significant numbers, toward the end of the nineteenth century, the hundreds of thousands of Arabs resident there saw that return as a challenge to their own religious supremacy. In some ways, then, the Israel–Arab conflict is based on a religious conflict that dates back at least 1300 years.

Politics, however, was perhaps even more important. The Jews who began to return to Palestine were motivated less by a religious quest than by the perceived need for a political homeland and refuge. Europe, where most Jews lived, was permeated by nationalism in the nineteenth century, and Jews absorbed this spirit. At first, the goal was expressed in national-cultural terms: to restore Hebrew as a living language of everyday national life; to work the land again after centuries of urban ghettoization; to live as a "normal" people with a land and culture of its own. Then, as pogroms against Jews resumed with unprecedented ferocity under Russian Czar Alexander III after 1881, the movement of Jewish nationalism became far more urgent and far more political. Persecuted Jews needed a refuge.

Assimilated Jews, living more contentedly in the USA and western European countries, at first discounted this argument. Even the Jews fleeing Russian pogroms headed mostly to the USA; only a comparative handful chose the more difficult, nationalistic route to Palestine. But then anti-Semitism resurfaced strongly in the 1890s in France. Assimilated Jews of western Europe were shocked. The Austrian-Jewish journalist Theodor Herzl (1860–1904) founded the modern political Zionist movement—"Zion" is a biblical designation for Jerusalem—to restore to Jews a political homeland in their ancestral land of Palestine.

Now a third identity—a colonial identity—entered the conflict. In 1917, during World War I, the British government issued the Balfour Declaration, proposing to redistribute the lands of the Ottoman Empire if Britain could conquer them:

> His Majesty's Government view with favour the establishment in Palestine of a
> national home for the Jewish people, and will use their best endeavours to facilitate
> the achievement of this objective, it being clearly understood that nothing shall be
> done which may prejudice the civil and religious rights of existing non-Jewish
> communities in Palestine.

Intentionally or not, this declaration inserted a colonial voice of divide-and-rule into the middle of the Middle East. Arabs and Jews simply followed through, playing their

The Camp David peace accords. In Maryland, September 1978, Israeli prime minister Menachem Begin, President Jimmy Carter, and Egyptian president Anwar Sadat relax during the historic Camp David peace talks that resulted in the 1979 treaty between Israel and Egypt. The Camp David Accords, documents signed by the leaders of Israel and Egypt, were a preliminary to the signing of the formal peace treaty between the two nations. The treaty returned the Sinai to Egypt.

assigned, antagonistic roles. As a result of the war, the end of Ottoman rule, and the beginning of British and French colonialism in the region, Arab nationalism took root. The two nascent nationalisms, Arab and Zionist, grew up together, and were soon fighting for control of the same land. Their numbers were, however, quite unequal. In 1920 there were only about 60,000 Jews and ten times that number of Arabs living in the area.

The Jewish immigrants—"pioneers" as they called themselves—came mostly from cities and small towns in eastern and central Europe. They had European educations, philosophies, technologies, and attitudes, and they usually viewed the Arabs among whom they settled as educationally backward and technologically primitive nomadic and farming peoples. Many of the Jewish settlers built egalitarian collective farms, kibbutzim, to maximize agricultural efficiency, achieve a social vision, and provide for their common defense. The Zionists argued, with a kind of colonial paternalism, that they could help reform and modernize the land and the people, but they took little account of the displacement of local society caused by their arrival and the anger it evoked. Armed Arab uprisings attempted unsuccessfully to halt and drive out Jewish immigration from the 1920s onward, with particularly severe attacks in 1929 and 1936.

The Holocaust marked the turning point. For Jews, that catastrophe re-affirmed the desperate need for a political state and refuge. They tended to (mis)identify the efforts of Arabs to block the creation of Israel, not as a struggle over control of land, but as a new Nazism, intent on root-and-branch destruction. This portrayal increased Jewish fear of, and opposition to, Arab concerns. Some Jewish immigrants also argued that their own suffering and desperation created the need for a small area to call their own that far outweighed any claims of the Arab inhabitants, who had, in any case, far more territory to call their own. The Jews did not seek armed conflict, but neither would they retreat in the face of armed opposition. Meanwhile Arabs asked pointedly: Why should Christian guilt over a Holocaust in Europe be expiated by assigning to Jews lands held by Muslims in the eastern Mediterranean? In Arab eyes, this was European colonialism parading as humanitarianism at Arab expense.

With United Nations' approval, Israel declared itself a state in 1948 in about one-half of the land of Palestine. Arab armies immediately attacked, but the state survived and even won some additional territory. Many Palestinians fled the new state, becoming the "wandering Jews" of the Middle East. Palestinians generally argue that they were forced out by armed intimidation; Jews claim that Palestinians followed their leaders' advice that they leave temporarily in order to return later in armed triumph. A great outpouring of revisionist historical writing by Israeli authors such as Benny Morris has provided documentary evidence that gave support to both claims. Whatever the immediate cause, some 600,000 Palestinians fled the borders of Israel at the time of the establishment of the state and the 1948 war. Another million stayed on as citizens, although many would say as second-class citizens, inside the borders of Israel.

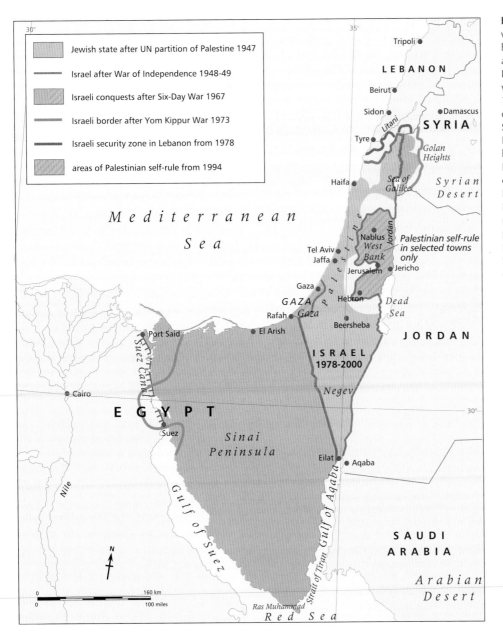

Israel and its neighbors. The creation, with Western support, of a Jewish homeland in Palestine in 1947 occurred at a time of increasing Arab nationalism. Israel's birth in 1948 was attended by a war and more followed in 1956, 1967, 1973, and 1982. Peace treaties exist only with Egypt, which regained the Sinai peninsula, and Jordan (1994). Beginning in 1987, an *intifada* (uprising) by Palestinians forced more attention on Israeli–Palestinian relations—an extremely vexed issue. In 1993, the Palestinian Liberation Organization and Israel began negotiations that would return land to Palestinian control and perhaps lead to a Palestinian state, while recognizing Israel's right to exist. So far these negotiations have proved fruitless and a second *intifada* began in 2000.

Israelis believed that the neighboring Arab states would—and should—absorb the exiles. After all, Israel had absorbed more than a million Jews who immigrated from Arab states after 1948, either pulled by the attraction of a Jewish homeland or pushed by fear of future reprisals by Arabs. But the Arab states chose to leave the Palestinians in refugee status, living in refugee camps, or seeking employment in the oil fields of the Persian Gulf region, or leaving the area entirely. The result has been a bitter irridentism, a desire to reclaim their homeland, represented among Palestinians primarily by the Palestine Liberation Organization (after 1996 the Palestine National Authority); militant hostility toward Israel; and unsettled refugee groups that threaten the stability of neighboring states.

Israel's 1967 conquest of the West Bank and Gaza Strip left one and a half million Palestinians under an increasingly harsh military occupation. Israel opened the lands conquered in 1967 to Jewish settlement, and about 400,000 Jews, under the protection of the Israeli army, came to settle among the 2 million Arabs of these areas. The Palestinians wanted to establish a state of their own in this land. Rejecting these territorial ambitions for a Palestinian state, the Israelis tightened the occupation. The Israeli–Arab conflict had two inter-related dimensions. The first was the internal struggle between two nations—Israel and a Palestine-striving-to-be-born—inhabiting a single geographical land. The second was the international strife between Israel and the surrounding Arab states. Through the 1970s and early 1980s, Arabs expressed their anger through violent attacks within Israeli borders as well as terrorist attacks against international travelers, especially in airports and airplanes, and against the Israeli athletes participating in the 1972 Munich Olympics. Israeli bombings of refugee camps were a common response.

The Israeli–Palestinian–Arab conflict had global implications. It inflamed the entire Arab world, which was the location of the world's greatest oil reserves. In 1973, when Israel and its neighbors fought another war, the oil-rich Arab countries, acting through the Organization of Petroleum Exporting Countries (OPEC) rationed and embargoed the export of oil to the United States and western Europe to demonstrate their anger at Western support for Israel and their power over the world's oil resources. OPEC repeated its restrictions through the 1970s, and the world economy went into a decline that lasted for several years. In addition, with the United States usually taking the side of Israel, and the USSR usually siding with the Arab nations, the Middle East conflict became a part of the global Cold War confrontation. Finally, militant Islamic groups pressured Arab governments to take a more active role in the conflict, threatening the stability of these states.

The decision by Anwar Sadat of Egypt to seek a peace treaty with Israel, finally signed in 1979, therefore signaled a significant breakthrough. Egypt was the largest and most powerful of the frontline states bordering Israel, so the treaty sharply diminished the likelihood that the local conflict would spread beyond its home region. When Palestinians in the West Bank and Gaza regions began an *intifada* (uprising) in 1987, employing both civil disobedience and low-intensity violence in a pattern of continuous demonstrations to disrupt Israeli control, the rest of the Arab world gave little practical assistance. Israel cracked down and hardened its positions.

Some renewed possibilities for peace opened in the early 1990s as the Soviet Union dissolved, ending the superpower rivalries that had helped militarize the Middle East. Also, the 1991 Gulf War in Iraq led to divisions and re-alignments among Arab states. New openings toward Israel appeared possible. Many observers looked to the USA to broker, or to impose, a peace agree-

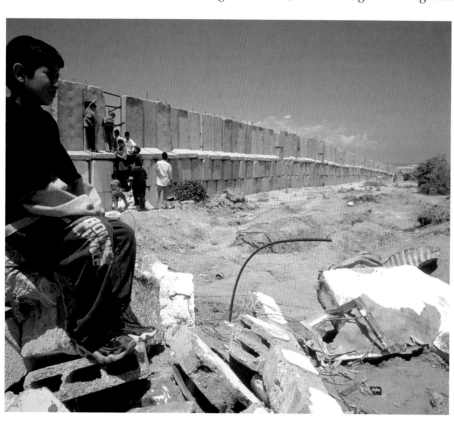

Children of the *intifada*, 2001. This wall separates Israelis and Palestinians in the Gaza quarter of Rafah.

ment in the region, but the United States, despite a great deal of public diplomacy, remained unwilling to assert itself, and when it did, it supported Israeli positions so strongly that it was seen more as an ally of Israel than as an "honest broker" between the two sides. US support for Israel seemed to be a product of historical sentiment toward the nation and its origins as well as of political lobbying both by Jewish voters and by many fundamentalist Christian groups, who saw the rebirth of Israel as part of God's plan for ultimately converting the Jews to Christianity. Religious as well as political identities in the United States had their influence on identities in the Middle East, and vice versa.

A breakthrough in the internal Israeli–Palestinian conflict appeared in 1993, when the government of Israel and the Palestine Liberation Organization signed an agreement—called the "Oslo accords" for the Norwegian city in which the agreements had been reached—to recognize each other, to cease fighting, and to extend at least limited self-rule to the Palestinians in Gaza and the West Bank. For the first time, each of the two combatants agreed publicly and in principle to recognize the identity and existence of one another. Until this point, the Palestinians had refused to recognize the legitimacy of the Jewish state and Israel had refused to recognize the legitimacy of the Palestinians' claim to their own state. Peace accords between Israel and the Palestinians opened the way for other Arab nations to normalize their relations with Israel. Jordan, under King Hussein, signed a peace treaty in 1994.

The euphoria did not last. A Jewish extremist assassinated Israeli prime minister Yitzhak Rabin, a sponsor of the peace agreement, in 1995. Later in the year Arab militants bombed several Israeli buses. The advocates for renewed violence on both sides were overwhelming the advocates for peace. The election of Ehud Barak as Israel's

SOURCE

The Geneva Accords: A Non-Governmental Plan for Peace

Intense peace negotiations between Israelis and Palestinians at Camp David in the United States in 2000 and in Taba, Egypt, in 2001 failed to produce peace agreements. Nevertheless, some of the representatives decided to continue to pursue a detailed framework for a peace agreement as a model of what might be achieved and to prove that responsible leaders on both sides could be partners in the search for peace. At the end of 2003, the Israeli Yossi Beilin and the Palestinian Abed Rabbo unveiled the agreements they had reached in their secret meetings in Geneva. They distributed copies throughout Israel and the Palestinian territories, claiming that at least 40 percent of each population accepted their framework for peace. Meanwhile the second Palestinian intifada *and Israel's harsh repression continued all around them, on the one hand mocking their efforts as utopian and, on the other, demonstrating dramatically the need for peace.*

We, the undersigned, a group of Palestinians and Israelis, endorse, on this day, October 12, 2003, a model draft framework final status agreement between the two peoples. At this point in time, after the Palestinian government and the Israeli government have accepted the Road Map [an international plan especially favored by the Americans], which includes reaching a final status settlement by 2005, based on a two-state solution, we consider it to be of utmost importance to present to the two peoples and the entire world an example of what such a final status agreement could include. This is proof that despite all the pain entailed in concessions, it is possible to reach an historical compromise which meets the vital national interests of each side. We present this model agreement as a package—which stands together as an integral whole.

In the near future we will launch a campaign whose goal is to convince both sides of the value of such an historical compromise in the spirit of this model framework agreement, designed to put an end to the protracted conflict ...

The decision to complete and later present this model draft agreement was not easy for any of us, however, we have decided to pursue this path since we believe that action of this type can serve as a source of hope after a long period of suffering, killing, and mutual accusations, that it can help build trust and facilitate the removal of the walls between our nations. In the context of the Road Map process, this draft agreement signifies a mutually acceptable and realizable endgame—to be reached by 2005, and as an answer to the skeptics and supporters of endless interim agreements. This agreement will bring about the creation of a sovereign Palestinian State alongside Israel, put an end to the occupation, terminate conflict and bloodshed, and end all mutual claims.

prime minister in 1999 seemed to favor peace agreements once more. Hopes were high that negotiations between him and the Palestinian leader, Yasir Arafat, sponsored by President Clinton at Camp David in 2000, would bring peace, but the dialogues broke down. Israelis lost heart. Even the "peace camp" lamented that Arafat did not want peace, that there was no "partner for peace" on the side of the Palestinians, that nothing short of the destruction of the Israeli state and identity would satisfy the Arabs. Arafat claimed that the proposed agreements simply did not meet his minimum demands for the creation of the new state of Palestine.

Leadership on both sides became more militant. Among the Palestinians, organizations dedicated to guerrilla warfare and terrorism against civilians gained increasing power and inspired a second *intifada* beginning in September 2000. Israel elected Ariel Sharon and his militant Likud Party over Barak and his more moderate Labor Party in 2001, symbolizing the return to hard-line militance rather than negotiated peace. Palestinian militants increasingly invoked the concept of Islamic *jihad*, or religious warfare. They recruited suicide bombers—people who are willing to die as they deliver bombs hidden on their bodies to explode in enemy locations—to attack Israeli military and civilian targets that they could not otherwise penetrate. Israeli leaders invoked ancient biblical references to Jewish control over the conquered territories and recent memories of the Holocaust, and they defended themselves with overwhelming, brutal power, including the use of assassination against specific militants. Between the beginning of the second *intifada* and mid-2004, approximately 1000 Israelis and 2500 Palestinians were killed. The Israeli occupation of the West Bank and Gaza continued harsh and disruptive of daily life. In return, the Palestinian *intifada* made it impossible for Israelis to rest in peace and security. Even efforts proclaimed to limit violence created antagonisms. Sharon began building a huge physical barrier to separate Jews from Palestinians, but the barrier ate deeply into land that Palestinians expected to be part of their state. The World Court condemned it totally, and the Israeli Supreme Court ruled that it had to be rerouted to be less disruptive to everyday Palestinian life. Palestinians selected new prime ministers thought to be more amenable to peace negotiations than Arafat, but Arafat remained the power behind the throne, and Israelis did not trust his intentions. The continuing conflict also introduced tensions into the relationships between the United States and the European Union. The United States generally supported Israeli positions, while the Europeans were more sympathetic to the Palestinians.

Ironically, and sadly, everyone seemed to know the basic outlines of what was needed for a peace agreement: mutual recognition of Israel and Palestine; an end of violence; national borders corresponding generally to the borders before the 1967 war, with minor territorial adjustments; and the dismantling of Israeli settlements in Palestinian territories. Indeed political leaders of the Israelis and the Palestinians, meeting as private individuals in Geneva intermittently between 2001 and 2003, drew up a plan for peace that expressed these basic principles. They claimed that a majority on both sides would accept them, but that political leadership on both sides would not allow it. In mid-2004 it appeared that everyone knew what might bring peace, but that not everyone wanted it, nor did they trust the other side to keep its agreements. Militant, oppositional, fierce, and fearful identities stood in the way.

Review Questions

- Literary critic Edward Said wrote that "the major contest in most modern cultures concerns the definition or interpretation of each culture." To what extent do the case studies of this chapter support Said's assertion?

- What are the means by which political leaders inflame, or tamp down, potential ethnic, religious, and cultural confrontations? Please give examples.
- Does this chapter seem to suggest that history repeats itself, or that historical change is often surprising because we never know what is coming next?
- To what extent does change in identity seem a natural phenomenon, in part because each new generation will have its own new way of looking at the past?
- What changes in political, economic, social, or cultural identities in the United States and the world currently seem to be most directly affecting your life?

Suggested Readings

With this chapter we are moving into contemporary times, and even into current events. In addition to television and radio news, and newspapers and the popular newsmagazines like *Time*, *Newsweek*, and *U.S. News and World Report*, two publications, serving an educated but not specialized readership, that are especially useful in tracking these events are:

Economist, a weekly review published in London and with extensive coverage of the United States and the entire world. Edited from a traditional liberal perspective—that is, favoring free markets and human rights as developed over the past centuries in Europe and the USA—the *Economist* covers the globe each week. Whatever one may think of its philosophical and political bias, the comprehensiveness and accessibility of its coverage cannot be matched in the English language.

New York Review of Books, published bi-weekly, takes the form of a tabloid of book reviews, but its reviews are lengthy and extensive explorations of subject areas. The particular book or books under assessment serve as a springboard for wide-ranging, thoughtful, and careful discussions of the subject matter. The authors are leading scholars in their fields.

BOOKS AND ARTICLES

Ayres, Alyssa and Philip Oldenburg, eds. *India Briefing: Quickening the Pace of Change* (Armonk, NY: M.E. Sharpe, 2002). The most recent, as of 2004, of a series published every year or two, of outstanding summary articles on developments in contemporary India. Various articles on politics, economics, social life, the arts, and culture.

Bearak, Barry, "Poor Man's Burden," *New York Times Magazine*, June 27, 2004. Descriptive analysis of Lula, as man and leader, and the problems he is encountering as president of Brazil.

China Development Brief. *250 Chinese NGOs: Civil Society in the Making* (Unpublished Report: China Development Brief, 2001). Underlines the importance of NGOs to China's progress—economic as well as political—and outlines the mission and accomplishments of 250 of them.

Chomsky, Noam. *Middle East Illusions* (Lanham, MD: Rowman and Littlefield, 2004). Chomsky takes to task everyone for failures in Middle East policy. He is especially critical of the United States for its uncritical support of Israel.

Crossley, Pamela Kyle, Lynn Hollen Lees, and John W. Servos. *Global Society: The World since 1900* (Boston: Houghton Mifflin, 2004). A fine, well-written history of the twentieth century, organized thematically rather than by nations or regions. Special emphasis on technology and useful references to websites for further research.

Das, Gurcharan. *India Unbound* (New York: Random House, 2000). A newspaper columnist and successful businessman reports on, and relishes, the opening of the Indian economy since 1991.

Edelstein, Jillian. *Truth and Lies: Stories from the Truth and Reconciliation Commission in South Africa* (New York: The New Press, 2001). Portraits and testimony—often quite moving—from individuals who spoke to the commission.

French, Howard. *A Continent for the Taking. The Tragedy and Hope of Africa* (New York: Knopf, 2004). A senior writer for the *New York Times* places the blame for Africa's current difficulties on self-interested political leaders in both Africa and the West, showing that there is plenty of blame to go around.

Gilbert, Mark and Jonathan T. Reynolds. *Africa in World History: From Prehistory to the Present* (Upper Saddle River, NJ: Prentice Hall, 2004). A useful survey. Up to date.

Gilbert, Mark. *Surpassing Realism: The Politics of European Integration since 1945* (Lanham, MD: Rowman and Littlefield, 2003). Step-by-step account of the building of the European Union with fascinating contemporary commentaries along the way.

Glenny, Misha. *The Balkans: Nationalism, War, and the Great Powers, 1804–1999* (New York: Viking, 2000). Comprehensive account of the Balkans and their somewhat unfortunate fate in the hands of the great powers, sometimes because of intervention, sometimes because of lack of intervention.

Gourevitch, Philip. *We Wish to Inform You that Tomorrow We will be Killed with Our Families: Stories from Rwanda* (New York: Farrar, Straus and Giroux, 1998). Brilliant journalistic reporting from the killing fields of Rwanda. Attempts to understand and explain the differences between Tutsis and Hutus.

Guillermoprieto, Alma, "Mexico City: 'The Morning Quickie,'" *New York Review of Books*, August 12, 2004, 40–43. Journalistic account of a Mexico not yet past the corruption of the PRI, not yet committed to a clean, functioning democracy, but able to mock, and therefore perhaps improve, its leadership.

Hughes, Neil C. *China's Economic Challenge: Smashing the Iron Rice Bowl* (Armonk, NY: M.E. Sharpe, 2002). Credits China with enormous, positive change economically and also politically, but argues that for China to continue to march forward she will have to introduce greater personal, political democracy.

Human Development Report 2003: Millennium Development Goals: A Compact among Nations to End Human Poverty (New York: Oxford University Press for the United Nations Development Programme, 2003). A survey of the nations of the world with an abundance of statistical tables and numerous, brief, specific topical discussions.

Hunt, Michael H. *The World Transformed: 1945 to the Present: A Documentary Reader* (Boston: Bedford/St. Martin's, 2004). An outstanding selection of primary documents with global scope and thematic breadth.

Jaffrelot, Christophe, "The Subordinate Caste Revolution," in Ayres and Oldenburg, pp. 121–58. Excellent, brief discussion of the rise of the lower castes in a silent, relatively peaceful revolution.

Kishwar, Madhu. *Off the Beaten Track: Rethinking Gender Justice for Indian Women* (New Delhi: Oxford University Press, 1999). The editor of one of India's leading feminist journals, Manushi, discusses the evolution of her thought in light of the possible and the ideal.

Meade, Teresa. *A Brief History of Brazil* (New York: Checkmark Books, 2004). Brief incisive account, with many insights presented through sidebars. Especially interesting on culture, music, and sports. Well-chosen illustrations.

Mishra, Pankaj, "India: The Neglected Majority Wins!" *New York Review of Books*, August 12, 2004, 30–37. A thoughtful report on the victory of the Congress and failure of the BJP in India's 2004 national election, taking great pleasure in poorer people asserting their political wishes.

Mukherji, Joydeep, "The Indian Economy: Pushing Ahead and Pulling Apart," in Ayres and Oldenburg. A professional economist's thoughtful, comprehensive, but brief assessment of the state of India's economy, about 1991–2002.

Nugent, Neill. *The Government and Politics of the European Union* (Durham, NC: Duke University Press, 5th ed., 2003). Detailed exposition of the institutional workings of the EU, with very useful historical prelude and concluding perspectives on the future.

Preston, Julia and Samuel Dillon. *Opening Mexico. The Making of a Democracy* (New York: Farrar, Straus and Giroux, 2004). Two *New York Times* reporters narrate the events that marked the contemporary "Opening of Mexico" from about 1968 to 2004. Readable, thoughtful, and engaged.

Rogel, Carole. *The Breakup of Yugoslavia and the War in Bosnia* (Westport, CN: Greenwood Press, 1998). Basic narrative supported by detailed chronology and primary documents to 1997. Critical of almost all participants and of NATO and the USA for years of appeasement.

Rosenberg, Rosalind, "The 'Woman Question,'" in Richard W. Bulliet, ed. *The Columbia History of the 20th Century* (New York: Columbia University Press, 1998).

Sen, Amartya. *Development as Freedom* (New York: Random House, 1999). Nobel Prize-winning economist stresses the significance of human development—health, education, and welfare—as the key issue in economic development, both as its cause and its result. Clearly and persuasively argued.

Sivard, Ruth Leger. *World Military and Social Expenditures 1996* (Washington: World Priorities, 16th ed., 1996). A useful compilation of statistical data revealing the colossal amounts spent by many nations of the world for military purposes, especially as compared with relatively smaller amounts for health, education, and other social purposes.

Tully, Mark and Gillian Wright. *India in Slow Motion* (New Delhi: Viking Penguin, 2002). Tully was the BBC's revered and respected correspondent from New Delhi for 25 years, and here continues to report with his partner. He is perceptive and direct about his observations, especially the toll that political corruption takes on Indian development.

Ullman, Richard H. ed. *The World and Yugoslavia's Wars* (New York: Council on Foreign Relations, 1996). Explores not only the wars but also the (lack of) responses by the European Community, the United States, and the United Nations.

⊚ World History Documents CD-ROM

28.4 Keith B. Richburg, "A Black Man Confronts Africa"
28.5 Alain Destexhe, "Rwanda and Genocide in the Twentieth Century"
29.3 Ethnic Cleansing in Northwestern Bosnia: Three Witnesses
29.4 Deng Xiaoping, "A Market Economy for Socialist Goals"
29.8 Henry A. Myers, "Now, in the Twenty-First Century"

GLOSSARY

Pronunciation guides for selected terms are enclosed in parentheses, with the stressed syllable appearing in capital letters.

asiento (a-SEE-en-toe) A contract between the Spanish crown and a private individual or sovereign power, by which the latter was granted exclusive rights to import a stipulated number of slaves into the Spanish American colonies in exchange for a fee. The British South Sea Company was granted a monopoly at the Treaty of Utrecht of 1713, a privilege that was relinquished for a lump sum in 1750.

balance of power In international relations, a policy that aims to secure peace by preventing any one state or alignment of states from becoming too dominant. Alliances are formed in order to build up a force equal or superior to that of the potential enemy.

Berlin Blockade In 1948 the Russians barred the entrance and exit of people and supplies to and from Berlin in an attempt to gain control of the city.

bourgeoisie (boor-zhwah-SEE) A French word that originally applied to the inhabitants of walled towns, who occupied a socio-economic position between the rural peasantry and the feudal aristocracy; with the development of industry, it became identified more with employers, as well as with other members of the "middle class," professionals, artisans, and shopkeepers. In Marxist theory, it refers to those who do not live by the sale of their labor, as opposed to the **proletariat**.

bourse stock exchange.

capitalism An economic system characterized by private or corporate ownership of the means of production and by private control over decisions on prices, production, and distribution of goods in a free, competitive market of **supply and demand**.

cartel An association of independent producers or businessmen whose aim is to control the supply of a particular commodity or group of commodities in order to regulate or push up prices.

Cheka (CHECK-a) The secret police of early Soviet Russia, established by the Bolsheviks after the Revolution of 1917 to defend the regime against dissidents. Criticized for its severe brutality, the agency was reorganized in 1922.

chonin City merchants and their collective class. During the Tokugawa shogunate this class grew in wealth, power, and sophistication.

client state A state that is economically, politically, or militarily dependent on another state. During the Cold War, states such as Cuba and Guatemala supported the policies of the USSR and the USA, respectively, while receiving extensive assistance from them.

collectivization A policy that aims to transfer land from private to state or communal ownership. It was adopted by the Soviet government in the 1920s and implemented with increasing brutality; by 1936 almost all the

peasants had joined the *kolkhozy* (large collective farms), although many resisted violently. The integration of agriculture into the state-controlled economy helped to supply the capital required for industrialization.

comprador (kahm-prah-DOOR) (Portuguese: "buyer") A Chinese merchant hired by Western traders to assist with their dealings in China. The comprador provided interpreters, workers, guards, and help over currency exchange.

concordat (kahn-KOR-dat) A public agreement, subject to international law, between the Pope as head of the Roman Catholic church and a temporal ruler regulating the status, rights, and liberties of the church within the country concerned.

contract labor Labor provided by workers under binding, legally enforceable contract, usually for a lengthy period, sometimes years, sometimes in organized gangs of laborers, and often for projects in distant locations. Compare **indentured labor**.

conurbation An enormous, complex city, made up of many parts, each of which is a small town or city by itself—a megalopolis.

creole (KREE-ol) In the sixteenth to eighteenth centuries, a white person born in Spanish America of Spanish parents. Excluded from the highest offices under the Spanish colonial administration, the creoles became the leaders of revolution, and then the ruling class of the new independent nations. The term creole is also used more loosely, with a wide range of applications.

daimyo (DIH-my-oh) The feudal lords of Japan, who by the sixteenth century controlled almost the entire country. Their constant warfare was finally ended in 1603 under the Tokugawa shogunate; they subsequently served as local rulers, joined to the **shogun** by oath. In 1868, when imperial rule was restored, their domains or **han** were surrendered to the emperor; in 1871 they were given titles and pensioned off.

dalit "oppressed person," a blunt term adopted by ex-untouchables to describe their status.

Dar al-Islam (DAHR ahl-is-LAHM) The literal meaning of the Arabic words is "the abode of peace." The term refers to the land of Islam, or the territories in which Islam and its religious laws (**shari'a**) may be freely practiced.

developed world Those countries that enjoy considerable wealth, derived largely from sophisticated industrialization, and characterized by high standards of living, healthcare, and literacy, advanced technological development, democratic constitutions, and world influence, as well as high labor costs and energy consumption. They comprise most of Europe, the United States, Canada, Japan, Australia, and New Zealand, the first areas to be industrialized.

developing world Those countries lacking advanced industrial development and money for investment, and with a low *per capita* income. Their economies are largely agrarian, often relying on one crop, with low yields. Labor is

plentiful, cheap, and unskilled; levels of literacy are low; poverty, disease, and famine have not been eliminated. They include most Asian countries, as well as Africa and Latin America. (*See* **third world**.)

divine right of kings A political doctrine influential in the sixteenth and seventeenth centuries. It held that the monarch derived his or her authority from God and was therefore not accountable to earthly authority. James I of England (1603–25) was a foremost exponent.

Duma (DOO-ma) The Russian parliament established by Nicholas II in response to the Revolution of 1905. Its powers were largely restricted to the judicial and administrative areas; the czar retained control over the franchise. The first two dumas (1906, 1907) were radical and soon dissolved; the third (1907–12) was conservative; the fourth (1912–17) became a focus of opposition to the czarist regime, particularly over its conduct of World War I, and enforced Nicholas's abdication in 1917.

econometrics The use of statistical techniques and mathematical models to analyze economic relationships. Econometrics may be applied by a government or private business to test the validity of an economic theory or to forecast future trends.

empiricism (em-PEER-eh-cism) The theory that all knowledge originates in experience; the practice of relying on direct observation of events and experience for determining reality. Often contrasted with rationalism on the one hand and with mysticism on the other.

enclosure acts Laws passed in England in the late 1700s to 1800s that converted public lands held in common into parcels of land to be sold to private owners.

encomienda (en-co-me-EN-da) A concession from the Spanish crown to a Spanish American colonist, giving him permission to exact tribute —in gold, in kind, or in labor—from a specified number of Indians living in a certain area; in return he was to care for their welfare and instruct them in the Catholic faith. The system was designed to supply labor for the mines, but it was severely abused and later abolished.

enlightened despotism A benevolent form of absolutism, a system of government in which the ruler has absolute rights over his or her subjects. It implies that the ruler acts for the good of the people, not in self-interest.

extraterritoriality In international law, the immunities enjoyed by the official representatives of a sovereign state or international organization within a host country; they are in effect "foreign islands," and thus exempt from prosecution, interference, or constraint.

fascism (FASH-ism) A political philosophy, movement, or government that exalts the nation over the individual, the antithesis of liberal democracy. It advocates a centralized, autocratic government led by a disciplined party and headed by a dictatorial, charismatic leader. The term fascism was first introduced by Benito Mussolini in Italy in 1919 and takes its name from the Latin word *fasces*, the ancient symbol of state authority, a bundle of rods bound around an ax.

feudal Refers to a social, military, and political system organized on the basis of land tenure and the manorial system of production. Property (the fief) was granted to a tenant (vassal) by a lord in exchange for an oath of allegiance and a promise to fulfill certain obligations, including military service, aid, and advice; in return, the lord offered protection and justice. Originally bestowed by investiture, the fief later became hereditary. Within the system, each person was bound to the others by a web of mutual responsibilities, from the king or emperor down to the serfs. Feudalism is particularly associated with medieval Europe, and with China and Japan. (*See* manorial economy.)

first world The advanced capitalist nations of the developed world, as opposed to the second world (countries with socialist state systems, particularly the former Soviet bloc) and the third world.

free market economy An economic system in which the means of production are largely privately owned and there is little or no government control over the markets, which operate according to supply and demand. The primary aim is to maximize profits, which are distributed to private individuals who have been encouraged to invest capital in an enterprise. The system is also known as a free enterprise economy or capitalism.

Führer German for "leader", the title taken by Hitler to assert his total control over Germany.

fundamentalist a person who believes in the literal truth of the bible as a revelation from God. Sometimes, more loosely, people of any religion who express intense devotion to their faith.

garden city A planned town combining work, residential, agricultural, and recreational facilities, and surrounded by a rural belt. This influential idea was the British planner Ebenezer Howard's solution to rural depopulation and the urban overcrowding of the industrial age. Letchworth (1903) in southeast England was the first example.

gazi (GAH-zee) A warrior or war leader in Islam, sometimes used as a military title among the Turks.

Girondins (juh-RAHN-dins) A French revolutionary group formed largely from the middle classes, many of them originally from the Gironde region. They were prominent in the Legislative Assembly (1791), urged war against Austria (1792), opposed the more radical Montagnards, and were overthrown in 1793.

glasnost (GLAZ-nohst) A Russian word meaning "openness," adopted as a political slogan by the Soviet leader Mikhail Gorbachev in 1986. It encouraged greater freedom of expression and genuine debate in social, political,

and cultural affairs; with perestroika, it heralded greater democracy and improved relations with the West.

guild A sworn association of people who gather for some common purpose. In the towns of medieval Europe, guilds of craftsmen or merchants were formed in order to protect and further the members' professional interests and for mutual aid. Merchant guilds organized trade in their locality and had important influence on local government. Craft guilds were confined to specific crafts or trades; they set and maintained standards of quality, regulated production and controlled recruitment through the apprenticeship system; they also had important social and religious functions. In India the guilds were associations of businessmen and producers who regulated weights and measures and prices and enforced quality control.

gulag (GOO-lahg) The acronym of Glavnoye, Upravleniye Ispravitelno Trudovykh Lagerey, the "Chief Administration of Corrective Labor Camps," a department of the Soviet secret police founded in 1934 under Stalin. It ran a vast network of forced labor camps throughout the USSR to which millions of citizens accused of "crimes against the state" were sent for punishment. The system was exposed by Alexandr Solzhenitsyn in *The Gulag Archipelago* (1973).

hacienda (ah-thee-EN-da) A large rural estate in Spanish America, originating with Spanish colonialization in the sixteenth century. The laborers, usually Indians, were in theory free wage earners, but in practice many became bound to the land through indebtedness to the owner. The owners (*haciendados*) controlled local and sometimes national government.

han In Japan, the territory or feudal estate controlled by a daimyo under the Tokugawa shogunate (1603–1868). Although legally subject to the central government, each *han* formed an autonomous and self-sufficient economic unit, with its own military forces. They were abolished in 1871.

harijan (har-YAH-jahn) A Hindu term meaning children of God, applied by Mahatma Gandhi to the poorest classes of Indian society, including the untouchables.

Huguenot Any protestants in France in the sixteenth and seventeenth centuries. Their legal status changed according to the wishes of the monarch on the throne at the time.

humanism A term applied to the intellectual movement initiated in Western Europe in the fourteenth century by such men as Petrarch and Boccaccio and deriving from the rediscovery and study of Classical, particularly Latin, literary texts. The humanist program of studies included rhetoric, grammar, history, poetry, and moral philosophy (the humanities); the humanist scholar aimed to emulate Classical literary achievements. The examination of Classical civilization formed the inspiration for the Renaissance. Although humanism attached

prime importance to human qualities and values, unlike its twentieth-century counterpart it in no way involved the rejection of Christianity.

indentured labor Labor performed under signed indenture, or contract, which binds the laborer to work for a specific employer, for a specified time, usually years, often in a distant place, in exchange for transportation and maintenance. The indenture is usually very restrictive and its conditions harsh. After the abolition of slavery in the nineteenth century, in many regions like the Caribbean, imported, indentured labor (from Asia) was employed extensively. Compare contract labor.

indulgences In the Roman Catholic church, the remission from the temporal penalty of an absolved sin, obtainable through good works or special prayers and granted by the church through the merits of Christ and the saints. The financial value often attached to indulgences in the late medieval church led to widespread abuse.

infitah An Arabic term meaning liberality and receptiveness to new ideas and arguments. In commerce, it implies expansion and freedom from restrictive rules and regulations.

irredentist An individual or group that seeks to restore territory to the state that once owned it.

Jacobins (jak-uh-bins) A French revolutionary party founded in 1789; the word derives from the popular name for the former Dominican convent in Paris, where meetings were held. It later became the most radical party of the Revolution, responsible, under Robespierre, for implementing the Reign of Terror and the execution of the king (1793).

janissary (JAN-ah-ser-ee) A member of the elite corps of Ottoman footsoldiers. Originally, in the late fourteenth century, they were Christian conscripts from the conquered Balkans who were forcibly converted to Islam and subjected to strict rules, including celibacy. Highly trained, they later became very powerful, frequently engineering palace coups; they were massacred after their insurrection in 1826.

jizya A tax levied on non-Muslims who were considered monotheistic people-of-the-book and therefore to be protected: Jews, Christians, and, later, Zoroastrians and Hindus.

keiretsu (kay-re-tsoo) Alliances of independent Japanese firms, either between large corporations in different industries or between a large corporation and sub-contractors. They are successors of the pre-war zaibatsu.

kulak (koo-LAK) A prosperous peasant in late czarist and early Soviet Russia. The leaders of local agricultural communities, kulaks owned sizeable farms and could afford to hire labor. They vigorously opposed Stalin's collectivization policy and were regarded as class enemies; large numbers were deported or executed, and their property confiscated.

laissez-faire (les-ay-FAIR) An economic policy of non-interference by government in the working of the market and the economic affairs of individuals. Proponents of the theory, which was developed in the eighteenth century, argued that an unregulated economy would work "naturally" at maximum efficiency and that the pursuit of self-interest would ultimately benefit society as a whole.

lateen (la-TEEN) A triangular sail affixed to a long yard or crossbar at an angle of about 45 degrees to the mast, with the free corner secured near the stern. The sail was capable of taking the wind on either side. The rig, which was developed by the Arabs, revolutionized navigation because it enabled vessels to tack into the wind and thus to sail in almost any direction; with a square sail, ships could only sail with the wind behind them.

libido, id In Freudian psychology, the aggressive force in humans largely representing the drive for sex and power.

madrasa (MEH-dress-eh) A traditional Islamic school of higher education, principally of theology and law, literally a "place of study." The madrasa usually comprised a central courtyard surrounded by rooms in which the students resided and with a prayer room or mosque, where instruction took place. Tuition, board, and lodging were free. Studies could last for several years and primarily consisted of memorizing text books and lectures.

manorial economy An economic system based on the manor, or the lord's landed estate, the most common unit of agrarian organization in medieval Europe. The manor comprised the lord's own farm (the demesne) and the land farmed by peasant tenants or serfs who were legally dependent on the lord and owed him or her feudal service on the demesne. The manor was not completely self-contained but it aimed more at self-sufficiency than at the market and supported a steady increase in population up to the fourteenth century.

maroonage A situation of slaves in the West Indian islands in the early eighteenth century. They organized their escape and sometimes lived in communities in inaccessible mountainous regions or forests.

mazombo A direct descendant of Portuguese settlers in the Americas.

Meiji restoration The reforms effected in Japan in the name of the emperor Mutsuhito (r. 1867–1912), who was known as the Meiji emperor. During his reign constitutional changes restored the emperor to full power, displacing the militarily powerful **shogun**, and Japan adopted many western innovations as it became a modern industrial state.

mercantilism An economic policy pursued by many European nations between the sixteenth and eighteenth centuries. It aimed to strengthen an individual nation's economic power at the expense of its rivals by stockpiling reserves of bullion, which involved government regulation of trade. Measures included tariffs on imports, the passing of sumptuary laws to keep demand for imported goods low, the promotion of thrift, and the search for new colonies, both as a source for raw materials and as a market for the export of finished goods.

mestizo (mis-TEE-zo) A person of mixed race. In Central and South America it usually denotes a person of combined Indian and European descent.

mir (MEER) A self-governing community of peasants in pre-revolutionary Russia having control over local forests, fisheries, and hunting grounds; arable land was allocated to each family according to size, in return for a fixed sum. The communes had elected officials and were responsible for the payment of taxes.

mita (MEE-tah) A system of forced labor in Peru, begun under Inca rule and continued by the Spanish colonists, by which Indian communities were required to contribute a set number of laborers for public works for a given period. Conditions were appalling, particularly in the mines, and many Indians perished. The system was abolished in 1821. (*See* **repartimiento**.)

monopoly The exclusive control over the production or supply of a particular commodity or service for which there is no substitute. Because there is no competition, the supplier can fix the price of the product and maximize profits.

Montagnards (MAHN-ton-yards) Members of a radical French revolutionary party, closely associated with the **Jacobins** and supported by the artisans, shopkeepers, and **sansculottes**. They opposed the more moderate **Girondins** and controlled the Legislative Assembly and National Convention during the climax of the Revolution in 1793–4.

mulatto (mah-LAHT-oh) In the Americas, a person of mixed race, usually with parents of European and African origin.

nabob (NAY-bahb) A British employee of the East India Company who made a huge fortune in India, often through corruption, in the eighteenth century.

neo-colonialism The control exercised by a state or group of states of the **developed world** over the economies and societies of the **developing world**. Although the latter countries may be legally independent, investment and economic control are often accompanied by political manipulation.

ninety-five theses Luther's exposition of his beliefs and his differences with the Catholic Church, posted publicly as a challenge to Church authority.

non-aligned nation A newly independent nation that chose not to align itself with either the USA or the USSR in the Cold War.

patrilineal The tracing of ancestry and kinship through the male line only.

patrilocal Residence by a couple in or near the home of the male's family or group.

Pax Americana Literally "American peace," a Latin phrase derived by analogy from Pax Romana (the peace enforced within the boundaries of the Roman empire by Roman rule) to designate the relative tranquility established within the American sphere of influence after World War II.

perestroika (pair-es-TROY-ka) A Russian word meaning "restructuring," used, like glasnost, to describe the reforms introduced by the Soviet leader Mikhail Gorbachev after 1985. It marked the development of a more flexible socio-economic system, distinguished by a move to a market-oriented economy, increased private ownership, and decentralization.

philosophes (fee-luh-ZAWFS) A group of eighteenth-century French writers and philosophers who emphasized the supremacy of human reason and advocated freedom of expression and social, economic, and political reform. They included Voltaire, Montesquieu, Rousseau, and Diderot, editor of the *Encyclopédie* (1751–72), which manifested their ideas. The *philosophes* influenced the ideals of the French Revolution and the American Declaration of Independence.

proletariat In Marxist theory, those who live solely by the sale of their labor, as opposed to the **bourgeoisie**. The term is usually applied to the wage workers engaged in industrial production.

proxy war A war waged between dependent, **client states** of larger, more powerful states that do not become directly involved in the fighting; for example the wars among Ethiopia, Somalia, and Eritrea, backed at different times in the 1970s and 1980s by the USSR and the USA. Civil wars between armed factions within a country, each backed by a different foreign power, as in the Congo in the 1960s, are also referred to as proxy wars.

Renaissance Literally "rebirth," a French term applied to the cultural and intellectual movement that spread throughout Europe from the fourteenth century. It was characterized by a new interest in Classical civilization, stimulated by the Italian poet Petrarch, and a response to the challenge of its models, which led to pride in contemporary achievement and renewed vigor in the arts and sciences. The new concept of human dignity found its inspiration in **humanism**.

repartimiento (ray-par-tee-mee-EN-toh) A system by which the Spanish crown allowed Spanish American colonists to employ Indians for forced labor, whether in agriculture or the mines. This had to be for the production of essential food or goods, and was for limited periods, but there was much abuse. (*See* **mita**.)

samizdat (SAHM-is-DAHT) From the Russian *sam-*, "self-", and *izdatel'stvo*, "publishing house." Literature printed (often in typescript) and circulated secretly to evade official suppression and punishment by the government; also this illegal, underground system of private publication.

samurai A member of the warrior class of feudal Japan, who became vassals of the **daimyo**. Characterized by their military skills and stoical pride, they valued personal loyalty, bravery, and honor more than life. During the peaceful years of the Tokugawa **shogunate** (1603–1867) they became scholars, bureaucrats, and merchants. The class was officially abolished in 1871.

sansculottes (sanz-koo-LAHT) (French: "without knee-breeches") In the French Revolution, members of the militant, generally poorer classes of Paris, so-called because they wore trousers rather than the knee-breeches of affluent society. The dress was also adopted by political activists. The name was proscribed after the fall of Robespierre in 1794.

sati (suttee) (sah-TEE) An ancient Hindu custom that requires widows to be burned on the funeral pyre of their husbands, or soon afterwards. The practice of self-immolation was officially abolished in British India in 1829.

satyagraha (sut-yah-grah-hah) A Hindi expression meaning "truth force," applied to Gandhi's policy of non-violent opposition to British rule in India.

scorched earth A strategy of defensive warfare, in which everything that might be of use to an invading army is destroyed by the defending army as it retreats. Practiced by Russia in its retreat before the armies of Napoleon and, later, of Nazi Germany; also practiced by the Chinese in the face of Japanese invasion in the 1930s and 1940s.

serf An agricultural worker or peasant bound to the land and legally dependent on the lord, characteristic of the **manorial economy** and the **feudal** system. Serfs had their own homes, plots, and livestock but they owed the lord labor, dues, and services. These services could be commuted to rent, but serfs remained chattels of the lord unless they were emancipated by him or her, or escaped. Serfdom declined in western Europe in the late medieval period, but persisted in parts of eastern Europe until the nineteenth century.

shari'a (SHAR-ee-ah) The "road" or sacred revealed law of Islam, based on the Quran and the traditional teachings of Muhammad. Since Islam does not distinguish between the religious and the secular spheres, Islamic law applies to every aspect of life. It covers such matters as marriage, divorce, inheritance, diet, and civil and criminal law.

shogun (SHOW-gun) The military dictator of Japan, a hereditary title held by three families between 1192 and 1867. Although they were legally subservient to the emperor, their military power gave them effective control of the country,

and they also took on judicial and administrative functions. The Tokugawa Shogunate (1603–1867) established a powerful centralized government at Edo (Tokyo). Imperial rule was restored in 1868.

shogunate The government of the shogun.

signares (SEEN-yahr-es) African concubines of French traders in the Senegambia.

Sikhs Members of a religious community founded in the Punjab region of North India by Guru Nanak in the sixteenth century. Sikhism combines *bhakti*, devotional Hinduism with Islamic Sufism. In the face of the militant opposition of its neighbors, Sikhs also became a militant armed group.

social contract A mythical, underwritten agreement made at an early stage of human development among citizens in creating a government, or between citizens and a ruler, which defines the rights and obligations of each party to the contract. The citizens accept the authority of the state; and the state agrees to act only with the consent of the governed. The idea goes back to Plato and became influential in seventeenth- and eighteenth-century western Europe through the writings of Hobbes, Locke, and Rousseau.

soviet A council, the primary unit of government in the Soviet Union at local, regional, and national levels, also adopted by other Communist regimes. Committees of workers' elected deputies first appeared in 1905 to coordinate revolutionary activities; they sprang up throughout the Russian Empire and were a crucial agent in the Revolution of 1917, forming the basis of Soviet administration thereafter.

Sufi (SOO-fee) In Islam, a member of one of the orders practicing mystical forms of worship that first arose in the eighth and ninth centuries C.E. Sufis interpret the words of Muhammad in a spiritual rather than a literal sense. Their goal is direct personal experience of God, achieved by fervent worship.

supply and demand In economics, the relationship between the amount of a commodity that producers are able and willing to sell (supply), and the quantity that consumers can afford and wish to buy (demand). The price fluctuates according to a product's availability and its desirability. Supply and demand thus controls a **free market economy**. In practice it is usually subject to some degree of regulation.

swadeshi (svah-day-shee) "Of one's own country," a Hindi word used as a slogan in the

Indian boycott of foreign goods, part of the protest against Britain's partition of Bengal in 1905. The Indian people were urged to use indigenous goods and to wear garments of *khadi*, homemade cloth.

swaraj (svah-raj) A Hindi word meaning "self-government" or "home rule," used as a slogan by Indian nationalists in their campaign for independence from British rule.

syncretism The mixture of different religious traditions. The term is also used to refer to hybridity in other areas, such as art and culture.

third world The countries outside the **first world** and the **second world** (countries with socialist state systems); more loosely, the **developing world**, which contains more than 70 percent of world population. The twenty-five least developed countries are sometimes characterized as "fourth world."

untouchables Members of the lowest castes of traditional Indian society or those outside the caste system; the "untouchable" groups were those engaged in "polluting" activities.

vodoun The popular religious cult of Haiti, as well as other areas of the Caribbean. It combines ritual elements from Roman Catholicism with theological and magical elements of West African origin. Vodoun ritual centers on animal sacrifice, drumming, and dance, and contact with a populous spirit world through trance.

yurt (YOORT) A portable dwelling used by the nomadic peoples of Central Asia, consisting of a tentlike structure of skin, felt or hand-woven textiles arranged over wooden poles, simply furnished with brightly colored rugs.

zaibatsu (zai-ba-tsoo) (Japanese: "wealthy clique") A large Japanese business corporation, usually under the control of a single family. A *zaibatsu* was a form of **cartel**, engaging in all important areas of economic activity and funded by its own bank. They emerged under the modernizing Meiji government (1867–1912) and were dissolved by the Allies in 1946 after World War II.

zemstvo (ZEMPST-voh) A rural council in the Russian Empire, established by Tsar Alexander II in 1864 and abolished in 1917. The assemblies, which operated at both district and provincial level, comprised the representatives of individual landed proprietors and village communes (**mir**). They were concerned with such matters as primary education, road building, agricultural development, and public health.

INDEX

SINGLE PC LICENSE AGREEMENT AND LIMITED WARRANTY